Marketing: Essentials 7e

Dana-Nicoleta Lascu, Ph.D.

Seventh Edition

Marketing: Essentials

Dana-Nicoleta Lascu
University of Richmond

The Quality Instructors Expect.
At Prices Students Can Afford.

Replacing Oligarch Textbooks since 2004

For more information, contact:
Textbook Media Press
info@textbookmedia.com

For permission to use material from this text
or product, submit a request online at
info@textbookmedia.com

Marketing: Essentials 7e
Dana-Nicoleta Lascu

Black & white paperback	ISBN: 978-1-891002-77-9
Black & white loose-leaf	ISBN: 978-1-891002-78-6
Four color paperback	ISBN: 978-1-891002-79-3
eBook access	ISBN: 978-1-891002-80-9

Textbook Media Press is a Minnesota-based educational publisher. We deliver textbooks and supplements with the quality instructors expect, while providing students with unique media options at uniquely affordable prices.

This book is dedicated to my husband, Bram, and my sons, Michael and Daniel Opstelten, with gratitude for their steadfast support and exuberance for everything marketing.

—Dana-Nicoleta Lascu

Brief Contents

Contents

Preface

Marketing is undergoing profound changes, as brands use technology to create strong relationships with consumers, ingeniously engaging them in meaningful relationships during a period of economic upheaval that has tempered consumer demand and created turmoil in the world of retailing. *Marketing: Essentials 7e* offers a comprehensive understanding of marketing in the midst of dynamic change for organizations and consumers, with new, up-to-date insights into the influence of environmental developments on firms' relationships to their target markets.

The 7th edition has been fully revised to offer insights into the most current marketing theory and practice, presenting memorable up-to-date examples throughout, and cases that offer relevant company examples illustrating the concepts covered. It provides an easy read to facilitate the understanding of complex concepts, with the goal of preparing tomorrow's marketing practitioners for a dynamic marketing world. As firms shift their primary focus to customer value and engagement, *Marketing: Essentials 7e* examines how marketing practitioners apply marketing intelligence, traditional marketing concepts and approaches, and the latest marketing strategies and tools to leverage new opportunities offered by social media, brand communities, and technology, and, in doing so, working with target consumers to write the new chapter of profitable firm-customer relationships.

Marketing: Essentials 7e reflects the authors' philosophy: offering memorable examples to help students understand marketing as a profession and the world of marketing around them – they are, after all, consumers. The authors share their own perspectives as consultants to several companies, including Fortune 500, as business owners, as marketing researchers, as world travelers, and as dedicated consumers.

In-Text Pedagogical Aids

Marketing: Essentials 7e enhances learning with the following pedagogical devices:

1. Each chapter opens with a Chapter Outline and a list of Chapter Objectives.
2. Smartly rendered four-color illustrations and photos throughout the online and PDF textbook versions clarify and enhance chapter concepts.
3. In all versions of the textbook (online, PDF, and print), key terms are highlighted and defined. Key terms are also defined in the text margins and listed in alphabetical order at the end of each chapter. A glossary at the end of each version of the textbook presents all the definitions alphabetically.
4. A comprehensive Summary at the end of each chapter reviews the Chapter Objectives, and content appropriate to each objective is summarized.
5. Review Questions at the end of each chapter allow students to check their comprehension of the chapter's major concepts.

6. End-of-chapter Discussion Questions suggest possible essay topics or in-class discussion issues.
7. Cases at the end of each chapter provide a wide range of scenarios and real-life situations, along with questions to help guide student analysis.

Media Options for Students

Marketing: Essentials 7e is available in multiple media versions: online, PDF, loose-leaf print, black and white paperback, and color paperback. The online version is bundled with all student purchases at www.textbookmedia.com because the publisher wants each student to have access to the online search function, which allows students to quickly locate discussions of specific topics throughout the text.

A premium version with web-assignments and gradebook functionality for instructors is also available through our partnership with SkyePack (www. Skyepack.com). Instructors can add to and customize the premium eBook with additional assignments, tests, and videos.

Ancillary Materials

Textbook Media is pleased to offer a competitive suite of supplemental materials for instructors using its textbooks. These ancillaries include a Test Bank, PowerPoint Slides, Instructor's Manual, and Video Labs.

This text comes with two Test Item Files, each with 100 or more questions. One Test Item File contains only true/false and multiple-choice questions, and it is ideal for instructors who want students to take online quizzes. In such cases, the other Test Item File can then be used for exams. The Test Item Files have been created by the authors and include questions in a wide range of difficulty levels for each chapter. They offer not only the correct answer for each question but also a rationale or explanation for the correct answer. The Test Item Files are compatible with all major LMS (learning management systems) vendors. The software allows the instructor to easily create customized or multiple versions of a test and includes the option of editing or adding to the existing question bank.

A full set of PowerPoint Slides, written by the authors, is available for this text. This is designed to provide instructors with comprehensive visual aids for each chapter in the book. These slides include outlines of each chapter, highlighting important terms, concepts, and discussion points.

The Instructor's Manual for this book has also been written by the authors and offers suggested syllabi for 10- and 14-week terms; lecture outlines and notes; in-class and take-home assignments; recommendations for multimedia resources such as films and websites; and long and short essay questions and their answers, appropriate for use on tests. The seventh edition of the Instructor's Manual offers a case for each chapter that can be used for testing, review, discussion, or a writing assignment.

The Video Labs that accompany this edition were selected by Dr. Clow. There are three to five videos per chapter, each with a brief description and length tally. Additionally, the Video Labs include student worksheets that instructors can assign. There's an instructor version of the worksheets that contains suggested answers.

Acknowledgments

We would like to express our gratitude to the staff at Textbook Media Press, who were the editorial team at Atomic Dog Publishing—our original publisher— for having the vision to put us together for this project and lead it through its 7th edition. We are very proud to be associated with the exceptional staff at Textbook Media Press. We would especially like to thank Ed Laube, Publisher and Founder, and Tom Doran, Founder and President at Textbook Media Press. Their steadfast support and guidance throughout the life of this textbook has been phenomenal. Over the years, many reviewers and adopters have provided valuable input in our different editions; we owe them a debt of gratitude for their helpful direction. We would also like to thank Lisa Pizzagalli, marketing associate at Deloitte, and Jason Cai, at University of Richmond, for their helpful research insights contributed to this latest edition.

About the Authors

Dana-Nicoleta Lascu is Professor of Marketing at University of Richmond. She has a Ph.D. in marketing from the University of South Carolina, a Master of International Management from the Thunderbird School of Global Management, and a B.A. in English and French from University of Arizona. She has published in journals, such as *International Business Review, Journal of Business Research, International Marketing Review, European Journal of Marketing, Journal of Global Marketing, Journal of Business Ethics, Journal of Global Business Advancement*, and authored *International Marketing 6e.* She is associate editor for the *Journal of Global Marketing,* a Regional Editor for the *Journal of Global Business and Technology,* and serves on the review board of several journals. Dr. Lascu was a simultaneous and consecutive translator and worked as an international training coordinator, teaching managerial and analytical skills to international business practitioners and civil servants. Dr. Lascu consulted with major U.S. and international corporations, and has lived, traveled, and lectured in Europe, Africa, Asia, and South America. She was a Fulbright Distinguished Chair in International Business in Austria, and a Fulbright Specialist in Mongolia. Dr. Lascu is a Fellow of the Academy of Global Business Advancement, and has received, among other awards, the Outstanding Faculty Award of the State Council for Higher Education of Virginia (SCHEV), her university's Distinguished Educator Award and Scholarly Activity Award, and an honorary doctorate from Ider University, Mongolia.

Kenneth E. Clow (deceased) was the Professor of Marketing at the University of Louisiana at Monroe, where he held the Biedenharn Endowed Chair in Business. He had a Ph.D. in marketing from the University of Arkansas. Before joining University of Louisiana, he was Dean at University of North Carolina at Pembroke, and MBA Director at Pittsburg State University. Dr. Clow's research activities were primarily in services marketing and advertising. He published more than 200 articles and six textbooks, including a second edition of *Marketing Management: A Customer-Centric Financial Approach 2e, Marketing Research Principles 3e, Services Marketing 2e,* and *Integrated Advertising, Promotion, and Marketing Communications 8e.* His articles were published in journals such as the *Journal of Services Marketing, Journal of Professional Services Marketing, Marketing Health Services, Journal of Business Research, Journal of Marketing Education, Journal of Restaurant and Foodservices Marketing, Journal of Hospitality and Leisure Marketing*, and *Journal of Marketing Management.* Dr. Clow also operated and owned a business in two states, with more than 40 employees, for over a decade.

Introduction to Marketing

PART 

Source: Rawpixel.com/Shutterstock

Scope and Concepts of Marketing

CHAPTER 1

Source: Rawpixel.com/Shutterstock

Learning Objectives

Ivelin Radkov/Shutterstock

After studying this chapter, you should be able to:

- Address the central role of marketing in the twenty-first century.
- Define marketing and identify its key concepts.
- Address the different marketing philosophies and explain them in view of the historical development of marketing.
- Discuss the key elements of the societal marketing concept and the importance of these elements in meeting the needs of consumers, society, and the organization.

Chapter Outline

Source: PKStockphoto/Shutterstock

1-1 Chapter Overview

Successful companies, such as Procter & Gamble, Nike, Microsoft, Siemens, and Apple, rely on marketing to ensure the success of their products and services in the marketplace. What is marketing? Many people—including some management professionals—think of marketing simply as advertising or selling. Indeed, promotion in the form of selling and advertising is omnipresent, arriving in neat packages in our mailboxes at home and at the office, or in our inbox, resonating on our television screens and radios, popping up in our e-mails and websites, calling for our attention from billboards on the side of the road, and enchanting us with memorable slogans, such as, "Just do it!" for Nike (for over 30 years), or "I'm Lovin' It" for McDonald's. Or, in times of the COVID-19 pandemic, using slogans to remind people to social distance, with Coke reminding people that "Staying apart is the best way to stay connected," or Nike similarly telling them "Play inside, play for the world," and keeping it safer. Promotion is part of marketing. It is an important marketing component.

Marketing is an integral part of life. It is pervasive, permeating many aspects of our daily existence, from our selection of the neighborhoods where we live, to the brands we purchase, to our choice of retailers and service providers, and to our selection of media. Marketing profoundly affects our decisions and features prominently in our lives. This chapter presents marketing as an engine of the modern economy and as an important determinant of our high standard of living. Section 1-2 addresses the importance of marketing in the twenty-first-century economy. Section 1-3 offers a definition of marketing and describes key marketing concepts. Section 1-4 examines the different marketing philosophies, and section 1-5 addresses the importance of markets, consumers, and consumer value.

1-2 The Importance of Marketing in the Twenty-First-Century Economy

Marketing constitutes an ever-growing, important driving force of today's modern society. In the United States there are more than 328 million consumers living in 112 million households, spending over $5 trillion on products and services, or two-thirds of the national **gross domestic product (GDP)**. Companies now spend over $1 trillion on marketing activities. The United States leads all nations in marketing expenditures.[1]

Gross domestic product (GDP) The sum of all goods and services produced within the boundaries of a country.

According to data published by the U.S. Bureau of Labor Statistics, retail salespeople and cashiers make up 6 percent of total U.S. employment, and more than 30 million Americans work directly within the marketing system, with salespeople accounting for the largest segment. There are almost 20 million business-to-business buyers. Marketing is a major contributor to jobs in the United States and throughout the world.[2]

Source: Truefelpix/Shutterstock

Marketing enhances economic development. Nations with higher proportions of their populations involved in marketing and with a developed marketing system also have a higher GDP. In the least developed countries, the focus of production is to satisfy basic needs, such as hunger and shelter. But in developed, high-income countries, marketing is manifest in all aspects of a company's operation, accounting for as much as 50 cents of every dollar spent on consumer products. Marketing enhances consumer well-being and quality of life. In many organizations, marketing practitioners represent consumers' interests, influencing the decisions about which products and services to offer. The marketing system then informs consumers about offerings through advertising campaigns and supports the delivery of goods and services in a manner that is convenient and affordable to consumers (see Figure 1-1). Competition leads to a broader spectrum of product choices and to an improved distribution system that reduces product costs.

As an important aspect of the daily life of a consumer, marketing informs the consumer about new products, their benefits, and their side effects. It offers choices of products, prices, and retailers. It entertains with well-executed commercials, it irritates with intrusive sounds that demand attention, and it attempts to satisfy many consumer needs and desires. What, then, is marketing?

FIGURE 1-1 This Advertisement for Iced Coffee Captures the Convenience and Affordability of the Product
Source: HstrongART/Shutterstock

1-3 Defining Marketing

Marketing Marketing is the activity, set of institutions, and processes for creating, communicating, delivering, and exchanging offerings that have value for customers, clients, partners, and society at large.

Markets All of the actual and potential consumers of a company's products.

Marketing is described by management guru Peter Drucker as "the most effective engine of economic development, particularly in its ability to develop entrepreneurs and managers."[3] He defines **marketing** as a systematic business discipline that teaches us in an orderly, purposeful, and planned way to go about finding and creating customers; identifying and defining **markets**; and integrating customers' needs, wants, and preferences. Marketing is also the intellectual and creative capacity and skills of an industrial society to facilitate the design of new and better products and new distribution concepts and processes.

In this textbook, we will adhere to the definition of marketing developed by the American Marketing Association:

> "Marketing is the activity, set of institutions, and processes for creating, communicating, delivering, and exchanging offerings that have value for customers, clients, partners, and society at large."
>
> Source: https://ama.org.

1-3a Needs, Wants, and Demands

Needs Basic human requirements such as food and water.

Successful marketers must be able to identify target consumers and their needs, wants, and demands. **Needs** are defined as basic human requirements: food, water, shelter and safety as well as social and self-esteem needs. Marketers attempt to address consumer needs with the different goods and services they offer.

Wants Needs that are directed at a particular product—for example, to meet the need for transportation, consumers may purchase an Uber or a bus ride.

Needs become **wants** when they are directed to a particular product. Wants are shaped by one's culture. Shelter in the United States typically consists of frame housing and built with brick or wood. In much of Europe, it consists of brick or cement block homes, whereas in sub-Saharan Africa, it consists of round huts made out of straw and/or mud. In each format, the home meets the consumer's need for shelter.

Self-esteem needs can be addressed in the United States and Europe through education or through luxury possessions, such as a home in the right neighborhood with the right furnishings or an automobile that qualifies as appropriate for the individual's aspirations. In sub-Saharan Africa, self-esteem needs are addressed by the number of cattle owned, and in many low-income countries, self-esteem is addressed by the number of servants helping with housework.

Demands Wants backed by the ability to buy a respective good or service.

Wants become **demands** when they are backed by the ability to buy. Discerning adults with deep pockets can buy S. Pellegrino mineral water or drive a Mercedes S-class, or take the Queen Mary ultramodern gigantic cruise ship, self-touted as the grandest, most magnificent ocean liner ever built, on a transatlantic voyage. Health-conscious moms who are pressed for time can purchase organic ready-made frozen food from various online vendors (**see Figure 1-2**).

FIGURE 1-2 Health-Conscious Moms Can Purchase Organic Foods from Various Online Vendors
Source: insta_photos/Shutterstock

1-3b Value, Quality, and Satisfaction

Companies are successful because they provide products of value. That value, defined as the overall price given the quality of the product, is especially important to consumers when they first purchase the product. Consumers vary in how they define value. To one consumer, a good value may be a cheap price. To another consumer, the value may be a quality product at a moderate price. To a third consumer, value may be an expensive product that conveys an image of prestige. Although consumers define value differently, each consumer makes a purchase because in the exchange process, he or she anticipates obtaining something of value.

Importantly, consumers monitor the price that other consumers pay for the same product and will readily switch to a lower-priced product. As a result, a number of websites have sprung up offering brand name merchandise at a lower price. In some cases, the lower price has alienated loyal consumers who have been paying full price.

Closely tied with the concept of value is quality, which is the overall product value, reliability, and the extent to which a product meets one's needs. Perceived quality has the highest impact on consumer satisfaction. As mentioned, successful companies sell products that are perceived to be of high quality relative to the price being charged. The quality of food served at a four-star restaurant is higher than that in a value meal at McDonald's. But for the amount a consumer pays at McDonald's, it is perceived to be a quality meal. Indeed, fast-food restaurants are quickly bridging the quality gap by providing healthier foods. For example, Hardee's sells a line of premium Thickburgers made from Angus beef, and Arby's is offering quality entrée salads and a line of low-carb wraps.

Companies that do not provide quality that is reflective of the price may get someone to try the product once, but more than likely that consumer will not come back. Word about poor quality offerings travels fast through websites such as Yelp, TripAdvisor, and service and product-specific sites such as Healthgrades for physicians. Products and service

Source: Sorbis/Shutterstock

providers with low ratings tend not to fare well. Product recall and the manner in which companies handle recalls have a direct impact on the companies' bottom line.

Satisfaction is the key to whether consumers or businesses engage in repeat purchase. If a consumer is satisfied with the taste and quality of a new flavor of potato chips, he or she will purchase them again. If not, that consumer will purchase another brand, and, often, disparage the product or service to others. The same is true for a business purchasing raw materials or components to manufacture a vacuum cleaner. The level of satisfaction is a function of the quality and perceived value and whether it adequately meets the need or want for which it was purchased.

1-3c Goods, Services, Ideas and Experiences

As the definition of marketing states, the primary focus of marketing is on the creation and distribution of goods, services, ideas, and experiences that satisfy consumer needs and wants. **Goods** typically refer to tangible items, such as food, automobiles and clothing. Industrial marketing, equipment, and component parts are examples of business goods. **Services** refer to intangible activities or benefits that individuals acquire but do not result in ownership. Hotel stays, restaurant meals, and attorney-prepared contracts are services. **Ideas** and **experiences** are concepts and experiences that consumers perceive as valuable because they fulfill consumer needs and wants. Watching a movie, riding Dumbo at Disneyland, and going on a kayak trip in the heart of the Grand Canyon fulfill consumers' needs for adventure and exploration. **See Figure 1-3** for more examples of goods, services, ideas, and experiences.

A restaurant is a service because consumers pay someone to prepare food served in a pleasant or unique atmosphere. Take for example the ubiquitous Shake Shack restaurant chain. Its genesis is in New York's glitzy Madison Square Park, but its positioning is that of a roadside burger stand. It sells itself as a neighborhood favorite.

Although there are differences in goods, services, ideas, and experiences, collectively they will be referred to as products. Products represent the first P of marketing. Marketing has four Ps that jointly shape the marketing strategy for a particular brand, as the chapters that follow illustrate.

Satisfaction A match between consumer expectations and good or service performance.

Goods Tangible products, such as cereals, automobiles, and clothing.

Services Intangible activities or benefits that individuals acquire but that do not result in ownership, such as an airplane trip, a massage, or the preparation of a will.

Ideas marketing Concepts that can be used to fulfill consumer needs and wants.

Experiences Personal experiences that consumers perceive as valuable because they fulfill consumer needs and wants.

1-3d Exchanges and Transactions, Relationships and Markets

Exchanges and transactions refer to obtaining a desired good or service in exchange for something else of value. Exchanges involve at least two parties that mutually agree on the desirability of the traded items. Shelter

1	A tennis racquet is a...	GOOD.
2	A beauty salon provides a...	SERVICE.
3	A political candidate is an example of an...	IDEA.
4	A dentist provides a...	SERVICE.
5	A trip to the beach is an...	EXPERIENCE.
6	Toothpaste is a...	GOOD.
7	A college textbook is a...	GOOD.
8	A college education is an example of an...	IDEA.
9	A haircut is a...	SERVICE.
10	Bungee jumping is an...	EXPERIENCE.

FIGURE 1-3 Examples of Goods, Services, Ideas, and Experiences

in New York City can be obtained by renting a tiny one-bedroom apartment for about $4,000 a month, renting a room at a hotel in Times Square in exchange for about $300 per night, renting a room at a hotel in Queens for about $150 per night, or going to a more affordable hostel. Other examples of exchanges involve voting for a particular political candidate for a promise of lower taxes or offering donations to charity in exchange for the comfort of knowing that others will be better off as a result. All of these are examples of transactions in which an exchange of something of value was given in return for something else of perceived equal value.

The exchange process is central to marketing. An exchange takes place between consumers and manufacturers or service providers. Consumers pay money for products produced by companies. In reality, the exchange is more complicated because it usually involves a complex distribution process and multiple exchanges:

- The first level of the exchange takes place between the manufacturer and a wholesaler: The wholesaler buys the product from the manufacturer.
- A second exchange takes place between that wholesaler and another wholesaler who is closer to the consumer; there could be several levels of wholesalers in the distribution chain, and at each level, an exchange will take place.
- Yet another exchange takes place between the wholesaler and the retailer where the target consumer will purchase the product.
- The final exchange takes place between the consumer and the retailer when the consumer pays the retailer for the product.

Product Any offering that can satisfy consumer needs and wants; products include goods (tangible products), services, ideas, and experiences; the first P of marketing.

Price The amount of money necessary to purchase a product; the second P of marketing.

Relationship marketing The process of developing and nurturing relationships with all the parties participating in the transactions involving a company's products; the development of marketing strategies aimed at enhancing relationships in the channel.

At each level, **products** (goods, services, ideas, or experiences) are exchanged for a monetary sum. Each product has a price (cost) at each level of distribution, with the consumer paying the final price for the good or service at the end of the distribution channel. **Price** is the second P of marketing.

At all these levels, important relationships of mutual benefit develop. Consumers develop loyalty or preference for the brand or the retailer. The retailer develops relationships with wholesalers, and wholesalers develop relationships with manufacturers. The manufacturer nurtures a relationship with all the parties involved in marketing its products and with the final consumer. This is known as **relationship marketing**, which is defined as the process of developing and nurturing relationships with the parties participating in the transactions involving a company's products. The parties involved in the exchange are part of the distribution process, which is referred to as **place**—the third P of marketing.

A market is the set of all the actual and potential buyers of a company's products. The company needs to understand its markets to produce goods that address the markets' needs and wants and to communicate with them effectively about their products. Communication with the market is accomplished through promotion in the form of advertising, personal selling, sales promotion, or social media. **Promotion** is the fourth P of marketing. Hence, product, place, price, and promotion—the four Ps of marketing, also known as the **marketing mix**—are used to address the needs and wants of consumers. The four Ps of marketing are illustrated in **Figure 1-4**.

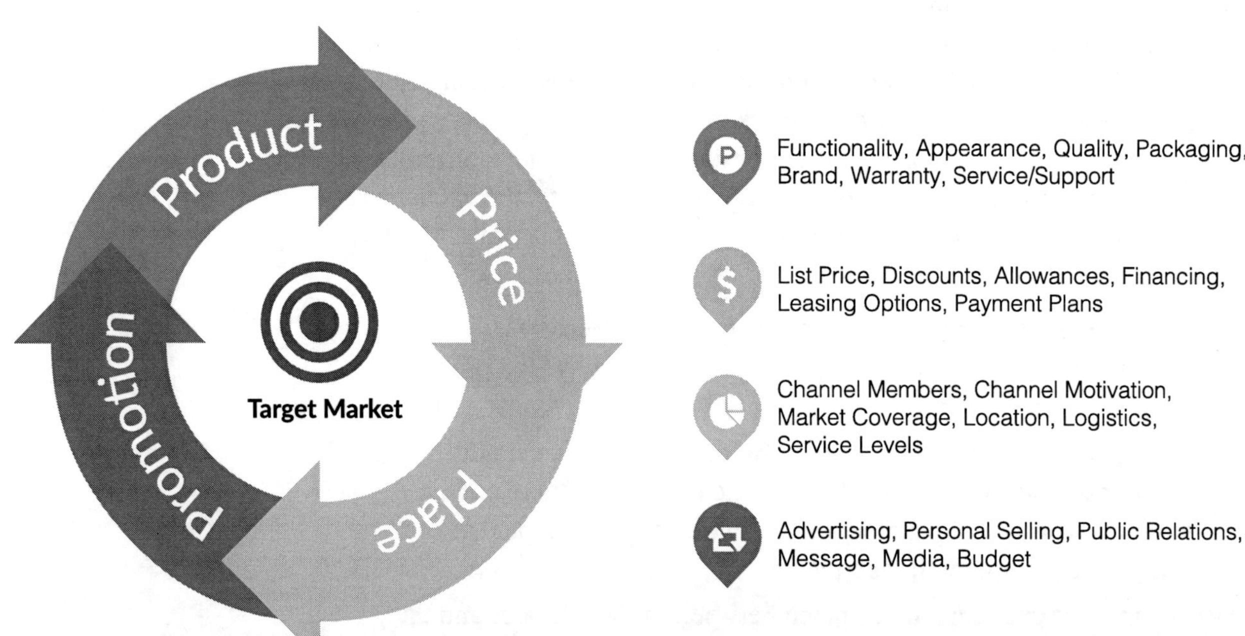

FIGURE 1-4 The 4 Ps of Marketing
Source: Martellostudio/Shutterstock

1-4 Marketing Philosophies

Firms can opt for one of five different approaches to marketing. The company can either:

1. Place a heavy emphasis on producing the best product it can, hoping someone will buy it.
2. Reduce costs through improved manufacturing processes and technological development, thus selling its products at a lower cost than its competition.
3. Put a heavy emphasis on selling its products to consumers and businesses, striving to convince customers of the superiority of its product.
4. Find out what customers want first and then develop a product that meets that want.
5. Produce and market the product in the way that will best benefit society.

1-4a The Product/Production Concepts

The **production concept** assumes that consumers prefer products that are easily accessible and inexpensive. For the company, the production concept focuses on strategies that reduce the cost of producing and delivering the product to consumers, or businesses. The production orientation works well for mass-market service organizations, such as fast-food providers and retailers that want to provide products to consumers at the very lowest price possible. Dollar General and the Dollar Tree are two retail chains that use the production concept.

The **product concept** assumes that consumers prefer products that are of the highest quality and optimal performance. Significant resources are devoted to research, product development, manufacturing, and engineering. The goal is to build a better product. Artesyn Technologies is a manufacturer of power supplies. According to the firm's mission statement "the goal of Artesyn Embedded Technologies is to maintain its position as a worldwide leading supplier in the power supply manufacturing industry by providing quality products and services which meet or exceed customers' current and future expectations."[4]

1-4b The Selling Concept

The **selling concept** assumes that when left alone, consumers will not normally purchase the products the firm is selling or will not purchase enough products. Accordingly, consumers need to be aggressively targeted and approached with personal selling and advertising to be persuaded to purchase the company's products. Although firms may focus on aggressive selling when they have excess inventories at the end of the year and new models must replace the old, companies are more likely to embrace the selling concept when their products are unsought goods, such as time-shares and insurance services. In the process of selling time-shares, companies such as Fairfield Resorts identify prospective buyers, approach them with an offer of two nights at the resort location, and then require those who choose

Place (or distribution) The physical movement of products from the producer to individual or organizational consumers and the transfer of ownership and risk; the third P of marketing.

Promotion Communication with a firm's market through advertising, personal selling, sales promotions, and social media.

Marketing mix Tools marketers use, consisting of product, price, place, and promotion, to deliver value to consumers and profits to the firm.

Production concept A marketing philosophy that assumes consumers prefer products that are easily accessible and inexpensive.

Product concept A marketing philosophy that assumes consumers prefer products that are easily accessible and inexpensive.

Selling concept Assumes that when left alone, consumers will not normally purchase the products the firm is selling or will not purchase enough products.

Source: JHVEPhoto/Shutterstock

to take advantage of the offer to spend about two hours in a hard-sell environment.

In today's economic downturn and uncertainty under a pandemic, department stores, most fighting extinction,[5] are adopting the selling concept, aggressively promoting discounts. Most of their advertising is promoting sales or coupons, at 15 percent off already discounted clothing. Beauty items are no longer limited to traditional gift sets or gifts with purchase; department stores now offer discounts even on rarely discounted premium brands. In a deluge of marketing communications, retailers are often assisted by manufacturers, who offer additional promotional incentives to consumers, which reinforces the selling strategy.

In both the time-share and the current retail examples, the focus is on persuading consumers to make purchases, rather than offering them goods that best fit their needs and desires. In the case of the time-shares, consumers might respond to the offer only to obtain the subsidized stay at the hotel. In the case of the retailers' blitz during the current pandemic, consumer response is likely to be short term, focused on the promotions offered.

1-4c The Marketing Concept

Marketing concept
A marketing philosophy that assumes a company can compete more effectively if it first researches consumers' generic needs, wants, and preferences, as well as good- or service-related attitudes and interests, and then delivers the goods and services more efficiently and effectively than competitors.

The **marketing concept** assumes that a company can compete more effectively if it first researches consumers' needs, wants, preferences, and attitudes towards specific products and brands. With this knowledge of the consumer, the firm is able to deliver the goods and services that consumers want more efficiently and effectively than the competition. This marketing philosophy entails a company-wide consumer focus across all functional areas.

At Arby's adopting the marketing concept is not limited to the product offering or the restaurant ambience. Arby's restaurants are located conveniently to target consumers, typically close to shopping centers that are frequented by its target market. Its prices are somewhat higher than those at a McDonald's or Burger King. Sandwiches, for example, cost more, but they are marketed as being of superior quality and match the taste desires of older Americans. Convenient locations, appropriate pricing, and well-targeted promotions are indicative of a consumer focus, hence reflecting a marketing concept philosophy. Following in its footsteps, McDonald's is now offering a McCafé line of smoothies and coffee-based beverages, and KFC (Yum! Brands) has developed a new fast-casual concept, with high-end finishes with natural, reclaimed wood, exposed brick and oversized windows, a place where customers can linger and have food served in real dishes.[6]

The marketing concept has five principal components that are essential to a company's performance. They are a market orientation, an integrated marketing approach, a focus on consumer needs, a value-based philosophy, and an organizational goal orientation—as illustrated in **Figure 1-5.**

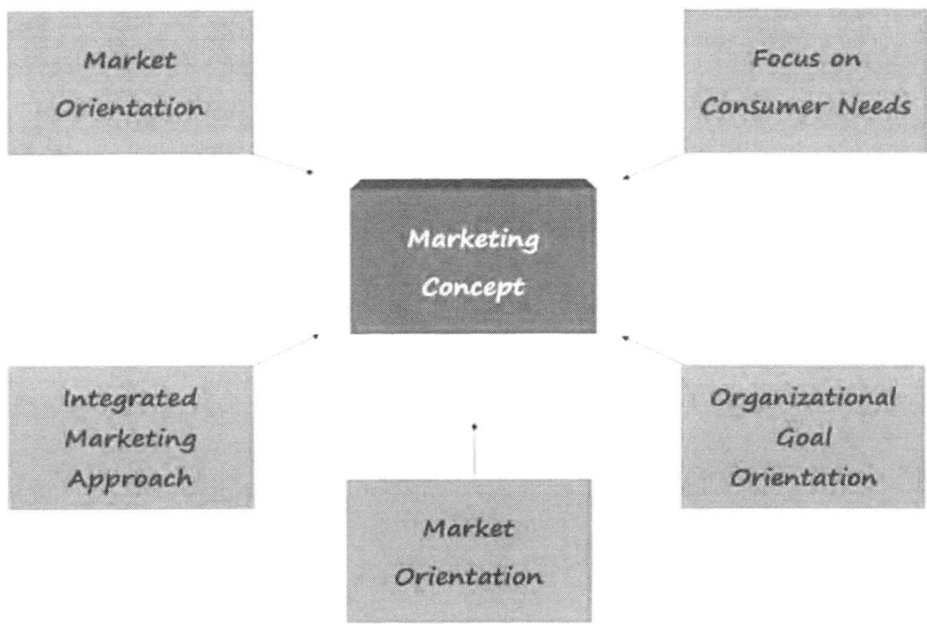

FIGURE 1-5 The Marketing Concept

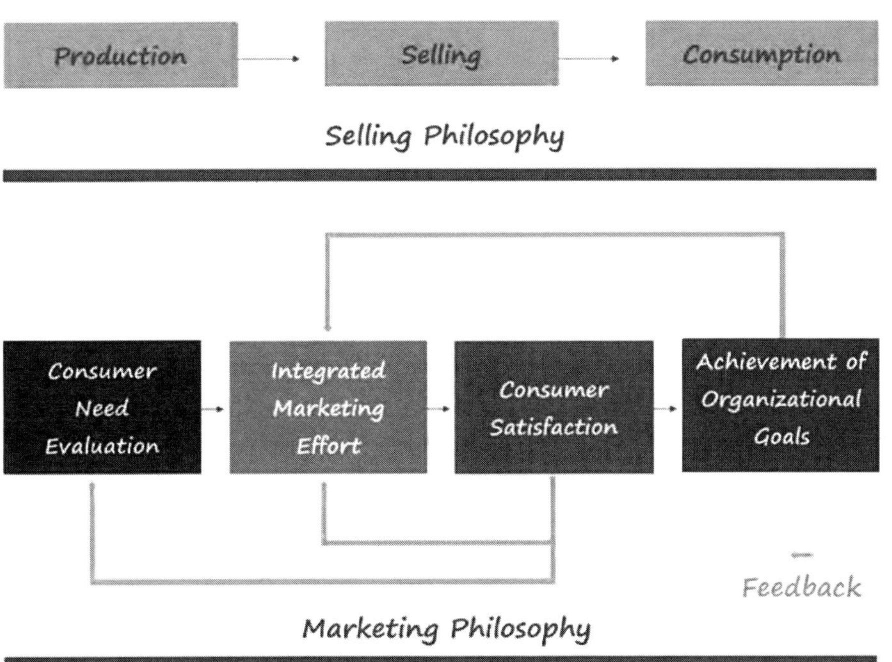

FIGURE 1-6 Selling versus Marketing Philosophies

The marketing concept is superior to the selling concept in two primary ways. First, the outcome of a focus on aggressive selling leads to short-term results (sales), whereas adopting the marketing concept leads to a long-term relationship with the customer. Second, selling's primary goal is to increase revenue, whereas the marketing concept has as its primary goal addressing customer needs and wants. Figure 1-6 illustrates the differences between a selling philosophy and a marketing philosophy.

1-4d The Societal Marketing Concept

Societal marketing concept A marketing philosophy that assumes the company will have an advantage over competitors if it applies the marketing concept in a manner that maximizes society's well-being.

The **societal marketing concept** assumes that the company will have an advantage over competitors if it applies the marketing concept in a manner that maximizes society's well-being. Companies today are expected to be good citizens of society. With the societal marketing approach, companies first research consumers' needs, wants, preferences, attitudes and personal interests. The goal is to deliver the good or service more efficiently than competitors, but in a manner that maximizes society's well-being.

Source: Joshua Small-Photographer

Arby's has established an exemplary record of following the societal marketing concept through its social involvement. The Arby's Foundation supports Big Brothers and Big Sisters of America, the Boys & Girls Clubs of America, and various other causes through donations from franchisees, suppliers, employees, customers, and sponsors. It also sponsors initiatives such as the Arby's Charity Tour, a series of amateur golf tournaments benefiting its national charities, and local youth mentoring organizations in cities where the tournaments take place. Ben & Jerry's, a Unilever subsidiary, positions itself as a supporter of social causes. The company ensures that none of its ice cream products are made with milk from hormone-fed cows and takes a strong stand against it. "We oppose recombinant bovine growth hormone" is a statement found on most of the Ben & Jerry's packages. It also supports environmental efforts, such as those involving Vermont's Lake Champlain Watershed, peace in the world, and other causes.

Cause-related marketing A long-term partnership between a nonprofit organization and a corporation that is integrated into the corporation's marketing plan.

Many companies, in the process of adopting the societal marketing concept, partner with nonprofit firms to engage in cause-related marketing. **Cause-related marketing** refers to a long-term partnership, between a nonprofit organization and a corporation, integrated into the company's marketing plan. Bank of America offers the Susan G. Komen Visa Signature credit card, donating a percentage of purchases to charity, and the Discover card allows users to give reward points to charities such as the American Red Cross and the American Society for the Prevention of Cruelty to Animals (ASPCA).[7]

Demarketing A company strategy aimed at reducing demand for its own products to benefit society.

Companies that subscribe to the societal marketing concept philosophy will, at times, engage in the **demarketing**, defined as reducing the demand for a product if it is in the best interest of society. Altria and other cigarette manufacturers offer information on the serious effects of smoking, quitting smoking, cigarette ingredients, and talking to children about not smoking. Casinos have signage with contact information for individuals who have a gambling problem. Anheuser Busch discourages underage drinking, and driving while intoxicated. Electric power companies may run ads in the summer encouraging consumers to reduce use of electrical power during extremely hot days. The goal for all of these companies is to demonstrate to consumers that they are responsive to the needs of society.

Demarketing for vice products, such as cigarettes and alcohol, although focusing the messages on vulnerable populations, such as children, the elderly, and the poor, demonstrates social concern on the part of the company and may diffuse public scrutiny of the sponsor's products and practices.

1-4e The History of Marketing Philosophies

The product/production concept, the selling concept, and the marketing concept can be traced historically to the **production era**, the **sales era**, and the **marketing era**—the periods when the respective philosophies were dominant. The production era, between 1870 and 1930, was characterized by firms focusing their attention on physical production and the production process. Firms attempted to fit products within their production capabilities, rather than focusing on customer needs. Output consisted of limited product lines, and because demand exceeded supply, competition was minimal. Retailers and wholesalers were only of peripheral concern because the products practically sold themselves.[8]

Production era Period between 1870 and 1930, when the primary focus of marketing was on producing the best products possible at the lowest price.

Sales era Period between 1930 and 1950, when the primary focus of marketing was on selling.

Marketing era Period from 1950 until the present, when the primary focus of marketing shifted to the needs of consumers and society.

Production efficiency led to a new phenomenon: overproduction. Companies turned to marketing professionals to sell their products during the sales era, between 1930 and 1950. The sales era was characterized by a focus on selling, which was based on the assumption that if the customer were left alone, he or she would not purchase the product or would not purchase enough products. Also, supply exceeded demand. With excess supply, companies had to persuade consumers and other businesses to buy their brand instead of the competitors'.

In the 1950s, scholars were concerned that marketers were not paying enough attention to customers' needs and wants. Thus, the marketing concept emerged as the dominant paradigm. It was agreed that the main task of the marketing function should not be "to be skillful in making the customer do what suits the interests of the business . . . but to be skillful in conceiving and then making the business do what suits the interests of the customer."[9]

1-4f Beyond the Marketing Philosophies: Avoiding Marketing Myopia

The danger of the product, production, and selling concepts is that they may lead to **marketing myopia**.[10] This term is attributed to Theodore Levitt, one of the most notable early marketing theorists, who noticed that marketers at the time (in the 1950s) were ignoring an important market—seniors. The term marketing myopia is defined as the tendency of marketing efforts to focus on products, production, or sales and ignore specific consumer needs or important markets.

Marketing myopia The tendency of marketing efforts to focus on products, production, or sales and ignore specific consumer needs or important markets.

Source: Lisa F. Young/Shutterstock

Even companies that embrace the societal marketing concept can experience other myopias, including "green marketing myopia," focusing too much on product greenness and environmental performance, and ignoring customer product satisfaction. Companies should address both—case in point, the Toyota Prius, yielding 44 miles to the gallon, but also an appealing, quirky-looking, distinctive car that was embraced by celebrities to project environmental awareness. Focusing on product greenness alone does not persuade consumers to buy.[11]

1-5 The Centrality of the Market and Consumer

Marketing managers today understand that their firms can no longer afford to limit their focus on the needs of their consumers and the needs of their organizations. The marketing concept alone cannot lead to optimal firm performance in the marketplace. Companies must be socially conscious. Younger consumers look to see what companies are doing, where products are being produced, and if the company is a good citizen. With social media, violations of this societal focus can be spread quickly to millions of people. Elements of the societal concept are illustrated in **Figure 1-7.**

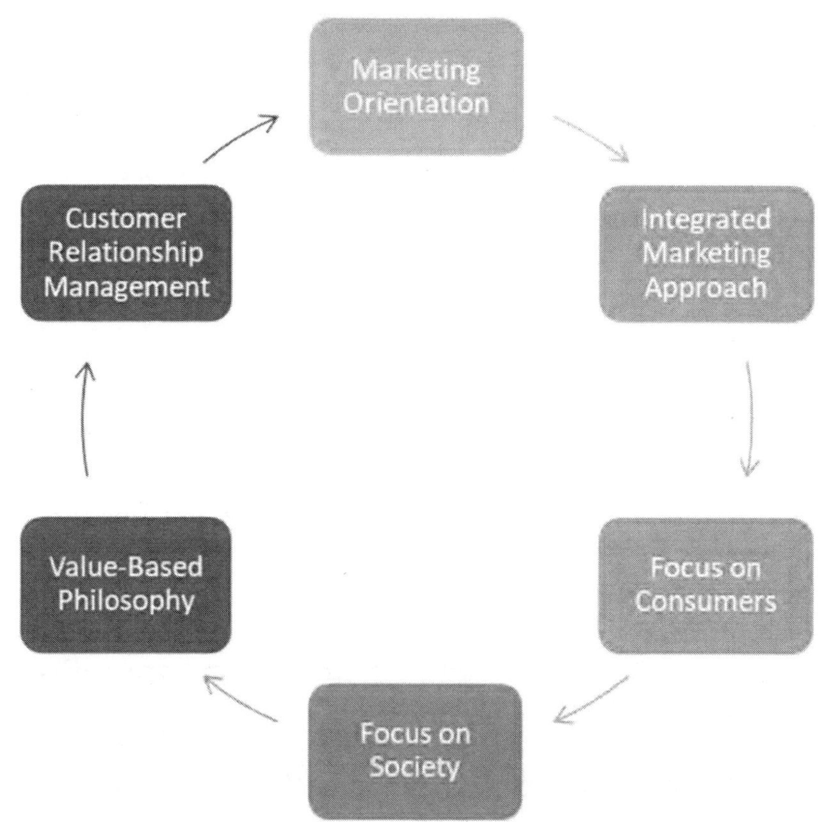

FIGURE 1-7 Elements of a Societal Marketing Orientation

1-5a A Market Orientation and an Integrated Marketing Approach

A **marketing orientation** is defined as a company-wide culture that encourages behaviors that will result in superior value to buyers. Companies should systematically seek marketing information at the organization level. This information should be disseminated to other departments, such as finance, research and development, engineering, manufacturing, and purchasing to ensure the entire organization can respond in a manner that best meets customers' needs. A marketing orientation also requires that the marketing function has considerable prominence in company-wide decision making, with the marketing vice president occupying a senior position in the firm.[12]

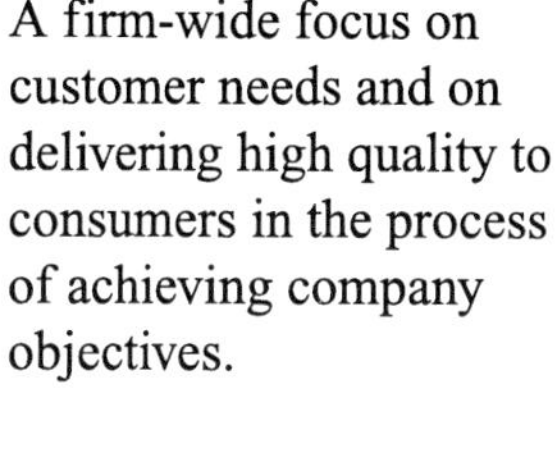

Marketing orientation A firm-wide focus on customer needs and on delivering high quality to consumers in the process of achieving company objectives.

A marketing orientation calls for an integrated marketing approach. Messages conveyed in advertising, through direct mail, on social media, and by salespeople must be consistent. In this information age, consumers (and businesses) use multiple sources of information. When accessed, it is vital that all of these sources convey the same message about a company. If the value proposition is based on price, then all information sources within the company must use this value proposition. If superior quality is the value proposition, then all communications must stress the brand's excellent quality.

1-5b A Focus on Consumer Needs

For optimal performance in the marketplace, marketers need to address consumer needs and wants more effectively than competitors. They have to employ a marketing strategy using the four Ps of marketing in a manner that optimally addresses consumer needs. This requires that companies:

- offer goods or services that satisfy consumer needs or wants
- offer a price the consumer perceives as fair in return for the value received
- make the product available at retailers that are conveniently located close to consumers, or that deliver directly to the consumers
- promote its marketing efforts through venues that effectively reach the target consumer.

Lululemon is known for its product innovation, loyal consumer base, and strong digital presence. While many apparel retailers, such as J. Crew, have had difficulty dealing with the COVID-19 pandemic—after all, apparel is not an essential product category—Lululemon has continued to thrive. The Canadian company, a market leader in the athleisure industry, offering relatively expensive, yoga-inspired athletic apparel, is known for its cult-like following. Although the brand has experienced many controversies in the past—a founder with outrageous

Source: JHVEPhoto/Shutterstock

world views, favoring child labor in developing countries, and clothing that was too revealing,—the Lululemon brand continues to thrive because it meets the needs of its target market. It sells, for about $90, the most popular leggings on the planet, to its younger target market. While competing brands recruit celebrity endorsers, Lululemon recruits brand ambassadors–local yoga instructors, elite athletes, or influencers—creating a strong, organic relationship between the brand and its followers.[13]

1-5c A Value-Based Philosophy

A value-based philosophy is essential to organizational success. Companies with a value-based philosophy ensure that their consumers' needs are addressed in a manner that delivers a good or service of high quality and value that ultimately leads to consumer satisfaction. It does so while also enhancing consumers' and society's quality of life. In fact, successful companies that adopt a value-based philosophy are also likely to invest in society, primarily for altruistic reasons that benefit society, not the company—even if, ultimately, there is an expectation of commercial return.[14]

Product quality, product value, and consumer satisfaction are interrelated, forming the basis for value judgment. One measure that addresses both quality and consumer satisfaction is the American Consumer Satisfaction Index.[15] This index is based on the following principles:

- Customer expectations occur when consumers anticipate product performance based on their experiences, on information received from the media, and on information from other consumers. Expectations influence the evaluation of good or service quality and predict how the good or service will perform on the market.
- Quality refers to overall product quality, reliability, and the extent to which it meets consumers' needs. Perceived quality has the greatest impact on satisfaction.
- Value refers to the overall price, given the quality of the product, and is important in the purchase decision.

Over time, the American Consumer Satisfaction Index has demonstrated that companies rating highly are more profitable and have greater shareholder value. These companies are in a better position to reach their organizational goals. Manufacturers, service providers, retailers, and wholesalers frequently conduct consumer satisfaction surveys to assess their own performance. Historically, consumer satisfaction has been defined as a match between consumer expectations and good or service performance:

- If a product or service performs better than expected, then consumers are likely to be satisfied and are likely to purchase the brand in the future.
- If performance matches expectations, consumers are somewhat satisfied. Psychologists refer to this as "satisficing" or "neutrality"—meaning that the consumer is satisfied but would switch to another good or service without much persuasion.

- If product performance does not meet consumer expectations, then consumers are likely to be dissatisfied and may never purchase the brand again. These consumers often engage in negative word-of-mouth communications about the brand or firm.

1-5d Customer Relationship Management

A cornerstone of most societal marketing practices is a process known as customer relationship management (CRM). **Customer relationship management** is a database application program designed to build long-term relationships with customers through the use of a personal and customized touch. The tenets of CRM are shown in **Figure 1-8.**

Customer relationship management (CRM) A database application program designed to build long-term loyalty with customers through the use of a personal touch.

Managing thousands and, often, millions of customers is a daunting task. CRM is a software management system designed to make this process more efficient and effective, using data analysis to understand customer preferences, allowing a company to personalize and customize its communication with each customer. Its goal is to provide a consistent and seamless conduit of communication with customers with the goal of enhancing the customer experiences. The database provides a unified customer view across the enterprise, tying together all interactions between the company and a particular customer. For example, the call center can find out about online transactions or direct mail pieces sent to a customer, and the customer thus does not have to repeat or re-enter information to engage in a new transaction.

CRM allows for multichannel marketing so that customers can deal with the firm when they want to and where they want to. The customer can go to a retail store during store hours to purchase a product, she can go to the website, or she can order the product by phone. Ultimately, CRM leads to more efficient customer targeting and retention, improving cost management and increasing profitability.

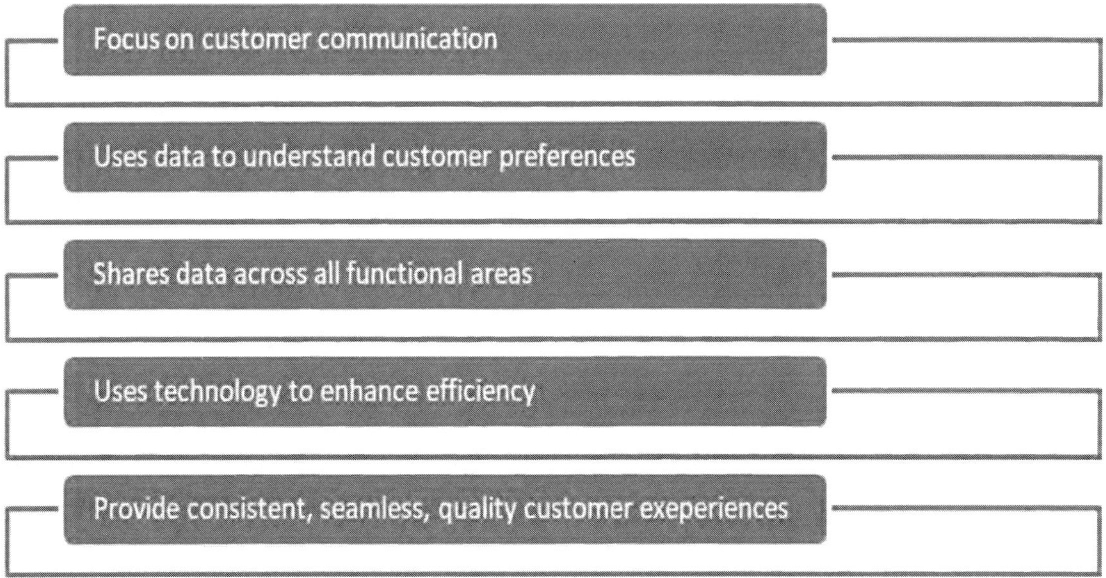

Focus on customer communication
Uses data to understand customer preferences
Shares data across all functional areas
Uses technology to enhance efficiency
Provide consistent, seamless, quality customer exeperiences

FIGURE 1-8 Tenets of Customer Relationship Management (CRM)

Customer lifetime value (LTV) The estimated profitability of the customer over the course of his or her entire relationship with a company.

Customer valuation theory (CVT) Assesses customer financial contributions to the firm—direct or indirect, or based on their scope.

For CRM to be profitable, companies must retain their customers for long periods. At the heart of customer relationship management is the concept of **customer lifetime value (LTV)**, an economic measure of the customer relationship to the firm which will promote customer referrals, positive social media influence, and feedback benefiting the firm (Kumar 2018). Its goal is to identify, maintain, and nurture profitable customers in order to build a relationship with them. It consists of an aggregate approach, involving measuring lifetime value from a segment, thus focusing on the effectiveness of the marketing plan, and the individual approach, measuring the LTV of one customer throughout his or her entire time with the company, helping the brand to create personalized strategies that target specific customer needs, and to identify the future profitability potential of consumers.[16]

Customer valuation theory (CVT) focuses on customer financial contributions to the firm—direct or indirect, or based on their scope—further confirming that LTV is the metric that most accurately captures a customer's potential value to the firm. To assess LTV, firms could measure exchange characteristics such as past customer spending level, purchase frequency, and past purchase activity. In business-to-consumer relationships, many other characteristics are assessed, such the average time between purchases, participation in loyalty programs, customer-initiated contacts, and consumer deal/coupon usage intensity.[17]

There are a number of approaches to calculating customer lifetime value. One approach is to use a historical approach, determining average revenue per user (ARPU), where:

$$\text{ARPU} = \frac{\text{Total profit for a chosen period}}{\text{Number of customers for a chosen period}}$$

If 30 Starbucks customers brought in \$1,860 over three months, then ARPU = \$1,860/30, or \$62. Then, ARPU (12 months) = ARPU (3 months) × 4 = \$62 × 4, or \$248 per year per customer. The historical customer lifetime value is the ARPU per year, or \$248 per year per customer.[18]

For digital marketing assessment purposes, Google Analytics offers detailed insights regarding how valuable different customers may be for your business based on their lifetime performance. One can calculate lifetime value of customers acquired through email or paid search. For example, you can compare customer lifetime values acquired through search, through social media, or email to identify which method brings the higher value customers. This will help the firm identify the most profitable target market where it should allocate its marketing resources.[19]

Summary

1. **Address the central role of marketing in the twenty-first century.**
   Marketing constitutes an ever-growing, important driving force of today's modern society. In the United States alone, there are more than 328 million consumers living in 112 million households, spending \$5 trillion on goods and services. A significant portion of all Americans are employed entirely or in part in assisting the marketing system to

perform its functions. Thus the broad marketing system is integral to a society's economic system, offering employment and income for millions working in the marketing field, enabling them to be productive and earn money needed for consumption. The system's mass-market efficiencies allow for lower costs, lower prices, and increased overall consumer access. Marketing enhances economic development, buyers' well-being, and general quality of life.

2. **Define marketing and identify its key concepts.**
Marketing is defined as the process of planning and executing the conception, pricing, promotion, and distribution of ideas, goods, and services to create exchanges that satisfy individual and organizational objectives. Important concepts in marketing are needs (basic human requirements), wants (directed to a particular product), and demands (wants backed by the ability to buy the respective product or service brand). The four Ps of marketing are products (goods, services, ideas, and experiences), price, place (distribution), and promotion. At each level of distribution between the manufacturer, wholesaler, retailer, and consumer, an exchange takes place: A desired good or service is obtained in exchange for something else. Exchanges involve at least two parties that mutually agree on the desirability of the exchange.

3. **Address the different marketing philosophies and explain them in view of the historical development of marketing.**
The production concept assumes that consumers prefer products that are easily accessible and inexpensive. The product concept assumes that consumers prefer products that are of the highest quality and optimal performance. The selling concept assumes that consumers left alone will not buy or not buy enough (they need to be aggressively sold to purchase). The marketing concept focuses on consumers' needs and works to create a good or service that matches those needs. The societal marketing concept is a philosophy that applies the marketing concept in a manner that maximizes society's well-being. Historically, the product/production concept can be traced back to the product era (1870–1930), when the focus was on products and production. The selling concept to the sales era (1930–1950), when the focus was on selling overproduction to consumers. The marketing concept occurred in the marketing era (1950–present), when the focus shifted to the needs of the consumer, and later, to the needs of society.

4. **Discuss the key elements of the societal marketing concept and the importance of these elements in meeting the needs of consumers, society, and the organization.**
The first two key elements are a market orientation and an integrated marketing approach, which is a firm-wide focus on customer needs and on delivering high-quality products to consumers. Important is the dissemination of marketing information across departments using an integrated marketing approach. The third and fourth key elements are a focus on consume r and societal needs. The fifth key element is a value-based philosophy that puts value, quality, and consumer satisfaction first. This is accomplished through the last key element, which is a customer relationship management approach to meeting the needs of customers.

Key Terms

Cause-related marketing (14)
Customer lifetime value (LTV) (20)
Customer relationship management (CRM) (19)
Customer valuation theory (CVT) (20)
Demands (6)
Demarketing (14)
Experiences (8)
Goods (8)
Gross domestic product (GDP) (4)
Ideas marketing (8)

Marketing (6)
Marketing concept (12)
Marketing era (15)
Marketing mix (11)
Marketing myopia (15)
Marketing orientation (17)
Markets (6)
Needs (6)
Place (or distribution) (11)
Price (10)
Product concept (11)
Production concept (11)
Production era (15)
Products (10)
Promotion (11)
Relationship marketing (10)
Sales era (15)
Satisfaction (8)
Selling concept (11)
Services (8)
Societal marketing concept (14)
Wants (6)

Discussion Questions

1. Review the concepts of goods, services, ideas, and experiences. Give two examples of each from your personal experience.
2. Identify a recent purchase you made based on a need. Identify a recent purchase you made based on a want. Explain the difference between the two.
3. Discuss a recent purchase you made in terms of its value, quality, and level of satisfaction. Explain the relationship among the three concepts.
4. Think of a recent purchase you made where you were dissatisfied. Explain why you were dissatisfied and the role that value and quality played in that dissatisfaction.
5. Examine the marketing philosophies presented in Section 1.4. For each of the companies or brands below, which of the marketing philosophies do you think the company (or brand) is using? Justify your answer.
   - AT&T cell phone service
   - DISH satellite TV service
   - Exxon gas
   - Apple (electronics)
   - Nabisco (cookies and crackers)
   - Reebok (shoes)
6. Philip Morris USA, the manufacturer of Marlboro and the creator of the legendary Marlboro Man, is attempting to reach consumers with pamphlets of information on the dangers of smoking. Does Philip Morris subscribe to the social marketing concept? Explain.
7. Is it important to you for a company to be involved in societal issues and concerns? Why or why not? Does it impact the brands you purchase? Explain. Are there brands you will not purchase because you feel they do not care about the environment and society? Explain.
8. Identify five brands that you believe provide good value to you. Explain why you consider the brands to be good values. Discuss the relationship of quality to price.
9. How important is customer service to you at a restaurant? Which is more important, good service or good food? Explain.

Review Questions

True or False

1. Marketing is a process of exchange at different levels.
2. The production concept assumes that consumers prefer products of the highest quality and performance.
3. The societal marketing concept assumes that the company will have an advantage over competitors if it is applied in a manner that maximizes society's well-being.
4. The selling concept assumes that, if consumers are left alone, they will normally purchase the product.
5. Overall product quality is a set of norms used by the manufacturer to meet the production specification.

6. The marketing concept emerged in the 1950s as a dominant marketing paradigm.
7. Either product or production orientation constitutes the best approaches to satisfying consumers.
8. The selling concept is superior to the marketing concept.
9. A market orientation is defined as a company-wide culture creating the necessary behaviors for delivering superior value to buyers.
10. Companies that adopt a value-based philosophy offer high-priced products.

Multiple Choice

11. Which of the following refers to demands?
    a. Basic human requirements
    b. Needs directed at a particular product
    c. Wants backed by customer ability to buy a product
    d. Obtaining a product in exchange for something else
12. A haircut is an example of a(n)
    a. good.
    b. service.
    c. idea.
    d. none of the above.
13. Demarketing is defined as a
    a. decline in retail distribution.
    b. reduction in demand for the company's own product for the well-being of society.
    c. process of changing advertisements in the media.
    d. none of the above.
14. The production era corresponds to
    a. 1850–1870
    b. 1870–1930
    c. 1930–1950
    d. 1950–present
15. Companies provide products of value. Value is defined as
    a. a low price guarantee.
    b. product quality at moderate price.
    c. an expensive product that conveys prestige.
    d. a product's overall price given its quality.
16. The marketing mix consists of the following four main components:
    a. product, people, place, and price.
    b. product, perception, price, and place.
    c. product, price, place, and promotion.
    d. prosperity, product, potential, and price.
17. Marketing myopia is defined as
    a. considering an important market segment.
    b. selling a new brand product within a short period.
    c. a marketing philosophy that is rooted in price and promotion.
    d. a tendency of marketing efforts to focus on product, production, and sales.
18. Elements of a societal marketing orientation are
    a. marketing orientation and integrated marketing approach.
    b. focus on needs of customers and society.
    c. value-based philosophy and customer relationship management.
    d. all of the above.
19. To gain a competitive advantage in the marketplace, a company should
    a. offer products that satisfy consumers at a perceived fair price.
    b. make products available to consumers.
    c. use effective promotion to reach a target consumer.
    d. all of the above.
20. Tenets of customer relationship management are
    a. focus on customer communication.
    b. using data to understand customer preferences.
    c. use technology to enhance efficiency.
    d. all of the above.

Answers: (1) True, (2) False, (3) True, (4) False, (5) False, (6) True, (7) False, (8) False, (9) True, (10) False, (11) c, (12) b, (13) b, (14) b, (15) d, (16) c, (17) d, (18) d, (19) d, (20) d

Source: ShotPrime Studio/Shutterstock

Maria Garza and her family own and manage Maria's Pizza. This has been a successful family business for the last six years, but recently has been running into trouble. They send coupons to their customers regularly in hopes that they return often and bring their families along. However, they have always had their share of customers who are problematic. They complain about the size of their drink or the temperature of the pizza and expect, in return, to receive a free drink or a free pizza in addition to the discount. These customers are the exception, but they are quite a nuisance. Maria is thinking about eliminating them from the mailing list because, even though they come to Mama's relatively often, they tend to be trouble. But somehow she is having difficulty reconciling this situation with the ingrained idea that the customer is always right.

Maria has done some research into how other businesses deal with this type of problematic customer. She has used various formulas to calculate customer lifetime value, including a tool provided by Harvard Business School. Through her research, Maria found out that many companies have problem customers. At Best Buy these customers are known as "devils." Best Buy classifies customers who are less demanding and spend money on expensive and new technologies as "angels." Customers who buy products, apply for rebates, return the purchases, and then buy them back at returned merchandise discounts are termed "devils." They request the company honor their lowest-price pledge by finding low-price deals on the Internet. The devils, according to the company, can wreak havoc on the company, and they should be discarded.

A marketing professor from a local university suggested to Maria that companies should manage customers like they would products, as investments. If customers are the most important assets of the business, then it makes sense to manage customers and allocate firm resources to those who are the most profitable. That made sense to her. Articles Maria read suggested that only the right customer is always right. These customers are satisfied, they derive value from the company and its offerings, they provide referrals, and they make money for the company. Maria has many of these customers. They are happy, friendly, love Maria's Pizza, and bring their families often.

An article Maria read stated that the majority of a firm's income comes from 20% of customers: those are the ones that need the most attention. It is a waste of company resources to spend much time on customers who contribute least to the company's income. It is even better to fire them since resources can be diverted to more useful activities. A customer's demand for low prices and deals destroys profitability and may create extra work for staff. Such a customer can be a negative influence on other customers as well as employee morale. Clearly, for Maria, the problematic customers are seriously eroding her business' profitability.

Case Questions

1. You have learned, throughout your experience as a customer, that the customer is always right. Did you ever do something that would lead one to conclude that you, as a customer, were wrong? Explain.
2. What are some problematic, but ubiquitous, consumer behaviors faced by restaurants?
3. When is it appropriate for a business to terminate a relationship? Discuss the situation Maria's Pizza faces, and suggest to Maria how she should handle these problem customers, beyond taking them off her mailing list.

4. Should Maria think about her best customers, the top 20 percent, and do something for them to increase their loyalty? Why or why not? If yes, what would you suggest?

Source: Based on Syed Balkhi, "When to fire a customer," CustomerThink, December 11, 2019. https://customerthink.com/when-to-fire-a-customer.

Case: JetBlue's Success

Source: EQRoy/Shutterstock

While airlines were reeling from the COVID-19 pandemic impact on air travel, JetBlue announced it was adding 30 new domestic routes to serve customers in markets where leisure and visiting friends and relatives travel (VFR) appeared to show signs of strength. The new routes offered JetBlue the opportunity to generate revenue, bring back aircraft that would otherwise sit idle, add flying opportunities to crewmembers, and do what JetBlue does best: keep its customers satisfied.

Over the years, JetBlue has been able to compete with airline market leaders Delta, United, and American by focusing on the consumer—having a customer-centric mindset and creating an enjoyable travel experience, thus differentiating itself against competing airlines. They consistently show customers how much they mean to the company through helpful gestures, such as being especially attuned to individuals' specific needs, ultimately earning their trust. They are also proactive, trying to mitigate customers' frustration that comes with traveling. For example, they post on social media, encouraging customers to arrive early when it is an especially busy travel day. Or they help frustrated customers with a calm, empathetic tone. In their attempt to further improve its customer service, they partnered with Gladly, a customer service platform, to create a new customer service system that would enhance the airline's interactions with flyers. Through the program, JetBlue staff has access to customers' contact information, past and upcoming flights, as well as all communications that they had with JetBlue, so they can engage in more personal interactions with flyers and be proactive in creating an enjoyable flying experience.

JetBlue offers many perks that help create a comfortable and memorable flight, including Direct TV, free movies, Sirius XM radio, as well as many other entertainment choices. It offers a range of complimentary snacks so that all flyers can find something that they like, and free highspeed WiFi, as well as power outlets. These benefits, combined with comfortable seats and a light-hearted, fun image, create an enjoyable flight and sets JetBlue apart from competitors, who offer much less—including less comfort, unless you pay for it—and require payment for in-flight food.

JetBlue's prices are very reasonable, but the cheap flights do not jeopardize flyers' experiences, as is the case with many low-cost airlines. Through its exceptional revenue management system, JetBlue is able to offer cheap flights while maintaining a profit. Two-day fare sales are common, offering customers one-way tickets for $44 and roundtrip flights for $88. Even with low prices, customers can still earn TrueBlue points under the company's loyalty program, and have good seats, but with less flexibility, while competitors American Airlines, United, and Delta basic economy fares require customers to give up early boarding, overheard space, and free carry-on bags.

Sources: BusinessWire, "JetBlue Will Add 30 New Routes, Launch Mint® at Newark," June 18, 2020, https://www.businesswire.com/news/home/20200618005531/en/JetBlue-Add-30-New-Routes-Launch-Mint%C2%AE. Blackiston, M., October 19, 2019, "Why JetBlue is the Best Example of Customer Service," www.successagency.com/growth/2017/10/18/

jetblue-best-customer-service. Deals, 2019, www.jetblue.com/deals/#/. Kaplan, D., March 28, 2016, "Can Gamification Change Millennials' Behavior? https://geomarketing.com/can-gamification-change-millennials-behavior-jetblue-has-the-answer. Pascus, B. September 28, 2016, "JetBlue is launching a basic economy fare to help it compete with Delta, United, and American," https://www.businessinsider.com/jetblue-to-add-basic-economy-fare-like-delta-american-and-united-2018-9; The JetBlue Story: Customer Service in an Industry Americans Hate. (2019, January 11), https://sharpencx.com/blog/jetblue-customer-service. Zhang, B. June 2, 2018, "How JetBlue, Southwest, WOW and other airlines can sell insanely cheap tickets and stay in business," https://www.businessinsider.com/how-airlines-can-sell-cheap-tickets-stay-in-business-2018-5.

Case Questions

1. How does JetBlue offer customer value? Explain.
2. Define the core product and the augmented product as offered by JetBlue. For which of the two offerings is JetBlue competing favorably with the market leaders American, United, and Delta? Explain.
3. Think back to your most recent experience with a competing airline. Did that experience differ from a JetBlue experience? How?

Endnotes

1. Deloitte, CMO Survey, https://cmosurvey.org/results/february-2019; Consumer Expenditure Survey, U.S. Bureau of Labor Statistics, http://www.bls.go, accessed July 9, 2020; www.ama.org, accessed June 9, 2020.
2. Ibid.
3. Peter Drucker, "Marketing and Economic Development," *Journal of Marketing* 22, no. 1 (July 1957–April 1958): 252–259.
4. www.artesyn.com, accessed June 20, 2020.
5. Sapna Maheshwari and Vaness Friedman, The Death of the Department Store. *The New York Times,* May 7, 2020.
6. Haley Cowthone, "First Look: KFC Debuts New Flagship Restaurant in Louisville," *BizJournals*, June 19, 2019.
7. Asia Martin, "8 Ways to Make Your Money Greener," *Forbes*, October 6, 2019, https://www.forbes.com/sites/advisor/2019/10/06/8-ways-to-make-your-money-greener/#d3e2b531314e.
8. Robert A. Fullerton, "How Modern Is Modern Marketing?" *Journal of Marketing*, 52, no. 1 (January 1988): 108–126.
9. J. B. McKitterick, "What Is the Marketing Management Concept?" in *Frontiers of Marketing Thought and Action*, ed. F. Bass (Chicago: American Marketing Association, 1957): 71–82.
10. Term coined by Theodore Levitt, "Marketing Myopia," *Harvard Business Review* (July–August 1960): 45–56.
11. Edwin Stafford and Antje Graul, "Marketing Myopia to Our 2020 Vision, 13 February, 2020, https://www.liebertpub.com/doi/10.1089/sus.2020.29178.ers.
12. Ajay K. Kohli and Bernard J. Jaworski, "Market Orientation: The Construct, Research Propositions, and Managerial Implications" *Journal of Marketing* 54 (April 1990): 1–18; Dana-Nicoleta Lascu, Lalita Manrai, Ajay Manrai, and Ryszard Kleczek, "Interfunctional Dynamics and Firm Performance: A Comparison between Firms in Poland and the United States," *International Business Review* 15, no. 6 (2006): 641–659.
13. Jim Edwards, "The long, strange history of Lululemon: North America's weirdest clothing brand," *Business Insider,* September 4, 2015, www.businessinsider.com/history-of-lululemon-2015-9; Theresa Rivas, "Lululemon Stock Is Rising Because Yoga Wear Has Legs," May 29, 2020, https://www.barrons.com/articles/lululemon-stock-is-rising-because-yoga-wear-has-legs-51590765568?mod=article_inline.
14. Marylyn Collins, "Global Corporate Philanthropy: Marketing beyond the Call of Duty?" *European Journal of Marketing* 27, no. 2 (1993): 46–55.
15. www.theacsi.org, accessed May 10, 2020.
16. Kumar, V., & Reinartz, W. (2016), "Creating Enduring Customer Value," *Journal of Marketing, 80*(6), 36–68.

17. Kumar, V. (2018), A Theory of Customer Valuation: Concepts, Metrics, Strategy, and Implementation. *Journal of Marketing*, *82*(1), 1–19.
18. Sharapa, M. (2019), "5 Simple Ways to Calculate Customer Lifetime Value", Medium, accessed at https://medium.com/swlh/5-simple-ways-to-calculate-customer-lifetime-value-5f49b1a12723 on June 15, 2020.
19. Google Analytics (2020). Lifetime Value Report, accessed at https://analytics.google.com/analytics/web on June 15, 2020.

The Environment of Marketing in the 21st Century

CHAPTER 2

Source: Rawpixel.com/Shutterstock

Chapter Outline

Learning Objectives

Ivelin Radkov/Shutterstock

After studying this chapter, you should be able to:

- Provide an overview of the marketing microenvironment and all of its components.
- Provide an overview of the sociodemographic and cultural environment components of the macroenvironment and related trends.
- Address the economic and natural environment components of the macroenvironment and the topic of economic development.
- Examine changes in the technological environment component of the macroenvironment.
- Address the political environment component of the macroenvironment and discuss indicators of political risk and company approaches to political risk management.

Source: Jacob Lund/Shutterstock

2-1 Chapter Overview

Marketing managers need to constantly monitor the environment, evaluating strengths and weaknesses related to the company, consumers and publics, suppliers, and the competition, which make up the **microenvironment**. Section 2-2 addresses the microenvironment. Management must screen the **macroenvironment** in order to be able to rapidly react to the threats and take advantage of the opportunities in the sociodemographic and cultural environment, the economic and natural environment, the technological environment, and the political and legal environment. Section 2-3 addresses the different components of the macroenvironment.

Microenvironment Environment of the firm, which includes the company, its consumers, suppliers, distributors, and other facilitators of the marketing function and competition.

Macroenvironment Environment of the firm, which includes the sociodemographic and cultural environment, the economic and natural environment, the political environment, and the technological environment.

2-2 The Microenvironment

A major function of marketing is to develop a company's customer base. Potential customers must be identified, targeted with appropriate marketing strategies, and persuaded to purchase a company's goods. Although this task may appear simple, it becomes daunting when the company's microenvironment is considered. Strengths and weaknesses of internal company dynamics, current and potential customers, suppliers, and competing firms can influence how successfully the marketing function is performed. It is the marketing department's responsibility to manage the components of the microenvironment, addressing their weaknesses and focusing on their strengths in a manner congruent with firm marketing and organizational goals.

2-2a The Company

Within the company itself, the marketing manager or marketing department will be involved in three arenas: battling for limited resources, seeking a voice in company strategies, and developing a marketing mindset. To succeed, the marketing manager must successfully interact with the various departmental representatives in the company to ensure the marketing function is appropriately stressed and promoted.

First is the battle for limited resources, where every department is seeking resources to carry out its role—most departments, including marketing, feel they do not have enough resources to accomplish their tasks. On average, firms spend around 11 percent of sales on the marketing function. Figure 2-1 shows the type of marketing activities of firms: 86.9 of firms engage in in social media marketing, and 52.6 percent spend on mobile marketing tools.[1]

	Number	Percent	95% CI
Direct expenses of marketing activities	142	92.8 %	± 4.1 %
Social media marketing	133	86.9 %	± 5.4 %
Brand-related expenses	123	80.4 %	± 6.4 %
Marketing employees	121	79.1 %	± 6.5 %
Marketing analytics	111	72.5 %	± 7.2 %
Marketing research	107	69.9 %	± 7.4 %
Other overhead costs associated with marketing	100	65.4 %	± 7.6 %
Customer experience expenses	90	58.8 %	± 7.9 %
Mobile marketing tools	86	56.2 %	± 8.0 %
Marketing training	83	54.2 %	± 8.0 %
Sales support tools	62	40.5 %	± 7.9 %
Sales employees	21	13.7 %	± 5.5 %
Total	1179		
Number of Cases = 153			

FIGURE 2-1 Marketing Budget Expenditures
Source: Based on "Topline Results," February 2020, www.cmosurvey.org, accessed May 20, 2020.

The second internal factor is gaining a share of the voice in developing corporate strategies. Because marketing strategies are derived from corporate goals and objectives, it is important that the marketing department be involved in their development—even in the development of the mission statement. By having a voice at the corporate level, marketing managers can ensure that top executives understand the marketing function and its important role in developing plans for the corporation. A decision to expand into another region or country will involve understanding the market potential and the capability of the firm to gain sufficient market share in order to make the expansion profitable. Marketing will influence decisions about production and product modifications based on understanding customers' needs.

The third internal company force involves developing a marketing mindset. Creating a company culture emphasizing delivering superior value to consumers—that is, creating a market orientation—is essential. Firms where marketing plays a prominent role require that marketing information be broadly disseminated and that the marketing department has access to information from other functional areas in the company—information then used to deliver high value to customers, resulting in better performance and higher customer retention.[2]

Every employee in the organization must understand who the firm's customers are and what is being promised to them. Although product quality is important, so is the manner in which customers are handled. A bad experience with a company worker could send the customer to competitors as quickly as a defective product. It costs six times more to gain new customers, than to keep existing ones, so it is imperative for employees to understand the marketing goals of the organization.

2-2b Suppliers, Distributors, and Other Facilitators of Marketing

Although it is the purchasing department that primarily deals with suppliers, this relationship is important to the marketing department. If the raw materials' and supplies' costs increase, it will result in price increases for the company. The marketing department must assess the price increase necessary to cover the additional costs, the impact on customer and competition. The marketing department may even have to communicate the price increase to customers and provide justifications. Supply disruptions, such as those created by the COVID-19 pandemic, a labor strike, or natural disasters (e.g., drought or hurricane), can affect the marketing function.

Similarly, a delay in product delivery can lead consumers to look for alternatives. The COVID-19 outbreak in March 2020 resulted in a rapid slowdown of China's manufacturing, with factories either closed or unable to attain full production capacity. China is the world leader in renewable energy investment, has built massive Lithium-ion manufacturing plants. The slowdown created supply shortages and production delays all over the world; as a result, companies like Fiat Chrysler narrowly avoided a shutdown, and Daimler, General Motors, and Ford, with plants producing parts in and around the Hubei province, the COVID-19 epicenter, were similarly impacted. As a consequence, automobile makers are now seeking independence from Chinese battery manufacturers, looking elsewhere for suppliers of Lithium-ion batteries.[3]

Although the marketing area is primarily looking toward customers, it must keep an eye on suppliers, distributors, and other factors to ensure that customers will always have the product when and where they want it and at the price they are willing to pay.

Distributors Intermediaries whose task is to ensure the convenient, timely, and safe distribution of the product to consumers.

Distributors are intermediaries whose task is to ensure the convenient, timely, and safe product distribution to consumers. Manufacturers rely on distributors to deliver, advertise and promote their products, and, often, to offer financing to other distributors down the channel or to the consumer. Often, they use the services of physical distribution firms, such as warehousing firms, transportation firms, and other facilitators of the marketing function, such as banks, insurance companies, advertising firms, and market research firms.

2-2c Customers and Publics

Source: wavebreakmedia/Shutterstock

Customers are essential to the firm, they are existing or potential groups of individuals who can have an impact on firm operations. Not all customers are alike; there are individual differences among customers, there are different types of customer groups, each requiring a different marketing plan. Primary customer groups are consumers, manufacturers, governments, institutions, other businesses, and retailers.

Because of differences in these customer groups, companies have to be diligent in developing their marketing plan. They must make sure that their marketing plan meets customer needs and, if more than one group is targeted, that additional marketing plans are developed. To understand these differences, think about the marketing of office supplies, such as pens, notebooks, paper, folders, and staplers. For consumers, a firm would need to advertise the location of its stores and the attributes of its products. If these companies were selling the office supplies over the Internet, then the site would be designed to be attractive and easy to use for consumers. If the company were selling office supplies to a manufacturer or another business, then it would require a salesperson calling on the customer. Once a relationship has been established, the business can then purchase the products online or by telephone.

Selling office supplies to the federal, state, or local government would require the office supply company to submit a bid. To make the sale, it would have to outbid its competitors either on price or some other designated criterion. Most institutions, such as schools and hospitals, also use a bidding process.

The marketing method used to sell to retailers depends on whether the office supplies are for resale or would be used by the retailer's employees. If the office supplies are for resale by the retail store, then the office supply business would have to compete with other firms on the basis of price and marketing deals it would offer the retailer to stock its brand. If the office supplies are just being used by the retailer and not resold, as would be the case with a florist or bakery, then the office supply firm may use salespeople for large retailers but would use a website, catalog, or direct mail for the smaller firms.

Source: James R. Martin/Shutterstock

For the international market, all of these scenarios are repeated, but they become more complex because of potential language and cultural differences. For each country, the office supply business would have to identify the marketing strategies that would work best in the respective market. Whereas online or billboard advertising may work in one country, sending direct-mail pieces or offering coupons may not be an option there if the mail system is unreliable and couponing is illegal.

In addition to consumers, the company has several publics that it must consider in its planning, entities that could potentially impact its ability to do business. Among them are: local communities; the local or national government; local, national, and international media; citizen-action groups and the public in general; external stakeholders such as banks and insurance companies; and internal stakeholders, such as employees and management. For example, companies must consider the local community where they operate and ensure that they project a desirable image; many firms create foundations to support local schools, art venues, and local events. Firms should be able to respond effectively to challenges from environmental groups or consumer action groups, or from media scrutinizing their actions.

2-2d Competition

In developing a marketing strategy, a company must take into consideration its competitors. The task of marketing is to meet the needs and wants of consumers more effectively and efficiently than competitors. Marketers must ask the question, "What do we offer customers that the competition does not or what do we do better than the competition?" When selecting a brand, consumers have choices and will readily compare one brand to another. The brand chosen will be the one the consumer feels is superior in some way or offers the best value.

In evaluating competitive forces, it is important to understand there are several layers of competition. Consider the case of Burger King **(see Figure 2-2)**. Burger King's primary competitors are those fast-food operations that sell hamburgers, such as McDonald's, Wendy's, and Hardee's. At a second level are fast-food franchises, such as KFC, Taco Bell, and Subway. These businesses sell products other than hamburgers but are still fast-food outlets. At a third level are all of the dine-in restaurants. Although they are not shown, you could argue for other layers, such as grocery stores that have a café serving hot lunch or dinner food or convenience stores, such as 7-Eleven, which offer sandwiches and wraps to go.

Source: testing/Shutterstock

The key to understanding the impact of competition on marketing is to examine it from the consumer's point of view. As a consumer, you are hungry. For Burger King to be considered as an option, you would think about it in terms of

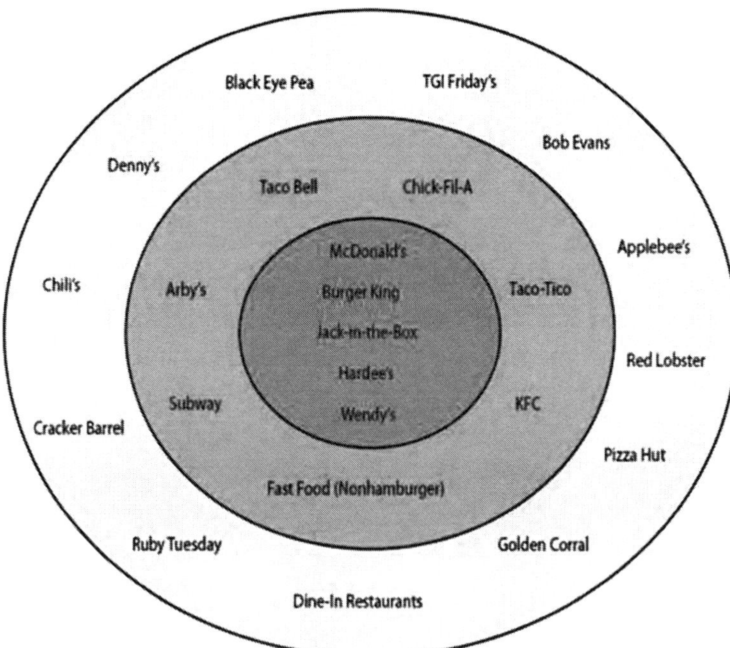

FIGURE 2-2 Burger King's Competitors

the competition. Do I want to eat at Burger King, McDonald's, Hardee's, or another fast-food outlet that sells hamburgers? Is there one close to me? If you decide you want chicken or Mexican food, then you may consider Burger King, but you would also consider all of the other options in the second layer. If you are not particular whether it is fast food or dine-in, then all of the options in layer three come into play. Consequently, in developing a marketing plan, Burger King would have to consider all of the options that you, as a consumer, would.

2-3 The Macroenvironment

The macroenvironment encompasses the elements of the broader environment that affect the firm. Marketing managers have no control over the macroenvironment, but must continuously monitor it to identify threats and opportunities that might impact the firm. The elements of the macroenvironment include the sociodemographic and cultural environment, the economic and natural environment, the technological environment, the political environment, and the legal environment. The legal environment is addressed at length in the next chapter, Marketing Ethics, Regulations, and Social Responsibility.

2-3a The Sociodemographic and Cultural Environment

The **sociodemographic and cultural environment** comprises many different elements, such as demographics, subcultures and cultures, and all other elements in the environment related to consumers' backgrounds, values, attitudes, interests, and behaviors. These variables constitute an

Sociodemographic and cultural environment A component of the macroenvironment that comprises elements such as demographics, subcultures, cultural values, and all other elements in the environment related to consumers' backgrounds, values, attitudes, interests, and behaviors.

Source: Iakov Filimonov/Shutterstock

important part of a marketing plan. Consider how many products are marketed based on the target consumer's gender, age, social class, or subculture. Even the same product may be marketed differently based on sociodemographic and cultural characteristics. For example, common products, such as deodorant, shampoo, and razors, are marketed differently to males than they are to females.

Demographics Statistics that describe the population, such as age, gender, education, occupation, and income.

Demographics are the statistics that describe the population, such as gender, age, ethnicity, education, and income. Demographic trends that will affect marketing include a slower population growth rate, an aging and more diverse population. Because individuals are waiting longer to get married and having smaller families than in the past, the U.S. population is not expected to grow as fast during the twenty-first century as it did during the twentieth century. The average age will increase, primarily a result of advances in medical knowledge. In addition, the diversity of the U.S. population will increase as a result of higher birth rates among minorities than among the Caucasian population. Immigration is also a factor in this increase in diversity, as the United States will continue to draw immigrants from around the world.

For many marketers, age is an important characteristic in examining the U.S. population. Spending habits, media preferences, and interests vary among the different age categories. **Figure 2-3** presents the main four U.S. generations and their respective dates of birth.

Generation Z Individuals born after 2001 that makes up approximately 25% of the U.S population, and are the most connected and sophisticated technological generation.

Generation Z **Generation Z** (also known as Generation Next) consists of individuals born between 1996 and 2015, and makes up approximately 25% of the U.S population. They are the most connected and sophisticated technological generation, and the most racially and ethnically diverse. They are brand influencers, social media drivers, and pop culture leaders. They were in line to inherit a strong economy with low unemployment; instead, COVID-19 has reshaped the social, political and economic landscape of the country, and they face an uncertain future—the oldest

U.S. Generation	Date of Birth	% of Population in 2020
Generation Z	1996 to 2015	25.3%
Generation Y	1981 to 1995	26.5%
Generation X	1965 to 1980	18%
Baby boomers	1946 to 1964	22.6%
Silent Generation	Prior to 1946	6.9%

FIGURE 2-3 Primary U.S. Generation Cohorts Based on Year of Birth (www.crmtrends.com)

entered into the job market during an economic meltdown not seen since the Great Depression.

Because Generation Z has grown up in the age of terrorism, climate change, and splintered homes, and their lives were upended by the Coronavirus, they tend to be realists and shun idealism. They have grown up on social media, but do not want to be tracked. Snapchat and other social media apps that allow communication, but not permanence, are attractive. They take multi-tasking to a new level and prefer to be on five screens at once, not just two.[4]

Generation Y Generation Y, also known as Millennials, Echo-Boomers, and Digital Natives, born between 1981 and 1995, have surpassed Baby Boomers as the largest living generation. They are also the most educated (23% have a college degree), and are racially and ethnically diverse. They are tech-savvy, value flexibility, speak their mind, and seek a work-life balance. As consumers, they are multitaskers, juggling e-mail while talking on cell phones, texting, and working online. They are also open to different cultures and international experiences. Their spending priorities revolve around appearance and fun.[5]

Generation X Born between 1965 and 1980, Generation X's focus is on the family and children. Food, housing, transportation, and personal services are the important categories for this market segment. Generation X-ers spend 78 percent more on personal services than the average consumer. They value convenience—time is at a premium as they strive to balance work and family—so they outsource daily tasks, such as house cleaning, lawn mowing, babysitting, and other domestic chores. They also value autonomy, flexibility, and a work-life balance, and expect clear goals and deliverables.[6]

Generation Y A segment of individuals born between 1978 and 2002; they spend substantial amounts on clothing, automobiles, and college education; they live in rental apartments or with parents.

Generation X A segment of individuals born between 1965 and 1977, whose focus is on family and children, striving to balance family with work, and outsourcing household chores and babysitting.

Baby boomers Born between 1946 and 1964, represent 22.6% of the population in the United States, but they account for almost half of the total spending, and the majority, 60 percent, own their own home; a considerable amount of their income is allocated to mortgage expenditures, home furnishings and renovation.

Baby Boomers Baby boomers, born between 1946 and 1964, are the second largest generation in United States (after Generation Y), but account for almost half of the total spending. Most are still in the labor force, more than any other preceding generation at that age. They spend primarily on the home and family—most own their home.[7]

Because most no longer have children at home, boomers spend considerably more on vacation and recreation, obtaining luxury items such as boats. Insurance and investments are also high-ticket items as they begin to think about their later years and retirement.[8] Some boomers' lifestyles resemble those of individuals 20 years younger: they refuse to acknowledge their senior status, refuse to

Source: IQoncept/Shutterstock

Source: goodluz/Shutterstock

Source: Nicholas Piccillo/Shutterstock

retire, perform daily exercise, and spend money on cosmetic surgery, clothing, and sports automobiles.[9]

In addition to the main generations, discussed above, there are two generations that represent about 7% of the population. One is the Silent Generation, seniors born before 1946 who uphold traditional values and have a strong work ethic. Their spending is primarily in the healthcare domain (medical supplies, medical services, among others), and on and household necessities, such as fresh produce. The second is the generation born after 2015, recently referred to as Generation Q (Quarantine), who came into the world just before the COVID-19 quarantine, and whose lives will likely be shaped by the pandemic and ensuing financial disruption, and the re-emergence of highly charged racial tensions.[10]

The United States is often described as a melting pot because of its multicultural composition. **Figure 2-4** shows the forecasted ethnic breakdown of the U.S. population in 2025. Already, over 40 percent of the population today non-white and this trend continues to grow. Nearly half of the population younger than age 25 is non-white. The United States is the third largest Spanish-speaking country

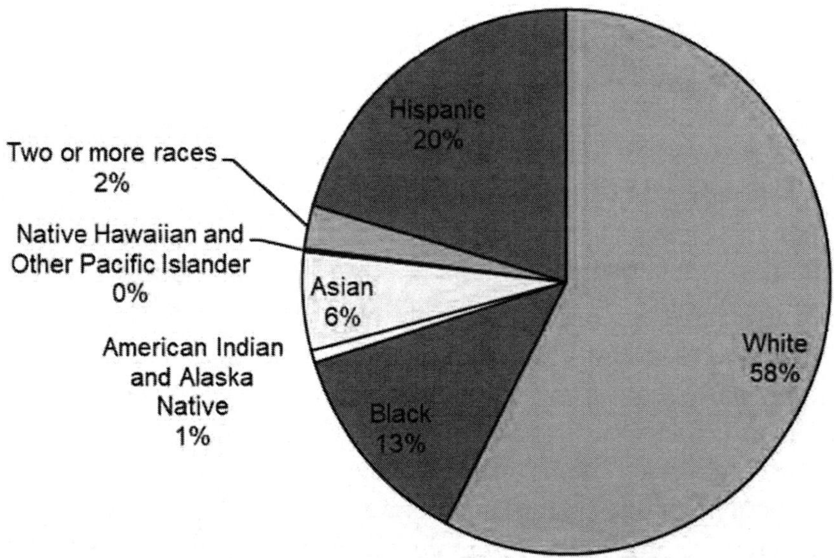

FIGURE 2-4 Ethnic Composition of the U.S. Population by 2025 (www.crmtrends.com)

Source: Kolett/Shutterstock

in the world. The Hispanic population in the last decade grew four times faster than the population as a whole.[11]

In the United States, the different subcultures are maintaining their old traditions but also building common traditions—a national culture. **Culture**, a society's personality, is a continuously evolving totality of learned and shared meanings, rituals, norms, and traditions among the members of an organization or society. The elements of culture are language, religion, cultural values, and norms. **Cultural values** are beliefs about a specific mode of conduct or desirable end state that guide the selection or evaluation of behavior. **Norms** are derived from values and are rules that dictate what is right or wrong, or acceptable and unacceptable.[12]

Cultures A society's personality and a continuously evolving totality of learned and shared meanings, rituals, norms, and traditions among the members of an organization or society. Elements include language, religion, cultural values, and norms.

Cultural values Beliefs about a specific mode of conduct or desirable end state that guide the selection or evaluation of behavior.

Norms Are derived from values and are rules that dictate what is right or wrong, acceptable or unacceptable.

Culture is continuously changing. Fierce individualism has been a dominant value in the United States. However, after the September 11, 2001, terrorist attacks and the Great Recession that followed, individuals turned to family and to nurturing relationships. The message resonating in the 1980s, "greed is good," sounds silly today. A focus on family has made a strong comeback in the past two decades. The COVID-19 pandemic and the ensuing financial crisis have also changed culture: older individuals in particular are cautious about attending or hosting events in closed spaces, or even going to malls to shop, large-scale events are less popular, and consumers are consuming less and saving more. The crisis moved retailing online rapidly and forcefully, with consumers seeking convenience, shopping from the comfort of their home.

Ethnic subcultures are shaping culture in the United States. Kimchi, dulce de leche, tacos, and sushi are part of the daily American fare. Salsa, hip-hop, and rap have wide appeal beyond the Hispanic-American and African-American subcultures. Telemundo and Univision have a large following among Spanish-language speakers, and Spanish-language radio stations are proliferating, serving a growing Hispanic population.

In Los Angeles, KBS America entertains with Korean dramas and shows targeting Korean-Americans.

Numerous niche cosmetics brands—Iman Cosmetics, Black Opal, Black Up, among others—and leading cosmetics brands—MAC and Lancôme, for instance—offer product lines specifically designed to address the needs of African-American women. Sensitized to the religious needs of consumers, companies cater to Jewish consumers with meat products labeled as Kosher, referring to the appropriate ritual slaughter of animals, or Pareve, meaning that it does not contain dairy, meat, or their derivatives, and to Muslim consumers with the Halal label, attesting to the appropriateness of the meat (no meat from hindquarters, no pork, and appropriate slaughter).

2-3b The Economic Environment

The economic environment encompasses all the factors in the environment that affect the use of resources, including natural resources, production of goods and services, and their allocation to individuals and organizations. The United States is an important participant in the world economy, but its dominant position is unstable. The world economy is especially affected by market blocs, such as the European Union (EU), and by developments in key emerging markets, like China. A pandemic resurgence in the U.S. sent Japan's Nikkei and the German DAX stock index tumbling as quickly as a trade impasse between China and the U.S. The 2020 recession abruptly put an end to the greatest economic expansion in history, decimated investments and retirement savings, and created an unemployment crisis, especially in the service industry—particularly in the leisure and hospitality industries and in the airline industry.

All companies are impacted by changes in the international economic environment, by the availability of raw materials in developing countries, by disruptions in important labor markets, and by the stability of international and local financial institutions. The local bakery and the mom-and-pop hardware store are affected by national and international economic cycles, by prices of raw materials from developing countries, by the local labor market, and by consumer income. Companies are also affected by developments in the international labor markets, and in consumer spending in the markets where they operate.

The economy affects consumer income and spending patterns. In periods of economic growth, consumers give in to their materialistic drive, purchasing products they may or may not need. In a slow economy, when companies reduce their workers' hours and the nation's payrolls shrink rapidly, consumers tend to be more cautious with expenditures. They deliberate over a purchase for weeks and then may decide against it. Retailers, who are already offering sales all year long, need to cut prices even further because customers do not respond to promotions unless they perceive that they are truly getting a great deal.

The income distribution across social class categories has important implications for marketing. Higher-income consumers are less likely to be affected by economic cycles. Their purchase patterns remain constant—they continue to spend on high-fashion clothing, gourmet food, cleaning services, exotic vacations, and country club memberships. Middle-class consumers are more vulnerable during economic downturns and could experience job loss or the threat of job loss. They are thus more likely to reduce consumption, limiting purchases to necessities. Lower-income consumers are hardest hit by an economic slowdown because part-time jobs or jobs requiring a lower skill level are likely to be cut.

2-3c The Natural Environment

The natural environment encompasses all the factors in the environment that affect the use of resources. Many resources are renewable or recyclable, such as timber. But some important natural resources, such as minerals, natural gas, and petroleum, are finite. Increased control over these limited resources by national governments has led to higher prices for oil and the need to evaluate alternative energy sources and technologies.

Other aspects of the natural environment have important repercussions on the economy and on the overall quality of life of consumers. Pollution in the form of greenhouse gases has led to global warming, accelerated biodiversity loss, and an overall change in the ecological equilibrium of oceans. Chemical spills and nuclear waste are compromising the water supply, and landfills are overflowing with packaging material, much of which is not biodegradable. Some of these environmental concerns are directly attributable to marketing efforts to create products that are convenient or attractive for consumers, such as excessive packaging, nonbiodegradable Styrofoam packaging, and disposable diapers. Marketing is also attempting to demarket (slow down or reduce) the use of environmentally harmful products. For example, fast-food companies

Source: Kat72/Shutterstock

have decided to limit the use of Styrofoam cups and containers, replacing them with paper bags and cardboard. Many products are now offered in environmentally friendly, recyclable packaging. In fact, many companies provide incentives for consumers who recycle their packages.

Topography, hydrology, climate, population, and environmental quality determine the status of a particular country as a viable trade partner. Topography is important because it determines access to the market and affects distribution decisions. For example, Holland has a flat terrain, allowing for efficient transportation. On the other hand, a mountainous terrain restricts access to markets. Lhasa is situated on the high-altitude Tibetan Plateau, in South-Western China. Access to Lhasa is restricted by surrounding high mountain ranges—driving from the city of Chengdu takes days. Traveling in the Andes is similarly challenging.

Hydrology determines access to local markets as well. Ocean access allows for the affordable shipping of goods to the local target market. Rivers and lakes offer access and potential for the development of agriculture and manufacturing. Hydroelectric power is essential for local development. In general, economic development is related to hydrology. In the Netherlands, the topography was altered to increase access by creating an effective network of human-made canals that cross the country in every direction allowing for easy access of goods to markets.

The protection of the environment has become an important concern, with increased pollution and global warming negatively affecting quality of life. Worldwide, there is a dire shortage of quality drinking water and a shortage of nonrenewable resources, particularly oil. Our food supply is also coming under scrutiny, more recently at the outset of the COVID-19 epidemic, when major meat processing plants were forced to close. Local and national governments have actively pursued several approaches for environmental protection. The U.S. Environmental Protection Agency has enacted and enforced regulations for environmental protection, ranging from improving the safety and reliability of the nation's drinking water, to enacting new rules regarding cleaner fuel from cars and fuel efficiency standards, to protecting critical streams and wetlands by ensuring that waters are protected under the Clean Water Act, to encouraging the development of alternative wind and solar energy.

Consumers themselves are demanding that firms control pollution, sell energy-efficient products, using minimal packaging that is recyclable. Allbirds appeals to consumers by providing shoes with the lowest possible carbon footprint. They replaced synthetics with natural and renewable materials, their logistics must follow stringent rules that keep emissions to a minimum, and for the rest of the energy used in manufacturing and distribution that they cannot mitigate, they purchase carbon offsets. Leading shoe manufacturers are adopting similar approaches, with Adidas partnering to offer shoes with yarn made from recycled ocean plastic and deep-sea fishing nets, while Reebok offers a sneaker made of 100% on top, a sole derived from corn, and insoles made from castor bean oil.

2-3d The Technological Environment

Technology is a primary driver of change in the environment. Our lives are changing dramatically and at a faster pace as a result of technology. Just in the past decade, the pharmaceutical industry has created numerous miracle drugs. For example, Trikafta has greatly improved the respiratory health of people with cystic fibrosis. Enzalutamide is the first effective hormone therapy for the treatment of advanced prostate cancer. Magnetic resonance imaging (MRI), laser, and endoscopic instruments have revolutionized diagnostics and treatment in medicine.

Technological change is taking place rapidly in all domains of human endeavor. Companies are under pressure to develop new and better products, with new technologies, to gain advantage over competitors, or simply to keep up. Billions of dollars are spent every year by corporations in research and development. The continued growth of research and development spending is largely attributed to industry's realization that structural and operational changes are not the only road to profitability. Continued investment in research and especially in development is required for long-term survival.

Research and development spending is also funded by the federal government and by universities and nonprofit research centers. The United States spends more on research and development than any other country in the world, more than $550 billion a year. Worldwide, the United States and China account for nearly half of the world's R&D total, with China spending over $500 billion yearly. However, more recently, a troubling trend has emerged. Corporate research and development spending is on

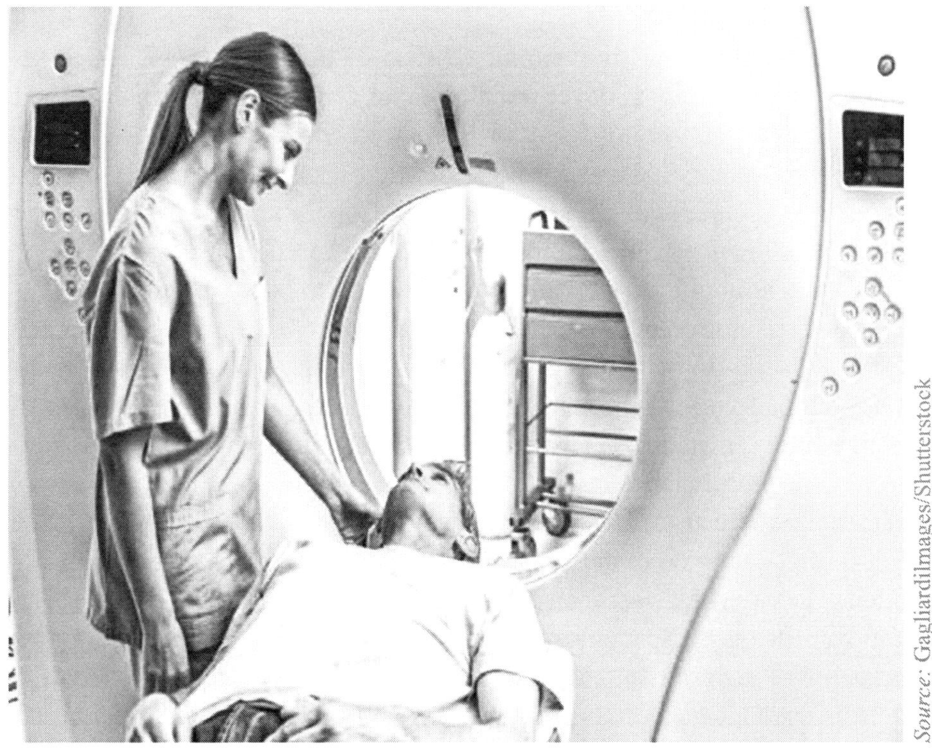

Source: GagliardiImages/Shutterstock

the decline. In particular, technology companies have cut back on R&D funding heavily. The National Science Foundation states that private sector funding for research and development has declined dramatically. Marketing experts cite global competition and the push for shareholder profits as a major culprit in this decline.[13] This general disengagement from R&D funding was most evident when the COVID-19 pandemic struck, in 2020, when scientists showed concern for the growing innovation deficit.

Technology is evolving rapidly, changing how consumers interact with each other, with their environment, and with products. The COVID-19 pandemic was a catalyst in redefining communication, determining how business is conducted and how people socialize, with meetings moved to the Zoom and other video conferencing platforms. Consumers are spending more time online, purchasing products for home delivery, banking, working. They also spend more time streaming movies, shows and other programming, rather than going to movies or watching television. They engage in social media to communicate with friends and family, with companies like Facebook creating different approaches to interaction, from Instagram to Messenger Rooms, which allow anyone with a Facebook account to create a video meeting and invite friends to join.

Global distribution is benefiting greatly from radio-frequency identification (RFID) technology, allowing companies to collect and manage data, to securely ship products. Technology helps consumers know where their shipment is at all times: with UPS, they can follow the delivery truck on a map and know precisely when it arrives closer to the destination so that they can prepare to receive it.

2-3e The Political and Legal Environment

Business must constantly scrutinize the political environment, which includes federal and local government policies as well as labor and political action groups that could have an impact on their operations. Multinational corporations have an even greater burden. They must evaluate political developments in the host country of operations and in the home country where the parent company is headquartered.

A poor economic performance and forecast are likely to lead to greater levels of risk for companies. Of particular concern are high inflationary rates and high unemployment rates, both of which could lead to higher taxes, regulatory restrictions, an increasingly active labor movement, and even political instability. The onset of COVID-19, followed by the 2020 recession, created substantial instability.[14] In this volatile background, anti-racial protests took over the country.

During downturns in the economy, federal, state, and local governments often resort to increasing taxes to provide a source of valuable revenue. The government may also reduce expenditures that facilitate industry performance. The government may spend less on improving the transportation infrastructure. It might reduce expenditures for the military or it might limit

Source: Halfpoint/Shutterstock

lucrative industry contracts on government-subsidized economic development projects.

Elections, especially those in which a change in the governing party occurs, usually signal a change in policies in general. The new policies may increase or decrease tax burdens or tighten or loosen industry regulations. In the United States, when a political party is elected that has a pro-business agenda, corporations quickly bring their wish lists to the new administration. Job creation, expansion, and product development are decisions often impacted by the attitude of the government towards businesses. Regulation and deregulation decisions have an impact on many businesses, especially in industries such as finance that tend to be regulated.

From labor unions to political action groups, many political forces, in addition to the government, can greatly affect a company's operations. In many countries, labor unions are very powerful and can readily influence national policies. In the United States, labor unions have lost some ground in recent years as a result a history of abuses and a strong economy that ensured solid bonuses for workers. Unions in the United States are organized under the umbrella of the American Federation of Labor-Congress of Industrial Organizations (AFL-CIO).

Consumer action groups can also affect company operations. Groups such as Public Citizen and other consumer groups are constantly monitoring companies to identify issues that may be of interest to consumers and those taking a stand. With the help of social media, action groups can present a veritable threat to business.

Companies have some control over the actions of labor and action groups. Although they cannot control market demand and derived demand for labor, companies can provide severance packages that are fair and seek placement for the employees who have been terminated. In addition,

Source: Diego G Diaz/Shutterstock

companies should be politically neutral and keep some distance from politics to avoid negative public sentiment. Being too closely associated with an administration or political party could result in a negative attitude toward the company and its products.

In fact, for many consumers, shopping has become a form of political activism, with consumers buying products from brands endorsing individuals they agree with, and refusing to buy brands that endorse those opposed. For example, the #grabyourwallet movement provides a list of companies with the goal of promoting equity and respect. The spreadsheet highlights why consumers should not purchase goods from a particular firm—the list covers brands whose CEO or representatives were donors or supporters of former President Trump.

Finally, corporations must protect themselves against corporate terrorism. Terrorist attacks against business interests culminated in the United States with the September 11, 2001, attack on the World Trade Center in New York City. Corporate terrorism has been on the rise in the past decades, with many U.S. interests being targeted worldwide. As a result, the cost of protecting corporations has increased greatly. Companies worldwide have reassessed their corporate preparedness programs to focus on protecting operations, finances, business strategy, brand reputation, and to maintain good corporate governance.

In addition to training employees in terrorism avoidance, companies can also purchase insurance against terrorist acts from private insurance companies. Cigna International's International Specialty Products & Services offers insurance products that cover kidnapping, detention (kidnapping without asking for ransom), hijacking, evacuation, business interruption and extra expenses, product recall expenses, and expenses arising from child abduction (e.g., hiring private investigators or posting rewards for information). The private and public sectors have learned to deal more effectively with terrorism, and a number of advances have mitigated terrorism risk: security controls, better political understanding, and a more efficient management of terrorism events when they take place. A company has several resources at its disposal to evaluate country risk. The Department of State, the Department of Commerce, and other governmental and nongovernmental agencies provide data on country political risk that are current and continually updated to reflect new developments in each country around the world.

All aspects of marketing are potentially under the scrutiny of the firm's legal environment. The next chapter, Chapter 3, Marketing Ethics, Regulations, and Social Responsibility, addresses the legal environment at length.

Summary

1. **Provide an overview of the marketing microenvironment and all of its components.**
   A major function of marketing is to develop a company's customer base. Potential customers must be identified, targeted with appropriate marketing strategies, and persuaded to purchase a company's goods or services. Although this task may appear to be rather simple, it becomes daunting when the company's microenvironment is considered. Strengths and weaknesses in internal company dynamics, current and potential customers and suppliers, and competing firms can influence how successfully the marketing function is performed. It is the responsibility of the marketing department to manage these various components of the microenvironment, addressing their weaknesses and focusing on their strengths in a manner that is congruent with the company's marketing and organizational goals.

2. **Provide an overview of the sociodemographic and cultural environment components of the macroenvironment and related trends.**
   The sociodemographic and cultural environment comprises elements, such as demographics, subcultures, and cultural values. Sociodemographic trends that will affect marketing in the future include a slower population growth rate, an aging population, and a more diverse population. Because individuals are waiting longer to get married and are having smaller families than in the past, the U.S. population is not expected to grow as fast during the twenty-first century as it did during the twentieth century. Although the growth is slower, the average age of the American population will increase. This is primarily a result of advances in medical knowledge. In addition, the diversity of the U.S. population will increase primarily as a result of higher birth rates among minorities than among the Caucasian population.

3. **Address the economic and natural environment components of the macroenvironment and the topic of economic development.**
   The economic environment encompasses all the factors in the environment that affect the use of resources, including the limited natural resources, the production of goods and services, and the allocation of goods and services to individual and organizational consumers. Marketing is an important driver of the economy. In turn, the economy has a profound impact on marketing decisions and on consumers, determining consumer income and

spending, borrowing decisions, and savings—which, in turn, affect the economy. There is a large degree of interdependence between the economies of the world.

4. **Examine changes in the technological environment component of the macroenvironment.**
   Technology is a major driver of change in the environment. Companies are under constant pressure to develop new and better products, with new technologies, to gain advantage over competitors, or simply to keep up. The continued growth of research and development spending is largely attributed to industry's realization that structural and operational changes are not the only road to profitability. The United States spends more on research and development than any other country in the world.

5. **Address the political environment component of the macroenvironment and discuss indicators of political risk and company approaches to political risk management.**
   Businesses must constantly scrutinize the political environment, which includes federal and local government policies and labor and political action groups that could have an impact on their operations. Companies can experience political risks attributed to economic performance, to government economic policy, to labor and action groups, and to corporate terrorism.

Key Terms

Baby boomers (37)
Cultures (39)
Cultural values (39)
Demographics (36)
Distributors (32)
Generation X (37)
Generation Y (37)
Generation Z (36)
Macroenvironment (30)
Microenvironment (30)
Norms (39)
Sociodemographic and cultural environment (35)

Discussion Questions

1. Comment on the following statement: "Strengths and weaknesses in internal company dynamics, current and potential customers, and suppliers and competing firms can influence how successfully the marketing function is performed."
2. Examine Figure 2-2, Burger King's competitors. Create a similar figure for your favorite brand of jeans. When you finish your figure, explain why you placed the various brands and products in the layers you did.
3. Compare Generation X with baby boomers. Can marketers target them similarly? Why or why not?
4. Which generation segment do you fit into? Explain your personal purchases and philosophies with what is contained in this chapter? In what ways do you fit the description? In what ways are you different? Be specific.
5. Pick two of the age groups discussed in this chapter. Compare and contrast their purchases of the following product categories and how it would impact the way brands would be marketed to each group.
   a. clothes
   b. vacation packages
   c. investment services
   d. house cleaning and lawn services
6. Pick one of products from this list. Discuss how a company would market to each of the age groups and ethnic groups mentioned Section 2-3.
   a. lawn service
   b. hiking boots
   c. Mexican restaurant
   d. condoms
   e. ski resort in Colorado
   f. mayoral political candidate

7. Economic interdependence exists today between countries of different levels of development. Assume that China and India experience a downturn in their economies. How could companies in the United States be affected by changes in the economies of these countries?
8. What are the factors driving up the costs of technology? Why is there a need for constant emphasis on research and development and technological change?
9. Describe indicators of political risk. Examine current events and identify some of the political risks that companies could encounter.
10. How can companies reduce political risk? Be specific, provide examples.

Review Questions

True or False

1. The political and legal environment is not a component of the macroenvironment.
2. To evaluate competitive forces, it is important to take into consideration several layers of competition.
3. Marketing managers do not typically have to consider limited company's resources.
4. Generation Y is a segment of consumers who spend heavily on clothing, automobiles, and college education.
5. Cultural norms are defined as beliefs about a specific mode of conduct or desirable end state that guide the selection or evaluation of behavior.
6. Since the United States became such a powerful leader in information technology, the fluctuations in the economy in the rest of the world barely affect its domestic market.
7. Middle-class consumers are less likely to be affected by downturns in the economy than high-class consumers.
8. Private industry is accountable for all the research and development spending in the United States.
9. Companies are usually not affected by terrorism acts, which are usually aimed at the public.
10. Companies have no control over the activities of labor and political action groups.

Multiple Choice

11. Which of the following categories relate to the microenvironment?
    a. strengths and weaknesses of the company
    b. consumers and suppliers
    c. wholesalers, facilitators of marketing functions, and competitors
    d. all of the above
12. The elements of sociodemographic and cultural environment are
    a. federal and local government.
    b. expenditures for different household items.
    c. labor and action groups.
    d. none of the above.
13. Which of the following consumer segments are more likely to have large proportions of disposable income and would tend to purchase luxurious items?
    a. generation Y
    b. baby boomers
    c. matures
    d. none of the above
14. Protecting natural resources is an important societal concern. The most appropriate action is
    a. demarketing the use of environmentally harmful products.
    b. outsourcing the production of harmful products to other countries.
    c. providing more power to environmental protection agencies.
    d. none of the above.

15. Which country spends the most on research and development?
    a. China
    b. United States
    c. Japan
    d. India
16. Which of the following is not a political risk that currently controls businesses?
    a. risk related to labor and political action groups
    b. risk related to competitive action
    c. risk related to terrorism
    d. risk related to government policies
17. During a period of poor economic performance, the government might reduce the expenditures that facilitate industry performance. What strategies are appropriate at this time?
    a. reducing the expenditures on the transportation infrastructure
    b. reducing the expenditures for the military
    c. limiting contracts on government-subsidized development projects
    d. all of the above
18. How could companies reduce the risk and/or costs of terrorism?
    a. by training their employees in terrorism avoidance
    b. by purchasing additional insurance against terrorism
    c. by considering the cultural, ethical, religious, and political issues of globalization
    d. all of the above

Answers: (1) False, (2) True, (3) False, (4) True, (5) False, (6) False, (7) True, (8) False, (9) False, (10) False, (11) d, (12) d, (13) b, (14) a, (15) b, (16) b, (17) d, (18) d

Case: House-Proud Consumers

Home remodeling is a $450 billion market, with remodeling spending generating 2.2 percent of national economic activity. Older generations spend most on upgrades, on average $7,524. Older generations are shelling out the most cash on upgrades. A report, which surveyed more than 1,000 homeowners across the U.S., found that boomers spent an average about $7,600 on remodeling, while Gen X-ers spent $6,600, and millennials just $5,700. Millennials are completing more projects than either Gen X-ers or boomers—because they cannot afford bigger homes, they are purchasing fixer-uppers they can upgrade instead.

Source: Breadmaker/Shutterstock

Improvements that improve comfort and quality of life are huge, with people adding a media or exercise room, outdoor fireplaces and cooking areas with granite countertops, steam showers, soaking tubs, Sub-Zero refrigerators, quiet Miele dishwashers, and generators to keep everything running doing power outages. Young couples prepare rooms for their soon-to-be-born children and then build an addition to accommodate their now larger family. Baby boomers reinvented the home as an expression of their tastes, comfort, and status and then sell it to buyers who tear it apart to renovate to their own tastes. Boomers then move to the Sunbelt and further renovate the houses they purchase to be able to age in place. They build elevators, or, eventually, they install electric chair lifts, widen doors and hallways, and, if feasible, they organize the entire living space on the ground floor. They upgrade lighting and install lever style door handles.

Renovation makes good sense. House prices have risen faster than the dollar-per-square-foot cost of renovating, which suggests that investing in your home is wise. The cost of buying a new home has escalated over the years, whereas the cost of remodeling has gone up minimally annually. Moreover, properties that are not properly maintained deteriorate. Kitchens and baths should be redone every 15 to 20 years to preserve the value of the house investment. Houses built in the 1960s had 1.5 baths, a small kitchen, and no family room, whereas today's new homes have three-four baths, great rooms, and huge master bedrooms with walk-in closets. The price of not keeping your home up to date is that it may eventually sell for significantly less than others of the same size, or it may linger on the market for months.

The house-proud constitute an attractive target market for home improvement stores, magazines, television programs, and contractors. These consumers rummage through expensive, glossy magazines for renovation and decoration inspiration—Kitchen and Bath, Elle Décor, Southern Living, Coastal Living, and This Old House. They spend hundreds of dollars on do-it-yourself books and videos, and call on friends and colleagues for contractor referrals. They tour appliance and furniture design showrooms and rummage through tiles in tile specialty shops. In the evening, they are glued to Home and Garden Television (HGTV) programs, such as This Old House, Weekend Warriors, Curb Appeal, and Before and After. These glossy magazines, books, and programs present a cornucopia of styles and choices—fanciful, practical, cutting-edge, and neotraditional. Direct-to-consumer retailers offer both mass-produced items as well as unique styles that can fit a wide range of incomes and social classes. The home design revolution is here to stay; despite the decline in renovations after the COVID-19 pandemic struck, more and more consumers working from home will spend to ensure they live and work comfortably.

Case Questions

1. Which demographic segments described in the text represent the best market for renovation businesses? Explain why.
2. What types of industries and businesses can take advantage of this trend for renovation? How should each industry or business market itself to this group?
3. What is the economic motivation behind renovation? How does consumer income influence this decision? How does the economic cycle influence it?

Sources: Andrea Riquier, "Home remodeling is a $450 billion market, and it's only going to get bigger, MarketWatch, March 15, 2019, https://www.marketwatch.com/story/home-remodeling-is-a-450-billion-market-and-its-only-going-to-get-bigger-2019-03-12; Emmie Martin, "How an overlooked part of owning a home can cost you and extra $6,000 or more a year," July 11, 2018, https://www.cnbc.com/2018/07/10/home-renovations-can-cost-homeowners-thousands-per-year.html.

Case: Huawei's Dilemma

Huawei Technologies Co., Ltd., is a Chinese technology giant, the world's largest provider of telecommunications equipment. It is also a manufacturer of consumer electronics, including laptops, tablets, wearable devices and smartphones—in 2020, Huawei surpassed Apple and Samsung to become the largest smartphone seller in the world. It has over 180,000 employees, with more than a third in China.

Worldwide, Huawei is under suspicion that the Chinese government could use its equipment to spy on other nations. The U.S. government blacklisted it, placing it on a list of foreign firms barred from receiving components from U.S. exporters without a license. Huawei was added in 2019 to the Entity List of the Bureau of Industry and Security, which imposes license requirements on companies doing business in the United States. The U.S. Government believes that Huawei has been involved in activities against U.S. national security, as well as against U.S. foreign policy interests. The U.S. also added 68 non-U.S. affiliates of Huawei in 26 different locations to the Entity List. Through the Entity List, the

Source: Ascannio/Shutterstock

Export Administration Regulations imposes constraints and limits license opportunities for exports, reexports, and transfers to the companies that are included in the restriction.

Huawei is believed to pose a threat to U.S. national security and foreign policy interests: it has been accused of violating the U.S. International Emergency Economic Powers Act, knowingly engaging in sales, directly and indirectly, of goods, technology and services from the United States to Iran and the government of Iran without obtaining a license. Huawei is also accused of stealing U.S. intellectual property, and thus it is considered a threat to national security. Huawei denies the accusation.

Being on the Entity List is considered a death penalty for businesses, because U.S. companies are no longer allowed to do business with Huawei. If Huawei and its affiliates want to purchase U.S. technology, they now need a U.S. government license. Since Huawei smartphones use Android technology and chips that are made by U.S. companies, its operations have been greatly compromised. For example, Google can no longer sell Android technology to the company unless it obtains a waiver from the Department of Commerce. Huawei has about 30 core suppliers in the U.S. from where it purchases parts that go into smartphone manufacturing as well as equipment for its telecommunications networks. networking. These companies include Qualcomm, Micron, Qorvo, and Skyworks, all of which are negatively impacted by these restrictions.

Case Questions

1. How is the political and legal environment affecting the market for telecommunications equipment in the United States? Explain.
2. Qualcomm is a competitor of Huawei. It is also a smartphone chip supplier to Huawei. How will Huawei's current situation, under U.S. government scrutiny, likely impact Qualcomm? Explain.
3. You have just bought a Huawei Y9 Prime smartphone on Amazon, for the low price of $230. Will the scrutiny that is currently affecting Huawei affect you? Why, or why not? Look up information online to find out if Huawei's situation will have any impact on Huawei smartphone users.

Sources: Kyle Almond, "A rare look inside Huawei, China's tech giant," CNN, 22 May, 2019, accessed at https://www.cnn.com/interactive/2019/05/business/huawei-cnnphotos/index.html, on July 4, 2020. Bureau of Industry and Security, May 16, 2019, "*Addition of Entities to Entity List*," https://www.bis.doc.gov/index.php/documents/regulations-docs/federal-register-notices/federal-register-2019/2393-addition-of-entities-to-entity-list-final-rule-rin-0694-ah86-on-public-display-at-federal-register-and-effective-5-16-19-1-2/file; Paletta, D., Nakashima, E., & Lynch, D. J. May 16, 2019, "Trump administration cracks down on giant Chinese tech firm, escalating clash with Beijing," *Washington Post*, https://www.washingtonpost.com/world/national-security/trump-signs-order-to-protect-us-networks-from-foreign-espionage-a-move-that-appears-to-target-china/2019/05/15/d982ec50-7727-11e9-bd25 c989555e7766_story.html?noredirect=on&utm_term=.6a85e930bff3; Reuters, January 24, 2019, "China's Fujian Jinhua to file complaint to be taken off U.S. export control list," *WSAU*, https://wsau.com/ news/articles/2019/jan/25/chinas-fujian-jinhua-to-file-complaint-to-be-taken-off-us-export-control-list.

Endnotes

1. "Topline Results," February 2020, www.cmosurvey.org, accessed May 20, 2020.
2. Dana-Nicoleta Lascu, Lalita Manrai, Ajay Manrai, and Ryszard Kleczek, "Interfunctional Dynamics and Firm Performance: A Comparison between Firms in Poland and the United States," *International Business Review* 15, no. 6 (2006): 641–659.
3. Power Technology, "Corona virus outbreak to impact China's battery storage production," March 20, 2020, https://www.power-technology.com/comment/battery-production-china-coronavirus.
4. Pew Research Center, "On the cusp of adulthood and facing an uncertain future: what we know about Gen Z so far, https://www.pewsocialtrends.org/essay/on-the-cusp-of-adulthood-and-facing-an-uncertain-future-what-we-know-about-gen-z-so-far; www.generationz.com/au, accessed August 8, 2017.
5. "All about Generation Y," Indeed.com, accessed at https://www.indeed.com/career-advice/finding-a-job/generation-y; "The Gen Y Budget," *American Demographics* 24, No. 7 (July/August 2002), S4.
6. "All about Generation X," Indeed.com, accessed at https://www.indeed.com/career-advice/finding-a-job/generation-x; "The Gen X Budget," *American Demographics* 24, No. 7 (July/August 2002), S5.
7. Richard Fry, "Baby Boomers are staying in the labor force at rates not seen in generations for people their age," Pew Research, July 24, 2019, https://www.pewresearch.org/fact-tank/2019/07/24/baby-boomers-us-labor-force; "The Younger Boomer Budget," *American Demographics* 24, no. 7 (July/August 2002), S6.8
8. "The Older Boomer Budget," *American Demographics* 24, no. 7 (July/August 2002), S7.
9. Elliot Gluskin, "Healthy, Adventurous 'Zoomers' Are Potential New Customers," *Bicycle Retailer & Industry News* 15, no. 10 (June 15, 2006): 38.
10. Paul Laudicina, "Generation 'Q': Casualty of the pandemic or vanguard of fundamental change? *Forbes*,June3,2020,https://www.forbes.com/sites/paullaudicina/2020/06/03/generation-q-casualty-of-the-pandemic-or-vanguard-of-fundamental-change/#29d879ac6e27
11. www.crmtrends.com/ConsumerDemographics.html, accessed May 20, 2020.
12. Milton J. Rokeach, The Nature of Human Values, New York: The Free Press, 1973.
13. Global R&D Funding Forecast, www.battelle.org/docs/tpp/2014_global_rd_funding_forecast.pdf.
14. World Economic Forum, *Global Risks*. Accessed on March 29, 2020.

Foundations of Marketing

PART 2

Source: Rawpixel.com/Shutterstock

Marketing Ethics, Regulations, and Social Responsibility

CHAPTER 3

Source: fizkes/Shutterstock

Chapter Outline

Learning Objectives

Ivelin Radkov/Shutterstock

After studying this chapter, you should be able to:

- Identify the ethical issues faced by marketers and discuss the pros and cons of each issue.
- Discuss the legislation and regulatory agencies that affect marketing.
- Describe the role of the Federal Trade Commission as it relates to marketing and discuss how it investigates complaints.
- Discuss the role of the Better Business Bureau in regulating marketing activities.
- Discuss the social responsibility of business firms and provide examples showing how a firm can demonstrate its social responsibility.

Source: Sergey Novikov/Shutterstock

3-1 Chapter Overview

A primary goal of marketing is to develop a customer base that will desire and purchase a firm's products. In this process, marketing materials are developed that will persuade consumers and other businesses to make a purchase. Ethical issues arise about the materials that are developed and about how they are transmitted and even to whom they are transmitted. For example, teenagers represent a huge market for processed food–and food advertising to teens almost exclusively promotes highly-processed food. Of teens aged 12 to 19, 21 percent are obese. According to the Center for Disease Control, obesity in adolescence likely leads to serious negative long-term physical and mental health outcomes, and increased risk of diabetes and heart disease. Marketing is seen as a culprit in encouraging the consumption of processed foods that leads to teen obesity. Ultra-processed foods are engineered to be deeply rewarding, and adolescents are vulnerable to addictive foods because their reward systems develop rapidly, culminating in adolescence, but the brain areas that provide brakes and restraints develop more slowly.[1]

This chapter discusses the ethical issues that arise when marketing material is developed to persuade consumers and businesses to purchase products. Section 3-2 presents both criticism of and a defense for marketing approaches. Because companies and organizations do act in unprofessional and even illegal ways, a number of laws have been passed to protect consumers and businesses. Section 3-3 addresses the legal environment of business, described in Chapter 2 as a component of the macroenvironment of the company. It is important to present the legal issues involved in marketing alongside ethics-related concerns and company self-regulation attempts. The section highlights the primary legislation that impacts marketing and the agencies that are responsible for regulating marketing activities. Of special importance to marketing is the Federal Trade Commission (FTC). This section closes with a discussion of industry regulatory agencies available through the Council of Better Business Bureaus (CBBB).

Section 3-4 presents the positive side of the ethical issue—social responsibility. Firms are expected to act in a socially responsible manner.

Ethics Philosophical principles that serve as operational guidelines for both individuals and organizations concerning what is right and wrong.

Morals Personal beliefs or standards used to guide an individual's actions.

3-2 Ethical Issues in Marketing

In understanding ethical issues in marketing, it is important to differentiate between ethics and morals. **Ethics** are philosophical principles that serve as operational guidelines for both individuals and organizations concerning what is right and wrong. **Morals** are personal beliefs or standards used to guide an individual's actions. Morals direct people as they make decisions about everything from personal conduct, to sexual behavior, to work activities, to family life, to interaction with other individuals. A person's feelings about companies can be based on his or her moral feelings. For example, numerous citizens believe the United States should not conduct business with countries that have a history of human rights violations or exploit child labor. Some will even boycott brands that operate in these countries.

Ethics help us as individuals and organizations to establish boundaries regarding acceptable and unacceptable conduct. Many leaders in organizations assert that they wish to be ethical in their decisions. Yet recent events with companies that have acted unethically have spurred the need for a higher level of ethical behavior within corporations. The public is now demanding that companies, their leaders, and their employees act in an ethical manner. How are your ethics? Before proceeding any further with this chapter, take "The Top Ten Test" on marketing ethics found in **Figure 3-1.**

Over the years, marketing has come under attack for questionable activities. Some of the major criticisms of marketing are listed in **Figure 3-2**. It is important to examine these criticisms in an introductory course in marketing. Although unfair and unethical behavior has occurred and will undoubtedly occur in the future, it is important to examine both sides of the issue and see how marketing can benefit society as a whole. If conducted in an ethical manner, marketing not only is a powerful force in the success of organizations but also can provide the opportunity for individuals to become more enlightened consumers of goods and services.

3-2a Marketing Causes People to Buy More Than They Can Afford

Marketing critics have voiced the concern that marketing persuades individuals to purchase goods and services that they do not need and cannot afford. Although it is true that millions of marketing dollars are spent to influence purchase decisions and sometimes people buy more than they should, the easy acquisition of credit and the overuse of credit cards make it possible to overbuy.

The average balance on a credit card is about $6,200, and most Americans have four credit cards. Moreover, credit card companies are offering customers more room to run into serious debt, by increasing the credit limit by 20% over the past decade, to $31,000. Middle-class families are burdened with a high cost of health care and education, so consumers rely on credit cards to cover emergency expenses and daily spending.[2] Post COVID-19 and the recession, credit card balances increased rapidly, as did the number of defaults.

Source: HAKINMHAN/Shutterstock

But should the entire blame lie with credit companies? No, not any more than it should be blamed on marketing. Overspending appears to be an epidemic, cultural change in our society caused by people seeking

Answer right or wrong to each of the following ethical situations. Be honest. Do not give the answer you think is right, but what you would do in that situation. No one will know your score, but you.

1. **Share the Glory**—You are writing the monthly status report to the board detailing the performance of your division. The talk in the corridor is about the incredible success resulting from an innovative strategic suggestion championed by a competitor in your division. Trouble is, you really dislike the guy. It is a personal thing. You deliberately fail to acknowledge his contribution and take all the glory yourself. Right or wrong?
2. **The Silent Kickback**—You are a consultant. A client, who trusts you implicitly, asks you to recommend a third-party vendor for a planned capital purchase. You provide a vendor recommendation but fail to mention that the vendor is going to commission you on the lead ... the classic 0-percent-off-the-top routine. Incidentally, the vendor in question does good work, and there is no fiddling with the pricing structure because of your referral fee. You choose not to say anything to your client about the arrangement. Right or wrong?
3. **He's Not in Right Now**—You do not use voice mail. Your assistant, who screens your calls, informs you that Mr. Unhappy, who has been trying to track you down for the past week, is on the line. You have time to take the call. Courtesy alone dictates that you take it, but you choose to blow it off with any one of the common excuses (i.e., he is in a meeting, he is on the phone talking to London). Right or wrong?
4. **Promises Not Kept**—You run a research firm and recently sold a proposed industry study to a group of clients based on the guarantee that you will be conducting interviews with 100 industry influentials. Because of timing and logistical difficulties, you complete only 75 of the interviews. However, you are still going to lose a ton of money on the deal. You priced the study too low to begin with, and it ended up absorbing more time than you had projected. Your clients, those who bought the study, have already prepaid and like the results even though you fell short of the guaranteed interview count. You choose to remain silent and not proportionally rebate your clients for the shortfall. Right or wrong?
5. **The Refund Not Refunded**—You are flying to meet a client in another city. At the last minute, you decide to extend the trip to visit a second client while you are on the road. The deal is that your clients always rebate you in full for travel expenses. You bill both clients for the full return airfare from your city to theirs, despite the fact that you were able to secure a multicity, discounted fare and in the process made money on the deal. Right or wrong?
6. **The Money-Back Guarantee**—Your sales literature clearly states that a dissatisfied customer is entitled to a full refund or credit irrespective of the reason or the cause. You do a job for a client, but because of contributory negligence on both sides and a lack of clear definition and cause of the problem, your client chooses to pay you and let the matter drop. You believe that you went above and beyond the call of duty in addressing the client's needs. But you still do not offer a refund. Right or wrong?
7. **The Plane Crash**—You are the marketing director of a major airline. One of your planes crashes because of airline negligence. You know that you have to expose the airline's insurance representatives to the next-of-kin as soon as possible to negotiate quick settlements. The longer the delay, the greater the risk that an attorney will get to them first and force protracted litigation in a class-action suit, which, in turn, will result in higher settlement costs. It does not feel right to force a confrontation with the next-of-kin at their moment of greatest vulnerability, but you do it anyway. Right or wrong?
8. **The Name Dropper**—You and I meet for the first time. During the meeting, you ask me to provide names of friends and associates, people who might be prospects for your product or service. You subsequently write them a letter, and in the opening paragraph, you mention that the referral came from me. The problem is, you did it without my permission. When I gave you the names, I neglected (and you deliberately failed) to mention the issue. Right or wrong?

(Continued)

FIGURE 3-1 The Top Ten Test of Right or Wrong

Source: From Alf Nucifora, "How Is Your Marketing Conscience?" Fort Worth Press, October 20, 2000. Reproduced with permission of the author. Alf Nucifora is a nationally syndicated marketing columnist and consultant. He can be contacted by phone at 415-332-1085 (Atlanta) or by e-mail at alf@nucifora.com. His website is www.nucifora.com.

9. **The Fake Request for Approval (RFP)**—You are the head of a young, aggressive advertising agency, and you would love to know how your competitors package and present themselves. Therefore, you fake an RFP for an imaginary account that is up for review, send it out, and specify that responses be mailed to a blind postal address. Your competition wastes precious time responding to a fictitious RFP, and you gain valuable insights into your competitors' psychology and marketing technique. Right or wrong?
10. **Fresh from the Faucet**—You are in the bottled water business. Unlike your competitors' products, your water does not come from a natural source. No gurgling springs for you. You take good old-fashioned town water, distill it, treat it, and package it with a fake, natural-sounding name, together with label artwork resplendent with waterfalls and bubbling brooks: A classic case of the reality not matching the perception. But it is great marketing. Right or wrong?

Results

If you answered "right" to 0–1 of the situations: Congratulations! You make good ethical decisions.

If you answered "right" to 2– 3 of the situations: Congratulations! You tend to make good ethical decisions, but at times you are not sure what is the correct course of action.

If you answered "right" to 4– 10 of the situations: Ethics is an important issue that you will want to study further. It is important not only to recognize ethical situations but also to make good ethical decisions.

FIGURE 3-1 **(Continued)**

Marketing causes people to buy more than they can afford.

Marketing overemphasizes materialism.

Marketing increases the prices of goods and services.

Marketing capitalizes on human weaknesses.

Marketing shapes inappropriate cultural values.

Marketing uses deceptive and misleading techniques.

Marketing violates consumer rights to privacy.

FIGURE 3-2 Ethical Issues in Marketing

immediate gratification. Few are willing to save and make a purchase only when they have the cash. This tendency to live beyond one's means, however, has been exacerbated by the opportunity offered by U.S. bankruptcy laws. Although many bankruptcies are caused by a major illness or loss of employment and are unavoidable, others are the result of overspending and inability to control personal gratification. This has resulted in an increase in personal bankruptcy filings in the United States.

3-2b Marketing Overemphasizes Materialism

Closely tied to the notion that people buy goods and services they cannot afford is the criticism that marketing has created a materialistic society. The debates center on one issue: Has the marketing of goods and services created an attitude of materialism, or has marketing merely responded to the materialistic desires of society?

Source: Monkey Business Images/Shutterstock

Underlying this argument is the assumption that materialism is wrong. In response, those who defend this aspect of free enterprise suggest that materialism, like many other things, is bad only if carried to an extreme. In comparing developing countries with the United States and other countries with high-consumption cultures, it is easy to show how materialism has created a positive impact on society and the standard of living people enjoy.

3-2c Marketing Increases the Prices of Goods and Services

Does marketing increase the prices of goods and services? Yes, it does. There is no doubt prices would be lower if marketing were eliminated. But before eliminating marketing expenditures, the following four factors must be considered:

- Marketing creates intangible benefits for a product.
- Marketing provides information that allows consumers to become better informed.
- A company can reduce its marketing efforts only if all the competitors within the industry do the same.
- Marketing is a significant contributor to the nation's gross domestic product (GDP).

Marketing can be used to create intangible benefits for goods and services. Consider the case of Nike shoes, Häagen-Dazs ice cream, Levi jeans, McDonald's restaurants, Tide detergent, American Express credit cards, and Southwest Airlines. Each of these brands conveys a meaning beyond the product category. Nike and Häagen-Dazs can command higher prices because of the brand name, which is the result of their marketing effort. McDonald's and Southwest Airlines enjoy a large market share in their respective industries because they have been able to position themselves in a highly competitive market as the low-cost provider. Tide and American Express are highly recognizable brands because of intensive advertising. Consumers purchase these brands and many others because of intangible benefits, such as the trust and quality that stands behind the name. Consumers know that every time they purchase Tide, it will perform.

Source: fizkes/Shutterstock

Through marketing, consumers have the opportunity to become better informed. Marketing can provide consumers with knowledge about specific brands and product categories. Until Rogaine advertisements appeared, consumers had no idea that there were products that could be used to prevent hair loss. Until Rogaine targeted some of its ads to females, consumers thought the product was only for men. Other forms of marketing communications such as point-of-purchase displays, product labels, and salespeople can provide valuable information to consumers to assist them in making wiser purchase decisions. For example, the advertisement for Family Care in Figure 3-3 provides information about its after-hours clinic for individuals who may be sick on the weekends or in the evenings.

Firms within highly competitive industries, such as soft drinks, automobiles, restaurants and athletic shoes, would like to reduce the size of their marketing budget. But if competitors do not reduce their marketing budget, it will be difficult for a firm to remain competitive with the firms in the industry. Figure 3-4 provides a list of the top eight restaurant chains by market share. Notice that advertising expenditures tend

FIGURE 3-3 Advertising Provides Important Information to Consumers
Source: Littlekidmoment/Shutterstock

Restaurant	Market Share	Ad Spend (millions)
McDonald's	7.0%	$687
Subway	2.0%	$347
Burger King	1.8%	$341
Taco Bell	1.8%	$422
Wendy's	1.7%	$258
Chick-fil-A	1.7%	$72
Domino's	1.1%	$363
Pizza Hut	1.0%	$204

FIGURE 3-4 Comparison of Market Share to Ad Spending for Top 8 Restaurants
Source: "Marketing Fact Pack, 2018 Edition," *Advertising Age*, December 17, 2018.

to be correlated with the market share. McDonald's has the highest market share, and also spends the most on advertising. Spending more does not necessarily mean that it will result in higher market share. Rather, to maintain a high market share, brands must continue to advertise and must advertise at a level commensurate with competitors. If Burger King chose to reduce its advertising expenditure, it is highly likely it would lose market share unless McDonald's, Wendy's, Subway, and Taco Bell also reduced their advertising dollars. If all of these brands agreed to reduce their advertising expenditures, then it is likely they would face collusion charges for restraint of free trade. We do not want competitors making agreements among themselves that will in any way hinder the free market system.

Figure 3-5 is a list of the top 10 mega-brands and how much each spends on advertising. It is interesting to note that in the top brands in terms of advertising spend, three are automobile brands and three are telecommunications companies.

Global advertising spend growth is at about 4% to 5%. Digital ad spend overtook television in 2017, with Google and Facebook accounting for about 85 percent of all digital ad spend—excluding China. Mobile internet ad spend accounts for 29% of all media expenditure. Television remains a dominant brand awareness channel, and, although its share has been slowly declining, it still accounts for over 30% of share.[3]

3-2d Marketing Capitalizes on Human Weaknesses

A sensitive ethical issue in marketing is the promotion of goods or services of a highly personal nature or during times of human vulnerability. For example, after the terrorist attacks of September, 2001, it was thought that some companies used patriotic themes to promote sales rather than

Brand	Ad Spend
Geico	$1,440
Verizon	$943
Ford	$894
Chevrolet	$817
T-Mobile	$777
Apple	$713
Samsung	$699
McDonald's	$687
AT&T	$632
Progressive	$622

FIGURE 3-5 Top Ten U.S. Mega-brands and Ad Spending
Source: "Marketing Fact Pack, 2018 Edition," *Advertising Age*, December 17, 2018.

to display genuine concern for the situation and victims of the attacks. Funeral homes and other similar services have been accused of taking advantage of grieving loved ones to encourage purchases beyond an individual's means.

Source: Cultura Motion/Shutterstock

In terms of personal services, marketers have been criticized for promoting the idea that happiness depends on physical attractiveness. Appearance is a critical issue, especially to females. To create an advertisement that feeds on insecurities about looks is considered by some to be unfair. Think about the various ads for weight loss programs. Most display both "before" and "after" pictures, with the person, usually a female, looking forlorn in the before photo, whereas the after shot depicts a much happier person.

In addition to weight loss programs, companies also offer consumers who are unhappy with their appearance services such as abdominoplasty (tummy tuck), electrolysis (hair removal), breast enhancements, and liposuction. All of these services are based on dissatisfaction with one's physical appearance. Critics say these efforts create unrealistic goals regarding personal appearance and cause people to examine self-worth in an unfair, shallow, and sexist manner.

Men have also been attracted by this desire to enhance their physical appearance as well as their desire to improve their sexual performance. Hair coloring products, hair transplants, face-lifts, penile enlargement programs, and erectile dysfunction treatments advertisements all feed on a person's insecurities. The issue here is similar to the first one that was raised about materialism. Is marketing driving human behavior or just responding to human desires? Is marketing responding to society's preoccupation with personal appearance, or is marketing taking advantage of a person's insecurities?

3-2e Marketing Shapes Inappropriate Cultural Values

In terms of marketing's influence on cultural values, several issues are at stake. For example, marketing has been attacked for promoting products that are not good for public consumption. Alcohol and tobacco, especially, are believed to have a negative impact on people and on society as a whole. This has led some activists to object to the advertising of these products. The first issue here is one of free speech and free enterprise. As long as the firms are not violating the law (e.g., selling to minors), then why should companies not have the same right to market their products as any other organization?

The second issue is more philosophical. Does the promotion of such products shape cultural values, and if so, then is it ethical to encourage individuals to consume a product (e.g., tobacco) that is known to be harmful to their health and results in millions of dollars of health care costs? If marketing, and especially advertising, indeed shapes cultural values, then it would appear that marketing should be regulated and controlled. The difficulty lies in the decision about who should determine what is appropriate and what is not appropriate. If, however, marketing just reflects the morals and values of our cultural environment, then regulating marketing would not be helpful in shaping cultural values.

To understand this dilemma better, consider the marketing of personal products, such as condoms, feminine hygiene items, male sex enhancement drugs, and underwear. In the 1960s, none of these products were advertised on television. Now all are advertised. Is this change a reflection of changing social and cultural values, or has the promotion of these

Source: NAS CREATIVES/Shutterstock

types of products molded social and cultural values to a point where this is now acceptable?

Many believe that advertisements are becoming more offensive, but outcry over companies' advertising is, in fact, becoming swifter and louder, amplified by social media; advertisers do think twice before injecting controversy that might affect the brand. A Peloton ad released for the holidays kicked off with a slim young mother discovering the $2,000+ stationary bike her husband bought for Christmas. She records herself riding the bike for a year, and then states that she did not realize how much the bike would change her. The campaign was met with instant ridicule; social media called the ad sexist and unrealistic. Gillette was met with backlash after it promoted the #MeToo movement by first depicting boys engaging in violent behavior and women harassed by men.

Over the years, sex and nudity have been the most troubling and controversial issues. Calvin Klein was heavily criticized for the level of nudity and sexual suggestiveness in its advertisements. The objections began years ago, when a 15-year-old Brooke Shields was featured in a Calvin Klein ad proclaiming "Nothing comes between me and my Calvins." People not only objected to Calvin Klein using a 15-year-old but also objected to the sexual innuendos of a 15-year-old not wearing underwear. The company pushed the envelope again with a series of television ads featuring underage girls asked about their bodies, magazine ads featuring partially clothed young models posing in sexy, suggestive ways, and a billboard showing boys and girls wearing only underwear.

Calvin Klein is not the only company using sex to sell its products. Sex is used overtly or subtly in many ads because it helps sell products. But in discussing the use of sex in marketing material, it must be kept in mind that what is offensive to one individual or group may not be to another. In a nation that proclaims freedom of speech and expression, sex in advertising is certainly controversial. Companies must carefully weigh whether they should use any marketing material that might be

Source: Gustavo Frazao/Shutterstock

controversial. Ultimately, it is the customers who decide if the advertisements are acceptable, and as long as controversy in ads increases sales, companies will likely continue to use it.

An especially controversial area of marketing is that of advertising to children. Advertisers spend more than $9 billion a year on marketing products to children ages 4 to 12. To attract children, advertising agencies and marketing managers are hiring child psychologists. They want to know what kids think and how best to reach them. Tweens, children between 9 and 13 years old, control an estimated $43 billion in spending power, and marketers that try to reach them will need to have a keen understanding of how these kids interact online. They are known as mobile mavens, who don't know a world without the social and mobile web. Their buying power is huge, at $1.2 trillion per year. Half of them have abandoned the Disney Channel and Nickelodeon in favor of streaming services, such as Disney+ and Netflix, making it increasingly difficult for marketers to reach them.[4]

Are children a fair target for marketers? Children have not reached maturity and do not have the reasoning power of adults. It is difficult for children to distinguish between fact and fiction. They are easily influenced and misled. They develop strong feelings toward brands at an early age and by the early teenage years, insist upon designer clothes and brand-name products. Although some would like to ban all advertising to children, others would like no restrictions at all, claiming First Amendment rights. Somewhere between these two extremes is the right answer.

3-2f Marketing Uses Deceptive and Misleading Techniques

For many consumers, the statement that "salespeople cannot be trusted" applies to more than just car salespeople. From the business-to-business perspective, many buyers feel that every salesperson will say and promise anything to make a sale. Often the relationship becomes adversarial, pitting buyers against sellers. Although it is true that some salespeople do use deceptive and misleading statements to sell, most do not. It is not in their best interests to do so. Salespeople rely on word-of-mouth communication from current customers to attract new business as well as repeat business from current customers. Dishonesty will be punished by customers who will make purchases elsewhere, tell others to avoid the business, and file complaints with agencies such as the BBB. The long-term benefits of being honest far outweigh the short-term benefits of high-pressure and deceptive sales tactics.

Source: pathdoc/Shutterstock

For the business-to-business sector, more serious ethical issues include gifts and bribery. To influence sales, purchasing agents and other decision makers within a company are often the recipients of gifts, meals, entertainment, and even free trips. From a personal ethics standpoint, many concerned leaders wonder if personal gifts should be accepted if they are designed to influence a business purchase decision.

Closely tied with the issue of receiving gifts is one that is even more complex and difficult. In many countries, bribery is an accepted practice. To obtain government permits and business contracts, it is a common practice to offer bribes. Without them, permits and business contracts are not granted or are difficult to obtain. In Germany, bribes were tax deductible until 1997—some forms of bribing were tolerated until 2002; versions of this practice persisted at Airbus, which recently used complex systems all over the world, hiding the payments as part of a pattern of worldwide corruption. Airbus eventually agreed to a record $4 billion settlement with France, Britain, and the United States in 2020.[5]

In the retail area, a marketing tactic occasionally used is **bait and switch**. When using bait and switch, retailers promote a special deal on a particular product, and then, when the consumer arrives at the store, they attempt to switch the consumer to a higher-priced item. Often, advertised specials are stripped-down versions of a product or the low end of a product line. Once consumers are in the store, salespeople will attempt to switch them to a better, more expensive model. This tactic becomes illegal under two conditions. The first is when the retailer does not stock enough of the sale item, with the intention of not having it in stock when the consumer arrives. The second is when the salespeople use undue pressure to influence the customer to switch. As one can see, the second would be harder to prove.

Bait and switch A marketing tactic in which a retailer promotes a special deal on a particular product and then, when consumers arrive at the store, the retailer attempts to switch them to a higher-priced item.

Deceptive or misleading advertising is even more difficult to judge. When does an advertisement become misleading or deceptive? A Botox ad promised that use of the product would reduce all wrinkles, although the Food and Drug Administration (FDA) had approved the product for use only between a person's eyebrows. Furthermore, the ad did not tell viewers that the result is temporary, and that, for lasting results, injections of Botox have to be taken every three to four months. Certainly, regulating authorities have concluded that this particular ad is deceptive and misleading.[6] Section 3-3 includes a more detailed explanation of the standards used in determining whether an advertisement is deceptive or misleading.

Another concern is ads that are legally not deceptive or misleading but are clearly biased. Consider the numerous ads for cologne and perfume. Many promote the idea that you will become instantly appealing to members of the opposite sex and that your dream mate will suddenly discover you. Most people would consider these events unlikely to occur, but the message is still there. Use the cologne or perfume and you will become more sexually attractive. How far can an advertiser go with themes like this before it becomes misleading? As you can see, that question is difficult to answer because everybody will have a different opinion about where that point is.

3-2g Marketing Violates Consumer Rights to Privacy

The more marketers understand about consumers, the more efficient they can become in developing marketing material that will influence their purchase behavior. Although age, gender, income, and education are important pieces of information, if marketers can learn about individuals' hobbies, interests, attitudes, and opinions, then it will be easier to design a message that will attract their attention. If marketers know where consumers shop and what they purchase, then the picture they have of those consumers becomes even clearer. To learn about what makes consumers act, the marketer must gather information. That is where the right-to-privacy issue comes into play. Consumers want to protect their personal information, but marketers need it to promote their goods and services.

Many firms and organizations collect consumer data and provide it (even sell it) to brokers, who sell it to businesses. Personal information (birth date, address, relatives, health and legal history) and preferences, affiliations, credit worthiness, and purchase behavior are available–at a cost. For example, a firm selling fishing equipment can purchase subscription lists from fishing magazines so that it can send direct mail to fishing enthusiasts. By targeting people who like fishing, the firm can reduce costs, and the material sent to the targeted individuals is more likely to be noticed and the probability of purchasing the fishing equipment increases.

The information-gathering source that has raised substantial controversy is the use of cookies. Through them, information can be gathered about what sites the user has visited, how long he or she was at each site, and any other activity he or she conducted online. This information becomes extremely valuable to marketers in understanding habits, interests, and purchases. Tied in with demographic data, this information is a gold mine for marketers. In discussing this controversy, it must be noted that marketers are interested in groups of people who fit a certain pattern, not individuals. It is not cost effective to market to every person with a different marketing message. However, it is cost effective to market to a group of consumers who have the same interests, habits, and purchase behavior. For example, the goal of the company that sells camping supplies is to obtain a database of people who would be inclined to purchase camping supplies. From this information, the company can better understand this group's thinking, interests, and attitudes, which can be used in preparing marketing communications material. Although it is important to protect the privacy of consumers, it is also important for consumers to understand how marketers are using the information.

3-2h Marketing's Role in Society

Although the criticisms of marketing have an element of truth, it is necessary to realize that marketing is an important ingredient of society and does perform a valuable role. Although marketing's primary function is to promote the purchase and consumption of goods and services, consumers

Source: Rawpixel.com/Shutterstock

have the opportunity to gather information that will allow them to make better decisions.

It is also important to remember that some marketing tactics may be legal but are still perceived by a large segment of society to be unethical or in bad taste. When one is making marketing decisions, it is important to keep in mind that individuals, groups, states, nations, and societies differ in their beliefs about what constitutes both ethical and unethical behavior, and about what should be considered legal or illegal. To help guide marketers in making ethical decisions, the American Marketing Association (AMA) adopted a statement of ethics, which is highlighted in **Figure 3-6**.

3-2i Individual Roles in Marketing Ethics

When thinking about individuals and ethical decisions that each person faces, one should consider the two extremes. At one extreme are marketing decisions that are viewed as unethical only by a few individuals because they do not have a serious impact on other people, firms, or society. At the other extreme are marketing decisions that are viewed as unethical by most people and do have a potentially lasting and serious impact on individuals, firms, or society.

Figure 3-7 provides a useful framework for examining how someone in marketing would make a decision that can carry some ethical ramifications. For purposes of illustration, suppose you are the marketing director of a video game company that wants to market a new video game to males ages 13 to 18. Although the game has some violence, the sexy attire of the female characters disturbs you. When you are preparing the marketing material for the game, your dilemma is how sexy to make the ads. More important, is using sex appeal even appropriate for this age group?

As illustrated in Figure 3-7, your decision is influenced by your personal background and experiences. If you grew up in a liberal environment

The American Marketing Association commits itself to promoting the highest standard of professional ethical norms and values for its members (practitioners, academics and students). Norms are established standards of conduct that are expected and maintained by society and/or professional organizations. Values represent the collective conception of what communities find desirable, important and morally proper. Values also serve as the criteria for evaluating our own personal actions and the actions of others. As marketers, we recognize that we not only serve our organizations but also act as stewards of society in creating, facilitating and executing the transactions that are part of the greater economy. In this role, marketers are expected to embrace the highest professional ethical norms and the ethical values implied by our responsibility toward multiple stakeholders.

Ethical Norms

As Marketers, we must:

1. Do no harm. This means consciously avoiding harmful actions or omissions by embodying high ethical standards and adhering to all applicable laws and regulations in the choices we make.
2. Foster trust in the marketing system. This means striving for good faith and fair dealing so as to contribute toward the efficacy of the exchange process as well as avoiding deception in product design, pricing, communication, and delivery of distribution.
3. Embrace ethical values. This means building relationships and enhancing consumer confidence in the integrity of marketing by affirming these core values: honesty, responsibility, fairness, respect, transparency and citizenship.

Ethical Values

Honesty–to be forthright in dealings with customers and stakeholders. To this end, we will:

- Strive to be truthful in all situations and at all times.
- Offer products of value that do what we claim in our communications.
- Stand behind our products if they fail to deliver their claimed benefits.
- Honor our explicit and implicit commitments and promises.

Responsibility–to accept the consequences of our marketing decisions and strategies. To this end, we will:

- Strive to serve the needs of customers.
- Avoid using coercion with all stakeholders.
- Acknowledge the social obligations to stakeholders that come with increased marketing and economic power.
- Recognize our special commitments to vulnerable market segments such as children, seniors, the economically impoverished, market illiterates and others who may be substantially disadvantaged.
- Consider environmental stewardship in our decision-making.

Fairness–to balance justly the needs of the buyer with the interests of the seller. To this end, we will:

- Represent products in a clear way in selling, advertising and other forms of communication; this includes the avoidance of false, misleading and deceptive promotion.
- Reject manipulations and sales tactics that harm customer trust.
- Refuse to engage in price fixing, predatory pricing, price gouging or "bait-and-switch" tactics.
- Avoid knowing participation in conflicts of interest.
- Seek to protect the private information of customers, employees and partners.

(Continued)

FIGURE 3-6 AMA's Statement of Ethics
Source: Reprinted by permission of American Marketing Association.

Respect–to acknowledge the basic human dignity of all stakeholders. To this end, we will:

- Value individual differences and avoid stereotyping customers or depicting demographic groups (e.g., gender, race, sexual orientation) in a negative or dehumanizing way.
- Listen to the needs of customers and make all reasonable efforts to monitor and improve their satisfaction on an ongoing basis.
- Make every effort to understand and respectfully treat buyers, suppliers, intermediaries and distributors from all cultures.
- Acknowledge the contributions of others, such as consultants, employees and coworkers, to marketing endeavors.
- Treat everyone, including our competitors, as we would wish to be treated.

Transparency–to create a spirit of openness in marketing operations. To this end, we will:

- Strive to communicate clearly with all constituencies.
- Accept constructive criticism from customers and other stakeholders.
- Explain and take appropriate action regarding significant product or service risks, component substitutions or other foreseeable eventualities that could affect customers or their perception of the purchase decision.
- Disclose list prices and terms of financing as well as available price deals and adjustments.

Citizenship–to fulfill the economic, legal, philanthropic and societal responsibilities that serve stakeholders. To this end, we will:

- Strive to protect the ecological environment in the execution of marketing campaigns.
- Give back to the community through volunteerism and charitable donations.
- Contribute to the overall betterment of marketing and its reputation.
- Urge supply chain members to ensure that trade is fair for all participants, including producers in developing countries.

FIGURE 3-6 (Continued)

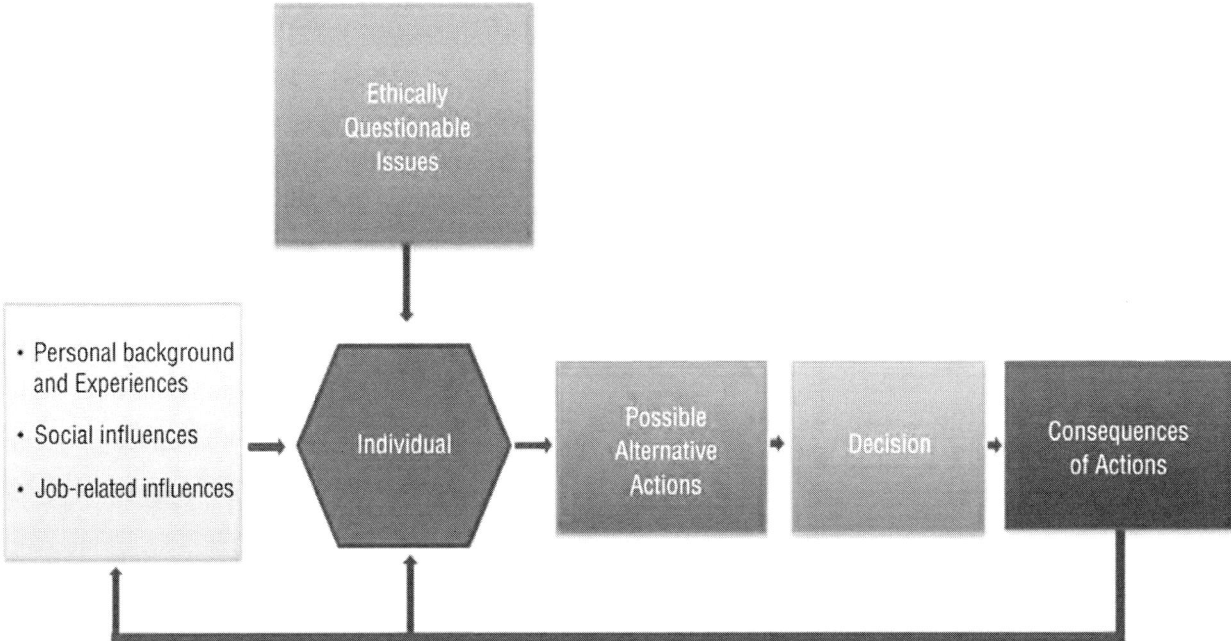

FIGURE 3-7 A Framework for Ethical and Unethical Decision Making

Source: fizkes/Shutterstock

where sexuality was discussed openly, you may not see an ethical dilemma at all. But if you grew up in a religious or conservative environment where sexuality was a taboo subject, you may feel sexuality is not an appropriate marketing appeal for young teenagers. If you were the parent of a teenage boy or a teenage girl, your feelings may be different than if you were 25 years old and have no children.

Although society and its views will have an influence on your decision, a more relevant influence will be the forces within your company. If you were just appointed the marketing director and your career will be influenced by the sales of this video game, your decision may be different than if you have been with the company for 20 years and have proven your ability to make good decisions. A major difficulty for employees in these situations is the attitude and beliefs of the company. If the chief executive officer (CEO) of this video game company feels it is not ethically wrong to use sex appeal for males between 13 and 18 years of age, then you will have less latitude to make an alternative decision.

In most ethical decisions, there are consequences to the decision. In this situation, your decision will affect the success of the video game. Although there is no guarantee that using sex appeal will increase sales, you suspect that teenage boys would be more inclined to pay attention to such an advertisement. However, if you take a stand and say no, will those in the company, especially your boss, respect your decision, or will you soon be looking for another job? Your decision and the consequences that occur as a result will then become part of your personal experience that will be used in future decisions.

3-3 Marketing Regulations

Because of the ethical issues discussed in the previous section, the federal and state governments of the United States have passed a number of laws to protect consumers from unethical corporate practices. These laws pertain to price fixing, free enterprise, food quality, fair interest

Legislation	Description
1890 Sherman Antitrust Act	Prohibits trusts, monopolies, and activities designed to restrict free trade.
1906 Federal Food and Drug Act	Created the Food and Drug Administration and prohibits the manufacture and sale of falsely labeled foods and drugs.
1914 Clayton Act	Prohibits price discrimination to different buyers, tying contracts that require buyers of one product to also purchase another item, and combining two or more competing firms by pooling ownership of stock.
1914 Federal Trade Commission Act	Created the Federal Trade Commission (FTC) to address antitrust matters and investigate unfair methods of competition.
1936 Robinson-Patman Act	Prohibits charging different prices to different buyers of the same merchandise and requires sellers that offer a service to one buyer to make the same service available to all buyers.
1938 Wheeler-Lea Amendment	Expanded the power of the FTC to investigate and prohibit false and misleading advertising and practices that could injure the public.
1946 Lanham Act	Established protection of trademarks.
1966 Fair Packaging and Labeling Act	Requires that manufacturers provide a label containing contents, who made the product, and how much of each item it contains.
1972 Consumer Product Safety Act	Established the Consumer Product Safety Commission (CPSC), which sets safety standards for products and ensures that manufacturers follow safety standard regulations.
1976 Hart-Scott-Rodino Act	Requires corporations wanting to merge to notify and seek approval of the government before any action is taken.
1990 Children's Television Act	Limits the number and times advertisements can be aired during children's programs.

FIGURE 3.8 Major Federal Legislation Affecting Marketing Activities

rates, product safety, deceptive advertising, and a variety of other issues. **Figure 3-8** lists the major federal legislation, along with a description of each.

Two overriding principles are behind the legislation mentioned in Figure 3-8. First is the objective of ensuring free trade and open competition among firms. Second is the need to protect consumers from unscrupulous actions of business firms. As businesses grew in size during the 1800s, the federal government realized that, if left unchecked, these businesses would create monopolies and eventually dominate the marketplace. With no competitors, the large businesses could dictate prices, distribution, and access to goods and services. Consumers would be forced to pay the price charged or do without, especially if no substitutes existed.

To prevent monopolies and trusts that could restrict trade, the Sherman Antitrust Act was passed in 1890. This was followed in 1914 by the passage of the Clayton Act and in 1936 by the Robinson-Patman Act. These last two acts were designed to prevent price discrimination by sellers. When businesses could no longer form monopolies or large trusts, they controlled buyers by using "tying contracts" and price discrimination. Charging small businesses more for the same merchandise and forcing them to buy an entire line of merchandise allowed the manufacturers to choose who would be allowed to purchase from them. The Clayton Act and Robinson-Patman Act prevented this type of behavior.

To protect consumers from unethical, deceptive, and misleading marketing tactics, the Federal Food and Drug Act, the Federal Trade Commission Act, the Wheeler-Lea Amendment, the Fair Packaging and Labeling Act, the Consumer Product Safety Act, and the Children's Television Act were passed. Although the focus of each piece of legislation was slightly different, the overarching principle of each was to ensure that consumers were treated fairly and protected from deceptive and misleading marketing practices.

Passing laws to prevent monopolies and to protect consumers did not ensure that businesses would comply. Using federal authorities, state authorities, and the court system became too burdensome. Therefore, a number of federal agencies were created to ensure that laws were upheld. **Figure 3-9** lists the primary federal agencies involved in regulating marketing activities and has a description of each agency's responsibilities. These various agencies were given the authority to set standards, investigate cases of wrong-doing, and punish those who did not comply. Although all are important, we will discuss only the FDA and the FTC because they are the most relevant to marketing.

3-3a Food and Drug Administration

The FDA has the responsibility of overseeing the sale of all food and drug products. Before a drug can be used by physicians or sold to the public,

Agency	Responsibility
Food and Drug Administration (FDA)	Regulates and oversees the manufacturing, distribution, and labeling of food and drugs.
Federal Communications Commission (FCC)	Regulates the television, radio, and telephone industries.
U.S. Postal Service (USPS)	Responsible for mail delivery and investigating mail fraud schemes and any other illegal marketing activities using the U.S. Postal Service.
Bureau of Alcohol, Tobacco, and Firearms (ATF)	Oversees the manufacture, sale, and distribution of tobacco and alcohol.
Federal Trade Commission (FTC)	Primary agency responsible for ensuring free trade among businesses and investigating false, deceptive, or misleading claims in advertising and other types of marketing communications.
Consumer Product Safety Commission (CPSC)	Sets safety standards for products used by consumers in or around their home.

FIGURE 3-9 Primary Federal Agencies Involved in Regulating Marketing Activities

the FDA must approve it. Strict tests and guidelines are used to ensure that there are no detrimental side effects. Occasionally, the FDA will allow doctors to use a drug under test conditions to measure its impact and side effects before it is released for public use.

For food products, the FDA is responsible for ensuring that food is safely processed and packaged. Because labels were often misleading, the Fair Packaging and Labeling Act was passed in 1966, requiring food products to have a label stating every ingredient in an order that corresponds to its relative content. Phrases such as "contains 220 calories per serving" have to be explained in terms of a serving size. Often, the typical serving size that an individual eats is not the same as that designated by a manufacturer. For example, low-fat granola stating it has 220 calories and three grams of fat per serving size must state on the label that a serving size is only two-thirds of a cup, not the two cups a typical person may eat at a meal.

Nutrition Facts

Serving Size 5 oz. (120g)
Servings Per Container 4

Amount Per Serving	
Calories	33
Calories from Fat	0
	% Daily Value*
Total Fat 0g	
Saturated Fat 0g	0%
Cholesterol 0mg	0%
Sodium 25mg	0%
Total Carbohydrate 16g	1%
Dietary Fiber 0g	5%
Sugars 1g	0%
Protein 2g	

Vitamin A 180% •	**Vitamin C** 15%
Calcium 5% •	**Iron** 2%

Percent Daily Values are based on a 2,000 calorie diet. Your daily values may be higher or lower depending on your calorie needs.

	Calories	2,000	2,500
Total Fat	Less Than	65g	80g
Sat Fat	Less Than	20g	25g
Cholesterol	Less Than	300mg	300mg
Sodium	Less Than	2,400 mg	2,400mg
Total Carbohydrate		300g	375g
Dietary Fiber		25g	30g

Source: Photo Melon/Shutterstock

3-3b Federal Trade Commission

The agency with the most impact on marketing is the Federal Trade Commission (FTC), ensuring free trade among businesses and investigating claims of false, deceptive, or misleading marketing communications. Such communications can stem from any type of marketing source, such as advertising, billboards, direct mail, corporate literature, oral and written communications by sales people, or social media. The Wheeler-Lea Amendment, passed in 1938, gave the FTC authority to investigate claims of false advertising and prohibit any marketing practice that might injure the public or be deceptive in any way.[7]

A firm can violate this law even when the company did not expressly intend to deceive or mislead consumers. According to the FTC, an advertisement or marketing communication is deemed to be deceptive or misleading when:

1. A substantial number of people, or the "typical person" is left with a false impression or misrepresentation that relates to the product; or
2. The misrepresentation induces people, or the typical person, to make a purchase.

A violation occurs if one or both conditions are met, and businesses and individuals can sue. For example, Nobetes advertising on Fecebook, YouTube, television, and radio featured a purported expert claiming that the drug controlled blood sugar. The claim was false and the expert was a paid actor, so a court banned Nobetes from selling or advertising the drug or any diabetes drug, and required Nobetes to provide a refund to consumers.[8]

Puffery When a firm makes an exaggerated claim about its goods or services, without making an overt attempt to deceive or mislead.

When investigating complaints, the FTC does not consider subjective or puffery claims to be a violation. **Puffery** involves exaggerated claims about a firm's offering, without making an overt attempt to mislead. Terms normally associated with puffery include words such as best, greatest, and finest. For example, in an advertisement, the FTC sees statements such as "most comfortable," the "easiest to use," and the "highest quality," as puffery and would take no action. However, when a company advertises that it is the "safety leader," then it becomes deceptive and misleading if indeed the company is not the safety leader. It must be able to back up this type of statement. Obviously, there is quite a bit of gray area when a claim about a false or misleading statement is made.

The FTC can receive a complaint from consumers, businesses, Congress, the media, even the FTC itself. Each entity can raise concerns about what appears to be an unfair or deceptive practice by a particular business, group of businesses, or even an industry. In the beginning, FTC investigations are often confidential, but they do not have to be. The initial confidential investigation protects both the FTC and the company being investigated if no violation has occurred. However, if the FTC believes a law has been violated or a marketing practice is viewed as deceptive or misleading, the first step in resolving the issue will be to issue a consent order. If the company agrees to the consent order, the firm agrees to stop the disputed practice but does not admit any guilt. Most investigations of the FTC end with a signed consent order.

An illustration of this process involves a California-based company, Nectar Brand LLC, which made the false statement in its promotional material that its mattresses were designed and assembled in the USA, when, in fact, they were imported from China, with no assembly in the United States. Under the FTC order, Nectar was prohibited from making unqualified U.S.-origin claims for its products, unless they could prove that this is the fact. As with all similar cases, when the Commission issues a consent order on a final basis, it carries the force of law with respect to future actions. Each violation of such an order may result in a civil penalty of up to $40,654. By signing the consent agreement, the firm agreed to stop the potentially "deceptive and misleading practices," while at the same time not admitting they were guilty of breaking any FTC regulations.[9]

If a consent agreement cannot be reached, the FTC may issue what is called an administrative complaint. A formal proceeding similar to a court trial is held before an administrative law judge. Both sides submit evidence and testimony to support their case. At the end of the administrative hearing, the judge makes a ruling. If the judge feels a violation has occurred, a cease-and-desist order is prepared. This order requires the company to immediately stop the disputed practice and refrain from any similar practices in the future. If the company is not satisfied with the decision of the administrative law judge, it can appeal the case to the full FTC commission.

The full commission holds a similar type of hearing in which evidence and testimony can be presented. The full commission can issue a cease-and-desist order if it believes the company is guilty or dismiss the case if it feels the administrative judge and previous rulings were incorrect. Companies not satisfied with the ruling of the full FTC commission can appeal the case to the U.S. Court of Appeals and even up to the U.S. Supreme Court. The danger in appealing to the Court of Appeals is that the court has the power to provide consumer redress, i.e., the power to levy civil penalties. Figure 3-10 summarizes the steps a complaint to the FTC can follow.

A complaint does not have to go to the Court of Appeals, however, for civil penalties to be assessed. A Georgia-based distributor of water filtration systems, iSpring Water Systems, LLC, made false claims that its water filtration systems were designed and crafted in the USA, when, in fact, they were wholly imported from China. This violation followed a previous similar violation. The distributor agreed to pay a $110,000 civil penalty to settle the FTC charges.[10] Rather than risk a greater penalty by appealing to the court system, firms like iSpring Water Systems, LLC will usually agree to consent orders.

In more severe instances of deceptive or misleading advertising, the FTC can order a firm to prepare corrective advertising. These situations

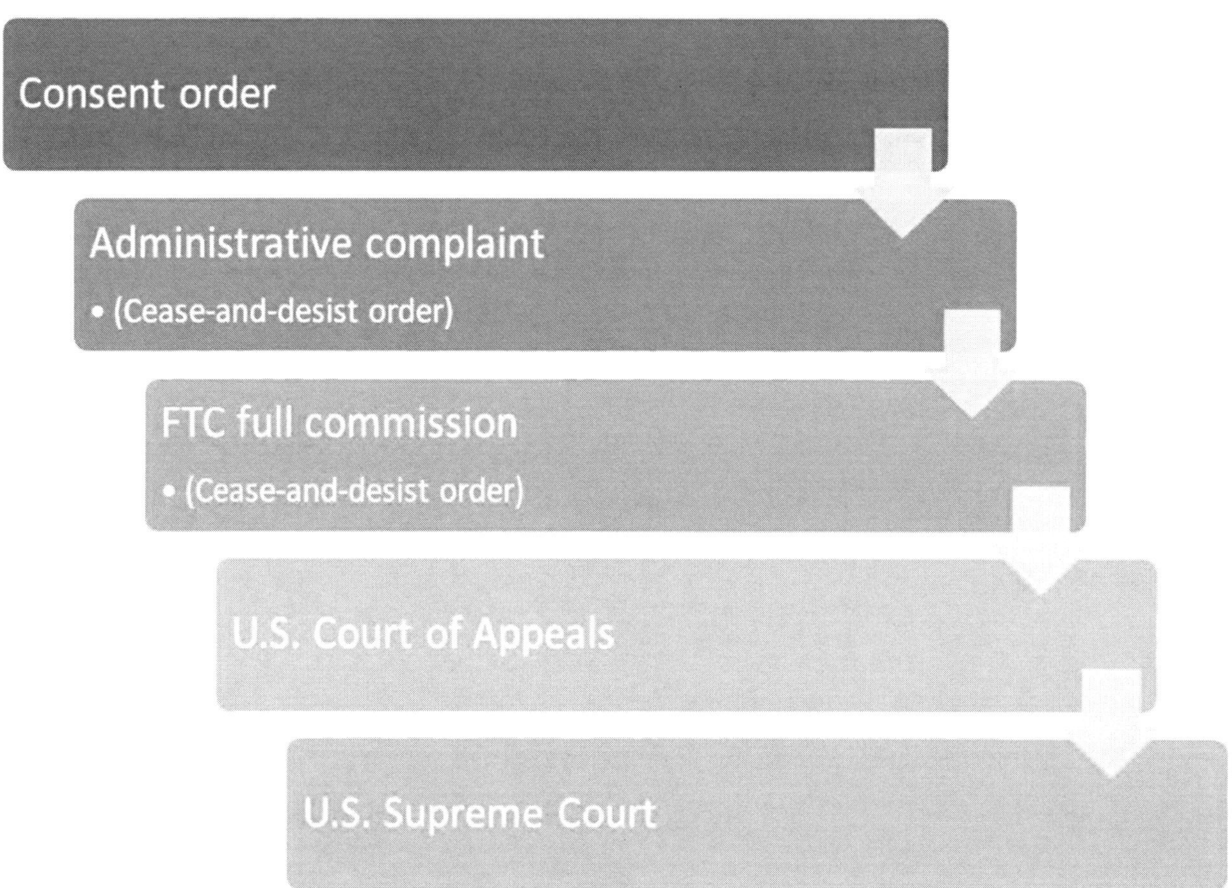

FIGURE 3-10 Steps in an FTC Complaint

are rare and occur only when the FTC believes that discontinuing a false advertisement will not be a sufficient remedy. In ordering corrective advertising, the FTC concludes that consumers believed the false or misleading information, and the goal of having the company issue corrective ads is to bring consumers back to a neutral state that existed before the misleading ads.

Corrective advertising orders are rare but were used by the FTC following a well-known judgment against Volvo Cars of North America. The company had created an advertisement showing a row of cars being destroyed by a monster truck as it ran over them. Only the Volvo was not smashed. After investigation, the FTC discovered that the Volvo automobile had been reinforced with steel bars to prevent it from being crushed. The FTC concluded that the ad would cause consumers to believe that Volvo was a safer automobile than it actually was. Consequently, the FTC not only ordered Volvo to discontinue the ad but also to run a new advertisement explaining how the car had been altered in the previous commercial. The FTC seldom orders corrective ads because in most cases, it is extremely difficult to eliminate the impact of a misleading ad and take consumers back to a neutral point.[11]

The FTC rules cover every aspect of marketing communications. Regardless of the type of communication, unfair or deceptive marketing communications are prohibited. Marketers must be able to substantiate claims through competent and reliable evidence. If a firm makes a claim about its product, it must be able to substantiate that claim. If a firm says, "Brand X reduces the symptoms of the common cold," it must be able to prove that Brand X does indeed reduce the symptoms of the common cold. In this case, an independent study would be the best substantiation. If the company performs the study itself, it must be careful to follow good scientific procedures. The FTC examines company-sponsored research more closely than research by an independent firm.

Because celebrities and experts are frequently used in advertisements to endorse a product, the FTC issued guidelines concerning the use of

Source: Zoriana Zaitseva

endorsements and testimonials. To not be deceptive, the following criteria must be met:

1. Statements must reflect the honest opinion, findings, beliefs, or experience of the celebrity or expert.
2. The accuracy of the endorser's claims must be substantiated by the advertiser.
3. If the advertisement claims the celebrity or expert uses the product, the person must in fact be a bona fide user of it.
4. The advertiser can use the endorsement only as long as it has good faith belief that the celebrity or expert will continue to hold the views expressed in the advertisement.[12]

3-3c Industry Regulations

Because of the volume of complaints, the federal regulatory agencies would have a difficult time investigating them all if it were not for the industry regulatory system. Although the various industry regulatory agencies have no legal power, they can reduce the load on the FTC and the legal system. Many allegations or complaints about unfair and deceptive marketing practices are handled and settled within the advertising and business industry. Although various industry agencies exist for monitoring marketing activities, the most common is the Better Business Bureaus and its three subsidiary agencies: (1) the National Advertising Division (NAD), (2) the Children's Advertising Review Unit (CARU), and (3) the National Advertising Review Board (NARB).

The Better Business Bureau (BBB) is a venue available to both consumers and businesses. Unethical business practices or unfair treatment can lead to the filing of complaints against a business with the BBB. The Bureau will compile a summary of charges leveled against individual firms. Although the charges are not investigated, they are kept on record for potential customers who want to learn about a particular business. When asked by an individual or business, the BBB will provide a carefully worded report that will raise cautionary flags about a firm that has received a great number of complaints and state the general nature of the complaints.

In 1971, the National Advertising Review Council (NARC) was formed by the Association of National Advertisers, the American Association of Advertising Agencies, the American Advertising Federation, and the BBB. The purpose of NARC is to foster truth, honesty, and accuracy in advertising through industry self-regulation. NARC also establishes policies and procedures for the NAD, the CARU, and the NARB. Figure 3-11 lists these industry agencies.

When complaints about advertising are received, the BBB refers them to either the NAD or the CARU. The agency concerned will collect information and evaluate data concerning the complaint to determine whether the complaint is legitimate. In most cases, the NAD and the CARU are looking for evidence of substantiation. If the firm's advertising claim is

FIGURE 3-11 Advertising and Business Industry Regulation Agencies

substantiated, then the complaint is dismissed. If it is not, the NAD and the CARU will negotiate with the business to modify or discontinue the advertisement. If the advertiser disagrees with the decision, then it can be appealed to the NARB. From there, the appeal would go to the FTC or other appropriate federal agency.

Complaints are often filed by a competitor because of unfavorable depictions of their brand versus the advertised brand. Such was the case when Procter & Gamble filed a complaint with the NAD concerning Unilever's ad for Degree Ultra's Clear Antiperspirant, which claimed:

> "Unless they're using New Degree Ultra-Clear, those white marks may just show up later."

> "Others go on clear. New Degree-Ultra Clear stays that way." "100% Little Black Dress Approved."

After viewing demonstrations of Unilever's brand (New Degree Ultra-Clear) and Procter & Gamble's brand (Secret Platinum Invisible Solid), the NAD stated that both brands left perceptible white residue, although the Procter & Gamble brand did leave substantially more than the Unilever brand. The NAD ruled, however, that leaving "substantially less residue" is significantly different than stating it "leaves no residue." Therefore, the NAD recommended that Unilever discontinue all television, website, and print advertising making such claims. Although Unilever disagreed with the NAD decision, they stated that it "fully supports the self-regulation program and will take NAD's opinion into consideration in future advertising."[13]

Not all of the NAD rulings are against the advertiser. The NAD determined that GlaxoSmithKline Consumer Healthcare provided a reasonable basis for its claim, appearing on the product package, that its Benefiber Healthy Balance relieves occasional constipation without causing diarrhea. The claim was challenged by Procter & Gamble, maker of the competing dietary supplement, Metamucil.[14]

In some cases, the advertiser is dissatisfied with the ruling of the NAD and appeals the decision to the NARB. Such was the case with NAD's recommendation that Bayer discontinue the claim that no other product works faster than Claritin-D, an allergy medicine. Bayer decided to appeal NAD's recommendation to the National Advertising Review Board.[15]

Most cases investigated by the NAD, the CARU, and the NARB are resolved. Occasionally, an advertiser refuses to participate in the self-regulation process or ignores the ruling. For example, the NAD investigated claims made by Spitz Sunflower Seeds that its brand was the "#1 sun-flower seed" and contained "all-natural ingredients." ConAgra filed the complaint because they believed their brand was the number one brand and they also believed the Spitz Sunflower brand did not use "all-natural ingredients." When Spitz Sales, Inc., refused to participate in NAD's investigation and provide substantiation for their claims, the case was referred to the FTC and the FDA for review. As noted previously, the FTC and FDA do have legal authority and can require Spitz Sales, Inc., to participate in the investigation. Spitz Sales also faced the risk of being forced to pay civil penalties. Because of this risk and the additional cost required to defend their case before the FTC or FDA, most companies willingly participate in the advertising industry's self-regulation system.[16]

3-4 Social Responsibility

Consumers today expect companies to act responsibly and to be good citizens. This can be done by producing environmentally safe products, by controlling for emissions and wastes that contaminate the environment, or by becoming involved in meeting the social needs of society. In the past, most corporations fulfilled the requirement of meeting the needs of society through philanthropy. Today's consumers have greater expectations–millennials more so than anyone else. Nielsen found that, globally, 66 percent of consumers are willing to spend more on a product if it comes from a sustainable brand; however, Millennials are even more dedicated to sustainable practices: 73 percent will spend more for sustainable brands, and 81 percent expect their favorite companies to make public declarations of their corporate citizenship. More than one in ten would switch brands to one associated with a cause. They want companies to be actively invested in the betterment of society; prioritize making an impact on the world around them; be honest about their efforts and about communicating them to the public; and they want companies to involve them in their good works, so that they can give back–time or money.[17]

Writing a check to a charity is merely philanthropy, and consumers no longer perceive it as sufficient. Companies are rethinking their approach to their societal engagement, and many have opted for cause-related marketing.

Cause-related marketing is a long-term partnership between a nonprofit organization and a corporation and is integrated into the corporation's marketing plan. Both parties must benefit from the relationship for it to be an effective cause-related marketing effort.

Cause-related marketing A long-term partnership between a nonprofit organization and a corporation that is integrated into the corporation's marketing plan.

To be successful with a cause-related program, the firm must demonstrate a genuine support for a cause. If it does not and if customers suspect

Source: Sk Elena/Shutterstock

Source: Prostock-studio/Shutterstock

a firm is using the nonprofit cause to benefit itself, it will backfire. To ensure that a cause-related program will work, a firm first must align itself with a cause that fits its mission and its products. Avon's support for breast cancer causes is a logical fit: it funded breast cancer education, breast screenings for millions of women, and spent considerable resources to raise breast cancer awareness.

How companies promote their cause is extremely important. If they spend millions to advertise their donation, consumers will see it as exploitation. If they mention it in their advertising, on point-of-purchase displays, and in their facility but do not overly emphasize it, consumers will accept it. Consumers are looking for a genuine relationship between the nonprofit organization and the company, not a gimmick by the corporation to boost its sales. One method of demonstrating this genuineness is getting employees involved. If employees do not support and believe in the cause, the public will be suspicious of the motives.

Summary

1. **Identify the ethical issues faced by marketers and discuss the pros and cons of each issue.**
   A number of ethical issues have been raised concerning marketing. First, marketing causes people to buy more than they can afford. Although some would feel this overspending is the result of marketing, others would claim marketing is just responding to what consumers want. Second, marketing overemphasizes materialism. Again, although some would argue that marketing creates materialism, others would say marketing is merely responding to materialistic desires. Third, marketing increases the prices of goods and services. Although this is true, marketing also provides information so consumers can make intelligent consumption decisions. Fourth is the criticism that marketing capitalizes on human weaknesses. Marketers would argue that they are just responding to personal needs. Fifth, critics would suggest that marketing shapes and encourages inappropriate cultural values. Marketers would contend that marketing responds to current cultural values and would not be effective in

promoting desires that do not conform to cultural values. Sixth, marketing uses deceptive and misleading advertising. Although some marketers do use deceptive and misleading advertising, agencies such as the FTC have been created to protect consumers. Lastly, critics contend that marketing violates consumers' right to privacy. Although marketers do gather personal information, it is used to better market to people's needs.

2. **Discuss the legislation and regulatory agencies that affect marketing.**
   A number of laws have been passed to protect consumers and to ensure free trade among businesses. Antitrust legislation includes the Sherman Antitrust Act, Clayton Act, Robinson-Patman Act, and the Hart-Scott-Rodino Act. Legislation to protect consumers includes the Federal Food and Drug Act, the Federal Trade Commission Act, the Wheeler-Lea Amendment, the Fair Packaging and Labeling Act, the Consumer Product Safety Act, and the Children's Television Act. These laws were passed to prevent misleading and deceptive marketing practices and ensure honest labeling of foods, drugs, and safe products for consumer use. From these acts, a number of agencies were established, including the FDA, FCC, USPS, ATF, FTC, and CPSC. Each of these agencies is responsible for regulating business and investigating activities of wrongdoing.

3. **Describe the role of the Federal Trade Commission as it relates to marketing and discuss how it investigates complaints.**
   The role of the FTC is to investigate activities that restrict free trade and claims of misleading or deceptive marketing communications. Complaints can be filed by consumers, businesses, Congress, the media, or the FTC itself. An advertisement or marketing communication is said to be deceptive or misleading if the typical person is misled. Any claims made by a company must be substantiated in some way. If the FTC finds that a violation has occurred, it can issue a consent order or a cease-and-desist order. It can also levy civil penalties. Appeals from the FTC go to a federal court of appeals.

4. **Discuss the role of the BBB in regulating marketing activities.**
   Complaints about advertising are referred to the BBB's NAD, the CARU, or the NARB. Complaints not settled by the NAD or CARU are referred to the NARB. Both operate similarly to the FTC but without obligatory power. However, in most cases, decisions by the NAD, CARU, or NARB are followed.

5. **Discuss the social responsibility of business firms and provide examples showing how a firm can demonstrate its social responsibility.**
   Businesses are expected to behave in a socially responsible manner and be supportive of societal needs. This social responsibility can be met through cause-related marketing programs.

Key Terms

Bait and switch (69)
Cause-related marketing (83)
Ethics (58)
Morals (58)
Puffery (78)

Discussion Questions

1. Marketing to teenagers has raised a number of ethical issues, as was discussed in the chapter opening. Do some research on the Internet or with an electronic database to find at least two articles that discuss the ethical issues in marketing to teenagers. Summarize what you find and compare it to your personal thoughts about advertising to teens.

2. Pick one of the ethical issues presented in Section 3-2. Talk to five people you know of various ages, genders, and ethnic backgrounds. Summarize how each felt about the issue you picked.
3. Pick one of the ethical issues presented in Section 3-2. Discuss how you feel about the issue. Find two articles from the Internet or an electronic database that either support or refute your view.
4. Look through the list of criticisms of marketing identified in Section 3-2. Which one concerns you the most? Why? Which one is of the least concern to you? Why? How does your age, gender, ethnicity, religious background, family, and environment impact your choices? Explain.
5. Pick one of the pieces of legislation listed in Section 3-3. Research its background and the impact it has on business.
6. Access the website of the FTC at http://www.ftc.gov. Review the press releases and past decisions. Find one that interests you to discuss. Write a report summarizing the case. Attach the case as a PDF to your summary.
7. If you came across an advertisement that you thought was misleading and wanted to report it, would you report it to the FTC or the BBB? Why?
8. What are your thoughts about email spam? What approach do you think the FTC should take towards spam? Would you be willing to turn in a friend, relative, or business associate who was violating the law? How much of a reward would it take?
9. What is your opinion of cause-related marketing? What causes do you support?
10. Do you modify your purchase decisions based on causes a company supports? Why or why not?

Review Questions

True or False

1. Ethics help individuals and organizations to establish boundaries regarding acceptable and unacceptable conduct.
2. Morals are personal beliefs or standards used to guide an individual's actions.
3. Marketing has been criticized for creating a materialistic society.
4. Bait and switch tactics used by retailers provide more product options to the consumer.
5. Personal information gathered through the Internet allows marketers to advertise specific products of interest to each individual.
6. To determine whether a company used deceptive or misleading advertising, the FTC will examine the company's intentions to design a deceptive and misleading ad.
7. The FTC does not have the power to levy civil penalties; only the U.S. Court of Appeals has this power.
8. Decisions by the NAD, CARU, or NARB cannot be appealed to the FTC or to the federal court system.
9. Historically, companies can choose not to follow NAD recommendations.
10. Cause-related marketing is a strategy used to promote a product line by advertising donations made to nonprofit organizations.

Multiple Choice

11. Easy consumer credit is partially to blame for which of the following criticisms of marketing?
    a. marketing causes people to buy more than they can afford.
    b. marketing increases the prices of goods and services.
    c. marketing capitalizes on human weaknesses.
    d. marketing violates consumers' rights to privacy.
12. Which of the following is an example of the criticism that marketing shapes inappropriate cultural values?
    a. an advertisement for weight-loss programs
    b. an advertisement offering a complete computer system for only $299
    c. an advertisement for Rogaine, a hair-growth product
    d. an advertisement for birth control pills

13. Which of the following statements defines the marketing role in society?
    a. marketing uses unethical methods to lure customers.
    b. marketing reduces tension between competing companies.
    c. marketing has a limited commercial role.
    d. marketing allows consumers to make better decisions.
14. The agency responsible for regulating the radio industry is the
    a. FDA.
    b. FCC.
    c. FTC.
    d. CPSC.
15. The legislation that prohibits false and misleading advertising is the
    a. Fair Packaging and Labeling Act.
    b. Lanham Act.
    c. Wheeler-Lea Amendment.
    d. Robinson-Patman Act.
16. The legislation that prohibits price discrimination to different buyers is the
    a. Sherman-Antitrust Act.
    b. Clayton Act.
    c. Fair Packaging and Labeling Act.
    d. Lanham Act.
17. When making a claim about a product, the FTC will look for
    a. puffery statements.
    b. substantiation of the claim.
    c. a testimony of an expert witness.
    d. overly complex claims.
18. Decisions by the NAD, CARU, and NARB are
    a. not binding, but most companies abide by decisions of the NAD, CARU, and NARB.
    b. binding only if ruled by the NARB.
    c. as binding as rulings of the FTC.
    d. none of the above.
19. Advertisers engage in puffery
    a. when the ad contains an obscene message.
    b. when the ad makes reference to a competitor's product.
    c. when the ad includes such words as "greatest," "finest," and "best."
    d. when the ad is obviously designed to mislead.
20. If the FTC believes that a company used unfair or deceptive practices, the first step in resolving the problem will be to issue a(n)
    a. consent order.
    b. administrative complaint.
    c. cease-and-desist order.
    d. judgment for approval by the federal court.

Answers: (1) True, (2) True, (3) True, (4) False, (5) True, (6) False, (7) False, (8) False, (9) True, (10) False, (11) a, (12) d, (13) d, (14) b, (15) c, (16) b, (17) b, (18) a, (19) c, (20) a

Case: The New Video Game

Normally, the initial marketing meeting for a new video game is not a big deal. However, this one was different for a number of reasons. Company sales had been flat. Combined with increased costs, profits had been down for the past two quarters. With the Christmas season approaching, Brad knew this was an opportune time to push a new product. Sales could be generated more quickly than at any other time of the year. The last two new video games had fallen under projected sales. Fingers were pointed at the marketing department, especially at Brad because he was the marketing manager, a position he had held for the past three years. But the CEO stood up for Brad, suggesting that maybe research and development had not done their homework in creating games that would appeal to the company's young male market.

Feeling some heat to produce a winner, Brad slid into his seat beside Amy, the new public relations director. She had made a huge impression on the management team in the four months she had been there. She was attractive, witty, and with a double degree in marketing and public relations from the University of Georgia, well qualified for the position she held. She had already earned

Source: fizkes/Shutterstock

the respect of the CEO and other top management personnel with the way she handled a recent negative press situation.

Across the table were the Vice President of Research and Development, Stewart Hanks, and two of the "techies" from the video game division. At the head of the table was Alex Olfermayer, the CEO. He had been with the company for 23 years and had served as CEO for the past seven. During his tenure, the company had grown from $3 million in annual sales to more than $9 million.

Brad turned his attention to Mr. Hanks, who explained the newest video game. It was based on the game player rooting out terrorists from around the world before they destroyed major American targets like the Pentagon and the White House. The terrorists were not easily identifiable, and if innocent people were killed, then the probability of the terrorists hitting American targets increased. Time and skill would be needed to beat the terrorists before the ultimate disaster hit, the assassination of the president.

Just listening to the description of the new game got Brad excited. As the video game team went through a simulated version of some of the graphics, Brad looked over at the CEO. He could see that he was also impressed. Brad had a gut feeling this was going to be a big winner.

When the presentation was over, the CEO expressed his enthusiasm for the game. Brad joined in the discussion, telling the group this would be an easy marketing sell. Turning to Amy, he asked her opinion. With a solemn look on her face, she replied, "Our competitor is already developing a similar game, but they are at least a month ahead of us in development."

"When is their game coming out? They've beaten us with the last three games, they're not beating us this time!" Mr. Olfermayer snapped.

"I don't know," Amy replied.

"Can you find out?"

"How do you know they are producing a similar game?" Brad asked before Amy could reply to the CEO's question.

"I know somebody who works over there."

"You need to get us the scoop on what is going on over there and when they plan to introduce their version. We have to make sure our game is better," the CEO replied.

"He's not going to tell me confidential information like that. He just happened to let it slip about this new game. It was just by accident I found out."

Looking at Amy, the CEO narrowed his eyes. "You find out about this game so we can beat them. We are not losing on another game." Turning to Brad, he continued as he stood up to leave the room. "You understand what I am saying, don't you?"

"Yes, sir," Brad replied.

Feeling the tension in the room, the research and development staff quickly slipped out behind the CEO. For a few minutes, neither Amy nor Brad spoke.

Turning to Amy, Brad asked, "Can you get the information?"

"It will cost $10,000."

"That's blackmail."

"How bad do you want it?" Amy replied coolly.

"Not bad enough to pay someone $10,000. It would be my head if an auditor ever found something like that, and I'm not going to Mr. Olfermayer with that type of request."

Standing up, Amy looked down at Brad, a sly grin on her face. "If $10,000 is too risky for you, then I'd settle for the associate marketing director's position."

"I already have someone in that position."

"So, what does that matter?" Amy replied as she walked out of the room.

Never in his eight years of working in a marketing department, in three different companies, had

Brad experienced anything like this. Looking out the window, he noticed his wife and two kids coming toward the building. He had almost forgotten this was his younger child's birthday. He could not afford to lose his job, at least not right now.

Case Questions

1. What options does Brad have for dealing with this situation? What are the ethical implications for each option?
2. If you were in Brad's spot, what would you do? Would your actions be different if quitting was not an option right now because of family concerns and financial obligations?
3. What is your evaluation of Amy and her approach to Brad's dilemma?
4. Although Amy does not report to you, should you have a talk with her boss about her? Should you talk with the CEO about Amy? What are the consequences of each action?
5. If Brad would make the decision to either give Amy the $10,000 or fire his current associate and give her the position, what would be the consequences of each decision?
6. Discuss the ethical implications of the newly proposed game.

Endnotes

1. Eden David, "Teens especially vulnerable to junk foodadvertising, experts say," February 28, 2020, https://abcnews.go.com/Health/teens-vulnerable-junk-food-advertising-experts/story?id=69060220.
2. Aimee Picchi, "Here's a top reason Americans are carrying an average credit card balance of over $6,200," USA Today, February 12, 2020, https://www.usatoday.com/story/money/2020/02/12/credit-card-debt-average-balance-hits-6-200-and-limit-31-000/4722897002.
3. JCDecaux, "Ad Spend Forecast Update 2018: DOOH, Google and Facebook drive growth," https://www.jcdecaux.com/blog/ad-spend-forecast-update-2018-dooh-google-and-facebook-drive-growth, March 20, 2020.
4. Mariel Soto Reyes, "Netflix is investing even more in kids-focused content after coming off of two Oscar nominations for animated films," Business Insider, February 11, 2020, https://www.businessinsider.com/netflix-investing-in-kids-content-2020-2; Sharon Goldman, "The Social Tween: Marketers Take Aim at Kids Raised on Smartphones and Facebook," Adweek, June 24, 2012, http://www.adweek.com/sa-article/social-tween-141314
5. Laurence Frost, Iain Withers, and Chris Prentice, "Record $4 billion Airbus fine draws line under pervasive bribery," Reuters, January 31, 2020, https://www.reuters.com/article/us-airbus-probe-france/record-4-billion-airbus-fine-draws-line-under-pervasive-bribery-idUSKBN1ZU1X4.
6. Lisa Stein, "Furrowed Brows," *U.S. News & World Report* 133 (September 23, 2002): 18.
7. The Wheeler-Leah Act, https://www.ftc.gov/public-statements/1938/05/wheeler-lea-act, accessed on April 15, 2020.
8. Federal Trade Commission, FTC refunds consumers who bought deceptively marketed and advertised Nobetes diabetes treatment supplement, August 21, 2019, https://www.ftc.gov/news-events/press-releases/2019/08/ftc-refunds-consumers-who-bought-deceptively-marketed-advertised.
9. Nectar Brand LLC agrees to settle FTC charges that company's claims about Chinese-made mattresses being assembled in USA are false, March 13, 2018, https://www.ftc.gov/news-events/press-releases/2018/03/nectar-brand-llc-agrees-settle-ftc-charges-companys-claims-about.
10. Federal Trade Commission, "Marketer of water filtration systems to pay $110,000 civil penalty for deceptive made-in-USA advertisements in violation of 2017 order," April 12, 2019, https://www.ftc.gov/news-events/press-releases/2019/04/marketer-water-filtration-systems-pay-110000-civil-penalty
11. R. Serafin and G. Levin, "Ad Industry Suffers Crushing Blow," *Advertising Age* 61 (November 12, 1990): 1,3.
12. Federal Trade Commission, "Use of Endorsers and Testimonials in Advertising," https://www.ftc.gov/enforcement/rules/rulemaking-regulatory-reform-proceedings/use-endorsements-testimonials-advertising, accessed on March 14, 2020.
13. National Advertising Division, "Unilever, P&G Participates in NAD Forum," October 4, 2006, available at www.narcpartners.org.

14. National Advertising Division, "NAD Findings Support the Claim that Benefiber Healthy Balance "Helps Relieve Occasional Constipation and Abdominal Discomfort Without Causing Diarrhea," April 30, 2020, available at www.narcpartners.org.
15. National Advertising Division, "NAD Finds Bayer Can Support Certain Claims for Claritin, Claritin-D; Recommends Advertiser Discontinue 'Nothing Works Faster' Claim–Bayer, Chattem to Appeal," April 23, 2015, available at www.narcpartners.org.
16. National Advertising Division, "NAD Refers Spitz Sales to the FTC and FDA," January 19, 2007 press release, available at www.narcpartners.org.
17. Sarah Landrum, "Millennials driving brands to practice socially responsible marketing," Forbes, May 17, 2017, https://www.forbes.com/sites/sarahlandrum/2017/03/17/millennials-driving-brands-to-practice-socially-responsible-marketing/#515452e14990

Consumer Behavior

CHAPTER 4

Source: one photo/Shutterstock

Chapter Outline

Learning Objectives

Ivelin Radkov/Shutterstock

After studying this chapter, you should be able to:

- Identify the elements of a consumer behavior model.
- Describe the different social influences that have an impact on consumer behavior.
- Describe the different psychological influences that have an impact on consumer behavior.
- Address the five stages of the consumer decision-making process.
- Describe variations in consumer decision making based on whether consumers engage in extensive, limited, or routine problem solving.

Source: Arina P Habich/Shutterstock

4-1 Chapter Overview

Product evaluations and purchase decisions dominate our lives as consumers. We define who we are through consumption. Take, for example, Cheri, a successful artist, who has recently built a 3,000 square foot home with the help of a local architect. Cheri had the living room rug designed to be identical to one of her paintings for about $8,500. She bought an antique grandfather clock for $900 at Goodwill, and placed it in the center of the living room. The adjoining kitchen combines expensive stainless-steel appliances with granite countertops and IKEA cabinets. The dining room is IKEA cheap chic, defined by functionality and simplicity. She considers IKEA home, she visits often for fun and for the food experience, then buys everything online to be delivered to her home.

Closets prominently display Cheri's designer wardrobe, dominated by black and gray Donna Karans and Armanis bought from a local boutique for about $3,000 per suit, and the occasional Hermès Birkin handbag, bought after deliberating whether she should buy on consignment from the RealReal. Her casual clothes come from discounters, such as T.J. Maxx, Marshalls, and Target, and the local Junior League thrift shop. Cheri purchases all her food at the affordable Food Lion supermarket, choosing the store brand, whenever available. She follows sales at online retailers and uses Honey to make sure she pays the lowest price. For dinner out, she goes to exclusive (preferably Michelin starred) restaurants.

Cheri's decisions require daily planning and decision making to project an image to the outside world, to others who see her on the street, and to her friends who visit her at home. It also involves cutting costs in areas that are not readily visible to others. Like Cheri, consumers cannot be easily placed into neat, well-defined categories. Individual motivations, interests, attitudes, and upbringing create complex individuals who may not be easily categorized.

This chapter presents a basic model of consumer behavior (Section 4-2), noting the personal and social (interpersonal) influences on behavior. Section 4-3 addresses social influences, such as cultures, subcultures, social class, individual roles, status, family, and reference groups. Section 4-4 addresses psychological influences, such as motivation, perception, learning, beliefs and attitudes, personality, and lifestyle. The stages of the consumer decision-making process are described in Section 4-5. Finally, Section 4-6 offers insights into variations in decision processes attributed to the extent of problem solving involved in the purchase and the level of consumer involvement.

4-2 A Consumer Behavior Model

Marketing managers carefully follow consumer behavior. From national department stores to local convenience stores to online large and small retailers, from large consumer goods manufacturers to small service providers, businesses strive to acquire timely information about their target consumers. Learning why consumers behave in a particular manner and how their behavior changes over time is essential to the company's bottom line.

Cheri's behavior described above was influenced by social factors, such as culture, social class, family, and reference groups. She is a single, upper-middle class professional, with upper-class tastes, but a middle-class budget. Although she can afford a larger home, unique furnishings, and an haute-couture wardrobe, she buys other products at discount to save money. Psychological influences also affect consumer behavior. Motivation, personality, lifestyles, beliefs, and attitudes, all influence how consumers behave. Cheri grew up in a materialistic culture and as a result, buys products that her friends or those that she aspires to have as friends approve of, and pays for them using a large amount of her discretionary income. She lives the lifestyle she aspires to, while cutting costs by purchasing less visible products from cheaper sources. Marketers need to understand what motivates consumers like her in their purchase behavior. What motivates them to purchase certain brands and shop at certain stores? What messages do consumers want to convey about themselves through the products they purchase? **Figure 4-1** illustrates the different influences exerted on consumer behavior.

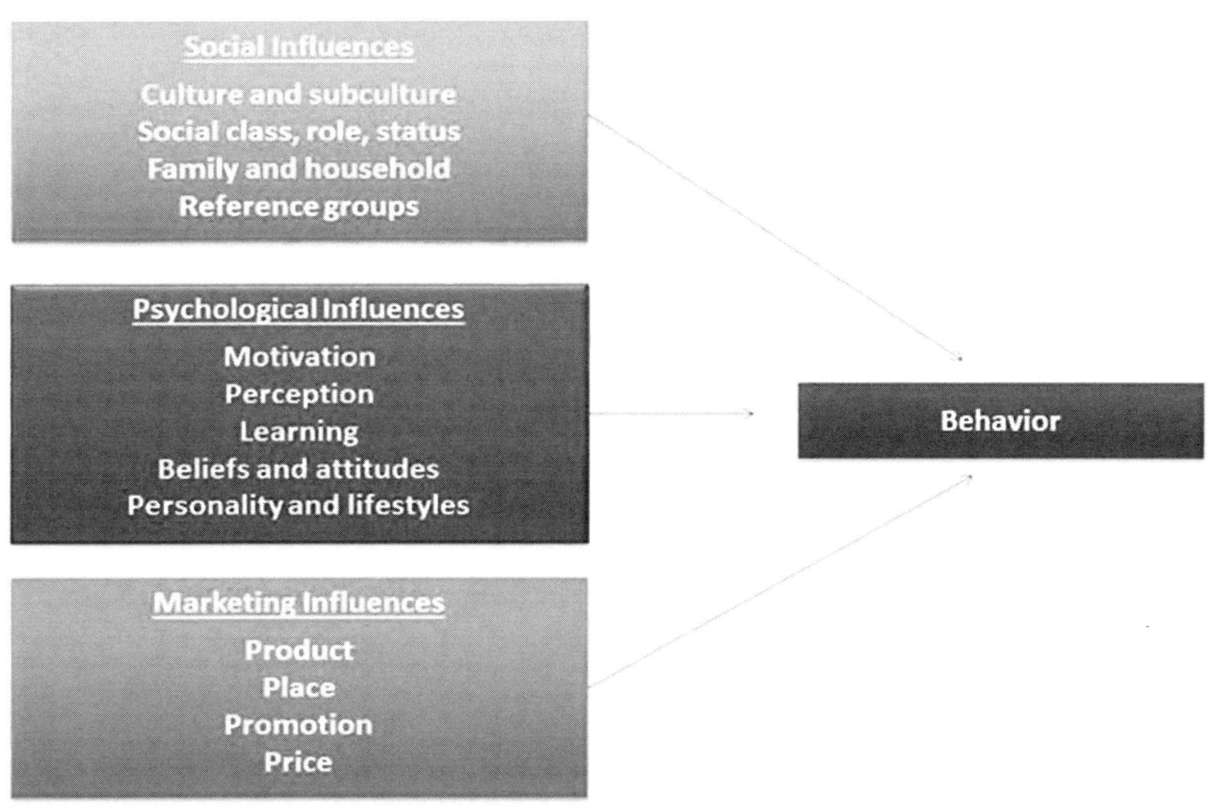

FIGURE 4-1 Model of Consumer Behavior

Sources: Adapted from George Fisk, "Reflection and Retrospection: Searching for Visions in Marketing," *Journal of Marketing* 63, no. 1 (1999) 115–121; William O. Bearden, R. E. Netemeyer, and Jesse E. Teel, "Measurement of Consumer Susceptibility to Interpersonal Influence," *Journal of Consumer Research* 15 (1989): 473–481; J. Paul Peter and James H. Donnelly, Jr., *A Preface to Marketing Management, 15th ed.*, 2019 (New York, NY: McGraw-Hill Irwin).

4-3 Social Influences on Consumer Behavior

The social influences examined in this chapter are culture; social class, role, and status; family and household; and reference groups. Culture is recognized as having an important influence on consumption and consumer behavior in general. Cultural influences are expressed in the consumption of goods and services for both personal use and business use. Similarly, social class, role, and status influence the types of goods and services consumers purchase. Friends and family are also likely to affect individuals' consumption, the brands that they purchase, the stores where they shop, and the media that they are exposed to.

4-3a Cultural Influences on Consumer Behavior

Values Important elements of culture defined as enduring beliefs about a specific mode of conduct or desirable end state.

Terminal values Values related to goals.

Instrumental values Values related to processes whereby one can attain certain goals.

Culture—a society's personality—is defined as a continuously changing totality of learned and shared meanings, rituals, norms, and traditions among the members of an organization or society. **Values** are important elements of culture. Values are enduring beliefs about a specific mode of conduct or desirable end state that guides the selection or evaluation of behavior. Values guide individuals' actions, attitudes, and judgments affecting their product preferences and their perception of brands. Cultures are set apart by their value systems. Western cultures place more stress on success, achievement, and competitiveness, whereas Eastern cultures are more likely to be concerned with social welfare. A sample of universally held values is provided in **Figure 4-2**. According to this classification, values can be related to goals (**terminal values**) or to the processes whereby one can attain those goals (**instrumental values**).[1]

Values are learned from those with whom individuals are in contact: family, friends, teachers, clergy, politicians, and the media. The United States

Instrumental Values	Terminal Values
Ambitious	A comfortable life
Broadminded	An exciting life
Capable	A sense of accomplishment
Cheerful	A world at peace
Clean	A world of beauty
Courageous	Equality
Forgiving	Family Security
Helpful	Freedom
Imaginative	Inner Harmony
Independent	Mature love
Intellectual	National Security
Logical	Pleasure
Loving	Salvation
Obedient	Self-respect
Polite	Social recognition
Responsible	True friendship
Self-controlled	Wisdom

FIGURE 4-2 Instrumental and Terminal Values

is a melting pot of different cultures that have blended together to create the American culture with its own values and beliefs. Learning a new culture, which most immigrants must do when they live in another country, is known as **acculturation**. Acculturation encompasses interaction with the culture and adaptation to the culture. It includes the **assimilation** of the new culture. Acculturation does not necessarily mean abandoning all home country traditions. It does not mean complete assimilation of the new culture. For example, recent Asian Indian immigrants to the United States are less likely to be assimilated in this culture because they maintain their original religious practices, language, food consumption, housing, friendship patterns, and contact with India. Although Indian Americans are not easily assimilated; they are, nevertheless, acculturated in the American culture.[2]

Acculturation The process of learning a new culture.

Assimilation Adapting to and fully integrating into the new culture.

Consumer acculturation refers to contact with a new culture and the resulting change for consumers in terms of their approach to consumption in the new environment. Asian Indian consumers consume fast food, shop at supermarkets, root for their favorite baseball team, and overall, successfully integrate in the American culture without necessarily being assimilated.

Subcultures **Subcultures** are components of the broad culture. They are groups of individuals with shared value systems based on some common background. Subcultures could be based on regional differences, ethnicity, religion, or social causes. For instance, Southern consumers have different lifestyles than Midwest consumers.

Subcultures Groups of individuals with shared value systems based on ethnicity or common background.

Subcultures are often based on ethnicity or nationality. Italian Americans maintain many of the traditions from their home country and have strong ties to the old country. Or subcultures can be based on religion—an important element of culture. Among the important ethnic and national subcultures in the United States are African Americans, Hispanic-Americans, and Asian Americans.

The African-American subculture makes up about 14% percent of the U.S. population. With an ever-increasing buying power, more than 50% have lived in the digital age their entire life. They are very influential on the economy and on pop culture, they spend almost 40 hours a week listening to music. African-Americans have the highest smartphone ownership and usage of any demographic group. They are fashion-conscious consumers, and they are brand loyal. They spend more than most U.S. consumers on online food shopping.[3]

Source: sirtravelalot/Shutterstock

Hispanics constitute the largest ethnic and racial group in the United States, accounting for 19 percent of the U.S. population. Their median age is lower (27) than that of non-Hispanics, and they have a longer life

Source: ESB Professional/Shutterstock

Source: Monkey Business Images/Shutterstock

expectancy; firms will have a long-term benefit if they serve this segment, as their buying power is expected to reach $1.9 trillion by 2022. They are very loyal to brands, and respond to those brands that create a meaningful dialogue with Hispanics. They are avid technology adopters and smartphone reliant, with 54% willing to pay more for top-quality electronics. More than 60% grew up in the internet age, and about 80% use it to gather product information and to buy products. They spend more than any other ethnic subculture on food at home, rented dwellings, apparel, gasoline, and public transportation.

More than half of Hispanic-Americans are of Mexican origin, with the rest coming from Central and South America and Puerto Rico. Although Hispanic-Americanss constitute a homogeneous group, they do share a number of traits: the Catholic religion, the Spanish language, and traditional values.[4]

The Asian-American ethnic subculture, which is 5.6 percent of the U.S. population, is the most heterogeneous subculture, consisting of ethnic and national groups with different languages and traditions—Chinese, Asian Indian and Pakistani, Filipino, Japanese, and Korean, among others. Their spending power is over $1 trillion, and they are the most affluent and educated U.S. population segment, with more than 50% holding a bachelor's degree or higher. They are digitally vocal influencers, most prefer to be reached through an app or the web on a smartphone, and spend 23 hours a week watching TV. Households are larger and often multigenerational, more than 91% use the internet to gather product information, and 87% make online purchases. They feel a sense of responsibility to the environment and their families' wellbeing.[5]

Consumer beliefs greatly influence consumer behavior. The dominant religion in the United States is Christian (over 70%), with Protestants accounting for about 47%. The Protestant religion stresses hard work and frugality and is linked to the development of capitalism and economic emancipation. Judaism, with its disdain for ignorance and sloth, stresses education. Jewish consumers in the United States (1.9%) are an important target market for educational and professional development. Islam encourages modesty and community, discourages behaviors deemed by Islamic law as forbidden. Practicing Muslim consumers (.9% in the U.S.) abide by it and shun the consumption of pork products and alcohol.

The Hindu religion (.75 in the U.S.)[6] encourages a family orientation and discourages the consumption of animal products—beef, in particular. Firms targeting these consumers need to be aware of the religious constraints and offer goods and services that address their special needs. For example, fast-food restaurants find that they can better serve their Asian-Indian consumers by offering ample choices of vegetarian food.

4-3b Social Class, Role, and Status Influences on Consumer Behavior

The position of individuals in society can be defined in terms of social class. **Social class** is the relatively permanent divisions within society that exist in a status hierarchy, with the members of each division sharing similar values, attitudes, interests, and opinions. Social class is evaluated as a combination of occupation, education, income, wealth, and personal values, which have a direct impact on consumption. Children are initially socialized in their parents' social class, engaging in activities characteristic of that class.

Social class Relatively permanent divisions within society that exist in a status hierarchy, with the members of each division sharing similar values, attitudes, interests, and opinions.

A brief examination of social classes in the U.S. reveals that there are three main social classes, upper, middle, and lower class, each with subcategories. The upper class is composed of the wealthiest Americans who either inherited money or earned it through business. They spend heavily, sometimes conspicuously, on luxury items and own expensive homes. The middle class is varied, with the upper middle class earning their money through successful careers founded on professional and graduate degrees. They live graciously, entertaining friends, emulating the upper class in their consumption. Members of the lower-middle social class have skilled jobs founded on technical training. They are price-sensitive, value homes and neighborhoods, and adhere to norms and standards. The lower class consists of employed individuals working in either skilled or semiskilled jobs, living routine lives, and with limited social interaction beyond family. Alternatively, they may be unemployed and on welfare. They have minimal skills and education, and buy impulsively, often on credit, and may live in substandard housing. In addition to differences in product preferences and consumption, each social class has other distinctive traits. For example, the upper classes have a broader social circle beyond their immediate community and family, whereas lower classes are more restricted to their home environment and to family life. Upper classes also participate more in activities outside the home, such as theater performances, than lower classes, which engage in physical activities for recreation.

Individuals' positions within a group can also be defined in terms of role and status. **Roles** are based on the activities people are expected to perform according to the individuals around them. In traditional families, women are expected to stay at home and take care of the daily functioning of the household. Women are traditionally assigned to the role of mother and maid. In a more modern rendition of this traditional role, women play

Roles The activities people are expected to perform according to individuals around them.

Source: Monkey Business Images/Shutterstock

Source: Syda Productions/Shutterstock

the role of soccer moms, carpool drivers, and Parent-Teacher Association (PTA) activists.

In many developing countries, this traditional role is in fact law. In the most traditional Islamic countries, such as Saudi Arabia, women were allowed to drive only recently and not permitted to be in public if unaccompanied by a male relative. In these countries, women's business activities are channeled toward interaction in a women-only or family-only environment. Personal services can be performed only by individuals of the same gender. Women can bank only at women's banks, can have their hair done only by other women, and so on. In less traditional Islamic countries, such as Pakistan, women share responsibility with men in business. It is noteworthy, however, that women play a more limited role politically, where only a few hold notable positions, and when they do, it is often by virtue of their father's position.

In today's Western cultures, women focus on careers, assuming the roles of professionals and managers. They leave traditional chores to individuals who are considered competent to handle them—maids, day cares, and personal shopping services. Gender roles are not as clearly defined, with children and the household becoming the responsibility of both parents, who take turns in fulfilling the roles that traditionally have been assigned to women. This is even more the case in today's society, transformed by the COVID-19 crisis, with children staying home with parents forced to work remotely.

Moreover, the make-up of the household is rapidly changing. While, in the past, most adults lived in married households, today, in the United States, there are 61.4 million opposite-sex married and 8 million opposite-sex unmarried partner households. There are also 543,000 same-sex married couple households and 469,000 same-sex unmarried couple households.[7]

Status The esteem which society bestows upon a particular role.

Status is defined as the esteem that society bestows upon a particular role. The role of soccer mom is lower than the role of marketing manager. A woman playing both roles will probably not stress the role of soccer mom in her professional circles for fear of lessening her status of manager. Status defines what products we consume and how we behave. Related to one's background is one's concern with status, or status concern—maintaining it or acquiring it—and with material possessions, or materialism. Individuals' concern with status is related to the values placed on symbols of status and on the attainment of high status. Often, the products consumed convey messages about the consumer in the same way that language does. Driving an expensive car advertises that one is a successful professional.

Status—like social class, to which it is related—is easier to transcend in high-income countries than in lower-income countries. In the United States, the Protestant ethic of hard work has led to centuries of individual prosperity and, at the individual level, status advancement. In the United States, it is not perceived as shameful for prominent politicians and businesspeople to refer back to their humble beginnings.

More recently, however, status and social class have become more dynastic than dynamic. The past two decades have seen a substantial increase in inequality in the United States, with real incomes of households in the lowest fifth (the bottom 20 percent) growing by 6.4 percent and the income of the top 1 percent growing 184 percent. This rise in inequality did not come with a commensurate rise in mobility. In fact, social sclerosis is evident for the middle and lower income population.[8]

4-3c Family and Household Influences on Consumer Behavior

For the majority of consumers, the family exerts the most influence on purchase behavior. Consumers continue to purchase the brands they grew up with. Somebody growing up with Ford automobiles will probably continue to purchase them as an adult. If a mother always bought a Butterball turkey for Thanksgiving dinner, her adult daughter will probably continue the Butterball tradition for her family.

Marketers are interested in how decisions are made in the family. Traditionally, food shopping has been the domain of women, whereas automobiles have been the domain of men. Those roles are greatly changing today, with men often taking charge of household purchases in households with dual-career couples. For decades, models of family decision making equated family decisions with husband-wife decisions and excluded or ignored the role of children. More recently, however, the influence of children has received ample attention from marketers, especially when the decision centered on less-expensive products and those products designed for the child's personal use. Yet children's documented buying power and influence on family purchase decisions extend beyond these products. Children are important influencers when it comes to decisions regarding family vacations, the family automobiles, furniture, and the family's live TV streaming services. Children even influence the brands of products used in daily consumption, such as food and grooming products. In a family household, there may be other decision makers, in addition to the family itself. The residential cleaning service

Source: Robert Kneschke/Shutterstock

may determine the brands of cleaning products and furniture polish. The family pet may have a preference of one brand of food over another. In nonfamily households, roommates bring with them their own families' consumption traditions. These household members exert an important influence on the types of goods and services consumed by an individual.

4-3d Reference Groups

Reference groups Groups that serve as a point of reference for individuals in the process of shaping their attitudes and behavior.

Associative reference groups Groups that individuals belong to.

Dissociative groups Groups that individuals want to dissociate from through their behavior.

Aspirational groups Groups that individuals aspire to join in the future—for example, by virtue of education, employment, and training.

Reference groups are defined as groups that serve as a point of reference for individuals in the process of shaping their attitudes and behavior. **Associative reference groups** are groups that individuals belong to. As a member of a group, an individual will adopt the group's behaviors, engage in similar activities, and purchase similar brand names as others in the group. For example, members of a sorority are likely to dress similarly, with a preference for the same brand names and retailers. **Dissociative groups** are groups that individuals want to dissociate from through their behavior. Lesbians are rarely dressed in pretty, frilly dresses, and they often reject the makeup and accessories preferred by heterosexual women. They tend to dissociate from the more traditional, submissive females through their style, which is simple, assertive, and natural. **Aspirational groups** are groups that individuals aspire to join in the future—for example, by virtue of education, employment, and training. Aspirational groups are important determinants of consumer behavior. Business students aspiring to work on Wall Street will acquire products that fit with their new profile—leather briefcase, designer suit, and other products associated with their coveted professional position.

Source: Djomas/Shutterstock

For Cheri in the chapter opening, Donna Karan and Armani outfits, expensive antiques, and the house on the lake reflect her desire to be accepted by refined locals of taste and means in the town to which she recently moved. In cases in which her products are visible and conspicuous, as in the case of clothing or the home itself, Cheri readily spends large amounts of money to signal her preferences to her aspirational group. Cheri distances herself from her associative group, her family on the farm in the Midwest, for purchases that will be seen by others. But for products that are privately consumed, such as food, Cheri purchases low-priced products and shops at low-priced retailers.

4-4 Psychological Influences on Consumer Behavior

Consumer behavior is likely to be influenced by the following psychological factors: motivation, perception, learning, beliefs, attitudes, personality, and lifestyles. The field of psychology has extensively examined these dimensions and their influence on individual behavior.

4-4a Motivation

Consumers are motivated by needs and wants. Needs were defined in Chapter 1 as basic human requirements. People are motivated to seek goods and services that satisfy their needs, and marketers attempt to address consumer needs with the different goods and services they offer. A need becomes a want when it is directed to a particular product—wants are shaped by one's culture. We may have a physiological need, such as something to drink, that can become a want—a desire for a particular brand: Coke. When a need is not satisfied, it becomes a **drive** (or motive), which is defined as a stimulus that encourages consumers to engage in an action to reduce the need. **Figure 4-3** illustrates motivation as a process that moves consumers from a latent need to the behavior that satisfies that need.

Drive (or motive) A stimulus that encourages consumers to engage in an action to reduce the need.

Consumers first experience a latent need, such as the need for food. The unsatisfied need becomes a drive or motivation to reduce hunger.

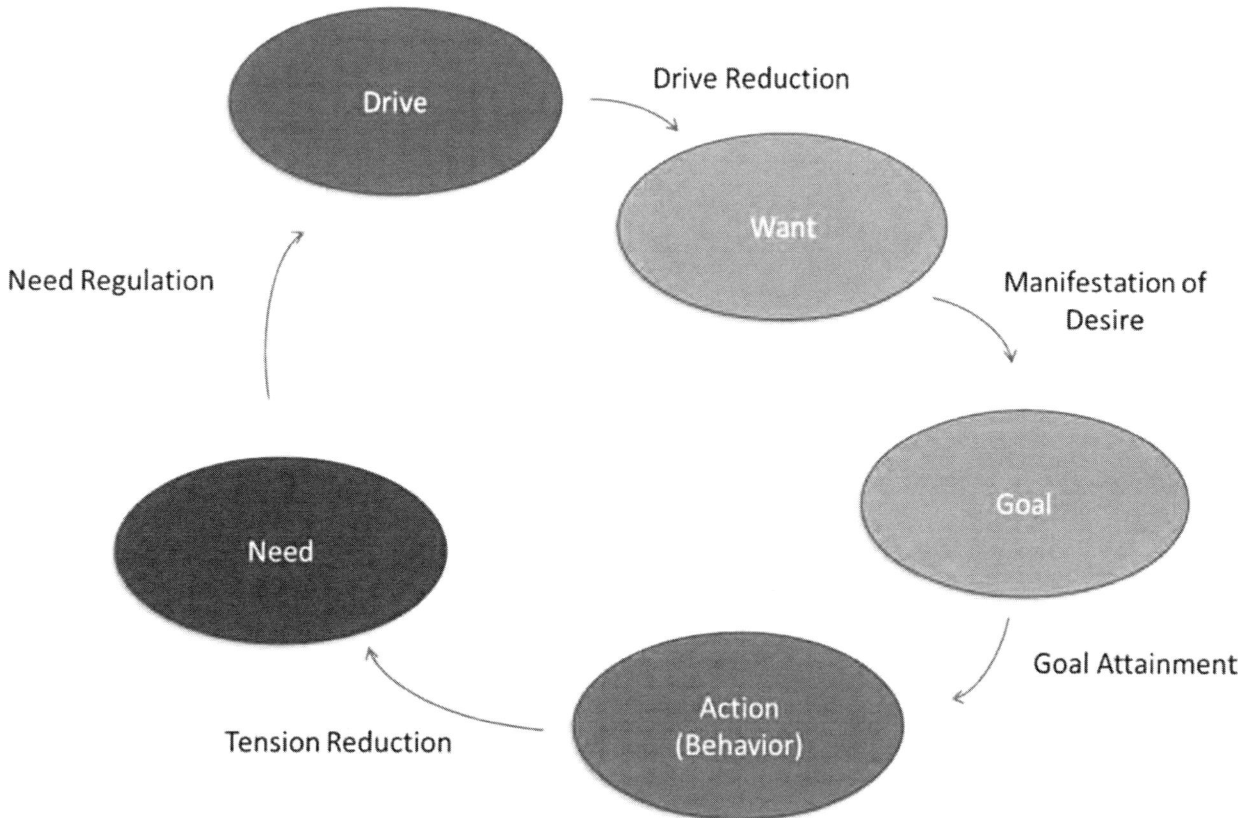

FIGURE 4-3 Motivation as a Process

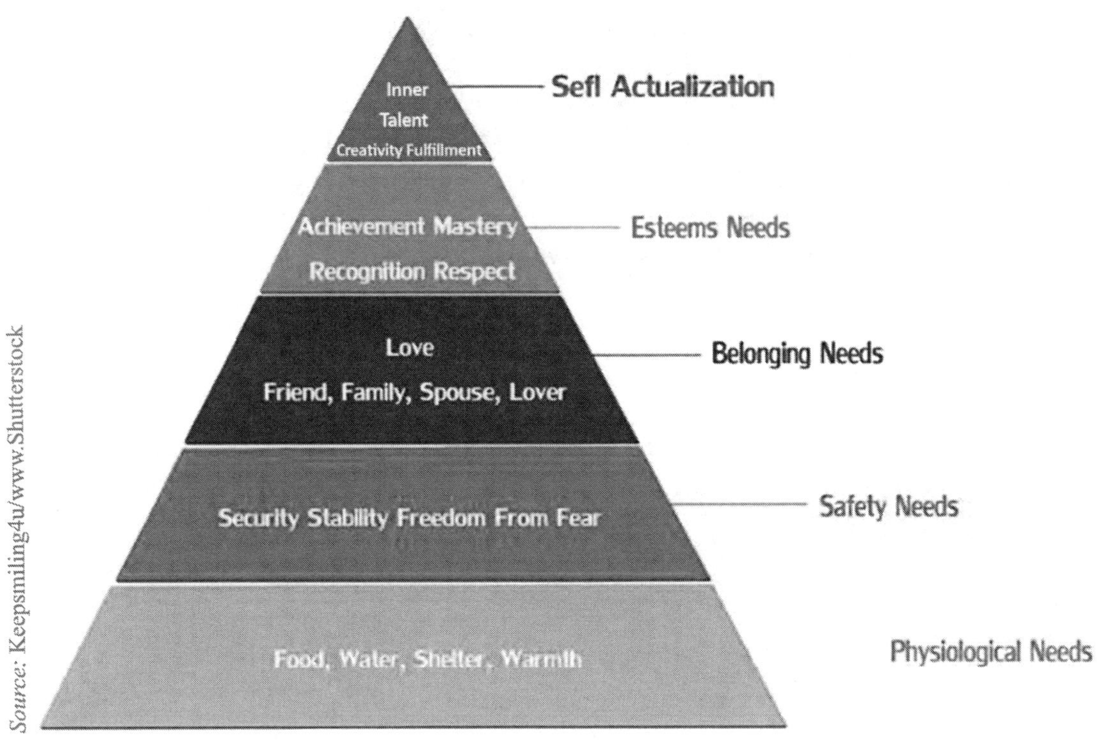

FIGURE 4-4 Maslow's Hierarchy of Needs

The need then translates into a want: a sandwich wrap. The consumer then has a specific goal—searching in his or her memory for various wrap sources—and decides to go to Wawa, a popular gas station convenience store. The behavior that reduces hunger involves eating the Wawa wrap.

One popular theory of motivation, Maslow's theory of needs,[9] explains individuals' motivation to engage in particular behaviors as a function of needs arranged in a hierarchy from the most urgent to the least urgent. Consumers need to satisfy their most urgent needs, such as food and drink, before they can satisfy higher-level needs. As soon as they satisfy their lower needs, their higher needs become more pressing.

The Maslow hierarchy of needs is illustrated in Figure 4-4 **(next page).** The most basic needs are physiological: the need for food, water, and sleep. At the next level are safety needs, such as the need for shelter and protection from danger or harm. Love, social, or belonging needs are at the following level—the need to be accepted by one's group, family, and friends. Once in a group, individuals crave self-esteem, status and appreciation, respect from others.

Finally, individuals need self-actualization, the need to accomplish and realize their own potential. Products can satisfy a number of needs at the same time. Cheri in our example has a strong social need. She needs to belong to an aspirational group defined as locals of taste and means. To satisfy this need, she purchases visibly consumed products, such as expensive antiques and top designer brands that are popular with this aspirational group.

Consumers can satisfy thirst needs with a can of Pepsi, iced tea, or tap water. They can satisfy hunger needs with a steak or a Snickers bar. They can satisfy safety needs with the right brand of tires. Love and belonging needs can be satisfied through attending a movie with friends or going to an amusement park with family members. An expensive home, furniture, clothes can be products that meet esteem needs by showing a person is successful. The top level, self-actualization, would involve the pursuit of goals that offer intrinsic satisfaction. The pursuit of education beyond what is necessary for one's career, or the pursuit of art or a craft solely for the pleasure it produces are examples.

4-4b Perception

Perception is the manner in which we collect, organize, and interpret information from the world around us to create a meaningful image of reality. Individuals form different images of the same stimulus because of differences in the perceptual processes. One such difference is attributed to **selective exposure**—the stimuli that consumers choose to pay attention to. Individuals are exposed to numerous advertisements every day. They see television, social media, and online ads. They listen to advertising on radio. Clearly, consumers could not possibly retain all the information from these different sources. They, therefore, selectively choose the messages they will pay attention to. The challenge for advertisers is to create ads that stand out from the multitude of messages consumers see on a daily basis.

Selective distortion involves consumers adapting information to fit their own existing knowledge or beliefs. For example, if a consumer believes that American electronics are inferior to Japanese electronics, then information in an ad that is contrary to this belief will likely be either ignored or distorted to fit into the consumer's current belief structure. After a purchase has been made, consumers often will distort information and evaluate the product to make it conform to their current beliefs and behavior.

Selective retention refers to consumers remembering only information about a good or service that supports personal knowledge or beliefs. An advertisement that does not support a person's current concepts is usually forgotten. A purchasing agent listening to a salesperson may remember only the portions of the conversation that reinforce his or her current beliefs about the vendor. To overcome selective retention, marketers must provide information that makes their good or service stand out from that of competitors, and getting beyond selective retention usually involves repeating the message over and over until the target audience makes the new information part of its current knowledge and belief structure.

Perception The manner in which people collect, organize, and interpret information from the world around them to create a meaningful image of reality.

Selective exposure The stimuli that consumers choose to pay attention to.

Selective distortion Consumers adapting information to fit their own existing knowledge.

Selective retention Remembering only information about a good or service that supports personal knowledge or beliefs.

Source: Monkey Business Images/Shutterstock

4-4c Learning

Learning Change in individual thought processes or behavior attributed to experience or new information.

Cues Stimuli in the environment, such as products or advertisements, that create individual responses.

Stimuli Cues in the environment, such as products and advertisements, that create individual responses.

Reinforcement Learning achieved by strengthening the relationship between the cue and the response.

Learning is defined as a change in individual thought processes or behavior attributed to experience or new information. It involves **cues** or **stimuli** in the environment, such as products and advertisements, which create an individual's response that will satisfy the person's drive. Cheri in our example has a drive to satisfy a social need—the need to be accepted locally by upscale consumers. Her response to this drive is conditioned by cues in the environment that confirm or reject her choices. Cheri may find it rewarding to see celebrities wearing outfits by her preferred designers, to note that these designers are available only in the most exclusive local shops, and especially, that her aspirational group approves of these designers. The outcome of these desirable cues is a reduction in the drive, known as **reinforcement**—referring to the reinforcement of the learning process, achieved by strengthening the relationship between the cue and the response. Repeated reinforcement creates a habit. Marketers are keen on making their brands habitual purchases.

4-4d Attitudes and Beliefs

Attitudes Relatively enduring and consistent feelings (affective responses) about a good or service.

Attitudes are defined as relatively enduring and consistent feelings (affective responses) about a product. A consumer may like Starbucks, Bose speakers, and Intel processors and dislike fast food, loud music in restaurants, and intrusive salespeople. Attitudes are difficult to change. Therefore, changing attitudes about brands can be quite challenging, depending on the strength of the attitudes. The more firmly held the attitude, the more difficult it is to change. Frozen yogurt has fought hard to be accepted as a health snack rather than as a sweet and unhealthy dessert. See Figure 4-5, illustrating how banks attempt to create and reinforce attitudes and beliefs about their brand.

Beliefs Associations between a good or service and attributes of that good or service.

Beliefs are associations between a product and attributes of that product. Examples of such beliefs could include: "Starbucks sells European-style, strong coffee," "Bose speakers are reliable because they are a product of German technology," "Intel processors only exist in quality computers," or "Fast food and smoking cause heart attacks." Marketers attempt to create positive attitudes toward their goods and services and to create beliefs that link their brands to desirable attributes.

U.S. firms have been successful in creating a positive brand-quality belief in the minds of Japanese consumers using advertising. As a result, Japanese consumers believe that English-sounding brands are superior brands, so many Japanese brands target Japanese consumers with English-sounding names.

4-4e Personality and Lifestyles

Personality An individual's unique characteristic patterns of thinking, feeling, and behaving.

Personality is defined as an individual's unique characteristic patterns of thinking, feeling, and behaving. [10]

Understanding personality traits is helpful in recognizing what consumers want in the products they purchase; after a careful study of target

Putman State Bank

Turning houses into homes since 1950

The Putman State of Mind

Whether you're a first-time homebuyer, looking to refinance your next home, or exploring other refinancing options, you can trust Putman State Bank to help you realize your goals.

FHA Loans
Rural Development Loans
VA Loans
Conventional Loans
Construction To Permanent Financing

The Bellevue Home Team
563-872-4774

Lisa Linn
Mortgage Loan Officer, Urban

Lori Ananda
Mortgage Loan Officer, Rural

Tony Blake
Mortgage Loan Officer, Duplex

FIGURE 4-5 This ad is designed to influence attitudes and beliefs about Putman State Bank

Sources: Images courtesy of fizkes and Ollyy/Shutterstock

consumer personality, brands are often positioned to appeal to those consumers. High-performance products, such as Porsche automobiles, Harley motorcycles, and Rossignol skis, attempt to appeal to high-sensation seekers looking for adventure and fun. Marketers endow brands with personalities that align closely with the personality of their target consumer groups: they attempt to offer brands that are congruent with those consumers' **self-concept**, that is, an individual's belief about himself or herself, including the person's attributes and who and what the self is.[11] Consumers reflect on the products and services that they consume, ensuring that they are congruent with their self-concept. Going to the hair salon, wearing professional clothes, driving a moderately conservative automobile is congruent with the self-concept of many mid-career professional women. Beyond the relationship between self-concept and brand choice is the concept of one's **extended self**, the idea that possessions contribute to the sense of self, as we learn, define, and remind ourselves of who we are by our possessions.[12] Cheri's possessions are part of her extended self, her unique furnishings, her couture collection, and, of course her art. Consumers engage in brand purchases in a way that is congruent with their perception as to who they are. Comedian Larry David drives a Prius, showing that he is concerned about climate change, and not very concerned with status. Comedian Bill Maher did not adopt a dog from a reputable breeder in Los Angeles; instead, he saved two older dogs from the pound; in doing so, he projects an image of a socially-conscious consumer. Actress Gwyneth Paltrow, through her lifestyle brand, Goop, defines herself as an enlightened new-age wellness goddess. You and I might purchase Target clothing to show that we are practical and not very brand conscious.

Self-concept An individual's belief about himself or herself, including the person's attributes and who and what the self is.

Extended self The idea that possessions contribute to the sense of self, as we learn, define, and remind ourselves of who we are by our possessions.

Lifestyles Individuals' style of living as expressed through activities, interests, and opinions.

Psychographics Categorization of consumers according to lifestyles and personality.

Innovators Psychographic group of individuals who are successful, sophisticated, and receptive to new technologies.

Thinkers Psychographic group of individuals who are educated, conservative, and practical consumers who value knowledge and responsibility. They look for durability, functionality, and value.

Achievers Psychographic group of individuals who are goal oriented, conservative, committed to career and family, and favor established, prestige products that demonstrate success to peers.

Experiencers Psychographic group of individuals who are young, enthusiastic, and impulsive. They seek variety and excitement, and spend substantially on fashion, entertainment, and socializing.

Lifestyles refer to individuals' style of living as expressed through activities, interests, and opinions. Marketers have made numerous attempts to categorize consumers according to lifestyles—this categorization and measurement is known as psychographics. **Psychographics** incorporate lifestyle and personality dimensions.

Strategic Business Insights provides a popular classification of lifestyles: The VALS typology categorizes respondents based on resources and on the extent to which they are action oriented. VALS categorizes consumers as:

Innovators—are successful, sophisticated, and receptive to new technologies. Their purchases reflect cultivated tastes for upscale products.

Thinkers—are educated, conservative, practical consumers who value knowledge and responsibility. They look for durability, functionality, and value.

Achievers—are goal-oriented, conservative consumers committed to career and family. They favor established prestige products that demonstrate success to peers.

Experiencers—are young, enthusiastic, and impulsive consumers who seek variety and excitement and spend substantially on fashion, entertainment, and socializing.

Believers—are conservative, conventional consumers who focus on tradition, family, religion, and community. They prefer established brands, favoring American products.

Strivers—are trendy, fun-loving consumers who are concerned about others' opinions and approval. They demonstrate to peers their ability to buy.

Makers—are self-sufficient consumers who have the skill and energy to carry out projects, respect authority, and are unimpressed by material possessions.

Source: Monkey Business Images/Shutterstock

Survivors—are concerned with safety and security, focus on meeting needs rather than fulfilling desires, are brand loyal, and purchase discounted products.

Knowledge about consumers' lifestyles is important. Marketers who learn about and adapt to changing consumer attitudes, interests, and opinions will have an advantage in the marketplace.

Believers Psychographic group of individuals who are conservative, conventional, and focus on tradition, family, religion, and community. They prefer established brands, favoring American products.

Strivers Psychographic group of individuals who are trendy and fun loving. They are concerned about others' opinions and approval, and demonstrate to peers their ability to buy.

Makers Psychographic group of individuals who are self-sufficient. They have the skill and energy to carry out projects, respect authority, and are unimpressed by material possessions.

Survivors Psychographic group of individuals who are concerned with safety and security. They focus on meeting needs rather than fulfilling desires, are brand loyal, and purchase discounted products.

4-5 The Consumer Decision-Making Process

Figure 4-6 illustrates the five stages in the consumer decision process. It should be noted, however, that not all consumers go through each stage every time they make a purchase. Certain stages may take more time and effort than others, depending on the type of purchase decision involved—as will be seen later in this section.

Let us, once again, use Cheri from the chapter opening to illustrate different stages of consumer decision making. Cheri is planning to entertain at Thanksgiving and has to engage in a number of purchases. On her most urgent shopping list, she has a new faucet for her guest bathroom, replacing the original faucet, which is a bit too basic for a transitional style bathroom. She also needs to purchase a turkey and the appropriate trimmings. These purchase decisions will be used to illustrate her decision-making processes, from problem recognition, to purchase, to post-purchase experiences.

4-5a Problem Recognition

The decision-making process starts when the consumer realizes that he or she has a particular need triggered by the difference between the actual state and a desired state. In the case of the guest bathroom faucet, Cheri has realized that her current faucet is too plain and that it does not convey her sense of style, which is reflected throughout the downstairs entertainment area. Her need for a new faucet is triggered externally. She has seen faucets with Victorian and contemporary designs at the

Problem Recognition

Information Research

Alternative Evaluation

Purchase

Postpurchase Behavior

FIGURE 4-6 The Consumer Decision Process

homes of many of her friends, in stores, and in restaurant bathrooms. A contemporary faucet and vanity at a friend's house may have suggested to her that she really needs to have a faucet that makes a statement in this room as well. She does not exactly know what she wants, but she knows that she wants something other than what she currently has in her guest bathroom.

Her need to have a Thanksgiving dinner is triggered internally. She has the need to socialize with new acquaintances she has met. She has a social need to belong to this group of individuals.

4-5b Information Search

Before making a purchase decision, consumers will search for information. They begin this search by first engaging in an internal information search, which involves thinking back to the different places where they have seen the product displayed or experiences that they themselves had with the good or service. If consumers have previously bought a product (or a particular brand), these consumers could simply engage in a repeat, habitual purchase, buying the same brand at the same store.

As previously mentioned, Cheri is a regular customer at Food Lion. Based on her experience, she knows that the store will carry some brand of fresh turkey, canned cranberries, stuffing, and walnuts for the stuffing. She also has seen pumpkin pie sold at the store. Cheri's mother used to shop at the last minute for products for the Thanksgiving dinner and she always delivered a great meal. Her mother was never keen on brand names—any brand of turkey was acceptable, as long as it was fresh. When the time comes, Cheri will spend about half an hour at Food Lion buying all the products she needs for the dinner.

Consumers could also engage in an external information search, taking time to read published information about a product, going through information brochures, searching the Internet, or asking friends about various brands. In her search for a new faucet, Cheri would most likely go to specialty stores that specialize in bathroom and kitchen fixtures to see what brands are available. She would also examine lifestyle and design magazines such as *Dwell,* as the Better Homes and Gardens Instagram blog, looking for faucet styles. Then, she will do extensive online searches to make sure that she gets the right product at the right price.

Source: Iakov Filimonov/Shutterstock

It is important for marketers to be aware of the information sources that their target consumers use. For bathroom sinks, for example, the most useful sources are those controlled by the manufacturer and its channel of distribution: Consumers rely on salespeople and manufacturer brochures for information. For turkey purchases, consumers are more likely to rely on retail advertising and on word-of-mouth communication for information. Marketers do not control the latter. Advertisements strategically placed in areas where consumers might need a particular product can trigger a need to purchase, for example, a cream that would pamper skin after lying in the sun.

4-5c Alternative Evaluation

In evaluating product alternatives, consumers compare the different brands and retailers to make sure that the brand they purchase best meets their needs. Often, this step occurs simultaneously with information search. For new product purchases, the alternative evaluation step is very important. Consumers typically use about five evaluation criteria in deciding on the brand that they are going to purchase. Among these criteria are those that a product must meet. For example, the faucet that Cheri is going to purchase must be stylish and unlike most of the other faucets on the market. There are no trade-offs for style and uniqueness. Other important criteria are performance and ease of use. In other respects, Cheri is flexible: Prices for faucets range between $20 and $130, but she is willing to go much higher. She is also flexible with regard to the location of the retailer, but she prefers the convenience of ordering the faucet.

In her search, Cheri finds brands such as Moen, FHP, Delta, Grohe, and Hansgrohe. The Moen and FHP brands appear to be rather simple, similar to the faucets that one can find in any public toilet. Grohe, a German manufacturer, seems to have more interesting designs in general, but its sink faucets are unremarkable. Cheri is particularly interested in the Philippe Stark models sold by Hansgrohe, another German manufacturer, under the brand name Axor and the Our Victorian brand sold by Delta.

Cheri finds out that the Axor faucet costs about $700 at the different specialty stores. She tries to find the brand at a lower price on the Internet, without success. All the sites direct buyers to retailers and none offer discounts. One such distributor is Duravit in Germany, which sells the complete Stark line, including toilets, sinks, and accessories. Lowe's, a home improvement store, does not carry the Stark collection. Home Depot, another large home improvement store, can obtain it at a lower price—$458. Cheri finds out that, if she orders the product at Home Depot, the store can put in a rush order so that the faucet can be installed before the Thanksgiving dinner.

Source: maxriesgo/Shutterstock

It is possible, however, that the alternative evaluation step may not be part of the decision-making process. For habitual purchases, consumers rely on their memory of a previous purchase and product experience and quickly decide which brand to purchase.

Cheri has organized many Thanksgiving dinners before, even when she used to live in a small city apartment while attending the Institute of Fine Art in New York. Although not a habitual purchase, a turkey is a turkey . . . with some caveats. First, her small convection oven would choke on anything larger than 20 pounds. Second, she would not consider buying a frozen turkey—her mother fervently believed that they could pose a health danger because they tend not to defrost evenly. And trimmings are trimmings—the store brand is just as good as any other competing national brand. Cheri thought that she could stop at the natural food store to purchase a farm-raised turkey on the way home from her studio in the city but quickly dismissed the idea. It involved complex logistics. Moreover, she believed that the turkey would probably not be as plump and juicy as one purchased at Food Lion.

4-5d Purchase

There are two important aspects to the purchase process: the purchase intention and the actual purchase. A number of consumer behavior models address the purchase intention and the purchase as two separate steps. Consumers may decide on a particular brand and on the outlet where the product will be purchased. These decisions reflect their purchase intentions. However, between the point where the purchase intention was formed and the actual purchase, there can be many intervening factors that could impede the purchase. The individual may have second thoughts about the brand or the importance of the purchase altogether. In our example, Cheri may decide that it is too expensive to purchase a new faucet and that she would be better off saving the money to purchase a new outfit. Or she may decide to buy the turkey from the organic food store, rather than from Food Lion, to make sure that she will serve the highest quality product—she can also share the information with her guests. If she were to purchase the turkey from Food Lion, then she would be reluctant to share information about the product's source with her guests.

Source: maxriesgo/Shutterstock

She may go to Home Depot with her best friend to make the faucet purchase. On a closer examination, however, her friend may notice that the Axor faucet does not spray water evenly. Cheri then could decide to purchase the Victorian style Delta faucet, which costs only $179. The job of marketers is to make sure that purchase intentions are translated into purchase behavior. Having a competent salesperson who will handle the order quickly, an appealing store environment with a pleasant atmosphere, and beautiful shiny fixtures could help the consumer to advance from intention to purchase.

4-5e Post-purchase Processes

The marketing task is not complete at the point where the client purchases the product. As mentioned in Chapter 1, satisfaction and dissatisfaction are important determinants of whether consumers will purchase the brand again. Marketing managers need to persuade consumers that they purchased a quality, reliable brand that addresses the needs consumers identified in the problem recognition stage and that it is better than the competition. Marketers must also address consumers' feelings of anxiety related to losing the freedom to purchase other brands or products that may or may not compete directly with the one chosen.

Expectations and Satisfaction As previously explained, consumers anticipate product performance based on their experiences, as well as information received from the media and from other consumers. They have expectations that influence the evaluation of good or service quality and predict how the product will perform on the market. Cheri expects that the Delta faucet she ultimately purchased will be of very high quality. She expects that the faucet will perform well, and more important, it will look lovely in her guest bathroom.

If a good or service performs better than expected, then consumers are likely to be satisfied. If satisfied, consumers are likely to purchase the brand in the future. If performance matches expectations, consumers are somewhat satisfied. If expectations are greater than performance, then there is a gap between expectation and performance and consumers are likely to be dissatisfied with the brand and may never purchase it again. These consumers are also expected to engage in negative word-of-mouth communication about the brand and switch to a competitor in the future.

Cognitive dissonance An anxiety feeling of uncertainty about whether or not the consumer made the right purchase decision.

Buyer's regret A feeling of anxiety related to the consumer's loss of freedom to spend money on other products.

If Cheri is satisfied with the Delta brand faucet, she may, in the future, spend thousands of dollars to purchase an entire Victorian style bathroom suite, from a formidable, wall-anchored toilet, to the geometric bathtub marvel, to the modest yet unique shower. If she is dissatisfied, she may return the product to the retailer for a full refund or just bad-mouth the brand to her friends, or post a negative product review if she does not want to go through the return process.

Source: Stephen VanHorn/Shutterstock

Cognitive Dissonance and Buyer's Regret **Cognitive dissonance** is an anxiety feeling of uncertainty about whether or not the consumer made the right purchase decision. This feeling is especially strong if the purchase is important and expensive and if the consumer does not have the option of returning the product if he or she is not satisfied with it. **Buyer's regret**

Stage	Faucet	Turkey
Problem Recognition	The need for a new faucet was triggered externally because of faucets Cheri had seen with Victorian and contemporary designs at the homes of many of her friends, in stores, and in restaurant bathrooms.	Cheri's need to have a Thanksgiving dinner party was triggered internally because she had the need to socialize with new acquaintances from her new environment.
Information Search	In her quest for a new faucet, Cheri looks externally for information at specialty stores and large home improvement stores to see what brands were available. She also read magazines looking for specifics about faucets.	Cheri conducted an internal search based on her memory of her mother shopping at Food Lion at the last minute for products for the Thanksgiving dinner. Her mother was never keen on brand names—any brand of turkey was acceptable if it was fresh.
Alternative	Cheri located several brands of faucets and spent considerable time evaluating each brand. Price, quality, and appearance were the major criteria she used.	Cheri spent little time evaluating the various brands of turkey. In fact, she never paid any attention to the brand name. She based her evaluation on the size and the appearance of the turkey.
Purchase	After careful consideration, Cheri purchased the Victorian style faucet made by Delta and sold at Home Depot.	Cheri purchased the turkey from Food Lion because that was the retailer she used for groceries and
Post-purchase	Cheri experienced both cognitive dissonance and buyer's regret. She worried her friends would not like the style she picked out, and if they did not, she did not have the money to buy another new set.	Cheri spent little time evaluating the turkey purchase because it tasted good and her company enjoyed it.

FIGURE 4-7 Cheri's Decision-Making Process for a Faucet and a Turkey

is related to cognitive dissonance, in that it is also a feeling of anxiety. The anxiety is related to the consumer's loss of freedom to spend money on other products. Spending $458 on a faucet will limit the amount that Cheri can spend when her favorite retailer carrying designer clothing has its end-of-year sale.

An important task of marketers is to reduce cognitive dissonance and buyer's regret by reassuring consumers that they made the right purchase. Post-purchase installation, service, warranties, advertisements, and direct-mail communications all serve to reduce consumers' cognitive dissonance and dispel any concerns the consumers may have about the purchase. Such communications may compare the brand favorably with competing brands and stress attributes that are important to the consumer. For example, Cheri would be delighted to receive a note from Delta congratulating her on her purchase or a telephone call from Home Depot reassuring her that it stands behind the Delta brand. **Figure 4-7** summarizes the consumer decision-making process for Cheri in the purchase of the faucet and the Thanksgiving turkey.

4-6 Variations in Decision Making

In the process of making purchase decisions, consumers can engage in **extensive problem solving**, going carefully through each of the steps of the consumer decision-making process. In this case, consumers will spend substantial amounts of time searching for information about the different brands and outlets where the product may be purchased. Extensive problem solving is typical for **high-involvement purchases** that have a high personal relevance.

Extensive problem solving Consumer decision making that involves going carefully through each of the steps of the consumer decision-making process.

High-involvement purchases Purchases that have a high personal relevance.

Cheri considers a faucet a high-involvement purchase because the faucet selected is important in projecting her sense of style to her aspirational group. She wanted the faucet to be unique, unlike all the other products on retailers' shelves and in her acquaintances' bathrooms. Cheri went through extensive problem solving when purchasing the Delta faucet, spending large amounts of time and energy to learn about the different faucet brands available on the market.

Consumers can engage in **limited problem solving** for products that are not especially visible or too expensive. In deciding to purchase the turkey at Food Lion, Cheri wanted to minimize the amount of time and effort dedicated to the purchase. Although buying a turkey was not quite a routine purchase, her once-a-year experience provided enough information to her that she did not need to ask around where she would find a reasonable product. She may have looked at the weekly advertisements from other supermarkets to note whether they offered a greater discount and she may have examined different brands of fresh turkey at Food Lion. Beyond that, her decision process was relatively simple: She selected the turkey brand, found the right size turkey, and purchased it.

Limited problem solving Consumer decision making that involves less problem solving. This type of decision making is used for products that are not especially visible, nor too expensive.

Consumers can also engage in **routine problem solving**. Consumers engage in routine problem solving for habitual purchase decisions involving products that they purchase frequently. Consumers routinely purchase Tropicana juice, Yoplait yogurt, Eggo waffles, Colgate toothpaste, and other similar brands. Consumers do not need to compare these brands with alternative product offerings if these brands have provided a satisfactory consumption experience. Routine problem solving is typical for **low-involvement products** (products with limited personal relevance, such as eggs, cheese, and other convenience goods).

Routine problem solving Consumer decision making whereby consumers engage in habitual purchase decisions involving products that they purchase frequently.

Low-involvement products Products with limited personal relevance.

Finally, consumers are greatly affected by situational influences. When purchasing products for personal private consumption, consumers are more likely to purchase discounted products or to buy store brands. When purchasing products with friends, consumers tend to engage in more limited problem solving in making their purchase decision. When purchasing a product for gift giving, consumers are likely to engage in extensive problem solving, both with regard to the brand and the retailer, ensuring that the product is impeccably packaged and presented.

Marketers need to take note of consumers' situational influences and steer their decision accordingly. Salespeople in boutiques and department stores often take special care to ensure that products targeted for gift giving are attractively wrapped and presented. For a review of the variations in decision making, see **Figure 4-8** on the following page.

Product	Cheri's action	Type of problem-solving situation
Faucet	**Cheri spent several days and a lot of time choosing just the right bathroom faucet.**	Extensive problem solving.
Turkey	**Cheri examined the various turkeys.**	Limited problem solving. She was at Food Lion and, after several minutes, picked the one that she thought would be the best.
Candy bar	**As Cheri was checking out, she noticed the rack of candy bars and picked out her favorite.**	Routine problem solving.
Stereo	**Wanting to get the right stereo, Cheri spent several weeks looking in stores and catalogs and online before she made a purchase.**	Extensive problem solving.
Soft drink	**Thirsty, Cheri went to the soda machine and bought Diet Coke, the same brand she almost always purchases.**	Routine problem solving.
McDonald's	**Cheri was hungry but did not have much time.**	Limited problem solving. She thought about which fast-food restaurants were on her way to work and because McDonald's was on the right side of the street and there did not appear to be a long line of cars at the drive-up window, she chose it.

FIGURE 4-8 Variations in Decision Making

Summary

1. **Identify the elements of a consumer behavior model.**
   The consumer behavior model addresses the influence of social and psychological factors that affect consumer behavior. Social influences, such as culture, subcultures, social class, roles, status, families, households, and reference groups, are instrumental in shaping individual attitudes, interests, opinions, and behavior. Psychological influences, such as motivation, perception, learning, personality, and lifestyles, as well as beliefs and attitudes, are likely to influence how consumers behave.

2. **Describe the different social influences that have an impact on consumer behavior.**
   Among the social influences that affect consumer behavior are culture, social class, role and status influences, family and household influences, and reference group influences. Culture includes the totality of learned and shared meanings, rituals, norms, and traditions among the members of an organization or society. Values are particularly important in that they guide individuals' actions, attitudes, and judgments and thus affect behavior. Values are learned from those with whom individuals are in contact: family, friends, teachers, clergy, politicians, and the media. Learning a new culture is known as acculturation. Subcultures are components of the broad culture; they are groups of individuals with shared value systems based on ethnicity or common background. Among the important ethnic and national subcultures in the United States are the African-American subculture, the Hispanic-American subculture,

and the Asian-American subculture. Social class, role, and status influences also have an important impact on consumer behavior. In the United States, the social classes are the upper class, consisting of upper uppers (old money) and lower uppers (new money); the middle class, consisting of upper-middle class (professionals) and lower-middle class (white collar); and the lower class, consisting of upper-lower class (blue collar) and lower-lower class (unskilled and unemployed). Additional social influences are exerted by one's family and household and by reference groups, especially by aspirational reference groups that one would like to belong to.

3. **Describe the different psychological influences that have an impact on consumer behavior.**
Consumer behavior is influenced by motivation, perception, learning, attitudes, beliefs, personality, and lifestyles. Consumers are motivated by needs and wants, which create a drive to engage in behavior. In the hierarchy of needs, physiological needs, such as food and water, are the most basic. They are followed by safety needs and social needs—for love and belonging. At the higher levels are the need for self-esteem and status in society, and at the highest level, the need for self-actualization—the need to accomplish and realize one's full potential. Perception is the manner in which we perceive the world around us, the manner in which we notice advertisements and products in a store. Learning, which involves changes in individual thought processes or behavior attributed to experience, influences consumer behavior. Attitudes and beliefs involve developing feelings about products and associations between a good or service and attributes of that good or service. Finally, individuals' enduring traits and responses to stimuli around them (personality) and individuals' style of living as expressed through activities, interests, and opinions (lifestyles) also influence consumer behavior. Marketers have devised modalities to cluster individuals based on personality and lifestyle through psychographic measurement.

4. **Address the five stages of the consumer decision-making process.**
The stages of the consumer decision-making process are problem recognition, information search, alternative evaluation, purchase, and post-purchase behavior. Problem recognition develops when there is a difference between the actual state and a desired state. It can be triggered externally, by advertising or store displays or by observing others consuming a product; or it can be triggered internally, through an individual need. Consumers could search for information internally, by searching their own memory about a product experience, or externally, by consulting magazines or salespeople. After evaluating the different brand and retail outlet alternatives, consumers typically develop the intention to purchase a product; barring any intervening events or concerns, the consumer engages in the purchase. After purchase, marketers need to ensure that consumers will be satisfied with their purchase by offering guarantees and prompt post-purchase service and by ensuring that the product functions optimally. They also have to reduce consumers' cognitive dissonance (the anxiety that consumers associate with the concern that they may not have bought the best product) and buyer's regret (the regret for the loss of freedom to purchase other products with the money).

5. **Describe variations in consumer decision making based on whether consumers engage in extensive, limited, or routine problem solving.**
Depending on the product purchased, consumers could engage in extensive problem solving, where they will go through each stage of the decision-making process. This is typical for products of high personal relevance—high-involvement products—that may have been expensive or may be closely tied to the consumer's self-image. Limited problem solving takes place in the case of products that are not especially expensive or important (low-involvement products), and only minimal problem solving takes place for routine purchase decisions, many of which are habitual.

Key Terms

Acculturation (95)
Achievers (106)
Aspirational groups (100)
Assimilation (95)
Associative reference groups (100)
Attitudes (104)
Beliefs (104)
Believers (107)
Buyer's regret (111)
Cognitive dissonance (111)
Cues (104)
Dissociative groups (100)
Drive (or motive) (101)
Experiencers (106)
Extended self (106)
Extensive problem solving (113)
High-involvement purchases (113)
Innovators (106)
Instrumental values (94)
Learning (104)
Lifestyles (106)
Limited problem solving (113)
Low-involvement products (113)
Makers (107)
Perception (103)
Personality (104)
Psychographics (106)
Reference groups (100)
Reinforcement (104)
Roles (97)
Routine problem solving (113)
Selective distortion (103)
Selective exposure (103)
Selective retention (103)
Self-concept (106)
Social class (97)
Status (98)
Stimuli (104)
Strivers (107)
Subcultures (95)
Survivors (107)
Terminal values (94)
Thinkers (106)
Values (94)

Discussion Questions

1. Look through the terminal values listed in this chapter. Pick the three that are the most important to you and drive your consumption behavior. Explain why and how they influence your purchases.
2. Look through the instrumental values listed in this chapter. Pick the three that best describe you and influence your consumption behavior. Explain why and how they influence your purchases.
3. Identify the subcultures that you are part of. How have these subcultures affected your consumer purchases? Be specific.
4. Discuss the impact of religion on your personal consumer purchases. What about your sexual orientation? How does that impact your purchase behavior? Provide specific illustrations.
5. Which social class do you belong to? How does this impact your purchase decisions?
6. Describe the role(s) that impact you. What about status? How does status impact your purchase behaviors?
7. Discuss the impact of your family on your consumer purchases? Which member or members of your household have the most impact on your purchase behavior? Why?
8. Identify your reference groups. What groups do you belong to (associative groups)? What types of products do you consume based on these affiliations? What groups do you aspire to belong to? What products do you consume or purchase by virtue of this projected affiliation?
9. Perception includes selective exposure, selective distortion, and selective retention. Give a recent example from your personal

experience of selective exposure, selective distortion, and selective retention.

10. Look through the VALS2 categories described in this chapter. In which group would you place yourself? Why? What type of purchase do you make as a result of that classification?
11. Identify a low-involvement product and a high-involvement product that you have recently purchased. Attempt to reconstruct the consumer decision-making process involved for each product.
12. Identify a recent high-involvement purchase you made. Discuss each of the five stages of the decision-making process in terms of the purchase. Especially highlight your mental thought processes and any influences that impacted the decision you made.
13. Identify products and brands that fit into each of the following categories: extensive problem solving, limited problem solving, and routine problem solving. Provide explanations for each product and brand you classified.

Review Questions

True or False

1. The consumer behavior model is based on social influences, such as culture, subculture, social class, individual roles and status, and family.
2. Values are defined as a continuously changing totality of learned and shared meanings, rituals, norms, and traditions among the members of society.
3. The lower-upper class accounts for 2 percent of the U.S. population; the class earned new money through business ventures and are most likely to show off their possessions.
4. Aspirational groups are groups an individual belongs to.
5. Selective retention involves consumers adapting the information to fit their own existing knowledge or beliefs.
6. A consumer's personality is expressed through activities, interests, opinions, and lifestyle.
7. The customer decision-making process consists of five stages: defining the desired social status, seeking information, searching for the best discounts, making the purchase, and postpurchase behavior.
8. The consumer decision process starts with the consumer realizing that a particular need is triggered by the difference between the actual state and the desired state.
9. Alternative evaluation is a necessary step in the decision-making process for all purchases.
10. When purchasing low-price products for personal private consumption, consumers tend to follow the extensive problem-solving pattern.

Multiple Choice

11. Which of the following categories relates to the psychological influences of consumer behavior?
    a. family and households
    b. personality and lifestyles
    c. individual roles and status
    d. culture and subculture
12. Which of the following categories relates to subculture?
    a. ethnicity and nationality
    b. age groups
    c. religion
    d. all of the above
13. Which of the following statements defines status?
    a. the products people consume and individuals' behavior
    b. activities people are expected to perform
    c. emphasis on the individual materialistic perception of success
    d. the esteem that society places upon a particular role

14. Which of the following are reference groups?
    a. aspirational groups
    b. associative groups
    c. dissociative groups
    d. all of the above
15. Reinforcement in the context of the learning process refers to
    a. strengthening the relationship between the cue and the response.
    b. change in the contents in an advertisement.
    c. applying more aggressive direct sales techniques.
    d. all of the above.
16. Which of the following characteristics describes the psychographic profile of the VALS group called "survivor"?
    a. focused on meeting needs rather than fulfilling desires
    b. sophisticated
    c. goal oriented
    d. b and c
17. When making a purchase, what information source do consumers use first?
    a. internal or external information sources
    b. internal information sources
    c. external information sources
    d. none of the above
18. Different factors could interfere and prevent the purchase in the ________ phase of the purchase process.
    a. purchase intention
    b. actual purchase
    c. post-purchase
    d. a and b
19. Which of the following statements describes cognitive dissonance?
    a. dissatisfaction with product performance
    b. consumers trying out a different brand each time when making a purchase
    c. anxiety feelings of uncertainty about the right purchase decision
    d. none of the above
20. The purchase of a new suit or dress will normally require
    a. extensive problem solving.
    b. situational problem solving.
    c. limited problem solving.
    d. routine problem solving.

Answers: (1) False, (2) False, (3) True, (4) False, (5) False, (6) False, (7) False, (8) True, (9) False, (10) False, (11) b, (12) d, (13) d, (14) d, (15) a, (16) a, (17) b, (18) b, (19) c, (20) a

Case: The Hispanic Market

Albertsons LLC is a supermarket chain with 2,252 locations in fifteen Western and Southern states. Because Hispanic-Americans account for 19 percent of the U.S. population, Albertsons sees it as an attractive market: Hispanic-Americans are the fastest-growing ethnic segment in the United States. The Hispanic population is setting pace to become the next demographic phenomenon, with Hispanics accounting for over half of the U.S. population growth from 2016 to 2020, and up to 80% by 2040. Their relatively younger age (27 versus 42 for non-Hispanic Whites) and longer life expectancy make them an attractive driving force in the U.S. economy for the next decades. Marketers are advised to put a premium on their main acquisition: as the Latinx slice of the population pie enlarges, so will their value to astute marketers who will jump at the opportunity to establish culturally-relevant ties in our hypersocial digital world.

To reach this important market segment, Albertsons hired Anton Estrada to design and direct the company's Hispanic-American marketing effort. Management believed that having someone of Hispanic-American background to develop the Hispanic-American marketing program would be a huge asset and increase their chances of succeeding.

Anton immediately began assessing the various markets where Albertsons operated stores. Although there were 60 million Hispanic-Americans in the United States, they were not evenly distributed throughout the states where Albertsons had stores. Anton was able to collect

Source: Monkey Business Images/Shutterstock

information regarding the states with the most Hispanic-Americans: there are over 15 million Hispanics in California, over 11 million in Texas, 5.6 million in Florida, 3.8 million in New York, and 2.2 million in Arizona.

Based on personal experience and facts he had learned in college, Anton knew that Hispanic-Americans tended to be more brand and store loyal than the population as a whole. If a retail store, such as a supermarket, treated Hispanic-Americans right, they would be loyal to that store. He also knew that Hispanic-Americans are willing to pay more money for a name brand product that they believe is of high quality, durable, and dependable.

In terms of grocery shopping, Hispanic-Americans prefer fresh food. Because they cook more from scratch, a greater percentage of their grocery money is spent on fresh fruit, vegetables, meat, poultry, fish, and eggs. Instead of shopping once a week like most Caucasians, Hispanic-Americans tend to shop more frequently, as much as four to five times a week. Furthermore, they spend an average of $133 per week on groceries compared with $91 for the non–Hispanic-American family.

A study by FMI (Food Marketing Institute) provided specific information about what store attributes were important to Hispanic-Americans. The percentages of Hispanic-Americans who rated the various store attributes as important or somewhat important are shown in the following table.

Store Attribute	Rate
A clean, neat store	98%
Fresh, high-quality fruits & veggies	97%
Fresh, high-quality meats & poultry	96%
Courteous, friendly employees	96%
Low prices	96%
Carry Hispanic foods	91%
Bilingual employees	88%
Bilingual signage	84%
Store active in Hispanic-American communities	84%
Bilingual packaging	82%

Now let us turn to the challenges faced by Estrada. Not all Hispanic-Americans are the same. Although most are from Mexico, many Hispanic-Americans are from Central and South America, Cuba, the Caribbean, Honduras, and Puerto Rico. Just as Caucasians are not all the same, neither are all Hispanic-Americans the same. Although they share a common Spanish language, they do not all share the same cultural views. Furthermore, the level of acculturation into the American culture varies considerably. Some are fully acculturated, whereas others have accepted and adopted little of the American culture. Some speak English well, others do not. Most, however, live in a world of dual languages. They watch and read both English and Spanish programs and magazines. Overall, 70 percent of Hispanic-Americans identify the Spanish language as the most important cultural aspect that they want to retain. However, four out of ten Hispanic-Americans prefer to use English, and 54 percent of Hispanic-Americans watch English-speaking television programs. The differences among the generations are evident with children growing up in the United States and Hispanic-Americans who have lived in the United States for a number of years, who show a higher level of acculturation than Hispanic-Americans who have recently moved to the United States.

Case Questions

1. Should Estrada develop a program that is used in all of the Albertsons stores or should he concentrate on only certain states? If only certain states, which states would you suggest? Also, within those states, should he concentrate only on certain stores? Explain your reasoning.
2. Because of the different nationality backgrounds of Hispanic-Americans, how does Estrada handle development of marketing materials?
3. What specific marketing recommendations should Estrada make to management to reach the Hispanic-American market?
4. Based on the information provided in this case, how has culture affected the Hispanic-American grocery shoppers and how does it impact the marketing approach Albertsons would use to reach them?

Sources: Fictitious case based on Nielsen, Descubrimiento Digital: the Online Lives of Latin-X Consumers, 2018m https://www.nielsen.com/us/en/insights/report/2018/descubrimiento-digital-the-online-lives-of-latinx-consumers; 2012 Statistical Abstracts of the U.S. Census Bureau, accessed at: http://www.census.gov/ data.html on June 1, 2020.

Endnotes

1. See Milton J. Rokeach, The Nature of Human Values: (New York: The Free Press, 1973); P. Kautish, A. Khare, and R. Sharma, "Influence of values, brand consciousness and behavioral intentions in predicting luxury fashion consumption," *Journal of Product & Brand Management*, 2020, doi.org/10.1108/JPBM-08-2019-2535.
2. Raj Mehta and Russell W. Belk, "Artifacts, Identity and Transition," *Journal of Consumer Research,* 17, 1991, 398–411; Lisa Penaloza and Mary C. Gilly, "Marketer Acculturation: The Changer and the Changed," *Journal of Marketing,* 63, no. 3, 1999, 84–104.
3. S.M. de Armas, S. M., and A. McCaskill (2018). *Descubrimiento Digital: The Online Lives of Latinx Consumers*, https://www.nielsen.com/content/dam/corporate/us/en/reports-downloads/2018-reports/the-online-lives-latinx-consumers.pdf.
4. Nielsen, Nielsen Examines the Digital Habits and Impact of Black Consumers, September 13, 2018, https://www.nielsen.com/us/en/press-room/2018/nielsen-examines-the-digital-habits-and-impact-of-black-consumers.html.
5. Nielsen, *Engaging Asian American consumers at the dawn of a new decade.* (n.d.). Retrieved June 10, 2020, from https://www.nielsen.com/us/en/insights/report/2020/engaging-asian-american-consumers-at-the-dawn-of-a-new-decade; Carpenter, M., & Scott-Aime, M. (2018). *Informed Influencers and Powerful Purchasers: The Asian American Consumer Journey*, https://www.nielsen.com/content/dam/corporate/us/en/reports-downloads/2019-reports/asian-american-diverse-intelligence-series-report.pdf.
6. Information on percentages from Pew Research Center, Religion and Public Life, accessed at https://www.pewforum.org/religious-landscape-study, March 13, 2020.
7. Bureau of the Census, Current Population Survey Annual Social and Economic Supplement, December 6, 2019, accessed athttps://catalog.data.gov/dataset/current-population-survey-annual-social-and-economic-supplement
8. This section based on: www.crmtrends.com/ConsumerDemographics.html, accessed March 8, 2020.
9. Maslow, A. H. (1943). A theory of human motivation. *Psychological Review, 50*(4), 370–96; Maslow, A. H. (1954). *Motivation and personality*. New York: Harper and Row; Maslow, A. H. (1962).
10. American Psychological Association, Personality, https://www.apa.org/topics/personality, accessed on March 8, 2020.
11. Baumeister, R. F. (1999). *Self-concept, self-esteem, and identity.* In V. J. Derlega, B. A. Winstead, & W. H. Jones (Eds.), *Nelson-Hall series in psychology. Personality: Contemporary theory and research* (p. 339–375). Nelson-Hall Publishers.
12. Belk, Russell (1988), "Possessions and the Extended Self," *Journal of Consumer Research,* Vol. 15, 140–166.

Business-to-Business to Behavior

Source: totojang1977/Shutterstock

Chapter Outline

Learning Objectives

Ivelin Radkov/Shutterstock

After studying this chapter, you should be able to:

- Identify the types of goods and services that businesses purchase.
- Identify the types of business customers.
- Explain the concepts of derived and joint demand and why it is important for the business-to-business market.
- Identify the types of buying situations and when each is used.
- Describe the concept of the buying center and the different roles employees can play.
- Discuss the factors that influence business-to-business buyer behavior.
- List the seven steps in the business-to-business buying process and explain what occurs in each step.

Source: Dennis Kartenkaemper/Shutterstock

5-1 Chapter Overview

Before the COVID-19 pandemic, private jets were reserved for business travelers and the world elite. Long lines at airports and high fares of commercial airlines caused business travelers to examine other options—hiring private charter jets, flying one of the new startups flying business travelers, or purchasing a jet plane or a share in a corporate jet. For the elite, private jets were something you read about in *Page Six*, with celebrities whisked away from black SUV to the Gulfstream.

The private aviation pitch has been efficiency and privacy, you are out of the airport five minutes after you land, and the baggage policy is that you are allowed to carry with you whatever is legal and you can fit through the door or can be pushed into the luggage compartment. With the pandemic and reports that not just the elderly are vulnerable, private travel has become a trading-up expenditure for both business and private travel. Where United and Delta will have difficulty in fully cleaning cabins between multiple daily flights, clocking 12 hours in the air per day, private jets barely reach 1,000 hours a year, and have enough time for thorough cleaning.

Corporate flight departments are seeking to buy extra flight hours as companies expand the number of executives who have access to private aviation. More firms are also signing up for new memberships that offer lower entry points, 10 hours, instead of 25 hours. Private jets reduce risk, flying with five or ten other people who can be screened in advance is safer than flying with 150 people. Since the price of airfare will likely rise with reduced schedules and regulations to keep the middle seat open, it may be that sharing a private flight or buying a seat end up being less expensive than airline travel.[1]

Although the marketing of goods and services to businesses has some similarities to the marketing to individual consumers, there are also some significant differences. This chapter addresses those differences. Section 5-2 begins with a discussion of the various types of goods and services purchased by businesses. They range from multimillion-dollar projects, such as new buildings and jet aircraft, to low-cost items, such as paper clips and copy paper.

Section 5-3 presents the different types of business customers and the way businesses determine demand for their products. In the consumer market, if a firm wishes to stimulate demand, it can offer a price discount, coupons, or some other promotion to encourage consumers to make a purchase. A supplier of raw materials, such as lumber to a furniture factory, cannot stimulate demand just by offering some type of special deal because the amount of lumber a furniture factory will buy depends on how much furniture it sells to retail stores, who in turn sell the furniture to consumers.

Section 5-4 examines the business-to-business purchase process itself. In many situations, more than one person is involved in the purchase decision, with each performing a different role. Some will be instrumental in making the decision, whereas others provide information or work out the details of the purchase. The section concludes with a discussion of the various factors that influence how individuals act within the business-to-business purchasing process and what affects the purchase decision that is made. The last section of the chapter, Section 5-5, identifies the seven steps of the business purchase process. The buying process begins with the identification of a need, goes through identifying potential vendors, and ends with the selection of a vendor who can meet the company's need.

5-2 Types of Business Goods and Services

In understanding business buyer behavior, it is helpful to identify the types of goods and services that businesses purchase. They include major equipment, buildings and land, accessory equipment, fabricated and component parts, process materials, maintenance and repair parts, operating supplies, raw materials, goods for resale, and business services (see Figure 5-1). Each of these requires a slightly different marketing approach and is purchased by a different kind of customer.

5-2a Major Equipment, Buildings, and Land

The purchase of buildings, land, and major equipment, such as factory machines, mainframe computers, and robotic equipment, requires considerable time and thought. Top management is almost always included

FIGURE 5-1 Types of Business Goods and Services

Source: Liz Van Steenburgh/Shutterstock

in the decision and often in the selection process because the cost of these items is high. These types of purchases are often the result of strategic decisions made by executive management, and financing is a significant consideration because few companies would have the cash to pay for them. In the case of major equipment, leases may be examined as an option because that could be more cost effective than a purchase. From a seller's standpoint, these types of purchases require a long period of time, often several months, and the involvement of the top management of the selling company.

5-2b Accessory Equipment

Accessory equipment consists of items used by a business but usually not directly involved in the production or sale of the firm's products. Accessory equipment would include furniture, computers, copy machines, forklifts and vehicles such as a company truck. These items are not purchased on a regular basis and therefore require some extra effort when the purchase is made. Because most are not high-ticket items, upper management is not normally involved in the selection but may be involved in the final approval. This would likely depend on the ticket price. For a high-quality scanner, top management probably would not be involved, but for a company semi-truck that may cost $120,000, it may be. At a minimum, a vice president will probably be involved in the truck purchase. As with major equipment, leases are sometimes considered rather than a purchase. For example, rather than purchase copy machines or a fleet of cars, these items may be leased.

5-2c Fabricated and Component Parts

Fabricated and component parts are identifiable products that are incorporated into another product. In automobiles, component parts include the spark plugs, the battery, the radio, and the tires. These parts are not made by the automobile manufacturer but are purchased from outside vendors and installed on the vehicle. Fabricated parts are a type of component part. However, the difference is that the fabricated parts are not as easily identifiable. For instance, most computer manufacturers use fabricated parts in building their computers. The processor, the camera, and the speakers used in your computer were purchased from various vendors. Your computer manufacturer just assembled them into a computer for you. Unless you are a computer

Source: Suradech/Prapairat/Shutterstock

wizard, the only fabricated part you can probably identify is the Intel processor.

Because fabricated and component parts become a part of a finished product, quality and dependability become important issues. If the motherboard on your computer or the radio in your automobile is of inferior quality, then it will reflect on the product being purchased. If you purchased a Mercedes, your expectations of radio quality would likely be different than if you purchased a Mini Cooper. Therefore, Mercedes is likely to purchase a higher-quality radio or stereo system. The key is to match the quality of the component part to the quality of the finished product.

The second important factor is dependability. Nineteen automakers, including Nissan, Infinity, BMW, and Honda, are recalling 70 airbag inflators made by the now bankrupt Japanese (now Chinese) firm Takata; this is the largest string of automotive recalls in U.S. history, affecting 100 million automobiles. The inflators use ammonium nitrate to create a small explosion that inflates the airbags, the chemical deteriorates when exposed to humidity and high temperatures, blowing apart the canister that is supposed to contain the explosion. The company, bankrupt since 2017, was bought by Chinese investors and is known as Joyston Safety Systems, operating in Michigan as Key Safety Systems. Repairs are still handled by the company, which is required to remain in business until all repairs are completed. These recalls reflect poorly on the automobile companies, which continued to use Takata airbags long after the initial recalls, a decade earlier. Firms must choose their suppliers carefully: poor product performance will not be attributed just to the supplier: it will reflect poorly on the BMW and Honda automobile brand as well. [2]

Source: Red Ivory/Shutterstock

5-2d Process Materials

Process materials are used in the manufacture of other products but lose their identity. Process materials include items such as cement, aluminum, steel, plastic, and wire. Because process materials are used in the building of other products, specifications are an important issue. The metal and plastic used in building a clothes dryer must meet certain grade, quality, and durability specifications. The grade of electrical wire required varies depending on whether it is used for the switch on the dryer's console or the cord that is plugged into the home's 220-volt electrical outlet.

As with fabricated and component parts, quality, delivery, and cost are important issues. Because process materials lose their identity, any defects will be directly attributed to the manufacturer. But it is also the case that because they lose their identity, they achieve a commodity status with buyers. The electrical wires used in the General Electric (GE) clothes dryer can be purchased from a number of firms that manufacture electrical wiring. The quality is often the same, so factors such as price, deals, and dependable delivery become more important in the purchase decision. GE would be inclined to go with the lowest cost as long as the firm can provide quality and dependable delivery. However, if another company offers GE a special deal on wire, GE may be willing to switch vendors. All of this is said with the understanding that dependable delivery is crucial. If the wire is not delivered to the GE factory in a timely manner, it could cause a shutdown of the assembly line and cost GE money. Therefore, buyers often build in penalties or fines if a supplier's failure to deliver their materials causes a production shutdown.

5-2e Maintenance and Repair Parts

Items such as oil, grease, lubricant, gears, switches, and motors are considered maintenance and repair parts. These items are needed to keep a machine running or to repair a machine when it is broken. Maintenance items are normally kept in stock and are replenished on a regular basis. As with process materials, maintenance items are often commodity products with no or little brand-name recognition. Because the brand of grease used on a machine is usually not a factor in the purchase decision, price becomes an important determinant.

Repair parts are not usually kept in stock unless they are items that break down often or may be extremely critical to an operation. For example, a mill that uses a large number of electrical motors will usually keep motor parts on hand so that a motor can be repaired quickly. It may even keep spare motors that can be switched out while the broken one is being repaired.

For accessory equipment, instead of the buyer taking handling all the repairs and keeping repair parts on hand, it may opt for a maintenance contract. Copiers are an excellent example. With the purchase of a Konika Minolta copier, a business may also purchase a three-year maintenance agreement whereby Konika agrees to maintain the copier and repair anything that is broken. These maintenance contracts are especially important for technical equipment requiring a specialized knowledge to repair.

5-2f Operating Supplies

Operating supplies tend to be low-cost items a company needs for day-to-day operations. Light bulbs, paper, pencils, paper clips, and cleaning chemicals would be examples. These types of products are purchased on a regular basis by the purchasing department's staff or secretarial staff. Price and convenience are usually the most important criteria in purchasing. Little effort or time is devoted to purchasing operating supplies.

5-2g Raw Materials

Raw materials are supplied by the agriculture, fishing, mining, and timber industries. Raw materials must go through some type of manufacturing process before they can be used in building a product. Timber must be cut into some type of board or chips before it can be used. Minerals must be mined and impurities taken out before the minerals can be used. Corn, wheat, and other agricultural products must be cleaned and processed before they can be used as ingredients in food or feed products.

Raw materials are purchased in bulk based on some type of grading process. The price a farmer will be paid for wheat is determined by the grade and quality of the wheat. When it is sold, it loses its identity because it is often mixed with grain from other sources. The mill that grinds the wheat into flour has no idea what farmer's wheat is used but does know the grade and type of wheat. Because the wheat has no brand identity, brokers, agents, and distributors are often used. General Mills does not want to deal with every farmer to purchase wheat for its needs. Therefore, it will deal with a broker or distributor who has purchased wheat from a number of sources and pooled it together.

Source: alexkich/Shutterstock

For a company like General Mills, the three most important factors in purchasing an ingredient like wheat are the price, grade or quality, and a dependable supply. Because wheat is graded by quality, General Mills will tend to go with the supplier offering the best price with an acceptable level of quality and delivery.

Because of the commodity nature of raw materials, online purchasing is preferred, with business-to-business auction marketplaces available for both buyers and sellers. Companies can sell excess inventory and liquidate stock they own and purchase materials and products for themselves. Sellers can post raw materials and other products on the site, inviting buyers' bids.

5-2h Business Services

Business services consist of professional services and operating services. Professional services would include legal counsel, medical services, certified public accountants (CPAs), auditing services, and consulting services. Operating services would include the telephone service, Internet provider, insurance carrier, lawn care service, janitorial service, and shipping services. Professional services tend to be hired for a particular situation or on retainer when they are needed. Operating services tend to be hired on contract to supply the service on a continual basis for a fixed period of time. For many companies, these types of services are let out for bid on a routine basis, often once a year.

In recent years, there has been a trend to outsource some of a company's operation to outside vendors. Large companies that have a cafeteria will often contract with an outside vendor, such as Aramark, to operate the food service for them. Other companies have outsourced human resource functions, information technology (IT) functions, and payroll. They believe doing this will allow them to obtain better service at a lower cost than if they did it themselves.

Marketing of a service to another business is a greater challenge than marketing a good because the business cannot see the service before making the purchase. Personal relationships and trust become more important. If the members of an office complex decide to hire a service to take care of their lawns, they must make decisions on proposals submitted and the work they believe the service will provide. Because of the risk of not knowing how well a service will perform, most companies do not switch service providers unless they are unhappy with their current provider. Seldom will coming in with a lower price be enough, unless the price is substantially lower than the company's current vendor. Even then, the company may have doubts whether the new service provider can provide the same service level at such a low price.

5-3 Characteristics of Business-to-Business Markets

As shown in **Figure 5-2**, business-to-business markets differ from consumer markets in a number of ways. Fewer buyers, larger purchase volumes, geographic concentrations, and a formal buying process are the major differences. A manufacturer of computer chips has a limited number of computer manufacturers who will buy its computer chips. Boeing has a limited number of airlines and other businesses that will purchase

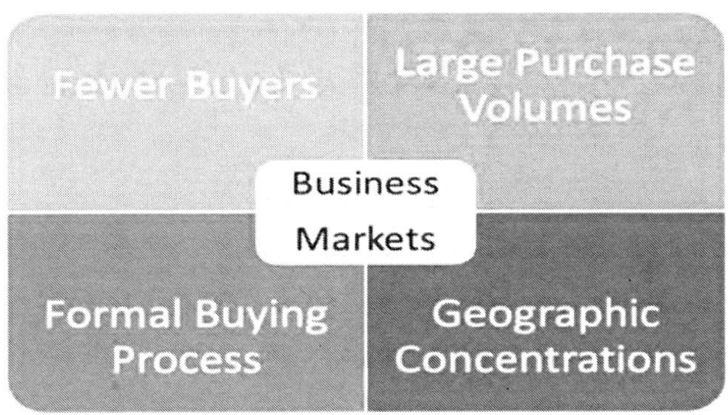

FIGURE 5-2 Characteristics of Business-to-Business Markets

its commercial large-body jets. Even a steel mill has a limited number of buyers of its products.

Because there are a limited number of buyers, the purchase volume of each is much higher. Dell, IBM, and other computer manufacturers will purchase computer chips by the thousands and will expect volume discounts and other services as a result of the purchase. If a computer chip manufacturer loses a large account like Dell, the loss can be devastating to the business. Because of the high cost of airplanes, a manufacturer like Boeing will not even start production until it receives an order from a major airline like Delta.

It is common for businesses to cluster in specific geographic areas. Most people know that the computer industry is concentrated in the Silicon Valley in California. That makes it easier for a company selling component parts because it can call on a number of companies within the valley **(see Figure 5-3).** It is not unusual for these suppliers to build offices and factories around their market. This has occurred around Walmart's office in Bentonville, Arkansas. Because of the size of Walmart and the size of the orders it places, a number of companies, such as Procter & Gamble, General Mills, and 3M, have built offices nearby to service the Walmart account. A similar scenario has occurred with Del Monte and its supplier of corrugated boxes used to ship Del Monte's food items. The supplier of Del Monte boxes has built a facility close to each factory.

5-3a Types of Customers

In developing an understanding of business buyer behavior, it is helpful to examine the different types of customers available to a business. A common classification system is the NAICS, North American Industry Classification System, used by the federal government. Figure 5-4 shows the 20 major categories of this system.

Not all of the customer types are viable customers for the different types of goods and services discussed in Section 5-2. These business customers also purchase varying quantities. For instance, manufacturers tend to purchase high volumes of raw materials, process materials, and component parts. A manufacturer of jeans will need sewing machines, cutting machines, and other types of equipment to make the jeans. It will

FIGURE 5-3 Business Clustered in Silicon Valley to Serve the Tech Industry

- Agriculture, Forestry, Fishing and Hunting
- Mining, Quarrying, Oil and Gas
- Utilities
- Construction
- Manufacturing
- Wholesale trade
- Retail trade
- Transportation and warehousing
- Information
- Finance and Insurance
- Real Estate, rental and leasing
- Professional, scientific and technical services
- Management companies
- Waste management
- Educational services
- Health care and social services
- Arts, entertainment and recreation
- Accommodations and food services
- Other services
- Public administration

FIGURE 5-4 NAICS Classification of Business Industries (https://www.naics.com)

also need cloth, buttons, zippers, and thread. To supply these important ingredients, the manufacturer must choose reliable suppliers.

To operate their business, wholesalers purchase buildings, accessory equipment, business services, and operating supplies. They do not purchase component parts, process materials, or raw materials. Because they serve as an intermediary between the producer and retailer, they will need some type of warehouse facility and offices. Forklifts and automated picking machines are primary needs.

Federal, state, and local governments represent huge opportunities for businesses. They purchase major equipment, land, and buildings. They purchase accessory equipment, maintenance supplies, repair parts, operating supplies, and business services. The major difference with government entities is the bidding process that must be used. Almost all governments have regulations that dictate how the bids have to be submitted and the manner in which the vendor is selected. For businesses willing to devote the time to submit bids, government contracts can be very lucrative.

Healthcare and educational organizations are similar to governments in the process they use to make purchases and in the types of products and services they purchase. Hospitals and schools are often the largest employers in the area. All need equipment, supplies, and services.

5-3b Understanding Business-to-Business Demand

Demand for business goods and services is not as easy to determine as for consumer products because of a concept called derived demand. **Derived demand** is the demand for a good or service that is generated from the demand for consumer goods and services. To illustrate, think about the demand for major appliances, such as refrigerators, stoves, washing machines, and dryers. The number of appliances that a retail store will order depends on the demand it sees in the consumer market. If it is planning a big holiday promotion and the economy is doing well, it may see an increase in demand and will therefore place a larger order with the various appliance manufacturers, such as GE, Whirlpool, and Maytag.

Derived demand Demand for a good or service that is generated from the demand for consumer goods and services.

A manufacturer's orders for metal, plastic, switches, motors, wires, and other parts used in the manufacturing of appliances depend on how many orders it receives from retailers such as Best Buy, Lowes, and other retailers that sell appliances. In turn, the suppliers of motors, electrical switches, metal, and plastic will order raw materials and processing materials based on the number of orders they receive from the appliance manufacturers. Thus, a company that makes plastic that is used in the manufacturing of major appliances depends on the demand that is derived all the way down from the consumer. The concept of derived demand is illustrated in **Figure 5-5**.

Because of derived demand in the business-to-business sector, it is much more difficult to predict demand and to control production the further distant a business is from the end user. The company that mines iron ore that is used for metal cannot stimulate demand by running an advertisement for metal. Consumers are not going to buy raw metals. The only way the demand can be stimulated is for other companies that use metal in their products to run ads, offer rebates, and create other special promotions for consumers.

Source: Bangkoker/Shutterstock

Because of the concept of derived demand, businesses face a much more volatile sales situation than consumer markets. Fluctuations and swings in demand are common

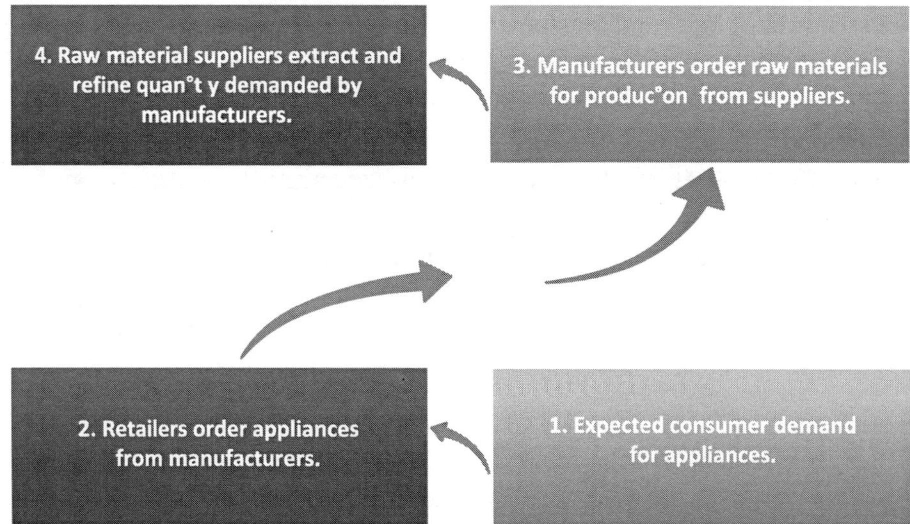
4. Raw material suppliers extract and refine quan°t y demanded by manufacturers.
3. Manufacturers order raw materials for produc°on from suppliers.
2. Retailers order appliances from manufacturers.
1. Expected consumer demand for appliances.

FIGURE 5-5 Illustration of Derived Demand for Major Appliances

and can be extreme. This fluctuation and wide swing in sales are due to a concept called the **acceleration principle**, which states that an increase or decrease in consumer demand for a product can create a drastic change in derived business demand. For example, a small increase of 10 to 15 percent in the demand for major appliances can cause as much as a 100 percent increase in the demand for major equipment to boost production of the appliances. Unfortunately, the reverse is also true. A 10 to 15 percent decline in orders for appliances can cause a complete collapse in the demand for the machines and equipment used in the manufacturing of appliances.[3]

Acceleration principle An increase or decrease in consumer demand for a product that can create a drastic change in derived business demand.

5-4 Business-to-Business Purchasing

In most cases, making purchases for a business is more complex than making personal purchase decisions. However, just like personal purchase decisions, not all business decisions are the same. Deciding on where to locate a plant or whether to build a $13 million building is certainly different than deciding where to purchase copier paper or ink pens. Purchase decisions vary because of the dollar value involved, the people involved in the decision process, and the amount of time spent making a decision. As would be expected, the decision on a $13 million building would involve more people and take more time than the decision about where to purchase office supplies.

5-4a Types of Buying Situations

Although business purchases tend to be more formal than consumer purchases, they do vary in terms of the number of people involved, the amount of time spent on making the decision, and the individuals who make the final decision. Business buying situations fall into one of three categories: new buy, modified rebuy, and straight rebuy.[4]

In a **new buy situation**, a business makes purchases for the first time. Land, buildings, and major equipment normally fit into this category. They are high-dollar purchases and will involve top management. It is not unusual for a new buy to take several months or even years. These complex decisions impact the strategic direction of the business and often require substantial research before a decision can be made. When buyers look for vendors, 53% rely on peer recommendations, 76% prioritize vendors based on such recommendations, and 84% of B2B purchases begin with a referral; buyers are also now better informed, making more online searches before buying or visiting the vendor's website. [5]

New buy situation
Purchases made by a business for the first time or purchases for which no one in the organization has had previous experience.

In a **modified rebuy situation**, a business makes occasional purchases. Modified rebuys occur in four different situations **(see Figure 5-6)**. The first is a situation in which the person making the purchase has limited buying experience with the product. It may be a vehicle or a forklift that is purchased every three to five years or a new computer system. Because of the limited experience, time will need to be taken to develop specifications and to examine the possibilities. The process is not as complex, however, as the new buy primarily because it involves lower dollar purchases with less impact on the strategic direction of the company.

Modified rebuy situation
Occasional purchases or purchases for which the members of the buying center have limited experience.

A second situation that involves modified rebuys is dissatisfaction with the current vendor. It can be the supplier of aluminum to a factory that manufactures aluminum cans, or it can be the janitorial service for a large office building. The current vendor may not be reliable with delivery, the quality of work may not be up to the firm's specification, or the current vendor may have increased prices. Regardless of the reason for the dissatisfaction, the business decides to solicit bids from other vendors. In many cases, these new bids are compared against the current vendor's contract. Depending on the reason for seeking new bids, the current vendor may or may not be allowed to submit a new bid.

The third situation that causes modified rebuys is the end of a contractual relationship. The firm is not dissatisfied with the current vendor, but at the expiration of the contract may seek new bids. Government and nonprofit institutions are often required by regulation or by-laws to seek

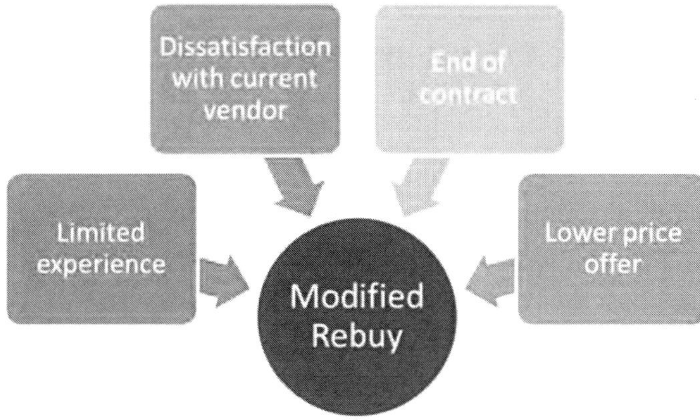

FIGURE 5-6 Modified Rebuy Situations

new bids at the end of each contractual period. The current vendor is allowed to rebid and often has the best chance of obtaining the contract unless the agency is required to go with the lowest bidder. This is often true for government entities.

Occasionally, a potential supplier will make an offer that is substantially lower than that of the current vendor (the fourth situation). When this situation occurs, the firm may decide to open the contract for bid, allowing the current vendor as well as others to bid. Alternatively, the firm may go to the current vendor and see whether it can reduce its prices to meet the new offer that the firm has received, or the firm may simply switch without giving the current vendor an opportunity to renegotiate. In all four cases, the firm making the purchase will have to study the specifications and spend some time making a decision. Although not as involved as the new buy situations, these modified rebuys do require some effort and time in making the best decision.

The last purchase situation is the straight rebuy in which a business routinely purchases from a vendor without modifying specifications or without renegotiating new terms. Purchasing office supplies for a large office building is likely to fall into this category. Supplies are purchased from a chosen vendor on a regular basis online, through a phone call, e-mail, or personal sales call. For a selling firm, this is the best situation. The buyer does not consider other firms, and as long as the buyer is pleased with the product and service, purchases continue on a routine basis.

5-4b The Buying Center

Buying center Group of individuals who are involved in the purchase process.

Business-to-business buying decisions often involve more than one individual. The group of individuals involved in the purchase process is called the **buying center**. This can be as few as one individual in a family-owned business or as many as 20 or more in a large corporation. The rank and roles of the various members of the buying center are determined by factors such as the dollar value of the purchase relative to the size of the company, the impact the purchase has on company operations, and the type of purchase situation. But within the buying group, regardless of size, there are five distinct roles. One individual can play multiple roles, or there can be a number of individuals within each role. The roles can also change over time and from one purchase situation to another. The roles in the buying center are gatekeeper, user, influencer, decider, and purchaser **(see Figure 5-7).**[6]

Gatekeeper Individual who is responsible for the flow of information to the members of the buying center.

The **gatekeeper** is responsible for the flow of information to the members of the buying center. This can be a secretary who screens phone calls and salespeople wanting to see the purchasing agent or other members of the buying center. It can be a member of the purchasing department who is responsible for gathering and filtering information. It could even be the purchasing agent. Not only does the gatekeeper screen access to the members of the buying center, but he or she may also be the one asked to

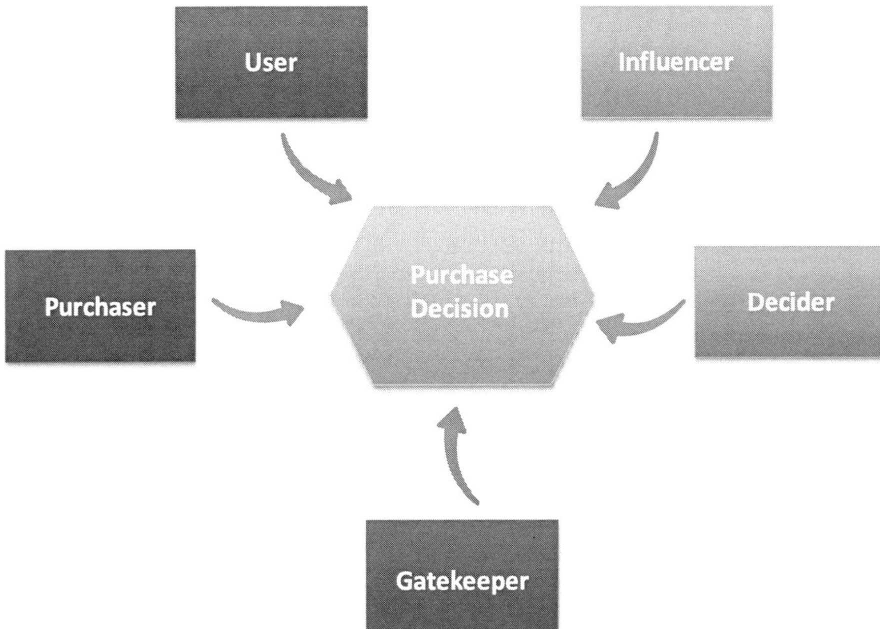

FIGURE 5-7 The Buying Center

gather information for the group. By having control over information, the gatekeeper will have a large impact on the decision that is made.

An important member of the buying center is the **user**. The user is the individual who actually uses the product or is responsible for the product being used. On a factory floor, it could be the shop supervisor, line supervisor, even one of the machine operators. The user's task is to provide information about the current product used and the current vendor. For a factory that uses plastic in building its product, the user will know if the grade of plastic currently being used is causing problems on the assembly line. If so, the information can be relayed to other group members. If several vendors are considered, the user will have insight on the different grades, types, and durability of the plastics being considered.

User An individual member of the buying center who actually uses the product or is responsible for the product being used.

The **influencer** is someone who can influence the decision, but may not necessarily use the product. It could be an engineer who knows the specifications that are required of specific process materials or fabricated parts. Through testing and information supplied by various vendors, the engineer could provide information as to which vendor is offering the best quality. The role of influencer can also be played by others in the company: a vicepresident, someone from the accounting, business or marketing department. Influencers have some stake in vendor selection and try to influence the purchase decision.

Influencer A member of the buying center who influences the decision but may not necessarily use the product.

The person making the final decision is the **decider**. This could be the president of the company, a vice president, the controller, the purchasing agent, or the secretary. The decider is the individual or individuals who decide which vendor to use and which products to purchase. This may be a routine process requiring little input from others in the buying center for a straight rebuy. However, in a new-buy situation, it may involve input

Decider The member of the buying center who makes the final decision.

Source: wavebreakmedia/Shutterstock

from many of people, and the actual decision is made by a group rather than a single person.

The **purchaser** is the one who makes the actual purchase. In a large company, this usually is someone in the purchasing department. In a smaller company, it may be the owner, the manager, or one of the other employees. Even for a large purchase, the president may make the decision, but it will likely be someone else who actually makes the purchase and works out the details of the purchase arrangement. In straight rebuy situations, the purchasing process may be automatic and just require a phone call, online submission form, or e-mail message.

Purchaser The member of the buying center who makes the actual purchase.

To understand how the buying center operates, suppose John Deere wants to purchase a hydraulic pump for a particular line of its tractors. Let's assume that John Deere is dissatisfied with the current supplier, which makes this a modified rebuy situation. Let us also assume that John Deere puts the item out for bids and has received offers from nine different companies. The purchasing agent for John Deere may ask an associate to screen the bid proposals to make sure each is legitimate. In the screening process, the associate purchasing agent is to make sure that the bidder has the capability of supplying the quantity of pumps that are needed each month, is financially solvent, and has experience selling hydraulic pumps to large manufacturers like John Deere. In this capacity, the associate purchasing agent is serving as a gatekeeper because he or she will control the information that is forwarded.

Assume that three companies are screened out, leaving six. The bid information is then sent to John Deere's engineering department. The members of the engineering department look through the specification information and suggest that two firms be eliminated because they are not sure that the durability and quality of the firms' hydraulic pumps will meet John Deere's standards. Although the decision to leave them in the pool or not is the purchasing agent's, the engineering department is serving the role of influencer by suggesting that two companies be dropped.

Source: Ms. Jane Campell/Shutterstock

After accepting the information of the engineering department, the purchasing agent reduces the list to four viable vendors. Each is contacted, asked to make an oral presentation to John Deere, and asked to provide three hydraulic pumps for testing by John Deere's engineering lab. At the presentation are two engineers, the plant foreman, the vice president of operations, and the associate purchasing agent. Two weeks after the presentation by the vendors, the buying center meets to make a decision. The engineers report the findings of their laboratory tests. At this point, the engineers will probably try to influence the decision on which brand should be used. The other individuals in the group may agree and a joint decision is made to accept the brand chosen by the engineers. But it is highly likely that someone in the group will make a different choice and urge the group to purchase a different brand. At this point, the group can discuss each vendor and come up with a consensus, or someone in the group may take the role of the decider and make the final decision. The decider could be the plant foreman or the vice president of finance. It could even be the purchasing agent or one of the engineers, but this situation is not as likely. Alternatively, it is possible that managers, experts, and users influence each other, using rational persuasion, inspiration appeals, consultations, or even personal appeals, such that each member can influence the final group decision.[7] After the decision is made, the purchasing agent will be designated the purchaser and charged with the responsibility of working out the details of the contract.

5-4c Influences on the Purchase Process

The behaviors of each member of the buying center are influenced by a variety of organizational, individual, social, and operational factors shown in Figure 5-8.[8] These factors influence the expectations of each member, the level of involvement in the purchase process, the role each person performs in the process, the person's level of participation in the decision, and the way the individual handles conflicting opinions.

Organizational Factors: Because members of the buying center work within an organizational structure, a number of organizational factors affect purchase decisions and the roles an individual performs within the buying center. Especially important are the organization's goals and objectives. Decisions must be made within the framework of these goals and objectives. For example, Walmart's goal of being the low-cost leader means that cost will be a major factor in purchase decisions. For FedEx, a major goal is fast delivery of packages. Therefore, decisions are made relative to how they may affect the speed of delivery. Although a purchase decision may be more cost effective, if it slows down the sorting process and packages do not reach

FIGURE 5-8 Influences on the Business-to-Business Purchasing Process

Source: Oleg Mikhaylov/Shutterstock

customers in time, customer service may decline, causing a loss of business.

A company's organizational structure has an impact on the various buying center roles. In an organization with a centralized structure, decisions are made by a few individuals, with others providing input or information. In a decentralized organization, decision making is moved down the organization, allowing more individuals to make decisions and be involved in decisions. Thus, in a decentralized organization, buying centers will tend to be larger, with buying center members participating more actively.

For many purchase situations, companies have a large number of options. Manufacturers who need to purchase nuts and bolts have a number of possible vendors, more than they have time to examine. To be able to eliminate possible vendors and narrow the list to a few that can be examined closely, most employees adopt some type of heuristic. **Heuristics** are decision rules adopted by individuals to make the decision process more efficient. For example, an individual within a buying center of a small manufacturer may decide that all large vendors should be eliminated. This decision could be based on his or her belief that a large vendor would not devote sufficient resources to a small account to provide good service and that, in an emergency, the vendor would neglect the small manufacturer to take care of larger clients.

Heuristics Decision rules that individuals adopt to make a decision process more efficient.

Because of the large amount of information available from each vendor and independent information that is available, buying center members often adopt a heuristic called satisficing. Satisficing is the process of making a decision that is satisfactory but not necessarily optimal. Often a buying center will make a decision when its members locate a vendor or arrive at a purchase decision that is satisfactory and meets the goals of the organization. It may or may not be the optimal solution. Individuals may feel making the optimal decision would require too much time or require additional resources and that the extra investment is not worth the possible payoff. Often, there is not time to solicit all the information needed before a decision must be made.[10]

Finances and budget constraints constitute organizational factors that impact the purchase decision. If engineers are involved in the buying center, it is not unusual for conflict to arise concerning which component parts or processes should be used. Engineers will push for the part or process that enhances the finished product, whereas the accountants will push for the lowest-cost part or process that will get the job done.

Again, the idea of satisficing will surface. If the $15 component part will suffice, then, from an accounting perspective, using it is wiser than using the $19 component part. The engineers will argue, however, that the $19 part will produce a superior product and fewer defects. However, if

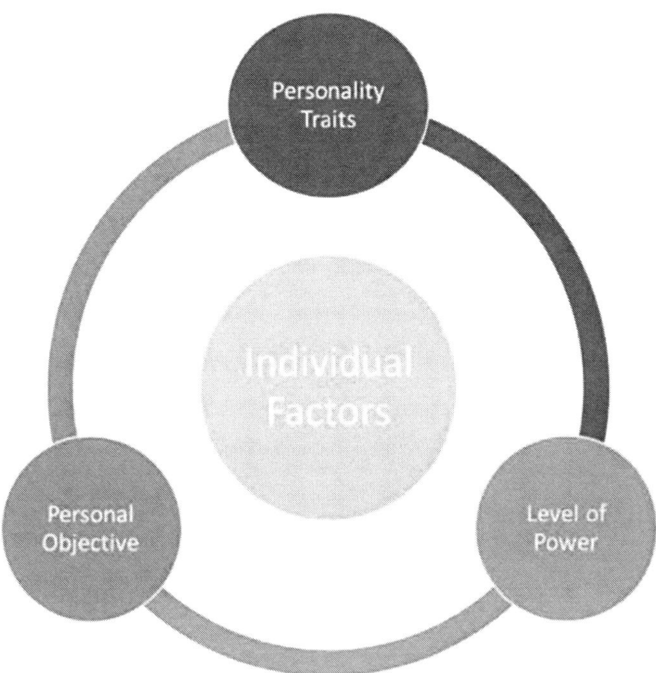

FIGURE 5-9 Individual Factors that Influence Members of the Buying Center

the $19 part will increase the cost of the product above the competition, the firm may have no choice but to use the $15 part. Financial constraints may restrict the company from using the better part.

Individual Factors: Although a number of individual factors influence each member of the buying center, the primary individual factors include personality traits, level of power, and personal objectives **(see Figure 5-9).**[11] Each factor influences how an individual acts within the buying center and how he or she reacts to other members of the buying center.

An individual's personality traits are an important factor in determining how a person behaves and interacts with others. A person who tends to be an extrovert will spend more time interacting with other members of the buying center than someone who is an introvert. However, an introvert is more likely to listen to a salesperson and gather more information than an extrovert. Another personality trait that is important is that of decisiveness. Some individuals are comfortable making decisions and recommendations, whereas others tend to be less decisive. They will wait and follow the recommendations of someone else. Decisiveness is closely tied with a person's level of risk taking and confidence. A person who is willing to take risks will be more likely to switch to a new vendor than someone who is risk averse. Individuals who have a high level of self-confidence will be more likely to share their opinion and persuade other members of the group that they are right, whereas a person who has a low level of self- confidence will tend to follow the recommendation of others. **Figure 5-10** summarizes these personality traits.

FIGURE 5-10 Personality Traits of Individuals in the Buying Center
Source: Dean Drobot/www.Shutterstock

In addition to personality traits, a person's level of power within an organization has an influence on how he or she behaves within a buying center. The higher ranking a person is in an organization, the more legitimate power he or she will have in each of the buying center roles. Others within the group will have a tendency to follow his or her suggestions, ideas, and decisions. This power tends to be formal and is based on the person's position in the firm. For instance, a vice president's comments are more likely to be accepted by the buying group than the comments of a shop foreman or a supervisor. This formal power, however, can be an impediment to an open discussion about a vendor, even if the person with the formal power strives for it.

All organizations include individuals with informal power. These people have earned the respect of coworkers because of their expertise or ability to make good decisions. Such an individual might be the shop foreman or someone who does not have the formal power but is highly respected by the other members of the buying center. Recommendations and comments made by this type of person will carry considerably more weight than others within the group.

Although we would like to believe that business purchase decisions are made on a rational basis and in terms of what is best for the firm; that is not always the case. Personal objectives, such as seeking promotions, building a good reputation with the boss, or making a rival look bad, will influence how a person acts within the buying center. Gifts or bribes offered by a salesperson can influence a purchase decision, especially in other countries where this practice is more common.

Employees tend to act in ways that enhance their personal career and personal objectives. These actions may not always be visible to other members of the group. The more that individuals have at stake in a purchase decision, the higher will be their involvement and the more forceful they will be in the decision-making process. Even individuals who tend to be introverts will exert a stronger voice in deliberations and decisions if they have a high stake in the outcome of the decision and their job performance will be affected by the purchase decision.

Social Factors: Closely tied with personal characteristics are social factors. Because individuals work within a social environment, social acceptance, norms, and rules of behavior will be factors in how members of the buying center interact with each other. Each person will have his or her own ideas of what is socially acceptable behavior and what is not. Each person will have his or her own ideas about how others ought to act and the roles they should perform within the group. Each business or organization tends to adopt over time a set of social norms. These norms are rules of behavior regarding the proper way to behave within the workplace. For example, most companies believe employees should treat others with respect and allow each person to express his or her views. With this open environment, better purchase decisions can be made. Although an open environment is ideal, social norms have developed in some companies that do not allow for open communication. Instead, it may be expected that individuals with formal power will not be questioned and that others are expected to demonstrate their loyalty by showing support for these individuals. Social norms are created in companies by management over a period of time. Employees learn what is acceptable and what is not acceptable. These norms affect the buying center because they influence how individuals interact with each other.[12]

Operational Factors: In the initial meeting of the buying process, members will make or discuss four operational factors, shown in Figure 5-11. During the first step, purchasing agents, engineers, users, and other members of the buying center bring their expectations to the process. These expectations are based on their past experiences with the various vendors and their knowledge of the purchase decision that is to be made. Their expectations are also based on the individuals who will be involved in the purchase decision and their past behaviors.

In the second step, various responsibilities or tasks are assigned. These may include collecting information, creating a list of potential vendors, obtaining information from other firms or individuals, examining a lease

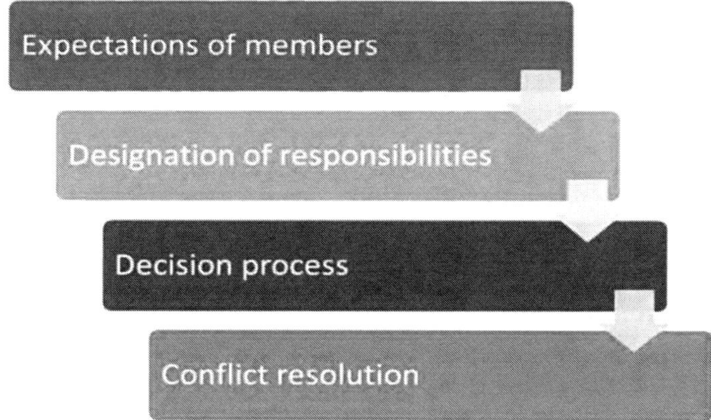

FIGURE 5-11 Operational Factors in the Buying Process

option versus making a purchase, and collecting specifications. Assigning these tasks is especially important as the price tag of a purchase increases and the number of individuals involved in the buying center increase.

In the third step, the responsibility for the decision is determined. Some decisions are autonomous, meaning that one person will make the decision, whereas others will involve multiple people and will be joint decisions. Factors determining who will be involved in the decision include the type of purchase decision, buying center makeup, social norms, relative cost of the purchase, and past experiences. Straight rebuy situations will tend to be autonomous, whereas new buys will tend to be joint decisions. Modified rebuys may go either way. If company executives or high-ranking personnel are in the buying center, joint decisions are less likely. Social norms that have been established and past experiences are usually followed unless they did not work in the past or someone specifically states, "We are using a different method for making this decision." Last, as would be expected, the higher the cost, the more likely it will be a joint decision.

In the last step, conflict resolution will be required if members of the buying center have different opinions about the decision. Social norms and past experiences will determine the conflict resolution method that will be used. It can vary from an open debate about the various vendors to someone taking charge and telling others what the decision will be.

After the decision is made, members of the buying center will use the results to develop their expectations of future purchase decisions. If a member of the group was not allowed to express his opinion or was put down by others when he tried to speak, it is likely he will be less involved in the next decision. If a member of the group took an autocratic approach when it was supposed to be a joint decision, it is likely that fewer people would participate in the next decision, and the process may become autonomous. Over time, these experiences often become the social norms for the company, at least in terms of how the buying center operates.

It is important to note that the buying process is rapidly changing with online buying. A rapidly-growing method for B2B marketing between vendors and buyers is social media. With a low barrier to entry, social media is a level playing field for vendors to vie for buyers, with marketers usually starting by casting a wide net of unobtrusive content via popular platforms such as Facebook, Instagram, or Twitter, and then moving to more specific content via B2B-inclined platforms. Social media gives customers access to information on suppliers' offerings and even buyers' experiences, thus helping both sides of the transaction gain more information to facilitate decisions. Since the role of influencers is essential in negotiations, sellers will need to find ways to win them over to increase the chance of being considered.[9]

5-5 The Business-to-Business Buying Process

The number of steps in the business-to-business process will vary, depending on the type of purchase situation. For a new buy situation, all seven steps listed in **Figure 5-12** are followed. For a modified rebuy

Step	New Buy	Modified Rebuy	Straight Rebuy
1. Identification of needs	X	X	X
2. Establishment of specifications	X	?	?
3. Identification of feasible solutions	X	?	–
4. Identification of feasible vendors	X	X	–
5. Evaluation of vendors	X	X	–
6. Selection of vendor(s)	X	X	–
7. Negotiation of purchase terms	X	X	X

FIGURE 5-12 Steps in the Business-to-Business Buying Process

situation, all seven may be followed, or the process may be reduced to five or six steps. For a straight rebuy, only two or three steps are involved.

To illustrate the steps in the business-to- business buying process, let us consider the case of a local office supply store, Dalton Office Supply. The retailer is contemplating the purchase of a delivery truck. The truck the firm currently has is 12 years old, has almost 200,000 miles, and is too small for the number of deliveries Dalton must now make every day. Because the last purchase was 12 years ago, this purchase situation would be a new buy for the current staff of Dalton.

5-5a Identification of Needs

The first step in the business-to-business buying process is the identification of a need. Although advertising and marketing can create desires and needs for consumers, this phenomenon is not as likely to occur in the business environment. In most cases, needs are the direct result of a firm's operation. A bakery needs flour, sugar, and other ingredients to bake its products, and when these ingredients run low, it is time to purchase more. Manufacturers must keep an eye on all of the components and materials used in the production process to make sure they have a sufficient quantity on hand to keep production going. In these types of situations, the purchase process is normally just a straight rebuy. The supplier is notified, and products are shipped to the manufacturer. This is an ideal situation for the supplier because no other vendors or options are even considered. With this type of purchase situation, the company will skip to the last step and negotiate terms of the purchase.

Source: Monkey Business Images/Shutterstock

Modified rebuy needs arise from dissatisfaction with the current vendor, a sales pitch by a potential vendor, or the need to purchase a product that is not purchased too frequently. The identification of a need with a new buy situation is the result of a strategic decision or the need to purchase a product that is seldom purchased.

5-5b Establishment of Specifications

The second step in the purchase process is the development of specifications. In straight rebuy situations, the specifications remain the same or are only slightly modified. In situations in which the specifications need a greater level of modification, a firm will usually enter into the modified rebuy situation, which involves examining other alternatives and vendors.

To ensure that vendor bids can be compared, it is important to establish specifications. When each vendor bids on the same set of specifications, a firm is able to compare bids and make a better decision. Sometimes firms are not sure what the specifications should be. This is especially true for new buy situations. A firm desiring to upgrade its computer system will often seek the help of vendors to establish the specifications. This makes the bidding process more difficult if the same specifications are not used by every firm submitting a bid.

In choosing a truck, Dalton developed two sets of specifications. The first are the specifications for the truck; the second are the purchase criteria. In terms of minimum specifications, the truck must be one ton with a box bed, power lift, and a diesel engine. The criteria that would be used for selecting the truck are listed in **Figure 5-13**. Notice that in addition to the required specifications, Dalton has identified three additional criteria that will be used in the process. The first is the level of business the truck dealer does with Dalton. This is a common practice in business and is known as **reciprocity**, which means that a business will purchase from businesses that in turn patronize them. Although it will not be the only criterion Dalton uses, it will favor a truck dealer that purchases office supplies from Dalton. Also used in the decision will be any personal experience the members of the buying center have had with the dealers. When this list is completed, the Dalton group is ready to move to the next step—identification of feasible solutions.

Reciprocity The practice of one business making a purchase from another business that, in turn, patronizes the first business.

5-5c Identification of Feasible Solutions

At the third step in the process, a business needs to examine various ways of handling the need. The three most common are to purchase the product

Required Truck Specifications

- One-ton box truck
- Power lift
- Diesel engine

Truck Specifications to Be Evaluated

- Fuel mileage
- Consumer report for quality
- Cost of repairs
- Warranty
- Price

Other Purchase Criteria

- Level of business with Dalton
- Brand name (preference for American brand)
- Previous personal experience with dealership

FIGURE 5-13 Truck Specifications Designated by Dalton Office Supply
Source: Rob Wilson/Shutterstock

from an external business, produce the product itself, or lease it. Companies examining shipping needs have the options of purchasing their own trucks, hiring an independent firm to ship the merchandise for them, or using a commercial service such as United Parcel Service (UPS).

Some decisions are more difficult. For example, suppose Avon has several pieces of equipment used in the production of lipstick that are quite old and labor intensive. For $200,000 to $300,000, Avon can automate the machine and virtually eliminate the human operators. Avon must compare the labor savings of a new machine to the cost of the machine and the level of production that will result. For a high-production item, the labor savings will likely exceed the cost of the new machine. However, for a low-production item, Avon may be better off keeping the old machine, repairing it, and paying out more in labor.

Another option, especially for equipment, land, and buildings, is leasing. This is something Dalton Office Supply could consider. Instead of purchasing a new truck, Dalton could lease a vehicle. The advantages would include always having a newer model that can be used. Because maintenance is the responsibility of the dealer, the company can expense the cost of the lease. Of course, the disadvantage includes not owning the truck. In addition, if the mileage exceeds the lease limits, there is normally a penalty. Dalton must carefully calculate the total cost of owning the vehicle over the life of the truck versus the cost of leasing.

5-5d Identification of Feasible Vendors

If the decision to use an external source is made, then someone must contact possible vendors and ask them to submit bids. This is one of the tasks of the gatekeeper, and in the process of identifying possible vendors, he or she controls the information flow. If the gatekeeper does not like a particular vendor, that vendor may never be notified. However, some possible vendors may be left out by accident. Just the process of selecting and notifying possible vendors may cause some to be eliminated. After possible vendors have been located, then someone must screen the list for firms that are not feasible. In this process, firms that may not be able to meet production schedules or that are too small may be eliminated. For example, if the process is the construction of a $20 million facility, small contractors with only a few employees do not have the capability of handling such a large job.

For Dalton, initial screening at this stage is to eliminate any trucks that do not have a diesel engine because that was set as a basic requirement. Suppose that in gathering information about the various dealers, the assistant manager finds two dealers who have trucks that meet the specifications but not the criterion of being current customers of Dalton. One has never been a customer; the other used to be a customer but gradually reduced purchases to less than $25 a month. Should these two possible vendors be eliminated? Suppose the dealer that has never been a customer has the lowest-priced truck. Because the assistant manager has been charged with the responsibility of gathering a list of possible trucks, he would have to make a decision. He can leave these two dealers on the list, he can eliminate them, or he can ask someone else in the buying center for advice. It is unlikely that he would call a meeting of the entire buying center. Instead, if he wants advice on what he should do, he will go to one of the influencers or the decider. In this case, that would be one or both of the store managers or the owner of Dalton. The person or people he would approach would depend a great deal on the organizational structure and the social norms for Dalton. If it is a company that encourages open communication and the owner is available, he may go straight to the owner and ask whether the dealers should be left on the list because the owner will ultimately make the decision. However, if the company social norms dictate a strong chain of command, then he will go to his boss, the store manager, for counsel.

5-5e Evaluation of Vendors

Evaluation of vendors normally occurs at two levels. The first level is an initial screening of candidates. This screening is different from the screening in the previous step. Vendors who make this list are qualified and meet the minimum specifications. Screening at this level entails evaluating how well a vendor meets the specifications and purchase criteria identified in step two. One or two individuals within the buying center may perform this initial evaluation screening, or the whole group may be involved. The person or persons responsible will largely depend on how many vendors are on the initial list, the type of buying situation, and the relative cost of the purchase. If there are a large number of vendors, normally one or two individuals will be asked to pare down the list. If it is a new buy situation, more individuals will be involved in the initial screening process than if it is a modified rebuy situation. The same is true for the relative cost of the purchase. The greater the cost, the more people are likely to be involved. The purpose of this initial evaluation screening is to reduce the list of feasible vendors down to a smaller manageable list.

Suppose, in our Dalton example, that the assistant manager has a list of nine dealers and 12 possible trucks in the two towns where the company has offices. It is possible that everyone involved in the decision will want to be involved in this initial evaluation screening. However, it is more likely that the assistant manager and another person or two will be asked to narrow the list. The user—in this case, the firm's truck driver—may be asked to work with the assistant manager, or it may be one of the store managers, or both. It is unlikely that Dalton's owner will be involved with this initial screening.

Source: Antonio Guillem/Shutterstock

The second level of evaluation is a vendor analysis. This is a formal evaluation of each vendor. **Figure 5-14** provides a vendor analysis for a supplier of denim cloth to a manufacturer of jeans. Each denim supplier

	Excellent	Superior	Acceptable	Inferior
1. Speed of delivery	_____	_____	_____	_____
2. Handling of emergency and rush orders	_____	_____	_____	_____
3. Quality of denim material	_____	_____	_____	_____
4. Availability of different colors/ styles	_____	_____	_____	_____
5. Handling of defective denim	_____	_____	_____	_____
6. Percent of denim that is defective	_____	_____	_____	_____
7. Purchase terms	_____	_____	_____	_____

FIGURE 5-14 A Vendor Analysis for Denim Suppliers for a Jean Manufacturer

will be evaluated on each of the seven criteria. This process will allow the jeans manufacturer to narrow down the list of feasible vendors.

During the vendor analysis, members of the buying center either visit the prospective vendor's site or have the prospective vendor make a presentation to the buying center. Typical questions asked during a vendor audit include:

- What are the vendor's production capabilities?
- What quality control mechanisms and processes does the vendor have in place?
- How closely does the vendor follow the processes?
- What is the defective material rate, and how does the vendor handle defective merchandise?
- What type of equipment is used, how old is the equipment, and how dependable is the equipment?
- What telecommunication and electronic data interchange (EDI) capabilities does the vendor have?
- Can the vendor handle order fluctuations?
- What is the financial stability of the company?
- How many customers does the firm have, and how many are competitors?
- What type of relationship does the vendor have with its suppliers? Will there be an interruption in supplies to the vendor that would affect the vendor's ability to fill orders?
- How stable is the vendor's labor pool? Will a strike or other labor problems cause an interruption in the ability to fill orders?

Source: SabOiga/Shutterstock

The primary purpose of the vendor analysis is to ensure that the vendor has the capability of meeting the supply demands of the purchaser. If the vendor is supplying denim for a manufacturer of blue jeans, the manufacturer must be sure that the supply of denim will be met, that the quality meets its specifications, and that special orders can be filled quickly. Because the production of the blue jeans cannot occur without the denim material, supply capability is crucial.

5-5f Selection of Vendors

Before a final selection is made, the business must decide whether it will go with one vendor or more. For Dalton, because only one truck will be purchased, only one vendor will be selected. But for a supplier of raw materials or component parts, the decision is more complicated. The advantage of choosing one vendor is lower prices through quantity discounts, but the disadvantage is that a greater risk occurs if, for some reason, the one supplier cannot fill all of the orders or is late with the shipment. If the business uses two or more vendors, then production information must be shared with multiple vendors. Sharing production schedules and sales data with suppliers assumes a high level of trust between the parties concerned. If more than one vendor is involved with a particular product, maintaining a high level of trust becomes more difficult. Each vendor is vying for a larger share of the business and can easily see from data it receives how much of the business it has and how much is being given to the competition.

5-5g Negotiation of Purchase Terms

In most purchase situations, the last step, negotiation, is merely a formality because most of the purchase terms have already been worked out during the evaluation and selection process. But for those terms that have not been agreed on, it will be the responsibility of the buyer to negotiate. Payment method, due date, size of order, delivery schedule, and method for handling defective merchandise are a few of the terms that will be agreed on at this stage. After a contract or agreement has been reached, the unsuccessful bidders are informed that the bidding process has been concluded and that a vendor has been chosen.

Although the buying process is over at this point for members of the buying center, evaluation of the purchase process occurs. It may be a formal evaluation, or it may be informal. Users will evaluate the decision based on the criteria used in the selection process. If the new vendor meets everyone's expectations, then for products used on a regular basis the company will move to a straight rebuy situation with the vendor. For both the buyer and seller, this relationship is the most desirable, and as long as it remains satisfactory for both parties, it will continue.

For products that are in the modified rebuy situation, the results of the purchase will be remembered by those involved, and the next time the product has to be purchased, the chosen vendor will have a greater chance of being selected. If Dalton purchases a Ford truck and is pleased with the truck's performance, then Dalton will be more likely to purchase a Ford truck the next time. Even in a modified rebuy situation, this will save members of the buying center a considerable amount of time.

For new buy situations, the results of the current purchase are of little value. If it is another 12 years before Dalton purchases another truck, it is likely that the company will spend the same amount of time during the purchase process. Most of the members of the buying center will be new, and the makes, models, and vehicle dealers will have all changed. It is very likely that the dealer the truck was purchased from will have a new owner, so there is no longer any guarantee of the same level of satisfaction. If the dealership is still owned by the same individual, personnel at the dealership have probably changed. That is why, for new buy situations, firms go through all seven steps, and decisions can take anywhere from a few months to a few years.

Summary

1. **Identify the types of goods and services that businesses purchase.**
   Businesses can purchase major equipment, buildings and land, accessory equipment, fabricated and component parts, process materials, maintenance and repair parts, operating supplies, raw materials, goods for resale, and business services.

2. **Identify the types of business customers.**
   The NAICS code identifies 20 different industries, such as construction, manufacturing, retail, transportation, finance, educational services, accommodations, food services, and public administration.

3. **Explain the concepts of derived and joint demand and why it important for the business-to-business market.**
   The demand for many business-to-business products is dependent, or derived, from the demand for consumer products. For example, the demand for parts that are used in the manufacturing of a washing machine is derived from the consumer demand for washing machines. For business-to-business markets, derived demand determines the demand for a product. Often, there is little a business-to-business firm can do to modify demand for its products.

4. **Identify the types of buying situations and when each is used.**
   Types of buying situations include new buy, modified rebuy, and straight rebuy. Organizations purchasing a product for the first time or products with which no one has any relevant experience are involved in a new buy situation. In a modified rebuy situation, a product is purchased infrequently and the organization has little experience with the product, or the organization is dissatisfied with its current vendor or receives an attractive offer from another firm it wants to consider. Modified rebuys can also occur at the end of a contract period. Straight rebuy situations occur when orders are placed with the current vendor without considering any other vendors.

5. **Describe the concept of the buying center and the different roles employees can play.**
   Many buying decisions within a business are joint decisions and involve more than one person. Members of the buying center can play the roles of gatekeeper, user, influencer, decider, and purchaser. The gatekeeper is responsible for filtering information to the other members of the buying center. The user is the individual who actually uses the product or oversees its use. Influencers are

individuals who have a significant influence on the decision but do not actually make the decision. The decider is the individual who makes the final decision. The purchaser is the one who negotiates the terms of the contract and actually makes the purchase.

6. **Discuss the factors that influence business-to-business buyer behavior.**
The behaviors of each member of the buying center are influenced by a variety of organizational, individual, social, and organizational factors. These factors influence the expectations of each member, the level of involvement in the purchase process, the role each person performs in the process, the person's level of participation in the decision, and the way the individual handles conflicting opinions. The organizational factors include the corporate goals and objectives, the firm's organizational structure, and the finances and budget of the firm. Individual factors that influence each member of the buying center are personality traits, level of power and personal objectives. Each factor influences how an individual acts within the buying center and how he or she reacts to other members of the buying center. Closely tied with personal characteristics are social factors. Because individuals work within a social environment, social acceptance, norms, and rules of behavior will be factors in how members of the buying center interact with each other. Organizational factors include expectations of members, designation of responsibilities of buying center members, the decision process used, and conflict resolution strategies.

7. **List the seven steps in the business-to-business buying process and explain what occurs in each step.**
The first step in the business-to-business buying process is identification of needs. They can be routine needs, such as those that are part of a manufacturing process, or rare needs, such as a new building. Once the need has been recognized, the next step is the establishment of objectives. For rebuy situations, this is routine and is the same that has been ordered in the past. For modified and new buy situations, time will need to be taken to determine both the product and purchase specifications. During the third step, feasible solutions are evaluated. They often include leasing and outsourcing or using an alternative material. After the decision is made to purchase the product, potential vendors are contacted. Once the list of possible vendors is narrowed down to a smaller, manageable list, evaluation of each vendor occurs. A vendor analysis and vendor audit are often a part of this evaluation. Based on the results of the evaluation, a vendor is selected. The last step is the negotiation of terms with the vendor.

Key Terms

Acceleration principle (132)
Buying center (134)
Decider (135)
Derived demand (131)
Gatekeeper (134)
Heuristics (138)
Influencer (135)
Modified rebuy situation (133)
New buy situation (133)
Purchaser (136)
Reciprocity (144)
User (135)

Discussion Questions

1. Discuss the difference between business buyers and consumers in purchasing airline tickets, automobiles, and cleaning supplies. Be specific.
2. Review the list of goods and services purchased by a business listed in Section 5-2. Pick one of the businesses below, then identify two examples for each of the categories.
   a. bakery
   b. manufacturer of electric leaf blowers
   c. pizza restaurant
   d. tree removal service

3. Discuss how the concept of derived demand and how it would be relevant to each of the following suppliers:
   a. supplier of sand to a concrete mixing company
   b. supplier of wire that is used in building electrical motors
   c. food processing factory that makes tomato paste that is sold to other businesses making various types of foods
4. For each of the following situations, discuss what type of buying situation it is and identify who might serve in each of the buying center roles:
   a. construction of a new 10,000-square-foot addition to a current 40,000-square-foot factory
   b. contract with a food service to manage the cafeteria at a university
   c. purchase of furniture for a new office complex that has just been built
   d. because of dissatisfaction with the last vendor, the selection of a new company to supply the flour used in baking pizza crusts for the retail food market
   e. the ordering of an extra 5,000 electrical switches used in the manufacturing of electrical space heaters that are sold to retail stores
5. During a recession, consumers reduce purchases. Identify five goods or services that you believe would decline in sales. What business-to-business markets would be adversely affected by the declines in consumer purchases?
6. How important is the Internet in identifying possible vendors for a business? Are companies located through the Internet viable vendors? How can a business determine whether a business is legitimate?
7. Assume you have been given the responsibility of searching the Internet for viable companies for one of the following purchase situations. Use the business-to-business section under business and economy at Yahoo or another search engine. Locate three feasible companies and discuss why each is a viable option.
   a. fresh fish for a retail grocery store
   b. circuit boards for a computer manufacturer
   c. electric motors to be used in electric leaf blowers
   d. translation services for a company wanting to do business in Argentina
   e. shipping company to transport grain to South America
8. Suppose you have been asked to locate feasible vendors for a restaurant seeking to upgrade its dining room furniture. Locate five different vendors on the Internet. Create a table with four columns. The first column should have the name of the possible vendor and the second column is the vendor's URL address. In the third column identify reasons to select the vendor and in the fourth column identify doubts you have about the vendor or reasons the firm should not be selected. Assume this is a chain of 25 restaurants located in the U.S. Southeast. When you finish with the evaluations, select one vendor and justify why that firm was chosen.

Review Questions

True or False

1. Top managers normally participate in the purchase of major equipment, buildings, and land.
2. To reduce the cost of a finished product, a manufacturer may use fabricated and component parts of inferior quality.
3. Two characteristics of business markets are fewer buyers and larger purchase volumes.
4. Derived demand is a business-to-business demand generated from the demand for consumer goods or services.
5. It is not unusual for a new buy to take several months or even several years to complete.
6. Purchasing office supplies for a large corporation is normally classified as a straight rebuy.
7. In the business-to-business purchasing process, the gatekeeper is responsible for screening the decisions made by the buying center.
8. The user in the buying center is the individual who actually uses the product or is responsible for the product being used.

9. If a group of engineers provides test data or information on quality and reliability, they can decide which vendor to choose.
10. Individual factors that influence the buying center are personality traits, level of power, and personal objectives.

Multiple Choice

11. A business hiring a law firm to handle a lawsuit would be an example of purchasing a(n)
    a. accessory equipment.
    b. operating services.
    c. business services.
    d. process services.
12. The fluctuations and wide swing in sales in business-to-business sales can be explained by the acceleration principle. The principle addresses which of the following?
    a. a small increase in the demand for a good can cause a huge increase in demand for production equipment.
    b. a 10 to 15 percent decline in orders can cause a complete collapse in the demand for the raw materials used in making a product.
    c. a and b.
    d. None of the above.
13. Business-to-business markets differ from customer markets in all of the following aspects except
    a. fewer buyers.
    b. large purchase volume.
    c. geographic concentration.
    d. informal buying process.
14. The number of batteries ordered by a Ford automobile manufacturing plant is determined by the number of new cars sold. This is an example of
    a. derived demand.
    b. joint demand.
    c. straight rebuy.
    d. direct demand.
15. A modified rebuy occurs in which of the following situations?
    a. limited buying experience with the product
    b. dissatisfaction with the current vendor
    c. switching to a new vendor by the end of the contractual relationship
    d. all of the above
16. Heuristics are decision rules adopted by the members of a buying center to
    a. make the decision process more efficient.
    b. select vendors based on location.
    c. avoid errors in vendors' evaluation.
    d. none of the above.
17. Satisficing is a heuristic decision rule that
    a. requires consideration of all known information in the final decision.
    b. satisfies the expectations and strategies of the top managers.
    c. is satisfactory but not necessarily optimal.

Answers: (1) True, (2) False, (3) True, (4) True, (5) True, (6) True, (7) False, (8) True, (9) False, (10) True, (11) c, (12) a, (13) d, (14) a, (15) d, (16) a, (17) c

Case: Briggs & Stratton

Briggs & Stratton is the world's number one maker of air-cooled gasoline engines used in lawn mowers, garden tillers, and other lawn equipment. Sales of these small gasoline engines account for about 86 percent of the total sales for Briggs & Stratton. In 2020, the company decided to sell its turf business to focus on its generator and commercial battery lines. The company is an innovator, receiving several patents, among them pressure washers with jet pumps, air filters, suspension systems, power-rake devices, and the Amplify Power management system, allowing standby generator owners to prioritize the division of power in their homes.

The company manufactures all of its 3 to 25-horsepower small engines in the United States. Factories are located in Alabama, Georgia, Kentucky, Missouri, and Wisconsin. It also has joint ventures with companies in Australia, Canada, China, India, Japan, New Zealand, and Latin America. The headquarters for Briggs & Stratton is located in Wauwatosa, Wisconsin.

A major component part of the gasoline engine is the spark plug. With the contract up for its

Source: Tim Evans/Shutterstock

current supplier, the Briggs & Stratton purchasing department in Wauwatosa, Wisconsin decided to put the contract up for bid. At the current production level, Briggs & Stratton purchases about two million spark plugs a year. Because of the size of the contract, Senior Vice President Paul Neylon and Vice President and General Manager of the Small Engine Division, Joe Wright, were asked to participate in the initial discussion.

The first decision that had to be made was who would be included in the vendor decision. At the first meeting, the group agreed that both Neylon and Wright should be involved in the decision. Neylon suggested, given the size of the contract, that Senior Vice President and CFO James Brenn should also be involved in the purchase decision— at least at the stage of selecting the vendor. Although the foreign joint ventures in China, India, or Japan would not be directly affected by the decision, Neylon suggested that the Vice President of International Operations, Michael Scheon, and the Vice President of European Operations should also be involved. His rationale for inclusion was that any changes in major suppliers in the United States would have ripple effects in the international operations and the same vendor chosen for the United States would be in the bidding for the international production facilities. Wright disagreed, saying that the Asian facilities are different because factories there tend to use local vendors, not U.S. firms.

Wright felt strongly that the buying center group should also include the plant managers at each of the five manufacturing facilities, an engineer from each facility, and the vice president of distribution, sales, and service, Curtis Larson. He wanted to know first-hand from each facility if there were any problems with the current vendor and what factors were important in the selection of a vendor. He also felt Larson was important because he could relay information about service problems with the engines and about whether the spark plug was a contributor to any service recalls or warranty repairs.

Leaving the final decision of who should be included in the buying center group to Wright, attention was turned to the possible vendors. Wright suggested they consider Autolite, Robert Borsch Corporation, ACDelco, NGK, Champion, Spitfire, and Kingsborne. Each of these brands had a good reputation, was dependable, and was large enough to handle the Briggs & Stratton account.

"We will need to develop the vendor analysis criteria for the site visit," suggested Neylon. "But the most critical decision is: Do we go with just one vendor, or do we use two or three? With five plants, we could potentially use up to five vendors. By allowing each plant the freedom to use a different vendor, we don't have such a high risk if there are problems with one vendor in meeting our production schedule. We could easily contact one of the others to fill in any slack."

Wright countered that he felt that strategy was not cost effective. First, he did not like the idea of each manufacturing facility choosing the brand of spark plugs. Second, he felt that by consolidating to one vendor, the company could negotiate a better price. Ordering two million from a single vendor would certainly be cheaper than breaking down the order to 400,000 from several vendors. Third, Wright did not want to share production data with four or five different vendors.

Although Neylon understood, he felt strongly that it was too risky to go with just one vendor. "At least use another vendor at one of the plants to ensure a backup vendor," he suggested.

Wright could see this was going to be a difficult decision and would take a long time to accomplish. It was also a critical decision that had significant ramifications for the entire company. He first would have to decide on how many people he wanted in the buying group and who they would be. He then would have to decide on the vendor analysis criteria and the vendor audit checklist. Lastly, he would have to decide about how many vendors to use.

Case Questions

1. Who should be in the buying center for this decision? Discuss which roles you think each person should play.
2. What organizational, individual, social, and operational factors do you believe will impact this buying center and the purchasing process? Explain why.
3. Develop a list of criteria you think should be included in the vendor analysis.
4. Should Briggs & Stratton use only one vendor or more than one? Justify your recommendation. What are the advantages and disadvantages to your decision?

Sources: Fictitious case based on Hoover's Company Profiles of Briggs & Stratton Corporation, January 7, 2017; www. briggssandstratton. com; Margaret Naczeck and David Schuyler, "Briggs and Stratton to sell power equipment business," Milwaukee Business Journal, May 6, 2020, https://www.bizjournals.com/milwaukee/news/2020/03/06/briggs-stratton-to-sell-power-equipment-businesses.html; Briggs & stratton (BGG) issued patent titled "pressure washers including jet pumps". (2020, May 21). *News Bites Consumer Durables & Apparel,* Proquest Database; Briggs & Stratton launches smart power management for standby: Amplify makes standby generator power management smarter. (2020, Jun 02). *PR Newswire*, Proquest Database.

Endnotes

1. David Gollan, "60 days that changes how we think about private jets," *Forbes,*" May 17, 2020, https://www.forbes.com/sites/douggollan/2020/05/17/60-days-that-changed-how-we-think-about-private-jets/#53ed75a129ad
2. Tom Krisher, "Takata recalls 1.4 million cars due to faulty airbags, including BMW, Honda, Toyota," *USA Today*, December 4, 2019, https://www.usatoday.com/story/money/cars/2019/12/04/takata-airbag-recall-2019-1-4-million-older-cars-recalled/2614475001.
3. Naimzada, A.K., Pecora, N. Dynamics of a multiplier–accelerator model with nonlinear investment function. *Nonlinear Dyn* 88, 1147–1161 (2017).
4. Philip Ruys, "A Development of theory of the Ricardo Effect," *The Quarterly Journal of Austrian Economics*, 20 (4), 297-335, 2017.
5. Diba, H., Vella, J. M., & Abratt, R. (2019). Social media influence on the B2B buying process. *Journal of Business & Industrial Marketing, 34*(7), 1482–1496.
6. Töllner, A., Blut, M., & Holzmüller, H. H. (2011). Customer solutions in the capital goods industry: Examining the impact of the buying center. *Industrial Marketing Management, 40*(5), 712–722; Patrick J. Robinson, Charles W. Faris, and Yoram Wind, "Industrial Buying and Creative Marketing," *Marketing Science Institute Series* (Boston: Allyn and Bacon, 1967).
7. Thanh Mai, N. T. (2019). Influence Strategies Affecting Organizational Buying Decisions: An Empirical Study in Vietnam Enterprises. *Journal of Science: Education Research, 32*(5E), 32–43.
8. Frederick E. Webster, Jr., and Yoram Wind, "A General Model for Understanding Organizational Buyer Behavior," *Marketing Management* 4 (Winter/Spring 1996): 52–57; Jagish N. Seth, "A Model of Industrial Buyer Behavior," *Journal of Marketing*, 37, October 1973, 51.
9. Diba, H., Vella, J. M., & Abratt, R. (2019). Social media influence on the B2B buying process. *Journal of Business & Industrial Marketing, 34*(7), 1482–1496.
10. Herbert Simon, *The New Science of Management Decisions* (Upper Saddle River, N.J.: Prentice-Hall, 1977).
11. Webster and Wind, A General Model; Doney and Armstrong, Effects of Accountability.
12. Marvin E. Shaw and Phillip R. Costanzo, *Theories of Social Psychology*, 2nd ed.: (New York: McGraw-Hill, 1982).

The Marketing Strategy

Source: Rawpixel.com/Shutterstock

Learning Objectives

Ivelin Radkov/Shutterstock

After studying this chapter, you should be able to:

- Identify the rationale for adopting a target marketing strategy.
- Identify the bases for consumer segmentation and offer company application examples.
- Identify the requirements necessary for effective market segmentation.
- Describe the three targeting strategies that companies use.
- Describe the six positioning strategies that companies can use to position their brands in the minds of target consumers.

Chapter Outline

Source: antoniodiaz/Shutterstock

6-1 Chapter Overview

With the exception of very narrow markets, one single company, however large its resources and capacity, cannot possibly serve all customers. Consumers are too numerous, and their needs and wants are too diverse. For example, social media took the global community by storm with the founding of Facebook. Founded in 2004, Facebook has over 2.6 billion active daily users worldwide.[1] However, today, teenagers in the U.S. view Facebook as their parents' and grandparents' social medium. While most teens continue to use Facebook occasionally, most are migrating to Snapchat, a photo messaging app that allows Apple and Android users to take photos, record videos, add text and drawings, and send them to recipients. Snapchat users control how long recipients can view their messages. They set the time up to ten seconds and send—then the message disappears forever. Moreover, Snapchat, founded in 2011, is among the fastest rising social media venues, lets you know if the recipients have taken a screen-shot. Snap Inc. reported a 20% year-on-year rise in Daily Active Users, with an average of more than 4 billion snaps created every day. At the onset of COVID-19, snaps and messaging rose by 30% compared to the previous year, and by more than 50% in geographic areas most heavily affected by the virus.[2]

Consumers have unique needs and different attitudes, interests, and opinions, and these can change with time. Given this diversity, it is important for companies to focus on those segments that they can serve most effectively and to design goods and services with these segments in mind—that is, to engage in target marketing. Companies use **target marketing** to:

Target marketing The process of focusing on those segments that the company can serve most effectively and designing products, services, and marketing programs with these segments in mind.

1. Identify segments of consumers who are similar with regard to key traits and who would respond well to a product and related marketing mix (market segmentation).
2. Select the segments that the company can serve most efficiently and develop products tailored to each (market targeting).
3. Offer the products to the market, communicating through the marketing mix the products' traits and benefits that differentiate the products in the consumer's mind (market positioning).

Market segmentation, targeting, and positioning constitute the focus of this chapter. Section 6-2 focuses on market segmentation, identifying the requirements for successful segmentation and the bases for segmentation. Section 6-3 addresses the three strategies used in targeting: differentiated, concentrated, and undifferentiated. Finally, Section 6-4 addresses the different approaches to positioning brands in relation to other competing products, based on product traits and benefits that are relevant to the consumer and Section 6-5 introduces the strategic plan.

6-2 Market Segmentation

Source: Andrey_Popov/Shutterstock

The marketplace is composed of consumers with unique needs and preferences. Firms find that it is difficult to satisfy all consumers. Consequently, they simplify their marketing task by appealing to those whose needs are most effectively met by their own offering. Market **segmentation** involves identifying consumers who are similar with regard to key traits, such as product-related needs and wants, and who would respond well to a similar marketing mix.

Not all market segments are financially feasible to explore because they are either too small or their characteristics are not that different from the population as a whole or other market segments. As will be seen in Chapter 7, most companies conduct some type of segmentation to identify profiles of different types of consumers that the company could target. Marketers are especially interested in consumer segments who are heavy product users.

Segmentation The process of identifying consumers or markets that are similar with regard to key traits, such as product-related needs and wants, and that would respond well to a product and related marketing mix.

Research found that, as eSports get bigger, they are starting to look less like the mainstream sports: they are more fashion involved, with an influx of luxury brand and streetwear collaborations: Louis Vuitton made a case for the eSports League of Legends World Championship trophy. These brand connections both legitimize eSports and offer luxury and streetwear brands the chance to successfully target gamers.[3]

For these brands, luxury and gaming combine to become the basis for segmentation. Yet other products are targeted at the mass market—the manufacturer mass-produces the product, promotes it, and distributes it widely. But even these products must be appropriately targeted.

6-2a Levels of Segmentation

As mentioned earlier, the marketplace consists of consumers with unique needs and preferences. Individual buyers have unique product needs, and a company that has all the resources available at its discretion—including time—can potentially target each prospective buyer individually. However, for most firms, that is difficult and costly: it is impossible to satisfy every consumer, and thus companies will simplify their marketing task by appealing to those consumers whose needs are most effectively met by their own offering. Some firms may not even segment the market at all, marketing to the masses. **Figure 6-1** identifies the three levels of segmentation: mass marketing, segment marketing, and micromarketing.

FIGURE 6-1 Levels of Segmentation

Source: chrisdorney/Shutterstock

Mass marketing is the shotgun approach to segmentation. It involves identifying the product-related preferences of most consumers and then targeting the product broadly to everyone. Mass marketing allows firms to subsequently target these consumers while incurring minimal costs. The outcome of this strategy is ultimately low prices for the consumer or high profit margins for the seller. Mass marketing is a rather difficult proposition in industrialized markets, where consumers are highly differentiated in their preferences. In the aggregate, there is a move from mass marketing to micromarketing. But the strategy that works best depends on industry. For fast-moving goods, for example, mass marketing should still be adopted because, for them, consumer demographics do not vary at an aggregate level.[4]

Mass marketing A shotgun approach to segmentation that involves identifying the product-related preferences of most consumers and then targeting the product broadly to everyone.

Segment marketing A process that involves identifying consumers who are similar with regard to key traits, such as product-related needs and wants, and who would respond well to a similar marketing mix.

Micromarketing A process that involves a microanalysis of the customer and customer-specific marketing.

Segment marketing involves identifying consumers who are similar with regard to key traits and who would respond well to a similar marketing mix. BMW offers the Mini to young consumers who have just finished college, the 300 series to young professionals, and the 500 and 700 series to mid-level professionals and families.

Micromarketing entails a microanalysis of the customer and involves customer-specific marketing. Micromarketers need more information about prospective customers than mass marketers. Therefore, they use databases to create and update customer information in a searchable form. In its most extreme form, micromarketing involves marketing to the individual, in effect, customizing the marketing mix to the needs of that individual. As such, micromarketing is more a targeting strategy than a segmentation strategy, unless it is a question of identifying the individuals who make it profitable for the firm to tailor its offerings.

6-2b Bases for Segmentation

Identifying individual market segments will enable a company to produce products that meet the precise needs of targeted consumers with a marketing mix that is appropriately tailored for the segment. The company typically conducts extensive marketing research to identify such segments. In the process of analyzing consumer demand and identifying clusters of consumers that respond similarly to marketing strategies, firms must identify those bases for segmentation that are most relevant for their goods or services. Figure 6-2 identifies the bases for segmentation that companies could use in the process of analyzing their markets.

Demographic Segmentation: Demographics are statistics that describe the population, such as age, gender, race, ethnicity, income, education, occupation, social class, life cycle stage, and household size. There are many differences among consumers with regard to demographic variables.

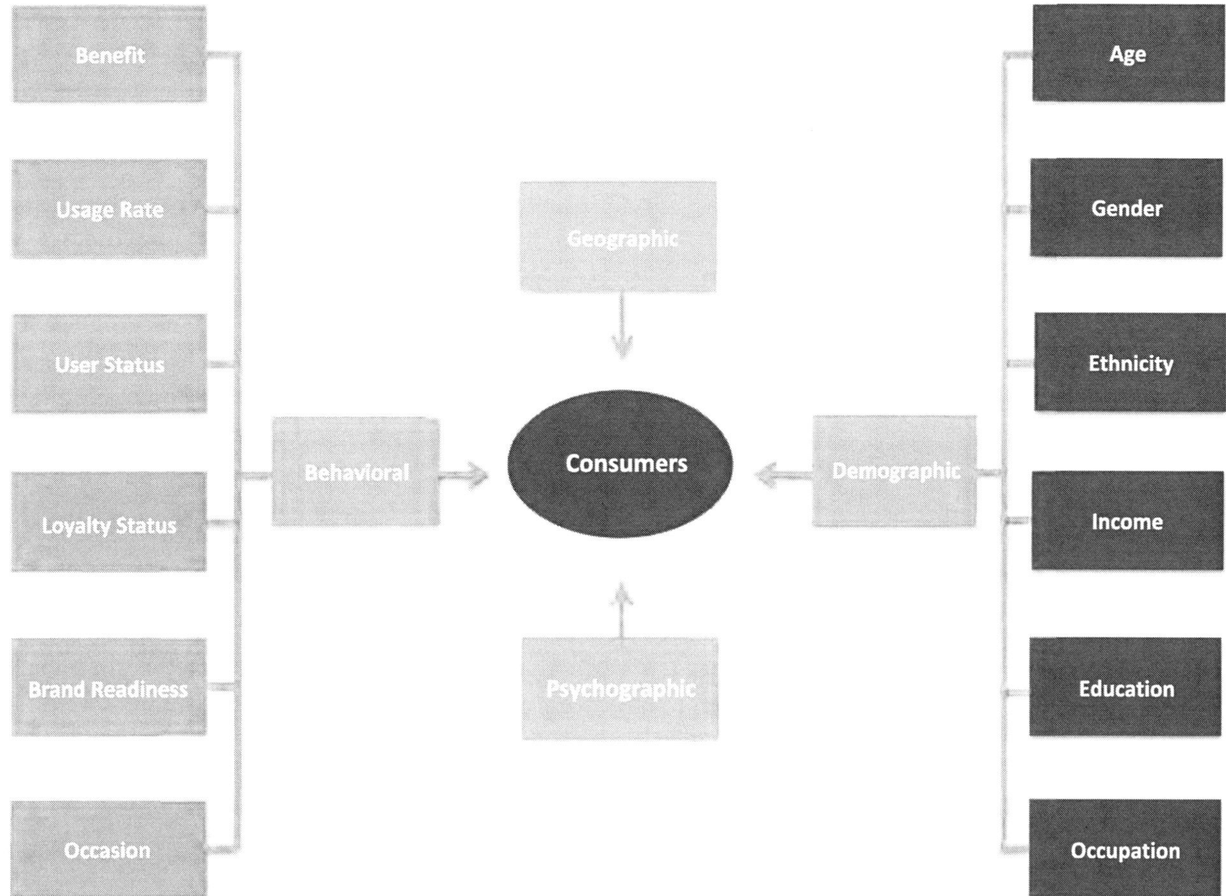

FIGURE 6-2 Basis for Segmentation

Demographic segmentation The process of identifying market segments based on age, gender, race, income, education, occupation, social class, life cycle stage, and household size.

Two major **demographic segmentation** variables are age and life cycle stage. As individuals age and enter different life cycle stages, their product preferences also change. In Chapter 2 an age categorization of socio-demographic groups examined Generations X, Y and Z, baby boomers, and seniors. Each of these categories has been identified as a viable target segment for certain products. For instance, Generation Y consumers tend to spend more on entertainment, whereas baby boomers and Generation X consumers' spending has a family focus. The needs and preferences of each segment vary substantially. Generations Y consumers (millennials) and Generation Z consumers have grown up in a media-saturated, brand-conscious world. The intense marketing efforts aimed at Generation Y have taught them to assume the worst about companies trying to coax them into buying something. Millennials just don't trust corporations and they are dismissive of marketing efforts, assuming businesses profit from war, spill oil in the gulf, and lobby to defund their healthcare; they care about social justice and quality of life, the things they see corporations taking away from them every day, so they are actively disengaged from marketing efforts. As a great brand, don't tell your story, let millennials tell theirs. Burberry, with their Art of the Trench campaign, created a platform for fashionistas to upload pictures of themselves in trenchcoats, and saw a 50% surge in sales. Millennials like to share opinions and buying experiences,

Source: aradaphotography/Shutterstock

and 68% are more likely to purchase after seeing a friend's post, and 84% say user generated content, even strangers' posts, influences what they buy.[5]

Products such as clothing, cosmetics, and hair products are among the obvious products that are tailored based on a person's gender. Companies may elect to target either men or women with their products. Yet often success in one category may compel the company to target the other gender. For instance, clothing brands such as Armani and Hugo Boss, which have traditionally targeted men, find their women's lines to be increasingly successful.

Even Nike, a company that has traditionally targeted hardcore sports guys, is now actively courting women. Nike has even plunged into the yoga market with everything from shoes to balance boards. The company's initiative towards women is an important strategic undertaking to reach the millennial segment. Nike has to target women differently than it targets men.

Targeting men and women with different products and marketing strategies makes good business sense. For example, women are socially engaged differently than men–see **Figure 6-3**. Notice that, platforms that allow more engagement at a personal level, Facebook and Instagram, attract a larger percentage of women, whereas, a concise conversation platform like Twitter attracts a larger percentage of men. Snapchat and WhatsApp are used by both men and women more or less equally, but Pinterest, used to curate and save content, is used by a larger percentage of women than men. Interestingly, a somewhat smaller percentage of women use LinkedIn for business connections and job search than men.

Social Media	Females	Males
Facebook	75	63
Instagram	43	31
LinkedIn	24	29
Twitter	21	24
Pinterest	42	15
Snapchat	24	24
YouTube	68	78
WhatsApp	19	21
Reddit	8	15

FIGURE 6-3 Percentage of Female and Male Use of Social Media
Source: Pew Center, Social Media Fact Sheet, June 12, 2019, https://www.pewresearch.org/internet/fact-sheet/social-media/#who-uses-each-social-media-platform

As seen in Chapter 4, subcultures constitute important markets of consumers with shared value systems that are based on common backgrounds. Marketing managers increasingly focus on specific ethnic segments, directing their marketing efforts to meet their specific needs, and creating communications that appeal to these segments. For example, Lexus has a number of television ads appealing to African Americans and to Hispanics, one with a Spanish-speaking announcer and a bilingual family. Tiffany, Louis Vuitton, and Gucci are advertising to millennial immigrants, as research found that this segment seeks quality and prestige in their luxury goods.[6]

Source: focal point/Shutterstock

Growth of the Hispanic-American population has challenged businesses to rethink their marketing strategies to this group. Marketers must be aware that Hispanic shoppers care about social responsibility, and 57% are more likely to purchase brands that support a cause, while 58% are willing to pay more for environmentally safe products. They are also using digital channels to interact with their favorite brands, with 44% reading digital grocery flyers or circulars.[7]

Product price is often a determinant of whether the company will target higher-or lower-income consumer segments. In general, luxury designers target their products at high-income consumers. Bvlgari, Fendi, Hermès, Prada, and Tiffany brands retail for prices prohibitive for middle-and lower-income consumers. The converse is not necessarily true. Lower-priced products do not necessarily appeal only to lower-income consumers. Walmart consumers come from all economic strata of society, all with the same goal: to get value at everyday-low prices.

Psychographic Segmentation: Demographics are closely linked to **psychographic segmentation**, which includes lifestyles, values, attitudes, interests, and opinions. It is difficult to describe psychographics without demographics. Cultural variables, such as religion, norms, and even language, influence consumer product preferences as well.

Psychographic segmentation The use of values, attitudes, interests, and other cultural variables to segment consumers.

One vehicle for segmenting consumers psychographically that was addressed in detail in Chapter 4 is the VALS (values and lifestyle framework) typology provided by Strategic Business Insights. The VALS typology categorizes respondents based on resources and on the extent to which they are action oriented. The VALS psychographic categories and their descriptors are listed in Figure 6-4.

Marketing managers must understand the psychographic and demographic makeup of their **target market** to effectively address its needs. The Fresh Market, a specialty food chain present primarily on the East Coast, uses a different appeal to consumers in the various neighborhoods where they have stores. Their merchandise mix varies to best address the needs of each neighborhood. For example, in their upscale neighborhoods, they carry prized French cheeses, such as Chaumes, Morbier, and Roquefort. In their more bohemian neighborhoods, they carry a wider

Target market Consumers or markets that are similar in aspects relevant to the company.

Experiencers

Self-expression—motivated consumers. High energy, like physical exercise, very social, younger, adventurous. They spend heavily on clothing, fast food, and music, and they like youthful activities.

Makers

Self-expression—motivated consumers. Practical, self-reliant, focus on family, work, and physical recreation. Interested in material possessions if they have a practical or functional use.

Survivors

Consumers with low resources and low innovation. Brand loyal.

Innovators

Consumers with highest resources and high innovation. Strong self-esteem, change leaders. Image is important, and they buy the finer things in life.

Thinkers

Ideals-motivated consumers. Well educated, high income, value oriented, with leisure activities centered within the home. Well informed about current events.

Believers

Ideals-motivated consumers. Conservative, modest incomes, favor established products and brands, with lives and leisure activities centered around their families, churches, communities, and nation.

Achievers

Achievement-motivated consumers. Successful, work oriented, politically conservative, favoring established products, with their satisfaction coming from their jobs and families.

Strivers

Achievement-motivated consumers. Very similar to achievers but with fewer economic resources. Style is important, and they like to emulate people they admire.

FIGURE 6-4 VALS Psychographic Categories

Behavioral segmentation The process of identifying clusters of consumers who seek the same product benefits or who use or consume the product in a similar fashion.

Benefit segmentation The process of identifying market segments based on important differences between the benefits sought by the target market from purchasing a particular product.

selection of natural foods. And in their ethnic neighborhoods, they attempt to carry products that appeal to their ethnic consumers.

Behavioral Segmentation: **Behavioral segmentation** is used to identify clusters of consumers who seek the same product benefits or who use or consume the product in a similar fashion. Behavioral variables include benefits sought, usage status, user rate, loyalty status, buyer-readiness stage, and occasion.

Benefit segmentation is defined as the process of identifying market segments based on important differences between the benefits sought by the target market. Marketers who understand the motivation behind consumer purchases will be able to send the appropriate message to the relevant market segments.

Source: BaLL LunLa/Shutterstock

Usage rate segmentation is defined as the process of segmenting markets based on the extent to which consumers are nonusers, occasional users, medium users, or heavy users of a product. Take for example Tesla owners. While Tesla created an affordable Model 3 to sell to new college graduates, nothing changed in terms of buyer demographics: the typical Tesla customer is male, in his 50s, owns his home and has a high household income, well over $100,00–probably also lives in California.[8]

Usage rate segmentation The process of segmenting markets based on the extent to which consumers are nonusers, occasional users, medium users, or heavy users of a product.

Brands will often target heavy users because of the volume of purchases they make. As a result, the competition for these heavy users may be intense. Therefore, a brand may decide to target medium users or even occasional users with the idea of increasing their level of purchase behavior.

User status segmentation is defined as the process of determining consumer status—as users of competitors' products, ex-users, potential users, first-time users, or regular users. Although the ideal consumer may be considered to be the regular user, companies should not limit their marketing efforts to just reinforcing the user behavior of a market. Introducing a product for the first time to a market of nonusers will create costly challenges for the company because they have to educate consumers about the brand and convince them to buy. But, these nonusers may present great potential. Krispe Kreme partnered with the Ferrero Group–makers of Nutella–to offer candy bar donuts, thus attracting consumers other than its donut aficionados. Cold Stone Creamery also collaborated with Ferrero to offer super-premium cookies. And Pizza Hut offers Mozzarella Poppers Pizza, with crispy mozzarella on top.

User status segmentation The process of determining consumer status—as users of competitors' products, ex-users, potential users, first-time users, or regular users.

Loyalty segmentation is defined as the process of segmenting the market based on the degree of brand preference, commitment, retention, allegiance, and the extent to which consumers engage in repeat purchases. Loyal consumers are valuable to companies. These are the consumers that the company does not need to persuade to buy its products. Marketing managers strive to create consumer loyalty by offering consistently high-quality goods and services. Marketers also tie the consumer to the brand by offering loyalty programs that direct an individual consumer's consumption to the company. Airlines and hotel chains ensure consumer loyalty by offering rewards tied to the extensive use of that airline or hotel chain. Retailers offer various promotions only to consumers who use their loyalty cards frequently. For instance, Overstock, an online retailer, sends almost daily promotions to its Club O members, and rewards them financially for their product reviews.

Loyalty segmentation The process of segmenting the market based on the degree of consumer loyalty to the brand.

Buyer-readiness stage segmentation is defined as the process of segmenting the market based on individuals' stage of readiness to buy a product. For laser-assisted eye (LASIK) surgery aimed at correcting

Buyer-readiness stage segmentation The process of segmenting the market based on individuals' stage of readiness to buy a product.

hyperopia, myopia, and astigmatism, the market can be segmented into the following consumer segments:

- Individuals who are not aware of the service
- Individuals who are aware of it and may need it in the future
- Individuals who are aware of it but will never need it
- Individuals who are interested to find out more about LASIK surgery
- Individuals who would like to have the surgery but cannot afford it
- Individuals who intend to have the surgery

A company such as Virginia Eye Institute, a heavy promoter of this type of surgery, will need to create different promotion campaigns for each of the consumer segments. For example, the Institute will need awareness campaigns for those who do not know about this type of surgery or that Virginia Eye Institute offers this surgery. Informational campaigns would be needed for consumers who might want additional information or lack knowledge of the procedure. Persuasive campaigns would be used for those who are still debating about whether they should have this type of surgery.

Occasion segmentation The process of segmenting based on the time or the occasion when the product should be purchased or consumed.

Occasion segmentation is defined as segmentation based on the time or the occasion when the product should be purchased or consumed. Champagne is normally consumed to celebrate a special occasion, on New Year's Eve, or at Sunday brunch. Cosmetics companies increase their advertising, promoting extensively before Mother's Day. Different types of candy are promoted for special occasions. For Halloween, candy is sold in large packages that include small portions. For Valentine's Day, candy is presented in heart-shaped packages. **Figure 6-5** summarizes the various behavioral segmentation strategies.

Geographic segmentation Market segmentation based on geographic location, such as country or region.

Geographic Segmentation: Geographic segmentation is defined as segmentation based on geographic location, such as region, state, or city. Small companies typically limit their marketing to segments within the proximity of the firm. Large companies may elect to target various regional segments differently, based on regional preferences. For example, Coke and Pepsi taste different in different parts of the United States and in the world—sweeter in the South of the United States and with a stronger lemon flavor in Europe.

Often, firms are organized geographically, with different divisions specializing in particular markets. Stihl, a manufacturer of chain saws, sells its products primarily to individual consumers in the southeastern United States and to professional loggers in the northwestern United States.

Retailers often use geographic segmentation by advertising to consumers within a specified distance from the retail outlets. Advertising to individuals 100 miles from a retail store is not likely to be effective. AdventHealth operates a number of hospitals in Florida and is a key provider of coronavirus care. The company has placed billboards like the one shown in **Figure 6-6**, along major interstate highways in Florida.

Multiattribute segmentation The process of segmenting the market by using multiple segmentation variables.

Multiattribute Segmentation: Multiattribute segmentation is defined as a process that uses multiple bases for segmenting consumers. Companies

Behavioral Segmentation	Definition	Typical Categories
Benefit segmentation	Market segments based on important differences between the benefits the target market seeks from purchasing a particular product	Varies
Usage rate segmentation	Market segments based on the extent, or quantity, to which consumers use a product	Nonusers; Occasional users; Medium users; Heavy users
User status segmentation	Market segments based on the current usage of a product	User of competing brands; Ex-user; Potential user; First-time users; Regular users
Loyalty status segmentation	Market segment based on the degree of brand preference, commitment, retention, and allegiance to a brand	No loyalty; Low loyalty; Medium loyalty; High loyalty
Buyer-readiness stage segmentation	Market segments based on individuals' stage of readiness to buy a product	Consumers who are not aware; Consumers who are aware of it but will never need it; Consumers who are aware of it and may need it in the future; Consumers who are interested and want to learn more; Consumers who are ready to purchase
Occasion segmentation	Market segments based on the time or the occasion when a product should be purchased or consumed	Varies

FIGURE 6-5 Behavioral Segmentation Strategies

rarely use only demographic variables in their segmentation approaches. Typically, they also add psychographic and behavioral variables to the demographic information to determine the best approach to reach their target market.

Many management consulting firms have come up with systems for segmenting consumers using multiple bases for segmentation: demographics, psychographics, and behavior. Two popular classification systems based on zip code are Claritas PRIZM (a Nielsen product) and Tapestry (offered by ESRI Business Information Solutions). PRIZM was the first lifestyle segmentation system and is still widely used. Based on the principle of "birds of a feather flock together" (i.e., that people of similar demographic and lifestyle characteristics tend to live near each other), PRIZM assigns every neighborhood in the United States to one of 67 clusters. Each cluster describes the predominant demographics and lifestyles of the people living in that neighborhood. For instance, a PRIZM segment called Blue Highways are lower-middle-class couples and families who live in isolated towns and farmsteads, where men hunt and fish, women

FIGURE 6-6 Coronavirus Care Billboard on I-95, a Major Highway in Florida
Source: marla dawn studio/Shutterstock

Source: wavebreakmedia/Shutterstock

enjoy sewing and crafts, and they all go to a country music concert. On the other hand, the segment Suburban Sprawl consists of a collection of middle-aged singles and couples living in the heart of suburbia who are members of the baby boom generation, hold decent jobs, and own older homes and condos, and pursue conservative versions of the American Dream. Both have similar household incomes—the median income is just under $50,000—and they have no children.

Tapestry is based on a similar principle and classifies neighborhoods into 65 market segments based on social, economic, and demographic characteristics. To illustrate consider Richmond, Virginia. An area in the center known as the Richmond Fan, a historic neighborhood housing a large university, has three primary segments: (1) college towns, representing on- and off-campus living, where convenience is important, residents eat out and order in; (2) metro renters, who are young, well-educated professionals in large cities, renters in high-rise units, living alone with roommates; and (3) dorms to diplomas, where most dwellers are college students. This segment is 44.5 percent white, 47.9 percent black, and the median income is just over $30,000.

6-2c Segmenting Business Markets

Relationship-seeking segment A market segment that consists of relatively sophisticated service users who believe that the user-provider relationship is important.

Price-sensitive segment The market segment that looks for low prices but also has low service requirements. It wants the work done at the lowest possible cost.

High-expectation service segment Market segment that is the most demanding and needs extensive customer focus, placing considerable demands on service providers while also wanting low prices.

Customer-focus needs segment Market segment willing to pay for higher-than-average service that is tailored to meet users' needs.

Business markets can be segmented based on similar variables used with the consumer market: geographic location, behavioral dimensions such as benefits sought, user status and usage rate, buyer-readiness stage, degree of loyalty, and other adapted dimensions. For example, instead of demographics, segmentation can take place based on firm size and industry sector.

The following are examples of four behavioral segments of business markets:[9]

- The **relationship-seeking segment** consists of relatively sophisticated service users who believe that the user-provider relationship is important. This segment has a "realistic" level of expectations for the service requirements and does not expect to pay a low price—these consumers understand the trade-off between service levels and price.
- The **price-sensitive segment** is looking for low prices but also has low service requirements. It wants the work done at the lowest possible cost.
- The **high-expectation service segment** is the most demanding and needs extensive customer focus, placing considerable demands on service providers while also wanting low prices.
- The **customer-focus needs segment** is prepared to pay for higher-than-average service that is tailored to meet users' needs.

6-2d Requirements for Successful Segmentation

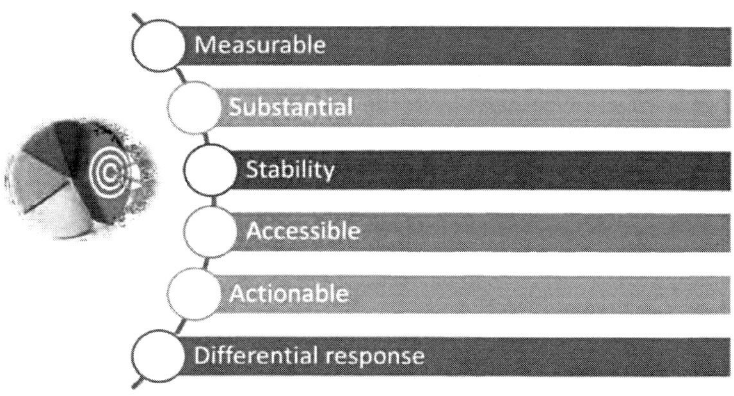

FIGURE 6-7 Characteristics for Effective Market Segmentation

Identifying the bases that the company will use for segmentation is important. Equally important is ensuring that the segments are large enough to warrant investment, that they are relatively stable over time, and that they are going to respond to the company's marketing efforts. For segmentation to be effective, marketing managers need to assess the characteristics listed in **Figure 6-7**.

Measurability refers to the degree to which an individual market segment is easy to identify and measure its relative size. In highly industrialized countries, such as the United States, it is easy to measure or estimate market segments. Government and marketing data are readily available to help companies in the process of making decisions. Census data are reasonably accurate, TV viewing data can be collected with the cooperation of cable companies, and shopping behavior can be evaluated by linking universal product code (UPC) data to loyalty cards' use.

Measurability The ability to estimate the size of a market segment.

Yet even in our data-rich environment, marketers will find that important segments may not be fully measurable. For example, a company advertising to Hispanic-American consumers can only partially estimate its reach in markets where there is a large seasonal and unregistered migrant population. Companies targeting products to gay and lesbian consumers find that only under five percent of the population self-identifies as gay and lesbian. Limiting targeting strategies to the self-identified segment ignores the larger LGBTQ+ segment that have not self-identified.

Substantiality is defined as the degree to which a segment is large enough and profitable enough to warrant investment. After measuring the size of a market segment, a company needs to determine whether the segment is large enough to earn a decent return on its investment. For example, it would not make sense for a retailer to position itself as specializing in selling clove cigarettes because the market for clove cigarettes is limited, even in large cities.

Substantiality The extent to which the market is large enough to warrant investment.

Stability is defined as the degree to which a segment's preferences are stable over time. This is an important consideration in an environment where products are in different life cycle stages and where preferences are continuously changing. For decades until the late 1980s, dealers of artifacts and antiques prominently displayed elephant tusks and rare leopard skins in Fifth Avenue and 57th Street store windows in Manhattan. Chinatown retailers experienced brisk sales of ornately carved elephant tusks. However, a change in public opinion took place after the U.S. government and various international organizations revealed the cruelty of these trades and stressed the distinct possibility that these animals may become extinct. The movie and book *Gorillas in the Mist*, also popular in the 1980s, further

Stability The extent to which preferences are stable, rather than changing, in a market segment.

convinced consumers that the trade in rare animals is cruel. The trade in objects made from rare animals fell out of favor with the consuming public, and this once-substantial market segment quickly diminished.

It is important to note that segments do change with time, especially early in the product life cycle or when new technologies appear. As discussed in the chapter opening, social media is changing rapidly, as new apps are developed that are capable of higher security, more creative interactions, and as technology is changing, allowing faster data processing and greater data storage, changing the way individuals communicate with each other and with brands.

Accessibility The ability to communicate with and reach the target market.

Accessibility is the ability to communicate with and reach the target market. Some markets cannot be accessed with marketing communications. A large proportion of children cannot easily be reached through marketing communication. Many children spend their weekdays in daycares that have a policy not to expose children to television or computer screens. At home, their parents may decide not to allow them to watch TV programs and stream, instead, educational videos. In their everyday lives, these children may never be exposed to children's advertising.

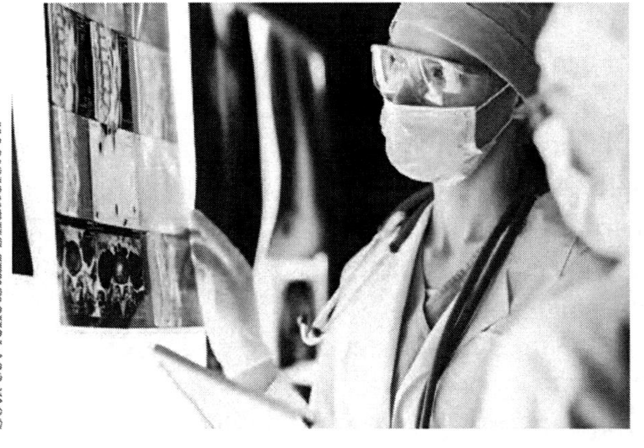

Source: lenetstan/Shutterstock

Working mothers are also difficult to target. Most have little time to spend online after working on a screen all day at work, or remotely, and have little time to watch TV, and see the ads. When they relax, they will likely spend time with their significant other, with children, or might stream programming. Marketers often reach them only relatively late during the consumer decision-making process, when they are already scrolling for product information, or already at the store, and they may have already made their purchase decision.

Actionability The extent to which the target market segment is responsive to the marketing strategies used.

Actionability refers to the extent to which marketers are capable of designing programs that can effectively serve the market segment. Do they have the product that the market needs? Are they pricing it based on the needs of the market? Small and large firms alike find that they have trouble predicting if their target segment is actionable when they go abroad. A small boutique Italian wine bar attempting to introduce authentic Italian wines in Germany finds that the market expects it to be primarily a restaurant. The largest retailer worldwide, Walmart, found that it could not compete effectively for consumers in Germany, where the market is saturated with low-service, low-priced local competition like Aldi and Lidl. An insufficient *a priori* assessment of actionability will often lead to failure.

Differential response The extent to which market segments respond differently to marketing strategies.

Differential response is defined as the extent to which market segments are easy to distinguish from each other and respond differently to company marketing strategies. If consumers are similar or have identical preferences—and this is hardly ever the case—there is no need for target marketing. Even the market for water is segmented into sparkling or still, based on its provenance, based on its mineral content, and so on.

6-3 Target Marketing Decisions

Source: Dmitri Ma/Shutterstock

Companies that have ample resources can, and often do, address the needs of all segments of consumers. Unilever and Mondelēz attempt to target all consumers with the various products they sell, filling the supermarket and discount store candy shelf space with what seemingly are competing brands–Dove, Magnum, etc. for Unilever, and Milka, Toblerone, Cadbury, and others for Mondelēz. Other companies, Boeing, for instance, choose to focus on one well-established brand, improving it continuously, offering alternatives under the same umbrella brand name. Not all companies have the resources of the companies mentioned here. Small and medium-size businesses can be successful by best addressing the needs of one or two segments or a small niche. One common trait of all these companies is that they research their consumers closely and target and position their products accordingly.

6-3a Differentiated Marketing Strategy

Companies that use a **differentiated marketing strategy** identify market segments that want different benefits from a product and target them with different brands, using separate marketing strategies. Some companies have the necessary resources to offer at least one brand to every conceivable market segment. Procter & Gamble offers a variety of laundry detergents to consumers all over the world: Bold, Cheer, Dreft, Era, Febreze, Gain, Ivory Snow, and Tide. To European consumers, the company offers combinations of the following brands: Ace, Ariel, Bonux, Dash, Daz, Dreft, Fairy, Febreze, Tide, and Vizir, among others.[10] Each of these laundry detergents appeals to a different market, consumers who want a detergent that has an excellent cleaning ability, consumers who need whitening, consumers who desire fabric softening agents in the washing process, consumers who want a product for sensitive fabrics or for babies' sensitive skin, and consumers who may be allergic. Such strategies, whereby companies offer brands for every market segment, require significant resources on the part of the company. It is more costly to develop a marketing strategy for each market segment than to address a single segment or to offer only one brand targeted at all consumers.

Differentiated marketing strategy A targeting strategy identifying market segments with different preferences for a particular product category and targeting each segment with different brands and different marketing strategies.

6-3b Concentrated Marketing Strategy

Not all companies can afford or want to offer something for each consumer. In fact, many companies select only one market segment and target it with one single brand, using a **concentrated marketing strategy**. Mont Blanc, a company manufacturing pens and fountain pens, offers a relatively limited product selection that it markets using the same theme—"the art of writing"—to all consumers worldwide. The product is targeted at the professional class.

Concentrated marketing strategy The process of selecting only one market segment and targeting it with one single brand.

Companies that cannot afford to compete in a mature market with an oligopoly may choose to pursue a small segment—a niche. This option may be the only one available for the company's limited resources. Retailers often use a niche strategy. The Body Shop caters to consumers who are environmentally concerned and who want to purchase natural products that have not been tested on animals.

6-3c Undifferentiated Marketing Strategy

Undifferentiated marketing strategy A targeting strategy aiming the product at the market using a single strategy, regardless of the number of segments.

An **undifferentiated marketing strategy** is one in which the product is aimed at the entire market using a single marketing strategy. The company using this strategy chooses to ignore differences between consumers and offers the entire market one single brand. Many bulk products are aimed at all consumers, regardless of demographics, psychographics, and behavioral differences. For branded products, this is difficult to achieve. Even salt brands offer low-sodium and kosher versions.

Using an undifferentiated strategy offers the company economies of scale in manufacturing and promotion and the ability to cut costs. Although this strategy may appear as the most efficient, marketers are aware that segment needs may be better served by tailoring offerings to various segments of the market. In that sense, manufacturers of branded products will benefit from using a differentiated strategy, if they can afford it; if not, they can offer a concentrated strategy, meeting the needs of a target segment more efficiently than they would those of the entire market.

6-4 Product Differentiation and Brand Positioning

Positioning entails placing the brand in the consumer's mind in relation to other competing brands, based on brand traits and benefits that are relevant to the consumer. Such a process involves identifying competitors, determining how the competitors are perceived and evaluated by target consumers and determining the competitors' positions in the consumers' mind. Based on this information, the firm must identify its value proposition used to differentiate the brand in the mind of consumers, and then position the brand relative to competitors.

6-4a The Value Proposition and Product Differentiation

Value proposition Proposition that convinces consumers to buy a firm's products and services over those of their competitors.

A company's **value proposition** convinces consumers to buy their products and services over those of their competitors. It is essential to have an appealing, excusive, and clear value proposition, so that all consumers know what they are benefitting when they buy a certain firm's offerings. Firms that lack a strong and clear value proposition attempt to compensate through offering an overwhelming amount of incentives. However, the incentive should only be a little extra something that helps consumers overcome doubts about purchasing the brand, not the entire reason for the customer to act; the value proposition should be the convincing factor for customers.[11] To achieve a strong value proposition, firms must differentiate their offer from their competitors' offers and excel in at least one value. It could match a competitor on every dimension except for an essential one, so that it can demonstrate to consumers this important difference.[12] This is the process of **product differentiation**: identifying an appealing, excusive, and clear value proposition based on the brand's competitive advantage. Next, the company must decide how to position its brand relative to competitors and communicate the information to its target market.

As shown in Figure 6-8, there are six approaches to the brand positioning strategy: attribute/benefit positioning, price/quality positioning, use or applications positioning, product user positioning, product class positioning, and competitor positioning.[13]

Brand Positioning Strategies
Attribute/ Benefit
Price/ Quality
Use or Application
Product User
Product Class
Competitor

FIGURE 6-8 Brand Positioning Strategies

Product differentiation Identifying an appealing, exclusive, and clear value proposition based on the brand's competitive advantage

6-4b Attribute/Benefit Positioning

Procter & Gamble focuses on product attributes and benefits to position many of its brands within a single product category. An **attribute/benefit positioning strategy** uses product or service attributes and benefits to position it in the consumer's mind relative to competitors' brands. The following are examples of product positioning by Procter & Gamble (www.pg.com):

- Cheer, in powder or liquid, with or without bleach, is positioned as protecting against fading, color transfer, and fabric wear.
- Dreft is positioned as a detergent that removes tough baby stains and protects garment colors.
- Gain, as a liquid and powder detergent, is positioned as having exceptional cleaning and whitening abilities.
- Tide, in powder or liquid, with or without bleach, is positioned as a laundry detergent with exceptional cleaning, whitening, and stain removal abilities.

Attribute/benefit positioning strategy Positioning that communicates product attributes and benefits, differentiating each brand from the other company.

Such precise positioning, which is reflected in the company's communication with its respective segments, clearly differentiates each brand from the other company brands and from those of competitors such as Unilever and Colgate-Palmolive.

6-4c Price/Quality Positioning

The **price/quality positioning** strategy positions goods and services in terms of price and quality. Manufacturers such as Toyota, Hyundai, and Philips, as well as retailers such as Walmart and Target, emphasize the value aspect of their offerings. Alternatively, goods and services can be positioned at the other end of the price/quality continuum, as the best product that money can buy. In addition to stressing high quality, such positioning also entails an exclusive distribution or access, an expert sales force and service, and advertising in publications aimed at an upscale market. Mercedes-Benz claims that, in a perfect world, everyone would

Price/quality positioning A strategy whereby products and services are positioned as offering the best value for the money.

drive a Mercedes. Kempinski Hotels and Resorts, an upscale German chain, reflect "the finest traditions of European hospitality," and are synonymous with distinctive luxury, style, nobility, and efficiency.

6-4d Use or Applications Positioning

Use or applications positioning The process of marketing a precise product application that differentiates it in consumers' minds from other products that have a more general use.

How a product is used or the various applications of a product are often used to position brands in the **use or applications positioning** strategy. Procter & Gamble's Era is positioned as a high-technology detergent that pretreats and washes fabrics to suspend dirt. This very precise application differentiates it in consumers' minds from other laundry detergents that have a more general use. Sometimes, the uses or applications differ from one market to another. A bicycle manufacturer would most likely position its offerings in Asia and Europe as efficient transportation, whereas in the United States, it would position them for high-performance recreation.

6-4e Product User Positioning

Product user positioning A positioning strategy that focuses on the product user, rather than on the product.

The **product user positioning** strategy focuses on the product user, rather than on the product. The marketing mix for the Jeep is targeted at the individual who wants to go places where trucks and cars do not have access. All product descriptions and advertising emphasize this aspect. The Jeep itself has the aspect of an all-terrain vehicle. GE Monogram appliances are aimed at those who have a Hatteras yacht, Barcelona chairs, and Noguchi tables. Phoenix Wealth Management is positioned to appeal to the woman who gives her broker investment ideas, who is taking her company public, or who earns more than her CEO husband.

Product class positioning A strategy used to differentiate a company as a leader in a product category as defined by the respective companies.

Competitor positioning strategy The process of comparing the firm's brand, directly or indirectly, with those of competitors.

6-4f Product Class Positioning

Pizza Hut has used the approach saying it is the best dine-in pizza establishment. It wants to be in the dine-in pizza product class, not the delivery business. Products using a **product class positioning** strategy differentiate themselves as leaders in a product category, as they define it. Milk, for most people, is considered a breakfast drink. For others, milk is consumed with cookies by children after school. To increase sales, the milk industry wants to reposition its product to be consumed at any time of the day, for any reason. Thus, it does not want consumers to put milk in the breakfast drink category. The milk industry wants milk to be a beverage. The danger, of course, of such a strategy is that now milk must compete with soft drinks, coffee, tea, and other drinks, instead of breakfast drinks like orange juice.

Source: Nathan Pang/Shutterstock

6-4g Competitor Positioning

When a firm compares its brand with those of competitors, it uses a **competitor positioning strategy**. Some comparisons are direct. Others are subtle. When Airbus asks readers of *The Financial Times* if they would be more comfortable with two or four engines when they are up in the air, it makes an implicit reference to Boeing, which has only two engines.

All positioning, ultimately, is relative to the competition, only not always explicitly so. Even symbols hint at competition. Merrill (Merrill Lynch) is bullish on the market (in its advertising, the bull used to be featured prominently—it still is referenced occasionally); its competitors don't. *The New York Times'* celebrated slogan coined in 1897, "All the news that's fit to print," implied that, if not published there, it is not newsworthy.

6-4h Positioning Maps

Positioning is all about perception—it is in the consumer's mind and is the consumer's perception of a brand relative to the competition. Brands can be mapped on a positioning map based on their attributes, allowing them to be compared relative to other brands with which they are competing. According to Trout and Ries, a company should ask the following questions:[14]

1. What place does a product occupy in most consumers' minds?
2. What place does the company want to occupy?
3. What competitors does the company have to defeat to occupy the position it desires?
4. Does the company have the resources to attain this position?
5. Can the company persist until it gets there?
6. Are the company's tactics supporting its positioning objectives?

Let us assume two attributes, price and strength of automobiles, where strength is defined as a tank-like safety quality, which offers the consumers the comfort (justified or not) that they will survive any collision. We are using only two attributes because they are easier to map than multiple attributes. However, marketers use three-dimensional maps routinely to position their brands. The two attributes, price and strength (or safety), will be mapped on the x and y axes, respectively, as shown in **Figure 6-9**.

We have four quadrants. The Range Rover Evoque has the highest price and strength as perceived by consumers. The Volvo also occupies a position, albeit a less-prominent one, in the high-price/high-strength quadrant. This position was achieved with extensive advertising over decades of Volvo attempting to convince buyers of the strength of its automobile. Jeep lies in the lower-price/high-strength quadrant. It is sturdy but more affordable than the Hummer or the Volvo. The BMW M-Models are very expensive and smaller automobiles, which, with their soft top, can be easily flattened by a collision with just about any sports utility vehicle. It occupies the low-strength/high-price quadrant. The Mitsubishi Mirage is perceived as cheaper and not as sturdy; therefore, it occupies the low-price/low-strength quadrant.

An automobile manufacturer can use this map in many ways, to determine its position on this positioning map or on another map with different attributes. It can also use the map to determine where, in consumers' minds, it should position its new models. By mapping all competing brands on

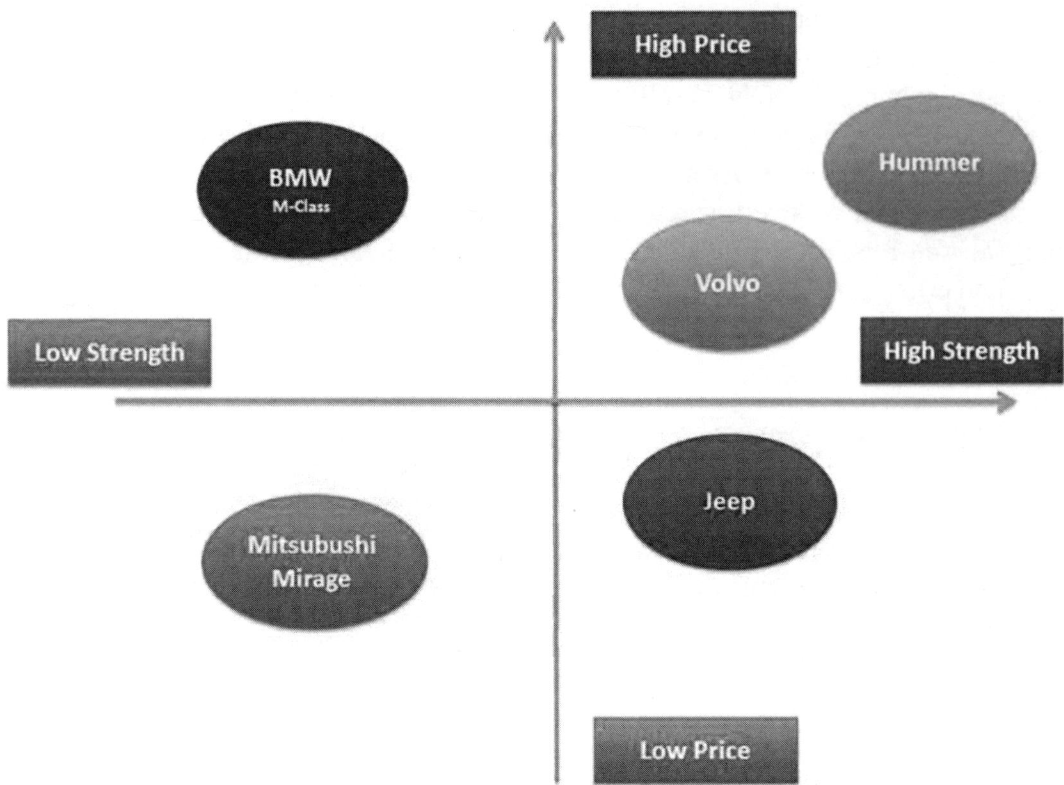

FIGURE 6-9 Positioning Grid

the price-strength dimensions, the company can identify gaps that are not addressed by competitors and offer a new model that fits in the respective position. Alternatively, if the company determines that the automobile is in an undesirable quadrant, from the consumer's point of view, it can advertise itself as occupying a different position—as long as that position is plausible.

6-5 The Strategic Plan

After completing segmentation, targeting, and positioning, the marketing plan is developed as an essential element of the overall corporate strategic plan, an effort to maintain a fit between the company objectives and capabilities and the continuously changing company environment (the marketing plan is part of the company strategic plan). A more detailed version of the strategic plan and marketing plan is offered in Appendix A.

The corporate strategic plan involves taking the following steps:

1. Articulating the mission statement, expressing the vision and principles of the company, a guide to what the company wants to accomplish in the marketplace. The mission should underscore the differentiating aspects of the business and the company's approach to its stakeholders: consumers, employees, and society.
2. Identifying company goals and objectives: stemming from the mission statement, objectives are expressed in terms of profit, sales, market share, and return on investment (ROI), or even societal outcomes. The primary firm goal is creating profit for the company and wealth for shareholders. Thus, increasing productivity and production,

maximizing consumption, and increasing sales are key objectives, accomplished with the appropriate marketing strategies. In the process of achieving organizational goals, companies must offer quality and value to consumers and businesses, leading to high customer satisfaction.

3. Managing the business portfolio, evaluating the different strategic business units of the company, and identifying products with great promise and in need of additional resources, those performing well in a mature market, and those that are not, which must be divested. In portfolio analysis, it is helpful to use portfolio matrices, such as the Boston Consulting Group matrix introduced in Chapter 8 to assess products in terms of their market and financial performance and potential.
4. Strategic business unit planning involves each unit developing its own mission statement, one that is more specific than the corporate mission statement, focusing on the brand and the strategic fit between its resources and the company goals, and conducting a strength, weaknesses, opportunities, and threats (SWOT) analysis. The SWOT analysis examines strengths and weaknesses related to the company, consumers, suppliers, intermediaries, other facilitators of marketing functions, and the competition, as well as threats and opportunities in the sociodemographic and cultural environment, the economic and natural environments, the technological environment, and the political and legal environments.
5. The marketing plan focuses on the good or service and involves the following steps:
   - Identifying marketing objectives defined in terms of dollar sales, units sold, or in terms of market share, brand awareness or customer traffic, depending on the type of business.
   - Defining the marketing strategy, engaging in segmentation, targeting, and positioning, and communicating through the marketing mix product traits and benefits that differentiate it in the consumer's mind from competitors' offerings—refer to previous sections on segmentation, targeting, and positioning.
   - Developing the marketing mix—the four Ps of marketing (product, place, price, and promotion)—that the company can use to influence demand for its products.
   - Marketing implementation, turning the marketing plan into marketing action programs to accomplish the marketing objectives. Implementation might consist of creating paid content to promote customer online engagement and television ads promoting a new product.
   - Marketing control, using procedures for evaluating the outcomes of the implemented marketing strategies and the corrective actions needed to ensure that the previously stated marketing objectives are met. For example, if the objective is to increase product awareness by 30 percent, the day-after recall (DAR) tests could be used to determine whether the

objective has been reached. If not, the corrective action could be the purchase of additional social media advertising or the development of a new advertising theme.

Marketing Return on Investment (Marketing ROI) A way of measuring the return on investment from the amount a company spends on marketing.

An important aspect of a marketing plan is assessment. One approach to assessment is calculation of the **Marketing Return on Investment (Marketing ROI)**, measuring the return on investment on the amount that a company spends on marketing. It is a standard by which all marketing investments, including advertising, direct marketing, social media, digital marketing, PR events, point-of-sale marketing, personal selling, branding, are assessed. To calculate Marketing ROI, divide the net marketing contribution (calculated as net sales minus cost of goods sold, minus marketing expenses) by marketing expenses–the higher the number, the better.[15]

One of the downsides of marketing ROI is that it helps recognize the incremental profits in short-term sales, but it underestimates the long-term benefits that marketing brings to brand value. This aspect is especially problematic for executives who might be impatient to see a return.[16]

Summary

1. **Identify the rationale for adopting a target marketing strategy.**
   Target marketing is used to identify segments of consumers who are similar with regard to key traits, who would respond to a particular marketing mix (i.e., to segment the market). The goal is to select the segments that the company can serve most efficiently and develop products tailored to each (i.e., to target the market). Once selected, companies should communicate through the marketing mix (i.e., positioning) the product traits and benefits that differentiate the product in consumers' minds.

2. **Identify the bases for consumer segmentation and offer company application examples.**
   Consumers are segmented based on demographics, which are statistics that describe the population, such as age, gender, ethnicity, education, income, and occupation. Psychographics refer to values, attitudes, interests, and other cultural variables used to segment consumers. Geographic location can be used to reach specific market segments. Behavior segmentation is composed of using variables such as usage rate and user status, loyalty status, and the benefits sought from purchasing the product or service. Business segments are based on some of the same criteria, with some adaptation. For example, demographic variables for businesses may consist of company size and industry sector. In addition, other behavioral variables could be used in the case of businesses. Examples are relationship-seeking segments, price-sensitive segments, high-expectation service segments, and customer-focus needs segments.

3. **Identify the requirements necessary for effective market segmentation.**
   For segmentation to be effective, segments must be easy to measure, substantial in size, stable over time, accessible via marketing communication and distribution, actionable through marketing strategies, and able to respond differentially from other segments to a company's marketing strategy.

4. **Describe the three targeting strategies that companies use.**
   The first strategy is differentiated marketing, whereby companies address the needs of different segments by offering them different brands and using different marketing mix strategies. Concentrated marketing addresses a single consumer segment that is large and stable enough to warrant the investment. With an undifferentiated marketing strategy a company can reap the

benefits of standardization by using the same strategy to market to all consumers.

5. **Describe the six positioning strategies that companies can use to position their brands in the minds of target consumers.**
Companies can position products by focusing on product attributes or benefits; by positioning the brand as a high-price/high-quality product or as the best value for the money; by positioning the brand based on use or applications; by positioning the brand based on traits of product use or by positioning it as the best product in its class.

Key Terms

Accessibility (168)
Actionability (168)
Attribute/benefit positioning strategy (171)
Behavioral segmentation (162)
Benefit segmentation (162)
Buyer-readiness stage segmentation (163)
Competitor positioning strategy (172)
Concentrated marketing strategy (169)
Customer-focus needs segment (166)
Demographic segmentation (159)
Differential response (168)
Differentiated marketing strategy (169)
Geographic segmentation (164)
High-expectation service segment (166)
Loyalty segmentation (163)
Marketing return on investment (marketing roi) (176)
Mass marketing (158)
Measurability (167)
Micromarketing (158)
Multiattribute segmentation (164)
Occasion segmentation (164)
Price/quality positioning (171)
Price-sensitive segment (166)
Product class positioning (172)
Product differentiation (171)
Product user positioning (172)
Psychographic segmentation (161)
Relationship-seeking segment (166)
Segmentation (157)
Segment marketing (158)
Stability (167)
Substantiality (167)
Target market (161)
Target marketing (156)
Undifferentiated marketing strategy (170)
Usage rate segmentation (163)
Use or applications positioning (172)
User status segmentation (163)
Value proposition (170)

Discussion Questions

1. Demographics and psychographics are often used in the process of conducting multiattribute segmentation. You have been hired by a new gardening magazine to identify the different market segments that the magazine could target. Conduct your segmentation analysis by identifying various segments of gardeners. Describe them in terms of demographics, psychographics, and behaviors.
2. Look at Figure 6-3. Identify the Internet segment that fits you. Discuss your usage situations and favorite materials. How closely does it fit the information provided in the figure? Identify the Internet segment of one sibling, your parents, and your closest friend. Discuss their usage situations and favorite materials as well.
3. Identify five products that you believe are segmented on the basis of gender. Identify what your think is the top brand in each product category. Explain why you think it is the top brand. Discuss how the brand is marketed to your gender.
4. Describe the different bases for behavioral segmentation. What are some of the relevant behavioral market segments for individuals who use a fitness center or gym? Describe a segmentation strategy a fitness center could

use based on benefit segmentation, usage rate segmentation, user status segmentation and occasion segmentation.

5. Marketing managers use a number of criteria to ensure effective segmentation. Assume that you are working for a manufacturer of children's hair care products. What are the criteria that you would use for effective segmentation?
6. Look at Figure 6-4, VALS Psychographic Categories. Which VALS category would you fit into? Why? How accurate are the characteristics listed in terms of your personal characteristics. Identify two close friends or relatives. Identify their VALS category and discuss each of their characteristics.
7. Go to ESRI's Web page at www.esribis.com and enter the following zip codes: 23220, 90210, 10022, and 23229. Type in your zip code. What makes of automobiles would sell well in these target markets? Explain. What other product categories should be targeted to these markets?
8. For each of the positioning strategies discussed in Section 6-4, identify a brand that uses the respective strategy not mentioned in the text. Explain your choice.
9. Go to YouTube and locate four advertisements. For each ad, identify the positioning strategy that is being used. Justify your answer and use screenshots to illustrate. Provide the YouTube URL with your answers.
10. Write down the names of the restaurants that are close to your college or where you live. Create a position grid using price and quality as the two dimensions. Place each restaurant on the grid. Discuss why the restaurants are placed where they are. Would the map be different if someone else drew it? Why or why not?

Review Questions

True or False

1. Market segmentation is defined as identifying the segments of consumers who are similar with regard to key characteristics and who would respond well to a product and related marketing mix.
2. The purpose of segmentation is to identify all consumers' needs and develop a specific marketing strategy for each segment.
3. User status segmentation is defined as the process of segmenting the markets based on the extent to which consumers are nonusers, occasional users, medium users, or heavy users of a product.
4. Multivariable segmentation is based on benefits sought and usage status.
5. Measurability for successful segmentation is defined as the degree to which an individual market segment is easy to identify and measure or the ability to evaluate the market segment's size.
6. Stability, as a basis for successful segmentation, is defined as the degree to which the segments are large enough to warrant the investment.
7. Companies that use a differentiated strategy identify or even create market segments that want different benefits from a product and target them with different brands.
8. A company that pursues a small market segment—a niche—is engaging in differentiation.
9. A company that offers a brand that is positioned as an advanced formula detergent that can suspend dirt engages in product user positioning.

Multiple Choice

10. Which of the following categories relate to selecting segments that the company can serve most efficiently and developing a product mix tailored to each segment?
    a. market segmentation
    b. market targeting
    c. market positioning
    d. all of the above

11. Demographic segmentation includes which of the following categories?
    a. motivation
    b. user status
    c. income
    d. none of the above
12. Companies that attempt to provide skin treatment products for baby boomers are engaged in which of the following types of segmentation strategies?
    a. behavior segmentation
    b. multiattribute segmentation
    c. segmenting business markets
    d. demographic segmentation
13. Two popular classification systems based on zip codes are PRIZM and ACORN. They aid in ___ segmentation.
    a. behavior
    b. geographic
    c. multivariable
    d. occasion
14. In segmenting business markets, the relationship-seeking segments are characterized as
    a. seeking low prices and accepting low service levels.
    b. understanding the trade-off between service levels and price.
    c. demanding low prices but extensive customer service.
    d. accepting higher prices to address their own specific needs.
15. Which strategy would offer the best value for the money spent on goods and services?
    a. price/quality positioning
    b. use or application positioning
    c. product user positioning
    d. competitor positioning

Answers: (1) True, (2) False, (3) False, (4) False, (5) True, (6) False, (7) True, (8) False, (9) False, (10) b, (11) c, (12) d, (13) c, (14) b, (15) a

Case: The World—Vegas Style

Source: Kobby Dagan/Shutterstock

Before 1990, the word elegance was never used in the same sentence as Las Vegas. The dominant traits of an earlier Las Vegas were excess and tackiness, not elegance. Vegas was about long-legged cocktail waitresses in Daisy-Duke tights, eating thick steaks, drinking scotch, and wearing gaudy fashions.

Las Vegas has fully outgrown its tacky past, creating fantasy excursions to faraway places: it is an opulent international oasis in the desert. The Bellagio Hotel, evocative of Italy—$1.8 billion cost—re-created Tuscany, and has an art collection; the atrium ceilings are covered with Dale Chihuly glass works. The Mandalay Bay—$950 million—has 3,700 rooms and a South Seas theme. The Venetian and Palazzo Towers—$1.3 billion—has 6,000 rooms and brings to mind Venice, complete with gondolas, and Italian melodies. The Paris Las Vegas—$760 million—has 2,900 rooms and an Eiffel tower that wanted to be as tall as the original, but was scaled down for the safety of descending airplanes.

Resort mogul Steve Wynn upped the ante with the Wynn Las Vegas, inspired by a Picasso painting he owns. This is a $2.8 billion resort, 50 story, 2,716-room hotel with an 18-hole golf course, an art gallery with Mr. Wynn's collection, 19 restaurants, and a Ferrari-Maserati dealership. The Wynn Las Vegas was the most expensive resort ever built in Las Vegas, topping the $1.8 billion Bellagio, another Wynn property. Built on the site of the old Desert Inn at the north end of the Strip, the Wynn Las Vegas is comparable in size to Bellagio, featuring an 111,000-square-foot casino with 2,000 slot machines and 136 table games, and a water-based entertainment complex.

In 2020, the COVID-19 crisis practically shut down the city, with all resorts and hotels closed. When they opened, almost three months later, under the Phase 2 Directive guidelines, requiring masks and social distancing, the resorts were packed. The vibe on casino floors was electric: gamblers at Venetian Las Vegas cheered as they raced through the doors, and, at Caesars Palace, actors dressed as Caesar and Cleopatra donned face masks and joined forces with Wayne Newton–Mr. Las Vegas–to welcome back guests. Visitors immediately started to embrace Vegas again, choosing between a gondola ride through an indoor canal at the Venice, a trip to the top of the Eiffel Tower, or an expensive dinner at the Wolfgang Puck eateries, delighting in one of the best restaurant cities in the United States. The Paris hotel, home of the French musical, Notre Dame de Paris, opened with can-can dancers and great fanfare.

Investors continue to bet on a bright future in the middle of the Nevada desert. Resorts World Las Vegas spent more than $4.3 billion to create a new resort on the Strip scheduled to open in 2021. It will have a new Elon Musk-designed underground transport system to whisk visitors from the complex to the Las Vegas Convention Center in under two minutes, with passengers transported in self-driving, all-electric Tesla vehicles. The resort will offer star-studded performances in a state-of-the-art 5,000-capacity theatre, a curated collection of exclusive retail boutiques, and the most technologically advanced, progressive approach to gaming the Las Vegas Strip has ever seen. It will house Hilton luxury brands Conrad and LXR, and a Hilton Hotel.

A unique city in the middle of the desert, Las Vegas draws numerous visitors attracted to gambling opportunities, conferences, entertainment, and the Strip's new hotels. Las Vegas does not share its visitors with any other attraction. They are captivated and captured by gambling, attending shows, and shopping. They want to take their morning stroll in Bellagio's botanical garden, splendid with blooms. These are the consumers who marvel at original paintings in the hotel's art museum, who dine in French restaurants, and who buy gowns in Vegas to wear proudly to a black-tie fund-raiser in Middle America.

Case Questions

1. Describe the different visitor market segments that Las Vegas appeals to. Use demographic, psychographic, behavioral, and geographic bases for segmentation in creating your descriptions.
2. What are the target markets of the new international hotels in Las Vegas? Go to the Bellagio Hotel and Casino website to find out more information about the hotel's target market.
3. What types of targeting strategies are these international hotels using? Be specific, explaining your reasoning.
4. What is the positioning strategy that the Wynn Las Vegas hotel is using to attract its visitors? Justify your answer.

Sources: Matt Villano, "Las Vegas reopened. People showed up," CNN, June 9, 2020, https://www.cnn.com/travel/article/las-vegas-is-back-coronavirus/index.html; Paul Szydelko, "Resorts World Vegas hopes to have Musk-designed transport system in place for its 2021 opening," *Travel Weekly,* June 16, 2020, https://www.travelweekly.com/North-America-Travel/Resorts-World-Vegas-eyes-debut-of-Musk-designed-transport-system-in-time-for-its-opening; Resorts World Las Vegas, accessed at https://www.rwlasvegas.com on June 20, 2020. Wynn Las Vegas, accessed at https://www.wynnlasvegas.com/?gclsrc=aw.ds&gclid=CjwKCAjw57b3BRBlEiwA1ImytkMpRGUHdKhaoAFfHOHpsPpG_YD6EBRg2WHxEgGDYi2YCo1P6MJrnhoCgngQAvD_BwE&gclsrc=aw.ds on June 20, 2020.

Endnotes

1. Facebook, "Facebook reports first quarter 2020 results, April 29, 2020, https://investor.fb.com/investor-news/press-release-details/2020/Facebook-Reports-First-Quarter-2020-Results/default.aspx.
2. Lizzy Hillier, "As usage soars, what are social media platforms doing to help support and inform users," Ecoconsultancy, May 21, 2020, https://econsultancy.com/coronavirus-as-social-media-usage-soars-what-are-platforms-doing-to-help-users-be-better-connected-informed-and-supported.
3. Ryan Nagelhout, "Streetwear and luxury brands are the future of gaming fashion," UPROXX, June 4, 2020, https://uproxx.com/gaming/gaming-fashion-streetwear-andbox.
4. G. Trinh, H. Khan, and L. Lockshin, Purchasing behaviour of ethnicities: Are they different? International Business Review (2018), https://doi.org/10.1016/j.ibusrev.2018.06.002.
5. Matt Haber, "Here is why millennials are ignoring your brand," *INC.*, May 19, 2017, https://www.inc.com/molly-reynolds/heres-why-millennials-are-ignoring-your-brand-and-what-to-do-about-it.html.
6. Sarah Ramirez, "5pc of advertising spend dedicated to multicultural audiences: ANA," August 9, 2019, https://www.luxurydaily.com/5pc-of-advertising-spend-dedicated-to-multicultural-audiences-ana.
7. Epsilon, "Why grocers need identity management for multicultural shoppers," August 18, v2019, https://us.epsilon.com/blog/multichannel-for-multicultural-shoppers-why-grocers-need-identity-management
8. Hedges & Company, "Tesla owner demographics: Income, age, gender and more, https://hedgescompany.com/blog/2018/11/tesla-owner-demographics, accessed on May 11, 2020.
9. Bill Merrilees, Rohan Bentley, and Ross Cameron, "Business Service Market Segmentation," *Journal of Business and Industrial Marketing* 14, no. 2 (1999): 151–164.
10. www.pg.com, accessed March 11, 2020.
11. Burstein, D. (2018). How to Consistently Increase Conversion. *American Marketing Association*. Accessed at https://www.ama.org/marketing-news/how-to-consistently-increase-conversion on March 10, 2020.
12. Jacobson, A. (2018). Value Proposition Archives. Retrieved from https://marketingexperiments.com/value-proposition, accessed March 10, 2020.
13. Adapted from David A. Aaker and Gary J. Shansby, "Positioning Your Product," *Business Horizons* 25, no. 3 (May/June 1982): 56–62.
14. Jack Trout and Al Ries, *Positioning: The Battle for Your Mind* (New York: McGraw-Hill, 2000).
15. Fu, F. Q., Phillips, J. J., & Phillips, P. P. (2018). Roi Marketing: Measuring, Demonstrating, and Improving Value. *Performance Improvement*, *57*(2), 6–13.
16. Amy Gallo, "A Refresher on Marketing ROI," *Harvard Business Review*, July 25, 2017, https://hbr.org/2017/07/a-refresher-on-marketing-roi

Marketing Research

Source: Rido/Shutterstock

Chapter Outline

Learning Objectives

Ivelin Radkov/Shutterstock

After studying this chapter, you should be able to:

- Define marketing research, provide a description of its scope, and offer examples of each type of research conducted in marketing.
- Describe the steps involved in the marketing research process.
- Introduce the concept of marketing analytics and describe the sales forecasting process.

Source: Liderina/Shutterstock

7-1 Chapter Overview

Marketing requires a thorough understanding of the product's target market and its ever-shifting preferences. Marketers must continuously monitor the market and its preferences through systematic marketing research. At its inception, Lego has been a toy aimed towards boys. It later studied girls' playing habits and developed a line targeted at girls—girls in go-carts, on horses, at the beach, as a friend for sea life, riding an octopus, and so on. More recently, Lego moved into the conference room, as businesses use Legos to improve problem solving, communication, knowledge sharing, and decision making. It is difficult for people to voice their feelings, opinions, even their ideas; using Lego Serious Play to build physical 3D models instead helps people express what they think without articulating in words. The method is thought to unlock imagination and come up with useful solutions, while playing with Legos.[1]

Without marketing research, Lego would never been able to successfully penetrate the broader market. This chapter defines marketing research in Section 7-2 and examines its broad scope within marketing across all components of the marketing mix (product, place, price, and promotion). Section 7-3 addresses the marketing research process and the different steps involved. Section 7-4 addresses the marketing analytics and big data.

7-2 The Scope of Marketing Research

Marketers need to constantly monitor the different forces affecting operations and the products that are sold. Marketing information can improve the chances of success in a complex global competitive environment. Research, however, does not provide all the answers, but it does provide solid information that marketing managers can use to make intelligent decisions. **Marketing research** involves the systematic design, collection, recording, analysis, interpretation, and reporting of information pertinent to a particular marketing decision facing a company.

Marketing research The systematic design, collection, recording, analysis, interpretation, and reporting of information pertinent to a particular marketing decision facing a company.

Marketing intelligence Results obtained from monitoring developments in the firm's environment.

Marketing research addresses both broad and specific issues that are relevant to a company. It ranges from monitoring developments in the marketing environment—or general **marketing intelligence**—to collecting data on the brand on social media and blogs, to anticipating a product's performance in the marketplace, to evaluating consumers' specific brand-related or advertisement-related attitudes. **Figure 7-1** highlights the scope of marketing research and the components of marketing research that will be examined.

FIGURE 7-1 The Scope of Marketing Research

7-2a Research of Industry, Market Characteristics, and Market Trends

Studies of industry trends, market characteristics, and market trends are conducted regularly by marketing research suppliers, such as Nielsen, and shared with subscribers, or by sponsoring associations, among many others. Packaged Facts, a leading publisher of market research in the food, beverage, consumer packaged goods, and demographic sectors, reported that affluent food shoppers shy away from conventional shelf-stable packaged foods in the center of the store and are more likely to be in the perimeter of the store buying bulk foods, organic fresh fruits and vegetables, hot rotisserie chicken, and prepared fresh seafood. When they do buy shelf-stable foods, they tend to be healthy, mostly organic versions of breakfast cereal and pasta, to choose healthier snacks, such as trail mix, or to select low-calorie soft drinks like unflavored sparkling water.[2]

Why would such data and information be valuable? First, understanding industry and market characteristics and trends will tell a firm what products should be produced and how those products should be marketed. For instance, to appeal to affluent consumers, Whole Foods can emphasize local provenance of their food, and Blue Apron **(see Figure 7-2)** can focus on offering healthy prepared meals with all of the ingredients already measured to the right proportions. All consumers have to do is mix, cook, and eat healthy.

7-2b Buyer Behavior Research

Buyer behavior research examines consumer brand preferences and brand attitudes. Marketers need to understand their consumers so that they can appeal to them effectively. For example, affluent food shoppers are far from monolithic, and yet different from less affluent shoppers. For example, Asians make up just 5% of the population of non-affluent food

Buyer behavior research Research examining consumer brand preferences, brand attitudes, and brand-related behavior.

FIGURE 7-2 Blue Apron makes cooking fun and easy by providing all of the ingredients to make a delicious meal
Source: Duplass/Shutterstock

shoppers but 12% of affluent food shoppers. Also, affluent food shoppers generally reflect the contrasting political and social environments of their surroundings: they live in the 25 largest Nielsen Designated Marketing Areas (DMAs) and are more likely to be liberal Democrats. They are more likely to buy organic fresh fruits and vegetables, and less likely to buy canned or jarred products. Also, they are more likely to drink flavored sparkling water. Affluent food shoppers are a key driver of grocery store profitability: they gravitate toward high-margin, value-added products and services.[3]

Brand awareness research Research investigating how consumers' knowledge and recognition of a brand name affects their purchasing behavior.

In developing strong brands, brand-name recognition and awareness are important. A component of buyer behavior research, called **brand awareness research**, investigates how consumers' knowledge and recognition of a brand name affects their purchasing behavior. Such studies are often conducted by companies to assess the position of their brands in the marketplace relative to the competition. For instance, Statista launched a study of luxury goods in the United States. A total of 900 respondents were approached online and asked about their familiarity, at least by name, with a set of 20 luxury brands. The researchers found that over 70% of respondents were familiar with Gucci, Chanel, Tiffany & Co., Michael Kors, and Louis Vuitton. Comparatively, Burberry has only a 62% familiarity[4] (**see Figure 7-3**). Burberry had its popularity and sales plummet in the 1990s, with upscale department stores dropping it altogether. With a carefully coordinated strategy, the brand made a comeback. Although it is in demand, it has yet to resonate with consumers as much as competing Gucci, Chanel, and other brands.

FIGURE 7-3 Familiarity with Luxury Brands
Source: Statista, Retail and Trade: Fashion & Accessories, January 6, 2020, ttps://www.statista.com/forecasts/876294/familiarity-with-luxury-accessory-fashion-brands-in-the-us

Other useful studies that belong to this category are consumer segmentation studies, which are conducted to identify profiles of different consumers that the company could target. Marketing researchers often attempt to identify those segments composed of consumers who are heavy product users. Some of those segments of consumers are easy to identify: parents are heavy users of baby shampoo, diapers, and baby food. Dog owners are heavy users of pet food, pet toothpaste, dental bones and chews. Other segments need more study. Who are the heavy users of manicure services? Women. Who are the women who prefer to have a professional dip manicure, rather than a gel, or a regular manicure? The answer here is more complicated and needs additional research. Who are the women who have opted for a do-it-yourself dip manicure? That is an even more complex question. After the onset of COVID-19, many women opted to cut and color their hair and do their own manicure. A dip manicure is more complex and requires skill; research on online sales of dip manicure sets could offer some insights.

In other examples, faced with stagnating sales, the milk industry conducted research to see how much milk girls drank and how much they should drink. Using this information, the Bozell Agency developed an advertising campaign to encourage girls to drink milk so their bodies would have the correct amount of calcium. Similarly, research has shown that children who include 100% fruit juice in their diet have higher quality diets, so the juice industry is using this information to increase consumption.

Source: Africa Studio/Shutterstock

7-2c Product Research

Most product research is directed to new product development. A brief overview will be given in this section, but a more thorough discussion is found in Chapter 8. Typical product research includes:

- Concept development
- Competitive product studies
- Brand-name generation
- Product packaging design
- Product testing
- Test marketing

Concept development research Studies that evaluate the viability of a new product and the composition of the other marketing mix elements in light of the product's intended target market.

Concept development research studies evaluate the viability of a new product and the composition of the other marketing mix elements in light of the product's intended target market. The cost to bring a new electronic product from concept to mass-manufactured product varies significantly, with highly complex products' introduction to market costing millions of dollars. The first iPhone cost $150 million to develop and bring to market. Given that about 80 percent of new products fail, and given the very high cost to develop new products, it is essential that companies test the product concept before they ever start investing money into actual product development.[5]

Brand-name generation The testing of brand names and logos.

Brand-name generation involves the development and testing of brand names and logos. These studies are used not only by companies manufacturing consumer goods, where their importance is obvious, but also by industrial marketing companies and agricultural goods companies. Companies usually start out with several brand names before narrowing them down to a shorter list for testing. Fortune 500 companies spend millions of dollars on brand name testing methodology, studies, and consultants. They test the pronounceability and the possible misspellings of their brands. Misspelled names, if intentional, might attract attention to the brand. Lyft is a misspelling of lift—as in catching a lift. Even Google is an intentional misspelling of googol, the number ten to the one-hundredth power, a reference to the many search results for your searches. Research can tell if misspelling the brand name appears to be accidental or merely off-putting to consumers.[6]

The annals of marketing are replete with examples illustrating the importance of testing a global brand name in all the countries where the product is to be sold. When Kraft spun off its international products under the Mondelēz International company name, it did so believing that, with the accent, it would be perceived as European, a combination of monde (meaning world in French) and an abbreviation of delizioso (meaning delicious in Italian). What they did not do is test it in Russian, where it means an obscenity. While the Mondelēz brands are sold as Toblerone, Milka, Cadbury, etc., advertising the corporate name in Russia is probably not a good idea. Brand name testing would have prevented this embarrassing situation.

Source: oxygen 8/Shutterstock

Product testing estimates product performance and preference in a given market, whereas **competitive product studies** are helpful in determining the overall product strategy for the product, the price that the market will bear for the respective product category, and the promotion that is appropriate in light of the competition. **Product packaging design** studies help firms determine consumers' reactions to various package designs, the extent to which the package adequately communicates information to the consumer, and the distribution implications of packaging decisions.

After a product has been developed, many companies will use **test markets** to fine-tune the marketing approach that will be used and to make modifications in the product itself. Test marketing involves testing new product performance in a limited area of a target market to estimate product performance in the overall market. Labatt, a Belgian-owned brewery in Toronto, Canada—the largest brewer in Canada—decided to go into the super-hot hard seltzer business, with 5% alcohol cherry lime, grapefruit, mango lemon and orange blackberry flavors, appealing with light and fruity flavors, low in calories, carbohydrates, and sugar. If successful, they will roll out shortly throughout the United States and Canada.[7]

Product testing Studies that estimate product preference and performance in a given market.

Competitive product studies Pricing studies that determine the price the market will bear for the respective product category based on a survey of competitors' prices.

Product packaging design Studies that evaluate consumers' reaction to a package, the extent to which the package adequately communicates information to the consumer, and the distribution implications of the package.

Test markets Evaluating product performance in select markets that are representative of the target market before launching the product.

7-2d Distribution Research

Types of distribution research are **channel performance and coverage studies**, which investigate whether existing channels are appropriate for the marketing task at hand. Channel performance and coverage studies are usually the first steps that a company undertakes in the process of channel design. The analysis involves identifying the threats, opportunities, strengths, and weaknesses that influence channel performance. Research evaluates competitors' share of existing channels, the profitability of each channel, market coverage, and the cost of each channel function. Research also evaluates changes in buying patterns, potential competitors, long-run cost, and new technologies, such as multimedia retail kiosks. Beyond that, research assesses what customers are seeking from the various channels.

Channel performance and coverage studies Studies investigating whether existing channels are appropriate for the marketing task at hand.

Plant/warehouse location study A study that evaluates the appropriateness of plant or warehouse location to ensure that it is in accordance with the needs of the company.

To evaluate the appropriateness of plant or warehouse locations to the needs of a company, a **plant/warehouse location study** can be used. Such research evaluates variables such as the cost of transportation, real estate, labor costs, the availability of power sources, and tax rates. Also important in the analysis is the proximity to the customer. Although it may seem like a minor detail, plants and warehouses located in the wrong places can add considerable costs to the price of a product and create a situation in which a company cannot compete effectively. A major reason Walmart has been so successful is its understanding of distribution costs and the need to minimize them through optimal locations of its distribution systems.

7-2e Promotion Research

Studies of premiums, coupons, and deals Studies that determine the appropriateness and effectiveness of premiums, coupons, and deals for a given target market.

Promotion research evaluates the extent to which the company effectively communicates with the market, the extent to which certain promotional strategies are appropriate for a particular market, and if the media used are appropriate for the intended message. **Studies of premiums, coupons, and deals** determine the appropriateness and effectiveness of these types of promotions for a given target market. Studies can be conducted to assess the effectiveness of a marketing campaign, such as the $5 appreciation bonus on a DoorDash delivery (**see Figure 7-4**).

A research study was recently conducted on mobile couponing. It found that not having a coupon available when needed is one of the biggest drawbacks to coupon use: over 77% of consumers indicated that they didn't have coupons available to them when needed. The other 23% expressed frustration that they didn't have coupons available via smartphones. Mobile engagement research shows that mobile coupons

FIGURE 7-4 Marketing research can be used to determine the effectiveness of this $5 appreciation bonus on DoorDash delivery
Source: David Tonelson/Shutterstock

create a sense of urgency and can be strategically delivered to drive consumers' behavior in real time, and thus be especially effective: 60% of consumers indicated that they would respond to a mobile coupon within a week. Creating urgency can be driven through the delivery of text messages and email.[8]

Advertising effectiveness research is frequently conducted to examine the effectiveness and appropriateness of advertisements aimed at individual markets. Advertising effectiveness can be evaluated by measuring viewers' recall of an advertisement such as the one below (see Figure 7-5), their attitude toward the ad, and the extent to which the ad persuaded the consumer to purchase the sponsor's product.

Advertising effectiveness research Studies conducted to examine the effectiveness and appropriateness of advertisements aimed at individual markets.

Media research is an important component of promotional research. Identifying the media that best fits with the company's target market and the company's advertising needs ensures that advertising dollars are well spent. It is critical that the product's target market match the viewing audience of the media being used. Nielsen is an important research provider in this category. It uses the National People Meter service to provide audience estimates for all national program sources, including broadcast networks, cable networks, Spanish-language networks, and national syndicators. It also provides local Nielsen ratings for television stations, regional cable networks, and Spanish-language stations in each of the 210 television markets it serves.

Media research Studies that evaluate media availability and the appropriateness of the medium for a company's message.

Other promotion-related research studies may address personal selling activities. Examples of such studies are **sales force compensation, quota, and territory studies**, which are crucial in helping to determine the appropriate sales and incentive strategies for certain markets. Sales force studies will also determine the performance of salespeople by territories, which will guide sales managers in placing salespeople in territories and redeploying salespeople to territories that may have greater potential.

Sales force compensation, quota, and territory studies Different studies pertaining to personal selling activities; they are crucial in helping to determine the appropriate sales and incentive strategies for certain markets.

FIGURE 7-5 Advertising effectiveness research can be used to test viewers' recall of this banner ad
Source: Tada Images/Shutterstock

Source: Jacob Lund/Shutterstock

7-2f Pricing Research

There are numerous types of pricing research. Pricing is a key determinant in research studies attempting to project demand, such as market potential studies, sales potential studies, and sales forecasts. Pricing research is also an important determinant in cost analyses, profit analyses, price elasticity studies, and competitive pricing analyses.

Pricing research reveals that, while product quality remains important today, the dealmaker is often the price tag. Decades ago, consumers were attracted by store atmosphere, the assortment of brand names, and customer service. That has changed drastically since high-income consumers no longer worry about being seen at discounters—they can have products delivered at home. Alternatively, high-net-worth consumers are confident enough to shop at discounters: celebrities like Britney Spears are fans of Target, the royal family shops at TK Maxx (U.K.'s version of T.J. Maxx), and even billionaires Mark Zuckerberg and Kylie Jenner shop at Costco.[9]

On the other hand, pricing research has persuaded companies to introduce down-market versions of their upmarket brands. For example, Procter & Gamble has introduced a cheaper cousin, Charmin Essentials, which is almost as squeezably soft as the original, and Bounty Basic, which is equally basic and not as fancifully packaged as the original. Research has determined that consumers are more deal prone now. Pricing research has also shown that attitudes have changed, and even well-off consumers flaunt their bargain-hunting abilities.

Pricing research can help companies find the optimal price that will help meet a company's pricing objectives—even when it comes to canned fruits and vegetables. Understanding pricing is essential for marketers. Consumers' need for a deal and price competition must be aligned with businesses' need to make a profit and with all of their other marketing mix strategies. **Figure 7-6** reviews examples of the various types of marketing research. It also highlights the operational and managerial uses of the research and the strategic use of the information.

Marketing Research
Operational Resources
Managerial Uses
Strategic Uses
Research of Industry, Market Characteristics, and Market Trends
Evaluate industry and market trends.
Modify product attributes and promotion to meet changes in the industry and market.
Ensure that the company is producing the product desired by the consumer.
Buyer Behavior Research
Understand why, how, and when consumers purchase the product.
Modify the promotional approach to ensure that the message matches the needs and interests of the target market.
Ensure that the product is being promoted to correct target market in the correct manner.
Product Research
Review current product features.
Assess new product features.
Use computerized design to devise new products.
Distribution Research
Monitor supply-demand imbalances.
Manage supply-demand imbalances.
Strengthen distribution channels.
Promotion Research
Evaluate effectiveness of promotions such as advertising, and consumer and trade promotions.
Adjust promotional methods and media outlets to ensure that the target market is being reached.
Ensure that the product is being correctly promoted.
Pricing Research
Measure consistency and accuracy.
Adjust prices to reflect elasticity.
Ensure long-run competitiveness.

FIGURE 7-6 Summary of Marketing Research

7-3 The Marketing Research Process

The marketing research process follows the steps outlined in Figure 7-7 **(next page).** The first step in the process is to define the issue or problem faced. The second step is to examine secondary data for relevant information. If the problem cannot be solved with secondary data, then a primary research study needs to be conducted. This is the third step. The fourth step involves analyzing the data, making recommendations, and implementing the findings of the research.

Marketing research can be done with in-house staff or through a marketing research firm. Using an in-house staff reduces the cost of the research, and staff members normally have a better understanding of the problem being researched and how it needs to be done. However, they are likely to lack the marketing research expertise that an outside vendor would have. It is because of this expertise that most companies look to outside vendors, especially for major research projects.

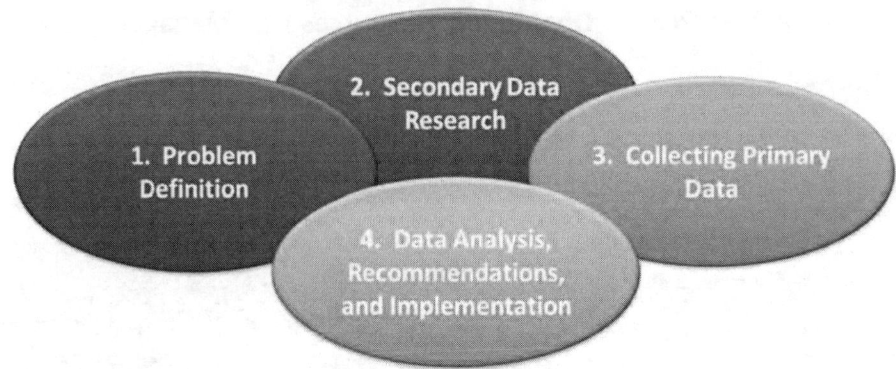

FIGURE 7-7 Steps in the Marketing Research Process

7-3a Problem Definition

The first step in the marketing research process requires that marketing managers and marketing researchers define the research problem and jointly agree on the research objectives. It is possible that the marketing manager does not have a clear idea of the research problem that needs to be investigated. They may know sales are declining or the company is losing market share, but not know why.

Exploratory research Research conducted early in the research process that helps further define a problem or identify additional problems that need to be investigated.

Descriptive research All research methods observing or describing phenomena.

Causal (experimental) research Research that examines cause-and-effect relationships.

To help in defining a marketing problem, researchers often conduct **exploratory research**, which is research conducted early in the research process to assist researchers in defining a problem or identifying additional problems that need to be investigated. In understanding the issue to be examined, researchers will also discuss the research approach that will provide the best answer. Marketers have two approaches that can be used: descriptive research and causal (experimental) research. **Descriptive research** involves observing or describing a phenomenon. For example, the study might involve collecting information about consumer privacy fears when ordering merchandise with a mobile phone. A descriptive study should also assess tangential issues, such as attitudes toward the product, brand, and price. **Causal (experimental) research**, however, examines cause-and-effect relationships.

7-3b Secondary Data Research

Secondary data Data collected to address a problem other than the problem at hand.

Internal secondary data Data previously collected by a company to address a problem not related to the current research question.

Researchers first must determine whether any information is available on the topic being researched. Researchers should start by examining **secondary data**, which are data collected to address a problem other than the problem currently facing the company. Secondary data offer the advantages of low cost and ready availability. The data that may be most relevant to the researcher's study, however, will most likely not exist, or if they do, they may be dated or unreliable.

There are two categories of secondary data. **Internal secondary data** are collected by the company to address a different problem or collected by the company to address the same problem, but in a different environment or for a different brand. Prior research reports on the company's other brands, sales figures for different territories, and inventory reports are types of secondary data.

External secondary data are defined as data collected by an entity not affiliated with the company. Relevant information may be available at companies' websites, trade association websites, marketing organizations, government websites, or various online research databases.

Source: Rawpixel.com/Shutterstock

Marketing organizations can also provide access to relevant data at a reasonable fee. Valuable secondary data is provided by marketing research firms, such as Nielsen, IQVIA, Gartner, Kantar, and others (**see Figure 7-8**). They offer extensive information to subscribers on different markets, products, and topics. Research firms can also be used to conduct specific brand or company research.

External secondary data Data collected by an entity not affiliated with the company.

Quality secondary data will help companies further refine problems and objectives and, if necessary, even redefine them. But even the highest-quality secondary data alone usually do not provide an answer to a specific research problem. Effectively addressing a research problem requires the collection of primary data.

7-3c Collecting Primary Data

Most marketing research projects involve the collection of **primary data**, which is information collected for a specific purpose to address the problem at hand. Collecting primary data requires substantial expertise

Primary data Data collected for the purpose of addressing the problem at hand.

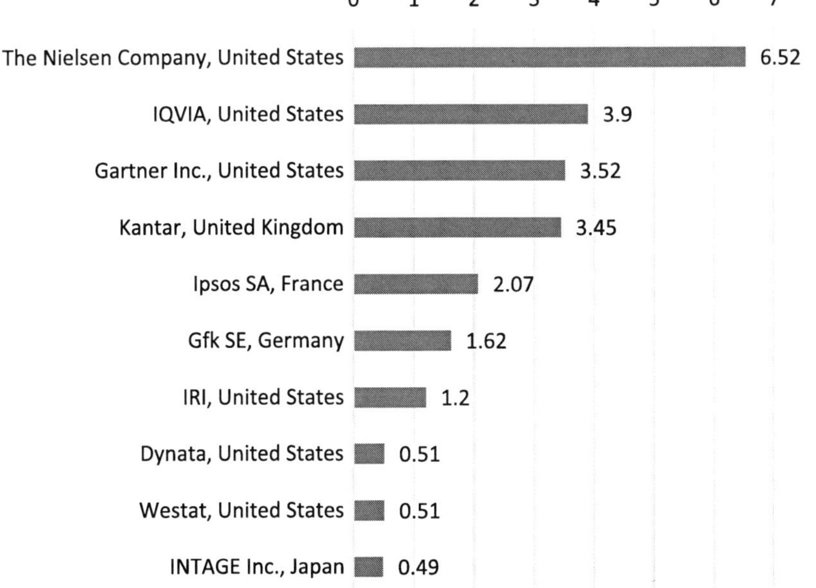

FIGURE 7-8 Top Global Research Providers by Revenue
Source: ESOMAR, Global Market Research 2019, page 96

in both instrument design and administration and, as a consequence, it is expensive and time-consuming. Collecting quality primary data requires a concerted effort on the part of marketing managers and researchers to identify the appropriate research approaches, data collection instruments, sampling plans, and contact methods that are capable of providing high quality data.

Qualitative research Research that involves a small number of respondents answering open-ended questions.

Quantitative research A structured type of research that involves either descriptive research approaches, such as survey research, or causal (experimental) research approaches, such as experiments in which responses can be summarized or analyzed with numbers.

The Research Methodology: When collecting primary data, researchers can use two different methods: qualitative research or quantitative research. **Qualitative research** typically involves a small number of respondents answering open-ended questions. Results are usually subjective because the researcher must interpret what respondents are saying. Alternatively, qualitative research could also involve observation that is not systematically structured but rather open to a subjective analysis; researchers might interpret consumers' comments on blogs, on brand communities, or on the brand's social media pages, and so on.

Quantitative research is a more structured approach involving responses that can be summarized or analyzed with numbers. Descriptive and causal (experimental) research approaches would use a quantitative research methodology, whereas exploratory research would typically use the qualitative methodology. It is interesting to note that, in certain countries, such as France and Italy, there is a preference for qualitative data as a complement to quantitative data, whereas in others, such as Germany, the United States, and Scandinavian countries, quantitative data are deemed as more valuable.

Focus group interviews A qualitative research approach investigating a research question, using a moderator to guide discussion within a group of subjects recruited to meet certain characteristics.

Qualitative research has been particularly useful either as a first step in studying marketing phenomena through exploratory research or as a means of exploring a marketing problem through various subjective techniques. Among the more popular qualitative research approaches are focus group interviews, depth interviews, and observation **(see Figure 7-9)**.

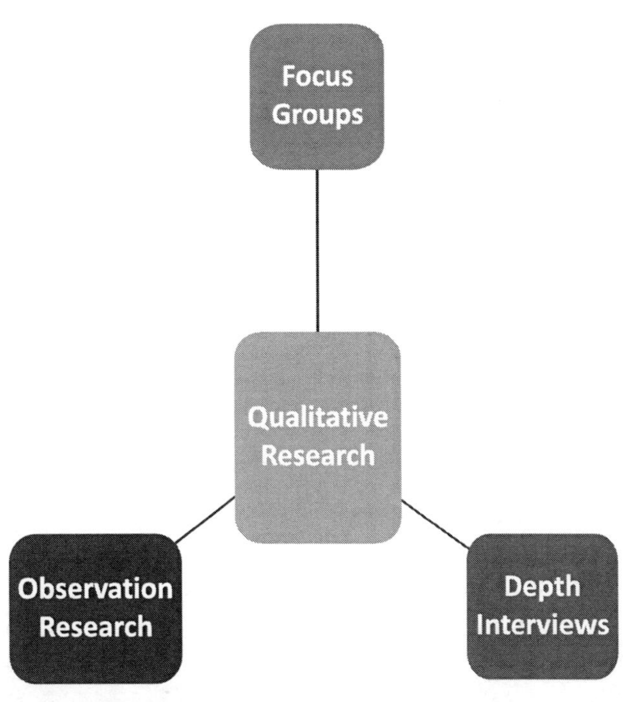

FIGURE 7-9 Popular Qualitative Research Methods

Focus group interviews typically involve six to twelve participants recruited to meet some previously decided characteristics, such as ethnic background, age groups, social class, and use of certain products. A moderator guides the discussion based on a pre-established agenda. Frequently, representatives of the sponsor observe the group's deliberations through a one-way mirror. A camera may also be used to record the group's deliberations. Focus groups are more often using videoconferencing, which is found to be acceptable in qualitative and mixed-method settings. After the onset of the COVID-19 pandemic, Zoom has turned into an important platform for qualitative data collection. Participants are usually offered a small financial reward or products for participating in the study.

Another approach that is helpful for collecting qualitative data is the **depth interview**. Depth interviews are one-on-one attempts to discover consumer motivations, feelings, and attitudes toward an issue of concern to the sponsor, using a loose and unstructured question guide. Depth interviews are typically used if the issue under study is a complex behavioral or decision-making consideration or an emotionally laden issue. Professional interviewers are typically well trained in keeping the respondent focused on the problem addressed and in handling complex interviewing situations. In addition to guiding respondents to address the problem investigated, interviewers can demonstrate the product and its features, and further probe into issues that are relevant to the research.

Depth interview A qualitative research method involving extensive interviews aimed at discovering consumer motivations, feelings, and attitudes toward an issue of concern to the sponsor, using unstructured interrogation.

Depth interviews can take place in person or via videoconferencing—these are referred to as personal interviews. Using interviewers to conduct research is very expensive and more time consuming than other research methods. However, the data they collect are normally more robust because interviewers can further address issues that come up during the interview. Consequently, the method offers insights that quantitative research approaches cannot provide.

Observational research (or observation) is a particularly useful research approach for gathering qualitative data. It is defined as a research approach in which subjects are observed interacting with a product and reacting to other components of the marketing mix and the environment. Researchers could observe consumers in the process of shopping, or read their review comments or their comments on the brand in brand communities or on the company's website or social media—numerous approaches are used in observational research. One method, known as **naturalistic inquiry**, is an observational research approach that requires the use of natural rather than contrived settings because behaviors take substantial meaning from their context. The researcher is directly involved in the data collection as a participant in the group whose verbal and nonverbal behaviors are observed. The analysis performed by the researcher is inductive, rather than deductive; that is, unlike in conventional research methods, the researcher does not rely on previous theory in the process of developing hypotheses, but rather develops theories from the data. **Ethnography**—the study of cultures—is largely based on naturalistic inquiry. Both academic researchers and practitioners have used this approach to better understand consumers and consumer motivations. This technique is frequently used by researchers who attempt to increase the validity of their studies by acquiring an intimate knowledge of a culture's daily life through personal observation.

Observational research (or observation) A research approach whereby subjects are observed interacting with a product and reacting to other components of the marketing mix and the environment.

Naturalistic inquiry An observational research approach that requires the use of natural rather than contrived settings because behaviors take substantial meaning from their context.

Ethnography The study of cultures.

Source: Olena Yakobchuk/Shutterstock

Source: PorporLing/Shutterstock

Quantitative research methods are structured research approaches involving either descriptive research, such as observation, survey research, and content analysis, or causal (experimental) research approaches, such as experiments. Observation, previously noted as a type of qualitative research, can also be quantitative when the subjects are systematically observed interacting with a product and reacting to other components of the marketing mix and the environment. An example of a quantitative observational method is the study of garbage (garbology). Garbology studies could examine if consumers' reported diet matches the packages identified in their garbage bins.

Pupillometric meter A physiological instrument used to measure eye movements and the dilation of a person's pupil.

Psychogalvanometer A physiological instrument that's attached to a respondent's fingers to measure an individual's perspiration level.

Physiological instruments can also be used as an observation method to measure a respondent's involuntary responses to stimuli. An instrument called a **pupillometric meter** can be used to measure eye movements and the dilation of a person's pupil. Another instrument, the **psychogalvanometer**, attached to a respondent's fingers, can measure an individual's perspiration level. These instruments are often used in advertising research to measure the physiological reaction to particular ads. Some researchers see these instruments as more accurate than verbal or written responses in which a respondent may give researchers the socially acceptable answer. These instruments are also useful for packaging research—not only to measure physiological reaction, but also to track eye movement across the package. Such research helps marketers identify whether people are paying attention to the ad and if they are focusing on the brand name and logo.

Survey research Descriptive research that involves the administration of personal, telephone, or mail questionnaires.

Survey research is the most widely used descriptive research methodology. It typically involves the administration of structured questionnaires in a personal interview, online, by telephone, email, or by mail (but mail questionnaires are becoming less and less common—they are discarded, they are slow…). The use of the questionnaires assumes that respondents are both capable and willing to respond to the questions. The most expensive survey method is the personal interview, a method that provides valuable data—although costs are going down if the interview is conducted via videoconference.

Such an interview would be highly structured, compared with the depth interview discussed in the qualitative research approach section. However, even a structured personal interview allows the interviewer to probe into issues that the respondent may raise or to answer questions, thus providing valuable additional information to the researcher.

Experimental research typically looks at cause-and-effect relationships, eliminating or controlling for other extraneous factors that may be responsible for the results and eliminating competing explanations for the observed findings. It requires the use of matched groups of subjects who are subjected to different treatments, to ascertain whether the observed response differences are statistically significant. Most of these studies are conducted within a laboratory or controlled environment. Although difficult to do, causal (experimental) research provides marketers with reliable data. Figure 7-10 summarizes the various research methods that can be used in collecting primary data.

Data Collection Instruments: Although electronic measurement devices are used to collect data, most data are collected using online questionnaires. In developing a questionnaire, researchers must come up with an appropriate format that will accurately collect the data. The questionnaire could use **open-ended questions**, which allow respondents to use their own words in responding to the questions. Alternatively, researchers can use **close-ended questions** that supply possible answers. It may be a **semantic differential scale**, which are questions anchored by words

Open-ended questions Questions with free-format responses that the respondent can address as he or she sees appropriate.

Close-ended questions Questions that supply possible answers.

Semantic differential scale Scale that is anchored by words with opposite meanings.

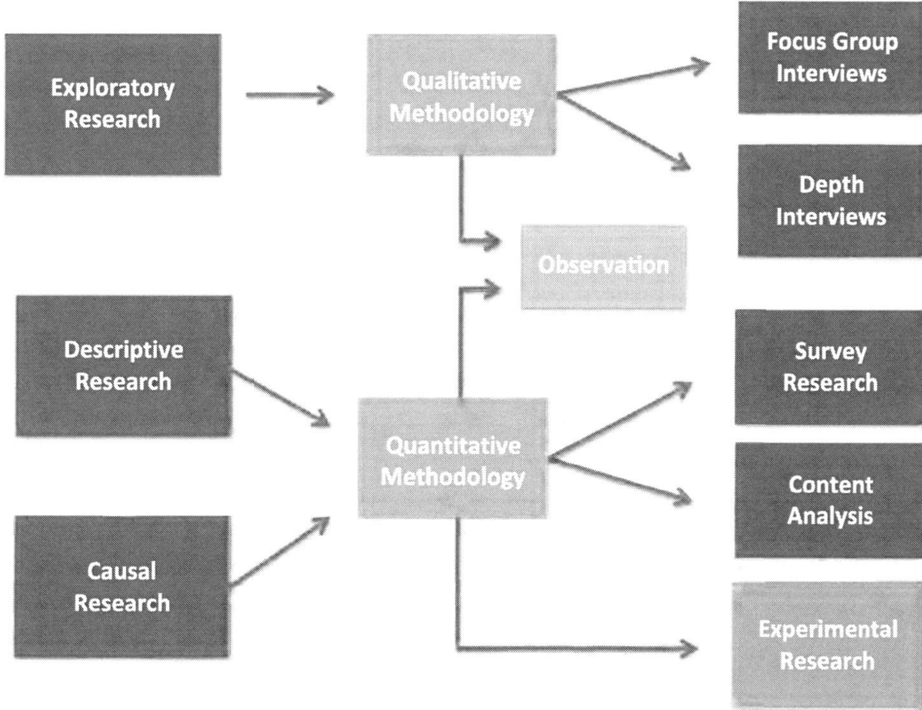

FIGURE 7-10 Primary Data Research Methods

with opposite meanings (good . . . bad, important . . . not important). Marketers often use a **Likert scale**, which is a series of statements that asks respondents to indicate their level of agreement or disagreement.

Likert scale A series of statements that asks respondents to indicate their level of agreement or disagreement.

A semantic differential questionnaire is illustrated in **Figure 7-11**. Notice that in this case, the respondent is asked to evaluate a particular television brand along the dichotomous criteria. The respondent is also asked to evaluate the leading competitor and the ideal rating for a 27-inch flat screen television. Charting all three measures on one graph allows researchers to determine how well their brand compares to the leading competitor and the ideal brand.

Sample A segment of the population selected for the study and considered to be representative of the total population of interest.

Sampling unit The individuals or groups included in the study.

Sample size The number of study participants.

Sampling procedure The procedure used in the selection of sampling units.

Random probability sample A sample in which each individual selected for the study has a known and equal chance of being included in the study.

Sampling Plan: The sampling plan calls for the marketing manager and researcher to jointly decide on the **sample**, that is, a segment of the population selected for the study and considered representative of the total population of interest. The first sampling decision is the selection of the **sampling unit**, which involves determining who will be included in the survey. Should the researcher interview anybody in the household, including children? Should the researcher interview only the driver? Should the sample include people from all over the United States or just certain regions? Should the sample include individuals from other countries?

Researchers must decide on the **sample size**—the number of individuals that will be surveyed. Ideally, a larger sample should be chosen to ensure that accurate results are obtained. The **sampling procedure** is how the sampling units will be selected. The goal is to select a sample that closely resembles the population being studied.

The most representative sample of a particular population is a **random probability sample**, in which each individual selected for the study has a known and equal chance of being selected. While ideal, this method is

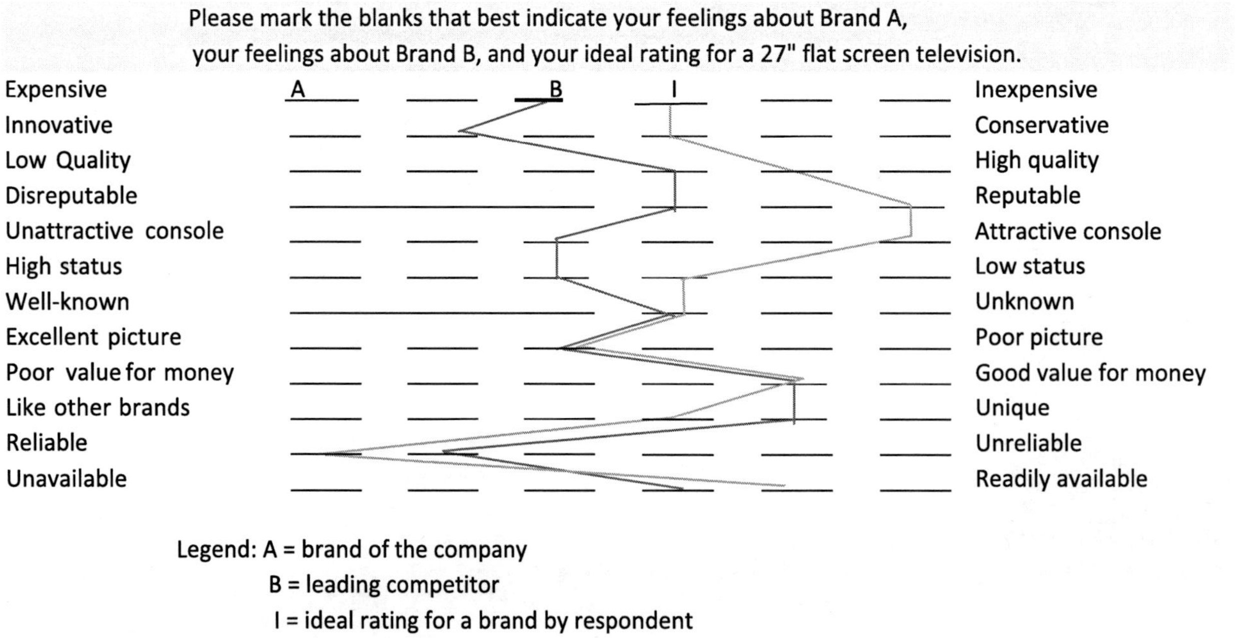

Please mark the blanks that best indicate your feelings about Brand A, your feelings about Brand B, and your ideal rating for a 27" flat screen television.

	A		B	I			
Expensive							Inexpensive
Innovative							Conservative
Low Quality							High quality
Disreputable							Reputable
Unattractive console							Attractive console
High status							Low status
Well-known							Unknown
Excellent picture							Poor picture
Poor value for money							Good value for money
Like other brands							Unique
Reliable							Unreliable
Unavailable							Readily available

Legend: A = brand of the company
B = leading competitor
I = ideal rating for a brand by respondent

FIGURE 7-11 Example of a Semantic Differential

difficult to manage because most sampling methods will exclude certain parts of a population. A less representative but easier method of selecting a sample would be to use a **convenience sample**, which is composed of individuals who are easy for the researcher to contact. Another sampling method that does not pose much effort for the researcher is a **judgment sample**, which is a sample of individuals thought to be representative of the population being studied.

Convenience sample Sample composed of individuals who are easy to contact for the researcher.

Judgment sample A sample of individuals thought to be representative of the population.

The most critical criterion in selecting a sampling technique is how well the sample represents the population under consideration. The population could be students at a university or all consumers who own a mobile phone. Although the ideal is to use a random probability sample, it is not always practical. Obtaining a random probability sample of students at a university may be possible, but it would not work for mobile phone owners. As long as the sample selected represents the population being studied, a convenience or judgment sample is adequate.

The last decision researchers must make, in terms of sampling, is the **sampling frame**—the list from which sampling units are selected. Examples of sampling frames are mailing lists or telephone books. Figure 7-12 reviews the sampling decisions that must be made.

Sampling frame The list from which sampling units are selected.

Collecting Data: Data can be collected using the various contact methods, such as email, Internet, telephone, mail, and personal interview. Figure 7-13 addresses the advantages and disadvantages of each type of

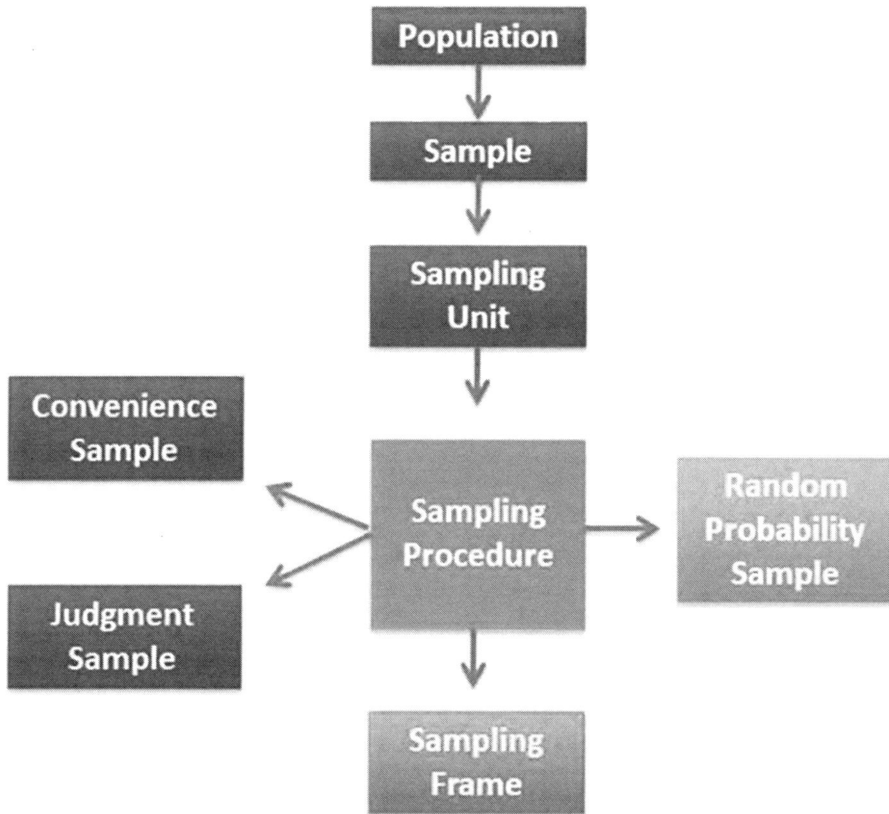

FIGURE 7-12 The Sampling Plan

Method	Advantages	Disadvantages
Mail	Inexpensive No interviewer effects Large amounts of data Reasonable sample control	Slow Low response rates Lack of flexibility
E-mail	Inexpensive No interviewer effects Reasonable amount of data Fast Reasonable sample control	Low response rates Lack of flexibility
Internet	Inexpensive No interviewer effects Reasonable amount of data Fast	Low response rates Not much flexibility Poor sample control
Telephone	Reasonable cost Few interviewer effects Reasonably fast Reasonable response rates Reasonable sample control	Lower amounts of data Higher cost
Personal and Focus Group Interviews	High flexibility High response rate Large amounts of data Reasonably fast High sample control	Expensive Large interviewer effects

FIGURE 7-13 Advantages and Disadvantages of Different Methods of Collecting Data

contact method. In the past, the traditional forms of data collection have been mail, telephone, and personal interviews. Email and online surveys are most common today.

The best method for a research study is a function of researcher needs, the size of the sample desired for the study, the amount of data needed, the time frame for the study, and the available budget. For a very large sample, using an online and email questionnaire is appropriate–even a mail questionnaire. Alternatively, if researchers want to further probe into a particular response, personal interviews offer more flexibility. A higher response rate is obtained with a personal interview than with other methods.

After the instrument is designed and the sample is selected, the researcher or research team is ready to collect the primary data. This expensive undertaking can be eventful. The data collectors need to be briefed appropriately. Researchers must decide how **nonresponse**—defined as the inability or refusal by a respondent to participate in the study—should be handled. In some instances, it makes sense to go back and identify the traits of the respondents who refused to participate to compare them with those of respondents who participated to be sure the sample who responded is the same as those who did not respond. For mail surveys, the nonresponse rate can be high, at 90 percent or even more. So for valid research, it is essential that individuals who participated in a study represent the population being studied and are not different from individuals who did not participate.

Nonresponse The inability or refusal by a respondent to participate in a study.

7-3d Data Analysis, Recommendations, and Implementation

Data collected should be coded, entered into the analysis program, and analyzed. Researchers will tabulate the results and put them in a form that is meaningful and that will answer the problems introduced in the beginning of the research process. To understand these last three steps in the research process, study **Figure 7-14 (on next page)**.

Notice in the first step of the analysis that 500 questionnaires were collected and that each questionnaire was numbered from A001 to A500. Each response was then coded and tabulated. The results of the tabulations appear on the right upper portion in Figure 7-14. Notice that out of the 500 respondents, 300 drink coffee, and 270 drink coffee in the morning. The lower portion of Figure 7-11 presents some of the analysis of the data. For instance, because 500 respondents took the survey and 300 said they drink coffee, we can say that 60 percent of the respondents drink coffee. Notice that 142 said they drink coffee two or more times per day. Because we know that 300 drink coffee, we can say that 47 percent of

Source: mimagephotography/Shutterstock

1. Do you drink coffee?	☐ Yes	01	300
	☐ No	02	200
2. In general, how frequently do you drink coffee? (Check only one answer.)	☐ Two or more times per day	03	142
	☐ Once per day	04	84
	☐ Several times per week	05	42
	☐ Once or twice per week	06	20
	☐ One to three times per month	07	12
	☐ Never	08	200
3. During what time of the day do you drink coffee? (Check all answers that apply.)	☐ Morning	09	270
	☐ Lunchtime	10	165
	☐ Afternoon	11	100
	☐ Dinnertime	12	150
	☐ Evening	13	205
	☐ None	14	200

Coding: Questionnaires numbered A001 to A500. Each response is labeled 01 to 14 (e.g., Morning is 09. Evening is 13.) Question 3 is a multiple response question.

Tabulation: Total responses are shown at right.

Analysis: Sixty percent drink coffee. About 28 percent drink coffee two or more times daily (representing 47 percent of all coffee drinkers); almost 25 percent of coffee drinkers (74 people) consume coffee less than once a day. Ninety percent of coffee drinkers consume coffee in the morning; only one-third consume it in the afternoon.

Recommendations: The coffee industry and individual firms need to increase the advertising geared toward noncoffee drinkers, as well as infrequent coffee drinkers. Emphasis should also be placed on lifting coffee consumption during afternoon hours.

Implementation: New, more aggressive advertising campaigns will be developed, and the annual media budgets devoted to increasing overall coffee consumption will be expanded. One theme will stress coffee's value as an afternoon pick-me-upper.

FIGURE 7-14 Data Analysis, Recommendations, and Implementation of Findings for a Coffee Study

coffee drinkers consume coffee two or more times per day (142 divided by 300). Likewise, we can say that 90 percent of the coffee drinkers consume coffee in the morning.

Based on this research and the analysis, a possible recommendation could be that the coffee industry and individual firms need to increase the advertising geared toward non-coffee drinkers because 40 percent of the sample does not drink coffee. For those who drink coffee, advertising could focus on drinking coffee in the afternoon, the period with the lowest consumption.

Implementation of the findings might include a more aggressive advertising campaign that is aimed at non-coffee drinkers. This would require an increase in the media budget and could also require an additional study

Source: sabthai/Shutterstock

to see what media outlets would be the best for reaching non-coffee drinkers. For the current coffee drinkers, to stimulate additional consumption, the theme that coffee is "an afternoon pick-me-upper" could be used.

7-4 Marketing Analytics

Marketing analytics refers to the coordinated collection of data, systems, analysis tools, and techniques designed to make sense of marketing information and to assess and forecast marketing performance. Marketers collect extensive data from various sources: sales, customer engagement on social media or directly with the company, customer reviews and discussions on brand communities, and customer response to marketing efforts, among others. Marketing analytics spending is expected to increase by 56% in the next three years—at present, only 37.7% of companies use marketing analytics in decision making. The larger the company in terms of sales revenue and the greatest the sales from the Internet, the higher the contribution of marketing analytics to company performance.[10]

Marketing analytics Refers to the coordinated collection of data, systems, analysis tools, and techniques designed to make sense of marketing information and to assess and forecast marketing performance.

Big data and analytics are likely to revolutionize marketing and sales. It will change how prices are defined and managed, it will inform sales managers what type of content is the most effective at each stage of a sales cycle, how Investments in Customer Relationship Management (CRM) systems can be improved, how to get greater customer responsiveness and gain greater customer insights, how to increase customer acquisition, reduce customer churn, increase revenue per customer and improve existing products, among others.[11]

Marketing analytics will likely greatly evolve beyond the following, more traditional forms of forecasting. Among them are simpler methods (sales force composite estimates, jury of executive opinion, and the Delphi method) that can be used to cross-validate the estimates given by the more sophisticated time series and econometric models.

Sales force composite estimates Research studies in which sales forecasts are based on the personal observations and forecasts of the local sales force.

Forecasts from **sales force composite estimates** are based on the personal observations and hunches of the sales force. Salespeople are in

Jury of expert opinion An approach to sales forecasting based on the opinions of different experts.

Delphi method A method of forecasting sales that involves asking a number of experts to estimate market performance, aggregating the results, and then sharing this information with the said experts; the process is repeated several times, until a consensus is reached.

Time series and econometric methods Methods that use the data of past performance to predict future market demand.

Point-of-sale (POS)-based projections Market projections based on the use of store scanners in weekly and bi-weekly store audits.

close contact with the consumer. Therefore, they are in the best position to learn about consumer desires and overall changing market trends. Forecasts from the **jury of expert opinion** are based on the opinions of different experts about future demand. The experts' opinions are then combined, and an aggregate demand estimation is offered. Another method, the **Delphi method**, entails asking a number of experts to estimate market performance, aggregate the results, and share this information with these experts. This process is repeated several times until a consensus is reached.

Among the more sophisticated forecasting techniques are time series methods, which use data of past performance to predict future market demand. Typically, these methods give more weight to more recent developments. They assume that the future will be similar to the past. Econometric methods, however, take into account different deterministic factors that affect market demand—factors that may or may not depend on past performance trends. **Time series and econometric methods** are dependent on the availability of historical data.

Important forecasting methods for retailers and other channel members involve **point-of-sale (POS)-based projections**, which are performed with the help of store scanners used in retail stores. Research suppliers increasingly use store scanners to assess market share and other relevant market dimensions. Weekly or biweekly store audits reveal the movement of goods within the store and from manufacturers and wholesalers.

Summary

1. **Define marketing research, provide a description of its scope, and offer examples of each type of research conducted in marketing.**
Marketing research involves gathering information for marketing decisions. It is wide in scope, covering industry research, market traits and trends, buyer behavior, and the marketing mix. Examples of product research are product testng, product package studies, and competitive product analysis. Distribution research covers areas such as channel performance and coverage and plant/warehouse location studies. Promotion research has a wide scope, with studies of premiums, coupons, and deals; advertising effectiveness; media research; and sales force analyses. Pricing research involves studies projecting demand, as well as market potential studies, sales potential studies, cost analyses, and profit analyses.

2. **Describe the steps involved in the marketing research process.**
The first step of the research process involves defining the research problem and setting the research objectives. This is usually done in conjunction with the research team and the marketing managers initiating the research. The development of the research plan involves deciding on the information sources—primary and secondary—and determining the appropriate research approach. The research approach may involve collecting qualitative data, using focus groups or observation methods, or collecting quantitative data, using descriptive (surveys) or causal (experimental)

research methods. They, in turn, determine the contact methods: mail, email, Internet, telephone, and personal interviews. The sampling plan must be determined: selecting the sampling procedure, sample size, frame, and unit. Finally, the researcher must collect, analyze, and interpret the information.

3. **Address marketing analytics describe the sales forecasting process.**
   Marketing analytics represent a coordinated approach to collecting and interpreting business and environmental data. Methods used in sales forecasting are sales force composite estimates, which are based on the personal observations or hunches of the sales force. The jury of expert opinion involves the aggregate opinions of different experts about future demand. The Delphi method entails asking a number of experts to estimate market performance, aggregate the results, share the information with the experts, and repeat the process several times until a consensus is reached. Time series and econometric models use data of past performance to predict future market demand. Marketers routinely use POS-based projections to estimate demand based on scanner data from retail stores.

Key Terms

Advertising effectiveness research (191)
Brand awareness research (186)
Brand-name generation (188)
Buyer behavior research (185)
Causal (experimental) research (194)
Channel performance and coverage studies (189)
Close-ended questions (199)
Competitive product studies (189)
Concept development research (188)
Convenience sample (201)
Delphi method (206)
Depth interview (197)
Descriptive research (194)
Ethnography (197)
Exploratory research (194)
External secondary data (195)
Focus group interviews (196)
Internal secondary data (194)
Judgment sample (201)
Jury of expert opinion (206)
Likert scale (200)
Marketing analytics (205)
Marketing intelligence (184)
Marketing research (184)
Media research (191)
Naturalistic inquiry (197)
Nonresponse (203)
Observational research (or observation) (197)
Open-ended questions (199)
Plant/warehouse location study (190)
Point-of-sale (pos)-based projections (206)
Primary data (195)
Product packaging design (189)
Product testing (189)
Psychogalvanometer (198)
Pupillometric meter (198)
Qualitative research (196)
Quantitative research (196)
Random probability sample (200)
Sales force compensation, quota, and territory studies (191)
Sales force composite estimates (205)
Sample (200)
Sample size (200)
Sampling frame (201)
Sampling procedure (200)
Sampling unit (200)
Secondary data (194)
Semantic differential scale (199)
Studies of premiums, coupons, and deals (190)
Survey research (198)
Test markets (189)
Time series and econometric methods (206)

Discussion Questions

1. Refer to the opening vignette about Lego. Describe the types of promotion-related research that could be conducted that would help the company more effectively promote its brand. Should Lego target girls, or mothers? What about fathers and grandparents? What type of research would you suggest for Lego to determine who they should target with advertising?
2. You have been hired by Procter & Gamble to conduct a study that investigates whether consumers are likely to purchase a new product: Dero Lux. Procter & Gamble envisages the product as a quality detergent to be used only on the highest-quality fabrics—silk, wool, and fine cotton blends. Take this study through all the steps of the research process and elaborate in detail on the investigation.
3. Assume a local business person wants to open a restaurant near your university. For each of the following types of research, identify research that would be beneficial, explain why it would be important, and describe what you would do.
   a. buyer behavior research
   b. product research
   c. promotion research
   d. pricing research
4. Assume a local business person wants to open a tanning salon near your university. From the various studies described in the chapter, identify four that you feel would be beneficial. Explain why you think they would be beneficial and describe what you hope to learn from the research.
5. What is the difference between qualitative and quantitative research approaches? Give examples of each that are not provided in the text.
6. Suppose your university wanted to know when, how, and why students use the computer labs on campus. Discuss how your university could use each of the following types of qualitative studies to gather this information.
   a. focus group
   b. depth interview
   c. observation research
7. Suppose the marketing department at your school wanted to survey students about why they chose marketing as a major. Which approach should they use—qualitative, quantitative, or both? Justify your answer. Then identify which research methods should be used, again justifying your answer. Lastly, discuss the sample that should be selected, how you would select it, and how you would guarantee it would be representative of marketing majors at your school.
8. Design a questionnaire using semantic differential questions that evaluates the portrayal of women in advertising.
9. Design a questionnaire using Likert questions that evaluates the portrayal of minorities in advertising.
10. One of the sororities at your school wants to study body image and how female students feel about their bodies and how that image impacts their lifestyle and performance in college. Discuss an appropriate sampling plan identifying a sampling unit, sample size, sample frame, and sampling method. Justify your choices. If the sorority decided on a survey instrument, what method of collecting data would be the best? Why? What would be the advantages and disadvantages of the method you selected if the goal was to have a sample that represented all female students at your school?

Review Questions

True or False

1. Channel performance and coverage studies are examples of distribution research.
2. Focus group interviews typically involve randomly selected groups of people who share their opinion about a product in front of TV cameras.

3. Observation is a type of research approach in which subjects are observed interacting with a product and reacting to other components of the marketing mix and the environment.
4. Exploratory research is conducted early in the research process. It is the research that helps to further define a problem or identify additional problems that should be investigated.
5. Observational analysis is a qualitative research method that utilizes descriptive research.
6. The questionnaires that use open-ended questions are based on semantic differential scales or Likert scales.
7. Marketing researchers should eliminate nonresponse cases—defined as the inability or refusal of respondent to participate in a study—because they do not provide conclusive information.

Multiple Choice

8. Marketing research addresses which of the following issues?
   a. monitoring developments in the market environment
   b. anticipating product's performance in the marketplace
   c. evaluating customer-specific brand-related or advertisement-related attitudes
   d. all of the above
9. ______research examines consumer brand preferences, brand attitudes, and brand-related behavior.
   a. buyer behavior
   b. purchase-related
   c. brand loyalty
   d. brand management
10. Advertising effectiveness research measures which of the following?
    a. viewers' recall of an advertisement
    b. viewers' attitude toward the ad
    c. the extent to which the ad persuaded the consumer to purchase the product
    d. all of the above
11. Which of the following categories relate to pricing research?
    a. cost analysis
    b. profit analysis
    c. competitive price analysis
    d. all of the above
12. Naturalistic inquiry is a method used in observational research in which information is gathered using
    a. a group of 6 to 12 individuals.
    b. natural rather than contrived settings.
    c. an analysis of verbal and nonverbal behavior.
    d. psychological instruments, such as the psychogalvanometer.
13. Which of the following types of research looks at cause-and-effect relationships and eliminates other extraneous factors that may be responsible for the results?
    a. observation
    b. content analysis
    c. descriptive research
    d. experimental research
14. Which of the following categories is used to determine who should be included in the marketing survey?
    a. sampling unit
    b. sampling procedure
    c. sampling size
    d. sampling frame
15. Which of the following methods asks a number of experts to estimate the market performance and then aggregates the results and shares this information with the same experts, repeating the procedure until a consensus is reached?
    a. jury of executive opinion
    b. analogy method
    c. delphi method
    d. time series model

Answers: (1) True, (2) False, (3) True, (4) True, (5) False, (6) False, (7) False, (8) d, (9) a, (10) d, (11) d, (12) b, (13) d, (14) a, (15) c

Source: NeonShot/Shutterstock

Karen Johnson is contemplating starting a modeling agency in Flagstaff, Arizona. She has previously worked for two top New York modeling agencies and believes that she has sufficient experience, both as a model and as a modeling agency employee, to create a successful agency of her own. Because Flagstaff is somewhat off the beaten path of these agencies, her scouting capabilities in this remote location and her connections in the fashion world may prove to be valuable for her new enterprise.

Although Karen has a feel for what fashion magazines and the fashion industry want in a model, she would like to create a better match between her models and the industry by creating for her models portfolios of photographs that present the prevailing "look"—what is considered the in-look. To better define the in-look, she has hired KD Research to perform a content analysis on the most recent advertisements that appeared on the websites and social media pages of the Vogue and Elle fashion magazines. KD Research recruited judges to fill out a questionnaire assessing the variables presented in the tables below. Each ad was individually evaluated by three judges considered experts on fashion modelling.

KD Research Questionnaire

Please look at each ad and indicate to what extent you believe that THE WOMAN IN THE AD appears to have the following characteristics by circling the corresponding number, as follows:

1. 1 = if the ad/woman DOES NOT AT ALL HAVE the respective characteristic
2. 2 = if the ad/woman DOES NOT QUITE APPEAR TO HAVE the respective characteristic
   3 = if the ad/woman APPEARS TO HAVE the respective characteristic
3. 4 = if the ad/woman HAS the respective characteristic
4. 5 = if the ad/woman DEFINITELY HAS the respective characteristic

The researchers then attempted to identify the characteristics that were the most prevalent in the ads. They calculated the averages for all the advertisements. **Figure 7-15** shows the results from KD Research.

Emotions / Expression	Mean	Standard Deviation
Soft	3.264	1.035
Poised	3.256	1.004
Confident	3.058	1.072
Youthful	3.019	1.124
Calm	3.001	0.898
Warm	2.977	1.042
Cool	2.975	1.037
Elegant	2.968	0.93
Daydreaming	2.947	1.099
Good girl	2.946	1.016
Seductive	2.901	0.959
Pensive	2.857	1.013
Proud	2.854	0.947
Sexy	2.826	0.988
Sophisticated	2.821	0.961

Emotions / Expression	Mean	Standard Deviation
Sexual	2.791	0.976
Loving	2.786	0.976
Self-loving	2.781	0.921
Snobbish	2.756	1.115
Natural	2.743	0.983
Smiling	2.731	1.135
Humble	2.686	1.031
Happy	2.679	1.007
Sassy	2.678	0.958
Mannequin	2.672	0.991
Demure	2.67	1.064
Anxious	2.641	0.954
Tease	2.623	0.937
Stiff	2.603	0.977
Superior	2.529	0.874

Emotions / Expression	Mean	Standard Deviation
Coy	2.496	0.884
Reluctant	2.456	0.951
Emotionless	2.438	1.175
Nostalgic	2.432	0.837
Caucasian	3.704	1.373
Hispanic	1.745	1.096
African American	1.314	0.818
Asian	1.29	0.67
Nothing	2.706	1.679
Reader	2.495	1.813
People	1.867	1.279
Object	1.832	1.153

FIGURE 7-15 KD Research Results of Prevalent Model Look in Fashion Magazines

Case Questions

1. Evaluate the research process that KD Research used. Was this an appropriate research approach? Why or why not?
2. Advise Karen on the prevailing "look" that she should create for her models.
3. In determining what individuals Karen should target for her modeling agency, she again wants to hire KD Research. Which research methodology should KD Research use? Why?
4. Using your response to Question 3, discuss what might have been the precise sampling plan. Describe the sampling unit, the sample size, the sampling procedure, and the sampling frame.

Endnotes

1. LEGO Friends, accessed at https://www.lego.com/en-us/themes/friends on March 12, 2020; Maish Nichani, "Using Lego models in user research—a case study," Pebble Road, December 6, 2016, https://www.pebbleroad.com/insights/using-lego-models-in-user-research-a-case-study
2. Packaged Facts, "Packaged shoppers: money isn't everything," https://www.packagedfacts.com/Content/Blog/2019/07/01/Affluent-Food-Shoppers-Money-Isn%E2%80%99t-Everything, accessed on March 10, 2020.
3. Ibid.
4. Statista, Retail and Trade: Fashion & Accessories, January 6, 2020, ttps://www.statista.com/forecasts/876294/familiarity-with-luxury-accessory-fashion-brands-in-the-us
5. John Teal, "The 10 Costs You'll Pay to Bring Your Hardware Product to Market," Entrepreneur, April 13, 2016, https://www.entrepreneur.com/article/270942
6. Kim Kohatsu, "4 top tips to test your business name with PickFu," *PickFu*, May 21, 2020, https://www.pickfu.com/blog/test-your-business-name.
7. Don Cazentre, "Labatt joins hard seltzer craze, test markets it in Upstate NY," NY Upstate, May 12, 2020, https://www.newyorkupstate.com/breweries/2020/05/labatt-joins-hard-seltzer-craze-test-markets-it-in-upstate-ny.html
8. GritDaily, "Why Consumers Want Coupons—And What Kind They Value Most," June 14, 2020, https://gritdaily.com/why-consumers-want-coupons-and-what-kind-they-value-most
9. Hillary Hoffower, "10 millionaires and billionaires who shop at Target, Costco, and other bargain-lover favorites," *Business Insider,* February 10, 2020, https://www.businessinsider.com/millionaires-who-shop-target-costco-walmart-tj-maxx
10. CMO Survey, February 2020, https://cmosurvey.org/results/february-2020
11. Louis Columbus, "Ten ways big data is revolutionizing marketing and sales," May 9, 2016.

PART 3 Marketing Mix Strategies

Source: Rawpixel.com/Shutterstock

Product Strategies

CHAPTER 8

Source: Fit Ztudio/Shutterstock

Chapter Outline

Learning Objectives

Ivelin Radkov/Shutterstock

After studying this chapter, you should be able to:

- Define and classify products into relevant categories.
- Address issues related to branding, such as the brand name, mark, logo, and character; brand sponsor; and brand strategy decisions.
- Address product packaging and labeling issues.
- Analyze the different dimensions of the product mix.
- Describe the new product development process and the different degrees of product newness.
- Examine the new product diffusion process and the different categories of product adopters.
- Address the different stages of the product life cycle.
- Examine the challenges involved in managing the product portfolio.

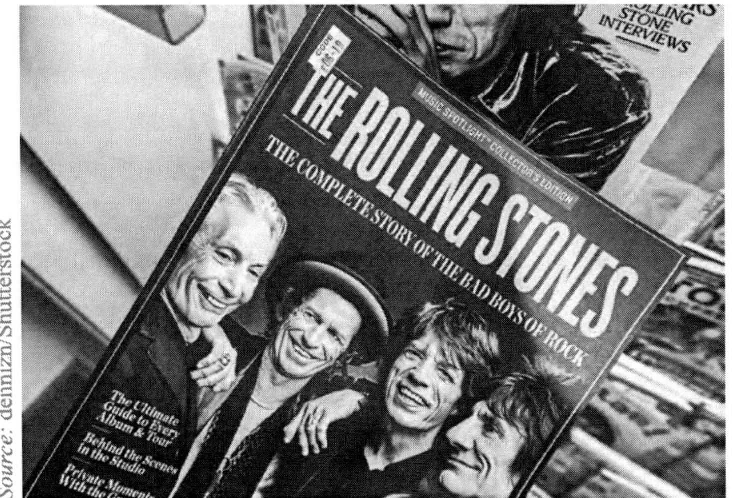

Source: dennizn/Shutterstock

8-1 Chapter Overview

Mick Jagger, Keith Richards, Charlie Watts, Ron Wood, and Brian Jones belong to a brand that is as much in demand today as it was 40 years ago: the Rolling Stones. The veteran rock band has managed to fill and rock the house at New York's Madison Square Garden, the Los Angeles Forum, and Toronto's Air Canada Centre, surviving more than four decades in a fickle, trend-driven, cutthroat, turbulent, insanely competitive music industry. Many consider the Rolling Stones "the greatest rock 'n roll band in the whole world ever." The band has generated more than half a billion dollars in revenues since 1989.

The Stones are, in fact, a brand, and their brand management skills are the reason for their remarkable success. From the beginning, the Rolling Stones positioned themselves strategically. They were not the Beatles or the Beach Boys—they were different, a little rougher, more in your face, and it paid for them to be a differentiated brand that stayed true to their original formula. The Stones also have developed business partnerships that are harmonious with their own, both in stature and shared relevance with their target audience—among their partners are Sheryl Crow, Anheuser-Busch, Microsoft, Sprint, and E*TRADE. Jagger readily understood the power of branding from the beginning of his career. He commissioned a graphic design student at the Royal College of Art in London to create the Stones' tongue logo, a design that was easy to reproduce and that could withstand the test of time. This is one of the strongest and most recognizable logos in the global market and their performances are as popular as ever–very little can derail them from their world tours (they had to cancel their 2020 tour because of the COVID-19 pandemic). The Stones' survival is attributed to a clear differentiation of their brand from that of the competitors, and consistency—staying true to their winning core product formula—over time. Most other similar music brands have not enjoyed the same resonant appeal over time.[1]

This chapter will address product-related issues—from new product development decisions, to managing the product portfolio in line with the company strategy and the demands of different consumers. Section 8-2 provides a product definition and addresses the different product dimensions and classifications. Section 8-3 addresses product decisions regarding branding, logos, trademark protection, and brand strategy. Section 8-4 addresses the packaging and labeling decisions of the firm while Section 8-5 examines product mix management decisions. Section 8-6 addresses the new product development process and Section 8-7 addresses product diffusion and the different types of adopters. Section 8-8 examines the product life cycle stages. Section 8-9 addresses issues related to the management of the product portfolio.

8-2 Product Definition and Classification

A Rolling Stones performance, merchandise sold at the concert, hair highlights at a hair salon, a burger at Burger King, and landscaping by the local landscaping service are all examples of products. A product is defined as any offering that can satisfy consumer needs and wants. As mentioned in Chapter 1, products include goods, which refers to tangible products, and services, which refers to intangible activities or benefits that individuals acquire but that do not result in ownership.

Core product The fundamental benefit, or problem solution, that consumers seek (expected or actual).

Expected (or actual) product The basic physical product, including styling, features, brand name, and packaging, that delivers the benefits that consumers seek.

Augmented product A product enhanced by the addition of extra or unsolicited services or benefits, such as a warranty, repair services, maintenance, and other services that enhance product use to prompt a purchase.

8-2a Core, Expected, and Augmented Products

Products can be conceptualized at three levels, as illustrated in **Figure 8-1**.[2] The **core product** is the fundamental benefit or solution that consumers seek. An individual who purchases aspirin is actually buying relief from headaches. Another individual buying an automobile is purchasing transportation. Individuals purchasing a massage are buying relief from muscle ache.

The **expected (or actual) product** is the basic physical product, including styling, features, brand name and packaging, which delivers those benefits. An individual purchasing a massage at her health club also expects to have a gentle masseuse with magic fingers, calming music, clean sheets, and clean covers. The consumer purchasing the automobile expects it to have comfortable seats, a reasonable radio, power steering, power windows, and in North America, air-conditioning and automatic transmission.

The **augmented product** is a product enhanced by the addition of extra or unsolicited services or benefits to the consumer to prompt purchase—such as warranty, repair services, maintenance, and other services that enhance the product's use. Most of the competition today takes place in the augmented product arena. A children's dentist provides a Mermaid toothbrush and fun-colored gel, sends a birthday card with a smiling cartoon character, and has toys ready for the tots in the waiting room. Some automobile dealers offer free service for three years for new cars. When all competitors offer extra or unsolicited services or benefits, that augmented product becomes the expected product. Turndown hotel service, where the bed is arranged for sleeping and a chocolate mint is placed on the pillow, becomes the expected product. Liquid washing detergents are expected to have a measuring cap indicating amounts required for different size loads. After the COVID-19 pandemic,

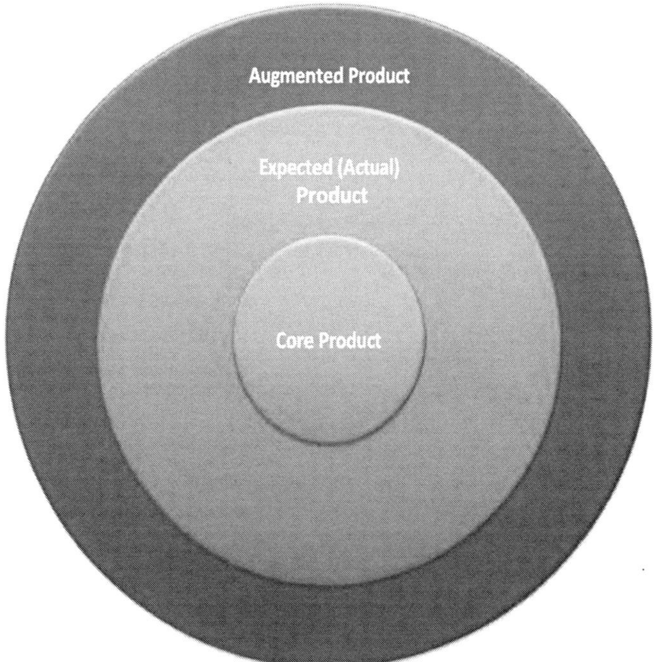

FIGURE 8-1 The Core, Expected and Augmented Product

consumers expect supermarkets to have disinfectant wipes or gel available.

8-2b Product Durability

Durable goods Tangible products that have a prolonged use.

Non-durable goods Tangible products that are consumed relatively quickly and purchased on a regular basis; they last less than two years.

Convenience goods Relatively inexpensive and frequently purchased products.

Impulse goods Goods bought without any earlier planning, such as candy, gum, and magazines.

Staples Goods that are bought routinely, such as milk, cheese, bread, and soap.

Durable goods are defined as tangible products that have a prolonged use. Automobiles, appliances, and furniture are types of durable goods that last over many years of use. Most definitions suggest that durable goods are goods that have a life of more than two years. **Non-durable goods** are defined as tangible products that are consumed relatively quickly, purchased on a regular basis, and last less than two years. Examples of non-durables are food, clothing, shoes, gasoline, and natural gas. Services are defined as intangible activities or benefits that individuals acquire but that do not result in ownership. Examples of services are medical care, legal counseling, accounting, and marketing services.

8-2c Product Classification

Marketing managers have classified consumer products into categories based on the level of risk attributed to the purchase and the amount of effort involved in purchasing the product **(see Figure 8-2)**.[3] **Convenience goods** are relatively inexpensive and frequently purchased. Relative to the other three categories, convenience goods are considered to have the lowest level of perceived risk and purchase effort. Examples of convenience goods are bread, milk, beer, and snacks. Convenience goods can be **impulse goods**, which are items bought without any prior planning, such as candy, gum, and magazines. Retailers place these products conveniently within reach of the checkout aisle. Other types of convenience goods are **staples**, which are products that are bought routinely, such as milk, cheese, bread, and soap. **Emergency goods** are convenience goods that are purchased to address urgent needs, such as candles, lanterns, and bottled water when a hurricane is announced and salt and snow shovels when snow is in the forecast.

Convenience Goods
- Impulse Goods
- Staples
- Emergency Goods

Preference Goods

Shopping Goods
- Homogeneous shopping goods
- Heterogeneous shopping goods

Specialty Goods

FIGURE 8-2 Product Classification

Preference goods are defined as products that become differentiated through branding and achieve some degree of brand loyalty. Preference goods are higher risk and higher in terms of purchase effort compared with convenience items. To indicate that a preference exists, the term *favorite* can be attached to the product category. For example, if one's favorite cola is Pepsi, one will most likely shop only in larger stores that are more likely to sell the brand than in smaller stores that could have an exclusive arrangement with Coke.

Source: Robert Kneschke/Shutterstock

Shopping goods are defined as goods that consumers perceive as higher-risk goods, which they are willing to spend a greater amount of purchase effort in searching for and evaluating. Among examples of shopping goods are home appliances, clothing, and furniture. Shopping goods can be classified further based on their degree of homogeneity. **Homogeneous shopping goods** vary little in terms of physical characteristics or functions but differ in terms of style and price sufficiently to warrant a search. Examples of homogeneous shopping goods are tires and stereo equipment. For homogeneous shopping goods, price is an important variable. After consumers decide on the desired characteristics of the good, the next step is to look for the lowest price. **Heterogeneous shopping goods** are products that vary significantly in terms of functions, physical characteristics, and quality. They require a physical evaluation by the buyer. These goods—clothing and furniture, for example—vary greatly in their characteristics. Retailers need to carry a wide assortment of these items to appeal to various individuals, and they need to have highly trained sales people to assist customers. For these products, price is not as important as other product characteristics.

Specialty goods reach the ultimate in differentiation and brand loyalty, where only the chosen brand is acceptable to the consumer. These goods are conceptualized as high risk and are distinguished from shopping goods primarily in terms of higher purchasing effort. Consumers are willing to wait, search high and low, and not settle for anything less. Examples of specialty goods are gourmet foods and designer clothes.

8-3 Branding

One of the most important roles played by marketing involves branding the product. Branding adds value to products because it makes products appear more distinctive and valuable.

A **brand** is defined as a name, design, symbol, or a combination thereof that identifies the product or the seller and is used to differentiate the product from competitors' offerings. A brand also serves as a guarantee to consumers that the product will be identical each time consumers purchase it, with the same features, design, and performance.

All products benefit from branding. Brands that have high consumer awareness and loyalty are said to have high brand equity (or brand franchise). **Brand equity (or franchise)** is defined as a set of brand assets and liabilities linked to a brand and its name and symbol, adding or subtracting

Emergency goods Goods purchased to address urgent needs.

Preference goods Convenience goods that become differentiated through branding and achieve some degree of brand loyalty.

Shopping goods Goods that consumers perceive as higher risk but for which they are willing to spend a greater amount of purchase effort to find and evaluate.

Homogeneous shopping goods Goods that vary little in terms of physical characteristics or functions.

Heterogeneous shopping goods Goods that vary significantly in terms of functions, physical characteristics, and quality.

Specialty goods Goods that reach the ultimate in differentiation and brand loyalty in that only the chosen brand is acceptable to the consumer.

Brand A name, design, symbol, or a combination thereof that identifies the product or the seller and that's used to differentiate the product from competitors' offerings.

Source: Rawpixel.com/Shutterstock

Brand equity (or franchise) Brands with high consumer awareness and loyalty.

Brand name The part of a brand that can be spoken; it may include words, letters, or numbers.

from the value provided by a product or service to a firm or to that firm's customers. Brand loyalty is an essential asset of brand equity. The epitome of brand equity is the Harley-Davidson aficionado who wears the Harley symbol as a tattoo.

Marketers have attempted to evaluate brand equity and establish the actual value of the brand. A widely accepted brand value ranking is compiled by Interbrand with the help of data from Citibank and currently is considered the most valuable indicator of the financial health of global brand leaders. The ranking is determined by a brand strength (based on factors such as leadership and market stability), financial and analyst reports, revenue, and profit figures.[4] Notice the two top brands, Apple is valued at over $234.2 billion, Google at $167.7 billion, Amazon at $125.3, and Microsoft at $108.8 (see **Figure 8-3**).

Rank	Brand	Value (Billions)
1	Apple	$234.2
2	Google	$167.7
3	Amazon	$125.3
4	Microsoft	$108.8
5	Coca-Cola	$63.4
6	Samsung	$61.1
7	Toyota	$56.2
8	Mercedes-Benz	$50.8
9	McDonald's	$45.4
10	Disney	$44.4
11	BMW	$41.4
12	IBM	$40.4
13	Intel	$40.2
14	Facebook	$39.9
15	Cisco	$35.6
16	Nike	$32.4
17	Louis Vuitton	$32.2
18	Oracle	$26.3
19	GE	$25.6
20	SAP	$25.1

FIGURE 8-3 The Top Brands Based on Brand Equity
Source: https://www.interbrand.com/best-brands/best-global-brands/2019/

8-3a Brand Identity

Selecting the instruments that identify the brand—that is, the brand name, the brand mark, the brand logo, and the brand character—are very important decisions. A **brand name** is defined as the part of a brand that can be spoken. It may include words, letters, or numbers. Toyota, McDonald's, Coach, and Delta Airlines are all brand names. Successful brand names have the following characteristics:

- They are easy to pronounce, memorable, and distinctive. Apple, Supreme, and ThinkPad are memorable names that are easy to pronounce. Distinctive fun names with memorable alliterations are Green Giant and Colgate Total.
- They suggest product traits or benefits. For example, Hefty bags suggest product strength. Other brand names that are indicative of product traits and benefits are Pampers, Huggies, Lean Cuisine, Healthy Choice, Taster's Choice, and Head & Shoulders.

- They are easy to translate into other languages. A number of international market research firms help companies test their names in international markets. In global marketing, the wrong brand name can make or break a product.

Source: Ratana21/Shutterstock

In addition to the brand name, there are other means for product identification. A **brand mark** is part of the brand that can be seen but not spoken. For McDonald's, the brand mark is the golden arches. A **brand logo** is a distinctive mark, sign, symbol, or graphic version of a company's name used to identify and promote its product. The Pepsi logo is the half-white, half-blue circle with a white curved dividing line. The Rolling Stones' logo consists of the well-known red lips and tongue. A **brand character (or trade character)** is a character that personifies the brand, such as Tony the Tiger for Kellogg's Frosted Flakes and Ronald McDonald for McDonald's. These elements together help build the brand's identity and are valuable and well-protected trademarks. A **trademark** consists of words, symbols, marks, devices, and signs that are used in trade to indicate the source of the goods and to distinguish them from competitors. A trademark is legally registered with the U.S. Patent and Trademark Office for use by a single company. Rights for a federally registered trademark can last indefinitely, as long as the owner continues to use it and continues to apply for renewal.

Brand mark The part of a brand that can be seen but not spoken.

Brand logo A distinctive mark, sign, symbol, or graphic version of a company's name that is used to identify and promote the company's product.

Brand character (or trade character) A character that personifies the brand.

Trademark Words, symbols, marks, and signs that are legally registered for a single company's use.

8-3b Protecting the Brand

Brand names are valuable assets to a company. Companies pay millions to protect their brand names from dilution by registering them anywhere they are present and defending them in court. Companies are proactive, rather than reactive, primarily because counterfeit merchandise harms the brand's reputation, its value, and company profits.

Fake goods account for 3.3% of global commerce. Yiwu, a city five hours from Shanghai, China, is one of the largest wholesale centers of China, where 200,000 distributors purchase up to 2,000 tons of goods daily, and it is also China's counterfeit capital, where Gillette razor blades, Prada, Bosch, Kimberly-Clark, and Nike are sold at a fraction of the genuine brand cost. Counterfeiters sell knockoffs of soft drinks and beer, car batteries, motorcycles, apparel, and even medicine. In 2019, Nike stopped selling on Amazon, citing fake products as a reason. A quarter of consumers have been tricked into buying knockoffs on Amazon, and many demand that the government and online sellers take action in preventing counterfeit sales online. Once consumers have bought fake products, more than half lose trust in the brand itself and 64% lose trust in the online marketplace where they bought it. The COVID-19 pandemic has only exacerbated the problem, with counterfeiters saturating social media feeds. A bipartisan bill in the U.S., the Shop Safe Act of 2020, aimed at curtailing counterfeits, has yet to be voted on.[5]

Source: dennizn/Shutterstock

Several factors contribute to the counterfeiters' success. First, consumers are willing to purchase counterfeit goods. Studies have shown, for example, that a large proportion of consumers are likely to select a counterfeit apparel item over a genuine good when there is a price advantage, primarily because function risks are low for apparel, whereas prestige gains are high. In this sense, products that are visible or consumed publicly are more likely to be in demand than products that are less visible or consumed privately. Second, the spread of advanced production technology makes it possible for counterfeiters to make perfect replicas of the original products. Frequently, neither the manufacturer nor the consumers can tell fakes from the real product. Third, supply chains are not adequately controlled. Traders use Internet chat rooms and unauthorized dealership networks to sell the products and mix counterfeit products with legitimate products sold on the secondary gray market. Finally, governments in many developing countries are reluctant to crack down on counterfeiters, especially when state-owned enterprises are involved in the operations. In the case of China, for instance, local governments hesitate to crack down on product pirates because they create thousands of jobs and keep the local economy going.[6]

Companies have used a number of strategies to combat counterfeiting. Lobbying the U.S. government, as well as the governments allowing counterfeiting, is a first step. Alternatively, companies could engage in a concerted action to combat counterfeiting by changing a product's appearance to differentiate authentic products from fakes. Budweiser embedded special images in its beer bottles that appear only when the product is chilled, rendering them difficult to copy. Microsoft included holograms on its software boxes and inside user manuals, but pirates quickly learned the trick. But the most successful attacks have been launched with the cooperation of governments of developing countries. In China, for example, a raid was launched by seven battery makers, including Gillette, Energizer, and Panasonic, with the help of 200 government agents, on two factories in a southwestern city. As a result of the raid, a total of 50 pieces of manufacturing equipment and three million counterfeit batteries were confiscated.[7]

8-3c Brand Sponsor Decisions

Brand sponsor decisions involve determining whether the brand should be sold as a manufacturer brand, also known as a national brand; a dealer brand, also known as a private label brand; a retailer brand; wholesaler brand; distributor brand; or as a generic brand. Brand sponsor decisions also involve determining whether the brand can be licensed or co-branded.

Branding today is more complex than ever. In the past, **manufacturers' brands (or national brands)**, defined as brands owned by a manufacturer, dominated retail shelves. Today, **private label brands**, defined as reseller (wholesaler or retailer) brands, abound on the retail shelves. Alongside the national megabrands, such as Procter & Gamble and Rubbermaid, there is now an increasingly large mix of store brands. In fact, retailers are major competitors to national brands. Kroger's Simple Truth private label has topped $1 billion in sales, Walmart has endless pages of its private label Great Value products online, and Whole Foods' 365 Everyday Value, Meijer's Meijer Gold, and Target's 36 private labels such as Archer Farms and Simply Balanced have a huge consumer franchise. Trader Joe's, Publix, Wegman's, Walgreens, CVS, Rite Aid, Family Dollar, DG, Giant Eagle and Raley's all sell under their names. Two thirds of consumers report that the private labels they bought were just as good if not better than the national brand and more than 40% say that they buy store brands frequently or always.[8] Private label brands are more profitable for retailers, compared with manufacturers' brands.

Manufacturers' brands (or national brands) Brands owned by a manufacturer.

Private label brands Reseller (wholesaler or retailer) brands.

For consumers, private labels represent a quality guarantee at a lower price, and thus they increase store loyalty and patronage. Retailers aggressively promote their brands, placing them side by side with national brands, offering consumers the choice of a lower price. Often, even the packaging is quite similar to that of the manufacturers' brands. This is an example of the **battle of the brands**, defined as a conflict between manufacturers and resellers to promote their own brands. In this battle, manufacturers' advantage lies in the consumers' preference for the manufacturer's brand. But to build this preference requires extensive expenditures on advertising. Retailers, however, have substantial bargaining power in this battle. They control the shelf space and manage it much like real estate, promoting their own brands by placing them, as mentioned, side by side with competing national brands to stress the price difference and offer consumers the option to purchase the product at a lower price. They have central displays with their own brands, creating convenience for consumers looking for that particular product category.

Battle of the brands The conflict between manufacturers and resellers to promote their own brands.

Generics Products that emphasize the product, rather than the brand of the manufacturer or reseller.

Licensing A process that involves a licensor, who shares the brand name, technology, and know-how with a licensee in return for royalties.

Generics, products that emphasize the product rather than the brand of the manufacturer or reseller, represent the third brand category. They are rarely, if at all, advertised. There is minimal expense associated with their manufacturing, packaging, and distribution, and their shelf location is confined to the bottom shelves in low-traffic areas. This strategy allows them to be significantly cheaper than branded product alternatives. Generics are popular in the drug industry, where the cost of certain brand-name products is often prohibitive for individuals living on low fixed incomes.

Source: wavebreakmedia/Shutterstock

Licensing involves the owner of the brand name allowing a manufacturer or a reseller to

FIGURE 8-4 Brand Sponsor Decisions

sell the product under the owner's brand name in return for a licensing fee. Numerous brands are licensed in the clothing industry. Oleg Cassini, Pierre Cardin, and Bill Blass have almost lost their cachet as high-quality exclusive brands as a result of extensive licensing. Barney, Teletubbies, Bob the Builder, and other popular children's programs have successfully licensed their popular brand names to create equally popular toys.

A fourth brand strategy is **co-branding**, which involves using the brands of two different companies on one single product. For example, American Express co-brands with Delta Airlines to offer the Delta Skymiles Credit Card. Breyer's Ice Cream Parlor brands are co-brand offerings with Almond Joy, Klondike, Reese's, Oreo, and Hershey's. Co-branding can be a profitable strategy for firms. Louis Vuitton co-branded with BMW to create the luggage of the future, crafted in carbon fiber for the newly launched BMW i8 (whose price starts at $150,000). This relationship could create the synergy needed for success for both the Louis Vuitton luggage set and the newly-introduced BMW hybrid sports car.[9] **Figure 8-4** summarizes the brand-sponsor decisions.

Co-branding Using the brands of two different companies on one single product.

Line extension The process of extending the existing brand name by introducing new product offerings in an existing product category.

8-3d Brand Strategy

In deciding on brand strategy, a company has a number of options as shown in **Figure 8-5**. A **line extension** involves extending the existing brand name by introducing new product offerings in an existing product category. Examples of line extensions are new flavors. For instance, Celestial Seasonings introduced a raspberry-flavored Green Tea, in addition to its already existing Green Tea. Pepsi introduced lime flavors for Diet Pepsi and regular Pepsi. Chickme created line extension by offering seven flavor combinations. New product forms are also popular line extensions. Most detergents introduced liquid versions that they sell in addition to the traditional powder versions. Added ingredients, such as Palmolive dish detergent with antibacterial soap, or removed ingredients, such as low-fat versions of products, are also examples of line

Line Extension
New Brand
Brand Strategy
Brand Extension
Multibranding
Family Brand

FIGURE 8-5 Brand Strategies

extensions. Size can be varied as well: Dove ice cream also offers bite-size versions of its popular ice cream. But companies must be careful not to sabotage their core brand with line extensions.

Another strategy involves introducing **brand extensions**—that is, using an existing brand name to introduce products in a new product category. The assumption, for brand extensions, is that the brand is quite successful and enjoys substantial consumer franchise. In fact, if a brand is well known and enjoys substantial consumer franchise, it is only natural for firms to attempt to leverage that into new products. Many strong brands, such as Disney and Taco Bell, have transformed themselves into megabrands through brand extensions. Crest toothbrushes, and Porsche and Harley-Davidson apparel and sunglasses are all examples of brand extensions. Dyson, known for its powerful, convenient, and well-designed cordless vacuum cleaners and air purifiers, successfully expanded into hair dryers that work without creating extreme heat.[10] It is important to note that the wrong extension could create damaging associations that may be expensive to change. Moreover, the decision usually involves an important strategic growth thrust, thus causing the company to lose substantial time and resources and to miss important opportunities.

Brand extensions The use of an existing brand name to introduce products in a new product category.

Family branding (or blanket branding) Branding strategy whereby one brand name is used for more than one product.

Multibranding Using different brand names for products that the firm sells in the same product category.

A third strategy is **family branding (or blanket branding)**, whereby one brand name is used for more than one product. Kodak, an imaging technology company, uses its name for all the products it sells, whether digital printing, graphics, entertainment, commercial film, or cameras—digital, drone, etc. Stihl sells chain saws for individual use and industrial use under the same brand name. Volvo sells automobiles and trucks under the Volvo umbrella name.

Source: Zety Akhzar/Shutterstock

The reverse of this strategy is **multibranding**, which involves using different brand names for products that the firm sells in the same product category. For example, Procter & Gamble sells an array of products in the laundry detergent category, positioned to address every imaginable laundry need. Tide, Cheer, Dreft, and Downy are some of P&G's brands.

Source: calimedia/Shutterstock

Yet another strategy involves creating new brands in new product categories for the firm. This strategy is often pursued through acquisitions. For example, when Kraft bought Jacobs Suchard, it expanded into the chocolate product category—a category consistent with its cookies and crackers. In the process, it acquired the Toblerone brand, as well as other famous European chocolate brands—Milka and Suchard, engaging in a large number of foreign acquisitions to penetrate even more new markets and new product categories before spinning off its confectionery and some of its food and beverage brands under the umbrella of Mondelēz International.

8-4 Packaging and Labeling

Package All the activities involved in designing the product container.

An important feature of the product is the **package**, which is defined as all the activities involved in designing the product container. Packaging is a very important product feature whose cost ranges from less than 10 percent for a simple plastic wrap to more than 50 percent for a fancy golden mirror that is part of a purse-size compact powder or an elaborate lipstick package. The package contains and protects the product during shipping, handling, and storage. The primary package may be a single container or wrapper. Bread, for example, is wrapped in one single plastic container. Almond Joy and Snickers bars are wrapped in a single wrapper.

The primary package may also be enclosed in a secondary package. For example, chewing gum is wrapped in a primary package for individual pieces of gum and a secondary package that holds five or more pieces of gum. An important consideration in designing the package is its storage. For example, products in round packages cannot be efficiently stored on the store shelves and result in substantial wasted space for the retailer, which manufacturers must take into consideration when designing the package. Ocean Spray comes in a square package that now fits in home refrigerator doors, saving valuable space.

The package contains the product label, which performs the following functions:

- Identifies the product or brand—it carries the brand name, logo, and brand mark.
- Describes the product in terms of ingredients or components, weight, or volume. For food products, the label contains nutritional facts, such as calories, fat, cholesterol, sodium, carbohydrates, sugars, and protein based on serving size and number of servings per package.
- Informs consumers when the product expires and classifies the product based on quality or size.
- Identifies the manufacturer or the distributor and has the UPC for easy inventory processing and scanning.
- Promotes the product. The label advertises the product to the consumer every time the consumer handles it. It is the last brand communication that reminds the consumer to purchase the product when it runs out.
- Directs the consumer on product use, offering recipes for food products or instructions on assembly and safety.

Packaging is a very important marketing function that must be appropriately coordinated with the company's marketing mix. Consumers expect that, if they pay over $200 for a one-ounce bottle of perfume, the package will be unique and plush, not just functional. And they react positively to creative and convenient packaging ideas, such as the Hershey's Kiss unique package and the self-serve soft drink 12-packs.

Source: mariakray/Shutterstock

8-5 The Product Mix

The product offering of a firm is usually diversified into various products to ensure a more stable income over time. The **product mix** is defined as the complete assortment of products that a company offers. One important dimension of the product mix is the **product line**, which consists of the related brands in the same product category. Companies use different line strategies to achieve market share and profitability goals. For example, companies engage in line extensions to target consumers who otherwise cannot afford a particular product or want different benefits. In the fashion realm, for example, numerous top-line designers attempt to increase their profits by targeting the masses with bridge offerings (secondary, more affordable lines): Escada with Laurel, Ann Klein with Anne Klein II, and Armani with Emporio Armani.

Product mix The complete assortment of the products that a company offers to its target consumers.

Product line The related brands the company offers in the same product category.

Product length The total number of brands in the product mix—all the brands the company sells.

Product width The total number of product lines the company offers.

Product depth The number of different offerings for a product category.

Other important product dimensions are the **product length**, which is the total number of brands in the product mix or all of the brands sold by the company. The **product width** is the total number of product lines the company offers and the **product depth** is the number of different offerings for a product category. To illustrate these product dimensions, consider Unilever, one of the largest global consumer product companies. Although Unilever is organized primarily into two divisions—the foods division and the personal care division—the company has a number of product lines that are addressed as separate strategic business units. **Figure 8-6** comprises the Unilever brands. The total product length, then, is 22. Counting the different product lines (culinary products, frozen foods, ice cream, margarine, tea, detergents, deodorants, shampoos, personal care, oral care, and fragrances), the total product width is 11. To explain product depth, Lipton tea comes in at least three variants: Lipton Yellow Label, Lipton Ice Tea, and Lipton Brisk. The depth of the tea category (the Lipton brand), therefore, is three. Product depth for the tea line is thus calculated by adding all the variants under the Lipton brand.

8-6 New Product Development

To maintain their competitive advantage and to ensure survival and growth, companies must develop and introduce new goods and services that meet the needs of their markets. New product development is a costly and risky

Product Area	Brand Names
Culinary Products	Ragu Spaghetti Sauce Hellmann's Mayonnaise Knorr Soups
Frozen Foods	Gordon's Tenders
Ice Cream	Breyers Ben & Jerry's
Margarine	I Can't Believe It's Not Butter
Tea	Lipton
Detergents	Snuggle
Deodorants	Sure Dove
Shampoo	Sunsilk Thermasilk Organics
Personal Care	Dove Vaseline Intensive Care Pond's
Oral Care	Mentadent Close-Up
Fragrances	Valentino Cerruti Calvin Klein

FIGURE 8-6 Unilever Products Targeted to the U.S. Market

process that involves the firm at all levels. The following are examples of risks and difficulties companies face when developing new products:

- Competitors could copy the good or service idea and deliver the final product to the market more swiftly and economically than the initial good or service developer.
- Target consumers might not respond as anticipated to the offering because it does not meet their needs, because they cannot afford it, or because they prefer to adopt a product later in the PLC stage, when the product is proven and more affordable.
- The government might impose restrictions on product-testing procedures.

Figure 8-7 illustrates the product development process. At each step, the process can be either terminated or continued. Consequently, a product that is commercialized will go through each stage to reach the product launching stage. Throughout the product development process, maintaining a strong market orientation is important, as is an understanding of what consumers want, of customer value, and of competitors.

8-6a Generating New Product Ideas

The first step in the new product development process is generating new product ideas—that is, systematically searching for ideas for new

FIGURE 8-7 Steps in the New Product Development Process

products. Depending on the products provided or company philosophies, ideas will be sought using different strategies. Most firms are driven by the marketing concept, and their product development decisions are based on identifying the needs, wants, and desires of consumers. For technology-driven firms, the focus is more likely to be on the product itself, and thus the research and development division may be responsible for developing product ideas. Even in this second instance, however, products are developed with the needs of the consumer in mind.

Companies use multiple sources for ideas. The most obvious sources for ideas are consumers, who can be observed as they interact in brand communities, on social media, and while interacting with them at the point of retail. Consumers can be queried about their reactions to products and about product preferences and needs. Marketing research firms can collect data on consumer preferences, behavior, and they can qualitatively assess their needs, gripes, complaints, and hassles. Good product ideas also come from consultants, research laboratories, universities, and other companies.

Crowdsourcing has become an important venue for sourcing new product ideas, with over 85% of top global brands reporting using it. It is the act of taking tasks traditionally performed by an employee or an outside service provider and outsourcing them to the community in the form of an open call. This community could range from experts and businesses not previously under consideration—or even known—by the company, to online communities. Anheuser-Busch, struggling as they lost

Crowdsourcing The act of taking tasks traditionally performed by an employee or an outside service provider and outsourcing them to the community in the form of an open call.

Source: Rawpixel.com/Shutterstock

customers to the popular craft beer companies, came up with Black Crown beer as a result of asking feedback on new flavors–this also created a buzz for the company. Lego even has a crowdsourcing business model allowing people to submit designs for new product sets.[11]

Internal idea sources are also useful. Brainstorming sessions represent a venue for conducting internal qualitative research and may also be used in the process of generating product ideas.

Finally, suppliers, channel members, and competitors could provide important product ideas. Chinese companies are often at odds with competitors for "borrowing" new product ideas: Motorola claimed Chinese company Hytera stole two-way radio technology, and T-Mobile US, Inc. claimed Huawei stole phone-testing know-how information. Products in the test market phase or just being launched are always vulnerable to having their ideas copied.[12]

8-6b Screening New Product Ideas

In the process of screening new product ideas, the goal is to ensure that the product fits well with the target consumers' needs, as well as with the overall mission of the organization. A checklist is usually developed to screen out product ideas that do not meet these criteria. Companies want products that are superior to current offerings and deliver unique benefits to users, offering new value to them, rather than a product that looks just like current offerings. There is a cost to switching and upgrading, and consumers must be persuaded that the new product is worth that cost.

8-6c Developing and Evaluating New Product Concepts

The next stage entails developing product concepts and determining how consumers will view and use the product. This information can be determined by having the target consumers test the idea to gauge its usefulness. Typically, the process involves developing a detailed description of the product and asking prospective consumers to evaluate it and to indicate their willingness to purchase the hypothetical product. Most often, this is done using a focus group of representative target consumers.

One method that is frequently used at this stage is conjoint analysis. In this method, respondents receive descriptions of different hypothetical products with varying levels of the same attributes, which they are then asked to rank. Analysts can determine the ideal combination of attributes, ascertain the importance of each attribute, and assuming the data were collected from a sufficiently large sample of the target population, even estimate market share.

The creation of new products ranges from minor changes to current products to radically different, new products. The degree of product newness refers to the extent to which a good or service is new to the market. Figure 8-8 identifies a common classification system of new products. **Radical innovations (or discontinuous innovations)** create new industries or new standards of management, manufacturing, and servicing, and they represent fundamental changes for consumers, entailing departures from established consumption. Examples of relatively radical innovations are the Internet and endoscopy. **Dynamically continuous innovations** do not significantly alter consumer behavior, but they represent a change in the consumption pattern. Mobile phones are an example of such an innovation. Tesla's new low-cost, longer lasting battery known as the "million-mile battery" promises to be one. The battery promises to last for a million miles before breaking down, allowing automakers to sell electric vehicles for the same prices as gasoline-powered ones, thus making them far more accessible.[13]

FIGURE 8-8 Classification of New Product Innovations

Continuous innovations have no disruption on consumption patterns and involve only product alterations, such as new flavors or a product that is an improvement over the old one. Continuous innovations are usually congruous, in the sense that they can be used alongside the existing systems: new Microsoft Windows versions will work with older computers. Most of the new products are continuous innovations.

Radical innovations (or discontinuous innovations) Innovations that create new industries or new standards of management, manufacturing, and servicing, and that represent fundamental changes for consumers, entailing departures from established consumption.

Dynamically continuous innovations Innovations, such as mobile phones, that do not significantly alter consumer behavior, but they represent a change in the consumption pattern.

Continuous innovations Innovations that have no disruption on consumption patterns and involve only product alterations, such as new flavors or a new product that is an improvement over the old offering.

8-6d Performing a Product Business Analysis

Performing a product business analysis includes calculating projected project costs, return on investment, cash flow, and determining the fixed and variable costs for the new product, while ensuring that the project fits with the company budget and profit goals.

8-6e Designing and Developing the Product

At this stage product design, defined as the aesthetic traits, style, and function of the product, is developed. Once the design has been created, prototypes of the new product are created. It is important that product prototypes precisely match the concept description developed in the earlier concept development and evaluation stage. If the company strays from the initial description, it is crucial that the revised product description be tested first. The product now acquires a name, a brand identity, and the marketing mix is developed. The cross-functional team developing the product—research and development, engineering, operations, marketing, and finance—must come together for this process.

Source: Rawpixel.com/Shutterstock

Source: eldar nurkovic/Shutterstock

8-6f Test Marketing

Test marketing a product can provide a good indication of how the product will be received when it is in the marketplace, but this stage can also be expensive, time consuming, and open to competitive sabotage. Firms have two options with test marketing: a simulated test market and a controlled test market.

Because eight out of ten products fail, **simulated test marketing** is often used to reduce the risks a company would incur in terms of marketing, sales, capital expenses, cannibalization of the original brand through a line extension and competitive reaction to the new product. In a simulated test market, participants might view marketing communications regarding the new brand and competitive brands, and be asked to comment on them. Or they could proceed to a simulated store stocked with the test brands and competitive brands where they could buy the brands at a discount. The proportion of individuals purchasing the test brand is then used to estimate product **trialability**, which is the number of individuals who would try a new product or brand for the first time.

Simulated test marketing Test marketing that simulates purchase environments in that target consumers are observed in the product related decision-making process.

Trialability The number of individuals that try a new product or brand for the first time.

Controlled test marketing Offering a new product to a group of stores and evaluating the market reaction to it.

Controlled test marketing involves offering a new product to a group of stores and evaluating the market reaction to it. In the process, different aspects of the marketing mix are varied—price, in-store promotion, placement in the store, and so on. A more informal controlled test involves asking a number of stores to carry the product for a fee. Depending on the outcome, the firm may decide to produce the product on a larger scale, or not.

A number of important decisions are involved in the full-blown actual test marketing, in which the product and related marketing mix are tested in a large test market area. Companies at this stage must decide on the cities that are most appropriate for testing the product based on the availability of retailers and the distribution and logistics service providers. For companies selling financial products and for companies that cannot afford large-scale testing in the marketplace, test marketing may be limited to direct mail or mobile phone offers. For example, MasterCard continuously tests new products by using email and direct mail.

Although test marketing can provide valuable information for the manufacturer, anticipating product performance in the short run, its usefulness is often questioned given the high expense it necessitates. In a rapidly changing competitive environment, being first in the market constitutes an important competitive advantage addressed earlier, the first-mover advantage. As such, a company is the first to attract consumers and to commit channel members for its new product. A company is also vulnerable to competitive reaction during the test-marketing stage. On one hand, the competition could appropriate the product idea and be the first to offer the product to the market. On the other hand, the competition could sabotage the new brand, cutting prices for all competitive offerings.

Define your target market
Access your target market
Find the users most likely to appreciate the product
Identify a success signal
Figure out how to launch to your next set of users

FIGURE 8-9 Steps in Launching a New Product

8-6g Launching the Product

Launching the product, also known as commercialization, involves introducing the new product to the full target market. Strategies for launching have an impact on the new product's long-term performance. New product launch steps are presented in Figure 8-9. It is important to define and access your target market to identify the users most likely to appreciate the product. After identifying a success signal, firms then leverage their experience to figure out how to market to the broader market.[14]

An important decision is the timing of the new product launch. Companies often gain the first–mover advantage by being the first to launch the new product. Alternatively, they could engage in later entry. The advantage of later entry is that a firm's competitors would have to incur the costs of informing the market about the new product and its features. Also, the company could market the product as a "me-too" product, reducing advertising costs significantly.

8-7 New Product Diffusion

Product diffusion Manner in which consumers accept new products and the speed of adoption.

Product diffusion refers to the manner in which consumers accept new products and the speed of new product adoption by various consumer groups. As shown in Figure 8-10, a number of factors influence the speed of product adoption.[15]

The first factor in consumers adopting a new product is relative advantage. The new product must offer some type of *relative advantage* compared with the other offerings available on the market, or consumers have little incentive to purchase the new item. The new product must be *compatible with the needs of consumers* and be observable (or communicable to others). Consumers must be able see or be told about the relative advantage or how it better meets a particular need than something they are

FIGURE 8-10 Factors Influencing the Speed of New Product Adoption

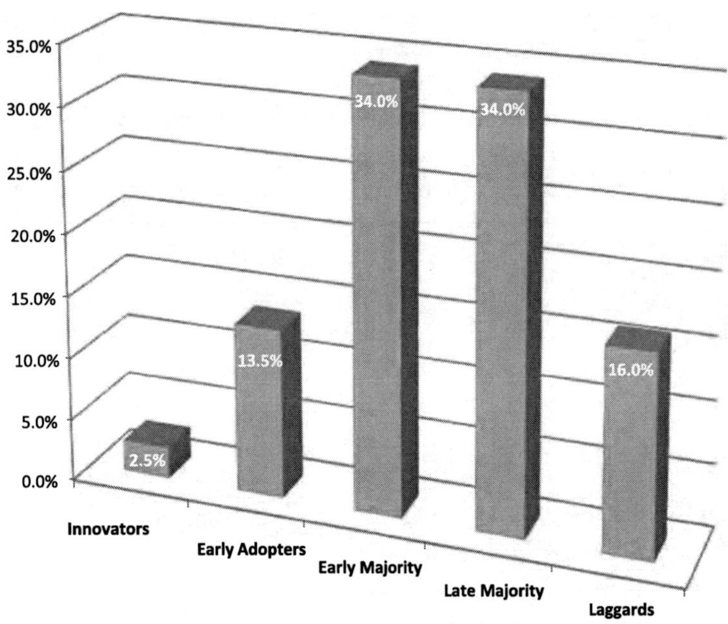

FIGURE 8-11 New Product Adoption Segments

currently using. Last, the new product needs a high level of trialability, which means consumers can try the product on a limited basis without making a purchase.

Target consumers can be segmented based on the manner in which they adopt new products throughout the respective products' life cycle. The segments and their relative size are shown in the graph in **Figure 8-11**.

Innovators (2.5% of the market) are risk takers and can afford to pay the higher price charged during the introduction stage of a new product. They are willing to accept risk and they like to be known as the first to try out new products among their peers.

Innovators Psychographic group of individuals who are successful, sophisticated, and receptive to new technologies.

Early adopters Consumers who purchase the product early in the life cycle and are opinion leaders in their communities.

Early majority Consumers who are more risk averse but enjoy the status of being among the first in their peer group to buy what will be a popular product.

Early adopters (13.5% of the market) are opinion leaders in their communities who take risks, but with greater discernment than innovators. For example, early adopters of electric vehicles tend to be socially conscious, more educated, with a higher income so they can afford the higher price. As battery technology improves and renders battery packs more affordable, electric vehicles will be adopted by the early majority.

Early majority (34% of the market) are more risk averse than individuals in the first categories but enjoy the status of being among the first in their peer group to buy what will be a popular product.

Late majority (34% of the market) are individuals of limited financial means who are likely to adopt products only if they are widely popular and the risk associated with buying them is minimal. The products themselves are much more affordable at this stage.

Laggards (16 percent of the market) are the last to adopt new products and often do so reluctantly. They tend to be risk averse and very conservative in their spending.

Source: aslysun/Shutterstock

8-8 The Product Life Cycle (PLC)

After new products are launched, marketers must ensure that their products perform well on the market long enough to generate sufficient profits that can be used to finance other products for the company. Products pass through distinct stages in their evolution, during which sales and profits rise and fall. In this evolutionary process, products require different strategies. The **product life cycle (PLC)** is defined as the performance of the product in terms of sales and profit over time. The PLC

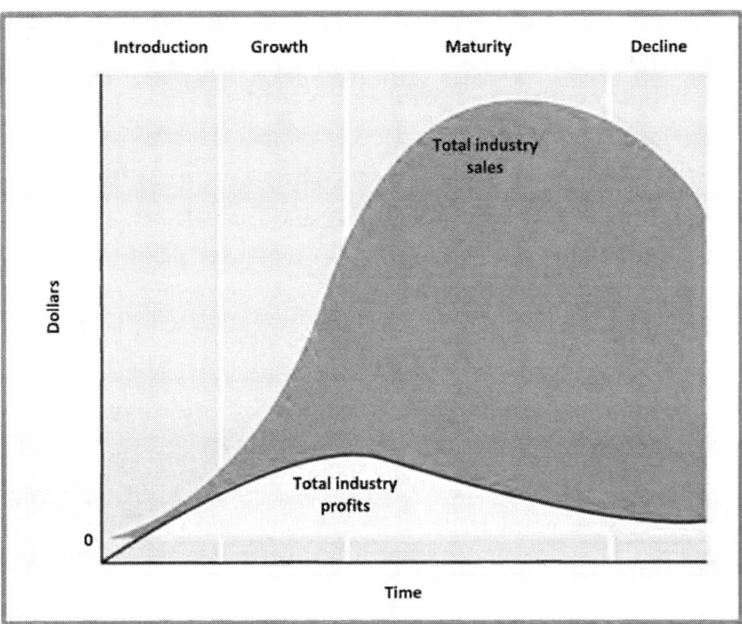

FIGURE 8-12 The Traditional Product Life Cycle

PLC Stage	Industry Sales	Industry Profit	Product Price	Promotion	Competi-tion	Target Market
Introduction	Low	Low	High	High	Low	Innovators
Growth	Increasing	Increasing	Decreasing	High	Increasing	Early adopters and early majority
Maturity	High and stable	Decreasing	Lower	Decreasing	High	Early and late majority
Decline	Decreasing	Decreasing	Low	Low	Decreasing	Late majority and laggards

FIGURE 8-13 Product Life Cycle Characteristics

can apply to a product category or to a particular brand. The traditional PLC is illustrated in **Figure 8-12**. The characteristics of each stage are explained in **Figure 8-13**, in terms of industry sales, profits, price, promotion, competition, and target market.

The **product introduction stage** is the PLC stage when the product is available for purchase for the first time. During this stage, products are developed in industrialized countries and supported by a firm's substantial research and development budgets and by highly skilled product research teams. To quickly recover the high costs of product development and launching, a firm markets products in industrialized countries to consumers who can afford the high prices that need to be charged. The firm at this stage still has control of the market. It is the only manufacturer or one of the few manufacturers of the product.

In the introduction stage, firms have negative or very low profits. They are attempting to recover the high product development costs. Sales

Late majority Consumers with limited means likely to adopt products only if the products are widely popular and the risk associated with buying them is minimal.

Laggards Consumers who are the last to adopt new products and who do so only in late maturity.

Product life cycle (PLC) The performance of the product in terms of sales and profit over time.

Product introduction stage Stage in the product life cycle when the product is available for purchase for the first time.

Growth stage Stage in the product life cycle characterized by increasing competition, with new product variants offered to the market, as well as rapid product adoption by the target market.

Maturity stage Stage in the product life cycle characterized by a slowdown in sales growth as the product is adopted by most target consumers and by a leveling or decline in profits primarily as a result of intense price competition.

Decline stage Stage in the product life cycle where products are rapidly losing ground to new technologies or product alternatives, and consequently, sales and profits are rapidly declining.

Style A general form of popular expression that could last for a longer period of time or that could be cyclical in nature.

Fashion A current style.

Fad A fashion that quickly becomes very popular and just as quickly disappears.

are low, but increasing. And the companies spend heavily on promotion to encourage product innovators to adopt the product and on developing a viable distribution channel for the product, if such a channel is not yet established.

The **growth stage** is the PLC stage characterized by increasing competition, with new product variants offered to the market, as well as rapid product adoption by the target market. Toward the end of this stage, the focus is on developing economies of scale in the manufacturing process. A standard is reached, and subsequently, price competition is intense. Sales increase rapidly, and profits reach their peak toward the end of this stage.

Usually the longest stage in the PLC is the **maturity stage**, which is characterized by a slowdown in sales growth as the product is adopted by most target consumers and by a leveling or decline in profits primarily as a result of intense price competition. At maturity, manufacturing moves to developing countries to save on labor costs. Products at maturity do not need as much promotional support. The cash they generate is used to promote products in the introduction and growth stages.

Products in the **decline stage** are rapidly losing ground to new technologies or product alternatives. Sales and profits are declining at this stage, and the firm is likely to cut back on production, distribution, and promotional support. Alternatively, management may decide that it is not worthwhile to maintain the product on the market because the costs of even minimal product maintenance are high and so they discontinue offering it.

Products vary in the length of time needed for them to go through the life cycle. Although most products go through the traditional life cycle, fashion, fads, and styles, for instance, have a much shorter cycle. For example, a **style** is defined as a general form of popular expression that could last for a longer period of time—even decades—or that could be cyclical in nature. The traditional home is an example of a style. It has traditional elements, such as molding, traditional mantle pieces, and modern bathrooms and kitchens. Louis XV is a furniture style characterized by slightly curved legs for chairs and tables. Current Louis XV designs are rendered in dark wood; the original style was popular gilded, white, or a combination thereof. The black-tie dress style for men has been a constant for more than a century, with small variations.

Source: Dean Drobot/Shutterstock

A **fashion** is defined as a current style. In the 1960s, polyester leisure suits and Nehru jackets became popular, followed by bell-bottom pants. In the 1980s, the dressy yuppie look became popular. In the past years, streetwear took the world by storm. A **fad** is a fashion that quickly becomes very popular and just as quickly disapears. The challenge for companies is to recognize early if something is going to be a fashion that is adopted by many, or fad that skyrockets to popularity, but then quickly

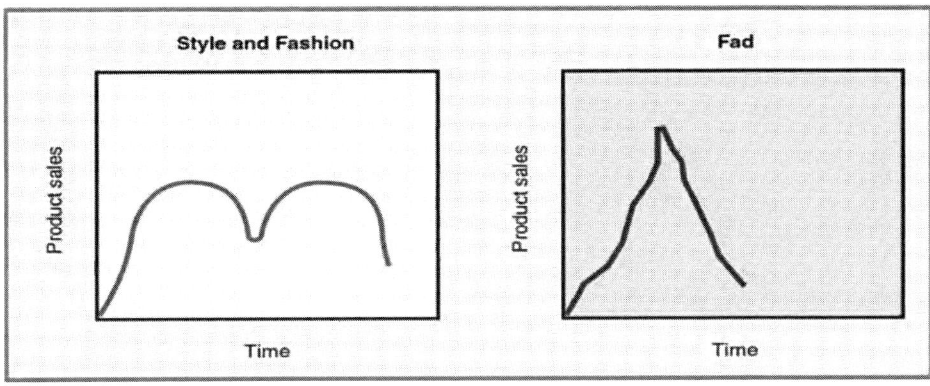

FIGURE 8-14 Style, Fashion, and Fad—Product Sales over Time

disappears leaving the company with thousands or millions of unsold products. Examples of fads are goat yoga–yoga conducted while goats wonder around–and ugly sneakers. **Figure 8-14** illustrates the sales of styles, fashions and fads over time.

8-9 Managing the Product Portfolio

The **product portfolio** is defined as the totality of products managed by the company as separate businesses. Product portfolio decisions are an important aspect of strategic planning. Companies periodically review their different businesses and make decisions on whether to acquire new ones or divest those that might be unprofitable, or that do not represent a good fit with the company. For example, PepsiCo decided to focus more on the Pepsi and Frito Lay brands and divest the restaurant business by spinning off its fast-food restaurants, Taco Bell, KFC, and Pizza Hut that now constitute Yum! Brands. And in the process of expanding their product portfolio, PepsiCo entered the health food industry by acquiring Stacy's Pita Chip Company and Duyvis in the Netherlands—primarily a nuts company. In its future expansion, PepsiCo is betting that the health food and convenience industry is an up-and-coming market and will be profitable for a long time to come.

Product portfolio The totality of products the company manages as separate businesses.

Companies must constantly evaluate their portfolios to make sure that they are appropriately allocating their resources to ensure overall firm success. Two models exist to evaluate portfolios: the growth-share matrix and the product-market matrix. The **growth-share matrix**,[16] discussed here, was developed by the Boston Consulting Group in the 1970s and remains one of the most popular bases for evaluating company product portfolios. The assumption of the matrix is that a company should have a portfolio of products with different growth rates and different market shares to be successful. High-growth products require cash inputs to grow, whereas low-growth products should generate excess cash, and both types of products are needed simultaneously.

Growth-share matrix Portfolio matrix developed by the Boston Consulting Group and one of the most popular bases for evaluating company product portfolios; it assumes that, to be successful, a company should have a portfolio of products with different growth rates and different market shares.

Products are evaluated on two dimensions: relative market share and industry growth rate. Evaluating each dimension in terms of high and low generates a 2 X 2 matrix, illustrated in **Figure 8-15**. A high relative

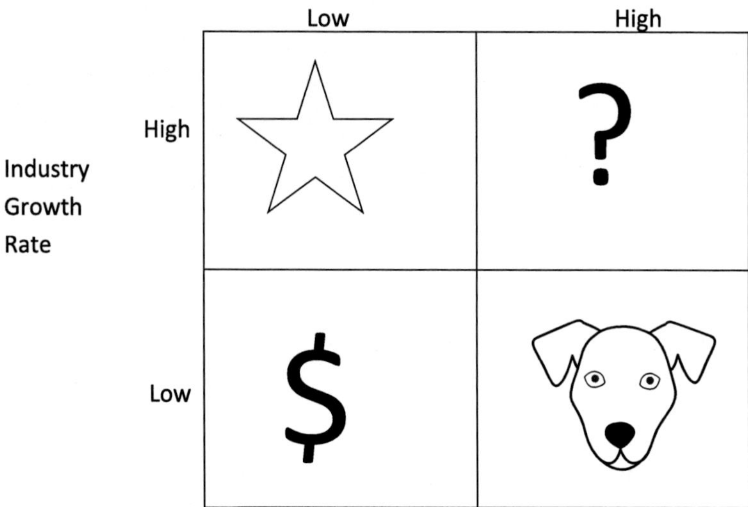

FIGURE 8-15 The Boston Consulting Group Matrix
Source: Adapted from Boston Consulting Group, https://www.bcg.com/about/our-history/growth-share-matrix.aspx; retrieved April 22

Stars High-share, high-growth products that create profits but require additional investment.

Question marks (or problem children) Low market share and high-growth products that require more cash investment than they generate.

Cash cows Products with high market share and slow growth that generate large amounts of cash, in excess of the reinvestment required to maintain market share.

Dogs Products with low market share and slow growth.

Product-market opportunity matrix A matrix used to identify future products and opportunities for companies.

market share would indicate that a particular brand has a high percentage of the market compared with competitors. A high industry growth rate would indicate an industry that is growing at a rate higher than 10 percent per year. A balanced product portfolio consists of **stars, cash cows,** and **question marks.** Companies should milk cash cows, and invest in other products. They should significantly invest in stars because they have great potential. They should invest in question markets if they have a chance of becoming a star; otherwise, they should divest. Companies should liquidate, reposition or divest **dogs**. All products either become cash cows or dogs eventually.

Most firms do rely on some type of matrix for portfolio planning. A drawback of relying on a particular model is that it keeps the firm focused on the matrix dimensions—in the case of the growth-share matrix, industry growth rate and market share. Other important market dimensions could be neglected in the analyses. Moreover, abandoning a product because it has become a dog may be premature. The dog could quickly become a star if the target market is actually becoming a niche market.

Another approach to evaluating products is the **product-market opportunity matrix.**[17] **Figure 8-16** identifies four strategies depending on market saturation and contingent on the firm's ability and desire to introduce new products.

The following is a brief summary of each strategy with corresponding examples:

- **Market penetration** is defined as selling more products to present customers without changing the product. Approaches include increasing the usage rate of current customers and attracting competitors' customers. Improving product visibility

FIGURE 8-16 The Product-Market Opportunity Matrix

through promotion and through securing better shelf space are two strategies that could be used to this end. Often, companies attempt to penetrate the market further by selling bundles of goods that might or might not be complementary. Research has demonstrated that consumers who buy products in larger packages are likely to consume more. This strategy, thus, might increase consumption.

- **Market development** is defined as increasing product sales by developing new markets for the company's existing product or by creating new product uses. Many companies increase their sales substantially by going international.
- **Product development** is defined as developing new products to appeal to the company's existing market. Apple could easily increase sales if they were to sell products other than those in their current portfolio. Apple devotees are rapid adopters of new company offerings.
- **Diversification** is defined as developing or acquiring new products for new markets. For example, Heinz Ketchup has developed a variety of new products to increase their revenues, including a fit-in-the door ketchup bottle and various new colors, such as purple and blue, to appeal to their younger audience.

Market penetration The process of increasing the usage rate of current customers and attracting competitors' customers to sell more products to present customers without changing the product.

Market development The process of developing new markets for the company's existing product or creating new product uses.

Product development The process of developing new products to appeal to the company's existing market.

Diversification Opportunity for expansion involving developing or acquiring new products for new markets.

Summary

1. Define and classify products into relevant categories.

A product, an offering developed to satisfy consumer needs, can be conceptualized at three levels. The core product is the fundamental benefit, or problem solution, sought by consumers. The expected or actual product is the basic physical product, including styling, features, brand name, and packaging, which delivers those benefits. The augmented product is a product enhanced by the addition of extra or unsolicited services or benefits to the consumer to prompt a purchase, such as warranty, repair services, maintenance, and other services that enhance product use. In terms of durability, products are classified as durables (tangible products that have a prolonged use, such as automobiles and appliances), nondurables (tangible products that are consumed relatively quickly and purchased on a regular basis), and services (intangible benefits or activities that individuals acquire but that do not result in ownership). Consumer products are classified into convenience goods, preference goods, shopping goods, and specialty goods. Convenience goods are inexpensive and purchased frequently and include impulse goods that are bought without earlier planning. Staples are bought routinely. Emergency goods are purchased to address urgent needs. Preference goods become differentiated through branding and achieve some degree of brand loyalty. Shopping goods are perceived as higher-risk goods that consumers are willing to spend a greater amount of purchase effort in searching for and evaluating. Specialty goods are highly differentiated and enjoy high brand loyalty, such that they are the only brand acceptable to the consumer.

2. **Address issues related to branding, such as the brand name, mark, logo, and character; brand sponsor; and brand strategy decisions.**
   A brand is a name, design, symbol, or a combination thereof that identifies the product or the seller and is used to differentiate the product from competitors' offerings. Brand marks are part of the brand that can be seen but not spoken. A brand logo is a distinctive mark, sign, symbol, or graphic version of a company's name and is used to identify and promote its product. A brand character or trade character is a character that personifies the brand, such as Tony the Tiger for Kellogg's Frosted Flakes and Ronald McDonald for McDonald's. These together help build the brand's identity and are valuable and well-protected trademarks. A trademark consists of words, symbols, marks, and signs that are legally registered for use by a single company. Brand sponsor decisions involve determining whether the brand should be sold as a manufacturer brand (a national brand), a private label brand, or a generic brand. Brand sponsor decisions also involve determining whether the brand can be licensed or co-branded. Brand strategies involve extending the existing brand name by introducing new product offerings in an existing product category, brand extensions, family (blanket) branding, multibranding, and creating new brands in new product categories for a firm.

3. **Address product packaging and labeling issues.**
   Packaging addresses all the activities involved in designing the product container. The primary package may be a single container or wrapper. The secondary package may enclose the primary package. The package contains the product label, which identifies the product or brand. It carries the brand name, logo, and brand mark; describes the product in terms of ingredients or components, weight, or volume. It informs consumers when the product expires. It classifies the product based on quality or size and identifies the manufacturer or the distributor. It has the UPC for easy inventory processing and scanning. The package also promotes the product because the label advertises the product to the consumer every time the consumer handles it.

4. **Analyze the different dimensions of the product mix.**
   The product mix is the complete assortment of products that a company offers to its target consumers. The product line consists of the related brands in the same product category. Other important product dimensions are the product length (the total number of brands in the product mix), the product width (the total number of product lines the company offers), and the product depth (the number of different offerings for a product category).

5. **Describe the new product development process and the different degrees of product newness.**
The new product development process starts with idea generation, inside and outside the company. The next step involves idea screening using predetermined criteria, followed by concept development and evaluation. Product business analysis determines the extent to which the product is likely to be viable. In the next stage—product design and development—product prototypes are developed and evaluated by target consumers. Test marketing involves great expense on the part of the company. It also leaves the company vulnerable to competitive idea theft. The final stage—launching—requires significant commitment to the product and to the target market. There are different types of new products: products that are new to an existing market or new to an existing company; new lines (i.e., new products or product lines to a company but for a company already operating in that market); new items in an existing product line for the company; modifications to an existing company product; and innovations.

6. **Examine the new product diffusion process and the different categories of product adopters.**
The new product diffusion process involves the following stages: innovators, early adopters, early majority, late majority, and laggards. Product diffusion begins when innovators try the product during the introduction stage of the PLC. If the product is successful, then early adopters will start using it. These are opinion leaders who others will follow. The early majority is ready to try the new product after it is established and prices have come down. The late majority purchases the product only during the mature stage of the PLC when competition is high, prices are lower, and product differentiation has occurred. The laggards resist the new product and buy only when older alternatives are not available.

7. **Address the different stages of the product life cycle.**
The first stage of the PLC is the introduction stage, when the product is first introduced to the market. The product most likely has no or only minimal competition, and it is targeted to innovators who are willing to try new products and spend substantial amounts for the product. The firm has negative profits in the sense that it is attempting to recover product development costs. In the growth stage, sales and profits are increasing rapidly, and more and more competitors are offering the product. In the maturity stage, there is a slowdown in sales growth as the product is adopted by most target consumers and as profits level off or decline primarily as a result of intense price competition. Products are rapidly losing ground to new technologies or product alternatives in the decline stage. Sales and profits are rapidly declining, and the firm is likely to cut back on production, distribution, and promotional support.

8. **Examine the challenges involved in managing the product portfolio.**
The product portfolio consists of the totality of products managed by the company as separate businesses. A popular matrix used for portfolio assessment is the Boston Consulting Group growth-share matrix. Its assumption is that a company should have a portfolio of products with different growth rates and different market shares to be successful. The matrix consists of cash cows, dogs, question marks or problem children, and stars. A product-market opportunity matrix is used to identify future products that companies should consider for their portfolio. Companies have the option to pursue one of four strategies: market penetration, market development, product development, and diversification.

Key Terms

Augmented product (217)
Battle of the brands (223)
Brand (219)
Brand character (or trade character) (221)
Brand equity (or franchise) (220)
Brand extensions (225)
Brand logo (221)
Brand mark (221)
Brand name (220)
Cash cows (238)
Co-branding (224)
Continuous innovations (231)
Controlled test marketing (232)
Convenience goods (218)
Core product (217)
Crowdsourcing (229)
Decline stage (236)
Diversification (239)
Dogs (238)
Durable goods (219)
Dynamically continuous innovations (231)
Early adopters (234)
Early majority (234)
Emergency goods (219)
Expected (or actual) product (217)
Fad (236)
Family branding (or blanket branding) (225)
Fashion (236)
Generics (223)
Growth stage (236)
Growth-share matrix (237)
Heterogeneous shopping goods (219)
Homogeneous shopping goods (219)
Impulse goods (218)
Innovators (234)
Laggards (235)
Late majority (235)
Licensing (223)
Line extension (224)
Manufacturers' brands (or national brands) (223)
Market development (239)
Market penetration (239)
Maturity stage (236)
Multibranding (225)
Non-durable goods (218)
Package (226)
Preference goods (219)
Private label brands (223)
Product depth (227)
Product development (239)
Product diffusion (233)
Product introduction stage (236)
Product length (227)
Product life cycle (plc) (235)
Product line (227)
Product mix (227)
Product portfolio (237)
Product width (227)
Product-market opportunity matrix (238)
Question marks (238)
Radical innovations (or discontinuous innovations) (231)
Shopping goods (219)
Simulated test marketing (232)
Specialty goods (219)
Staples (218)
Stars (238)
Style (236)
Trademark (221)
Trialability (232)

Discussion Questions

1. Examine the concepts of core, expected, and augmented products. Give an example of each concept in relation to a product you recently purchased.
2. Review the product classifications presented in the chapter. Provide two examples of each that are not given in the textbook.
3. If you were going to list the top five brands for you personally, what would they be? Explain why you chose these particular brands.
4. Identify three brand characters and three brand logos. What makes these characters and logos memorable?

5. Think of brand names for medicine that you do not normally take. What traits of these brand names made them memorable?
6. Go to Unilever's home page and access the brands sold to consumers in the United States. Comment on the product depth, width, and length.
7. Many products are advertised in the United States as "new and improved." What does this description mean in terms of new product classifications?
8. Recall the last time you remember a product launch that was accompanied by aggressive advertising. What brand was advertised? What traits of the introductory communication campaign do you recall?
9. Describe the PLC and the activities involved at each stage. Offer examples of products at each of the four stages.
10. Differentiate between a fad and a fashion. Can a fashion be really a fad? When can marketing managers find out whether this is the case? Can marketing managers influence fashion and fads? Explain.

Review Questions

True or False

1. The expected, actual product is enhanced by the addition of extra and unsolicited services or benefits to the consumer, which help promote the purchase.
2. Impulse goods are those products bought routinely, such as groceries.
3. Manufacturing brands are also sold as private labels.
4. Licensing involves the owner of the brand name allowing a manufacturer or reseller to sell the product under the owner's brand name in return for a licensing fee.
5. Packaging has a minimal influence on a product's purchase price.
6. Companies' success depends on internal research and brainstorming sessions to generate new product ideas.
7. Test marketing involves offering a new product to a group of stores or on a limited basis to see how it will perform.
8. Innovators and early adopters constitute the majority of consumers throughout the life cycle of a product.
9. The maturity stage of the PLC is characterized by increasing competition, with new product variations offered to the market, and rapid market adoption.

Multiple Choice

10. The set of brand assets and liabilities linked to a brand and its name is
    a. brand equity
    b. brand image
    c. brand identity
    d. the brand trademark
11. Which of the following categories characterize brand names? Brand names
    a. are easy to pronounce and memorize.
    b. suggest product benefits.
    c. are easy to translate into other languages.
    d. all of the above.
12. The battle of the brands is defined as
    a. a conflict between manufacturers and retailers to promote their own brands.
    b. a similarity in packaging of manufacturers' and retailers' brand products.
    c. the selling of the retailer brand at a lower price than the national brand.
    d. all of the above.
13. Which of the following categories is related to the product mix?
    a. product length
    b. product width
    c. product depth
    d. all of the above

14. The product introduction stage is characterized by
    a. negative or low profits.
    b. rapid product adoption.
    c. high level of competition.
    d. all of the above.
15. Which of the following groups in the growth-share matrix is characterized by low market share and high-growth products that require more cash investment than they generate?
    a. cash cows
    b. dogs
    c. question marks (or problem children)
    d. stars

Answers: (1) False, (2) False, (3) False, (4) True, (5) False, (6) False, (7) True, (8) False, (9) False, (10) a, (11) d, (12) a, (13) d, (14) a, (15) c

Case: GoPro Cameras

In July 2014, investors coughed up $437 million in the camera maker at the company's initial public offering, with GoPro valued at almost $3 billion at the time. That is quite impressive for a company that made its profit by making just one camera and gadgets for the camera, to mount it everywhere, on people, babies, eagles, you name it. Early sales and profits surged during the early stages of the product's life cycle. GoPro made the world's most versatile cameras that produce high-definition video photography. The cameras are small, lightweight, waterproof, wearable, and gear-mountable.

Switching from a GoPro is a low-cost proposition for consumers who like to purchase the newest gadget to record their latest adventures. Switching to a new, more established brand, like Cannon, is not exactly a stretch. GoPro could either create more and more innovative cameras to keep customers interested, or hold content captive. Apparently, GoPro is doing both, spending 12 percent of revenue on R&D, creating, among others, a gooseneck and a bracket that works with night-vision goggles, and packaging its videos into its media platform. The company already has content deals with Virgin America and Xbox Live. Moreover, last year, people loaded to YouTube 2.8 years' worth of video with GoPro in the title. However, individuals making videos with a GoPro will not hand them over for free.

Source: Mauricio Graiki/Shutterstock

GoPro's latest venture is in drone photography. The venture has met some obstacles, causing a recall of the company's drones. But, renewed effort, R&D dollars, and determination have created a successful drone camera product launch. GoPro believed drone photography is now in the growth stage of the product life cycle and expands the company's target audience beyond thrill seekers and extreme sports enthusiasts. In order to reach only where a drone can, its HERO 9 Black camera is the newest in GoPro's flagship range, and quite simply the most powerful and feature-rich action camera in the world right now. It is a super-versatile action camera that boasts a sleek frameless design, the most effective image stabilization available, an intuitive user interface with superb new preset modes, and its all-but-bombproof construction you can expect from GoPro (including waterproofing to 30+ ft. without a case).

Case Questions

1. Is the GoPro camera a fad, fashion, or style? Explain.
2. What life cycle stage would you attribute to the GoPro camera? Justify your answer.
3. Comment on the degree of product newness for the GoPro drone camera.
4. Examine the five categories of new product adopters. Which group is now adopting the

GoPro camera? What about the drone camera technology? Explain your rationale for both.

5. If you were in charge of product development at GoPro, what new products would you investigate for the future? Why?

Sources: Adapted from Ruth Hamilton, "How's this for a Father's Day gift? GoPro HERO8 drops to cheapest price ever," Smarter Living, accessed at https://www.t3.com/us/news/hows-this-for-a-fathers-day-gift-gopro-hero8-drops-to-cheapest-price-ever on June 4, 2020; Kyle Stock, "GoPro Goes Big, but Customers Are Still Free to Jump," Bloomberg Businessweek, June 26, 2014.

Endnotes

1. www.rollingstones.com, accessed February 10, 2020; Ian Mirlin, "The World's Greatest Rock 'n' Roll Brand," *Marketing Magazine* 107, no. 43 (October 18, 2002): 16.
2. Theodore Levitt, "Marketing Success through Differentiation—Of Anything," *Harvard Business Review* (January–February, 1980): 83–91; Levitt, T. (1983). *The marketing imagination.* New York: Free Press. Kotler, P. (2016). Principles of marketing. Boston: Pearson.
3. Casey Donoho, "Classifying Services from a Consumer Perspective," *The Journal of Services Marketing* 10, no. 6 (1996): 33–44.
4. Interbrand, Best Global Brands 2019, https://www.interbrand.com/best-brands/best-global-brands/2019
5. See Forbes, "The counterfeit problem and how retailers can fight back in 2020, https://www.forbes.com/sites/forbestechcouncil/2020/03/17/the-counterfeit-problem-and-how-retailers-can-fight-back-in-2020/#4cce42131f32; Fast Company, "Counterfeiting is a billion dollar problem. COVID-19 has made it far worse," May 4, 2020, https://www.fastcompany.com/90500123/counterfeiting-is-a-billion-dollar-problem-covid-19-has-made-it-far-worse; CNBC, "A new bill could make e-commerce companies for counterfeits sold on their platform, March 2, 2020, https://www.cnbc.com/2020/03/02/shop-safe-act-2020-cracks-down-on-counterfeits-on-ecommerce-platforms.html; Washington Post, "How Amazon's quest for more, cheaper products has resulted in flea market fakes, November 14, 2019, https://www.washingtonpost.com/technology/2019/11/14/how-amazons-quest-more-cheaper-products-has-resulted-flea-market-fakes/?arc404=true
6. Dexter Roberts, Frederik Balfour, Paul Magnuson, Pete Engardio, and Jennifer Lee, "China's Pirates: It's Not Just Little Guys—State-Owned Factories Add to the Plague of Fakes," *Business Week* no. 3684 (June 5, 2000): 26, 44.
7. Brandon A. Sullivan and Steven M. Chermak, "Product Counterfeiting and the Media: Examining News Sources Used in the Construction of Product Counterfeiting as a Social Problem," *International Journal of Comparative and Applied Criminal Justice,* Vol. 30, 4, 15 November 2013, 295-316; Dexter Roberts, Frederik Balfour, Paul Magnuson, Pete Engardio, and Jennifer Lee, "China's Pirates: It's Not Just Little Guys—State-Owned Factories Add to the Plague of Fakes," *Business Week* no. 3684 (June 5, 2000): 26, 44.
8. Louis Biscotti, "Private labels roar at retail," *Forbes*, May 2, 2019, https://www.forbes.com/sites/louisbiscotti/2019/05/02/private-label-brands-roar-at-retail/#16e7e9e78990
9. Louis Vuitton, "Louis Vuitton and BMW partner to create luggage of the future, April 2, 2020, https://uk.louisvuitton.com/eng-gb/articles/louis-vuitton-bmw-i-partner-to-create-luggage-of-the-future
10. Clay Chander, "Dyson CEO: $400 Supersonic Hair Dryer Has Been 'Very, Very Successful,'" *Fortune*, March 18, 2019, https://fortune.com/2019/03/18/dyson-ceo-jim-rowan
11. Jessica Day, "How to Use Crowdsourcing for Product Innovation," *Idea Scale*, June 28, 2016, https://ideascale.com/how-to-use-crowdsourcing-for-product-innovation
12. Industry Week, "Motorola Claims Chinese Rival Stole Wireless Radio Technology," November 2, 2019, https://www.industryweek.com/technology-and-iiot/article/22028539/motorola-claims-chinese-rival-stole-wireless-radio-technology
13. Sean O'Kane, "Tesla's readying a 'million mile' battery that could greatly lower the cost of EVs," *The Verge*, May 14, 2020, https://www.theverge.com/2020/5/14/21258650/tesla

-million-mile-battery-catl-china-kilowatt-hour -cost-range-improvement

14. Patrick Campbell, "The 5 Step Process to Perfecting Your Product Launch Strategy," ProfitWell, June 14, 2020, https://www.profitwell.com/blog/product-launch-strategy
15. Everett M. Rogers, Diffusion of Innovations, 5th Edition, 2003 Diffusion of Innovations, 5th Edition, Free Press, New York, NY.
16. Boston Consulting Group, The Growth Share Matrix, accessed at https://www.bcg.com/about/our-history/growth-share-matrix.aspx on June 1, 2020.
17. H. Igor Ansoff, "Strategies for Diversification," *Harvard Business Review* 35 (September–October 1957): 113–124.

Services Marketing

Source: Jirapong Manustrong/Shutterstock

Chapter Outline

9-1 Chapter Overview
9-2 The Service Sector
9-3 Characteristics of Services
9-4 The Purchase Process for Services
9-5 Service Quality
Case: First Eastern Shore Bank

Learning Objectives

Ivelin Radkov/Shutterstock

After studying this chapter, you should be able to:

- Discuss the impact of the services sector on the gross domestic product and what has led to the growth of the service sector.
- Identify the four unique characteristics of services and how each affects the marketing of services.
- Explain the components of the purchasing process for services.
- Identify the factors that affect the purchase decision during the prepurchase phase of the purchase process.
- Discuss the relevant elements of the service encounter and why they are important.
- Describe the postpurchase evaluation of services and its impact on future purchase behavior.
- Discuss how service quality is measured.
- Describe an effective service recovery process.

Source: MinDof/Shutterstock

9-1 Chapter Overview

Digital cameras and smart phones have replaced traditional cameras, as consumers readily embrace easy picture taking and sharing of pictures. With the traditional camera technology, individuals dropped off their film at the local drugstore to be processed. With digital photography becoming mainstream, drugstores were forced to adapt the services they offer, and many left the photo-processing business altogether. Consumers today make their own prints rather than rely on a commercial photo-processing service. Most save, store, and keep their images in digital format, which has led to online photo printing services to become the new standard. Newer sites like Snapfish and Shutterfly and traditional providers like Walgreens and CVS offer online photo services such as storage, sorting, editing, sharing, and printing of photos. They also provide software that allows people to edit and touch up images, or the service will do it for them; they can even print large, high quality canvases for wall mounting. With new technology ranging from digital cameras to high-quality camera phones, such as the three-cameras iPhone 12 Pro Max come changes in services supporting the technology. Printing from film is in the decline stage of the product life cycle (PLC), but this decline has spurred a whole new industry, now in its growth stage: digital online photography services. Another service is likely nearing decline: the photography studio: nowadays, everyone is a photographer, taking high-resolution portrait and low-light photos and manage their photo collection with Snapfish and Shutterfly.

Services are an integral part of the U.S. economy. They furnish the majority of jobs and contribute the major portion of the nation's gross national product (GNP). Some marketers would consider that marketing of goods and services is the same, whereas others will contend that it takes a different marketing approach. Although it is true that the principles are the same, the unique characteristics of services discussed in Section 9-3 do make it apparent that the application of those principles may vary. Services face some unique challenges that often require a different approach–the purchase process for services is described in Section 9-4. Understanding how services are purchased, consumed, and evaluated is critical to understanding how services are marketed. Section 9-5 presents the concept of service quality, how it is measured, and what happens when a service failure occurs.

9-2 The Service Sector

When you think of services, it is helpful to think of a continuum with pure services at one extreme and pure goods at the other extreme. A pure service does not have any type of good attached to it. Examples would include personal fitness training, legal services, medical services, and driver education instruction. A pure good is something that is sold without any type of service component attached, such as a computer,

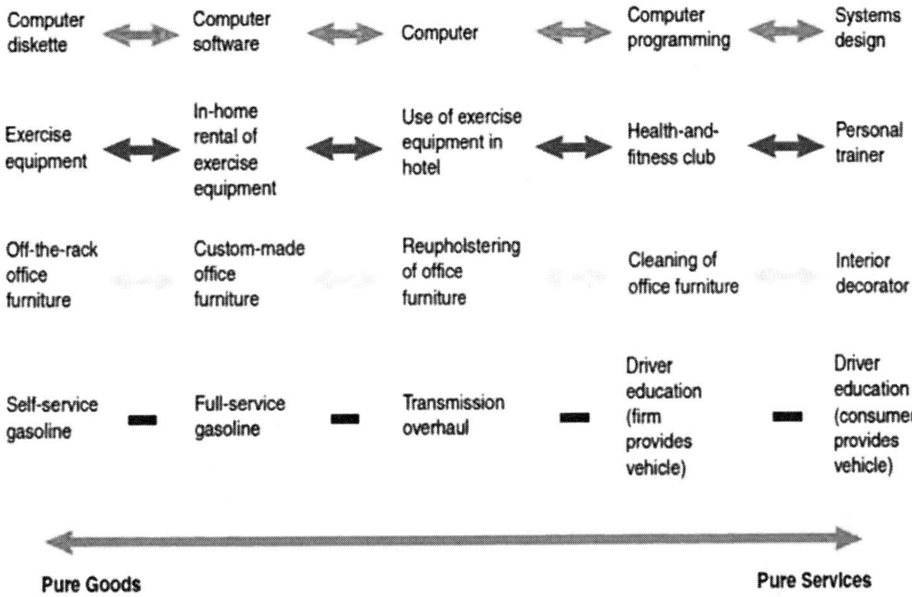

FIGURE 9-1 The Goods and Service Continuum

exercise equipment, socks, or gasoline at a self-serve convenience store. Most products fall somewhere between a pure service and a pure good. A restaurant is a service because you are paying the business to prepare the food (a good) for you. Computers are a good, but if you have difficulty with your computer, you can call a toll-free number for assistance, contact the company online, or call a local computer repair company. Figure 9-1 illustrates this goods and services continuum.

Services are a vital component of the U.S. economy and that of most industrialized nations. The service sector in the United States accounts for almost 80% percent of the country's gross domestic product (GDP); within services, finance, insurance, and real estate, what we refer to as Wall Street, accounted for a fifth of the total economy. On the other hand, manufacturing's share to GDP is 11 percent, while agriculture, mining, utilities, and construction accounts for 8.1 percent of GDP.[1]

Figure 9-2 highlights the size of the service sector in a few countries throughout various regions of the world. The GDP is the sum of all goods and services produced within the boundaries of a country. In the United States the GDP would include the production by U.S.-owned and foreign-owned firms. Goods and services produced by U.S.-owned firms outside the country are not calculated in the GDP of the United States.

Between 2018 and 2028, the service sector in the United States is expected to have the most job growth, with professions such as personal care aides, food preparation and serving workers including fast food, registered nurses, and home health aides growing the most in terms of number,[2] reflecting needs of an aging population—see Figure 9-3 for information regarding the top ten professions with the highest growth.

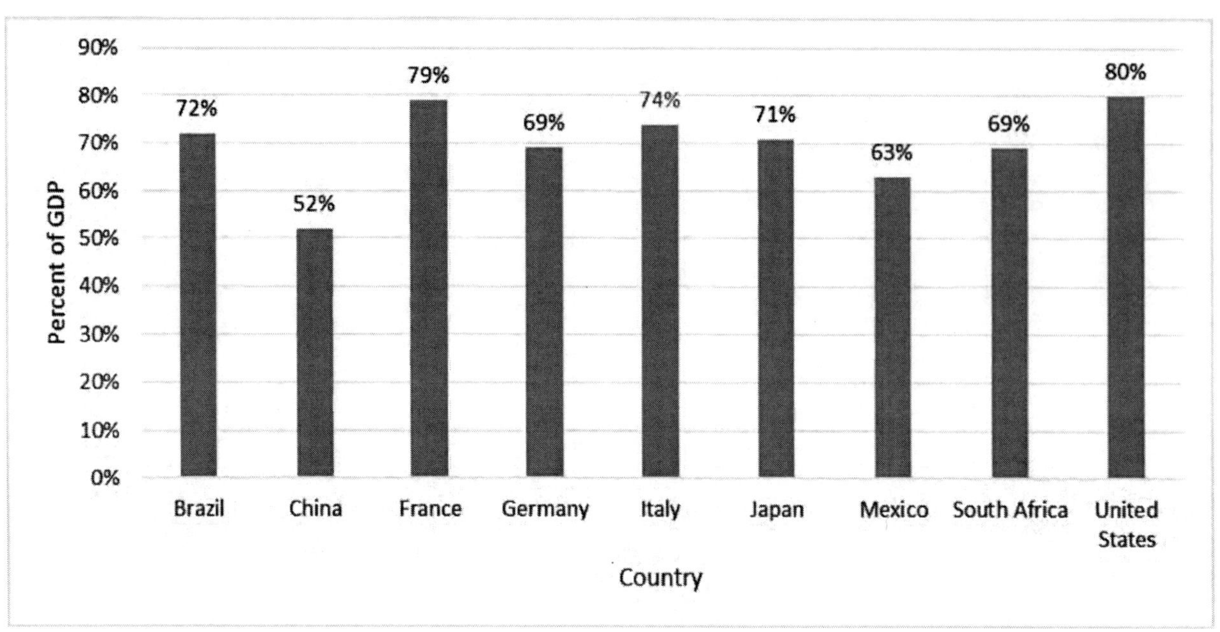

FIGURE 9-2 The Service Sector as a Percentage of the GDP in Select Countries
Source: CIA Fact Book, accessed at https://www.cia.gov/library/publications/the-world-factbook/fields/214.html May 22, 2020

Rank	Occupation	2018	2028	Number	Percent
1	Personal care aides	2,421.2	3,302.1	881.0	36.4
2	Food prep and serving workers, including fast food	3,704.2	4,344.3	640.1	17.3
3	Registered Nurses	3,059.8	3,431.3	371.5	12.1
4	Home health aides	831.8	1,136.6	304.8	36.6
5	Cooks, restaurant	1,362.3	1,661.3	299.0	21.9
6	Software developers, applications	944.2	1,185.7	241.5	25.6
7	Waiters and Waitresses	2,634.6	2,804.8	170.2	6.5
8	General and operations managers	2,376.4	2,541.4	165.0	6.9
9	Janitors and cleaners (not maids, housekeeping)	2,404.4	2,564.2	159.8	6.6
10	Medical Assistants	686.6	841.5	154.9	22.6

FIGURE 9-3 The 10 Occupations with the Largest Employment Growth in Terms of Numbers (in thousands)
Source: https://www.bls.gov/emp/tables/occupations-most-job-growth.htm, accessed May 23, 2020

The service sector's rapid growth is primarily the result of nations shifting from a manufacturing-based economy to a service-oriented economy. This shift is attributed to the move to an information society, to an aging population, longer life expectancies, increased leisure time, higher per-capita income, increased time pressure, more women in the workforce, sedentary lifestyles, changing social and cultural values, and advances in technology **(see Figure 9-4)**. The aging population and increase in life

- Advances in computers and telecommunications
- Aging population
- Longer life expectancies
- Increased leisure time
- Higher per-capita income
- Increased time pressure
- More women in workforce
- Sedentary lifestyles
- Changing social and cultural values
- Advances in technology

FIGURE 9-4 Factors Influencing the Shift to a Services Economy

expectancy have spurred the need for medical services, nursing homes, and limited-care facilities. More women in the workforce has resulted in families with higher incomes, which translates into more discretionary income to spend on leisure-type goods and services, such as entertainment, dining out, and vacations. With both work and family responsibilities, individuals are stressed for time. Consequently, services that save time, such as housecleaning and lawn care, are in higher demand.

Advances in technology have led to a rise in the demand for maintenance and computer-related services. Even automobiles have become more computerized, requiring skilled mechanics. Because of cultural and social changes, society no longer places a stigma on individuals who hire businesses to take care of personal chores. Society no longer expects mothers to stay home to care for their children, cook the meals, and clean the house, or men to mow the lawn and do home repairs.

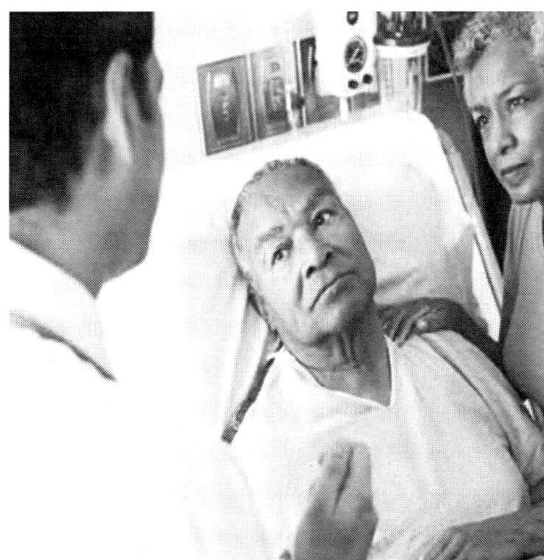

Source: Monkey Business Images/Shutterstock

The service sector is a critical component of our economy, and the successful marketing of services requires an understanding of how services are different from goods. Although the principles of marketing are the same, the application of those principles will be different for a service operation.

9-3 Characteristics of Services

Intangibility The lack of tangible assets of a service that can be seen, touched, smelled, heard, or tasted before a purchase.

Perishability The inability of a service to be inventoried or stored.

Inseparability The simultaneous production and consumption of a service.

Variability The unwanted or random levels of service quality customers receive when they patronize a service.

Services possess four inherent characteristics not found in goods: Intangibility, perishability, inseparability, and variability **(see Figure 9-5).**[3] **Intangibility** refers to the lack of tangible assets that can be seen, touched, smelled, heard, or tasted before a purchase. **Perishability** refers to the inability of a service to be inventoried or stored. **Inseparability** is the simultaneous production and consumption of a service, and **variability** is the unwanted or random levels of service quality customers receive when they patronize a service. These characteristics create unique marketing challenges for services not only in terms of attracting new customers but also in retaining current customers.

9-3a Intangibility

Services vary in the degree to which they are intangible. Services such as a music concert, legal counsel, medical treatments, and a college education are highly intangible. The service cannot be seen, touched, smelled, heard, or tasted before the purchase. However, for each of these services, tangible items are used to perform the service: chairs, a stage, as well as instruments, and loudspeakers for a concert; office, desks, law books, computers for legal services; medical instruments and equipment for a medical practice; and buildings, classrooms, overhead projectors, cameras, and computers for a university. The actual outcome of these services, however, cannot be seen until the service is performed or the event has taken place.

Some services offer a tangible good with their service, but the service itself is still intangible because consumers are purchasing the service, not

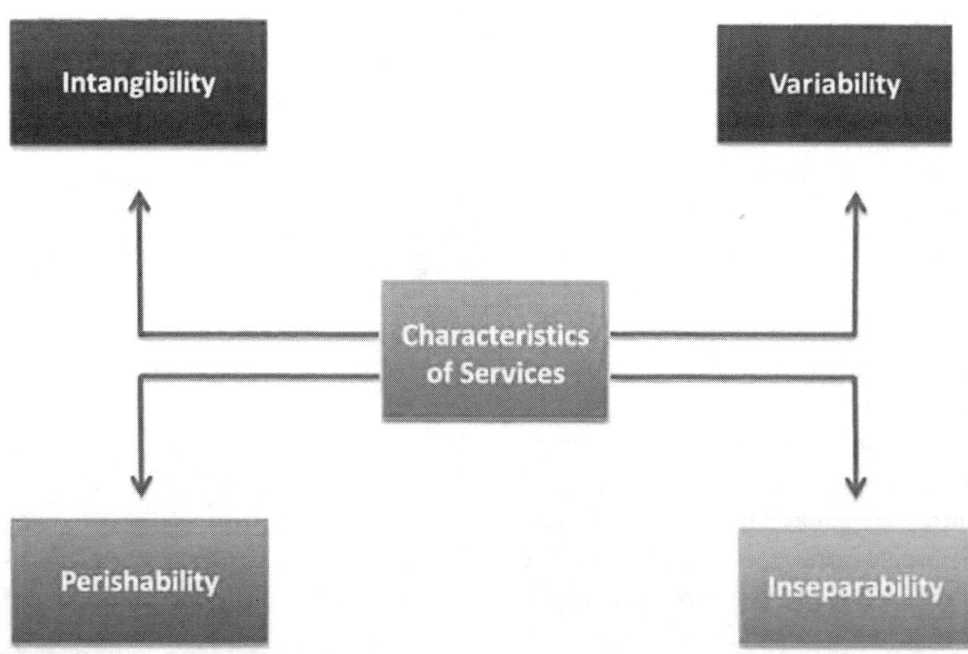

FIGURE 9-5 Characteristics of Services

Source: ImageFoto/Shutterstock

the good. For instance, restaurants offer food and a dentist uses crowns and other materials to perform his or her work. In the case of the restaurant, consumers are paying the restaurant to prepare the food for them. An evaluation of the service is based on how well the restaurant prepares the food and serves it. In the second case, patients are paying the dentist to repair a tooth, not just to supply the tooth crown and other materials. The quality of both services will be based on how well the service is performed as well as how consumers are treated by the service personnel.

Because of intangibility, consumers have greater difficulty in judging the quality of a service before purchase. A good can be examined in advance, offering consumers some idea of what they are purchasing. Services are much more difficult to examine in advance. The haircut you receive at a beauty salon cannot be known until the beautician performs the work. This intangibility makes the purchase of a service a higher risk.

To reduce the purchase risk consumers face, service firms strive to reduce the level of intangibility through the strategies shown in **Figure 9-6**. Attorneys can feature tangible assets such as their building, their office, or other personnel in an advertisement that will convey high quality legal services. A college can feature its facilities, students, athletes, and professors. Using testimonials of students for a college and clients for a legal practice can reduce the level of risk and intangibility.

Personal sources of information and word-of-mouth communications are excellent ways of making a service appear more tangible. Employees can talk about the service. A beautician, through communicating with the customer, can reduce the intangibility of getting a haircut. An attorney, during an initial visit, can discuss the process he or she will use in handling the case. Because a service is intangible, the communication becomes an important element in marketing the service. Although word-of-mouth communication from one customer to another is the best,

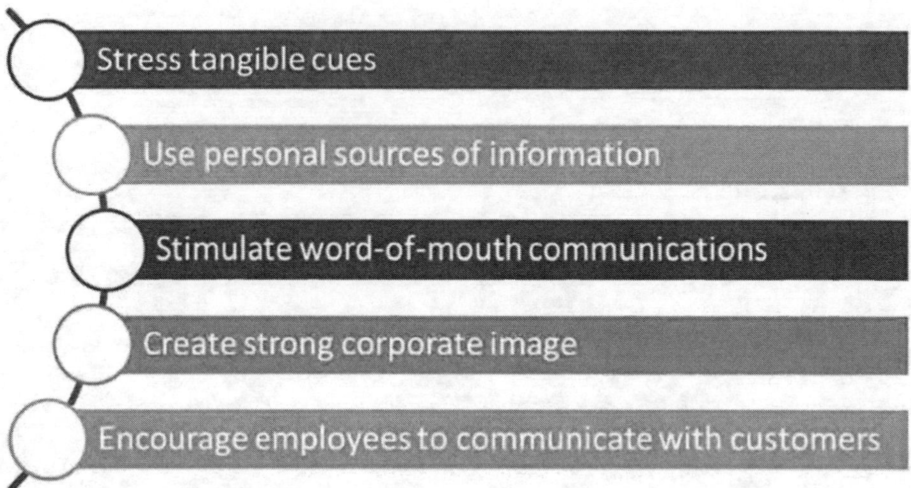

Stress tangible cues
Use personal sources of information
Stimulate word-of-mouth communications
Create strong corporate image
Encourage employees to communicate with customers

FIGURE 9-6 Strategies to Reduce the Intangibility of Services

anything a service can do to communicate with consumers about the service will help reduce the intangibility.

9-3b Perishability

The second characteristic of services is perishability. If a sweater does not sell today, a retailer can keep it and sell it at a later time. If the sale occurs much later, the retailer will sell it at a discount but, most likely, will still cover the cost of the sweater. This feature allows firms to mass-produce goods and store them in warehouses and in retail stores until consumers are ready to make a purchase. For services, this is not possible. Airlines that had to ground their fleet during the COVID-19 pandemic will never be able to recover the lost revenue.

The situation was similar for concert and sporting events. The Kennedy Center (John F. Kennedy Center for the Performing Arts in Washington, D.C.) cancelled its schedule from March to December, 2020. The National Football League was advised not to play or to play in a bubble format, with players isolated and tested every day. The National Collegiate Athletic Association cancelled the March Madness men's Division I basketball tournament because of the virus, but the National Basketball Association started playing in late summer of 2020, as did Major League Baseball. In Europe, the German Bundesliga soccer games started early, in May.[4] All these events were attended in stadiums with stadiums' capacities greatly reduced. Sports teams will never be able to recover the lost revenue due to reduced stadium capacities, nor for lockdown periods, when all sports events were cancelled.

In normal situations, to reduce the negative impact of perishability, services can develop strategies to deal with fluctuating demand through simultaneously making adjustments in demand, supply, and capacity. The goal is to achieve parity among the three. At the optimum, demand will equal supply, which in turn will equal capacity.

Perishability for Beyoncé concerts can be managed in a number of ways. First, demand can be reduced through increasing ticket prices. As prices are increased, the number of people willing to pay the higher prices declines. Second, demand at various locations can be managed through a website that indicates sold-out concerts and locations where tickets are still available. This will shift some of the demand to locations where empty seats are still available. Beyoncé can manage the supply side of perishability by increasing the number of live concerts, thus allowing more people the opportunity to see her perform. The capacity component can be managed by finding larger facilities. Using all three components simultaneously, Beyoncé can maximize her revenue from the live concerts while providing fans the opportunity to see her perform. Her goal would be to fill every location to capacity with no empty seats and no fans turned away because the concert was sold out.

For a restaurant, the same principles apply. Demand can be managed through advertising, special promotions, and pricing. Having a higher dinner price will reduce demand during the evening dinner hours, whereas having a lower lunch price will stimulate demand at lunchtime. Advertising specials for breakfast meals will encourage people to eat breakfast at the restaurant. Supply can be managed by hiring part-time employees during meal times. Unlike the Beyoncé concerts, a restaurant does not have the ability to expand its physical capacity. The number of customers it can have at any one time is controlled by the seating capacity of the facility.

Managing perishability is critical to the success of a service. When demand is less than supply, revenue is lost and the firm has excess capacity. A facility or equipment that is not used to capacity increases the total average unit costs to operate. For example, a movie theater that has a capacity of 175 will have a higher total average cost per customer to operate when the theater averages only 90 people per night, compared with 160 per night. Fixed costs remain the same, but the theater has fewer customers to spread the costs over.

When demand exceeds capacity, potential revenue is lost. Because the facility is filled or equipment is being used to its full capacity, businesses often do not worry about the customers who are turned away. But if customers cannot get tickets to a basketball game or make an appointment with an attorney, they will seek other alternatives. The basketball fan may switch to another sport and never come back to watching basketball games, and the person seeking legal counsel may choose another attorney. In the long run, these lost customers can be detrimental to a firm that may need them during a later time, when demand is less than supply.

Source: Drazen Zigic/Shutterstock

9-3c Inseparability

Goods can be produced in one location, warehoused in another, and then sold at a later time in a retail store; services cannot. For example, getting a cavity filled in a tooth involves a patient going to a dentist and being present while the service is being performed. Because the service must be performed and consumed at the same time, the quality of the service is highly dependent on the ability of the service provider and the quality of interaction between the service provider and the customer.

To reduce the importance of the customer-employee interaction, service firms look for methods of automating their service through the use of machines, computers, or other technology. The more that a service can be automated, the less it will be reliant on human performance, and the greater will be its availability to consumers. Banks mostly rely on automated teller machines (ATMs) and online banking to conduct business. Both provide efficiency for the bank and convenience for the customer since they are available 24/7. Neither requires employees to perform the transaction at the time it is desired by customers. As a result, the cost involved for a bank to handle transactions is reduced.

Service providers such as hair salons have a more difficult situation because they have a high degree of inseparability. Customers are involved in the production of the service, other customers are usually present, and centralized mass production of the service is not possible. Because of the importance of the customer-service provider interaction, it is essential for service businesses like hair salons and restaurants to reduce any negative consequences that might be due to the inseparability. These negative consequences can be reduced if companies emphasize the selection and training of employees. Training should include how to perform the service, as well as how to interact with customers. This training will increase the probability of a positive interaction between the customer and the service provider. During the COVID-19 pandemic, hair salons enforcing appropriate protocols for disinfection, distancing, and mask coverage instilled confidence and provided reassurance to consumers that they would be safe and protected during the interaction with the service provider.

Because of inseparability, the number of customers that a hair salon can serve is limited by the time required for each haircut and the size of the facility, and, during the COVID-19 pandemic by regulations requiring distancing and having one customer per service provider. If a hair salon has six beauticians and six chairs, then only six customers can be served at one time unless other customers are under the hair dryer or waiting for a perm to set. A hair salon can reduce the negative impact of this inseparability and serve more customers by opening multiple sites. Because customers have to be present for the service, this strategy offers customers multiple sites to receive the service. The multiple-site strategy will also reduce the number of customers present at any one time in a facility. This should allow employees more time with each customer, increasing the quality of service and interaction with the customer.

9-3d Variability

The last unique characteristic of services is variability. Variability is primarily caused by the human element (although machines may malfunction). Each employee will perform a service in a slightly different way with various levels of quality, and even the same employee will provide different levels of service from one time to another. In getting a haircut, the outcome will differ if you use a different beautician each time you go to a salon. The outcome also will vary from one time to another even if the same person is cutting your hair.

Although machines are much more reliable, differences in service can occur. If the computerized testing equipment at an auto repair facility does not operate properly, it may not detect a problem with an engine or it may misdiagnose the problem. However, when these problems do occur, the problems often are not with the computerized equipment but with the person operating the equipment.

Although most variability is caused by the service provider, it also can be caused by a variance in the inputs. Computer consultants staffing hotlines face the challenge of dealing with the various levels of knowledge and expertise customers bring to the service process. The same would be true for a consulting service handling situations for various clients.

Because of this variability characteristic of services, standardization and quality control are the primary methods used to ensure a consistent level of quality across different service providers and across different service experiences with the same provider. A restaurant such as McDonald's will industrialize operations. In this context, **industrialization** refers to the use of machines and standardized operating procedures to increase the productivity and efficiency of a business. Hamburgers, French fries, and other foods are prepared in advance and put in warming bins. By producing these items in advance, more customers can be served during peak demand times. Employees are also trained to follow a specific procedure in preparing each food item. Through standardization and industrialization, customers can expect the same quality of food and service at all of the McDonald's locations.

Industrialization The use of machines and standardized operating procedures to increase the productivity and efficiency of a business.

Source: Iakov Filimonov/Shutterstock

Keep in mind that variability refers to unwanted or random variations in service quality. Thus, a restaurant like Outback Steakhouse will use industrialization and standardization procedures to improve productivity, but customers do not all want their food exactly the same. The cooking of steaks must be customized to meet the customer's desire, or a dish that has shrimp on it may be cooked without the shrimp upon a customer's request. Customers at Outback want food prepared differently. What they do not want is unwanted or random variance in quality. Therefore, to reduce this unwanted or random variability, it is the responsibility of the wait staff to ask how food items are to be prepared. This will ensure that the particular requests of each customer are met and the unwanted variability in the service does not occur.

To be successful, service businesses must understand the characteristics of intangibility, perishability, inseparability, and variability. For examples of all four unique characteristics of services, see **Figure 9-7**.

9-4 The Purchase Process for Services

Because of the unique characteristics of services, it is beneficial to examine the services purchase process. When you understand the process consumers use in choosing and evaluating a service, developing an effective marketing approach will be easier. The purchase process for services can be divided into three phases: the prepurchase phase, the service encounter, and the postpurchase phase. During the prepurchase phase, consumers evaluate alternatives, make a purchase decision, and finalize a brand choice. At some point after the decision is made, the consumer will move into the second stage, the service encounter, which is the actual interaction point between the customer and the service provider. Sometimes, the service encounter immediately follows the decision, whereas at other times, it may occur later. For example, when you are on vacation, deciding to patronize a particular restaurant and stopping to eat at the restaurant could be virtually simultaneous. At most other times, the decision to patronize a particular restaurant may be made hours or even days in advance. During the service encounter, the service is performed or provided to the customer. Because of the inseparability of services, what goes on at the time of consumption has a significant impact on the way customers evaluate the quality of the service and their future purchase decisions. The last phase of the services purchase process is the postpurchase evaluation, which begins upon completion of the service. During this phase, consumers make evaluations concerning the quality of service, their level of satisfaction or dissatisfaction, and future purchase intentions.

9-4a Prepurchase Phase

During the prepurchase phase, consumers evaluate alternatives and make purchase decisions. A number of factors affect the evaluation and decision. These factors can be grouped into internal factors, external factors, firm-produced factors, and perceived risk.

Intangibility

Definition: Lack of tangible assets that can be seen, touched, or smelled before the purchase.

Business-to-business example: A professional janitorial service cannot be seen, touched, or smelled before the service. A firm hiring a professional janitorial service will have to rely on what the janitorial service tells it about the services to be performed.

Consumer example: The food at a restaurant cannot be seen, touched, or smelled before the service. The waiter or waitress can describe the food, and the restaurant may have a picture of the food on the menu or a written description of the particular dish, but consumers cannot actually see what will be served to them.

Strategies to reduce negative impact: Intangibility can be reduced by stressing tangible cues when marketing the service, using personal sources of information, stimulating word-of-mouth communications, creating a strong corporate and brand image, and encouraging employees to communicate with the customers during the service.

Perishability

Definition: Inability of a service to be inventoried or stored.

Business-to-business example: The janitorial service cannot be inventoried or stored. Every day or week, depending on the contract, the service will have to be performed again. The same set of tasks will be performed each time the building is serviced.

Consumer example: The food is prepared when the customer places the order. Some food may be cooked in advance, but the actual order is prepared only after it is ordered. It cannot be inventoried or stored for a later time.

Strategies to reduce negative impact: The service firm has to develop strategies to deal with demand, supply, and capacity. The goal is for demand and supply to match, which should be close to the capacity of the firm. For example, when demand is high, the restaurant will need to expand supply by hiring additional wait-staff and cooks.

Inseparability

Definition: Simultaneous production and consumption of a service.

Business-to-business example: The janitorial service cannot be separated from the individuals doing the service, and it must be performed at the customer's place of business.

Consumer example: The restaurant prepares the food for a customer when it is ordered. The customer consumes the food at the restaurant, and the customer's perception of quality will be partly due to the customer's interaction with the restaurant employees.

Strategies to reduce negative impact: It is important for the service firm to hire competent employees and then train them to perform the service. The service firm needs a process for managing customers so customers will have positive feelings about the interaction between employees and themselves. Inseparability can also be managed by having additional restaurant locations and by offering carryout and home delivery services.

Variability

Definition: Unwanted or random levels of service quality that customers receive when they patronize a firm.

Business-to-business example: The quality of the service will depend on who does the work and how well they are trained.

Consumer example: The quality of service will depend on how well the cook prepares the food. Even the same cook may not prepare the food exactly the same way each time.

Strategies to reduce negative impact: Standardization and quality-control measures can reduce the variability of services. Standardization means that customers will tend to receive the same quality of service, regardless of who performs the service and when. In addition, if machines can be incorporated into the service, machines tend to be more consistent, in terms of quality production, than humans.

FIGURE 9-7 Understanding the Unique Characteristics of Services

Internal Factors

For most purchase situations, internal factors are the most critical. Internal factors consist of individual needs and wants of the consumer, past experience,

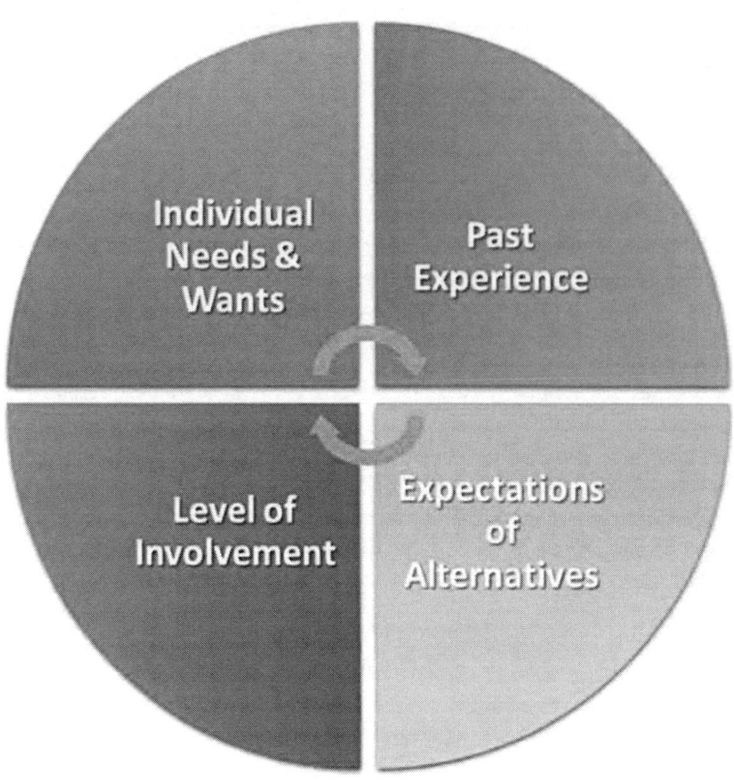

FIGURE 9-8 Internal Factors That Affect the Prepurchase Phase

expectations of the service alternatives, and level of purchase involvement **(see Figure 9-8)**. To understand these elements, assume that you are looking for a vacation spot for spring break. The most important internal element in the decision will be your particular needs and wants. What do you want to do during spring break? What types of activities do you want to participate in? If you want to go swimming, then you will likely choose the beach or a lake. If you want to go scuba diving, you may choose a resort that teaches scuba diving or has excellent scuba facilities. If you are interested in nightclubs, you will choose a larger city, but if you want peace and quiet, you will choose an isolated, out-of-the way location. If you want to snow ski, you will look for a place in the mountains. If you want to explore another country, then you may choose Europe or South America.

Source: Samot/Shutterstock

Your past experience will factor into this decision. If your past experience with a particular location was positive, then you will be more inclined to go back to the same place. If your past experience was negative, then it is highly probable that you will choose a different place for your spring break. The expectations of the various spring break locations will factor into your evaluation and decision. These expectations are based on past experiences, word-of-mouth communications from others, and promotional materials produced by the various resorts and spring break locations. The higher the expectations you develop for a specific location, the greater the likelihood you will choose that location. Of course, the reverse would also be true: The lower the expectations you have for a location, the less likely it will be chosen.

The last internal factor affecting your purchase decision in the prepurchase phase is the level of your involvement. Involvement refers to the level of mental and physical effort exerted by a consumer in selecting a good or service.[5] In high-involvement purchase decisions, consumers spend considerable time searching for information, both internally and externally. They are also inclined to spend more time in deliberating and weighing the various alternatives. In contrast, in low-involvement purchase decisions, consumers spend minimal time searching for information and in deliberation. In many cases, it becomes a habitual purchase that is performed with little thought. For example, selecting a car wash would be considered a low-involvement situation and would involve little thought or deliberation. In most cases, consumers patronize the car wash facility closest to them or one they have patronized in the past. Unless you are going back to the same location for spring break, it is likely that selecting a spring break location will be a high-involvement decision that will require searching for information and then carefully evaluating the alternatives.

External Factors

The external factors that influence the purchase decision during the prepurchase phase are the competitive options available, the social context of the purchase, and word-of-mouth communications **(see Figure 9-9)**. Going back to our example of a place for spring break, your decision will be influenced by the competitive options available to you. Some options will come from your own memory, others from individuals around you, and yet others through your external search for information on the Internet or

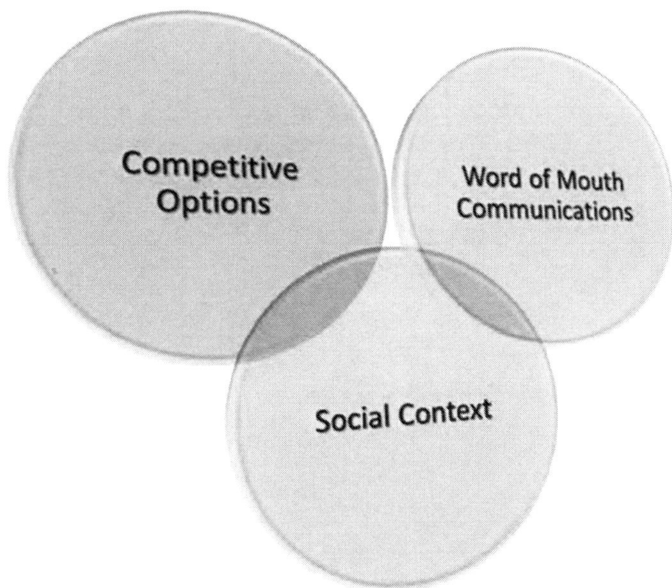

FIGURE 9-9 External Factors That Affect the Prepurchase Phase

other sources, such as an advertisement. If scuba diving is on your agenda for things to do, your options will be more limited because not all resorts and spring break locations are ideal for scuba diving.

For spring break, the social context of the purchase is usually very important. In fact, it may have a greater influence than even your own personal desires. If you want to spend spring break with college friends or family members, where you go will depend on where they want to go. Your choice will be more of a group decision than your individual decision unless you can convince everyone within your group to choose the location you desire.

An important impact on purchase decisions are assessments shared by acquaintances, known as word-of-mouth communications (WOM), as well as trusted reviews and comments in online communities, known as electronic word-of-mouth communications (eWOM). When selecting a service, consumers ask others for recommendations regarding destinations, believing that others' communications are more reliable than company communications. In choosing a spring break location, students will seek information from individuals who went on spring break last year, and they will read others' reviews to find out where they went, and how they liked it. While internal information may help narrow the list of possible locations to a smaller subset, external information can help students develop more concrete views of each location and influence choice.

Firm-Produced Factors

The firm-produced factors affecting the purchase decision include promotions, pricing, and distribution **(see Figure 9-10)**. From a consumer's viewpoint, firm-produced factors are the least reliable because consumers realize

FIGURE 9-10 Firm-produced Factors That Affect the Prepurchase Phase

that the goal of the firm is to consumers to make a purchase. From the service firm's perspective, firm-produced factors are its primary method of reaching consumers with information and persuading them to purchase its service. Firms have several forms of promotion that can be used, such as advertising, sales promotions, and personal selling. Testimonials are especially useful for services.

FIGURE 9-11 This Advertisement for a Fitness Club is Designed to Influence Consumers During the Prepurchase Phase
Source: HstrongART/Shutterstock

Service organizations can provide consumers with information that can be used as they make decisions about what service to purchase and which vendor to patronize. For spring break locations, advertising on college campuses and in newspapers in the area is an effective way to communicate with the target market. Social media, television, and radio ads can be used during the winter months to encourage students to start thinking about spring break and to book their location early. Often, special deals encourage college students to act. Special deals also encourage consumers to join a fitness club **(see Figure 9-11)**.

Pricing is an important element of the prepurchase evaluation process. Consumers often compare the prices charged by competing firms. For services, more so than for goods, prices are seen as an indicator of quality. An attorney who charges $200 per hour is normally perceived as more competent than an attorney who charges $75 an hour. A carpet-cleaning service that charges $49.99 per room will be seen as superior to one that charges $19.99 per room. This does not, however, mean that consumers will choose the higher-priced firm. They may choose the lower price for one of several reasons. They may not have the money to pay a higher price. They may feel the higher-priced service is overpriced. They may rationalize that, although the service quality will not be as good, it is still a good value for the price being charged.

For services, **service distribution** is defined as the availability and accessibility of a service to consumers. It would include the firm's physical location, its hours of operation, and its access availability. A bank may operate several branches and place ATMs at various locations. Although actual bank hours are limited, customers have 24-hour-a-day access to their accounts through ATMs and online banking.

Service distribution The availability and accessibility of a service to consumers.

Perceived Risk

The last factor in the prepurchase phase is perceived purchase risk. Because of the unique characteristics of services, the purchase decision for services is perceived to be a higher risk than for goods. Before a purchase, consumers will seek a means to reduce the risk involved in the decision, primarily through obtaining additional information. Consumers use the internal factors, external factors, and firm-produced factors just discussed to reduce this purchase risk.

Risk has two components: uncertainty and consequences. **Uncertainty** is the probability that a particular outcome or consequence will occur.

Uncertainty The probability that a particular outcome or consequence will occur.

Risk	Definition
Performance	The chance that the service will not perform or provide the benefit expected
Financial	The amount of monetary loss incurred if the service fails
Time-loss	The amount of time lost as a result of a service failure
Opportunity	The risk of losing other choices when one choice is selected
Psychological	The chance that the service will not fit the individual's self-concept
Social	The chance that the service will not meet the approval of others
Physical	The chance that the service will actually cause physical harm

FIGURE 9-12 Types of Perceived Purchase Risk

Consequence The degree of importance or danger of the outcome itself.

Consequence is the degree of importance or danger of the outcome itself. For example, there is risk in heart surgery. The uncertainty is the unknown probability of the surgery not being successful, and the consequence, if the surgery does not go well, is death or serious side effects. Because the procedure is now well developed and the probability of something going wrong during the surgery is low, most patients no longer view heart surgery as a high-risk medical procedure, even though the seriousness of the consequences is high.

In the purchasing of services, there are seven types of risk. They are performance risk, financial risk, time-loss risk, opportunity risk, psychological risk, social risk, and physical risk **(see Figure 9-12)**.

Performance risk The chance that the service will not perform or provide the benefit for which it was purchased.

Performance risk is the chance that the service will not perform or provide the benefit for which it was purchased. For example, in the selection of a spring break location, there is the risk that the services the resort promises to provide are not available or are performed poorly. For an automobile repair service, performance risk would be the garage not fixing the problem properly.

Financial risk The amount of monetary loss the consumer incurs if the service fails.

Time-loss risk The amount of time the consumer lost as a result of the failure of the service.

Financial risk is the amount of monetary loss incurred by the consumer if the service fails. Money invested in personal tutoring that does not help a student is money poorly spent, or money lost. Money spent on a haircut that is not satisfactory is lost. In addition to the financial loss, there is the possibility of time loss. **Time-loss risk** refers to the amount of time lost by the consumer as a result of the failure of the service. If a consumer has to return to a garage to have his or her car repaired again because the problem was not taken care of the first time, then the consumer has lost the time required to drop off the vehicle and pick it up. In addition, the consumer could not use the vehicle during the time it is in the shop the second time it is being repaired.

Opportunity risk The risk involved when consumers must choose one service over another.

Psychological risk The chance that the purchase of the service will not fit the individual's self-concept.

Opportunity risk refers to the risk involved when consumers must choose one service over another. After a spring break selection is made, the opportunity to go to other locations is lost. You will never know if the other locations would have been better or worse. **Psychological risk** is the chance that the purchase of the service will not fit the individual's self-concept, and **social risk** is the probability that a service will not meet with approval from others who are significant to the consumer making the purchase. Choosing a resort that friends do not like is a high risk for the person who values friendships. Choosing a resort that does not meet with your self-concept is equally risky. The last type of risk that consumers of services face is **physical risk**. Physical risk is the probability that a service will actually cause physical harm to the customer. Medical procedures, such as plastic surgery, have physical risk.

Social risk The probability that a service will not meet with approval from others who are significant to the consumer making the purchase.

Physical risk The probability that a service will actually cause physical harm to the customer.

During the prepurchase phase, consumers evaluate the type and extent of risk involved in the purchase decision. They will often compare service firms to see how much risk would be involved with each option. It is normally the uncertainty component being examined because the consequence component is usually the same. The first step most consumers take in reducing prepurchase risk is to examine their own personal experiences. The tendency is to patronize service firms they have used in the past because they know what type of service will be received. People tend to use the same hair stylist because they know what to expect. Only if they are unhappy with the last haircut will they be inclined to switch.

To further reduce risk, consumers will often seek the opinion of others, such as friends, relatives, business associates, or experts in the field. When looking for a dentist, consumers usually ask other people for recommendations. When looking for spring break locations, the opinions of others will be valuable. The higher the perceived risk, the more likely that the opinion of someone else will be sought. Consumers will sometimes seek service-produced sources of information during the deliberation stage or information-collecting stage. Before deciding on a spring break location, you may collect information on several resorts. Common sources of information include advertising, promotions, and the Internet.

Service firms must be aware of the risk consumers perceive during the prepurchase phase and take appropriate steps to reduce it. It is important to understand the difference between the uncertainty component and the consequence component. To reduce the uncertainty component, services must reduce the perceived probability of a service failure. It is important to recognize that the perceived risk may not be the same as the actual risk. Although the actual risk of a parachute not opening for a skydiver is extremely low, most consumers perceive the risk to be relatively high. Airlines face a similar problem in that it is statistically safer to fly than it is to drive one's own automobile, yet most people perceive flying to be riskier. In both cases, the perception is that risk is greater than in reality, but consumer decisions are based on the perception, not reality. Therefore, firms must deal with reducing the perceived risk consumers have, regardless of what the actual risk may be.

Source: fizkes/Shutterstock

Communication is a key in reducing the uncertainty component of risk. Through advertising, brochures, and certification, the perceived probability that something will go wrong can be reduced. Having a strong brand name is extremely beneficial. Most travelers feel more comfortable eating at a brand-name restaurant, such as Outback Steakhouse, than at a restaurant with an unfamiliar name. The brand-name restaurant is perceived to be more likely to have consistent quality at all of its restaurants. The traveler has no idea what to expect at an unknown local restaurant.

Reducing the consequence component of risk is achieved by having quality control standards and procedures. Applebee's can reduce the consequence of food poisoning, or just a meal that tastes bad, by ensuring that all of its cooks and employees follow established quality control standards and specific operating procedures.

9-4b Service Encounter

Service encounter The second stage of the service purchase process, which is the actual interaction point between the customer and the service provider.

The second stage of the service purchase process is the **service encounter**, which is the actual interaction point between the customer and the service provider. In most cases, the service provider is a person, but it can also be a machine, as in the case of a bank's ATM. Usually, the customer and service provider interaction are in person— as would be the case with a dental procedure. However, it can occur over the telephone—as would be the case with a call center employee helping a customer with a computer problem. In both of these cases, the quality of the service encounter depends on the service environment and the service personnel or the service machine providing the service.

The service environment consists of the tangible elements of the facility, the facility's atmosphere, other customers who are present at the time of the service, and the service personnel **(see Figure 9-13)**. Tangible

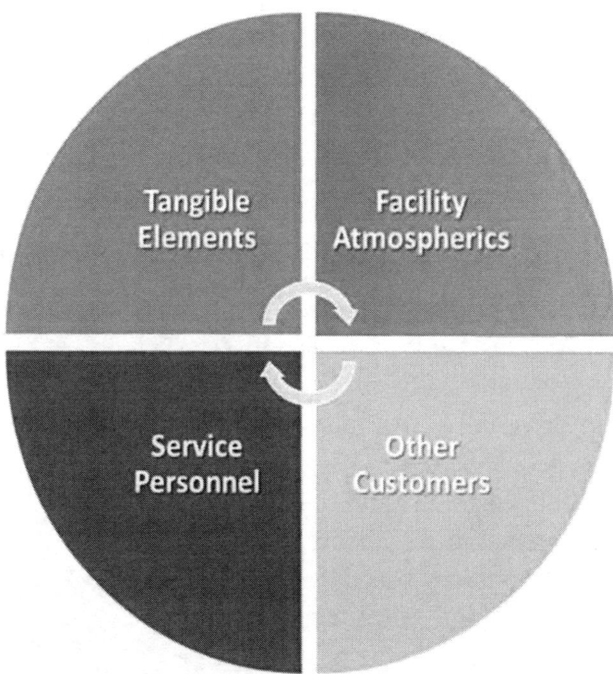

FIGURE 9-13 Components of the Service Encounter Environment

elements include, for example, the furniture, signs, brochures, and the equipment and tools being used to perform the service.

The atmospheric elements include such things as the office decor, the cleanliness of the facility, and intangible elements like noise, sound, and odors. (Atmospherics are further addressed in the discussion of the retail environment in Chapter 10.) All of these elements affect how customers react to service situations. If a restaurant is cold, consumers are likely to have a lower evaluation of the service. If a dental office is dirty, it will affect patients' evaluation of the dental care they are to receive. If a bakery has the smell of freshly baked cookies, it will positively influence the consumer's evaluation of the pastry just purchased. In all of these cases, the evaluation of the service is affected by intangible elements that are not part of the service itself. The actual service may be performed well, but customers can go away unhappy or extremely pleased because of an intangible element.

If other customers are present during the service encounter, they can affect the quality of the environment. This is especially true for entertainment services such as sports, theme parks, movie theaters, and concerts. A rowdy fan can destroy the fun of others watching a game. A customer talking at a movie theater can aggravate other viewers to the point they may not even stay for the whole movie.

In service encounters in which service personnel and customers have direct interaction, the conduct of the service personnel becomes a critical factor. If service personnel are polite and show genuine interest in the customer, their behavior will increase the level of customer satisfaction. If service personnel are indifferent or rude, their behavior can create customer dissatisfaction. The food at a restaurant can be excellent, but if the service is poor, it will reflect negatively on the entire experience. For many services, the conduct of the service personnel is as important or more important than the service itself.

To ensure a positive service environment, many firms use a concept called **blueprinting**, which is the process of diagramming a service operation.[6] Through blueprinting, every step in the purchase process, from the first contact the customer has with a firm to the completion of the service, is diagrammed. Through this blueprinting process, the firm can see how customers and the firm interact. They can see which steps are not being performed efficiently and where improvements need to be made. The blueprint shows at what times during the service are the service environment, other customers, and service personnel involved. By carefully blueprinting every step in the purchase process, a firm can manage the entire experience to increase the probability the customer has a positive experience. Figure 9-14 illustrates a blueprint for an X-ray process.

Blueprinting The process of diagramming a service operation.

Each block in the blueprinting diagram is a "moment of truth" when the customer or patient interacts with the service. The total experience is the sum of each of the contact experiences or moments of truth. If one link in the experience is bad, it will result in the negative evaluation of the whole experience.

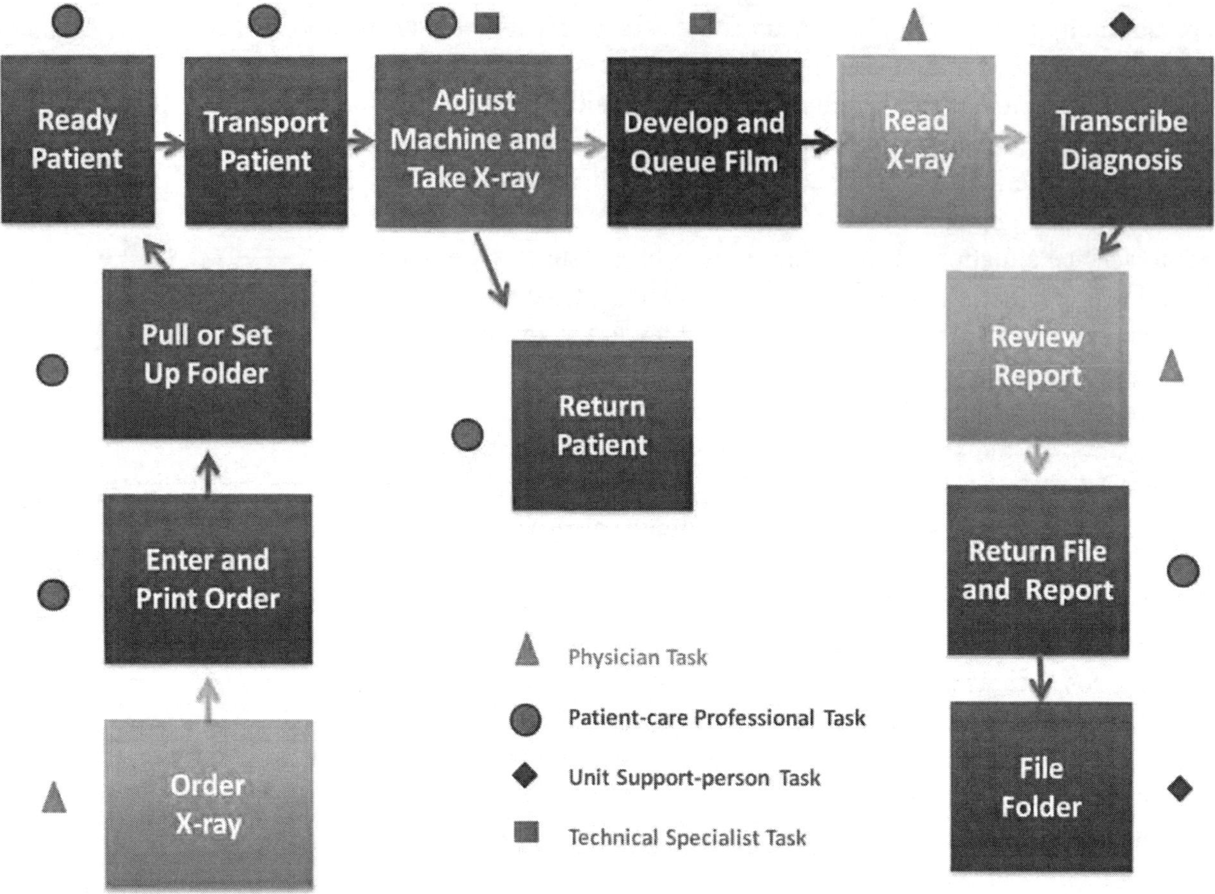

FIGURE 9-14 Blueprint of an X-Ray Medical Process

9-4c Postpurchase Phase

The third stage of the purchase process is the postpurchase phase. During this stage, customers will evaluate the quality of service and their level of satisfaction or dissatisfaction. For satisfied customers, future actions include repeat purchases, customer loyalty, and positive word-of-mouth communications. For dissatisfied customers, future actions include switching vendors and negative word-of-mouth communications, or actions directed toward the service provider **(see Figure 9-15)**.[7]

Technical service quality The outcome of the service.

Functional service quality The process whereby the service was performed.

In evaluating service quality, consumers evaluate two components: the technical quality and the functional quality.[8] **Technical service quality** is the outcome of the service, and **functional service quality** is the process whereby the service was performed. For a restaurant, the technical service quality is the food and drinks that are served, whereas the functional service quality is the interaction with the people providing the service. For both components, a consumer will compare the perceived level of service quality that was received to the level of service expected. If expectations are met or exceeded, then consumers are satisfied. If expectations are not met, then consumers are dissatisfied.

In cases in which expectations are not met, the level of customer dissatisfaction will be determined by how and where customers attribute the cause of the service failure or poor service. The process of deciding

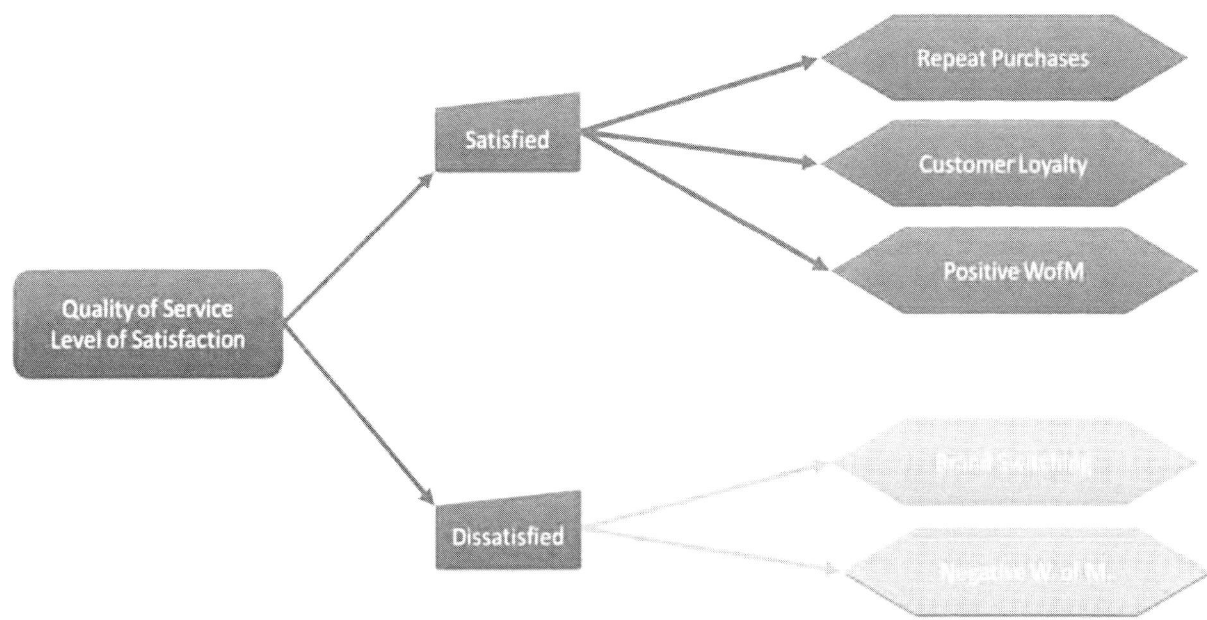

FIGURE 9-15 Postpurchase Evaluation Outcomes

the cause of the poor service is called **attribution theory**.[9] Customers look at two factors in determining attribution: First, was the cause of the service failure controllable, and second, could the firm have prevented the service problem? If either factor is confirmed, then the customer will attribute the service problem to the firm and blame it for what occurred.

Attribution theory The process of deciding the cause of a service failure or poor service.

To illustrate, suppose you are at your wedding and the wedding cake arrives one hour late. If the delay is caused by bad weather, such as ice or snow storm, you are less likely to be dissatisfied because the bakery does not have any control over weather conditions. However, if the cake is delayed because the bakery failed to bake and deliver the cake in a timely manner, before the storm hit, then it is likely that you will be dissatisfied because you will feel the bakery is at fault and the delay could have been prevented.

Customers who are dissatisfied with a service are likely to choose another firm the next time they purchase that particular service. Few customers actually voice a complaint to the manager or service personnel. The customer may be unhappy with the haircut or the food that was served at a restaurant but will usually not say anything to anyone at the service. In fact, research has shown that 90% of customers will not voice a complaint but not use the service again. Of those, 13% will tell about their negative experience to 15 more people[10] and the information could quickly end

Source: Sergey Ryzhov/Shutterstock

up on social media. The negative word-of-mouth can be devastating to a business, because a post on social media can be seen by thousands.

For customers who are satisfied, typical future behaviors include repeat purchases, firm loyalty, and positive WOM and/or eWOM communications. Satisfied customers tend to patronize the same firm and, over time, become loyal to that firm. If a person likes the way a service mows the lawn or cleans the house, that person will continue to use the service. He or she may even engage in positive word-of-mouth communications, although usually it does not involve as many people as negative word-of-mouth communications.

9-5 Service Quality

A critical component of future purchase behavior is the evaluation of the service a consumer receives. If customers are satisfied with the quality of service, they likely will patronize the firm again. If they are not satisfied, they likely will not patronize the firm in the future. Because future purchase behavior is largely determined by this service experience, it is beneficial to examine how a service business can measure service quality.

9-5a Measuring Service Quality

Gap theory Method of measuring service quality that involves measuring the gap between expectations and customers' evaluation of the service.

In making an evaluation of service quality, customers will compare the service they received to what they expected. This method of measuring service quality is called the **gap theory** because you are measuring the gap between expectations and customer evaluations of the service. Past research has indicated that consumers make this evaluation along the five dimensions of tangibles, reliability, responsiveness, empathy, and assurance listed in **Figure 9-16.**[11]

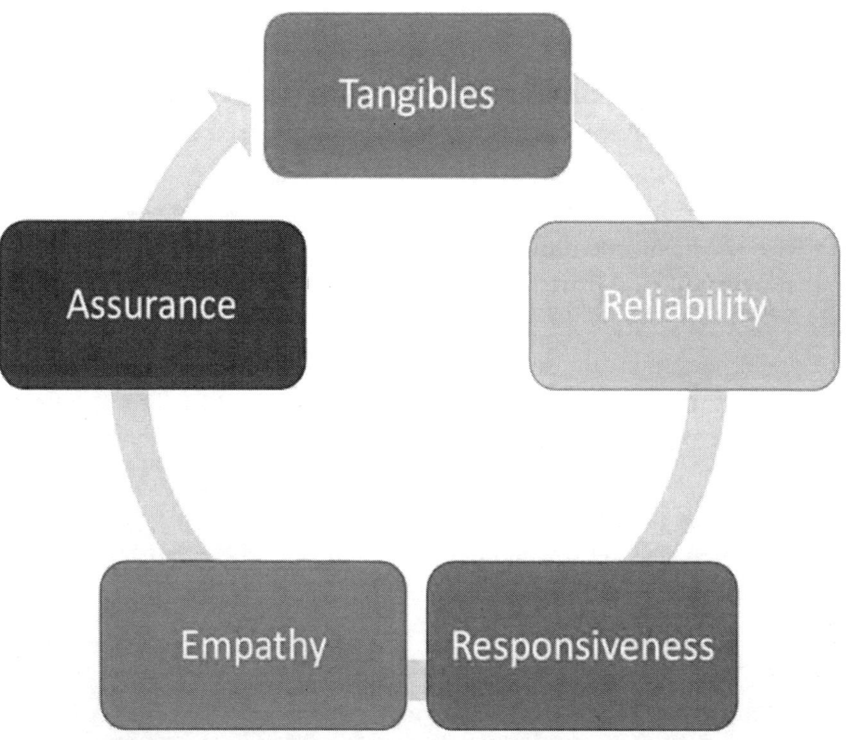

FIGURE 9-16 Dimensions of Service Quality Evaluation

Tangibles refer to the service provider's physical facilities, equipment, and the appearance of employees. **Reliability** is the ability of the service firm to perform the service promised dependably and accurately. **Responsiveness** is the willingness of the firm's staff to help customers and to provide them with prompt service. **Empathy** refers to the caring, individualized attention the service firm provides each customer. **Assurance** refers to the knowledge and courtesy of the employees and their ability to inspire customers to trust and have confidence in the service provider.

To illustrate these dimensions, suppose you have contacted a company to clean the carpets in your home. The tangibles are the appearance of the equipment being used and the personnel doing the work. If the equipment is old and worn, you may be inclined to believe that the quality of service the company provides is not as good as it would be for a company that has new, clean equipment. If the service is scheduled for 2:00 P.M. and the company shows up an hour late, the response will negatively impact your evaluation of the service quality. If, however, you called a company because of a water pipe break and service technicians are able to get out to your house in the afternoon or the first thing the next day, this quick response would have a positive impact on your evaluation. Employees who are knowledgeable and responsive will enhance your evaluation of the firm's service, whereas employees who do not know how to get particular stains out of your carpet or are rude will have a negative impact. In fact, a rude service technician can create a negative evaluation of the service even though the actual outcome of the service may be satisfactory. Empathy would be the caring, individualized attention the service should provide. It may be moving some furniture at no additional cost, or spending extra time on a particular spot in your carpet. How you evaluate the quality of service of the carpet-cleaning firm will be a summation of all five dimensions. The firm may do well on four of the five, but doing poorly on one dimension can create a negative overall evaluation of the service.

In measuring service quality using the gap theory, a service firm has two options. First, it can ask consumers about their expectations before the service and then ask the same series of questions after the service. Subtracting the two scores will give a gap score for each dimension, as well as for the overall service. An alternative method of using the gap theory methodology is to ask customers to evaluate the service along the five dimensions as it relates to what they expected. For example, a question about empathy would read, "The service technician demonstrated he cared about me as a customer." This latter method requires surveying customers only once and will yield similar results.

Instead of using a gap analysis to measure service quality, a company can use internal measures. For airlines, internal measures are such items as the percentage of on-time flights, number of baggage claims, and number of customer complaints. By tracking these measures over time, an airline can see whether its level of service is increasing or decreasing. It can also

Tangibles The service provider's physical facilities, equipment, and appearance of its employees.

Reliability The ability of the service firm to perform the service provided in a dependable and accurate manner.

Responsiveness The willingness of the firm's staff to help customers and to provide prompt service.

Empathy The caring, individualized attention the service firm provides to each customer.

Assurance Refers to the knowledge and courtesy of the employees and their ability to inspire customers to trust and have confidence in the service provider.

Source: Dundanin/Shutterstock

compare its data to that of other airlines to see how it stands. These comparative data are especially helpful because they will indicate areas for improvement. If an airline ranks first in the number of baggage claims per 1,000 passengers, then it needs to look at ways of improving its baggage-handling process. If it does not address the problem, passengers are likely to start flying on other airlines

The advantage of using internal measures of service quality is that weaknesses as well as strengths can be identified. Weaknesses need to be improved to remain competitive, and strengths can be marketed as a reason to patronize the firm. The airline that ranks first in percentage of on-time flights can advertise this as proof of its dependable and reliable service.

9-5b Service Failure and Recovery

Service failures Instances in which a service is either not performed at all or is poorly performed.

Service failures are defined as instances in which a service is either not performed at all or is poorly performed. Customers are not only dissatisfied, but they may be extremely angry. When service problems occur, customers are less likely to purchase from the firm again in the future and in many cases will tell others about the bad experience. For both reasons, services must develop methods for dealing with service failures.

Service firms must realize that a service failure does not automatically result in firm-switching behavior and negative word-of-mouth communications. Customers can be recovered. The manner in which service failures are handled will have a greater impact on future purchase behavior than the original bad experience. Firms often have a second chance to make things right. However, if a firm fails the second time around, the backlash is even stronger because the firm, in essence, has failed twice. This process of attempting to regain a customer's confidence after a service failure is called **service recovery**.

Service recovery The process of attempting to regain a customer's confidence after a service failure.

A successful service recovery program can overcome most service failures and diminish the negative impact of the original poor or failed service. The more quickly a service problem is handled, the more likely the customer can be recovered and will purchase from the firm again. If the service problem can be corrected at the time of the service encounter, the negative impact of the experience is almost always diminished. The longer it takes to correct the problem, the less likely it can be resolved satisfactorily and the less likely the customer will be to purchase again.

Employees should be trained to defuse a customer's anger as quickly and tactfully as possible. This requires attentive listening and acknowledging the customer has a right to feel annoyed. Listening will allow customers to vent their anger and explain why they are unhappy. Admitting the firm made a mistake, if indeed this happened, will offset any attribution directed to the firm. It is harder to be mad at someone who admits he or she made a mistake. By agreeing that the customer had a right to be upset and dissatisfied, employees demonstrate empathy and understanding. With this groundwork, the recovery process is ready to move into the resolution stage.

Source: Iakov Filimonov/Shutterstock

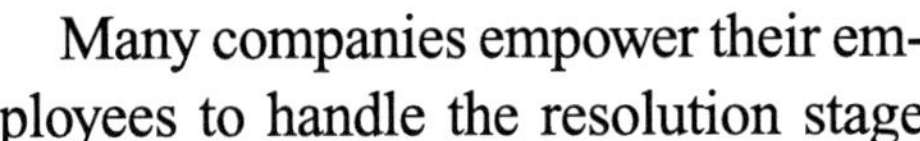

Many companies empower their employees to handle the resolution stage and correct the wrong. The Ritz-Carlton goes even further: its "Gold Standards" enable the company's employees to deliver the exceptional service that its refined customers have come to expect. Employees are trained to break routine to solve problems and own them until they are resolved. They must anticipate customer needs and are empowered to resolve any customer concern in any way possible–they have up to $2,000 per customer per day they can spend on service recovery, without a supervisor's approval.[12]

Successful service recovery programs empower employees to correct the wrong. They trust employees to make the right decision. After the customer has made a suggestion, the service employee is then ready to negotiate a viable solution to the problem. The goal of the resolution is twofold. First, the firm wants to eradicate the negative experience and change the dissatisfaction into some type of satisfaction. Second, the firm wants that customer to return and purchase again. With these goals in mind, the employee should negotiate a solution that satisfies the customer and is feasible for the firm.

If the problem cannot be corrected at the time it is discovered, then customers need to be informed. The customer needs to be kept up to date on the progress that is made. If the same employee can deal with the customer through the whole service recovery process, it will increase the chances of a positive outcome. In the business-to-business area, keeping customers informed through one contact person is very important. Too often, either the problem is passed around or it is assumed that the customer knows what is happening.

Summary

1. **Discuss the impact of the services sector on the gross domestic product and what has led to the growth of the service sector.** Services are a vital component of the U.S. economy and that of most industrialized nations. The service sector in the United States accounts for just under 80 percent of the country's gross domestic product (GDP). The preponderance of services in a nation's economy is typical of most developed

countries in Western Europe and is growing in Asia. The service sector's rapid growth is primarily the result of nations shifting from a manufacturing-based economy to a service-oriented economy. A major stimulus in this shift is the movement to an information society spurred by the computer and advancements in telecommunications. Additional factors contributing to the growth of the service sector are an aging population, longer life expectancies, increased leisure time, higher per-capita income, increased time pressure, more women in the workforce, sedentary lifestyles, changing social and cultural values, and advances in technology.

2. **Identify the four unique characteristics of services and how each affects the marketing of services.**
   Services possess four inherent characteristics not found in goods: intangibility, perishability, inseparability, and variability. Intangibility refers to the lack of tangible assets that can be seen, touched, smelled, heard, or tasted before a purchase, which renders a service relatively difficult for a consumer to evaluate before a purchase. Perishability refers to the inability of a service to be inventoried or stored. This means that one of the goals of marketing is to manage demand so it equals supply and capacity. Inseparability refers to the simultaneous production and consumption of a service, which requires marketing the service at the time and location of the service provider. Variability refers to the unwanted or random levels of service quality that customers receive when they patronize a service. Because of this variability, promises made in advertising and other marketing materials are not always kept; this reflects negatively on the service operation.

3. **Explain the components of the purchasing process for services.**
   The purchasing process consists of three phases: the prepurchase phase, the service encounter, and the postpurchase phase. During the prepurchase phase, consumers evaluate alternatives, make a purchase decision, and choose a particular brand. At some point after the decision is made, the consumer will move into the second stage, the service encounter, which is the actual interaction point between the customer and the service provider. The last phase of the services purchase process is the postpurchase evaluation, which begins upon completion of the service. During this phase, consumers make evaluations concerning the quality of service, their level of satisfaction or dissatisfaction, and future purchase intentions.

4. **Identify the factors that affect the purchase decision during the prepurchase phase of the purchase process.**
   During the prepurchase phase, the factors that affect the purchase decision are internal factors, external factors, firm-produced factors, and perceived risk. Internal factors consist of individual needs and wants of the consumer, past experience, expectations of the service alternatives, and the overall level of purchase involvement. The external factors that influence the purchase decision during the prepurchase phase are the competitive options available to consumers, the social context of the purchase, and word-of-mouth communications. The firm-produced factors affecting the purchase decision include promotions, pricing, and distribution. The types of perceived risk that can affect the purchase decision are performance risk, financial risk, time-loss risk, opportunity risk, psychological risk, social risk, and physical risk.

5. **Discuss the relevant elements of the service encounter and why they are important.**
   The service encounter is the actual interaction point between the customer and the service provider. The quality of the service encounter depends on the service environment and the service personnel or service machine providing the service. The service environment consists of the tangible elements of the facility, the facility's atmosphere, and other customers who are present at the time of the

service. All of these components of the service encounter affect a customer's evaluation of the service being delivered, as well as the interaction between the customer and service personnel.

6. **Describe the postpurchase evaluation of services and its impact on future purchase behavior.**
During the postpurchase phase, customers evaluate the quality of service and their level of satisfaction or dissatisfaction. For satisfied customers, future actions include repeat purchases, customer loyalty, and positive word-of-mouth communications. For dissatisfied customers, future actions include switching vendors and negative word-of-mouth communications.

7. **Discuss how service quality is measured.**
In the process of evaluating service quality, customers will compare the service they received to what they expected along the five dimensions of tangibles, reliability, responsiveness, assurance, and empathy. Using this method of measuring service quality, companies can ask consumers about their expectations before the service and subsequently ask the same series of questions after the service. Subtracting the two scores will give them a gap score for each dimension, as well as for the overall service. An alternative method is to ask customers to evaluate the service along the five dimensions as it relates to what they expected. Instead of using a gap analysis to measure service quality, a company can use internal measures, such as the number of lost baggage claims or percentage of on-time deliveries.

8. **Describe an effective service recovery process.**
A successful service recovery program is designed to overcome service failures and diminish the negative impact of the original poor or failed service. The more quickly a service problem is handled, the more likely the customer can be recovered and will purchase from the firm again. Employees should be trained to defuse the customer's anger as quickly and tactfully as possible. Normally, all this requires is attentive listening, admitting that the firm made a mistake, and acknowledging that the customer has a right to feel annoyed. Once this is accomplished, it is time for the resolution stage. Many companies begin the resolution stage by asking the customer what the firm can do to correct the problem. Once the customer has made a suggestion, the service employee is then ready to negotiate a viable solution to the problem.

Key Terms

Assurance (271)
Attribution theory (269)
Blueprinting (267)
Consequence (264)
Empathy (271)
Financial risk (264)
Functional service quality (268)
Gap theory (270)
Industrialization (257)
Inseparability (252)
Intangibility (252)
Opportunity risk (264)
Performance risk (264)
Perishability (252)
Physical risk (265)
Psychological risk (264)
Reliability (271)
Responsiveness (271)
Service distribution (263)
Service encounter (266)
Service failures (272)
Service recovery (272)
Social risk (265)
Tangibles (271)
Technical service quality (268)
Time-loss risk (264)
Uncertainty (263)
Variability (252)

Discussion Questions

1. What type of camera or cameras do you own? What types of photography service businesses do you use? What do you foresee as the future for photography and photography-related service businesses?
2. The majority of new jobs in the future will be in the service sector. Using the Internet and an electronic database, locate at least three articles that discuss future employment and the service sector. Will the service jobs in the future be primarily minimum-wage jobs at service businesses like restaurants, or will they be high-dollar jobs that require a college degree?
3. Select one item from the list of factors contributing to the growth of the service sector discussed in Section 9-2. Using the Internet and an electronic database, locate two articles that discuss the factor selected. What types of service industries have benefited in the past, and what types of service industries will benefit in the future? What do you see in the future for the contributory factor you chose in terms of its impact on the service sector?
4. Think about the restaurant industry and your personal dining habits. Compare your eating-out habits with those of your parents and grandparents. What changes do you see among the three generations in terms of dining out, purchasing takeout, and eating at home? How has food that is purchased for home consumption changed?
5. For each of the following services, discuss the degree of intangibility, perishability, inseparability, and variability inherent in each service. Pick one service and discuss strategies for reducing the negative impact of each unique service characteristic.
   a. automobile repair service
   b. dentist
   c. fast food restaurant
   d. lawn service
6. Suppose you wanted to go somewhere on spring break. Discuss each of the internal factors that impact the prepurchase phase as it relates to your decision on where to go for spring break
7. Suppose you wanted to go out to a local nightclub Saturday night. Discuss each of the external factors that impact the prepurchase phase as it relates to your decision on where to go.
8. Suppose you want to go to a musical concert that is located in a large city near you. Discuss each of the types of perceived risk in purchasing a ticket to this concert that costs $125. Also consider traveling costs and other expenses related to the concert purchase.
9. Suppose you decide to spend a week on a vacation at a resort in Miami Beach, Florida. Discuss each of the perceived risks involved in making the decision. What would be the uncertainty and consequence factors involved in the decision?
10. Consider a recent dining-out experience. Describe your service encounter experience. Discuss each element of the service encounter phase presented in Section 9-4b in terms of your experience. How did each element affect your evaluation of the service?
11. Identify a recent personal service failure situation in which the service was poor or not performed at all. Did you complain to anyone at the service? Why or why not? Have you told any of your friends, relatives, or others about the experience? How many have you told? Did the service make any attempt to make things right with you (i.e., use a service recovery process)? If so, describe the outcome. If not, what could the service have done to correct the situation?

Review Questions

True or False

1. Because medical treatment of elderly patients requires special equipment and facilities, such a treatment cannot be characterized as a service.
2. Perishability is directly related to the demand for a particular service. Demand can be managed through advertising, special promotions, and pricing.
3. Variability is a unique characteristic found in most services.
4. Involvement refers to the level of mental and physical effort exerted by a consumer in selecting a good or service.
5. The service encounter is the actual interaction point between the customer and the service provider and consists only of tangible elements.
6. Using the gap theory to evaluate service quality involves measuring the gap between customer expectations and customer evaluation of the service.
7. An alternative to the gap analysis as a measure of service quality is using internal measures performed by the company.
8. After a service failure takes place, dissatisfied customers will be reluctant to make another purchase from the same company despite a successful service recovery program.

Multiple Choice

9. The simultaneous production and consumption of a service is
   a. intangibility
   b. perishability
   c. inseparability
   d. variability
10. What is the most critical group of factors that affect the prepurchase phase?
    a. Internal factors
    b. External factors
    c. Firm-produced factors
    d. Risk
11. The social context of a purchase is a(n) factor that impacts the prepurchase phase.
    a. internal
    b. firm-produced
    c. external
    d. perceived risk
12. The probability that a particular outcome will occur refers to which component of risk?
    a. uncertainty
    b. consequences
    c. opportunity
    d. performance
13. To ensure a positive service environment, many companies use the concept of blueprinting, which reveals
    a. every step in the purchase process.
    b. steps where the service is not performed in an efficient manner.
    c. how customers and service personnel interact in the environment.
    d. all of the above.
14. The process of how a service is performed is
    a. technical service quality
    b. functional service quality
    c. the gap theory
    d. attribution theory
15. The service staff's willingness to help customers and to provide prompt service is an example of
    a. validity
    b. reliability
    c. responsiveness
    d. assurance

Answers: (1) False, (2) True, (3) True, (4) True, (5) False, (6) True, (7) True, (8) False, (9) c, (10) a, (11) c, (12) a, (13) d, (14) b, (15) c

Case: First Eastern Shore Bank

Looking down his attendance list, Thomas Lauden, the Vice President of Marketing for First Eastern Shore Bank, checked off the names. Present were branch managers Brenda Neely and Charles Jones, Vice President of Retail Operations Kristen Hammersmith, Vice President of Consumer Loans

Mingshing Liu, and marketing staff members Theresa Hanks and Ollie Jenkins. Lauden called this meeting to discuss the bank's marketing program. Because of declining profits and the emergence of two new banks on the Eastern Shore, First Eastern Shore Bank's number of customers had actually declined for the first time in 30 years. Lauden began the meeting by presenting the financial statement for the past year for the 12 facilities in the First Eastern Shore Bank system. All but two had profits decline, and all but four had fewer customers.

Lauden continued by presenting data from the American Bankers Association, showing what customers value in a bank. Trust was at the top of the list, with 83 percent of the respondents indicating it was very important. Reasonable fees were second, competitive interest rates were third, convenience was fourth, financial strength fifth, and reputation sixth, followed by personal attention, up-to-date technology, investment expertise, and a wide range of products and services **(see Figure 9-17)**.

Jones was the first to speak. "We have no control over interest rates or fees really. Our fees are similar to those of other banks. So we can toss those out."

"I don't think we should toss them out if they are important," countered Hanks. "If they are important to customers, then we should discuss our fees in the marketing material."

"But what value is it if our fees are the same as those of every other bank? There is no value in promoting something that does not provide a competitive advantage for us or at least makes us stand out from the competition," Jones argued.

"I'm not so sure about that. Maybe our fees are the same and maybe our interest rates are the same, but how do people know that if we don't promote it?" Hammersmith interjected.

"So from this list, it would appear to me we ought to promote the idea of trust, that we have reasonable fees, competitive interest rates, convenience, and financial strength," Neely spoke up.

"But how do you promote trust? What can you say in an advertisement that conveys that message?" Jones asked.

Smiling, Lauden looked at Hanks and Jenkins as he replied, "That's what I pay my staff to figure out."

Putting another slide on the overhead **(see Figure 9-18)**, Lauden continued. "I think this slide is even more startling. When people were asked if their bank was committed to meeting their financial needs, look at the results. The younger the respondent, the less likely they were

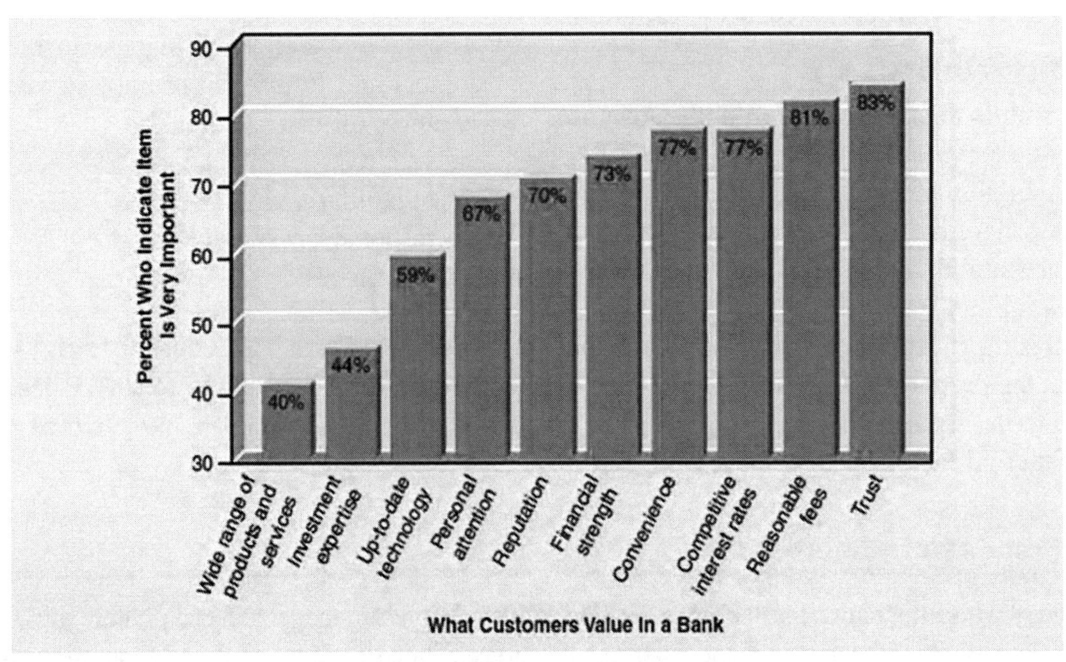

FIGURE 9-17 Survey of What Customers Value in a Bank

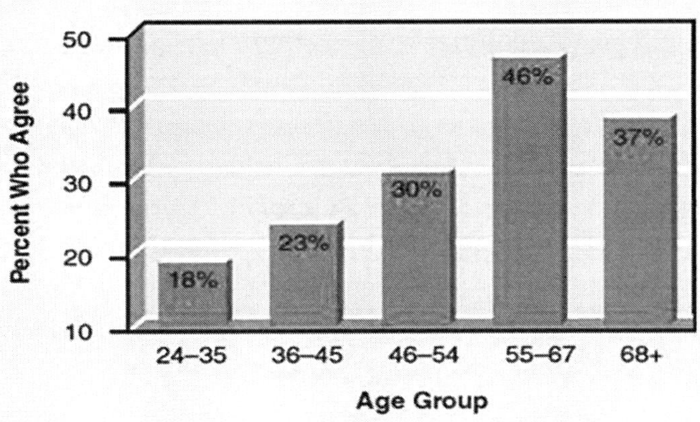

FIGURE 9-18 Banks' Commitment to Meeting Customers' Financial Needs by Age
Source: "Customer Views about Banks," *ABA Banking Journal*, 93 (September 2001), pp. 6-7.

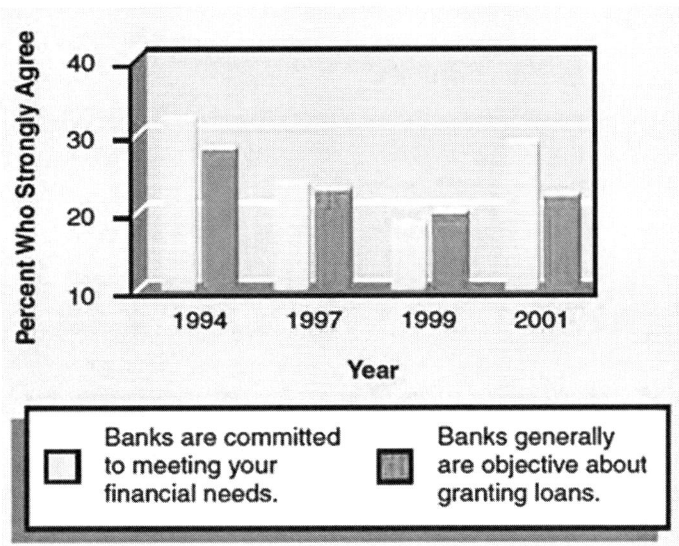

FIGURE 9-19 Survey of Banks' Commitment to Customer Financial Needs

to agree. That means that it's the younger generation that does not believe that we are committed to meeting their financial needs."

"And they are our future customers," mused Hammersmith.

"The percentage of 24- to 35-year-olds is half of the percentage of retired people," Ollie pointed out. "In fact, the real problem appears to be the 24- to 45-year-old age group."

"Before we go any further," Lauden suggested, "let me show you the next slide, which looks at the overall percentages over time **(see Figure 9-19)**. First is the statement that banks are committed to meeting your financial needs. Notice that 31% strongly agreed in 2000, which dropped to a low of 17% in 2005 and is now up to 28%. For the statement that banks generally are objective about granting loans, the percentage for strongly agree was 27% in 2000, which dropped to 19% in 2005, and is now at 21%."

"I thought we were doing a better job of granting loans to all of the different demographic groups," Liu spoke. "But this information indicates that is not the perception. Do you think we need to include more minorities in our marketing material?"

"That may be a good idea. Have we examined all of our marketing material to see how minorities, women, retirees, and even college students are represented?" Mingshing asked.

"We have, but not formally," Ollie replied.

"I don't think that is a real issue with us. What I do sense is that we are not attracting the under-30 individual, especially males. We seem to do better with females in that age category," Hammersmith pointed out.

"Do you think it's because they have higher expectations or maybe they are just harder to please? What do you think is the issue?" Mingshing asked.

Lauden responded, "I think they have options, especially Internet options that the older consumer does not have. I also believe they are not as interested in developing a personal relationship with their bank as are older consumers. Look who's in the lobby. Almost everyone out there is over 50. Look who's at the ATM, the drive-up window, and banking with us online. It's almost the opposite."

"I think Tom has a valid point," Jones spoke up. "If our goal is to reach the younger consumer, then we must promote the technology, the online access, the ATMs. That's what they want to see."

"And my experience from the loan area," Mingshing shared, "is that they are concerned about interest rates and reasonable fees. But before we go further on this, let me give you some information I found in my research. We are talking about gaining new customers, but shouldn't we be just as concerned about retaining our current customers? I read that it costs about six or seven times more money to get a new customer than to retain a current customer. I also read that the longer a customer stays with a company, the more profitable they become. They buy more and require less of our time. Here, let me show you some more interesting facts."

Moving to the overhead, Mingshing put up a slide with the following information:

- There is little correlation between satisfaction and retention.
- From 65 to 85 percent of defectors were satisfied with their previous service.
- For those dissatisfied, the primary reasons for leaving were failure to deliver a service as promised and being treated in an unprofessional manner.
- For those satisfied, the primary reasons for leaving were because of perceived better prices or a better value package from a competitor.

Mingshing continued, "As we develop our marketing plan, we need to think about our current customers and encourage them to stay with us. It makes no sense to spend our marketing budget trying to gain new customers if we are losing them as fast as we gain new ones. If the information I read is correct, we have to gain at least six new customers to just break even on the cost of losing one current customer."

"In the study you read, what was the key to retaining customers?" "Contact with the bank," Mingshing answered.

"But how do you do that if 70 percent of our business is transacted at the ATM, drive-up, online, or by phone?" objected Hammersmith.

"That's the challenge," Mingshing countered.

"So, do we develop a marketing plan to seek new customers, or do we put our money into keeping our current customers?" Jenkins asked.

"Can we do both? Why does it have to be either or?" asked Neely.

Case Questions

1. How do the service characteristics of intangibility, perishability, inseparability, and variability fit into this discussion of marketing a bank?
2. Using all of the information presented in this case, what theme would you suggest for marketing of the First Eastern Shore Bank to the under-30 consumer? Why?
3. Can you target new customers and use the same set of ads to encourage current customers to stay with the bank? Why or why not?
4. What should the bank do about the customers they are losing?
5. If trust is an important value to bank customers, how can that message be conveyed to customers who bank primarily using the ATM, drive-up, or online banking?

The case is fictitious; *sources*: Serena Dorf, "7 Effective Bank Customer Retention Strategies," Payments Journal, November 28, 2018, https://www.paymentsjournal.com/7-effective-bank-customer-retention-strategies; Thomas J. Healy, "Why You Should Retain Your Customers,"

America's Community Banker 8 (September 1999): 22–25; "What Customers Value Most," *ABA Banking Journal 93* (September 2001): 17; "Customer Views about Banks," *ABA Banking Journal* 93 (September 2001): 6–7.

Endnotes

1. Deloitte Insights, "Changing the lens: GDP from the industry viewpoint," July 2019, https://www2.deloitte.com/us/en/insights/economy/spotlight/economics-insights-analysis-07-2019.html; CIA World Factbook, accessed at https://www.cia.gov/library/publications/the-world-factbook/fields/214.html May 22, 2020.
2. U.S. Bureau of Labor Statistics, https://www.bls.gov/emp/tables/occupations-most-job-growth.htm, accessed May 23, 2020.
3. Valarie A. Zeithaml, A. Parasuraman, and Leonard L. Berry, "Problems and Strategies in Services Marketing," *Journal of Marketing* 49 (1985): 33–46.
4. ESPN, Coronavirus cancellations and reactions in sports, accessed on June 19, 2020, at https://www.espn.com/espn/story/_/id/28871525/coronavirus-cancellations-reactions-sports
5. Judith Lynne Zaichkowsky, "Measuring the Involvement Construct," *Journal of Consumer Research* 12 (December 1985): 341–352.
6. G. Lynn Shostack, "Understanding Services through Blueprinting," in *Services Marketing and Management,* eds. T. Schwartz, D. Bowen, and S. Brown (Greenwich, Conn.: JAI Press, 1992): 75–90.
7. M. Fetscherin, "The five types of brand hate: How they affect consumer behavior," *Journal of Business Research* 101 (2019) 116–127; Diane Halstead, Cornelia Droge, and M. Bixby Cooper, "Product Warranties and Postpurchase Service," *Journal of Services Marketing* 7, no. 1 (1993): 33–40; Mary Jo Bitner, "Evaluating Service Encounters: The Effects of Physical Surroundings and Employee Responses," *Journal of Marketing* 54 (1990): 69–82.
8. F. Ali, K. Hussain, R. Konar and H-M Jeon, "The Effect of Technical and Functional Quality on Guests' Perceived Hotel Service Quality and Satisfaction: A SEM-PLS Analysis," *Journal of Quality Assurance in Hospitality & Tourism*, 2017, VOL. 18, NO. 3, 354–378; Christian Gronroos, *Service Management and Marketing* (Lexington, Mass.: Lexington Books, 1990): 37–39.
9. Valerie S. Folkes, Susan Koletsky, and John Graham, "A Field Study of Causal Inferences and Consumer Reaction: The View from the Airport," *Journal of Consumer Research* 13 (March 1985): 534–539.
10. Andrea Stojanovic, "What do Customers Want?–37 Customer Service Statistics," SmallBizGenius, August 2, 2019, https://www.smallbizgenius.net/by-the-numbers/customer-service-statistics/#gref
11. Material in the following paragraphs based on seminal work by A. Parasuraman, Valarie A. Zeithaml, and Leonard L. Berry, "SERVQUAL: A Multiple-Item Scale for Measuring Consumer Perceptions of Service Quality," *Journal of Retailing* 64 (Spring 1988): 12–40.
12. Nagesh Belludi, "How Ritz-Carlton Goes the Extra Mile," Right Attitudes, April 13, 2020, https://www.rightattitudes.com/2020/04/13/ritz-carlton-gold-standard-customer-service-book-summary

Retailing and Channel Strategies

CHAPTER 10

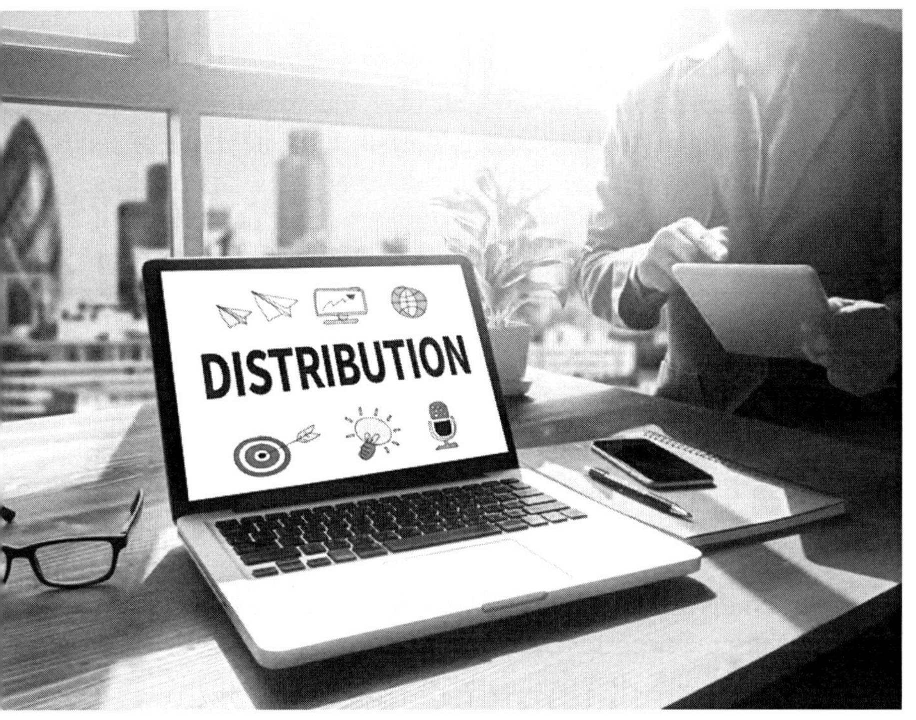

Source: one photo/Shutterstock

Chapter Outline

Learning Objectives

Ivelin Radkov/Shutterstock

After studying this chapter, you should be able to:

- Define distribution and identify the different channel functions and dimensions.
- Identify issues related to channel management, such as channel organization, administration, and relationships.
- Examine the different logistics functions.
- Provide an overview and description of the general merchandise retailing category and offer examples and illustrations.
- Provide an overview and description of the food retailing category and offer examples and illustrations.
- Provide an overview and description of the non-store retailing category and offer examples and illustrations.
- Address issues related to merchandise and service mix, location, atmospherics, and future trends in retailing.

Source: Nestor Rizhniak/Shutterstock

10-1 Chapter Overview

Kathleen King rented a bakery in downtown Southampton, New York, in 1979 for $350 a month and spent the winter perfecting her recipes and readying them for mass production. She then opened her doors when the summer crowd descended upon Southampton, and her all-natural cookies, pies, cakes, and other baked goods were an instant hit. In 2010, she decided to focus her expansion efforts on wholesaling: her goods were distributed to about 100 gourmet shops on Long Island, in New York City, and in other states. She also sold through popular upscale grocery chains all over the East Coast. Kathleen's Bake Shop changed its name to Tate's Bake Shop, in honor of her father. Her primary distributor at the time was Bay View Distributing. Kathleen's Bake Shop took on the role of manufacturer or producer, selling baked goods through a wholesaler, Bay View Distributing, to gourmet retailers and directly to Fresh Market gourmet grocery stores on the East Coast. After ups and downs, Kathleen eventually sold her share of the business in 2018 to Mondelēz International, allowing the company to operate Tate's as a separate standalone business to maintain the authenticity of the brand, maintaining its Bake Shop in Southampton and its headquarters in Long Island. However, the brand now benefits from Mondelēz distribution, with its cookies sold at supermarkets, discounters, and wholesale clubs.[1]

This chapter addresses distribution, including retailing, with Section 10-2 discussing the need for distribution channels and the different channel functions, Section 10-3 examining the different channel dimensions, such as direct and indirect channels, channel length and width, and the intensity of distribution, Section 10-4 addressing channel management, and Section 10-5 addressing logistics functions, such as transportation and inventory control. Section 10-6 addresses full-service and limited-service wholesalers and examines the different types of agents and brokers, Section 10-7 different retailing formats, and Section 10-8 addresses retailing merchandise and service mix decisions, atmospherics, and location. Section 10-9 reviews trends related to life-cycle, technology, competition, and international expansion.

Channels of distribution The totality of organizations and individuals involved in the distribution process who take title to or assist in the transferring of goods from the producer to the individual or organizational consumer.

Intermediaries (or middlemen or channel members) The organizations or individuals involved in the distribution process.

10-2 Distribution and the Channel Functions

Marketing managers understand that the planning of product distribution is among the most important tasks they need to undertake to ensure market success. Distribution involves establishing the **channels of distribution**, defined as the totality of organizations and individuals involved in the distribution process who take title to or assist in the transferring of goods from the producer to the individual or organizational consumer. The organizations or individuals involved in the distribution process are known as **intermediaries (or middlemen or channel members)**.

The goal of intermediaries is to offer support for the activities involved in delivering products for the enhanced benefit of the customer. In that sense, intermediaries are active participants in the **value chain (or supply chain)**, the chain of activities performed in the process of developing, producing, marketing, delivering, and servicing a product for the benefit of the customer. Today, many firms partner not just with the channel members or intermediaries, but also with their suppliers to provide optimal efficiencies that enhance profits, as well as customer benefits.

Value chain (or supply chain) The chain of activities performed in the process of developing, producing, marketing, delivering, and servicing a product for the benefit of the customer.

Using intermediaries entails relinquishing control over the marketing mix to a channel member. It also means paying for the channel member's services. Why do manufacturers use distributors to sell their products? Why do they not handle distribution themselves? The answer is that distributors cut down on the cost of distribution, while conveniently providing the desired assortment to consumers at a lower price. The following are the advantages of using intermediaries:

- Intermediaries deliver convenience to consumers. Intermediaries help distribute the product to a location that is convenient to the consumer.
- Intermediaries carry and store the product.
- Intermediaries assume risk in the delivery process. Intermediaries typically carry not just the title to the product, but also the risk for the product while it is in their possession, or even beyond.
- Intermediaries reduce the cost of the product delivery process by reducing the number of transactions needed to deliver the product to the final consumer. **Figure 10-1** illustrates how using a wholesaler can reduce the number of transactions, cutting down on the cost of transportation and handling. In the first scenario, there is no wholesaler; it would take 25 transactions to create an assortment of goods from each of the five manufacturers for each of the five retailers. Introducing a middleman in the second scenario reduces the number of transactions to ten. That, in fact, means fewer shipments are loaded, unloaded, and insured; fewer trucks are used in the transportation of the goods; and less paperwork is filled out by the firms.
- Intermediaries provide an assortment for retailers and, ultimately, for consumers.
- Intermediaries buy products in bulk from manufacturers, at a discount, then break bulk to sell smaller quantities to retailers.
- Intermediaries conduct research for the manufacturer and the channel about changing consumer needs and behavior.
- Intermediaries provide credit to other channel members or to consumers, which facilitates transactions.

Source: Zapp2Photo/Shutterstock

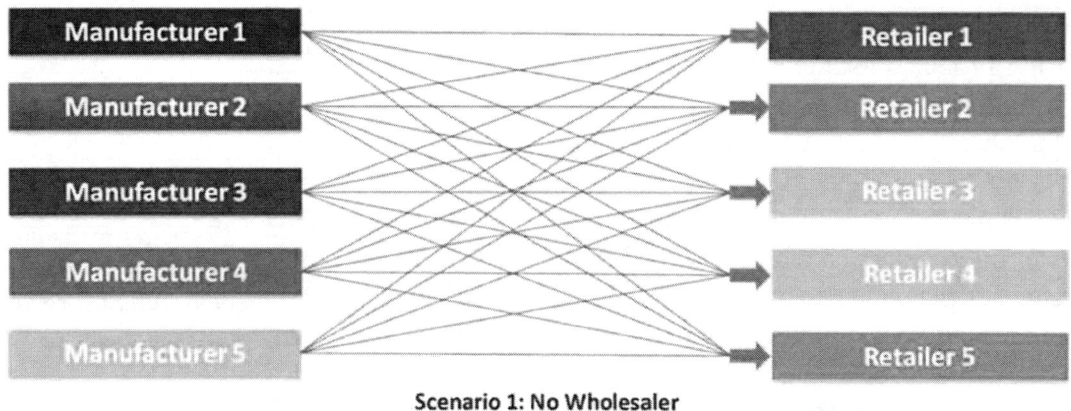

Scenario 1: No Wholesaler

Assume that each retailer needs an assortment of goods from each manufacturer.
The total number of transactions conducted without a wholesaler is 25.

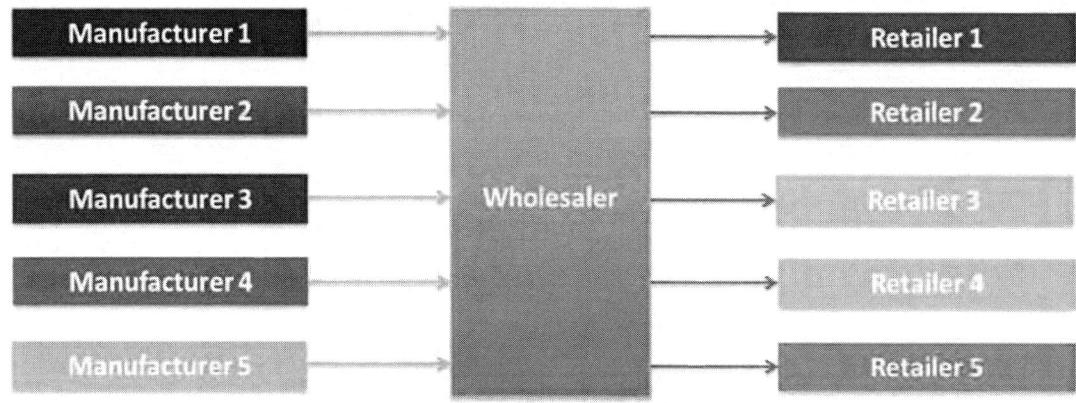

Scenario 2: One Wholesaler

Assume that each retailer needs an assortment of goods from each manufacturer.
The total number of transactions conducted with a wholesaler is 10.

FIGURE 10-1 A Role of the Wholesaler Is to Reduce the Number of Transactions within the Supply Chain

- Intermediaries often pay for part of the advertising and sales support expenditures of the manufacturer or retailer to promote the product.

10-3 Channel Dimensions

Direct channel of distribution A channel that has no intermediaries; the manufacturer sells directly to the final consumer.

Indirect channel of distribution A channel that involves one or more intermediaries between the manufacturer and the consumer.

A **direct channel of distribution** has no intermediaries. The manufacturer sells directly to the final consumer. In the chapter opening, Kathleen selling her baked goods at her Tate's Bake Shop in Southampton, New York, is an example of a direct channel of distribution. In the direct channel, Kathleen has close customer contact and full control over all aspects related to marketing her products.

An **indirect channel of distribution** involves one or more intermediaries between the manufacturer and the consumer. When Kathleen sells her chocolate chip cookies to the Amish Market in New York City, she uses an indirect channel of distribution, with Bay View Distributing acting as wholesaler. She sells the product directly to the Fresh Market, a retailer, and thus she uses an indirect channel of distribution since the retailer is between Kathleen and consumers who purchase her bakery goods. These channels are illustrated in **Figure 10-2**.

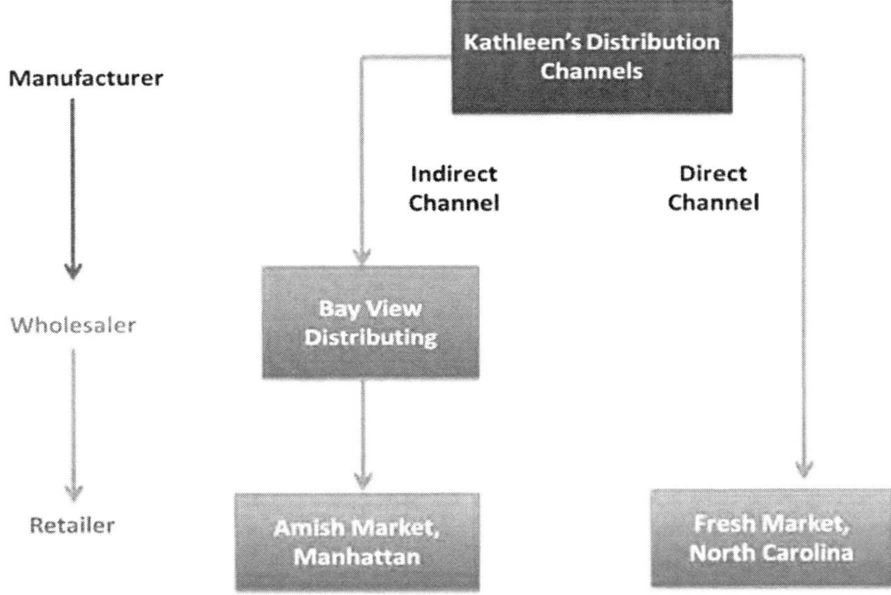

FIGURE 10-2 Two of Kathleen's Distribution Channels

An indirect channel does not allow Kathleen close contact with consumers, and she has no control of the marketing. But the indirect channel allows her to increase her presence in the different markets and to increase her sales. It also reduces her marketing expenses and the risk involved in selling in the different locations where she has a presence.

Companies must decide on the number of intermediaries at each level of distribution. An **intensive distribution strategy** has as goal full market coverage, with the product available to all consumers; it aims at achieving high total sales but is able to recover only low per-unit profits as a result of channel expenses. Staples, such as milk, colas, beer, and snacks, are using an intensive distribution. Mondelēz Tate's Bake Shop cookies currently have an intensive distribution, sold at supermarkets, discounters and wholesale clubs, among others.

An **exclusive distribution strategy** offers a high control of the intermediaries handling the product and thus of the marketing strategy by limiting their number to just one or two per geographic area. This type of distribution is intended to create prestige for the company's products and strong distributor support and service in return for high per-unit profit. Designer clothes, such as Prada, Dior, and Armani, and sleek electronics, such as Bang & Olufsen, are distributed to retailers using an exclusive distribution strategy.

A **selective distribution strategy (see Figure 10-3)** lies in the middle between the two, intensive and exclusive distribution, in terms of control, service, and profits. Firms using this strategy have some control over marketing, limiting distribution to select resellers in each area. At the same time, the company has a reasonable sales volume and profits. Kathleen initially used a selective distribution strategy, selling at gourmet shops in Manhattan and Long Island, but not at regular supermarkets or upscale supermarkets.

Intensive distribution strategy A strategy that has as its purpose full market coverage, making the product available to all target consumers when and where consumers want it.

Exclusive distribution strategy A distribution strategy that offers a high control of the intermediaries handling the product and thus of the marketing strategy by limiting their number to just one or two per geographic area.

Selective distribution A strategy whereby firms have some control over the marketing strategy by limiting distribution to a select group of resellers in each area, while, at the same time, the company can achieve a reasonable sales volume and profits.

FIGURE 10-3 The publishers of this textbook, Textbook Media, use a selective distribution strategy that allows students to purchase the book from the company directly or at their bookstore
Source: https://www.textbookmediapress.com/how-it-works

10-4 Channel Management

In managing the channel of distribution, companies first consider the channel structure. Decisions must be made with regard to channel organization and administration, as well as channel strategies, such as vertical or horizontal integration. Second, channel relationships must be examined. The use of power in the channel and conflict management constitutes important channel dynamics that can lead to the success or failure of the channel.

Contractual channel arrangement A contract between intermediaries that defines all the tasks that each channel member must perform with regard to production, delivery strategy and terms of sale, territorial rights, promotional support, the price policies of each intermediary, and contract length.

10-4a Channel Organization and Administration

A channel of distribution consists of one or more independent intermediaries, in which each is a separate entity whose goal is resource or profit maximization. Because of this potential conflict among channel members, a mechanism must exist that assigns marketing responsibilities and addresses channel-wide strategic objectives. **Figure 10-4** highlights the primary methods of channel organization and administration.

Channels of distribution adopting a **contractual channel arrangement** spell out in a contract all the tasks that must be performed by each channel

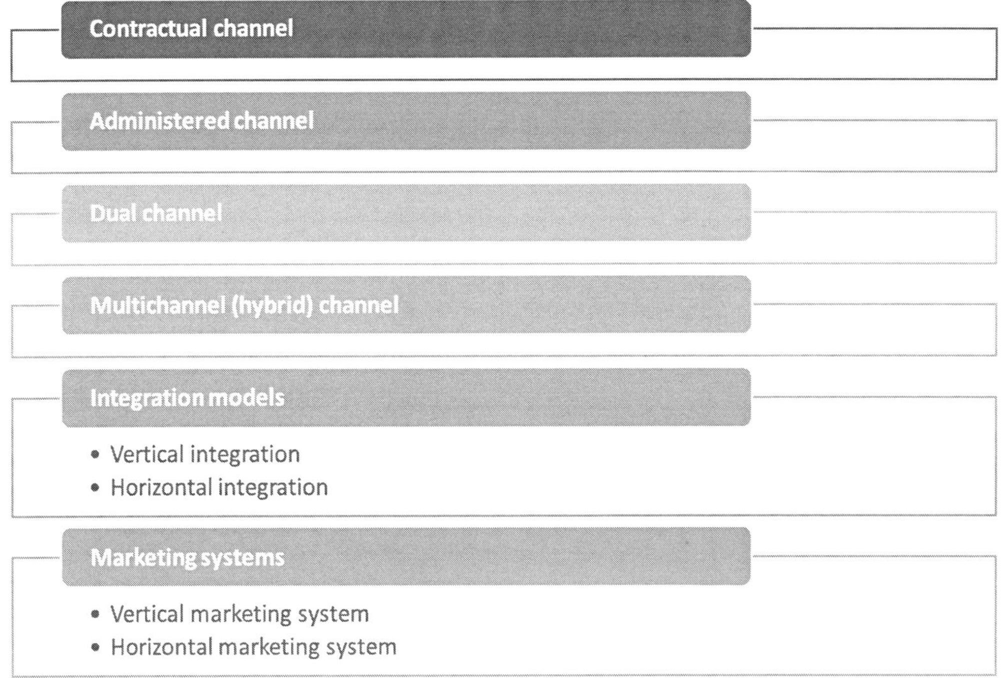

FIGURE 10-4 Methods of Channel Administration

member with regard to production, delivery, terms of sale, territorial rights, promotional support, the price policies of each intermediary, and contract length. Channels adopting an **administered channel arrangement** have a dominant member of the distribution channel in terms of size, expertise, or influence coordinating the tasks of each channel member. The dominant member, known as the **channel captain**, can be at any level of the distribution channel. A manufacturer with a strong brand pull, such as Coca-Cola or Colgate-Palmolive, could be the channel administrator. Many powerful wholesalers, such as SUPERVALU, dealing with smaller manufacturers or retailers can act as channel captains. Hybrid structures, such as Costco, a leading warehouse club that sells both to final consumers and resellers, also can administer the distribution channel.

Administered channel arrangement An arrangement between intermediaries such that a dominant member of the distribution channel in terms of size, expertise, or influence coordinates the tasks of each member in the channel.

Channel captain The dominant member of a channel of distribution.

A **dual channel of distribution** is employed by firms that use two different channels. For example, Kathleen uses a dual channel of distribution, selling (1) through a wholesaler to gourmet shops and (2) selling directly to the Fresh Market retail chain. In another illustration, the Donna Karan collection is distributed exclusively, whereas her bridge brand, DKNY, is distributed selectively. It is thus likely that two different channels are used to distribute the two brands: an exclusive distribution channel for the Donna Karan collection and a selective distribution channel for the DKNY brand.

Dual channel of distribution The use of two or more channels of distribution to appeal to different markets.

A firm can also use a **multichannel distribution system**, also known as a hybrid marketing channel. Before the Internet, multichannel marketing was popular primarily in business-to-business environments. With multiple channels, customers have an expanding menu of purchase and communication options. For example, you can purchase an Abbyson leather sofa directly from their website, or from online retailers Overstock,

Multichannel distribution system (or hybrid marketing channel) The use of multiple (more than two) channels of distribution, thus offering customers multiple purchase and communication options.

Source: Jeff Bukowski/Shutterstock

Wayfair, and Walmart (online only), or you can go to BJ's Wholesale Club and purchase it in the store.

Channel members can strengthen their position in the channel through **vertical integration,** by acquiring or merging with an intermediary in the channel—a supplier or a buyer. Such integration offers the channel member more control in the channel. Zara, a popular clothing retailer, makes more than half of its clothes in-house, rather than relying on a network of suppliers. Its competitor, H&M, however, buys clothes from hundreds of firms. Starting with basic fabric dyeing, almost all of Zara's clothes take shape in a design-and-manufacturing center in Spain, with the sewing done by seamstresses from 400 local cooperatives. This setup allows designers to closely follow which items are in demand, and on the basis of this real-time data, they place orders and ship the inventory directly to the stores twice a week. This eliminates the need for warehouses and for keeping large inventories. In 2020, however, after the onset of the COVID-19 pandemic, Zara found itself forced to temporarily shut down 3,700 stores and eventually write off obsolete inventory to the tune of over $324 million.[2]

Vertical integration The acquisition or merger with an intermediary in the channel that is either a supplier or a buyer.

Horizontal integration An acquisition or merger with an intermediary at the same level in the distribution channel.

Vertical marketing systems (VMS) Intermediary marketing systems that consist of manufacturers, wholesalers, and retailers in the same channel who have partial VMS ownership acting as a unified whole.

Horizontal marketing systems (HMS) Intermediaries at the same level of the distribution channel pooling resources and achieving partial ownership of the system, achieving economies of scale, and playing on their individual strengths.

Trading companies Complex marketing systems that specialize in providing intermediary service and reducing risk through extensive information channels and financial assistance.

Horizontal integration, involving an acquisition or merger at the same level in the channel, also increases channel member strength. An example is a manufacturer buying another manufacturer, a wholesaler acquiring another wholesaler at the same level in the distribution chain, or a retailer purchasing another retailer. This strategy, may trigger antitrust investigations and create long-term problems for the firms involved.

An important development in distribution has been the emergence of **vertical marketing systems (VMS),** which consist of manufacturers, wholesalers, and retailers in the same channel acting as a unified whole. VMS typically involve partial ownership. An example is the wholesaler SUPERVALU purchasing Rainbow Foods grocery stores, and then co-owning these stores, now known as Cub Foods, along with other wholesalers. Vertical marketing systems benefit from greater coordination achieved through common ownership.

Horizontal marketing systems (HMS) consist of intermediaries at the same level of the distribution channel pooling resources and achieving economies of scale, thereby playing on their individual strengths. At the wholesale level, Mitsui and Mitsubishi, large integrated trading companies, are using their bottling and distribution systems to bottle and distribute all Coca-Cola products in Japan. **Trading companies** are complex marketing systems specializing in providing intermediary services, risk reduction through extensive information channels, and financial assistance. Trading companies have been very successful in Japan and South

Korea. Japanese trading companies have operations all around the world, ranging from finance to distribution, technology, mining, oil and gas exploration, and information. They act as intermediaries for half of Japan's exports and two-thirds of its imports. They have changed from pure traders to more sophisticated investment holding companies. The biggest and the best of the traders are members of **keiretsus**, which are families of firms with interlocking stakes in one another. Here, the trading companies' role is to act as the eyes and ears of the whole group, spotting business trends, market gaps, and investment opportunities. The top trading companies in Japan are Itochu, Sumitomo, Marubeni, Mitsui, Mitsubishi, and Sojitz.[3]

Source: imtmphoto/Shutterstock

Keiretsus Japanese families of firms with interlocking stakes in one another.

10-4b Channel Relationships: Conflict and Power

Intermediaries sometimes disagree on channel goals, on their roles in the channel of distribution, or on the channel rewards. One area of potential conflict is the manufacturer's use of a **pull strategy**, whereby the manufacturer first focuses on consumer demand through extensive promotion, expecting that consumers will request the brand through the channel. The alternative, a **push strategy**, focuses on intermediaries, providing the necessary incentives for them to cooperate in marketing the product to the final consumer. Manufacturers typically use both strategies because using only a pull strategy would create conflict in the distribution channels.

Pull strategy A strategy whereby the manufacturer first focuses on consumer demand through extensive promotion, expecting that consumers will request the brand through the channel.

Push strategy A strategy that focuses on intermediaries, providing the necessary incentives for them to cooperate in selling the product to the final consumer.

Channel conflict can be reduced through the appropriate use of power. **Reward power** refers to power over the channel members based on anticipation of special privileges, such as financial rewards for engaging in a particular desirable behavior. Reward power in the form of slotting fees offered by the manufacturer to the retailer will be exerted only as long as the slotting fees are paid. When the manufacturer ceases to pay slotting fees, the products will be removed from the retailer's shelf, unless other types of power exist concurrently. Coercive power refers to power over channel members based on the ability of one or more intermediaries to remove privileges for noncompliance. An example of **coercive power** involves the threat of elimination from the channel of distribution for noncompliance with a particular channel policy. Reward power and coercive power are less persuasive than the other forms of power because when the reward or coercion factors are removed, channel members' behavior reverts to one that is focused on individual goals.

Reward power Power over the channel members based on an anticipation of special privileges, such as a financial reward for conducting a particular behavior.

Coercive power Power over channel members based on the ability of one or more intermediaries to remove privileges for noncompliance.

Type	Definition
Reward power	Power over the channel members based on the anticipation of special privileges
Coercive power	Power over channel members based on the ability of one or more intermediaries to remove privileges for noncompliance
Expert power	Power over the other channel members based on experience and knowledge that a channel member possesses
Referent power	Power over the other channel members based on the close match in terms of values and objectives that members of the channel share
Legitimate power	Power over the other channel members by virtue of an intermediary's status or position in the channel

FIGURE 10-5 Types of Channel Power

Expert power Power over the other channel members based on experience and knowledge that a channel member possesses.

Referent power Power over the other channel members based on the close match in terms of values and objectives that members of the channel share.

Legitimate power Power over the other channel members by virtue of an intermediary's status or position in the firm.

Logistics (or physical distribution) All the activities involved in the physical flow and storage of materials, semi-finished goods, and finished goods to customers in a manner that is efficient and cost effective.

Expert power refers to power over the other channel members based on experience and knowledge that a channel member possesses. **Referent power** refers to power over the other channel members based on the close match in terms of values and objectives shared by members of the channel. **Legitimate power** refers to power over the other channel members by virtue of an intermediary's status or position in the channel. A channel captain has legitimate power over the other channel members by virtue of its position and role in the channel. **Figure 10-5** reviews the various forms of channel power.

10-5 Logistics: Overview and Functions

Logistics is defined as all the activities involved in the physical flow and storage of materials, semi-finished goods, and finished goods to customers in a manner that is efficient and cost effective. The logistics function can be handled by any entity in the distribution channel—the producer, intermediaries, or the customer. An important trait of distribution is that it should meet customers' needs in terms of convenient and timely access to the product at a fair cost.

Logistics costs in the United States are about 8 percent of the gross domestic product (GDP), reaching $1.64 trillion. To put it into perspective, logistics as a share of GDP was 18% in 1979, before the trucking deregulation.[4] These costs vary greatly by industry sector and by company size and location. For example, retailers that offer wide assortments will spend more on logistics as transportation and storage costs increase. A critical decision in this regard is whether the manufacturer seeks to have an intensive, selective, or exclusive distribution. Logistics involve the primary functions shown in **Figure 10-6**, which are discussed in the next sections.

10-5a Transportation

Transportation is an important factor that marketers must consider. The choice of transportation determines whether products arrive at their destination on time and in good condition. The cost of transportation is also an important consideration because transportation costs can increase the product price. **Figure 10-7** shows the breakdown of the primary modes of

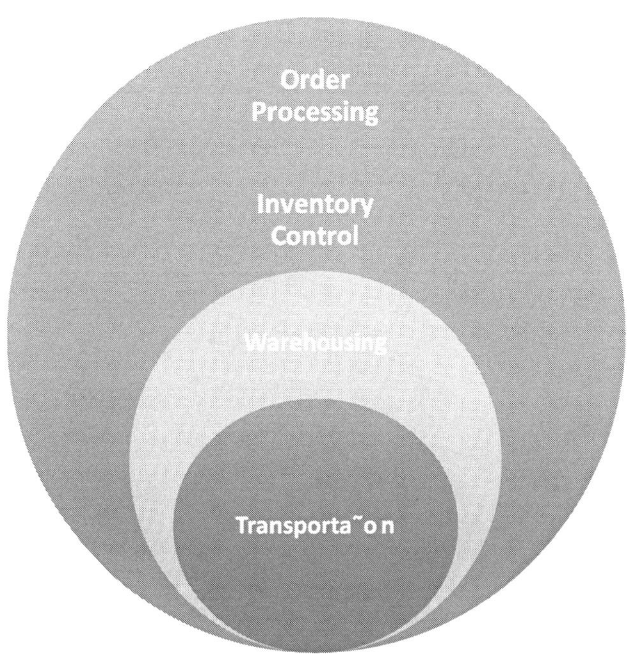

FIGURE 10-6 Logistic Functions

Means of Transportation	Area Coverage	Cost	Speed	Product	Domestic Traffic Vol. (ton-miles of freight)
Truck	High	Higher	Higher	Perishables, clothing, cement, furniture, appliances, electronics, automobiles	2,023,456
Rail	Higher	Medium	Lower	Coal, cement, oil, grain, lumber, automobiles	1,674,784
Air	Highest	High	High	Jewelry, perishables, electronics, semiconductors, wine, spirits	14,417
Water	Low	High	Low	Coal, cement, oil, grain, automobiles	489,000
Pipeline	Low	Lower	Low	Oil, gas, chemicals, semi-liquid coal	882,444

FIGURE 10-7 Characteristics of Different Modes of Transportation
Source: Bureau of Transportation Statistics, U.S. Ton-Miles of Freight, https://www.bts.gov/us-ton-miles-freight, accessed on March 7, 2020

freight transportation: truck, railway, air, waterways, and pipeline. Notice that in terms of volume, the highest percentage of products is moved by rail. See **Figure 10-8** for a graphical illustration of the volume distribution of the different transportation modes.

Trucks transport smaller shipments over shorter distances than the other freight carriers. Most local transportation is handled by truck, and thus trucks handle a substantial proportion (almost one-third) of all traffic

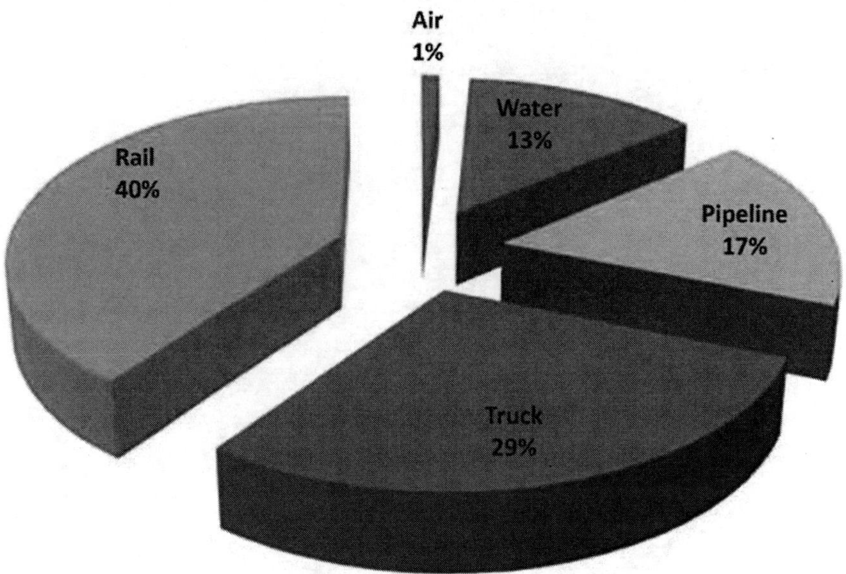

FIGURE 10-8 Volume Distribution of Modes of Transportation

in the continental United States annually. Trucks offer high flexibility, taking products from the factory directly to the destination. Their rates are competitive with the other modes of intracontinental transportation in the United States, and they offer fast service on shorter routes compared with the other modes of transportation. Trucks can carry a wide array of products, from perishables to clothing, furniture, appliances, electronics, cement, and automobiles.

Railways continue to be an important mode for freight transportation in the United States. They transport over long distances high-weight, high-volume products that have a low per-pound value, such as coal, stone, cement, oil, grain, and lumber, but also more expensive products, such as large equipment and automobiles. Railways are a low-cost mode of relatively low-speed freight transportation. They do not offer the flexibility that trucks do, however, because their mobility is restricted to areas designated for freight handling.

Air freight accounts for a smaller percentage of intracontinental transportation in the United States. Air carriers offer high-speed, high-cost shipping that is ideal for perishable products, such as cut flowers. It also works well for low-volume, lower-weight, high-value products, such as jewelry and electronics, or for documents that necessitate prompt delivery. Companies such as FedEx base much of their business on air transport, banking on their capability to deliver products overnight.

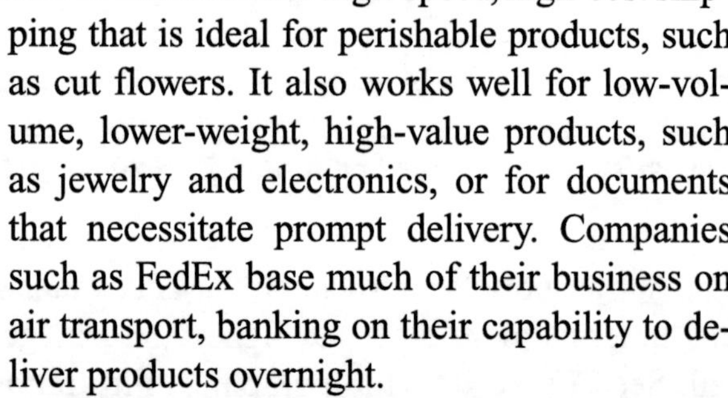

Source: newroadboy/Shutterstock

Tankers, barges, and other freighters in the inland and coastal waterways continue to play a role in domestic traffic. However, water transportation is essential for international trade, accounting for a substantial proportion of international traffic. Waterways are used for transporting high-weight, high-volume products that have a low per-pound value, such as coal, stone, cement, oil, grain, lumber, and petrol, over long distances.

Pipelines are a low-cost mode of transporting liquid or semiliquid products from the source to the target market in a continuous manner, in which there are no interruptions and intermediate storage is not necessary. Pipelines are expensive to maintain; among them are the Trans Alaska Pipeline, Basin, and Wolverine Pipeine.

Firms often resort to **intermodal transportation**, using two or more different transportation modes—a combination of truck, rail, air, and waterways. Intermodal transportation has been greatly facilitated by containerization. Goods can be placed into containers at the factory, taken by truck to a train loading facility, transported to a port, and loaded aboard a ship. After crossing the ocean, the containers are loaded on a truck and transported to their final destination. All of these maneuvers can be accomplished using the initial containers, thus providing greater protection for the products, which do not have to be shifted individually from one vessel to another—and at lower cost because loading the individual products from/into vehicles is more expensive than using containers.

Intermodal transportation Transportation using two or more different transportation modes—a combination of truck, rail, air, and waterways.

10-5b Logistics Facilitators

Moving goods from the place of origin, normally a manufacturer, to the place of sale, normally the retailer, requires some type of facilitation. The two most common logistics facilitators are freight forwarders and the hub-and-spoke distribution center.

Freight forwarders are specialized firms that collect shipments from different businesses, consolidate them for part of the distance, and deliver them to a destination, in what is typically a door-to-door service. Many freight forwarders are adapting to fit the needs of their corporate customers. Many pursue different value-added techniques, such as developing distinctive competencies in terms of geography, type of business, or specific commodities. It may be shipping museum art or zoo animals. Other freight forwarders will handle shipping for specific industry sectors such as health care, fashion, electronics, or perishables. Freight forwarding is becoming increasingly important as a result of the rapid globalization of business.

Freight forwarders Specialized firms that collect shipments from different businesses, consolidate them for part of the distance, and deliver them to a destination, in what is typically a door-to-door service.

Hub-and-spoke distribution centers are designed to speed up warehousing and delivery by channeling operations to one center (hub) that is particularly well equipped to handle the distribution of products to their destination. The idea of a hub location is to consolidate traffic from different origins and send it directly to different destinations, thus achieving economies of scale on hub-to-hub links. Such designs have been popular with airlines as well. A package can make several hub stops before arriving at destination. FedEx and UPS have successfully used the hub and spoke model over the years. The FedEx central hub is Memphis, where it is building a $1.5 billion World Hub with huge conveyor bridges and state-of-the-art equipment.[5]

Hub-and-spoke distribution centers Distribution centers designed to speed up warehousing and delivery, by channeling operations to one center (hub) that is particularly well equipped to handle the distribution of products to their destination.

Source: View Apart/Shutterstock

10-5c Warehousing

Warehousing is defined as the marketing function whereby goods are stored, identified, and sorted in the process of transfer to an intermediary in the distribution channel or to the final consumer. **Inventory** is the amount of goods being stored. Warehousing is necessary when the speed of production does not match demand or consumption. A wholesaler normally gets a break on price for bulk purchases, but may have to store products before there are enough retail orders or reorders. The concern, in this regard, is that the cost of storage is significantly lower than the price break the wholesaler received from purchasing the product in bulk, allowing for a profit. Or the wholesaler may have to stock extra products to have them available for immediate delivery to ensure customer satisfaction. If the product is not immediately delivered, the customer may order products from a different wholesaler in the future.

Warehousing The marketing function whereby goods are stored, identified, and sorted in the process of transfer to an intermediary in the distribution channel or to the final consumer.

Inventory The amount of goods being stored.

Private warehouses Warehouses that are owned or leased and operated by firms storing their own products.

Public warehouses Independent facilities that provide storage rental and related services.

Distribution centers Computerized warehouses designed to move goods.

Companies can use different types of storage facilities. **Private warehouses** are owned or leased and are operated by firms storing their own products. They are used by intermediaries at all levels of distribution: manufacturers, wholesalers, and retailers. These intermediaries typically need to have storage on a regular basis. **Public warehouses** are independent facilities that provide storage rental and related services. Public warehouses are used by firms that cannot afford to have their own facilities or that do not have a need for storage on a regular basis. International companies doing business in the United States periodically tend to use public warehouses rather than private warehouses. This is especially true in cases in which they have to store their products in customs-privileged facilities, such as foreign trade zones.

Distribution centers are computerized warehouses designed to move goods. They receive goods from different producers, take orders from buyers, and distribute them promptly. One of the largest distribution centers for electronic components and computer equipment is the Phoenix, Arizona–based Avnet Inc. It has the capability of serving customers ranging from IBM, Fujitsu, Intel, and Hewlett Packard to mom-and-pop shops in the technology market, who demand to have zero-inventory. To keep a handle on inventory, to increase shipping capacity, and to reduce errors, the company has rolled out Optum Inc.'s MOVE warehouse management system at its 400,000-square-foot Chandler, Arizona, logistics center. This distribution center handles distribution for

Source: Petinov Sergey Mihilovich/Shutterstock

more than 40,000 customers who do not want any inventory: they expect Avnet to control that.[6]

In addition to the storage function, many warehouses engage in product assembly and packaging. This applies in particular to warehouses located in free trade zones. A **foreign trade zone (FTZ)** is a tax-free area in the United States that is not considered part of the United States in terms of import regulations and restrictions. Products can be shipped to an FTZ, stored and assembled there, and then shipped to the United States or another country. Such products are not assessed duties and cannot be subjected to tariffs or quotas unless they enter the United States. FTZs are usually located in or near a port of entry and operated as a public utility by a public entity. In Virginia, for example, there are five foreign trade zones, including one at the Dulles International Airport serving the Washington, D.C., area and another, at the Virginia Port Authority in Suffolk.[7]

Foreign trade zone (FTZ) Tax-free area in the United States that is not considered part of the United States in terms of import regulations and restrictions. Also called a free trade zone.

10-5d Stock Turnover

A central aspect of inventory management is **stock turnover**, defined as the number of times per year that the inventory on hand is sold. The stock turnover annual rate is calculated as follows:

Stock turnover The number of times a year that the inventory on hand is sold.

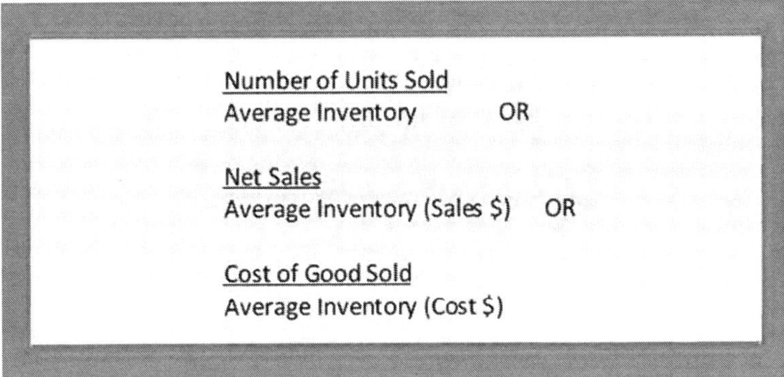
Number of Units Sold / Average Inventory OR

Net Sales / Average Inventory (Sales $) OR

Cost of Good Sold / Average Inventory (Cost $)

A high stock turnover rate is a goal that allows companies to perform optimally in terms of inventory carrying costs. But, with a high turnover rate there is the risk of not having merchandise items in stock when customers want to purchase them. Reducing the stock turnover rate will help ensure stockouts do not occur, but it will increase inventory carrying costs.

10-6 Wholesaling

Wholesaling encompasses all the activities involved in buying and handling the goods intended for sale to resellers or other organizational users. Wholesalers sell goods and services to manufacturers, to other wholesalers, to retailers, to the government, and to nongovernmental organizations. As mentioned in Section 10-2, wholesalers provide the advantages of distributing the product down the channel of distribution to a location that is convenient to consumers, warehousing it in the distribution process. California Almonds, for example, are distributed all over the country by the wholesaler. Wholesalers take risks for products in their

Wholesaling All the activities involved in buying and handling the goods intended for sale to resellers or other organizational users.

Wholesalers

- Merchant wholesalers
- Rack jobbers

Agents

- Manufacturer agent
- Selling agent
- Purchasing agent

Brokers

FIGURE 10-9 Types and Levels of Wholesaling

possession. They reduce the number of transactions needed to deliver a wide product assortment to retailers and, ultimately, to consumers. They buy products in bulk from manufacturers at a discount and then break the bulk to distribute smaller quantities to retailers. **Figure 10-9** identifies the various levels and types of wholesalers.

Merchant wholesalers Independent intermediaries who take title to and possession of products distributed to resellers or organizational consumers.

Rack jobbers Wholesalers that manage the store shelves carrying their products.

Agents Intermediaries who represent buyers or sellers; they do not take possession of or title to the merchandise, and they work based on commission or fees.

Manufacturers' agent (or manufacturers' representative) Representative who works as the company's sales representative, representing noncompeting manufacturers in a particular market, and is paid on a commission basis.

Merchant wholesalers are independent intermediaries who take title to and possession of products they distribute to resellers, such as retail stores. Merchant wholesalers can provide a full range of distribution tasks, such as product delivery, warehousing, sales force assistance, credit, research, planning, installation and repair assistance. These full-service wholesalers sell primarily to retailers, either to general merchandise retailers or to specialty stores. Other merchant wholesalers offer a limited array of services. They normally provide delivery and storage, but may not provide services such as sales force assistance, credit, research, planning, installation and repair assistance.

The second category of wholesalers are called **rack jobbers**, who manage the store shelves carrying their products. They assemble point-of-purchase displays and determine product prices. They take title to the products they sell on consignment but are allowed to take unsold items back to the manufacturer or wholesaler selling the product.

Agents represent buyers or sellers. They do not take possession of or title to the merchandise and they work based on commission or fees. A **manufacturers' agent (or manufacturers' representative)** usually works as the company's sales representative representing manufacturers in a particular market, and is paid on a commission basis. Manufacturers' agents can represent one or more noncompeting manufacturers. They are typically hired by small-and medium-sized businesses that cannot afford their own field force but need the sales function covered. They sense, they have a specified territory and must adhere to specific order-processing procedures.

Source: ESB Professional/ Shutterstock

A **selling agent** has an exclusive arrangement with the company, representing all of its operations in a particular market and acting as the sales or marketing department of the firm. Selling agents do not take title to the goods and are usually paid a percentage of sales. Given their broad responsibilities, their commission is higher than that of manufacturers' representatives. They are common for the clothing and furniture industries.

Purchasing agents have a long-term relationship with a buyer. They select, receive, and ship goods to buyers and are paid on a commission basis. Purchasing agents know their markets well and are familiar with the needs of their customers. Examples of purchasing agents are smaller agents in Italy who purchase designer clothes that are not very popular in the United States but are regarded as solid in Europe. Purchasing agents scour the garment districts in Milan and Rome and bring the newest designs to U.S. buyers in the New York or West Coast garment districts or to another location in Europe.

Brokers bring buyers and sellers together. They too do not take possession of or title to the merchandise, and they work based on commission or fees. Brokers will often locate firms that have not previously been considered viable customers. In addition to bringing buyers and sellers together, brokers may also negotiate through the selling process. Brokers can reduce overall selling expenses because they know the market and understand the needs and wants of various buyers as well as the products being offered by the seller.

Selling agent Agent that holds an exclusive arrangement with the company, represents all its operations in a particular market, and acts as the sales or marketing department of the firm.

Purchasing agents Agents with a long-term relationship with buyers who select, receive, and ship goods to buyers and are paid on a commission basis.

Brokers Intermediaries who bring buyers and sellers together; they do not take possession of or title to the merchandise, and they work based on commission or fees.

10-7 Retailing and Retail Formats

Most consumers think of grocery stores and discount stores as retailers because they are stores that sell products to consumers for final consumption. Yet retailing has a much broader spectrum that includes vending machines, catalog sales, manufacturers' outlet shops, wholesale clubs, Amway salespeople, and websites selling products. **Retailing** comprises all the activities involved in the final stage of distribution—selling goods and services to consumers for their consumption. Retailers perform the following distribution functions:

Retailing All the activities involved in the final stage of distribution—selling goods and services to consumers for their consumption.

- Create convenience for consumers. Retailers offer assortments of goods and services from different manufacturers. Consumers do not have to go to each manufacturer's outlet or wholesaler distributing the manufacturer's product; instead, they shop at a conveniently located single retail outlet.
- Inform consumers about products through salespeople in the store, advertisements, and point-of-purchase displays. This process is part of the **shopper marketing** effort, focusing all marketing activities on improving consumers' shopping experience to drive sales in-store or online, at the point of purchase.

Shopper marketing Focusing all marketing activities on improving consumers' shopping experience to drive sales in-store or online, at the point of purchase.

- Serve the other channel members (manufacturers and wholesalers). Retailers place individual products, rather than bundles, on the shelves (i.e., they break bulk), mark product prices, store the products, and take ownership of the products, while assuming all related risks (e.g., theft, loss).

The three main retail formats are general merchandise retailing, food retaiing, and non-store retailing (**Figure 10-10**). The top U.S. retailers in terms of revenue belong to the first two categories - the top ten are listed in **Figure 10-11**. However, many of the general merchandise retailers and

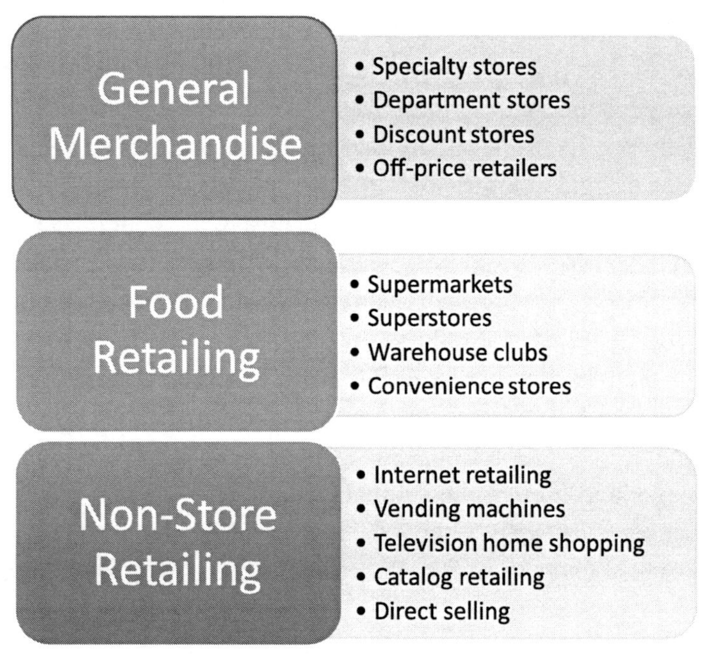

General Merchandise
• Specialty stores
• Department stores
• Discount stores
• Off-price retailers
Food Retailing
• Supermarkets
• Superstores
• Warehouse clubs
• Convenience stores
Non-Store Retailing
• Internet retailing
• Vending machines
• Television home shopping
• Catalog retailing
• Direct selling

FIGURE 10-10 Retail Formats

Rank	Company	Revenues (Billions)	Number of Stores
1	Walmart Stores, Inc.	$387.66	5,263
2	Amazon	$120.93	490
3	Kroger	$144	3,035
4	Costco	$101.43	523
5	Walgreens	$98.39	9,451
6	The Home Depot	$97.27	1,969
7	CVS Health	$83.79	9,954
8	Target	$74.48	1,844
9	Lowe's Cos. Inc.	$64.09	1,723
10	Albertsons Co.	$59.71	2,249

FIGURE 10-11 Top Ten Retailers by Revenue
Source: Kantar Retail; published by the National Retail Federation

food retailers also sell through their websites, which places them in the non-store category as well.

10-7a General Merchandise Retailing

General merchandise retailers are composed of specialty stores, department stores, discount stores, and off-price retailers. Approximately 55 percent of all retail sales are made in this category.

Specialty Stores Specialty stores offer a narrow product line and wide assortment. In this category are clothing stores, which are usually further specialized into women's, men's, or children's clothing stores, such as Gap and Victoria's Secret; bookstores such as the local apparel retailer or Barnes & Noble's chain; smaller local home improvement stores, or large chains such as Lowe's and Home Depot, and many others.

The largest of these stores (e.g., Barnes & Noble, Office Depot, and Lowe's) offer a huge selection of products in the category in which they are specializing. These are known as **category specialists (category killers)** and carry a narrow variety of merchandise but offer a wide assortment. Traditionally located in suburbia, category specialists are now migrating to urban areas. For example, Home Depot has two large stores in prime locations—one in midtown Manhattan and another in the Flatiron district, where one can often see people carrying large bags with the Home Depot logo.

Category specialist or (category killers) Large specialty stores that carry a narrow variety of merchandise but offer a wide assortment.

Specialty stores are expanding at the expense of all forms of non-food retailing. Specialty store chains are taking market share away from traditional department stores in the United States because they can offer a greater depth of merchandise within a product category. Shoppers looking for a new camera, stereo, kitchen utensils, or clothing will find more brands and selections in a specialty store than they would in a department store. Stores like the Indigo Company succeed because they offer a better selection of merchandise than other types of stores, or unique items.

Department Stores Department stores offer a broad variety of goods and wide assortments. Among the products they carry are the latest fashions for men, women, and children; household appliances and electronics; kitchenware; china; home furnishings; and toys and games. Department stores most often serve as **anchor stores (or generator stores)**, situated at the end (anchor) positions in malls to generate consumer traffic. Outside the United States, department stores typically also have large supermarket sections, and some may even carry fresh produce.

Anchor stores (or generator stores) Department stores situated at the end (anchor) positions in malls to generate consumer traffic.

It is typical for department stores to have numerous leased departments—sections that are centrally located in the store and that are leased to another retailer. Cosmetics counters at most department stores are leased departments, where the cosmetics companies pay rent to be able to sell their products using their own sales staff. The Estée Lauder counter at Nordstrom's department store is such an example: Its staff is hired, trained, and paid by Estée Lauder. Leased departments create traffic for the department store, bringing in clients to purchase products that are complementary to the store's offerings.

Department stores have suffered substantial losses in the past decade, mostly attributed to consumers opting for shopping on multiple channels looking for the best price for the same product. After trying on Bernie Mev Drake shoes, which cost $80 at Nordstrom, shoppers can find that DSW sells them online for under $40 with free shipping; it is easy for consumers, to search for better deals on the same product, even while shopping. Department stores, which tend to charge higher prices, are being replaced by online retailers, online or brick-and-mortar discounters, and category specialists. Discounters, off-price retailers, and category killers can purchase large volumes of merchandise and sell it at a lower price than department stores, which puts a squeeze on the profit margins for department stores. Moreover, renting mall space is more expensive than for stand-alone facilities. In good times, department stores do reasonably well. In bad times, shoppers look for discounts elsewhere. With each serious downturn in the economy, the department store customer base is eroded, imperiling its existence. The COVID-19 pandemic marked an existential crisis for department stores, with J.C. Penney and Neiman Marcus filing for bankruptcy, Macy's closing stores and cutting corporate staff, Lord & Taylor firing its executive team, and Nordstrom canceling orders and putting off paying its vendors. With department stores taking up 30% of mall square footage, the future looks grim for malls as well.[8]

Discount Stores Discount stores sell high volumes of merchandise, offer limited service, and charge lower prices. Discount stores are divided into two categories: all-purpose discount stores, which offer a wide variety of merchandise and limited depth, and category specialists (category killers), which carry a narrow variety of merchandise and offer a wide assortment. The all-purpose category is dominated by Walmart and Target.

Off-price retailers Retailers that sell brand-name and designer merchandise below regular retail.

Category specialists, also known as category killers, stores with category dominance, are large stores carrying a narrower merchandise variety of but a wide assortment. Office Depot, Home Depot, Barnes & Noble, and IKEA are examples.

Source: Chekyravaa/Shutterstock

Off-Price Retailers **Off-price retailers** sell brand-name and designer merchandise below regular retail prices. The products they sell may include overruns, irregular products, and products from previous seasons. Off-price retailers include:

- Factory outlet stores, for designers such as Ralph Lauren, Liz Claiborne, and Jones New York.

- Department store outlets, such as Off Fifth for Saks Fifth Avenue, or Nordstrom Rack for Nordstrom's.
- Close-out retailers, such as T.J. Maxx and Marshalls.
- Single-price retailers, such as the Dollar Store and Dollar General.

10-7b Food Retailers

Food retailers consist of the conventional supermarkets, supercenters, warehouse clubs, and convenience stores. Conventional **supermarkets** are self-service retailers with annual sales higher than $2 million and less than 20,000 square feet of store space. Conventional supermarkets, such as Kroger, Food Lion, Publix, and Fry's, account for almost half of all supermarket sales and offer a one-stop grocery shopping opportunity to consumers. **Superstores** are food retailers with more than 20,000 square feet of space and at least $17 million in sales. However, the superstore category nonfood items account for at least 25 percent of sales. A number of all-purpose general discount stores, Walmart, for example, have been transformed into superstores to facilitate one-stop shopping for consumers. In their enhanced formats, these stores carry an extensive food selection in addition to broad non-food product lines.

Warehouse clubs (or wholesale clubs) require members to pay an annual fee and operate in low-overhead, enormous warehouse-type facilities. They offer limited lines of brand-name and dealer-brand groceries, apparel, appliances, and other goods at a substantial discount. They sell to consumers as well as to small businesses. The top U.S. warehouse clubs are Sam's Club (part of Walmart), Costco, and BJ's. As seen earlier in this chapter, Costco ranks third in terms of sales revenue, and a typical Costco warehouse is jammed with consumers loading their shopping carts at any time of day.

Convenience stores are small retailers located in residential areas convenient to consumers. They are open long hour, usually 24 hours a day, 7 days a week. The stores carry limited lines of high-turnover necessities, such as milk, coffee, soft drinks, beer, bread, medicine, and gasoline; and offer the possibility of a one-stop shopping experience. Formats of convenience stores vary from small, independent retailers to chains such as 7-Eleven and Wawa. Convenience stores are able to compete with supermarkets by selling other products, such as gasoline, propane gas tanks, and other products. Most convenience stores now sell some type of food, such as sandwiches. A number of convenience stores lease space to fast food franchises, such as Subway.

Supermarkets Stores that carry an extensive food selection and drug products, as well as nonfood items (which account for at least 25 percent of sales), combining supermarket, discount, and warehouse retailing principles.

Superstores Large retailers, such as combination stores or hypermarkets, that sell food, drugs, and other products.

Warehouse clubs (or wholesale clubs) Stores that require members to pay an annual fee and that operate in low-overhead, warehouse-type facilities, offering limited lines of brand-name and dealer-brand groceries, apparel, appliances, and other goods at a substantial discount.

Convenience stores Small retailers that are located in residential areas, are open long hours, and carry limited lines of high-turnover necessities.

10-7c Non-store Retailing

Non-store retailing is by far the fastest growing category. Online retailing is rapidly increasing for the on-line only category, such as Amazon, Overstock, Gilt.com, and Zappos, and for store retailers of all types, such as Walmart, Target, Costco, and Lowe's. This trend has become more pronounced since the onset of the COVID-19 pandemic. Non-store retailing

Source: Rawpixel.com/Shutterstock

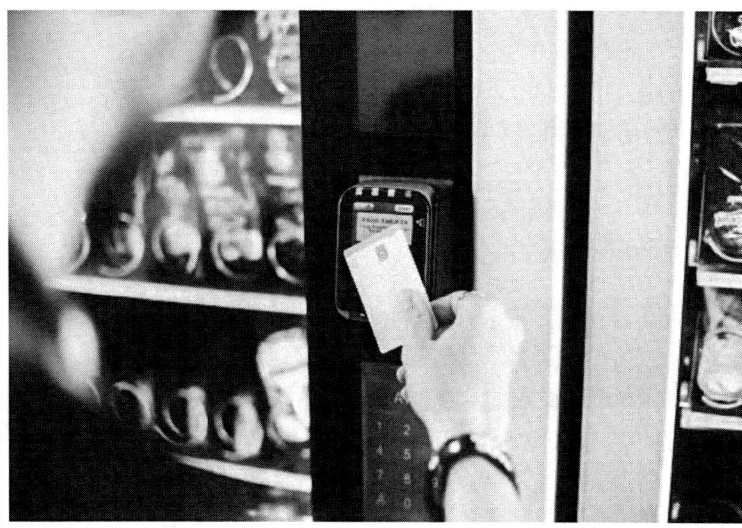

Source: Nacho7/Shutterstock

also includes vending machines, television home shopping, catalog retailers, and direct marketers.

Internet retailing (or e-commerce) has become an essential retail format. The Internet retailing category includes both traditional retailers and a seemingly endless array of online retailers, such as Amazon, Horchow, Wayfair, Zappos, Zulily, and many others. Traditional retailers are pursuing additional market penetration online, creating convenience for customers, and market diversification, selling to new customers. Online retailing offers opportunities to retailers to target beyond their consumer base and geographic regions. Online retailing will be addressed in depth in Chapter 13, Digital and Social Media Marketing.

Vending machine retailing today is very different than just a few years ago. Consumers can use credit cards or cellphones for purchases, in addition to cash. They are located in proximity to consumers, allow for 24-hour access, and eliminate the need for salespeople. In the United States, they primarily sell beverages and food items. In Japan, they are very popular and sell just about anything one can think of, including beer, sausage, rice, life insurance, eggs, cameras, pantyhose, and condoms. In Munich, Germany, vending machines for fresh flowers are located in the center of town.

Internet retailing (or e-commerce) Selling through the Internet using web-based tools to increase market penetration and market diversification.

Television home shopping Retailing through cable channels selling to consumers in their homes, through infomercials, and by direct-response advertising shown on broadcast and cable television.

The **television home shopping** category includes cable channels selling to consumers in their homes, infomercials, and direct-response advertising shown on broadcast and cable television. The primary television shopping networks in the United States are QVC and the Home Shopping Network (HSN). All sell products to consumers in a format that approximates that of a talk show with a primary focus on the product and on making the sale. Infomercials also have a talk-show format, often featuring celebrities or other appropriate spokespeople who, during half-hour-long television programs, attempt to sell a product. They also sell their products online.

Catalog retailers Retailers selling products through mail catalogs.

Catalog retailers are very popular in high-income countries, and most products are sold through catalogs. Gardeners ordering from one catalog retailer will find themselves on the list of many other catalog retailers, such as Heirloom Roses, Wayside Gardens, and Edible Landscaping.

Most gardening catalog retailers offer a colorful website as an alternative to the equally colorful catalog.

In the **direct selling** retail format, a salesperson, typically an independent distributor, contacts a consumer at a convenient location (e.g., his or her home or work-place), demonstrates a product's use and benefits, takes orders, and delivers the merchandise. Retailers involved in direct selling are Avon Products, Nu Skin, Mary Kay Cosmetics, and Cutco knives, among others. **Network marketing (or multilevel marketing)** is a variation on direct selling that involves signing up sales representatives to go into business for themselves with minimal start-up capital. Their task is to sell more "distributorships"—that is, to identify more sales representatives from their own personal network, to buy the product, and to persuade others to buy the product. Among successful network marketing firms are Amway and Herbalife.

Direct selling Selling that involves a salesperson, typically an independent distributor, contacting a consumer at a convenient location (e.g., his or her home or workplace), demonstrating the product's use and benefits, taking orders, and delivering the merchandise.

Network marketing (or multilevel marketing) An alternative distribution structure, using acquaintance networks for the purpose of distribution.

10-8 Retailing Decisions

Retailers need to make a number of important decisions to most effectively appeal to their target market. They need to determine the merchandise assortment, the types of services that need to be offered, the store characteristics likely to appeal to their target consumers, and the store location that is most appropriate for their customers **(see Figure 10-12).**

Merchandise mix The product assortment and brands that a store carries.

10-8a The Merchandise Mix and the Service Mix

Retailers need to determine the optimal **merchandise mix**, which is the product assortment and brands that will be carried by the store. Related to the merchandise mix is the **service mix**—the different types of services that will be offered to the retail customers. Decisions such as product assortment and service are important aspects of marketing that necessitate extensive evaluation on the part of retailers.

Service mix The different types of services offered to retail customers.

For example, Martin's Super Markets carry the typical supermarket fare that most of its competitors carry. In addition, it features gourmet products, such as specialty cheeses. Martin's also has dinner packages with complete entree, dessert, and bread, waiting to be picked up and served on the dinner table and hot gourmet food in its cafe´. It has one section dedicated to natural foods and another to international foods. In terms of customer service, Martin's staff actually takes customers to the location of the merchandise on the shelf and, if their groceries do not fit neatly in a small grocery bag, carries them to customers' automobiles.

Today, many retailers attempt to increase their merchandise mix to become a one-stop shopping

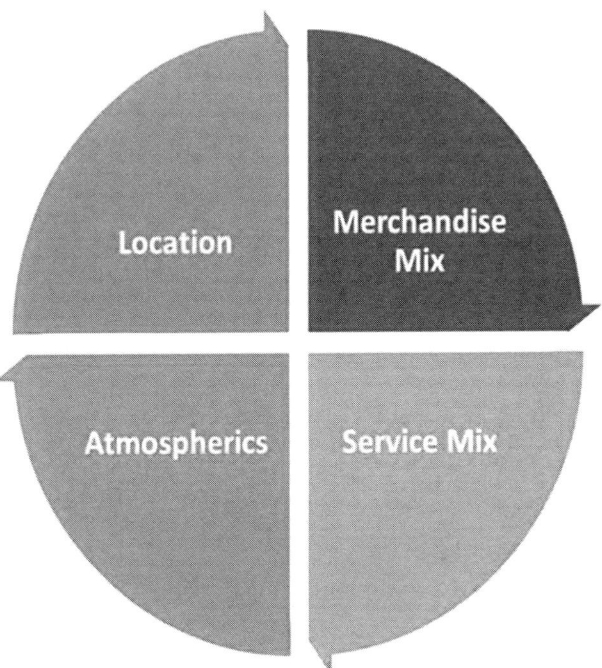

FIGURE 10-12 Retail Decisions

experience for consumers. In the process, they add products that are not related to the existing merchandise mix, which is known as **scrambled merchandising**. Scrambled merchandising expands a firm's competitive base. A wine shop could add gourmet products and fresh bread from a local baker and produce from local farmers, thus competing with other gourmet stores, bakeries, and supermarkets. An antique dealer could carry designer pillows and sheets, thus competing with department stores. A home-improvement warehouse could carry furniture, thus competing with furniture stores. From the consumer's point of view, one-stop shopping is clearly an advantage. Inside Indigo carries small furniture items and home decor specialties, along with its clothing and jewelry lines.

Scrambled merchandising Scrambled merchandising involves retailers adding complementary product categories not included in the existing merchandise mix and more services to create one-stop shopping convenience for target consumers.

Assuming that the retailer's traditional consumers do purchase the additional products added to the merchandise mix through scrambled merchandising, there is still the possibility that the same consumers may eventually become confused as to the precise business of the retailer. There is also the danger that the retailer will descend into the spiral of retailing. To illustrate, suppose a supermarket adds a line of health and beauty aids to increase its profit margins. Drugstores, because they are losing customers now, will add a product to their merchandise line, such as greeting cards, stamps, magazines, and office supplies. Because of this, stationery stores are being threatened, so to remain competitive, they add gift items, toys, novelties, perfume, and inexpensive jewelry. Consumers no longer need to go to a stationery or gift store for gift specialties, so to maintain their customers, stationery and gift stores add candy, party supplies, a deli, and perhaps a small cafe′. What do the supermarkets do now that some of their business is leaving? They need to add new scrambled merchandise. **Figure 10-13** illustrates this self-perpetuating nature of scrambled merchandising.

10-8b Atmospherics

Atmospherics refer to the physical attributes of the store or non-store retailer. For a brick-and-mortar store, atmospherics include lighting and music tempo, the fixtures and other displays, colors, and store layout. It is all the store characteristics that create the overall mood and image for the store. For example, the Bloomingdale's department store is divided into what appears to be smaller boutiques. Individual designers or groups of designers have their own chambers, which are vividly lit. Perfumes are omnipresent, as are individuals ready to spray any of the passers-by with the newest olfactory attraction. Bookstores, including Barnes & Noble, offer reading areas and cafés with armchairs for quiet reading. Online, atmospherics are eye-catching: Bloomingdales' offers a celebratory, opulent holiday website, with hefty coupons for large purchases, and elegant outfits parading on the screen, inviting you to click.

Atmospherics The general atmosphere of the store created by its physical attributes, including lighting and music tempo, the fixtures and other displays, colors, and store layout.

10-8c Location

A critical decision for retailer success is location. It is important for a retailer to be located close to its customer base. Retail location determines

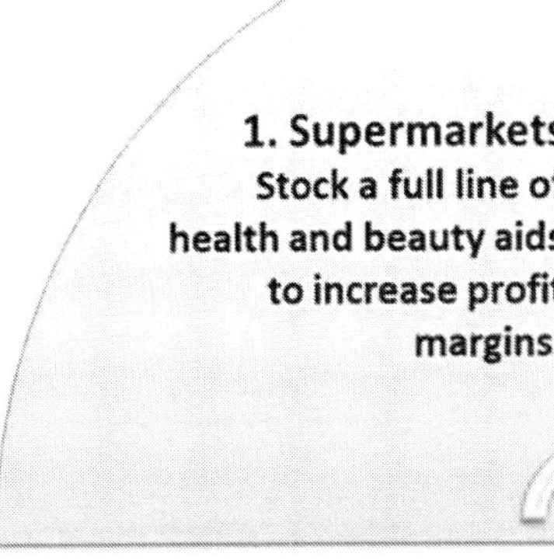
1. Supermarkets
Stock a full line of health and beauty aids to increase profit margins.
2. Drugstores
Lose health and beauty aid sales. They scramble into greeting cards, stamps, postcards, magazine, and ballpoint pens.
3. Stationery Stores
Lose sales in traditional lines. They scramble into gift items, toys, novelties, perfume, and inexpensive watches.
4. Gift Stores
Lose sales in traditional lines. They scramble into gum, candy, baked goods, deli gift packs, and paper goods for parties.

FIGURE 10-13 The Self-Perpetuating Nature of Scrambled Merchandising

in a large part the customer mix and the competition. In the past, most stores used to be located in **central business districts**, in the middle of busy downtowns, and often close to movie theaters and banks. In many urban areas, central business districts continue to thrive as the commercial and cultural heart of the city.

Secondary business districts are shopping areas that form at the intersection between two important streets, consisting primarily of convenience and specialty stores. **Neighborhood business districts** meet the needs of the neighborhood and tend to be located on a main street of a neighborhood; typically, they have a supermarket, a drugstore, and several smaller retailers.

Shopping centers consist of a group of stores that are planned, developed, and managed as one entity. **Regional shopping centers** consist of at least 100 stores that sell shopping goods to a geographically dispersed market. They tend to have three or four anchor stores or generator stores and with other retailers between. Customers are drawn from the entire area to its stores. **Community shopping centers** have fewer than 40 retailers, with a department store, a supermarket, and several smaller specialty retailers. **Neighborhood shopping centers** have between 5 and 15 retailers and serve the neighborhood, providing convenience in the form of a supermarket, discount store, and other

Central business districts Business districts located in the commercial and cultural heart of the city, in the middle of busy downtowns, and close to movie theaters and banks.

Secondary business districts Shopping areas, consisting primarily of convenience and specialty stores, that form at the intersection between two important streets.

Neighborhood business districts Business districts that meet the needs of the neighborhood and that tend to be located on a main street of the neighborhood; typically, they have a supermarket, a drug store, and several smaller retailers.

Shopping centers Groups of stores that are planned, developed, and managed as one entity.

Regional shopping centers Shopping centers that consist of at least 100 stores that sell shopping goods to a geographically dispersed market.

Community shopping centers Shopping centers with fewer than 40 retailers, containing a department store, a supermarket, and several smaller specialty retailers.

Neighborhood shopping centers Shopping centers that have between five and 15 retailers and that serve the neighborhood, providing convenience in the form of a supermarket, discount store, laundry service, and other smaller specialty stores.

smaller specialty stores. In Europe, neighborhood shopping centers are likely to have a small pedestrian zone that cannot be accessed with automobiles. These neighborhoods are created for a walking rather than a driving.

10-9 Trends In Retailing

Retailers operate in a rapidly changing environment. New retailers need to be innovative and proactive to survive. Established retailers can easily fail if they do not keep up with retailing trends and practices. Moreover, the Internet has radically changed retailing practices. For existing retailers, it has created new possibilities for reaching old and new consumers, but it has also created new competition.

10-9a Shortening Retailer Life Cycles: The Wheel of Retailing

Wheel of retailing A model that describes how stores evolve from innovative low-margin, low-cost, and low-price operations and, in seeking to broaden their customer base, they add services, upgrade facilities, and thus increasing costs and prices; and, in the process, lose their initial customers, who move on to new low-priced retailers, and become conventional retailers.

New forms of retailing are emerging and rapidly reaching maturity. Whereas the department store took a century to reach maturity, new formats, such as warehouse clubs and Internet retailing, have reached maturity in less than a decade.

The **wheel of retailing** partially illustrates the evolution of retailing. It describes how stores that start out as innovative low-margin, low-cost, and low-price operations seek to broaden their customer base by adding services, upgrading facilities, and thus increasing costs and prices. In the process, they lose their initial customers, who move on to new low-priced retailers, and become conventional retailers. Ultimately, these conventional retailers fall off the wheel because they are replaced with more innovative retailers climbing up on the wheel. The wheel of retailing is illustrated in **Figure 10-14**.

FIGURE 10-14 The Wheel of Retailing

The wheel of retailing could explain the decline and disappearance of many department stores today. They lost their middle-class customer base, who decided to go online for lower prices, rather than attentive customer service. Higher-end department stores and select specialty stores have met with a swift decline–among them are Bonwit Teller, FAO Schwartz, Barney's, and Bergdorf Goodman.

10-9b Technology-Based Developments

Technology is facilitating the retailing function, eliminating the need for salespeople, and increasing the accuracy of transactions. Pumping gas today is largely a self-service transaction, as is banking. Optical scanners have greatly facilitated the checkout process, ensuring accurate calculation and facilitating inventory control. At many stores today, consumers can scan their own merchandise items and pay for them with credit cards, thus lowering the cost of human resources for the retailer.

The Internet enables traditional retailers to further penetrate their current market, offering convenience to loyal customers. It also allows them to diversify and expand their market to consumers who otherwise would not normally use the respective retail establishment, even to consumers in international markets interested in the retailer's offering.

In other developments, retailers are attempting to use technology to create brand experiences. **Shoppertainment** is the logical blend of retailing and leisure that increases the guests' length of stay and, very importantly, the total spending on the retailer's premises. World retail brands and consumer product companies in the new millennium are aiming to create entertaining in-store environments that delight customers and increase the likelihood of repeat visits and spending.

Shoppertainment Blend of retailing and leisure that increases the length of stay and total spent with a retailer.

10-9c The Broadening Competitive Base

Retailers are facing increasing competition from competitors who are not in the same retail category. This trend is attributed primarily to online diversification, and scrambled merchandising, which provides one-stop shopping convenience to consumers and increases store profits. For example, in the past, gourmet coffee was available only at gourmet shops and coffee houses. Today, you can purchase gourmet coffee at gourmet shops, at gourmet coffee houses, at many supermarket chains, at wholesale clubs, at drugstores, and over the Internet. Consumers can purchase books at bookstores, at discounters such as Walmart, at Internet sites such as Amazon.com, at supermarkets, and at drugstores.

Source: adriaticfoto/Shutterstock

10-9d International Expansion of Retailers

Retailers are rapidly expanding internationally to gain competitive advantage and to increase sales, profits, and overall firm performance. As they expand beyond their home-country borders, retailers also can take advantage of cost savings and learn from experiences in a way that could further enhance home-country operations. Among retailers who have relatively recently moved to the United States are German food discounters Aldi and Lidl, giving Walmart serious competition. Retailers from the United States are expanding in Latin America, Asia, and Europe. It would be inconceivable to see a large metropolitan city in a European emerging market without a Carrefour, a French hypermarket, a Metro, a German warehouse club, or Aldi, a German discount supermarket.

Retailers expanding internationally must be aware of different regulations in the countries where they operate. Even in the European Union, where regulations are slowly becoming uniform, there are differences. French companies, for example, rarely offer an extra product free because the amount companies are allowed to give away is limited to seven percent of the total value. In Germany, bundling offers, such as offering three products for the price of two, are illegal, and cash discounts to the consumer are limited to a particular percent, depending on the product. Although these rules are no longer as strict, they have nevertheless created business practices that are entrenched and are unlikely to change quickly.

Furthermore, retailers expanding internationally must be aware of different retail practices from one market to another. Consumers in the United States prefer to shop less frequently and purchase products in bulk, whereas, in Europe, consumers go to the supermarket, the butcher, or the baker daily, or every other day, buying in smaller quantities. This has somewhat changed after the onset of the COVID-19 pandemic, with Europeans shopping less frequently and buying larger fridges than the under-counter versions to store larger amounts of food.

Supermarkets in the United States play quiet contemporary music, whereas supermarkets in Asia tend to be bright and loud, with salespeople creating excitement by announcing sales. In many emerging markets, buying at farmers' markets means buying at bargain prices, whereas in most high-income countries, consumers pay a premium price at outdoor markets for what is sold as organic food.

Summary

1. **Define distribution and identify the different channel functions and dimensions.** Distribution planning is the planning of the physical movement of products from the producer to individual or organizational consumers and the transfer of ownership and risk. It involves transportation, warehousing, and all the exchanges taking place at each channel level. It involves establishing the channels of distribution and managing other

intermediaries involved in distribution. Intermediaries are active participants in the value chain (or supply chain), the chain of activities performed in the process of developing, producing, marketing, delivering, and servicing a product for the benefit of the customer. An intensive distribution strategy has as its purpose full market coverage, whereas exclusive distribution has as a goal of high-level control of the intermediaries handling the product, and thus the marketing strategy, by limiting their number to just one or two per geographic area. Selective distribution opts for some control over the marketing strategy by limiting distribution to a select group of resellers in each area; at the same time, the company has a reasonable sales volume and profits.

2. **Identify issues related to channel management, such as channel organization, administration, and relationships.**
Intermediaries can opt for a contractual channel arrangement, which spells out in a contract all the tasks that must be performed by each channel member with regard to production, delivery strategy and terms of sale, territorial rights, promotional support, the price policies of each intermediary, and contract length. Intermediaries can also have an administered channel arrangement, which has a dominant member of the channel in terms of size, expertise, or influence that coordinates the tasks of each channel member—the channel captain. Firms can also use a dual channel of distribution, or multichannel distribution, appealing to different markets; this strategy is also known as multimarketing. Channel members can strengthen their position in the channel through vertical integration (by acquiring or merging with an intermediary in the channel—a supplier or a buyer). Alternatively, they can increase intermediary strength in the market through horizontal integration, which would involve an acquisition or merger at the same level in the distribution channel.

3. **Examine the different logistics functions.**
Logistics involve the following primary functions: transportation, warehousing, and inventory control. In terms of transportation, firms must decide whether to ship products by truck, water, rail, air, or pipeline, or a combination of these methods—known as intermodal transportation. These decisions depend on the type of product involved, on the urgency of delivery, and on how much the firm can afford to pay for the shipment. Companies must also decide on warehousing, which involves deciding where goods are stored, identified, and sorted in the process of transfer to an intermediary in the distribution channel or to the final consumer. There are different types of storage facilities that companies can use. Private warehouses are owned or leased and operated by firms storing their own products. Public warehouses are independent facilities that provide storage rental and related services. Public warehouses are used by firms that cannot afford to have their own facilities or that do not have a need for storage on a regular basis. Firms must also determine how to optimally manage their inventories. Inventory control involves ensuring that there is a continual flow of goods to customers that matches the quantity of goods with demand. Reducing inventory costs is essential because high inventories may result in products becoming stale, or large stocks of last year's models may hurt sales of new models.

4. **Provide an overview and description of the general merchandise retailing category and offer examples and illustrations.**
In the general merchandise retailing category are a number of retailers. Specialty stores, offering narrow assortments and deep product lines, are rapidly increasing their presence internationally. Department stores (general retailers that offer a broad variety of goods and deep assortments) are experiencing somewhat of a decline, whereas discount stores are rapidly expanding, with great success. Walmart, Kmart, and Target, in particular, have made great strides in attracting consumers. Category specialists, specializing in one product category, are also very successful.

5. **Provide an overview and description of the food retailing category and offer examples and illustrations.**
   Food retailers include conventional supermarkets, which are dominated by national and regional chains. Superstores are large combination stores (food and drug); in the rest of the world, they are known as hypermarkets. Warehouse clubs are becoming very popular worldwide, and many U.S. retailers in this category are doing very well. Convenience stores abound, with many chains developing in conjunction with gas stations.

6. **Provide an overview and description of the non-store retailing category and offer examples and illustrations.**
   Non-store retailing is one of the areas with the highest growth and unlimited opportunities. Internet retailing has vastly expanded opportunities for small and medium-sized retailers all over the world. Vending machines are increasing in sophistication and have different formats and capabilities in each market where they are available. Television home shopping is attracting more audiences, and today also offers opportunities to brick-and-mortar retailers to expand. Catalog retailers are still strong, expanding rapidly on the Internet. Direct selling and network marketing continue to gain ground, especially in developing countries.

7. **Address issues related to merchandise and service mix, location, atmospherics, and future trends in retailing.**
   Retailers need to make a number of important decisions in order to most effectively appeal to their target market. They need to determine the merchandise assortment that they should carry, the type of service that they should offer, the store characteristics likely to appeal to their target consumers, and the store location that is most appropriate for their customers. Among the trends in retailing are the shortening of the retailer life cycle, with new forms of retailing quickly emerging and rapidly reaching maturity; technological changes that facilitate inventory control and the overall retail transaction, as well as access, facilitated by the Internet; broadening of the competitive spectrum, with many stores expanding beyond their traditional product mix; and rapid internationalization to take advantage of new opportunities and increase retailers' bottom line.

Key Terms

Administered channel arrangement (289)
Agents (298)
Anchor stores (or generator stores) (301)
Atmospherics (306)
Brokers (299)
Catalog retailers (304)
Category specialist (or category killers) (301)
Central business districts (307)
Channel captain (289)
Channels of distribution (284)
Coercive power (291)
Community shopping centers (307)
Contractual channel arrangement (288)
Convenience stores (303)
Direct channel of distribution (286)
Direct selling (305)
Distribution centers (296)
Dual channel of distribution (289)
Exclusive distribution strategy (287)
Expert power (292)
Foreign trade zone (ftz) (297)
Freight forwarders (295)
Horizontal integration (290)
Horizontal marketing systems (hms) (290)
Hub-and-spoke distribution centers (295)
Indirect channel of distribution (286)
Intensive distribution strategy (287)
Intermediaries (or middlemen or channel members) (284)
Intermodal transportation (295)
Internet retailing (or e-commerce) (304)
Inventory (296)
Keiretsus (291)
Legitimate power (292)

Logistics (or physical distribution) (292)
Manufacturers' agent (or manufacturers' representative) (298)
Merchandise mix (305)
Merchant wholesalers (298)
Multichannel distribution system (or hybrid marketing channel) (289)
Neighborhood business districts (307)
Neighborhood shopping centers (307)
Network marketing (or multilevel marketing) (305)
Off-price retailers (302)
Private warehouses (296)
Public warehouses (296)
Pull strategy (291)
Purchasing agents (299)
Push strategy (291)
Rack jobbers (298)
Referent power (292)
Regional shopping centers (307)
Retailing (299)
Reward power (291)
Scrambled merchandising (306)
Secondary business districts (307)
Selective distribution (287)
Selling agent (299)
Service mix (305)
Shopper marketing (299)
Shoppertainment (309)
Shopping centers (307)
Stock turnover (297)
Supermarkets (303)
Superstores (303)
Television home shopping (304)
Trading companies (290)
Value chain (or supply chain) (285)
Vertical integration (290)
Vertical marketing systems (vms) (290)
Warehouse clubs (or wholesale clubs) (303)
Warehousing (296)
Wheel of retailing (308)
Wholesaling (297)

Discussion Questions

1. The chapter-opening vignette introduces Kathleen King as the owner of Tate's Bake Shop. Describe and categorize all the distribution activities she is involved in.
2. Assume that you are working for a large competitor of Kathleen's (see opening vignette), one that would like to dominate this particular niche market—the gourmet bakery market. Devise a distribution plan for your company that would effectively compete with Kathleen in her target market.
3. Suppose you are the marketing manager for a large bakery on the outskirts of Greenwich, Connecticut. Your job is to determine the logistics involved in shipping cookies and other baked goods to San Francisco, California; Oahu, Hawaii; and Boise, Idaho. What mode of transportation could you use for each destination? Explain why.
4. Refer to your and your family's shopping habits. How often do you shop at department stores? What products do you typically purchase there and why do you shop there as opposed to other types of stores? Do the department stores in your hometown appear to be doing well? Explain.
5. Examine the various types of retail stores. Which category or categories do you shop at the most? Provide specific examples.
6. Make a list of the various types of general merchandise retail categories discussed in the text. For each category, discuss your personal shopping behavior. Identify a store or stores that you regularly patronize. Which category of general merchandisers do you patronize the most? Why?
7. Do you shop at convenience stores often? Why or why not? What types of products do you typically purchase at convenience stores?
8. How often do you shop online? What types of products do you typically purchase online? Would you say your online shopping has increased over the last few years or decreased? Why?
9. Pick your favorite retail store. Discuss the store's merchandise mix, service mix,

atmospherics, and location. How important are each of these to you? Explain.

10. How important is atmospherics in your choice of a retail store? Explain. Pick one retail store you patronize because of the atmospherics. Explain why. Pick another store where you will not go because you dislike the atmospherics. Discuss why.
11. Think of your personal shopping behavior. Rank the following in terms of importance to you in the selection of a retail store: merchandise mix, service mix, atmospherics, location, and brands sold within the store. Explain the rationale for your ranking.
12. Think of your personal shopping experiences. Identify the five retail stores where you shop the most. Explain what you like about each store and why you patronize it. Is there anything you dislike about the five stores? Explain why and how it impacts your shopping decisions.
13. Look through the non-store retail formats identified in the chapter. Discuss each type of non-store retailing in terms of your personal experience. What types of products have you or do you purchase from each? How often do you use each? What factors impact your purchase decision with each type?

Review Questions

True or False

1. A direct channel of distribution might have one or two intermediaries.
2. The strategy for selective distribution is full market coverage, making the product available to all consumers when and where they want it.
3. The channel captain is the dominant channel member in the administered channel arrangement.
4. Trading companies are complex marketing systems specializing in providing intermediary services, risk reduction, and financial assistance.
5. Because logistics can be handled by any entity in the distribution channel, operational expenses for logistics are rather low.
6. Stock turnover is defined as the number of times per year that an inventory on hand is sold.
7. Category specialists offer great product depth and narrow product breadth.
8. The wheel of retailing illustrates how stores that start out as innovative low-margin, low-cost operations seek to broaden their customer base by adding services and increasing prices. In the process they lose their initial customer base and become conventional type retailers; soon they fall off the wheel as more innovative retailer chains replace them.
9. A reason for retailers to expand internationally is to increase sales and profits by taking advantage of new consumer markets.

Multiple Choice

10. Which of the following is a component of distribution planning?
    a. planning of the physical movement of products
    b. transfer of ownership and risk
    c. transportation, warehousing, and all exchanges at each channel level
    d. all of the above
11. Which distribution strategy aims at full market coverage, making products available to all consumers at the right place and the right time?
    a. intensive distribution
    b. exclusive distribution
    c. selective distribution
    d. contractual distribution
12. Multimarketing or selling through warehouse and retailer chains is an example of
    a. vertical integration.
    b. dual channel of distribution.
    c. horizontal integration.
    d. vertical marketing system.
13. Which type of power is based on a close match in terms of values and objectives shared by other channel members?
    a. coercive power
    b. expert power
    c. referent power
    d. legitimate power

14. Which stores most often serve as anchors in the mall, generating traffic for the stores situated in between?
    a. all-purpose discount stores
    b. category specialists
    c. department stores
    d. off-price stores
15. Which of the following categories create atmospherics in a retail store?
    a. lighting and music tempo
    b. interior fixtures and displays
    c. store layout and color selection
    d. all of the above

Answers: (1) False, (2) False, (3) True, (4) True, (5) False, (6) True, (7) True, (8) True, (9) True, (10) d, (11) a, (12) b, (13) c, (14) c, (15) d

Case: Shipping European Hot Water Radiators

Jane Whitman has spent her junior year in college in a study-abroad program in Germany. It was a frigid winter, and the large apartment she shared with five roommates was toasty for the whole month of February, when the thermometer never climbed above freezing. The apartment was equipped with hot-water heaters that stood flat against the wall and looked like contemporary art, and at the same time, they did not intrude into the space. Jane's parents live in an old Baltimore neighborhood of Victorian-era homes, where they heat their home with heavy, ornate cast-iron radiators, which will soon need to be replaced. In Jane's experience, the cast-iron radiators are not in any way superior to these more modern counterparts, which heat much faster. Jane decided to go to Baumax, a home-improvement warehouse in Berlin, and to her surprise, she found various brands of modern radiators selling for less than $50. In comparison, cast-iron radiators cost hundreds, even thousands of dollars, and they are available mostly in poor condition at architectural salvage firms that charge a lot for discarded goods that must be refinished.

Jane hoped to find similar hot water radiators for her parents' home through distributors in the United States for a comparable price. She searched the web and found that, indeed, there were radiant hydronic heaters selling in the United States. One of the most popular brands is Runtal Radiators, the world leader in this product category. They offer sleek and decorative European Style panel radiators in different formats: baseboard, wall panels, column radiators, and vertical panels. They claim to have invented the Europanel radiator in Switzerland more than 50 years ago. She quickly found a distributor for Runtal, but the prices they charged were around $700 for the radiator alone, without the hardware. She could ship the German off-brand (Baumax) radiators to Baltimore and the price for delivery duty paid would still be below half of what the Runtal distributors charged.

Source: Marcos Mesa Sam Wordley/Shutterstock

Her parents had talked to neighbors about Jane's new venture: purchasing modern replacement radiators from Germany, and many indicated that they too were interested in this product. Soon, Jane's order swelled to 122 radiators. Jane quickly came to the realization that this might just be the small business that she would like to be involved in during her senior year in college and, possibly, beyond. She quickly embarked on a study of shipping options and attempted to understand the industry.

Her first challenge was to decide whether she should ship by air or by ocean freight. Air freight was a possibility. Air freight was growing, which meant prices were going down. But the cost was still high compared to ocean vessels. The new ocean container ships offered prices that were much lower, but also slower. However, using modern containerization did increase the speed of moving merchandise through various modes of transportation, such as rail, truck, and ocean vessels.

Jane approached one of her roommates, a marketing major, with this information, and asked her for help with ideas on how to transport 122 radiators—and, possibly, many more if this becomes a successful business.

Case Questions

1. You are Jane's roommate. Discuss the advantages and disadvantages of the different modes of transportation. Indicate what transportation venues are not appropriate for this shipment.
2. Advise Jane on the appropriate mode for transporting the radiators—air or ocean freight. Justify your recommendations.
3. Jane found that hardware for doors and bathrooms is much cheaper in Germany than in the United States. Advise her whether, in the long term, she should use air or ocean freight based on the developments described previously.
4. If Jane wants to have the radiators sold through a retail outlet in the United States, which type of outlet would be the best? Justify your choice.
5. Would it be feasible for Jane to sell the radiators directly to consumers through the Internet? Explain why or why not?
6. If Jane decided to sell directly to consumers via the Internet, discuss the issues she would face in shipping the radiators. Would she use a freight forwarder? Why or why not?

Source: www.runtalnorthamerica.com, accessed on July 27, 2014.

Endnotes

1. www.tatesbakeshop.com, accessed on March 10, 2020; Mondelēz International, "Mondelēz International to Acquire Tate's Bake Shop," May 6, 2018, https://ir.mondelezinternational.com/news-releases/news-release-details/mondelez-international-acquire-tates-bake-shop; Gail Buchalter, "Out of the Nest–Now," *Forbes* 149, no. 11 (May 25, 1992): 64.
2. Carrie LaFrenz, "Zara owner shuts 3,700 stores, writes off inventory," *Financial Review,* March 19, 2020, https://www.afr.com/companies/retail/zara-owner-shuts-3700-stores-writes-off-inventory-20200319-p54bnf; "Business: Floating on Air," *The Economist* 359, no. 8222 (May 19, 2001): 56–57.
3. Hanna Makino, "How to enter the Japanese market–business partner models and other options," Switzerland Global Enterprise, June 18, 2020, https://www.s-ge.com/en/article/export-knowhow/20202-c2-japan-market-entry.
4. John Shulz, "The State of Logistics in 2019: What's Next," *Logistics Management,* July 20, 2019, https://www.logisticsmgmt.com/article/state_of_logistics_in_2019_whats_next.
5. Jacon Steimer, "FedEx construction costs for $1.5B world hub Memphis, January 16, 2020," Memphis Business Journal, https://www.izjournals.com/memphis/news/2020/01/16/what-fedex-has-spent-so-far-on-construction-for-1.html.
6. Avnet, accessed at https://www.avnet.com/wps/portal/us on March 2, 2020; Brian Albright, "Better Distribution, Fewer Errors," *Frontline Solutions* 3, no. 13 (December 2002): 13–14.
7. Department of Commerce, U.S. Foreign-Trade Zones, https://enforcement.trade.gov/ftzpage/letters/ftzlist-map.html#virginia, accessed on March 2, 2020.
8. Sapna Maheswari and Vanessa Friedman, "The death of the department store: very few are likely to survive," *The New York Times,* May 7, 2020, https://www.nytimes.com/2020/04/21/business/coronavirus-department-stores-neiman-marcus.html.

Pricing Strategies

CHAPTER 11

Source: Indypendenz/Shutterstock

Chapter Outline

Learning Objectives

Ivelin Radkov/Shutterstock

After studying this chapter, you should be able to:

- Define pricing and examine the external and internal influences on pricing decisions.
- Examine the different price objectives: sales-based, profit-maximization, and status quo.
- Address the pricing strategies: cost-based, demand-based, competition-based, and combination pricing.
- Address strategic marketing applications in relation to pricing, such as price variability, price psychology, price discounting, and product-related pricing.
- Address strategies that companies use to change prices.

Source: Monkey Business Images/ Shutterstock

11-1 Chapter Overview

In a recent survey of 1,884 Americans between the ages of 13 and 21 (Generation Z), researchers found that price was the most important factor when deciding whether to purchase items from a particular brand for 60% of the respondents. A distant second, at 18%, were shared values. Generation Z consumers refuse to pay full price for anything—their spending habits were passed down to them by their parents, who were shaped by the 2007-2009 Great Recession.[1]

Pricing is a central marketing strategy element because of its effect on product positioning, market segmentation, demand management, and market share dynamics. Setting prices is a complex undertaking. Numerous internal and external variables, such as the nature of the product, the location of production plants, the type of distribution system used, and the economic climate must be evaluated before determining the final price of products and services.[2]

This chapter addresses challenges that firms face when setting prices. It also addresses the impact of the competitive, political and legal, and economic and financial environment on pricing decisions. Section 11-2 offers a definition of pricing and addresses external and internal influences on pricing. Section 11-3 discusses the different price objectives: sales-based, profit-maximization, and status quo objectives. Section 11-4 examines the cost-based, demand-based, competition-based, and combination pricing strategies. Section 11-5 addresses strategic marketing applications in relation to pricing, such as price variability, pricing psychology, price discounting, and product-related pricing, whereas Section 11-6 examines issues related to changing the price.

11-2 Influences on Pricing Decisions

Price is defined as the amount of money necessary to purchase a good or service. Everything and everyone has a price. A marketing manager's price is his or her salary, which accounts, in part, for the individual's ability, work experience, education, and training. Chief executive officers (CEOs) of large multinationals have a much higher price than supervisors in an industrial supply firm. A hamburger has a price, which captures various costs incurred in obtaining and processing the ingredients, in paying labor costs, for franchise royalties, facility rent, and advertising. Pets have a price, from a $100 spaying fee for an adorable half-breed street puppy from the local SPCA to $14,000 for a superb Hyacynth Macaw parrot.

In today's economy, price plays an essential part. Many products are standardized in the mature marketplace of the United States, and competition stands ready to chip away at company profits by offering the same product at a lower price. A business can use its pricing strategy wisely to reach its objectives and maximize its revenue. In fact, price is the only element of the company's marketing mix that produces revenue. Product, place, and promotion, the other elements of the marketing mix, represent costs to the firm. This section addresses the different external and internal influences on price decisions.

11-2a External Influences on Price

The primary external influences on price are consumers, economics, competition, and the government.

Consumer Influences on Price Consumers play an important role in determining the final price of products. According to the **law of demand**, consumers purchase more products at a lower price than at a higher price. For each price the company may charge, there will be a different level of demand. This relationship is illustrated in the **demand curve**, which portrays the number of units bought for a particular price in a given time period. **Figure 11-1a** shows the demand curve for most products: As price increases, the quantity demanded decreases. Marketing managers can influence the price-quantity demanded relationship to a certain extent. For example, they could increase promotion for the product. This would lead to an increase in the quantity demanded, as illustrated in **Figure 11-1b**, causing a shift in the entire demand curve.

Law of demand Economic law whereby consumers are believed to purchase more products at a lower price than at a higher price.

Demand curve Curve that portrays the number of units bought for a particular price in a given time period.

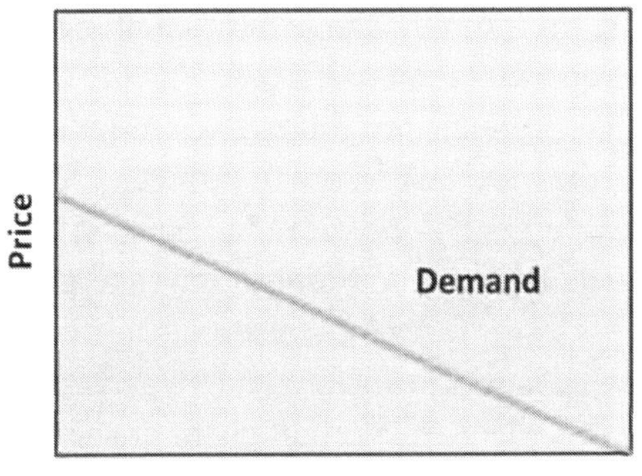

Quantity Demanded
(a) As the price increases, quantity demanded decreases.

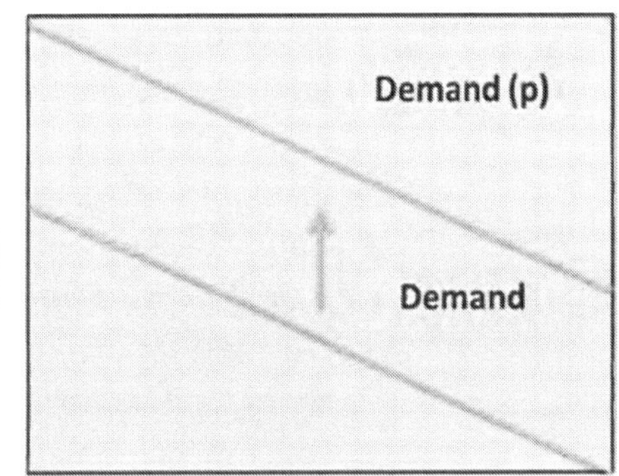

Quantity Demanded
(b) Promotion leads to a shift in the demand curve.

FIGURE 11-1 Demand Curves

However, consumers may or may not be sensitive to price changes. For example, introducing a high excise tax on cigarettes has not led to a change in cigarette demand, regardless of the tax imposed. Cigarette users view cigarettes as necessities and are thus not likely to give up smoking as a result of price increases. Demand for cigarettes is inelastic; it does not respond to price changes. **Price elasticity** is defined as buyer sensitivity to a change in price. The formula for calculating price elasticity is:

Price elasticity Buyer sensitivity to a change in price.

$$\text{Price Elasticity of Demand} = \frac{\text{Percentage Change in Quantity Demanded}}{\text{Percent Change in Price}}$$

or

$$\text{Price Elasticity of Demand} = \frac{\dfrac{\text{Quantity 1} - \text{Quantity 2}}{\text{Quantity 1}}}{\dfrac{\text{Price 1} - \text{Price 2}}{\text{Price 1}}}$$

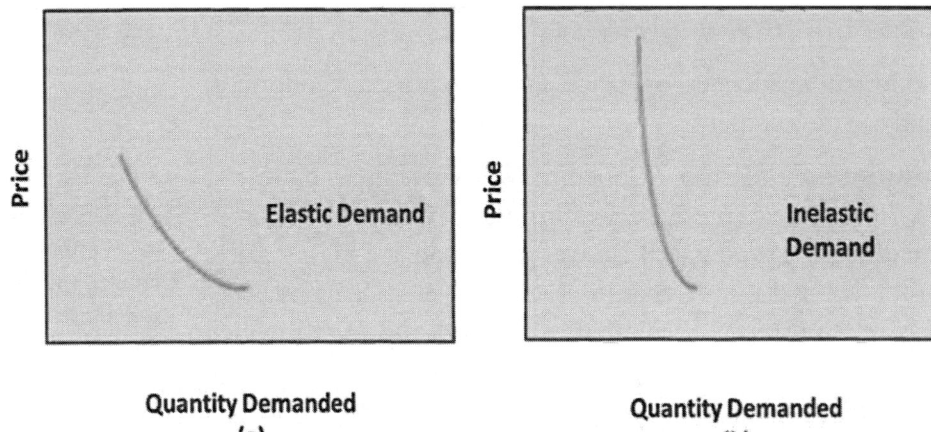

FIGURE 11-2 Demand Elasticity

The formula calculates the percentage change in demand for each percentage change in price. Demand is elastic if a small change in price results in a large change in demand **(see Figure 11-2a)**. For cigarettes, demand is inelastic; that is, for a small change in price, there is only minimal, if any, change in the quantity demanded **(see Figure 11-2b)**.

If consumers believe that products are relatively similar and there are many product substitutes, they are less likely to purchase at high prices. Thus, for these consumers, demand is elastic. Marketers who understand elasticity price their products and run their promotions accordingly. Delta Airlines, for example, offers lower fares for consumers to fly across country in October or February because the airline understands that, for these consumers, demand is elastic. They are more likely to travel if airfares are discounted. Business travelers, however, must travel on short notice and their travel cannot be postponed until prices are lower. For these consumers, who cannot purchase tickets in advance, airlines maintain high prices during these months, despite the seasonal slowdown in the business.

In addition to a consumer's financial situation, other consumer behavior-based determinants explain price-related behavior. Deal-prone consumers are more likely to respond to deals than consumers who are not deal-prone. Similarly, consumers loyal to a brand will purchase that brand even if prices increase—up to a point. Consumers loyal to a retailer will pay higher prices for the privilege of shopping there because they prefer special treatment.

Source: ALPA PROD/Shutterstock

Martin's Super Markets offer extra services to consumers. Employees carry the products to the shopper's automobile and load them in the trunk. Consumers who ask about the location of a product are taken to the aisle that has the product, and the employee will pick up the product off the shelf for them. Despite the fact that Martin's charges higher prices, the stores are busy at all hours. Martin's consumers are willing to pay higher prices for the extra service and atmosphere.

A company's pricing decisions are also influenced by customer profitability, spending potential, and retention. As addressed in Chapter 1, companies are increasingly focusing on customers' lifetime value—that is, the estimated profitability of the customer over the course of his or her entire relationship with the company. Companies realize acquiring new customers takes greater effort and costs more than retaining old customers. Under this assumption, a particularly valuable customer is one who has a profitable relationship with the company. Over time these customers add value to a company because they buy more products and purchase more often.

Economic Influences on Costs and Price Economic factors, such as inflation, recessions, and interest rates affect pricing decisions because they impact the cost of producing a product. An inflationary environment places strong pressures on companies to lower prices. Pricing competitively may mean that companies are not producing a profit. During inflationary periods, firms often find that they must decide between maintaining a competitive presence in a market and weathering the downside of the economic cycle or abandoning the market, which is a high-cost, high-risk proposition.

The cost of materials, supplies, and labor are some of the costs that are not within a firm's control. For example, several factors affect the cost of gasoline. Price increases can be caused by rising crude oil costs (the raw material that accounts for 40 percent of the retail price for gas). Supply chain issues could also affect prices. After the onset of the COVID-19 pandemic, some prices in stores, from supermarkets to all-purpose discounters, went up for different reasons. Supermarkets had to deal with unprecedented demand, while, at the same time, food production facilities, such as meat-processing plants, had to shut down due to the pandemic. Disruptions in supply chains were common: China's lockdown to contain the disease, affecting large swaths of its population, led to factories slowing down production; U.S. firms dependent on parts from China had to look for alternative, more expensive sources.

Political turmoil in one or more oil-producing countries can reduce the supply available. The price can also be affected by the risk premium accompanying the political or economic uncertainty in the Middle East. Environmental regulations, such as the tough Clean Air Act requirements for reformulated gasoline and the proliferation of distinct fuel blends, can create price increases. Similarly, summer is the time of both the highest motor fuel demand and the imposition in metropolitan areas of costly environmental regulations designed to fight smog. In Europe, consumers are paying higher prices for gasoline, even when the market price is low, as a result of high taxes.

Competitive Influences on Price Pricing strategies must take into consideration both the competitive environment and the firm's position relative to competition. Firms can control prices only if their product is in the early stages of the product life cycle and they are one of the market leaders. During the maturity stage of the product life cycle, the competitive

Source: Arina P Habich/Shutterstock

field is broad, characterized by products that are relatively similar. In this type of market, individual firms have little control over price. Therefore, the goal of firms is to keep product prices low, for example, by moving production to a low-labor-cost country. In the maturity stage, companies can still maintain some control over price if their products are well differentiated and have a high degree of brand franchise.

Finally, in certain markets, such as utilities, the government regulates prices to ensure access to the services for all consumers. Utilities can also be owned and operated by the government. In planned economies, such as those of China, North Korea, and Cuba, the government sets most prices.

Pure competition Market that consists of many buyers and sellers, where no buyer or seller can control price or the market.

Monopolistic competition Market that consists of many buyers and many sellers with products that vary.

Oligopolistic competition Market that consists of few sellers who dominate the market.

Pure monopoly Market that consists of only one seller.

An economics perspective describes four different types of markets based on competition. **Pure competition** characterizes a market that consists of many buyers and sellers, where no buyer or seller can control price or the market. In this environment, marketing plays a minimal role. Because sellers can sell as much as they want and buyers can buy as much as they need, perfect market information is available to both buyers and sellers, and the product sells for about the same price in the marketplace. Although pure competition is difficult to accomplish, commodities come the closest to pure competition.

Monopolistic competition is a market that consists of many buyers and sellers and products that vary greatly in the same product category. Products are differentiated based on price, style, flavor, and other characteristics important for the final consumer. Coffee is this type of category, with many brands, such as Maxwell House, Folgers, Nescafé Taster's Choice, Starbucks, store brands, regional distributor brands, and even ethnic brands. These brands are differentiated, and price changes for one brand may not lead to a change in pricing strategy for another.

Oligopolistic competition markets consist of a few sellers who dominate the market. Change in the strategy of one seller will directly affect the other sellers in the marketplace. The automobile industry and the airline industry are characterized by oligopolistic competition. In terms of pricing, the airlines follow similar pricing strategies. Similar prices are seen for the same type of consumer: leisure traveler, business traveler, or off-peak traveler. If one airline lowers prices, typically, all the airlines follow suit.

Source: wavebreakmedia/Shutterstock

Pure monopoly characterizes a market that consists of only one seller. This seller could be the government, for planned economies, or a government-owned utility company, in the case of market economies. In the United States, the government owns and operates the U.S. Postal Service. Other examples of monopolies are private regulated monopolies, such as local power companies, and unregulated monopolies, as in the case of pharmaceutical companies' drugs that are under patent protection. Regulated monopolies are often required to maintain lower prices to ensure access to all consumers. Unregulated monopolies can charge any price the market will bear, but often they do not do it because they need brand-loyal consumers or because of concern that the government may interfere.

The Government's Influence on Price The government plays an important role in pricing. The government has enacted legislation to protect competitors, channel members, and consumers from unfair strategies. **Figure 11-3** identifies some of the ways the government regulates pricing. The primary goals of these laws are to ensure fair competition and to protect consumers from unscrupulous business practices.

Legislation, such as the Robinson-Patman Act, prohibits **price discrimination**, which is charging different prices to different buyers of the same merchandise.

It also requires sellers that offer a service to one buyer make the same service available to all buyers. This law applies to consumer markets, business markets, and the channel of distribution. A related law is **resale price maintenance**, which prohibits manufacturers from requiring retailers to charge a particular price for their brands. They are allowed to print a suggested retail price on the product package or attached label, but cannot require that the item be sold at that price.

Legislation such as the Federal Trade Commission Act and the Sherman Antitrust Act addresses all types of unfair competition, including **price fixing**—an agreement between channel members at the same level

Price discrimination The practice of charging different prices to different buyers of the same merchandise.

Resale price maintenance Prohibits manufacturers from requiring retailers to charge a particular price for a product.

Price fixing Agreement among channel members at the same level in the channel of distribution to charge the same price to all customers.

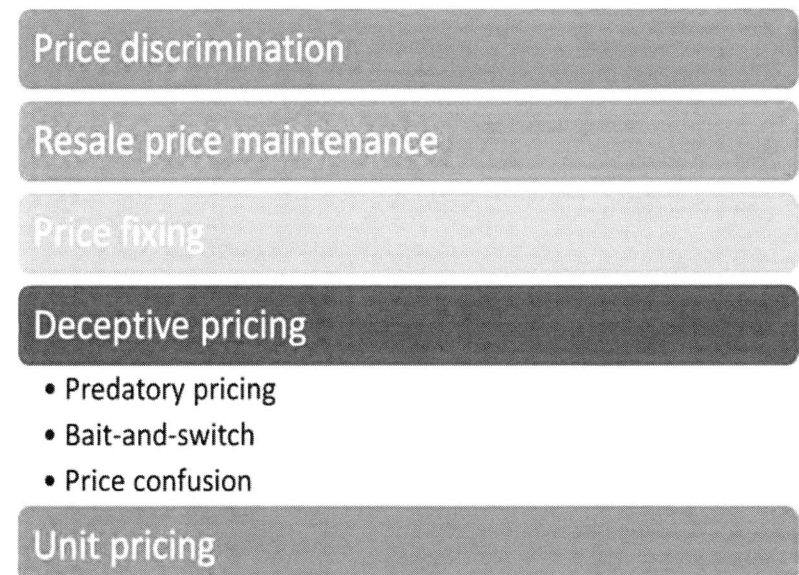

Price discrimination
Resale price maintenance
Price fixing
Deceptive pricing
• Predatory pricing
• Bait-and-switch
• Price confusion
Unit pricing

FIGURE 11-3 Pricing Federal Regulations

Deceptive pricing Strategy used by sellers who state prices or price savings that may mislead consumers or that are not available to consumers.

Predatory pricing Pricing strategies used to eliminate small competitors and to deceive consumers.

Dumping Selling products below cost to get rid of excess inventory or to undermine competition.

Bait and switch A marketing tactic in which a retailer promotes a special deal on a product and then, when consumers arrive at the store, the retailer tries to switch them to a higher-priced item.

Price confusion Strategies to confuse consumers so that they do not quite understand the price that they ultimately have to pay.

Unit pricing Pricing that allows consumers to compare among prices for different brands and for different package sizes of the different brands.

in the channel of distribution to charge the same price to all customers. This law prevents large businesses from colluding on a price to inflate prices so they can earn greater profits.

Stating prices or price savings that may mislead consumers or that are not available to all consumers is **deceptive pricing**. Unfair pricing tactics can include predatory pricing, bait-and-switch tactics, and price confusion strategies. **Predatory pricing** is charging prices below cost to eliminate competitors. One way to do this is through **dumping**, which is selling products below cost to get rid of excess inventory or to undermine competition. **Bait-and-switch** strategies advertise items at a low price. However, when customers arrive, they are told that the store is out of stock, and the retailer attempts to sell them a higher-priced item. The last type of unfair pricing is **price confusion**, which firms use to confuse consumers, so that they would not quite understand the price that they ultimately have to pay. Examples are a wireless company charging for calls that go unanswered for more than 30 seconds, hotels charging a connectivity fee for access to the phone and funeral homes charging for various services that are not explained.

Many states also require retailers to engage in **unit pricing**—that is, pricing that allows consumers to compare between prices for different brands and for different package sizes of the different brands. For instance, consumers have a difficult time determining if a larger box of cereal is actually a better buy. If unit pricing is not shown, the larger box may actually cost more per ounce than a smaller box.

Because of the potential for fraud and deception with pricing, the federal government has passed a number of pieces of legislation that monitor pricing of products. Some of the major legislation that affects pricing is shown in **Figure 11-4**.

Legislation	Description
1890 Sherman Antitrust Act	Prohibits trusts, monopolies, and activities designed to restrict free trade. Bans predatory pricing (i.e., charging prices below cost to eliminate small competitors).
1914 Clayton Act	Prohibits price discrimination to different buyers, tying contracts that require buyers of one product to also purchase another item, and combining two or more competing firms by pooling ownership or stock. Bans predatory pricing.
1914 Federal Trade Commission Act	Created the Federal Trade Commission (FTC) to address antitrust matters and investigate unfair methods of competition. Addresses price fixing and price advertising.
1936 Robinson-Patman Act	Prohibits charging different prices to different buyers of the same merchandise and requires sellers that offer a service to one buyer to make the same service available to all buyers.
1938 Wheeler-Lea Amendment	Expanded the power of the FTC to investigate and prohibit practices that could injure the public, and false and misleading advertising. Addresses price advertising. Bans bait-and-switch advertising.
1966 Fair Packaging and Labeling Act	Requires that manufacturers provide a label containing the contents, what company made the product, and how much of each item it contains. Allows for fair price comparisons.

FIGURE 11-4 Major Legislation Affecting Pricing

11-2b Internal Influences on Price

Internal factors, such as the firm size, organizational structure, and industry, determine who in the company makes pricing decisions. In smaller organizations, it is usually the owner or the top managers, whereas in larger organizations, pricing is decided by the brand manager or negotiated in a business-to-business setting. In a market-oriented company, pricing is based on information shared with the marketing department by the other functional areas, such as finance, engineering, or sales–these departments may even be allowed direct input in pricing.

Costs are also important determinants of price. In pricing products, companies need to take into consideration all product costs and determine a fair rate of return on investment. A company has **fixed costs**, which do not vary with the amount of output, such as building rent, maintenance, and permanent staff costs. It also has **variable costs**, which vary with the output, such as raw materials, packaging, and shipping costs. Variable costs and fixed costs make up total costs at a particular level of production. Production costs typically fall as a function of experience: as companies acquire more experience, they realize economies of scale. This leads to lower costs and greater profits for the company since the item can be sold at a lower price.

Fixed costs Costs that do not vary with the amount of output.

Variable costs Costs, such as raw materials, packaging, and shipping costs, that vary with the amount of output.

Sales-based pricing objectives Attempts to increase sales volume and market share relative to competitors.

Penetration pricing Pricing strategy whereby firms initially price the product below the price of competitors to quickly penetrate the market at competitors' expense and acquire a large market share, and then gradually raise the price.

11-3 Setting Pricing Objectives

Firms set their pricing objectives in line with the company goals. Thus, different firms in the same industry may have different pricing objectives predicated on firm size, in-house capabilities, and focus on profit, sales, or government action. Sales-based objectives focus on increasing sales volume; profit-based objectives focus on the total return on investment; and status quo objectives focus on maintaining a good relationship with customers, channel members, and regulatory bodies **(see Figure 11-5)**. Companies may elect to have more than one goal. A firm that focuses on **sales-based pricing objectives** attempts to increase its sales volume and its market share relative to competitors. The premise of this strategy is that sales growth will lead to dominance in the marketplace achieved at low per-unit cost. Companies often introduce new products with sales-based objectives in mind. To achieve high sales a company may resort to **penetration pricing**, whereby firms price the product below the price of competitors to quickly penetrate the market at competitors' expense and acquire a large market share, and then gradually raise the price. The Microsoft Surface Duo, an innovative phone that can turn into a tablet and fits

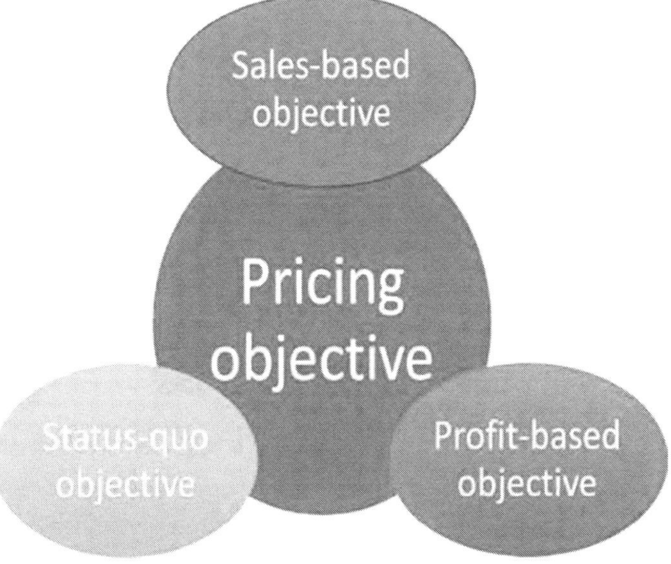

FIGURE 11-5 Pricing Objectives

in one's pocket, has two Gorilla Glass displays at 5.6-inches each and unfolds into an 8.3-inch tablet. The product is priced above $1,000, but, with incentives, it could cost under $750, a penetration price point where it could successfully compete with the iPhone.[3]

Penetration pricing is used when consumers are sensitive to price, as well as when the company has achieved economies of scale in manufacturing and distribution, and can afford to sell the product at lower prices. The price must be low enough to minimize competition.

Profit-maximization pricing objectives Attempts to maximize the gross margin on each unit of a product sold, while simultaneously providing value to consumers.

Skimming A pricing strategy whereby the product is priced higher than that of competitors.

A firm that focuses on **profit-maximization pricing objectives** attempts to maximize the gross margin on each unit of a product sold, while simultaneously providing value to consumers. Companies estimate the demand and costs at different prices and will select the price that will produce the maximum profit or return on investment. Companies often introduce new products with profit-maximization objectives in mind using a **skimming** strategy, whereby the product is priced above that of competitors. The focus of the company is on immediate profit, rather than on long-run performance. This strategy is most effectively used early in the product life cycle when competition is minimal (once there is substantial competition, there is a high likelihood that competitors will undercut the price) or when there is a high degree of brand loyalty. In general, consumers responding to skimming strategies are more concerned with quality, uniqueness, and status, rather than price. In turn, the product's image and quality must warrant the product's high price. The iPhone, until recently, used a skimming strategy, pricing their phones above competitors' prices, in line with the brand's stellar reputation for innovativeness and quality. In 2020, during the COVID-19 pandemic, they decided to use a penetration pricing strategy, selling an ultra-cheap phone, the iPhone SE, for $399.

Status quo–based objectives Pricing designed to maintain a firm's current position in the market.

Firms may set **status quo–based objectives** when they are facing too much competition, when they want to refrain from disrupting the channel with changes, or when they do not want to be scrutinized by the government. Such objectives are used to minimize the impact of competitors, government, or channel members and to avoid sales decline. This strategy does not mean that the firm does not change prices—it must match competitors' price reductions or price increases. It should be noted that status quo–based objectives can be adopted only in the short-term, to weather a particular condition or challenge. Companies must be proactive to be able to optimally meet the needs of their target consumers. A firm must coordinate its pricing strategy with its product image, with product design, and with its promotion and distribution strategy to optimally address target market needs. Prices

Source: goodluz/Shutterstock

need to mesh with the entire product line and compare favorably with the competition. Coordinating pricing strategies with the overall marketing strategy is complex. Price is a flexible element of the marketing mix that can be changed quickly to respond to new market developments, unlike the product, distribution, and promotional. The pricing strategy also poses a challenge: even companies de-emphasizing price in positioning, opting for a quality positioning, need to be mindful of how they use price to communicate. A price that is not high enough may cause consumers to question quality. Pricing the product too high may cause consumers to switch to competitors because they feel it is overpriced.

Cost-based pricing Pricing strategy whereby the firm sets the price by calculating merchandise, service, and overhead costs and then adds an amount needed to cover the profit goal.

Price floor The lowest price a company can charge to attain its profit goal.

Cost-plus pricing Pricing strategy that involves adding a target profit margin to total costs.

11-4 Price Calculations

Firms have several options when calculating the actual price of a good or service. The primary approaches to determining the price are cost-based, demand-based, or competition-based **(see Figure 11-6)**. At times companies will combine these approaches into what is known as combination pricing.

FIGURE 11-6 Methods of Determining the Price of a Product

11-4a Cost-Based Pricing

In **cost-based pricing**, the firm sets the price by calculating merchandise, service, and overhead costs and then adding an amount needed to cover the gross margin goal. Cost-based pricing is relatively easy to calculate because there is no need to take into consideration the estimated price elasticity of demand or the reaction of competitors to price changes. Moreover, costs are easier to estimate than demand elasticity, competitive reactions, and market conditions. The firm's goal is to obtain reasonable profits, using a specified **price floor**, that is, the lowest price a company can charge and attain its margin goals. The cost-based pricing techniques are cost-plus, markup, traditional break-even analysis, and target profit pricing **(see Figure 11-7)**.

FIGURE 11-7 Cost-Based Pricing Methods

Cost-plus pricing is relatively simple: It involves adding a target profit margin to total costs. Let us assume that a "boutique" nursery selling unique plants tailored to business customers' needs in the eastern United States wants to earn a $20,000 profit margin. The variable cost for each plant is $100, fixed costs are estimated to be $30,000, and the nursery anticipates growing and selling 4,000 of these plants. The price for each plant is calculated as follows:

Variable Cost:	**$100 per plant**
Fixed Costs:	**$30,000**
Number of Plants Produced	**4,000**
Desired Profits	**$20,000**

$$\text{Price} = \frac{\text{Fixed Costs} + \text{Variable Costs} + \text{Profits}}{\text{Number of Units Produced}}$$

$$\text{Price} = \frac{30{,}000 + (4{,}000 \times 100) + 20{,}000}{4{,}000} = \$112.50 \text{ per plant}$$

This method evaluates profits (margins) as a function of costs and the price is not linked to demand. There is no accounting for excess capacity, and there is no attempt to lower costs because profits remain the same regardless of costs. This strategy is appropriate for custom-made products, such as furniture and equipment. Typically, the nursery gets orders for a number of plants from customers, calculates the price using the cost-plus method, and sends invoices to the businesses placing the order after calculating the total costs.

Markup pricing A variant of cost-plus pricing, with a markup used to cover selling costs and desired profit margin.

Markup Pricing **Markup pricing** is a variant of cost-plus pricing, with a markup used to cover selling costs and desired profit margin. The markup can be based on costs or selling price. Using the markup pricing approach on costs, suppose the nursery wants to earn a 20% margin on each of the plants sold. The nursery would use the following method to calculate the price of each plant.

$$\text{Price} = (\text{Unit cost} * 20\%) + \text{Unit cost} = (\$100 * 20\%) + \$100 = \$20 + \$100 = \$120$$

Based on costs, the margin would be $20 per plant. This $20 margin is added to the costs of $100 to yield a selling price of $120 per plant.

With the markup pricing off selling price, the 20% is calculated from the selling price rather than costs. This method is often used by retailers to determine selling prices. With this method the selling price would be $125 per plant. The following approach is used:

$$\text{Price} = \frac{\text{Unit costs}}{1 - \text{Markup percentage}} = \frac{\$100}{1 - 20\%} = \frac{\$100}{80\%} = \$125.00$$

Accountants, contractors, and other service providers use this strategy to determine price. It is a method commonly used for pricing at the different levels of the channel of distribution as well. It is a very popular method. First, costs are easier to calculate than demand. Second, this method is based on costs, which are more stable than demand. Third, expenses, trade discounts, and markdowns are expressed as a function of sales or unit prices—and so are markups. Fourth, competitive price data are readily available, whereas cost data are not. Markup pricing thus facilitates comparison with the competition. Lastly, when all competitors use this method, prices tend to be similar. Thus price competition is minimized.

Break-Even Analysis **Break-even analysis** identifies the number of units the company needs to sell or the total number of dollars it needs to make on sales to break even with regard to costs, given a particular price. If the sales exceed the break-even quantity, the company earns a profit; if sales come short, the company has a loss. The break-even point can be calculated in terms of the number of units sold or in terms of sales dollars. Let us assume that an art book publisher is planning on publishing a catalog for a new contemporary art exhibition that will travel to numerous museum venues. The variable cost for printing the catalog is $15 per book, the fixed costs are $130,000, and the selling price of each catalog is $70 per book. To cover the variable and fixed costs the museum would need to sell 2,363 books or catalogs. The break-even in sales dollars is $163,456. The calculations for this break-even analysis follow:

Break-even analysis Identifies the number of units the company needs to sell or the total number of dollars it needs to make on sales to break even with regard to costs, given a particular price.

Variable Cost:	**$15 per book**
Fixed Costs:	**$130,000**
Price of Each Book	**$70**
Desired Profits	**$40,000**

$$\text{Break-even Point (Number of Units)} = \frac{\text{Fixed Costs}}{\text{Unit Price} - \text{Variable Costs per Unit}}$$

$$\text{Break-even Point (Number of Units)} = \frac{\$130{,}000}{\$70 - \$15} = 2{,}364 \text{ books (Units)}$$

$$\text{Break-even Point (Sales Dollars)} = \frac{\text{Fixed Costs}}{1 - \dfrac{\text{Variable Costs per Unit}}{\text{Price}}}$$

$$\text{Break-even Point (Sales Dollars)} = \frac{\$130{,}000}{1 - \dfrac{\$15}{\$70}} = \$165{,}456$$

The break-even point can also be calculated by taking into account the amount of the profit margin targeted by the firm. With this method, the profit margin target is considered a fixed cost. Notice to earn the $40,000 desired profit, the museum would need to sell 3,091 units, or $216,365.

$$\text{Break-even Point (Number of Units)} = \frac{\text{Fixed Costs} + \text{Desired Profit}}{\text{Unit Price} - \text{Variable Costs per Unit}}$$

$$\text{Break-even Point (Number of Units)} = \frac{\$130{,}000 + \$40{,}000}{\$70 - \$15}$$

$$= 3{,}091 \text{ books (Units)}$$

$$\text{Break-even Point (Sales Dollars)} = \frac{\text{Fixed Costs} + \text{Desired Profit}}{1 - \dfrac{\text{Variable Costs per Unit}}{\text{Price}}}$$

$$\text{Break-even Point (Sales Dollars)} = \frac{\$130{,}000 + \$40{,}000}{1 - \dfrac{\$15}{\$70}} = \$216{,}365$$

Break-even analysis is used by many types of businesses, including intermediaries at different levels of the channel of distribution. The company can create a break-even chart, which shows the total cost and total revenue expected at different sales volume levels. Break-even analysis has many of the shortcomings of cost-based pricing: It does not take into consideration demand, and it assumes that customers will purchase at the given price, that no purchase discounts will need to be offered over time, and that costs can be fully assessed a priori.

Target profit pricing A pricing strategy used by capital-intensive firms, where the formula used to calculate target profit pricing takes into consideration a standard volume of production that the firm is expected to achieve.

Target Profit Pricing Target profit pricing is used by capital-intensive firms, such as automobile manufacturers, public utilities, and theme parks. The formula used to calculate target profit pricing takes into consideration a standard volume of production that the firm is expected to achieve. For most firms, that target is more than 90 percent of plant capacity. Assume that a motorcycle company has invested $120 million for a new manufacturing plant with a 30 percent target return on investment (ROI). Over the first four years, its production is estimated to be 70,000 units. Its average total costs for each motorcycle are $8,500 at a production level of 70,000 units.

Investment Cost	$120,000
Target ROI	30 Percent
Standard Volume (number of units per year)	70,000
Average Cost per Unit	$8500

To calculate the selling price for the motorcycle, the firm uses the following approach:

$$\text{Price} = \frac{\text{Investment Cost} \times (\text{Target ROI Percentage} + 1)}{\text{Standard Volume (Units per Year)}}$$

$$+ \text{Average Costs per Unit (at standard volume)}$$

$$\text{Price} = \frac{\$120{,}000{,}000 \times 1.30}{70{,}000} + \$8500 = \$10{,}728.57 \text{ (Selling Price)}$$

Target profit pricing is likely to understate the selling price for firms with low capital investments. It also assumes a standard volume that may not be achievable by the firm or, if achieved, does not account for the possibility that there may not be enough demand for the units.

11-4b Demand-Based Pricing

Demand-based pricing takes into consideration customers' perceptions of value, rather than the seller's cost, as the fundamental component of the pricing decision. As such, price is considered as part of the marketing mix before assessing the costs involved. Whereas cost-based pricing is product driven, demand-based pricing is consumer driven. For demand-based pricing, firms identify a **price ceiling**, which is the maximum amount that consumers are willing to pay for a product. The ceiling is contingent on the elasticity of demand, which itself is contingent on the availability of product substitutes and urgency of need. Demand estimates are much less precise than cost estimates because they are based on research of consumers' willingness to pay for the product at different price levels and on consumers' perceptions of product value. In highly competitive situations, firms need to lower prices, which, in turn, requires companies to keep costs low. When there is minimal competition, firms can afford to increase prices and obtain high profits from sales.

Demand-based pricing Pricing strategy that takes into consideration customers' perceptions of value, rather than the seller's cost, as the fundamental component of the pricing decision.

Price ceiling The maximum amount that consumers are willing to pay for a product.

One type of demand-based pricing is modified break-even analysis, which combines break-even analysis with an evaluation of demand at various price levels. This approach assumes that as the price increases demand will decrease in an elastic demand environment, where there are many product substitutes and competition is intense. It should be noted, however, that demand estimates are not always going to be on the mark, so this approach, although taking into consideration likely demand, is not as precise as the cost-based, traditional break-even approach.

Another approach is **differential pricing**, which involves charging different prices based on product features, time of sale or consumption, season, or place. For instance, at a baseball stadium seats are priced differently based on location. Front row seats near the field and dugouts cost more than upper level seats or bleacher seats. Concerts and theatrical productions use a similar pricing structure.

Differential pricing Pricing strategy that involves charging different prices based on product features, time of sale or consumption, season, or place.

Source: Joseph Sohm/Shutterstock

11-4c Competition-Based Pricing

Many firms choose to use competitors' prices, instead of demand or product costs, to determine the prices of their products. This method is useful when firms compare themselves to companies with similar products that have similar demand patterns and costs. Competition-based pricing may mean that the firm prices its products at the level of competition, above the prices of competition, or below the prices of competition. Pricing at the level of competition does not lead to competitive retaliation because it does not affect competitors. Pricing below competition, however, is likely to elicit some level of competitive response.

In an oligopoly, typically one firm, or a few firms, tend to be the first to announce price changes, and the rest of the firms follow. This is known as **price leadership**. These firms tend to be the market leaders with well-accepted leadership positions in the industry.

Price leadership The tendency of one firm or a few firms to be the first to announce price changes, with the rest of the firms following.

Another form of competition-based pricing is **bid pricing**, which involves competitive bidding for a contract, whereby a firm will price based on how it believes competitors will price, rather than based on demand or costs. The firm that bids lowest typically wins the contract. Most federal, state, and local governments, as well as numerous other organizations, require competitive bidding. In almost all cases, the bidding is secret and all bids are opened at one time, at the conclusion of the bidding price. The contract usually is awarded to the lowest bidder, but there are situations where other criteria may be used in the selection in addition to price.

Bid pricing Pricing that involves competitive bidding for a contract, whereby a firm will price based on how it believes competitors will price, rather than based on demand or costs.

11-4d Combination Pricing

Combination pricing is often used in practice. Firms might use cost-based pricing to establish the lowest acceptable price—the price floor—and then use demand and competition-based approaches when pricing their products for intermediaries or for the final consumer. For example, a manufacturing firm might determine the maximum price that consumers are willing to pay for its products—the price ceiling—and then work backward to the product cost to determine the target profit it should achieve.

11-5 Strategic Marketing Applications

It is easy to reduce prices in order to boost sales. But, for long-run success there must be a solid marketing strategy behind pricing decisions. This section addresses pricing concepts such as price variability, pricing psychology, price discounting, and product-related pricing decisions.

11-5a Price Variability

Consumers prefer and expect prices to be relatively stable for the most part. **Customary pricing**, whereby a firm sets prices and attempts to maintain them over time, is a strategy used to address this expectation. One of the primary reasons for increasing prices is inflation. In this case, manufacturers are forced to pass price increases on to the final consumer.

Customary pricing Pricing strategy whereby a firm sets prices and attempts to maintain them over time.

Another reason is excessive demand. In this situation, increasing prices to lower demand may work against the firm at some point because consumers may move on to competitors who charge lower prices or to product substitutes. And, when the cost of ingredients increases, manufacturers prefer to alter product size or the product ingredients, rather than alter the price. Candy in the checkout aisle has relatively constant prices over time.

Source: FUN FUN PHOTO/Shutterstock

Certain products, however, are priced to change. Prices at gas stations change almost daily, in direct response to changes in crude oil costs or to changes in driving behavior. In the summer, the cost of gas goes up. Gas stations practice **variable pricing**, changing their prices in response to changes in cost or demand.

Variable pricing Strategy of changing prices in response to changes in cost or demand.

A more extreme version of variable pricing is **dynamic pricing**, also known as surge pricing. Dynamic pricing is a strategy whereby much higher prices are charged depending on demand. Princeton Review was found to be twice as likely to charge Asian Americans higher test-preparation prices than other customers, regardless of income. More recently, Lyft and Uber were found to increase ride-hailing prices when riders were picked up or dropped off in neighborhoods with a low percentage of people over the age of 40, people with a high school education or less, and in areas where houses were priced under the median in the region.[4]

Dynamic pricing A strategy whereby much higher prices are charged depending on demand.

Similarly, the state of Virginia charges drivers much higher toll prices during congestion. For example, the price to travel on the I-66 Express Lanes was $44 one way, while the price at times without congestion for the same distance is around $5.

Flexible pricing is a strategy that allows a firm to set prices based on negotiation with the customer or based on customer buying power. Real estate, automobiles and furniture are often purchased using flexible pricing. Seldom do customers pay the sticker price, but instead negotiate a price. The same is true for antiques and art pieces. The price placed on the item is the starting place for price haggling. Some consumers take great pride in getting the price of products reduced.

Flexible pricing Pricing strategy that allows a firm to set prices based on negotiation with the customer, or based on customer buying power.

11-5b Pricing Psychology

Psychological pricing refers to setting prices to create a particular psychological effect. One of the dimensions involved in psychological pricing is the **reference price**, the price that consumers carry in their mind for a particular product or brand. Reference prices can be created or influenced by previous purchase experiences, by advertising, or by the manufacturer's suggested retail price or list prices.

Psychological pricing Setting prices to create a particular psychological effect.

Reference price The price that consumers carry in their mind for a particular product or brand.

Price is often used as a signal for quality. Consumers tend to believe that higher prices are associated with better quality, especially in cases in which quality is difficult to evaluate. This is especially true for services that cannot be seen or touched prior to the purchase.

Prestige pricing Strategy based on the premise that consumers will feel that products below a particular price will have inferior quality and will not convey a desired status and image.

Prestige pricing is a strategy based on the premise that consumers will feel that products below a particular price will have inferior quality and will not convey a desired status and image. Thus, the idea is to use a high price to indicate the prestige image of the product. Social and psychological impact of the brand is important. The brand name becomes synonymous with prestige.

11-5c Price Discounting

Price discounting involves reducing the price for purchasing a particular product. The discount can be based on purchasing large quantities, for responding to a promotion, for paying cash, or responding within a set timeframe. **Figure 11-8** identifies the primary methods of discounting.

Quantity discount A discount method where both consumers and intermediaries typically get a price break when they purchase larger quantities of a particular product.

Trade discount A price incentive offered by manufacturers and wholesalers to make a purchase or stock a particular brand.

A common method of discounting is the **quantity discount**. Both consumers and intermediaries typically get a price break when they purchase larger quantities of a particular product. Purchasing a mega-pack of Huggies diapers results in a per-unit price that is almost two thirds of that paid for a small package. Purchasing a package of eight Bounty paper towel rolls is significantly cheaper than purchasing eight separate rolls of identical size. The goal of the firm is for consumers to respond to the price incentive by purchasing the product and then to increase consumption, that is use more paper towels for more household chores or change the baby more often.

In the distribution channel, manufacturers and wholesalers often will offer **trade discounts**, which is some type of price incentive to make

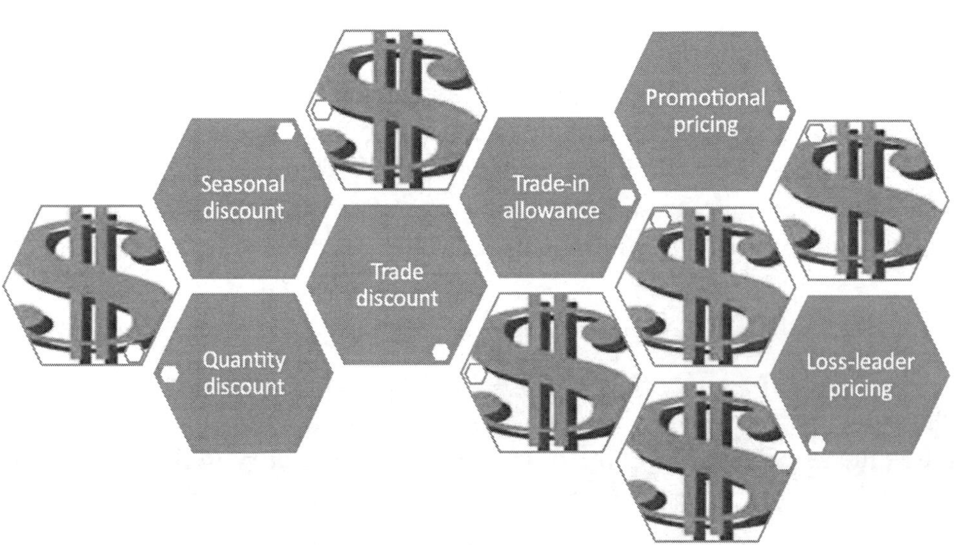

FIGURE 11-8 Methods of Price Discounting

purchase or stock a particular brand. The most common trade discount is a price-off, but it can also be a bonus pack where the channel member receives extra merchandise for making the purchase. In almost all cases, the channel member offering the trade discount will stipulate a minimum quantity, such as 1,000 cases, and a specific timeframe, such as within the next 60 days.

Source: zhu difeng/Shutterstock

For a number of goods and services, **seasonal discounts** are offered. Consumers can benefit from seasonal discount by going to a resort in the off-season. Retailers will offer seasonal discounts on lawnmowers in the fall and winter to move the merchandise. Another form of discounting is the **trade-in allowance**. Most vehicles are purchased with a trade-in, thus reducing the price of the new car.

Seasonal discount Discounts offered by retailers to promote off-season sales.

Trade-in allowance A form of discounting where an item is purchased with a trade-in of a similar item, thus reducing the price of the new item.

Another form of price discounting is **promotional pricing**, which reduces prices temporarily to increase sales in the short run. Special event sales, cash rebates, low- or zero-interest financing, and free maintenance are all examples of promotional pricing strategies. One strategy that retailers use and that manufacturers find problematic if it involves their brand is **loss-leader pricing**, whereby the firm advertises a product at a price that is significantly less than its usual price. The goal is to create traffic in the stores for consumers to purchase higher-margin products. Eggs for 99 cents before Easter and turkeys for 59 cents a pound before Thanksgiving are typical loss leaders. The problem with loss-leader pricing and with promotional pricing in general is that it can hurt the brand in the long term. Consumers will expect to find the brand at the reduced price and will refuse to purchase it at its regular price. Also, if the product is available for a very low price, consumers may come to question its quality relative to the competitors' product.

Promotional pricing Strategy that reduces prices temporarily to increase sales in the short run.

Loss-leader pricing Pricing whereby the firm advertises a product at a price that is significantly less than its usual price to create traffic in the stores for consumers to purchase higher-margin products.

11-5d Product-Related Pricing

With regard to the product component of the marketing mix, pricing can be used for numerous purposes. **Product line pricing** involves creating price differences between the different items in the product line, such that specific price points are used to differentiate between the items in the line. For instance, instead of selling products for one price, using one version of a product, the firm may identify different market segments and price products differently for the respective segments. Segmented pricing, in this case, adjusts prices to allow for differences in the products. Designers offer collection lines (Ralph Lauren, Anne Klein) at higher prices and the bridge lines (Polo, Anne Klein II) at lower prices. The differences between the prices of the different lines are easily observable—thus

Product line pricing Pricing that involves creating price differences between the different items in the product line, such that specific price points are used to differentiate among the items in the line.

Source: lxdbzxy/Shutterstock

Source: Markus Mainka/Shutterstock

the price points are distinct. Ralph Lauren shirts retail for more than $100, whereas Polo shirts can be bought for less than $60.

Men's Warehouse will offer suits at different pricing levels, such as $200, $400, and $600. As the examples illustrate, product line pricing is popular in the clothing industry, where designs are greatly differentiated. With multiple product lines, companies can appeal to different market segments, increasing their profit opportunities. Problematic with product line pricing is the likelihood that markdowns taken on the higher-priced merchandise will blur the distinction between the different lines.

Other product-related dimensions of pricing include **accessory pricing**, which addresses pricing of accessories and other optional products sold with the main product. Accessories for a bed set are neck pillows, decorative pillows, valances, and other products that have the same design and that would look lovely when used with the main product. Printers are often sold at a low cost, but ink cartridges are priced higher. Thus, companies like HP make their profit on the ink cartridges, not the actual printer.

Accessory pricing Pricing of accessories and other optional products sold with the main product.

Bundling Pricing of bundled products sold together.

Bundling refers to the pricing of bundled products sold together. A company can sell a product, warranty, delivery, and installation together in one bundle. Bundling is used in the fast food industry with value meals and in the transportation industry with vacation packages. The concept behind bundling is to encourage consumers to spend more money overall, than if they purchased each item separately.

11-6 Changing the Price

Companies often find that they have to make price changes to remain competitive. In inflationary times, they must pass along costs to consumers. When competition is intense and competitors are slashing prices, the company must go along with the price cuts to avoid losing customers. Cutting prices, however, is not always the solution. In addition to diminishing profit margins, such strategies might bring about price wars with competitors trying to hold on to their market share, crippling the entire industry.

Companies can use a number of methods to pass on increases in costs to the consumers. First, the company can communicate openly the reason for the price increase. Gas companies rely on the media to communicate this information. Because the media are perceived as unbiased, this type of communication is very valuable. The gas companies themselves do not need to justify the price increase to the consumer. Retailers can also communicate price increases to consumers. In times of shortage as a result of drought or other natural phenomena, retailers will communicate the reason behind the high prices of produce. Another method for increasing prices is to do so without the consumer immediately noticing by eliminating price promotions, by adding more expensive items to the product line and eliminating cheaper ones. The company can change to lower-cost ingredients and reduce the quantity, without altering the package.

One important concern of the firm is the reaction of competitors to price changes. Usually, if more than one competitor follows suit in lowering the price, all the others will follow suit. If more than one competitor follows suit in raising the price, it is uncertain whether the others will do so, leaving the firm that initiated the price increase at a disadvantage, unless the firm repositions itself as a higher-quality prestige brand.

Summary

1. **Define pricing and examine the external and internal influences on pricing decisions.**
   Price is the amount of money necessary to purchase a good or service. Among external influences on price are consumers, who, according to the law of demand, purchase more products at a lower price than at a higher price. Economic factors, such as inflation, recession, and interest rates, also affect pricing decisions because they affect the cost of producing a product. The costs of materials, supplies, and labor are some of the costs that are not within a firm's control. Intermediaries also affect product prices, as does competition. In a competitive environment where there is pure competition, the effect is not as great as in an oligopolistic environment. Yet another external influence on the firm is exerted by the government, which takes action against unfair pricing practices, such as price discrimination, resale price maintenance, price fixing, and various deceptive pricing practices. Deceptive practices include predatory pricing, which involves charging prices below cost to eliminate competitors. Other deceptive practices include bait-and-switch and price confusion.
2. **Examine the different price objectives: sales-based, profit-maximization, and status quo.**
   Sales-based pricing objectives focus on increasing the sales volume. One way a company can increase sales for its company is through penetration pricing, selling the product for a low price in order to gain market share. Profit-based objectives focus on the total return on investment. With this strategy, a company introducing a new product can use a skimming strategy, pricing the product high to recoup investments quickly in the early stages of the life cycle. Status quo objectives focus on maintaining a good relationship with customers, channel members, and regulatory bodies. This strategy cannot be maintained long-term. Companies may elect to have more than one objective.
3. **Address the pricing strategies: cost-based, demand-based, competition-based, and combination pricing.**
   For cost-based pricing, a firm sets the price by calculating merchandise, service, and overhead costs and then adding an amount needed to cover the profit goal. Cost-based pricing is easy to calculate because it does

not take into consideration the price elasticity of demand or the reaction of competitors to price changes. The cost-based pricing techniques are cost-plus, markup, target, and break-even analysis. Demand-based pricing takes consumers' perceptions into account and their potential response to the product at different price levels. With demand-based pricing, firms identify a price ceiling, which is the maximum amount that consumers are willing to pay for a product. This amount is contingent on the elasticity of demand, which itself is contingent on the availability of product substitutes and urgency of need. Demand estimates are less precise than cost. When there is minimal competition, firms can increase prices and obtain higher profits. Many firms use competitors' prices, instead of demand or product costs, to determine the prices of their products. This approach is useful when firms compare themselves to similar companies with similar products that have similar demand patterns and similar costs. Pricing at the level of competition does not lead to competitive retaliation because it does not affect competitors. Pricing below competition, however, is likely to elicit some level of competitive response. Companies can also use combination pricing or a combination of these strategies.

4. **Address strategic marketing applications in relation to pricing, such as price variability, price psychology, price discounting, and product-related pricing.**
   With regard to price variability, companies can use customary pricing, keeping the same price over time. They can also use variable pricing, changing their prices in response to changes in cost or demand, and flexible pricing, which allows a firm to set prices based on negotiation with the customer, or based on customer buying power. Psychological pricing refers to setting prices to create a particular psychological effect. Price is often used as a signal for quality. Prestige pricing is a strategy based on the premise that consumers will feel that products below a particular price will have inferior quality and will not convey a desired status and image. Price discounting involves reducing the price for purchasing larger quantities, for responding to a promotion, or responding earlier than a particular set time. The goal in price discounting is for consumers to respond to the price incentive by purchasing the product, and then to increase consumption in the long term. Intermediaries can benefit from trade discounts. Consumers can benefit from seasonal discounts, or they can qualify for a trade-in allowance for turning in their old product when they purchase a new one. Promotional pricing reduces prices temporarily to increase sales in the short run. Loss-leader pricing, whereby the firm advertises a product at a price that is significantly less than its usual price to create traffic in the stores for consumers to purchase higher-margin products, may pose problems to the brand in the long term. With regard to product-related pricing, product line pricing is used to distinguish between lines of similar products. Accessory pricing involves pricing of products used with a particular product, such as ink cartridges for printers. Price bundling refers to pricing of a group of products sold together at a set price.

5. **Address strategies that companies use to change prices. Companies often find that they have to make pricing changes to remain competitive.**
   In inflationary times, firms must pass along costs to consumers. When competition is intense and competitors are slashing prices, the company must go along with the price cuts to avoid losing customers. Companies can use a number of methods to pass increases in costs on to the consumers. First, the company can communicate openly the reason for the price increase. Retailers and manufacturers can also communicate price increases to consumers. In times of shortage as a result of drought or other natural phenomena, retailers will communicate the reason behind

the high prices of produce. Another method for increasing prices is to do so without the consumer immediately noticing: by eliminating price promotions; by adding more expensive items to the product line and eliminating cheaper ones; and by changing ingredients and lowering the quantity, without altering the package.

Key Terms

Accessory pricing (336)
Bait and switch (324)
Bid pricing (332)
Break-even analysis (329)
Bundling (336)
Cost-based pricing (327)
Cost-plus pricing (327)
Customary pricing (332)
Deceptive pricing (324)
Demand-based pricing (331)
Demand curve (319)
Differential pricing (331)
Dumping (324)
Dynamic pricing (333)
Fixed costs (325)
Flexible pricing (333)
Law of demand (319)
Loss-leader pricing (335)
Markup pricing (328)
Monopolistic competition (322)
Oligopolistic competition (322)
Penetration pricing (325)
Predatory pricing (324)
Prestige pricing (334)
Price ceiling (331)
Price confusion (324)
Price discrimination (323)
Price elasticity (319)
Price fixing (323)
Price floor (327)
Price leadership (332)
Product line pricing (335)
Profit-maximization objectives (326)
Promotional pricing (335)
Psychological pricing (333)
Pure competition (322)
Pure monopoly (322)
Quantity discount (334)
Reference price (333)
Resale price maintenance (323)
Sales-based pricing objectives (325)
Seasonal discount (335)
Skimming (326)
Status quo–based objectives (326)
Target profit pricing (330)
Trade discount (334)
Trade-in allowance (335)
Unit pricing (324)
Variable costs (325)
Variable pricing (333)

Discussion Questions

1. Demand for certain products is price inelastic. Identify three goods or services that you would purchase at practically any price. Would most consumers consider your choices to be inelastic? Why or why not?
2. Demand for most products is price elastic. Identify three products that you would purchase in a greater quantity or more frequently if the price were lower. Would most consumers purchase more of those same products? Why or why not?
3. On a continuum where pure monopoly is at one end and pure competition is at the other, where would you place the following industries: automobiles, airlines, mobile phones, clothing, dine-in restaurants, and dentists? Explain.
4. Have you experienced personally, or known someone who has experienced, some form of deceptive pricing? Explain the situation and explain why you believe it was deceptive pricing.
5. Recall your recent shopping experiences. What product accessories have you bought? How were they priced relative to the main product

6. Access the website of Ray-Ban sunglasses at www.ray-ban.com. Which pricing objective do you believe Ray-Ban is using? Why? What types of psychological pricing strategy would you advise the company to use for its products? Why?
7. A retired person has decided to make bird houses for some extra income. Use the following information to calculate the selling price using the cost-plus pricing method.
   - Variable costs per bird house: $14.00
   - Fixed costs: $170.00
   - Number of bird houses being built: 40
   - Desired profit: $500.00
8. A retired person has decided to make bird houses for some extra income. Use the following information to calculate the selling price using the markup off costs pricing method. What would be the selling price if markup off selling price was used?
   - Variable costs per bird house: $14.00
   - Fixed costs: $170.00
   - Number of bird houses being built: 80
   - Desired profit: $1.000.00
9. A retail store pays $6.65 for a bag of horse feed. The store wants to mark it up 30%. Using the markup off selling price pricing method, calculate the selling price.
10. A manufacturer of televisions is planning to spend $300,000 on an advertising campaign. A television costs $120.00 to build and sells for $160.00. How many television sets must the manufacturer sell to break-even on the advertising campaign?
11. Refer to the information in Question 10. Suppose the manufacturer wants to earn $200,000 in profit with the advertising campaign. How many televisions must the manufacturer sell to break even on the advertising campaign including the $200,000 desired profit margin?
12. The cost of building a theme park is $8 million. The company wants to earn a 20% return on investment. The company estimates 400,000 people will visit the theme park during the next three years and that variable costs per visit will be $25.00. Using the target pricing method calculate the price the theme park will need to charge for each visitor.
13. Access each of the following websites. For each site discuss the level of price elasticity you believe is present for that product, the factors that most influence prices, type of competitive market (pure competition, etc.), price objective being used, and any price discounts that you observe. For each be sure to justify or explain your rationale.
    a. Taco Bell (www.tacobell.com)
    b. Guess (www.Guess.com)
    c. John Deere (www.deere.com)

Review Questions

True or False

1. According to the law of supply and demand, consumers purchase fewer products at a lower price than at a higher price.
2. The demand curve portrays the number of units bought for a particular price in a given time period.
3. Monopolistic competition characterizes a market that consists of many buyers and sellers, where no buyer or seller can control price or the market.
4. Legislation such as the Robinson-Patman Act prohibits charging different prices to different buyers of the same merchandise and requires sellers that offer a service to one buyer to make the same service available to all buyers.
5. Predatory pricing and dumping are examples of price fixing.
6. In pricing their products, companies need to take into consideration all product costs to obtain a fair rate of return on investment.
7. Skimming involves firms initially pricing the product below the price of competitors to quickly penetrate the market at competitors' expense and acquire a large market share, and then gradually raise the price.

8. In cost-based pricing, the firm sets the price by calculating merchandise, service, and overhead costs and then adds an amount needed to cover the profit goal.
9. Cost-plus pricing is a variant of cost-based pricing, with a markup used to cover selling costs and profits.

Multiple Choice

10. A market that consists of few sellers who dominate the market is a(n)
    a. pure monopoly.
    b. monopolistic competition.
    c. oligopoly.
    d. monopoly.
11. A market that consists of many buyers and sellers and products that vary greatly in the same product category is a(n)
    a. pure monopoly.
    b. monopolistic competition.
    c. oligopoly.
    d. monopoly.
12. Manufacturers are prohibited from requiring retailers to charge a particular price for a product; they are thus prohibited from
    a. price discrimination.
    b. price fixing.
    c. resale price maintenance.
    d. engaging in odd pricing.
13. The price that consumers carry in their mind for a particular product or brand is known as
    a. referent pricing.
    b. reference pricing.
    c. referral pricing.
    d. none of the above.
14. A strategy that allows a company to set prices based on negotiations with the customer is
    a. differential pricing
    b. flexible pricing
    c. prestige pricing
    d. target profit pricing
15. A strategy whereby the firm advertises a product at a price that is significantly less than its usual price to create traffic in the stores for consumers to purchase higher-margin products is known as
    a. loss-leader pricing.
    b. reference pricing.
    c. odd pricing.

Answers: (1) False, (2) True, (3) False, (4) True, (5) False, (6) True, (7) False, (8) True, (9) False, (10) c, (11) b, (12) a, (13) b, (14) b, (15) a

Case: The Business Side of Exhibition Catalogs

Karen James, a talented curator and art businesswoman with noteworthy art exhibitions on her resume, is in the process of planning a traveling exhibition of German expressionist painters throughout the United States. She has received commitments, pending adequate insurance, for a number of paintings. To date, Karen has received financial support commitments from two nonprofit foundations—the Goethe Institute and the Institut für Auslandsbeziehungen—to underwrite the cost of transportation of the art pieces from different museums and private lenders to the museums where the art will be exhibited. She is still working with museums to ensure their commitment. She has been able to secure only a handful of venues for the exhibit: a midsize museum in central Maryland with a reasonable contemporary art collection, but with only a small gallery of expressionist paintings, and a small museum in New York City specializing in German expressionist art. She has also been able to persuade one other museum in the Midwest to host the exhibition.

Source: Lakov Filiminov/Shutterstock

In planning the traveling exhibition, Karen needs to cover two additional costs. One is the cost of the exhibition catalog, which she will co-author. She will have 4,000 copies printed and delivered at a cost of $30 each.

Another cost is for insurance. This cost is likely to present the most problems. According to Lisa Dennison, a deputy director of the Solomon R. Guggenheim Museum in New York and its chief curator, "the rising value of art, coupled with the escalating cost of insurance premiums are making these . . . shows prohibitive. This, along with falling attendance, has been one of the most serious repercussions of September 11." The art lost in and around the World Trade Center, about $10 million worth of pieces by Calder, Miro, and Lichtenstein, may constitute just a fraction of what could be lost in another massive attack. Collectors also fear for their art, and some insist that museums obtain extra insurance before they agree to lend their art. More recently, artists and collectors have demanded additional earthquake insurance, which museums and galleries rarely carry because it is prohibitively expensive. Karen's total insurance bill will be high, at $18,000 ($13,000 for the New York museum and $5,000 for the other two museums).

Karen also has personal expenses in developing the traveling exhibition. She estimates these personal expenses are $27,000. She has negotiated to receive $62,000 from the three museums, regardless of exhibit attendance, to help offset her expenses. But, the $62,000 will not cover the total costs. Now she must decide the price that she should charge the museums for the catalogs.

Case Questions

1. If Karen's fixed expenses are $120,000 for the catalog, $18,000 for insurance, and $27,000 for personal expenses, how much must she charge the museums for the catalog to break even?
2. If Karen wanted to make a total of $100,000—which includes the $62,000 that she was able to negotiate with the museum—how much would she have to charge the museum for the catalogs?
3. What are some of the shortcomings of the method you used to calculate the prices of the catalogs in questions 1 and 2?
4. From Section 11-4, discuss each of the major methods of pricing as it would relate to Karen's pricing of the catalog. Which method should she use? Why?

Sources: Daniel Grant, "Artists: Is Your Work Insured in Your Gallery?," Huffington Post (May 22, 2012), accessed at http://www.huffingtonpost.com/daniel-grant/artists-is-your-work-insu_b_1535342.html; Carol Vogel, "Fear of Terror a Complication for Art Exhibits," *New York Times* (February 25, 2003): A1, A20.

Endnotes

1. Mary Hanbury, "Gen Z is leading an evolution in shopping that could kill brands as we know them," Business Insider, July 2019, https://www.businessinsider.com/gen-z-shopping-habits-kill-brands-2019-7.
2. Ravi Dhar and Rashi Glazer, "Hedging Customers," *Harvard Business Review* 81, no. 5 (May 2003): 86–92.
3. Rob Enderle, "Samsung Galaxy Fold vs. Microsoft Surface Duo, Techspective, October 19, 2019, https://techspective.net/2019/10/12/samsung-galaxy-fold-vs-microsoft-surface-duo.
4. Kyle Wiggers, "Researchers find racial discrimination in 'dynamic pricing' algorithms used by Uber, Lyft, and others," VentureBeat, June 12, 2020, https://venturebeat.com/2020/06/12/researchers-find-racial-discrimination-in-dynamicpricing-algorithms-used-by-uber-lyft-and-others.

PART 4

Marketing Communications

Source: Rawpixel.com/Shutterstock

Integrated Marketing Communications

Source: one photo/Shutterstock

Chapter Outline

Learning Objectives

Ivelin Radkov/Shutterstock

After studying this chapter, you should be able to:

- Discuss the concept of integrated marketing communications.
- Identify the various marketing communication elements.
- Identify the elements of communication and the importance of AIDA.
- Discuss the various factors that affect the relative mix of communication elements in an integrated marketing communications plan.
- Identify the various types of advertising.
- Describe the appeals that can be used in designing an advertisement.
- Differentiate between the three types of message strategies.
- Discuss the advantages and disadvantages of the primary media (with the exception of digital).

Source: aslysun/Shutterstock

12-1 Chapter Overview

In most purchases, whether a cup of coffee or a fast car, emotions are a critical part of the decision. Brand loyalty is built on emotions, not facts! Consumers like ads that make them laugh, make them smile, make them feel good. Thus, the Super Bowl ads with horses, puppies, and other animals touch a heart string. Advertising and marketing communications are an integral part of creating those emotions that lead to positive brand feelings.

The fourth component of the four Ps of marketing is promotion—all forms of external communications directed toward consumers and businesses, with the goal of developing customers. Recently, marketers have been pushing to integrate all forms of promotion, or communication, to ensure that the company speaks with one voice. Section 12-2 presents the concept of integrated marketing communications (IMC), and the principal channels of an IMC program are discussed in Section 12-3. Marketing communications are based on an understanding of the communication process, addressed in Section 12-4. For an effective IMC plan, a firm must decide which elements of communication it needs to use to communicate effectively with customers; the mix will vary depending on firm objectives and the budget allocated for marketing. Section 12-5 discusses the communication mix and the elements that influence how the marketing package is developed. Advertising is an important component of integrated marketing communications (IMC) and is presented in Section 12-6 and Section 12-7. The last section of the chapter (Section 12-8) discusses the media selection process and the advantages and disadvantages of the primary media.

12-2 Integrated Marketing Communications

Integrated marketing communications (IMC) The coordination and integration of all marketing communication tools, avenues, and sources within a company into a seamless program designed to maximize the communication impact on consumers, businesses, and other constituencies of an organization.

Integrated marketing communications (IMC) has been around for decades, promoting the coordination of all of the marketing functions and activities. Although the concept may have been discussed in marketing articles, few companies practiced IMC until the beginning of the 21st century. Integrated marketing communications has now become the key term and key guiding principle in developing marketing communications. What is **integrated marketing communications (IMC)**? It is creating a unified, seamless experience for consumers to interact with the brand, combining all marketing communication, including advertising, sales promotion, public relations, direct marketing, and social media, through their own mix of tactics, methods, channels, and activities, so that all work as a unified force, ensuring all messaging and communications strategies are consistent and centered on the customer.[1,2] It involves communicating through **paid media**, such as traditional advertising, direct marketing, and online ads, **earned media**, such as organic search, public relations, and influencer marketing, and **owned media**, such as social media, company websites, customer service, and direct marketing through channels that include email and mobile devices.

Paid media Media the company pays for such as traditional advertising, direct marketing, and online ads.

Earned media Media exposure earned through organic search, public relations, and/or influencer marketing.

Owned media Media owned by the company, such as social media, company websites, customer service, and direct marketing through channels that include email and mobile devices.

Coca-Cola decided to wade deeply into polarizing issues in a campaign that is in line with its broader integrated marketing communications effort to position itself as a purpose-led brand. It had already previously tackled sustainability and LGBT rights. Now it is taking on social media misbehavior, asking viewers to consider listening to different perspectives, creating a message that emphasizes empathy and meaning. The campaign, entitled "Open," created by Wieden+Kennedy, set in an angry nasty city, implores viewers to ask themselves if they are wrong to be sanctimonious. Its tagline is "Everything is better when we're open." While the campaign launched in Europe, Coca-Cola has undertaken an integrated marketing campaign around its position as a purpose-led brand, putting the traditional view of the customer as buyer to bed, and working to create engagement, based on the premise that consumers support companies whose brand purpose aligns with their beliefs.[3]

By unifying messages around its purpose-led brand and by using multiple media to communicate its position, Wieden+Kennedy increased the chances that the consumer would be exposed to its new theme. Integrating all communication will likely result in a greater impact than using different themes.

Customers, both individuals and businesses, are becoming more socially conscious, opting for brands that share their philosophy—they expect social activism on the part of the companies they support. In general, consumers are better informed, more price conscious, and more demanding than in the past. Reaching these customers requires a consistent marketing message at every point of customer contact. IMC is a holistic approach that involves everyone in the company articulating the same message. For this integration to work, it must occur at three levels. First, there must be open communication vertically within the company, from the employees who interact with customers and perform the day-by-day work to the chief executive officer (CEO). Second, there must be horizontal communication, across functional areas and departments. Third, there must be communication to customers and stakeholders who have an interest in the company.

Source: designmer491/Shutterstock

FIGURE 12-1 Advertising Is a Cost-Effective Method to Reach a Brand's Target Consumers
Source: Julian Prizont-Cado/Shutterstock

12-3 Communication Channels

An organization has many potential venues of communication. Traditionally, the promotional mix included advertising, sales promotion, trade promotion, personal selling, and public relations. With an integrated approach, other components of communication have also become important, such as digital marketing, direct response marketing, and social media.

Advertising Any form of paid communication directed to an organization's customers or other stakeholders.

Practically every organization uses some type of advertising to promote its products. **Advertising** is any form of paid communication directed to an organization's customers or other stakeholders. Outlets for advertising include the traditional media, such as radio, television, magazines, newspapers, and billboards, as well as the Internet and social media. Advertising has a major advantage: it is a cost-effective vehicle for reaching your audience (see **Figure 12-1**). It is able to reach a large number of people with a single message. Although the cost may be high for a television ad (as much as $5.6 million for a 30-second Super Bowl spot), the relative cost per person reached is very low since that message has the potential to reach over 100 million people. While a direct-mail piece to consumers may cost as much as $2 per person, a television advertisement that costs $250,000 but reaches 2.5 million people costs only ten cents per person.

Public relations (PR) A communication venue that addresses issues an organization faces and represents the organization to the public, media, and various stakeholders.

Whereas, advertising is aimed primarily at customers, **public relations** is aimed at the general public and stakeholders of an organization. Public relations (PR) addresses issues faced by an organization and represents the organization to the public, media, and various stakeholders. The PR department normally handles any event that occurs that has a direct or indirect impact on the public or stakeholders. If an accident occurs at a factory, the PR department will deal with the media and provide information to the public. If a new product is introduced, it is the responsibility of the PR department to send out a news release. If the quarterly earnings are above or below the projection, it is the PR department that deals with Wall Street and other investors.

Publicity is usually an outcome of public relations that is produced by the news media and is not paid for or sponsored by the business involved. A newspaper article about Coca-Cola, Beyond Burger, or any other organization would be publicity. The company has no control over what is being said. It is the responsibility of the PR department to monitor the media and the environment that surrounds a firm—especially the macro-environment—for events that may affect the organization. Businesses should monitor articles that are written about the firm. Rather than react to events, it is better if a business is prepared for them and can act proactively. If a strike in South America is going to interrupt the supply of coffee to Starbucks, the PR department can alert Starbucks's management so another source of coffee beans can be contacted or an alternative plan can be developed. If an article is going to appear in the *Wall Street Journal* about the labor practices of a company, then the firm can be better prepared to counter possible misconceptions.

Publicity A form of public relations produced by the news media but not paid for or sponsored by the business concern.

To stimulate sales, companies will often use either sales promotions or trade promotions or both. **Sales promotions** (often called consumer promotions) are incentives used to encourage end users to purchase a product. **Trade promotions** are incentives directed toward channel members to encourage them to purchase, stock, or push a product through the channel. Both are short-term tactics used by firms to stimulate sales, demand, or inquiries.

Sales promotions Incentives to encourage end users or consumers to purchase a product.

Trade promotions Incentives directed toward channel members to encourage them to purchase, stock, or push a product through the channel.

Sales or consumer promotions include offers such as coupons, premiums, sweepstakes, and contests. Most consumer promotions offer some type of price incentive or additional gift or merchandise to encourage consumers to make a purchase. Coupons offering $1.00 off a bottle of shampoo or 50 cents off a box of cereal are found in almost every Sunday newspaper across the United States. According to Inmar, 80% of shoppers indicate that coupons (digital or paper) changed their behavior in some way, with 37% buying sooner than they would have, 35% buying a brand they would not have otherwise purchased, 35% buying more than they would normally buy, and 24% buying an alternative product within the brand than they would have otherwise because of a coupon.[4]

Source: ISyda Productions/Shutterstock

Trade promotions involve channel members. Similar to consumer promotions, trade promotions are designed to encourage immediate activity. It may be a discount or price-off offer if a retailer will purchase a certain number of cases of cereal by the end of the month. It can be an offer for a free case of motor oil if the retailer will purchase 200 cases within the following 30 days. It may be a commitment to pay 75 percent of the cost of a retailer's advertisement in a newspaper if the manufacturer's product is prominently featured. Because of intense competition among manufacturers for retail shelf space, trade promotions have become extremely important in the marketing of products.

Personal selling A direct communication approach between the buyer and seller with the express purpose of selling a product.

Personal selling is an important component of marketing, especially for companies that sell to other businesses, the government, or institutions. It is also important for consumer products, such as real estate, insurance, and high-ticket items like automobiles and furniture. **Personal selling** is a direct communication approach between the buyer and seller with the express purpose of selling a product. In most cases, personal selling takes place between two individuals, but it can also take place between teams of individuals. With large corporate purchases, it is not unusual for the selling organization to use a team approach in selling its products. Even with consumer sales, teams may be used, but it is usually with the buyer, in the form of a couple or family. Home and automobile purchases are normally joint decisions, and vacations may involve the entire family.

Figure 12-2 contrasts advertising, the publicity component of PR, personal selling, and sales promotion on factors such as audience, message, cost, sponsor, flexibility, control over the content and placement of the message, credibility, and major goal. An example is also given of each type of promotion as it would relate to Amazon Echo.

Database marketing The collection, analysis, and use of large volumes of customer data to develop marketing programs and customer profiles.

Direct response marketing The promotion of a product directly from the manufacturer or seller to the buyer without any intermediaries involved in the transaction.

Digital technology has facilitated the development of customer databases, which can be used for database marketing programs and direct marketing programs. **Database marketing** refers to the collection, analysis, and use of large volumes of customer data to develop marketing programs and customer profiles. **Direct response marketing** is the promotion of a product directly from the manufacturer or producer to the buyer without any intermediaries involved in the transaction. Because of the development of computerized customer databases, most direct response marketing today uses the information stored in company or commercial databases. Both approaches have gained prominence with the increased use of computer technology.

Internet (digital) marketing The promotion of products through the Internet.

The rise of computer technology has also given birth to **Internet or digital marketing**, which is the promotion of products through the Internet. According to the U.S. Census Bureau, approximately 75 percent of Americans have access to the Internet at home or have a smartphone with Internet access. As shown in **Figure 12-3** (see page 352), overall Internet usage decreases with age, with 87.5 percent of Americans under 25 having Internet at home, have a Smartphone, or have both. That number falls to 58.4 percent for individuals 55 and older. The largest decrease is in the use of Smartphones going from 67 percent for individuals 34 and under to 23.3 percent for individuals 55 and older. Because of the impact the Internet currently has on marketing and the tremendous impact it could have in the future, all of Chapter 13 is devoted to this topic.[5]

Factor	Advertising	Social Media	Publicity Form of Public Relations	Personal Selling	Consumer Promotions
Audience	Mass	Targeted	Mass	Small (one-to-one)	Varies
Message	Uniform	Specific	Uniform	Specific	Varies
Cost	Low per viewer or reader	Low per viewer or reader	None for media space or time; can be some costs for media releases and publicity materials	High per customer	Moderate per customer
Sponsor	Company	Initially the company; then users/reviewers	No formal sponsor (media are not paid)	Company	Company
Flexibility	Low	High	Low	High	Moderate
Control over content/ placement	High	Low (initial message controlled by sponsor, but the social media takes effect)	None (controlled by media)	High	High
Credibility	Moderate	High	High	Moderate	Moderate
Major goal	To appeal to a mass audience at a reasonable cost, and to create awareness	To reach specific demographics with independently reported message	To reach a mass audience with independently reported message	To deal with individual consumers, resolve questions and close sales	To stimulate short-run sales, to increase impulse purchases
Example	T.V. ad for Amazon Echo	Facebook Page Reviews on Yelp	Magazine article describing the unique features of Amazon Echo in typical home	Retail personnel explaining how Echo works in a kitchen setting	A digital coupon for $10 off the price of Amazon Echo

FIGURE 12-2 Characteristics of Major Forms of Marketing Communications

Social media is an integral element of marketing communication plans **(see Figure 12-4)**. Social media allows brands to communicate with customers in real time. This instant communication creates the potential to generate buzz and excitement for a brand. More sophisticated interactions with customers can be readily achieved through blogs, websites

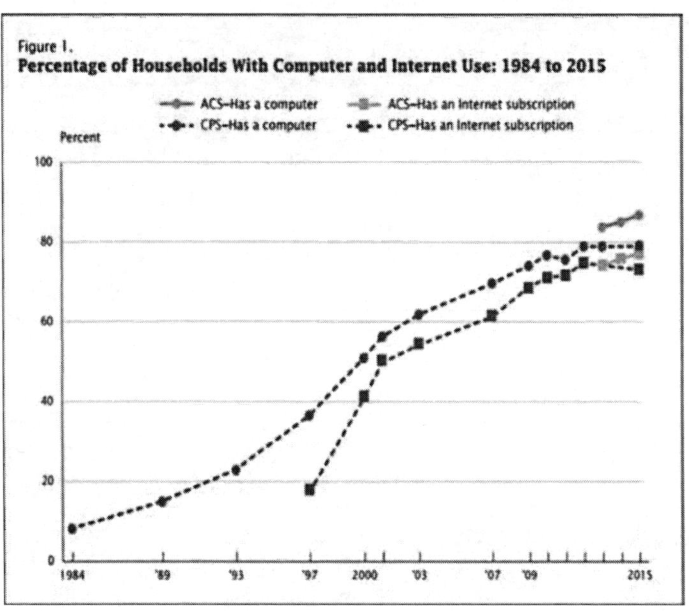

FIGURE 12-3 Internet and Smartphone Usage in the United States
Source: U.S. Census Bureau: https://www.census.gov/content/dam/Census/library/publications/2017/acs/acs-37.pdf

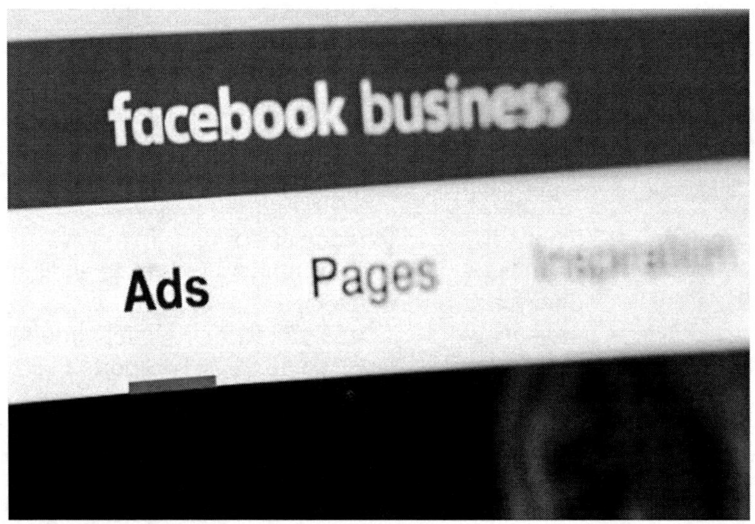

FIGURE 12-4 Social Media Is Now an Integral Part of Every Brand's Marketing Strategy
Source: PixieMe/Shutterstock

and social media advertising. At the same time, negative word-of-mouth and other developments which can quickly damage a brand can be addressed in a tactful manner that reduces any potential harm. Social media is no longer just an option for marketing communications: brands and businesses must develop social media marketing plans or be left behind by competitors, and must think beyond Facebook or Twitter. Colgate toothpaste, for example, launched a hashtag challenge called "Smile Challenge" that covered India, Malaysia, Singapore, Thailand, and the

Philippines over six days, with a customized smile sticker that can detect and virtually score the TikTok user's smile. A hundred content creators in the five countries were also invited to film and upload videos for the challenge, encouraging users to upload their own versions on TikTok. The campaign produced 1.6 million user-generated videos, 2.5 billion total video views, and there were 53,000 videos generated by users and 26 million video views.[6]

12-4 The Communication Process

The key to successful marketing is communication. Someone must send a message, and someone must hear and understand the message. The challenge is developing a message that will get the attention of consumers or businesses and that will then move the recipient to respond in the desired manner. With all of us being bombarded by hundreds of marketing messages each day, getting noticed is difficult. Then, if a message is noticed, will the message be interpreted correctly, in the manner the advertiser or business intended?

12-4a Model of Communications

Marketing communications function similarly to other types of communication between two parties. Someone sends a message; someone else receives it. With marketing, however, the message does not always have to be sent through a person. It can be sent using television, magazines, the Internet or social media **(see Figure 12-5)**. The channel of communication contains a series of six sequential stages, as illustrated in **Figure 12-6**.

The message begins with a **source**, which is the organization that originates a marketing communication. The source can be the company itself,

Source The organization that originates a marketing communication message.

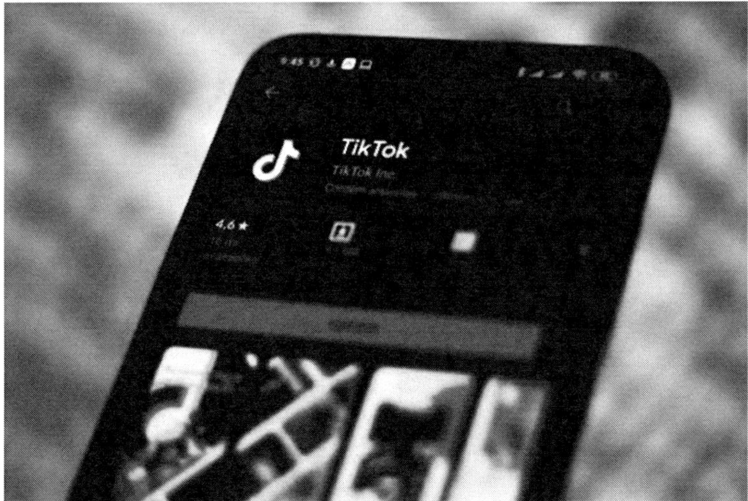

FIGURE 12-5 Advertisers Send Messages through Social Media to More Effectively Target Their Audiences
Source: rafapress/Shutterstock

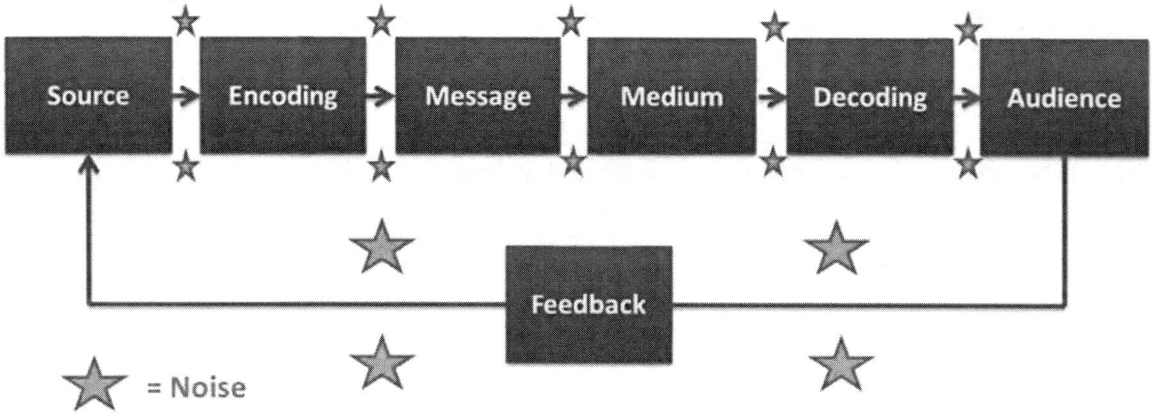

FIGURE 12-6 The Communication Process

or it can be the advertising agency that represents the company. For the "Got Milk?" series of advertisements, the source was the Bozell Agency, hired by the milk industry to develop the advertising campaign. The goal of the campaign was to encourage consumers to drink more milk. With the rise in popularity of soft drinks and other types of drinks, the consumption of milk had declined. To reverse this trend, the milk industry hired the Bozell Agency to create a series of ads to stimulate interest in drinking more milk.

Encoding The process of transposing the objective or goal of a marketing communication concept into an actual marketing communication piece, such as an advertisement, brochure, or sign.

The second step in the communication process is **encoding**, which is the process of transposing the objective or goal of a marketing communication concept into an actual marketing communication piece such as an advertisement, brochure, or sign. With the "Got Milk?" campaign, the creative staff working on the milk industry account wanted to convey the message that drinking milk is fashionable and cool. Therefore, they chose a series of celebrities that were well liked by consumers and not only showed them with a glass of milk, but also with a white milk mustache. In addition, copy was added to explain the importance of drinking milk and the fact that milk is a good source of calcium for bones.

Message The completed marketing communication piece.

When the encoding process is complete, a message has been created. The **message** is the completed marketing communication piece. It may be a 30-second advertisement for television, a point-of-purchase display for a retail store, an interactive website, or a post on a social media site. If the message is done well, it will embody the objectives and goals of the creatives who developed it. In the milk advertisement shown in Figure 12-8, the message was the importance of calcium for both the pregnant mother and the unborn baby, and that milk provides that calcium.

Medium The venue the source uses to send a marketing communication message to its intended audience.

Once the message has been created, it must be sent to the consumer. The **medium** is the venue used by the source to send a marketing communication message to its intended audience. The medium may be television, radio, the Internet, an envelope, or a sign on the side of a city bus. The choice of medium is important because, if the intended audience does not receive or see the marketing message, they cannot react to it.

Decoding The process of interpreting the meaning conveyed in a marketing message.

Once a consumer is exposed to an advertisement, **decoding**, the process of interpreting the meaning conveyed in a marketing message, begins.

FIGURE 12-7 Billboard Sign for the Snoring Center
Source: Roman Sigaev/Shutterstock

If the consumer interprets the message the way that it was intended in the original encoding process, then effective communication has taken place, and the agency has effectively communicated the message.

Audience Individuals who observe a marketing communication and decode the message.

The **audience** is defined as the individuals who observe a marketing communication and decode the message. It is the individuals who see the ads during a television show, in a magazine, or on a billboard. It is the shopper who sees a point-of-purchase display in a grocery store. It is the person at home who receives a direct-mail piece offer. For effective communication to take place, the audience who receives the marketing communication needs to match the audience for which it was designed. If the ad shown in **Figure 12-8** were intended for females 20 to 30 years old, but 80 percent of those who saw the advertisement were males older than 50, the advertisement did not reach its intended target. The message the agency wanted to send to the 20- to 30-year-old female was never received.

Feedback The response of the audience to the message.

The last step in effective communication is **feedback**, which is the response of the audience to the message. For the milk advertisement, the feedback may be the increased consumption of milk or a more positive attitude toward drinking milk. For the Snoring Center ad, it is visits to the Center's website. For advertising and many types of marketing communications, feedback is informal and indirect, making it difficult for marketers to know how effective the communication was, or even if the

FIGURE 12-8 An Advertisement for Milk Highlighting the Importance of Calcium for Both the Mother and the Unborn Baby
Source: Lucky Business/ Shutterstock

intended audience received the message. For personal selling, however, the salesperson can watch the buyer and listen to his or her reaction. Feedback is immediate, allowing the salesperson to modify the message to ensure that the decoding is taking place as intended.

The last factor in the channel of communication is **noise**, which is anything that interferes with the audience receiving the message. It can occur anywhere along the channel of communication. It may be someone talking during the airing of a radio advertisement. It may be someone getting something to eat during a television commercial. It may be that the models in the ad distract a viewer, who might not even hear the message. It may be a shopper is distracted and not listening to what a salesperson is saying. Noise prevents the audience from seeing or reading a marketing message or from comprehending the intended message correctly.

One form of noise interfering with the ads is clutter. When reading an article online, ads may compete for your attention, with some even blocking the article, while your firm's ad may attract attention less intrusively. For those reading magazines, they will find that there are more pages devoted to advertisements than to content.

12-4b AIDA Concept

Source: Luciano Mortula - LGM/ Shutterstock

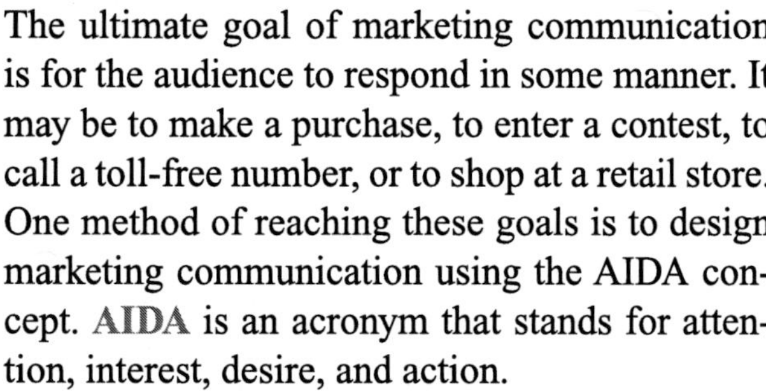

The ultimate goal of marketing communication is for the audience to respond in some manner. It may be to make a purchase, to enter a contest, to call a toll-free number, or to shop at a retail store. One method of reaching these goals is to design marketing communication using the AIDA concept. **AIDA** is an acronym that stands for attention, interest, desire, and action.

Before consumers or a business can be influenced to make a purchase, the marketer must get their attention. If it is a salesperson making a sales call, then a smile, a handshake, and a friendly greeting can gain a buyer's attention. If it is a television commercial, the viewers' attention might be gained by having the volume louder; having an attractive person appear on the screen; playing a familiar tune; or using a tranquil scene. For an online ad, attention may be garnered through a unique, psychedelic array of colors; a large, bold headline; an eye-catching scene; or a well-known celebrity. In order to get viewers' attention, the advertisement in **Figure 12-9** for Sabula Independent Bank used a Dachshund in full color to contrast with the black ink and white background in the rest of the ad.

Noise Anything that interferes with the audience receiving the message.

AIDA An acronym that stands for attention, interest, desire, and action.

Once the marketer has the person's attention, the next step is to develop interest. The attractive model, the Dachshund, or a familiar tune may catch your attention, but if you do not stop and read the advertisement, the message will not be received. Taglines and written or verbal copy must then express the concept or idea that the advertiser wishes to express to develop your interest in the product. The advertisement for Sabula Independent Bank used the headline "Here's the Long and Short of It" to tie in with the picture of the Dachshund and the content copy of the ad. The agency that designed the ad is hoping the headline, with the picture, will garner your attention long enough that you will be interested in reading the rest of the ad. A salesperson has an advantage over media advertising because once the salesperson has your attention, he or she can adjust the sales presentation to build interest in the product and answer any questions you may have.

Once a person's interest has been gained, the third step is to build desire. A purchasing agent for a large company may have four or five vendors from whom she can purchase raw materials. The salesperson has to convince the purchasing agent why his company should be selected. In contrast, it is more difficult for an advertiser to present a message that will lead the viewer from just being interested in the product to wanting to purchase it. A sales representative talking about the product benefits would have an easier time developing desire than if someone just read the advertisement itself.

FIGURE 12-9 To Grab the Viewer's Attention, a Dachshund Dog in Full Color Was Contrasted to a Black and White Ad
Source: gcafotografia/Shutterstock

The last step in this process is action. This is the decision to make the purchase. For the purchasing agent, it may be signing a contract with a supplier. For the person seeing the Sabula Independent Bank ad, it may be going to the bank and securing a home equity loan.

The amount of time a person will spend in each step will vary widely. For high involvement decisions, such as purchasing furniture, clothing, or a vehicle, it may take a marketer a long time to develop desire. For candy bars, simply using a point-of-purchase display near the checkout stand may be enough to urge someone to make a purchase. The time from attention to action may be only a few seconds. If it takes longer, the person is likely to decide that the candy bar has too many calories and that he or she can get by without it. **Figure 12-10** summarizes the use of AIDA for an exercise bicycle in a retail sales situation and with a television advertisement.

12-5 The Communication Mix

In developing an integrated marketing plan, the marketing manager must decide on the relative mix of communication tools. How much will be

Attention ⟶ Interest ⟶ Desire ⟶ Action

AIDA Concept	Retail Sales Situation	Television Advertisement
Attention	A store sign offering $25 off catches your attention.	A well-built young man appears on the screen wearing only shorts.
Interest	A sign by the exercise bike highlights the low cost and features of the bike.	You have been wanting an exercise bike, and this is a model you have not seen before, so you want to see what it looks like and what features it has.
Desire	You sit on the bicycle, and it feels more comfortable than any others you have tried.	After seeing the TV ad, you check the Internet to see where the closest retail store is located and what the Web site says about the bike.
Action	**When a salesperson tells you that the bike can be purchased now and, if for any reason, you don't like the bike, you can return it within 30 days for a full refund, you decide to purchase it.**	**Having thought about the exercise bike, you see another advertisement. You decide this is the right bike and make a decision to purchase it, using the toll-free number listed on the TV screen.**

FIGURE 12-10 Using the AIDA Concept to Sell an Exercise Bike

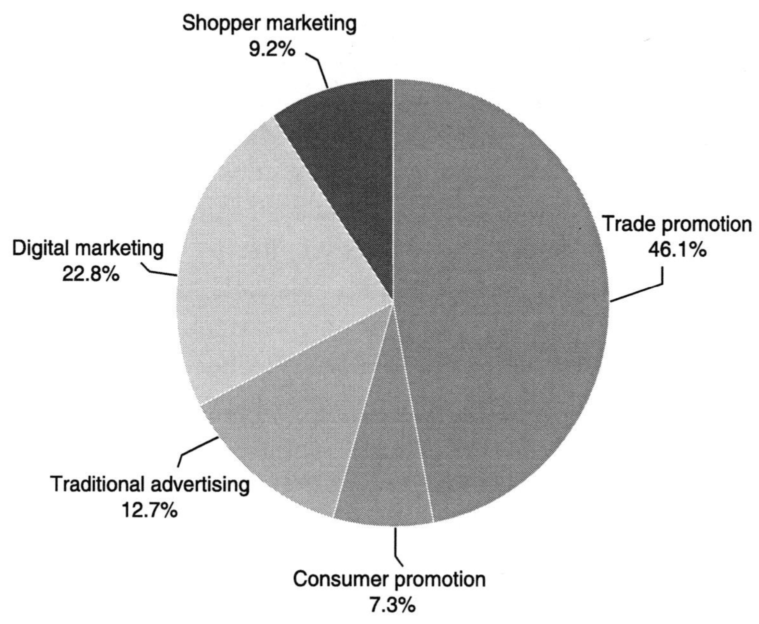

FIGURE 12-11 How Marketing Dollars Are Used

spent on advertising? How much will be spent on trade promotions and sales promotions? How much will be spent to support personal selling? Will social media be used? Will the company use database marketing? How will the Internet be used? The answer to these questions depends on a number of factors that will be discussed in this section. But first, it is interesting to examine how current marketing budgets are used **(see Figure 12-11)**. Because of the pervasive nature of advertising, students tend to believe that most of a company's marketing budget is spent on advertising. This is not true. Spending on promotions accounts for more than half of the marketing budget, with trade promotion representing 46.1% and consumer promotion representing 7.3% of the marketing budget. Traditional advertising continues to fall and now represents 12.7% of the marketing budget, while digital marketing accounts for 22.8%. Shopper marketing—marketing communications at the point of sale (see Chapter 10)—is 9.2 of the marketing budget.[7]

12-5a Business versus Consumer Marketing

The communication mix for business-to-business marketing tends to be different than for consumer marketing. Business-to-business marketing relies more on personal selling, trade promotions, digital marketing and telemarketing, whereas consumer marketing relies more on advertising, social media and consumer promotions. Because businesses are more concentrated and make larger volume purchases, using a salesperson makes sense. One salesperson may account for annual sales in the millions of dollars. Also, because of the high volume of a single purchase, it is important to use the best means of communication: personal selling. For consumers, however, it would not be financially feasible to use a salesperson, except for large ticket items. Advertising and social media can reach more people with a message at a much lower cost per person.

12-5b Communication Objectives

A major factor in how marketing dollars are allocated and the mix of communication tools is what the firm wishes to accomplish. An IMC plan is often oriented toward a single objective. It is possible, however, for a program to accomplish more than one objective at a time, but this may be confusing to potential customers. Communication objectives can be classified into the six major categories illustrated in **Figure 12-12**.

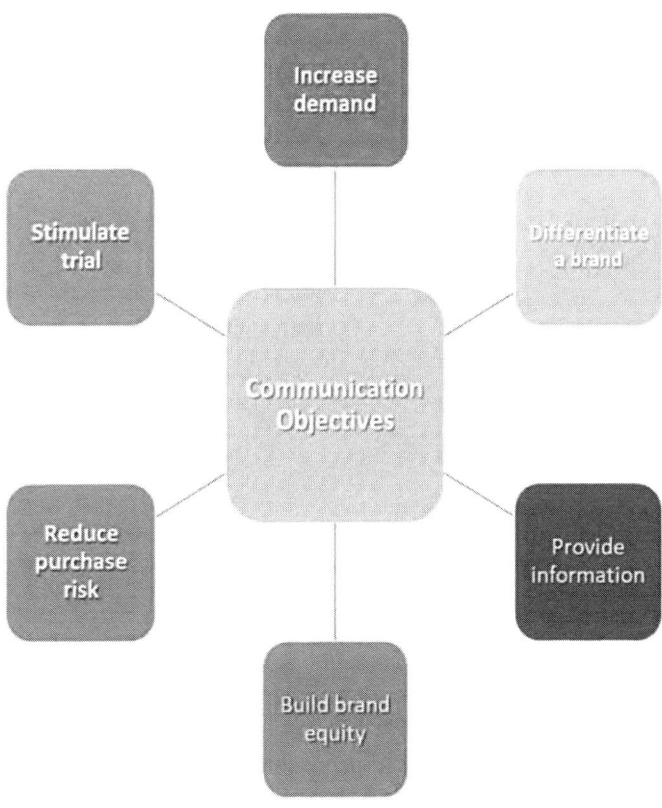

FIGURE 12-12 Communication Objectives

Each objective requires a different approach, and each requires a different mix of communication elements. Although any of the communication elements, such as advertising, can be used to accomplish any of the objectives, other forms of communication such as consumer (or sales) promotions or personal selling may work better for a specific objective. The optimal results occur when the communication tools are used together, integrating them into one common theme. For example, to reduce purchase risk, a firm may use advertising coupled with a $2-off coupon and a special point-of-purchase display. The combined effect of using all three elements together is greater than if only one were used.

Increase Demand To increase demand, firms usually turn to trade and sales promotions. Offering wholesalers and retailers price discounts, quantity discounts, and bonus packs encourages them to purchase more of a product because they can increase their margins. For example, if a manufacturer of picture frames offers retail stores a 10 percent discount on purchases made by October 1, many of the stores will boost their orders. They can then either pass the savings on to the customer through cheaper prices, or they can charge the customer the same amount, increasing their profit by 10 percent. In most cases, retailers use the latter strategy. Retail prices stay the same. To make the increase in demand more dramatic, manufacturers may offer a manufacturer's coupon to consumers at the same time they are offering the channel discount. Giving a discount to both consumers and channel members drastically reduces the profit margin for manufacturers, but it will create a short-term burst in sales.

Advertising is the least effective promotional element to directly increase demand but can serve a valuable support function. An advertisement on television, in a newspaper, or on the Internet can alert consumers to a manufacturer's coupon or a special price offer. A direct-mail piece sent to wholesalers and distributors can alert them to the trade discount being offered. For more of an impact, the manufacturer could have its salespeople offer customers special trade discounts. In these situations, channel members will often either increase the order they had planned or make a special purchase.

Differentiate a Product The proliferation of brands has created a situation in which most consumers as well as businesses have multiple choices. In many cases, there is little difference between the various brands. If this is perceived to be so by the buyer, then price becomes the determining factor. To avoid situations in which buyers make purchase decisions entirely on price, companies strive to differentiate their product from the competitors' product. Benefits and features not available from competitors are stressed. If there are few or no actual differences, companies will often strive to create a psychological difference.

Source: leungchopan/Shutterstock

The best communication tool used to differentiate a product is personal selling. A salesperson has the opportunity to explain a product's features and benefits. The message can be tailored to each buyer, and questions can be answered. For business-to-business markets and high-end consumer products that use salespeople, this method is very effective once the salesperson has the ear of a prospective buyer. But in situations in which personal selling is not possible, a product can be differentiated effectively through advertising. Through an ad, a firm has the opportunity to highlight a product's features and benefits and to show how a particular brand differs from competing brands.

Trade promotions and consumer promotions are not effective in differentiating a product, unless the differentiation is based on price. If a brand is positioned as the low-cost option, then using trade promotions and consumer promotions can be valuable. But, if the differentiation is based on a benefit or feature, then using numerous trade and sales promotions can actually make it more difficult to differentiate a brand. If Pringles chips are promoted as not being greasy, but the company uses coupons extensively, consumers are likely to see Pringles as a cheap brand of potato chips rather than a brand that has been differentiated in another way.

Provide Information Salespeople and advertising are effective at providing potential customers with information. Salespeople are able to modify the information to meet the needs of individual customers. A retail salesperson can provide a shopper with information on major appliances and features of each brand. A field salesperson can inform clients about a special upcoming sale or a new product recently introduced. Advertising is also an excellent means of providing information. Retailers use advertising on a regular basis to inform customers of their location, their operating hours, and the brands they carry. Advertising can be used to promote special events like a Labor Day sale; the introduction of a new brand, such as Vanilla Coke; or the grand opening of a new business. Trade and consumer promotions are good venues for providing information because each offers some type of incentive to encourage action on the part of the consumer or business.

Build Brand Equity For long-term survival, brands must develop a certain level of brand equity that allows them to stand apart from competitors. As mentioned in Chapter 8, brand equity is defined as a set of brand assets and liabilities linked to a brand and its name and symbol, adding or subtracting from the value provided by a good or service to a firm or to that firm's customers. Brand equity is built on two foundations: quality and awareness. The quality must match or exceed the relative price being charged. The quality of food served at McDonald's does not match that of food served at Outback Steakhouse, but it meets the standard relative to the price. If McDonald's did not produce quality fast food items, it could not stay in business. Part of McDonald's brand equity, however, is not only its food but also its service, convenience, and standardization.

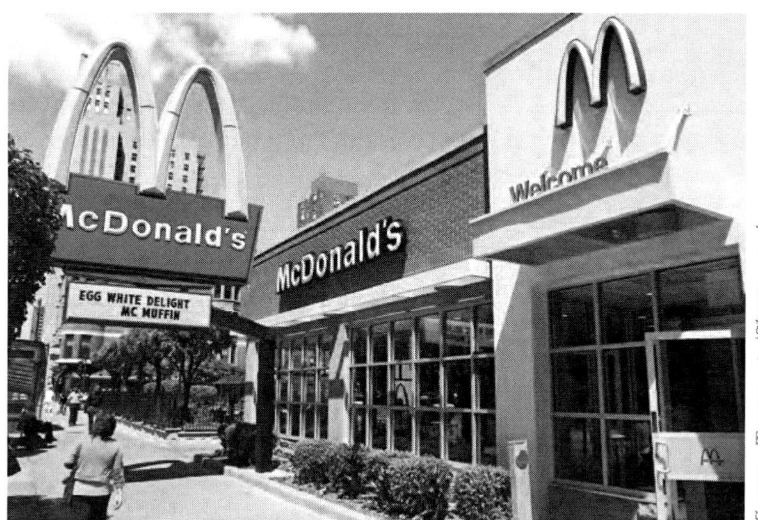

Source: Tupungato/Shutterstock

Source: YanLev/Shutterstock

The other factor in building brand equity is awareness. Although awareness does not equate to brand equity, you cannot have a high level of brand equity without awareness. McDonald's, Campbell's Soup, Walmart, Nike, and Toyota are all well-known and have a high level of awareness. Takata airbags are also well-known, but because of quality issues, it lacks a high level of brand equity.

About the only way to develop a high level of brand awareness is through advertising. Television, radio, digital, and print advertising are major avenues for making people aware of a particular brand. For many brand ads, little information is given. The focus is not on differentiating the product, but on building an awareness of the brand name and reminding consumers of the brand. The goal is to build a strong brand name. If awareness and a brand name are backed by quality products, then brand equity will develop, leading to loyal customers.

Reduce Purchase Risk Reducing purchase risk is important for new products, new brands and for gaining new customers of current brands. Personal selling is the best communication tool to accomplish this objective, offering the salesperson the opportunity to answer objections and explain features that will reduce the buyer's perceived risk. If safety is a factor, the salesperson can explain the safety features. If performance is a factor, the salesperson can explain the performance features and how the brand will provide the benefits the customer wants.

Consumer and trade promotions also reduce purchase risk. Both are effective because they offer the buyer an incentive, normally a price reduction, to purchase. A 25% discount reduces purchase risk. Sampling can reduce purchase risk even further: If a potential customer can use a gym free for a week, then the risk of buying a membership is reduced. The customer has a good idea of the benefits of membership and can more readily tell if it is a lifestyle fit.

Although advertising can be used to reduce purchase risk, it is not very effective for this purpose. Viewers know that the ad is going to promote a product and its features, so it will have little effect on their perceived risk of making a purchase. In rare cases, however, an advertisement may point out a feature or statistic that will be effective in reducing purchase risk. Airlines have tried to reduce the perceived risk of flying for those who are afraid by pointing out that it is statistically safer to fly than to drive. The ads have virtually no impact on perceived risk because people who fear flying may think that they would be the statistics.

Stimulate Trial To build new brands and to rejuvenate stagnant brands, companies will want to stimulate trial. Consumer promotions are the best means for accomplishing this objective. Coupons, sweepstakes, contests, and sampling are excellent methods of getting someone to try a product. Food manufacturers will often offer free samples of their food at grocery stores so people can try it. If they like it, there are coupons readily available that allow the consumers to purchase the product at a reduced price.

Trade promotions are relatively ineffective in stimulating trial. Wholesalers and retailers are reluctant to try new products unless they know consumers will buy them. The trade incentive would have to be substantial, reducing the wholesaler's and retailer's risk, before they would stock an item that no one may buy. For established companies like Procter & Gamble, General Foods, and Kellogg's, retailers are more likely to take the risk because they know that these companies thoroughly test a product in advance, and their history indicates that they have solid products. But even in these cases, the retailer will want the manufacturer to tie the trade promotion into some type of consumer promotion or advertising.

Advertising and personal selling have moderate success in stimulating trial. Advertising could create interest in the product, but stimulating trial would be slow. If advertising is tied with consumer promotions, then its effectiveness increases dramatically. The same is true for personal selling. A salesperson has some impact on stimulating trial, but it takes a trade or consumer promotion offer for the buyer to persuade one to purchase. Take, for example cosmetics: after the onset of the COVID-19 pandemic, consumers were reluctant to go to a cosmetics counter for a free makeover. Trying on different lipstick colors or foundations was only possible with virtual tools: using your webcam, you could find the best foundation shade for your skin or the perfect Pure Color Envy Lipstick shade at the Estee Lauder website. While browsing to find an ideal shade, consumers see various promotions flashing at the top of a screen: free shipping, 15% off for joining their email list, or a gift bag with lipstick, mascara and other goodies valued at $145, free if you spend $45. Spend $45 for two lipsticks and you get a free gift worth three times as much—a no brainer option that will persuade the consumer to purchase. **Figure 12-13** summarizes the strength of each communication element for each of the communication objectives.

12-5c Push/Pull Marketing Strategies

Push/pull marketing strategies relate to how manufacturers market their products. With a push marketing strategy, the manufacturer attempts to push the product through the channels with the belief that if the product is available in retail outlets, consumers will purchase it. With a pull marketing strategy, the manufacturer builds product demand at the consumer level with the belief that consumers will go to retailers and demand that the product be stocked. Manufacturers seldom use either one or the other; instead, they use a combination. Thinking of push/pull marketing strategies along a continuum provides a better understanding of how they work together and what types of communication elements are best suited for each.

Communication Objective	Advertising	Trade Promotions	Consumer Promotions	Personal Selling
Increase demand	Slow, takes time	Excellent for encouraging distributors and retailers to purchase more; impact is immediate and short term	Excellent for encouraging end users to request the product; impact is immediate and short term	Good for items that are sold almost entirely by field salespeople, but poor for retail sales, because the salesperson is dependent on someone coming into the store
Differentiate a product	Excellent	Poor, because differentiation is almost always based on price, not product features	Moderate for encouraging end users to request the brand, but may create price-related differentiation rather than differentiation based on product features	Excellent, because the salesperson has the ability for two-way communication and can often demonstrate how the product is different from that of a competitor
Provide information	Excellent	Poor, because it depends on the type of trade promotion, and the trade offer normally overshadows the information	Poor, because it depends on the type of consumer promotion, and the promotional offer normally overshadows the information	Excellent, because there is two-way communication and the buyer can ask questions
Build brand equity	Excellent	Poor, because most trade promotions focus on some type of price incentive	Poor, because most consumer promotions focus on some type of price incentive	Moderate, because salespeople's primary goal is to sell a product, not to build its equity
Reduce purchase risk	Poor, because advertising can reduce risk only through talking about the features and benefits of the product	Good, because wholesalers and retailers can receive price incentives to make a purchase	Good, because consumer promotions can reduce the financial risk; excellent if the firm can use sampling or trial purchase incentives	Excellent, because the salesperson has an opportunity to answer questions and demonstrate the product
Stimulate trial	Moderate to good success if tied with a sales promotion	Poor, because of so many new products being introduced	Excellent, through offering consumers some type of incentive	Moderate success because of ability to answer questions and demonstrate the product

FIGURE 12-13 Communication Objectives and Communication Elements

Manufacturers who place the greatest emphasis on a push strategy will primarily use trade promotions and personal selling. Trade promotions provide incentives to channel members to stock an item and to push it through the channel. Personal sales calls on retailers and wholesalers will then enhance this process. For a pull strategy, the emphasis will be on advertising and consumer promotions. Advertising builds awareness and brand identity, and consumer promotions offer consumers incentives to try the product. Figure 12-14 summarizes these relationships.

In the past, pharmaceutical companies relied exclusively on a push strategy. Samples of new drugs were offered to physicians and advertisements were taken out in medical journals to get physicians to prescribe a drug to patients. Recently, however, drug companies have turned to a pull strategy, advertising to consumers on social media, showing consumers relevant ads about their personal health—while disavowing the practice of targeting ads to people based on their medical conditions. Spending on Facebook mobile ads alone by pharmaceutical and health-care brands

Push Strategy	Communication Element	Pull Strategy
Low	Advertising	High
High	Trade promotions	Low
Low	Consumer promotions	High
High	Personal selling	Low

FIGURE 12-14 The Communication Elements and Push/Pull Marketing Strategies

reached a billion dollars in 2019, nearly tripling over two years. Many more people will see ads for a drug designed to treat their particular health condition in the intimate setting of a social media feed.[8]

12-5d Product Life Cycle

The stage of the product life cycle (PLC) has a strong impact on marketing communications and the elements used. During the introductory stage, the goals of businesses introducing a new product are to promote industry demand and brand awareness, and to stimulate trial. Advertising works best for promoting industry demand and building awareness. For a business-to-business product, personal selling will also work well. Consumer promotions stimulate trial purchases. Normally, trade promotions will not work because channel members are uncertain about the projected consumer demand.

When the product moves to the growth stage, marketing dollars continue to be spent on advertising, but the objective is to develop brand preference and to differentiate the product from the competition, rather than build industry demand, unless the company has substantial market share. As more consumers appear to be interested in automobiles with self-driving traits, such as lane-keeping assist, and self-parking capabilities, automobile manufacturers are turning to advertising. Memorable ads, such as those for the Hyundai Sonata "smart park," differentiating the brand from competition, are becoming more frequent.

Because of increasing demand, dollars are shifted from consumer promotions to trade promotions. With growing consumer demand, companies will spend more on encouraging channel members to push their brand rather than the competition's brand. Because consumers want the product, there is little need for consumer promotional offers.

When the product hits maturity, competition becomes intense. About the only way a company can increase market share is to take it away from the competition. In this environment, expenditures in all four areas are high. Advertising is needed to differentiate the product. Trade promotions are needed to encourage channel members to place a greater emphasis on a particular brand. Consumer promotions are needed to encourage consumers to choose a particular brand over the competition. Personal selling is needed to highlight the advantages of one brand over another.

Marketing Communication Element	Introductory Stage	Growth Stage	Maturity Stage	Decline Stage
Advertising	Moderate, to develop awareness of a new product and build industry demand	High, to develop brand name and brand awareness	High, to differentiate the product from the competition	Low, because demand is declining and a new product or technology has taken its place
Trade Promotions	Low, because consumers are not familiar with the new product, and for retailers, it would be a high risk	Moderate, since consumers are demanding the product, and manufacturers do not need a high level of trade promotion to push their product	High, to encourage channel members to stock and push the firm's product	Low, because with declining demand, there is no need to encourage channel members to stock the product
Consumer Promotions	High, to encourage trial usage of the product	Low, since consumers are demanding the product, and few sales incentives are needed for purchasing	High, to encourage consumers to choose a particular brand over the competition	Low, because sales promotion incentives will not encourage consumption
Personal Selling	High for business-to-business salespeople because they can explain the new product, but low for consumer products since the salesperson would have to wait for the customer to come to them	Moderate, since salespeople serve primarily as order takers with consumers and businesses demanding the product	High, to encourage customers to purchase a particular brand	Low, because few people or businesses want the product

FIGURE 12-15 Marketing Communications and the Product Life Cycle

The reverse situation occurs when the product moves into the decline stage. It does not make sense to advertise, use trade or consumer promotions, or personal selling. Firms reduce marketing expenditures, planning to pull out of the market and discontinue the product. **Figure 12-15** summarizes the marketing communication elements as they relate to the PLC.

Rank	Company	Advertising in billions
1	Comcast	$6.12
2	AT & T	$5.36
3	Amazon	$4.47
4	Proctor & Gamble	$4.3
5	General Motors Co.	$3.14
6	Walt Disney Co.	$3.13
7	Charter Communications	$3.04
8	Alphabet (Google)	$2.96
9	American Express	$2.8
10	Verizon Communications	$2.68

FIGURE 12-16 Top Ten U.S. Advertisers
Source: Business Insider, "10 biggest advertisers that spent more than $1 billion so you'd buy their products," October 4, 2019

12-6 Advertising

Advertising is all around us. We see it on TV, view it on the Internet, hear it on the radio, view it in magazines, and see it on our social media feeds. It is on billboards, the sides of buses, and even in public bathrooms. It is an important part of marketing communications. Ad spending in the United States is now over $390 billion per year.[9]

Companies spend millions, with several spending billions of dollars on advertising. The largest advertiser in the United States is Comcast, spending over $6.1 billion annually. AT&T, Amazon, and Proctor & Gamble are second through fourth with expenditures in excess of $4 billion.[10] **Figure 12-16** shows the top ten U.S. advertisers.

It is important for marketers to remember that advertising is just one component of the

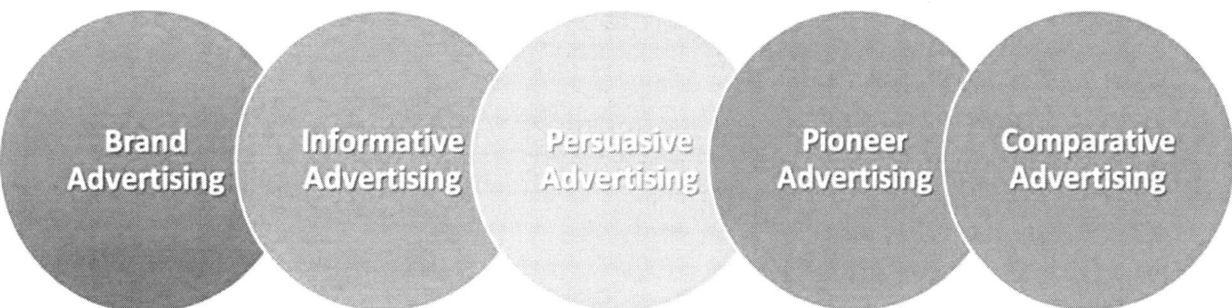

FIGURE 12-17 Types of Advertising

communication mix, and it must fit the overall IMC objectives, and not drive the marketing campaign. Too many marketers fall into the trap of thinking that advertising can solve all of their problems and thus put it into a lead role. For some IMC campaigns, advertising should be in a lead role, but for others, it needs to provide a supporting role.

Brand advertising An advertisement designed to promote a particular brand with little or no information in the advertisement.

Informative advertising An advertisement designed to provide the audience with some type of information.

Advertising can perform a number of functions, shown in Figure 12-17. In examining the different types of advertising, you must keep in mind that a good advertisement may have components from more than one category. These categories exist only for the purpose of discussion and to assist in understanding how advertisements are created.

Brand advertising is designed to promote a particular brand and typically provides little or no information in the advertisement. Figure 12-18 is an advertisement for Putman State Bank. The ad provides little information about the bank other than identifying the different loans available. The primary goals of brand advertising are to develop a strong brand name and to build brand awareness, with the purpose of building brand equity.

Informative advertising is designed to provide the audience with some type of information. It may be a retail store informing the public of its address, phone number, or operating hours. It may a brand introducing a new product or version, such as Apple when each new version is introduced. It may be a baseball team informing fans of an upcoming home series and what team they are playing.

The most common form of product advertising is **persuasive advertising**, which is designed to persuade viewers' thinking in some way. Among the most persuasive of those ads are promotions

FIGURE 12-18 This Advertisement for Putman State Bank Illustrates Brand Advertising
Source: (top photo) fizkes/Shutterstock

FIGURE 12-19 Among the Most Persuasive Marketing Communications are Endorsements by Influencers: When this Beauty Influencer Promotes a Brand, her Followers will Take Note
Source: Amnaj Khetsamtip/Shutterstock

Persuasive advertising An advertisement designed to persuade viewers' thinking in some way.

Pioneer advertising An advertisement designed to build primary demand for a product.

Comparative advertising An advertisement that compares the featured brand with another brand, either named or implied.

by influencers—either in an ad, or on their blog (**Figure 12-19**). Influencers have changed product advertising, and their paid endorsements have become the norm in marketing to consumers.

The least-used type of product advertising is pioneer. With **pioneer advertising**, the goal is to build primary demand for a product. It is normally used only in the introductory stage of the product life cycle (PLC). Because the product is new, consumers have to be convinced to buy it. After the product moves into the growth stage of the PLC, advertisers switch to another type of advertising, unless they are the industry leader. Even in those cases, they must be careful because pioneer advertising builds demand for the product category, which means the ad will also help the competition. Pfizer used pioneer advertising to introduce Viagra. The first ads were designed to build demand for the product—the Viagra name was not even mentioned. Men with impotency problems were just encouraged to see their physician and told that there was a drug available that would help.

The last type of product advertising is **comparative advertising**, which compares the featured brand with another brand, either named or implied. Advertisers have to be careful with comparative ads to ensure that they do not violate the FTC rule regarding substantiation of claims. The ads must compare similar products, and any claims made in the advertisement must be substantiated. Because companies do not like to see their brand ridiculed in an ad or portrayed as inferior, most companies examine comparative ads very closely to ensure that they are not violating the law. Comparative ads can be successful, however, especially for new brands. When a new brand is compared to a well-known brand, the new brand will gain recognition and brand equity. Seeing the two brands together in the same ad encourages consumers to consider the two brands as equals.

12-7 Advertising Design

The creative design process begins with information obtained from a client about the objectives of the advertisement or the ad campaign, the target audience, and any message themes that should be included. The advertising objective would be related to the communications objectives previously discussed. For example, if the communication objective were to build brand equity, then the advertising objective might be to increase brand awareness by 25 percent over the four months of the advertising campaign. If the brand already has a high level of awareness, then the objective may be to increase brand preference by 10 percent over the life of the advertising campaign. Notice that with advertising objectives, the objective needs to be specific, measurable, and have a specific timeframe.

In addition to the advertising objective, advertisers must know who the target audience will be in terms of demographics, psychographics, and lifestyle. A brand awareness advertisement aimed at teenage females is going to be designed differently than one aimed at females older than 60. Psychographics will provide information about the target audience's activities, interests, and opinions. This information is as important as the demographics. If the creative knows about the target audience's lifestyle, such preference for outdoor activities that includes hiking, boating, and fishing, this information will help in designing an effective ad. The more advertisers know about how the audience thinks and behaves, the easier it is to design an effective ad.

In advertising campaigns, message themes are often carried over from one ad to another and even from one campaign to another. Capital One has the tagline "What's in Your Wallet?" in most of their ads, and Home Depot's ad emphasizes "How Doers Get More Done". The message theme is a method of ensuring that ads and campaigns are connected and that consumers hear a consistent message.

Once the advertiser is in possession of the background information from the client, she is ready to start working on the ad or the ad campaign. The next set of decisions involves the appeal and the message strategy. Although these decisions will be discussed independently, the creative normally makes the decision about each simultaneously, as they are interrelated.

Advertising appeal The design a creative will use to attract attention to and interest in an advertisement.

12-7a Advertising Appeals

The **advertising appeal** is the design advertisers will use to attract attention to and interest in an advertisement. The six primary types of appeal are shown in **Figure 12-20**. The appeal chosen will depend on the objective of the ad, the target audience, and how the creative wants to convey the message to the intended audience. Almost every product can be advertised using any of the six appeals, and an advertisement can use two or three appeals together. For instance, in creating advertisements

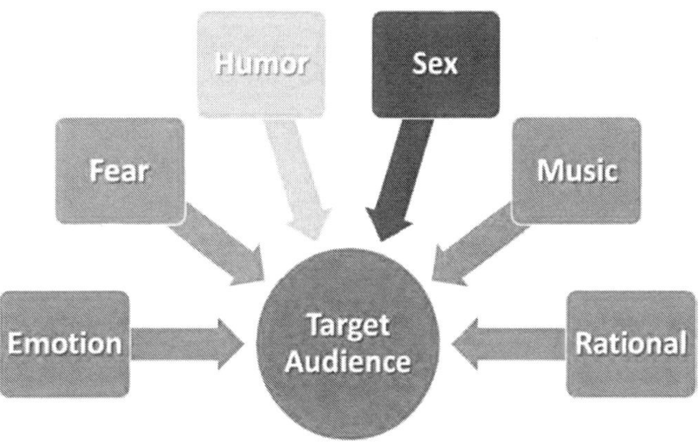

FIGURE 12-20 Types of Appeals

for the milk industry, Goodby, Silverstein & Partners used a deprivation approach with a humor appeal. Bozell, however, used a variety of appeals in its print ads. Some ads used an attractive, sexy model. Others used a rational approach in talking about the importance of milk in providing calcium. Some used an emotional approach, as in the "Got Milk?" ads.

Emotional appeals are an excellent method of building brand preference and brand loyalty. The goal is to build a bond between the brand and the consumer, just as you would between two people. Because of the capacity to use both sight and sound, TV and Internet videos are most suited for emotional appeals. Facial expressions, body language, and voice inflections can all be used to demonstrate feelings.

Fear appeals are used for many products such as insurance, fire alarms, deodorant, and mouthwash. With insurance, the fear focuses on what happens if an accident occurs and the person is not insured. With deodorant, the fear focuses on social rejection. Fear appeals work because they increase viewer's attention, interest, and persuasion. Skin care products advertise their ability to address one's fear of aging. More people remember an ad with a fear appeal better than one with a rational, upbeat argument. But, advertisers must be careful to calibrate the amount of fear they induce. If the fear level is too low, viewers will not be paying much attention to the ad; if too high, then they will tune the ad out or switch channels. The most effective fear ads are somewhere in between.[11] See **Figure 12-21** for an illustration of this concept.

Humor is used in almost half of all TV advertising, helping create very effective ads, making them more enjoyable, involving, and memorable. However, if the humor distracts from the brand and from conveying the communication to consumers, it can impede the ad's effectiveness. Perceptions

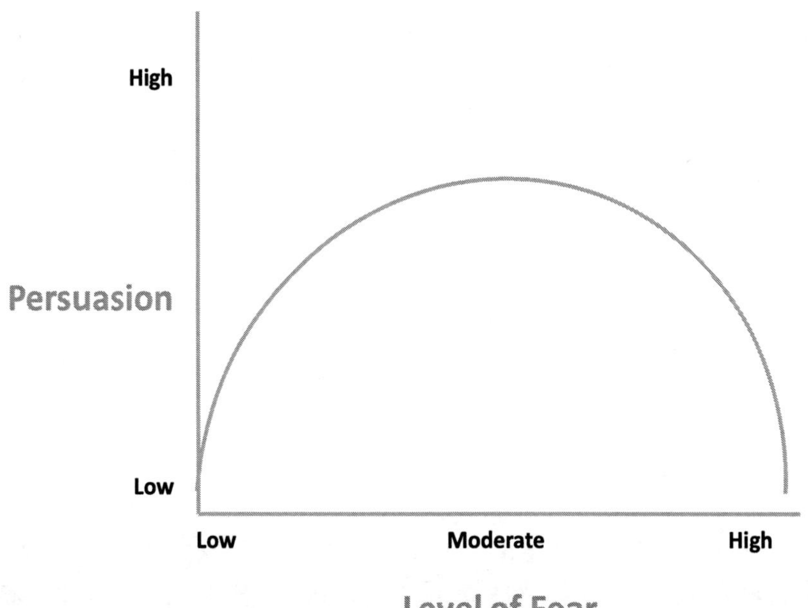

FIGURE 12-21 The Relationship between Fear Intensity and Persuasion

of humor are different around the world and also across different audiences, limiting the ability of the campaign.[12] Perceptions of what might be funny can also change with time. At the time of the COVID-19 pandemic, KFC was tone-deaf introducing an ad with people sensuously licking their fingers; it would have been funny at any other time.

Source: TonyV3112/Shutterstock

Humor does have **intrusion value**, the ability to break through clutter and gain a person's attention. People like to laugh, and they enjoy watching ads that are humorous. Humor also provides a way to escape from reality through a comedic view of life. But if the humor is too strong, then the viewer will remember the ad but not the brand advertised or of the message being conveyed. It is important to tie the humor to the brand and the message.

Advertisers use sex appeal for a variety of products. Research has shown that sex and nudity in an advertisement increases viewer attention, regardless of the audience gender or the gender of the models in the ad. The danger, however, is that brand recall for ads with sex appeal is usually lower: although sex appeal gains attention, if not done carefully, the sex appeal may interfere with remembering the brand advertised or the message conveyed.[13] Sex appeals work best for products in some way related to sex. For instance, Guess ads use sex appeal effectively because the clothes advertised are designed to enhance one's appearance. Using sex appeal to sell office furniture or life insurance will not be as effective because the products do not have a natural relationship with sex.

Intrusion value Advertising that has the ability to break through clutter and gain a person's attention.

Music is an important component of broadcast ads because it helps to gain people's attention and link them emotionally to the brand being advertised. Music, like humor, has a strong intrusion value and can capture the attention of an individual who is not paying any attention to advertising on the TV, Internet, or the radio. Music has become a common element and a crucial feature in advertisements, as advertisers use it to appeal to consumer emotions: making consumers smile, laugh, cry and feel nostalgic. The choice of which type of music is used is a conscious and creative decision that needs to be strategic.[14] With this type of appeal, advertisers like to use popular tunes that people have already developed an affinity for with the hope that the same feelings will be transferred to the product being advertised. To use a popular song in the ad, however, can cost anywhere from $25,000 to $500,000 plus per year. The typical range for a well-known song is $75,000 to $200,000 for a one-year national usage in the United States, on television and radio.[15]

Rational appeals are used in many advertisements, especially in print ads and for business-to-business ads. The premise of a rational appeal is that consumers will stop, look at the ad, and be interested in reading the copy or listening to what is being said. Unfortunately, with the large number of ads everyone is exposed to daily, it is much harder to get a person's attention using a rational appeal. However, if a person is interested in a product, then the rational appeal is the most effective means of conveying information and

FIGURE 12-22 Very Expensive Anti-Aging Creams Should Use Rational Appeals to Promote the High-Involvement Product and to Persuade Consumers That They Are Worth the High Cost
Source: Lucky Business/Shutterstock

promoting the brand's benefits. It is also an effective means of advertising high-involvement products about which consumers may want to obtain additional information. If a consumer will stop and pay attention to an ad using a rational appeal, the chances are good that the information will be understood and become a part of the person's memory. Very expensive anti-aging creams (**Figure 12-22**) use rational appeals to promote a high-involvement product to consumers and persuade them that they are worth the high cost.

12-7b Message Strategies

Cognitive message strategies The presentation of rational arguments or pieces of information to consumers.

The message strategy is the primary tactic an advertisement will use to deliver a message. The message strategy is what is being said, whereas the appeal is how it is being said. For example, a person may say "look at that" and by the inflection of the person's voice relay fear, shock, love, emotion, or just a matter-of-fact, rational statement with no emotion. Message strategies fall into three categories: cognitive, affective, and conative **(see Figure 12-23)**.

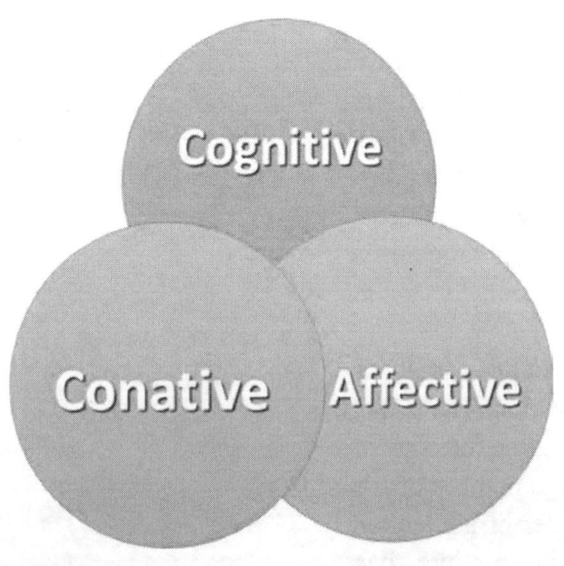

FIGURE 12-23 Types of Message Strategies

Cognitive message strategies are the presentation of rational arguments or pieces of information to consumers. The message focuses on key product attributes or important customer benefits. Shoes with DMX technology may be described as comfortable. A fishing boat may be featured as being designed for bass fishing with live wells for fish, and ergonomically-designed cockpits. With a cognitive message strategy, advertisers will assume the audience will read or listen to the ad, pay attention to the message, and cognitively process the information. The goal is to develop cognitive knowledge and beliefs about the brand by presenting information about the product's attributes and benefits the consumer can receive from the brand.

The cognitive message strategy works well with a rational appeal. However, often advertisers will use an emotional, fear, or sexual appeal to get the person's attention, and then use a cognitive message to explain the product's benefit. With this contrasting approach, the visual element or the headline is normally used to grab attention; then the body of the ad is used to explain the product.

Affective message strategies are designed to invoke feelings and emotions within the audience. They are based on the belief that if consumers react emotionally to an advertisement, their response will affect their attitude toward the ad, which will then be projected toward the brand. An advertisement that elicits warmth and love will usually create a liking for the ad, which will enhance positive feelings toward the brand. Affective emotions can work in the reverse as well. An advertisement that creates anger or disgust will create a negative feeling toward the ad and, in turn, a negative feeling toward the brand. This strategy is often used for political advertising, portraying an opponent in a negative light. Affective message strategies are used in conjunction with emotional, fear, humor, sex, and music appeals. Seldom will an affective message strategy be coupled with a rational appeal. Figure 12-24 illustrates how an affective message strategy builds a favorable attitude toward the brand.

Conative message strategies are designed to elicit some type of audience behavior, such as a purchase or inquiry. They are normally tied with a promotion that is offering a coupon, a price-off, or some other special deal. An advertisement for Cheerios with a 50-cent coupon and an opportunity to enter a special sweepstakes would be a conative message strategy because the goal of the ad is to have consumers purchase a box of Cheerios and to enter the contest. The advertisement in Figure 12-25 by the Willow Tree Medical Center uses a conative message strategy.

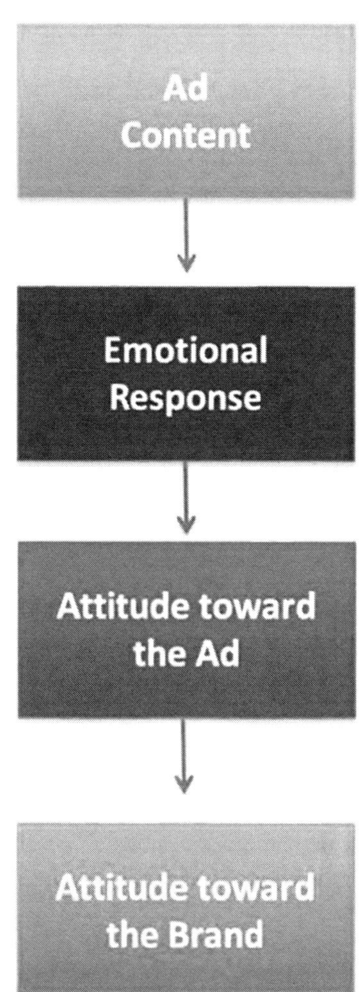

FIGURE 12-24 The Mediating Effect of Emotions on Communication Cues and Attitude toward the Brand

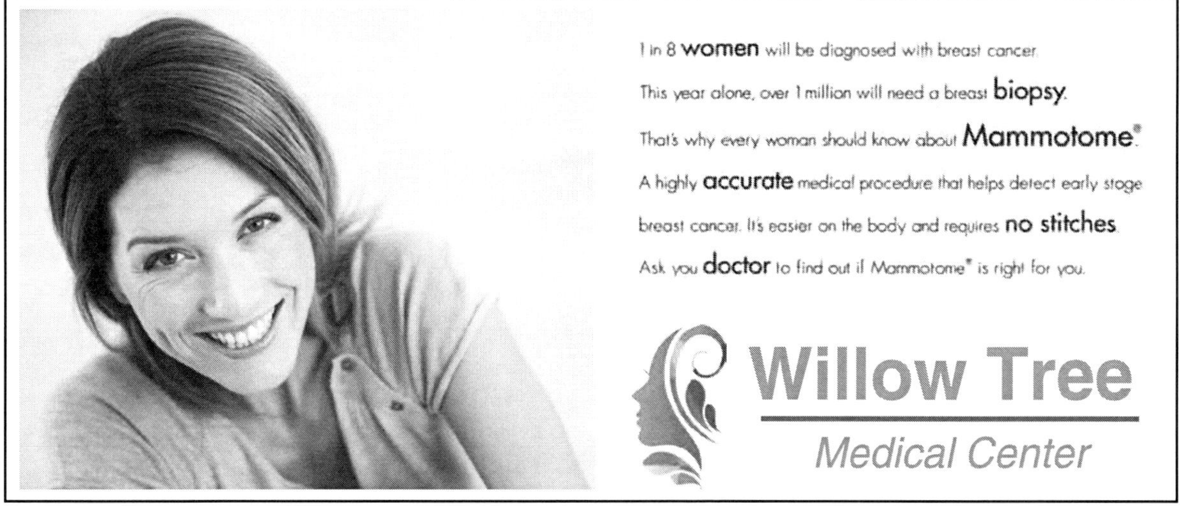

FIGURE 12-25 This Advertisement by Willow Tree Medical Center Uses a Conative Message Strategy

12-8 Media Selection

Affective message strategies Messages designed to invoke feelings and emotions within the audience.

Conative message strategies Messages designed to elicit some type of audience behavior, such as a purchase or inquiry.

Media selection is a critical component of advertising. If the correct medium is not selected, the target market will not hear the message. Understanding the target audience in terms of media behavior is important. Just as research is conducted to understand consumer behavior in terms of purchasing products, research must be conducted to understand media behavior. How much advertising should be allocated to each medium, such as radio, TV, newspapers, the Internet, and so forth? More important, if the members of a particular target market watch TV, which shows do they tend to watch?

Figure 12-26 presents the breakdown by media of the $263.11 billion spent on advertising media buys in the United States. Notice that the largest category is for digital, 58.7%. Approximately 70% of the digital advertising is for mobile ads. Until 2017, television was the largest category. It is now second, accounting for 27.4% of ad spending. Print media, newspapers and magazines, make up smaller shares.[16]

12-8a Broadcast Media

Broadcast media consist of television and radio. TV provides excellent opportunities for creating effective advertisements because both visual images and sounds can be incorporated simultaneously. TV also has the advantage of having high **reach**, defined as the number of people, households, or businesses in a target audience exposed to a media message at least once during a given time period.

Reach Number of people, households, or businesses in a target audience exposed to a media message at least once during a specific time period.

Just one TV advertisement can reach millions of consumers. For example, an advertisement on American Idol reached 18.4 million households, and an advertisement on CSI reached 11.1 million households. Each week, Nielsen Media Research publishes the Nielsen ratings for TV shows.

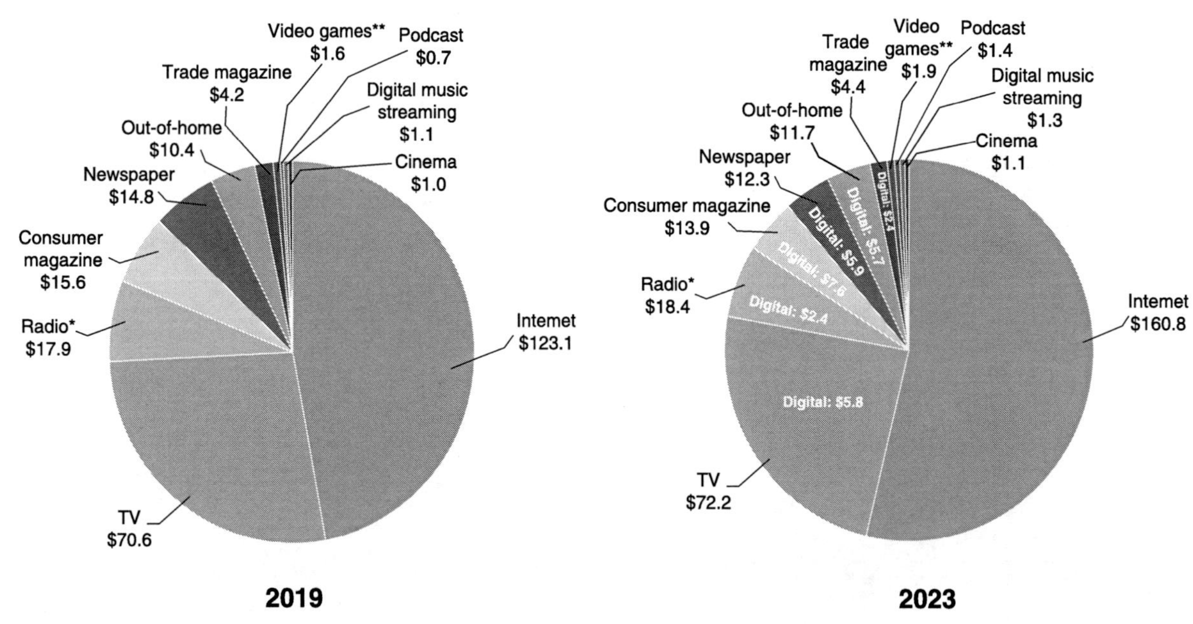

FIGURE 12-26 U.S. Ad Spending by Media
Source: https://www.emarketer.com/topics/topic/ad-spending

Nielsen ratings are an important factor in how much it costs to advertise on a TV show. The higher the Nielsen rating, the more it will cost. The average cost of a 30-second ad on network TV during prime time is approximately $130,000. But, the cost can vary widely depending on the number of viewers each show garners, based on Nielsen rating. Figure 12-27 presents the cost of a 30-second ad on various television shows across the major networks. Notice the most expensive television show was Sunday Night Football, at $685,277.[17]

Source: Monkey Business Images/Shutterstock

To be able to compare across media and even across TV shows, advertisers use **cost per thousand (CPM)**, which is the cost of reaching 1,000 members of a media vehicle's audience. Thus, if, for Sunday Night Football, the Nielsen rating for a particular week was 11.4, indicating 11.4 million households watched the show, then the cost per thousand (CPM) would be $60.11, that is, $685,277 / 11,400.

Cost per thousand (CPM) The cost of reaching 1,000 members of a media vehicle's audience.

The high reach of television combined with the relative low cost per thousand helps to explain why the Super Bowl has become the showcase of new advertising each year and brands are willing to pay over $5.6 million for just 30 seconds of exposure. Viewership is now over 100 million, which means the CPM is around $40.00. A large percentage of Super Bowl viewers tune in to see the new ads. While they may watch the football game, their primary interest is the new ads. Social media explodes during and after each game with comments about the various ads

TV Channel	Television Show	Cost for a thirty-second ad
NBC	Sunday Night Football	$685,277
FOX	Thursday Night Football	$540,090
NBC	This Is Us	$359,413
FOX	The Masked Singer	$201,583
NBC	The Voice (Monday)	$192,983
ABC	Grey's Anatomy	$186,026
NBC	The Voice (Tuesday)	$179,951
FOX	9-1-1	$172,215
NBC	New Amsterdam	$172,085
FOX	Empire	$171,187

FIGURE 12-27 Cost of 30-Second Television Ads for Various Shows
Source: https://www.statista.com/statistics/275158/cost-of-a-30-second-tv-spot-during-select-tv-shows-in-the-us; Kantar Media; Advertising Age, October 2019

Source: Alessandro DYD/Shutterstock

and, by the next morning, the best and worst ads of the Super Bowl are announced. For advertisers, in addition to people watching the advertisement during the game, additional exposure is gained through the social chatter and the ratings of the Super Bowl ads by various organizations and websites. To ensure strong brand exposure, brands are spending in excess of $1 million to produce the ads and will spend nearly a year in planning the strategy around the ad. Thus, as soon as one Super Bowl ends, brands and their advertising agencies begin work on the next one.

However, television has some major disadvantages. Clutter remains the primary problem, especially on network programs. Most TV networks now have 14 to 16 minutes of advertising per hour. Within each commercial break, between 8 and 15 commercials are packed together. Many viewers simply switch channels during long commercial breaks or use the time to get something to eat or go to the bathroom. DVRs are used to record shows and allow viewers to skip the commercials.

Although radio may not have the glamour appeal of TV, it does offer the advantage of intimacy. Listeners can develop an affinity with the DJs and other radio personalities. This closeness grows over time, especially if the listener has a conversation with the DJ during a contest or when requesting a song. The bond that develops means the DJ will have a higher level of credibility, and goods or services that are endorsed by the DJ will be more readily accepted. Moreover, certain market segments, such as Hispanics, are most effectively reached through radio.

Radio is also mobile. People can take radios with them wherever they go. They can listen while at the beach, at home, at work, or on the road in between. Radio stations tend to have well-delineated target markets based on their formats, such as talk radio, country music, rock, pop, oldies, and so forth. This means that a company that wants to advertise on country music stations can find stations all across the country.

Radio has some disadvantages. The short exposure time of most radio advertisements makes it difficult to comprehend what has been said. This is especially true for radio, because people are often involved in other activities, such as working on a computer or driving a vehicle. In many cases, the radio is simply background noise used to drown out other distractions. For national advertisers, producing a national radio advertisement is challenging because there are only a few large radio conglomerates and national networks available. To place a national advertisement requires contacting a large number of stations and companies that may own a handful of the available radio stations. For a summary of the advantages and disadvantages of TV and radio advertising, see **Figure 12-28**.

Advantages	Disadvantages
Television	
1. High reach	1. High level of clutter
2. High frequency potential	2. Low recall
3. Low cost per contact	3. Short ad duration
4. High intrusion value	4. High cost per ad
5. Creative design opportunities	
6. Segmentation through cable channels	
Radio	
1. High recall potential	1. Short ad duration
2. Segmented target markets	2. Low attention
3. Flexibility and short lead time in ad production	3. No national audience
4. Intimacy with DJs	4. Difficulty in buying national time
5. Mobility of radios	5. Target duplication in large metropolitan areas
6. Excellent for local businesses	
7. Low cost per contact	

FIGURE 12-28 Advantages and Disadvantages of Broadcast Advertising

12-8b Print Media

The primary print media are newspapers and magazines. As shown in Figure 12-26, newspapers and magazines account for 4.9 percent of total expenditures,[18] with each generating half of that ad revenue. While newspaper and magazine readership continues to decline, both remain important venues for advertisers.

Retailers rely heavily on newspapers because they offer geographic selectivity (i.e., access to the local target market area). Sales, retail hours, and store locations are easy to promote in a newspaper ad. Newspapers have relatively short lead times, which allow retailers the flexibility to change ads frequently and keep ads current. They can quickly modify an ad to reflect recent events or to combat a competitor's actions.

Newspapers tend to have a high level of credibility because people rely on newspapers for factual information in stories. This carries over to a greater level of credibility for newspaper advertisements. Because readers take time to read a newspaper, they tend to pay as much attention to advertisements as to the news stories. This increased audience interest allows advertisers to provide more copy detail in their ads.

Source: Syda Productions/Shutterstock

An advantage of magazines is the ability to precisely target audience segments. Specialized magazines aimed at specific target markets are more common than general readership magazines. Advertising in these specialized magazines allows advertisers to reach a greater percentage

Advantages	Disadvantages
Newspapers	
1. Excellent for local businesses	1. Poor buying procedures
2. High flexibility	2. Short life span
3. High credibility	3. Poor quality reproduction
4. Strong audience interest	4. Limited ad design creativity possible
Magazines	
1. High target audience segmentation	1. Declining readership
2. High reader interest	2. High level of clutter
3. High color quality	3. Long lead time to design ad
4. Long life	4. Little flexibility
5. Multiple frequency	5. High cost

FIGURE 12-29 Advantages and Disadvantages of Print Advertising

of their audience. Individuals reading *Brides* magazine will pay more attention to ads about weddings than someone reading *People*, so advertising wedding products in *Brides* magazine is likely to be more effective.

Most magazines offer high-quality color reproduction capabilities that allow creatives more freedom in designing advertisements. Color, headlines, and unusual images can be used to attract attention. Magazines such as *Glamour, Elle*, and *Cosmopolitan* will use scratch and sniff ads to entice women to smell a particular brand of perfume or cologne.

Both magazines and newspapers are facing tough times with declining readerships, with their readers defecting to Internet options. Rather than read a hard copy, consumers are turning to the publications websites or social media. This is especially true for younger consumers. For a summary of advantages and disadvantages of print media, see **Figure 12-29**.

Summary

1. **Discuss the concept of integrated marketing communications.**
IMC is the coordination and integration of all marketing communication tools, avenues, and sources within a company into a seamless program designed to maximize the communication impact on consumers, businesses, and other constituencies of an organization. IMC is a holistic approach that involves everyone in the company articulating the same message. There must be open communication vertically within the company, horizontally across functional areas and departments, and outward to customers and stakeholders who have an interest in the company. IMC involves communicating to four primary groups: customers, channel members, employees, and stakeholders.

2. **Identify the various marketing communication elements.**
The marketing communication elements include the traditional promotional mix of advertising, sales or consumer promotions, trade promotions, personal selling, and PR. But with the integrated approach, other

components of communication have also become important, such as Internet, database, and direct marketing. Possible communication outlets include traditional venues such as radio, television, newspapers, and magazines, but also the Internet, billboards, transit signs, store signage, and social media.

3. **Identify the elements of communication and the importance of AIDA.**
The six steps in communication are the source, encoding, message, medium, decoding, and audience. For communication to occur, the source, which for IMC is normally a business or an ad agency, encodes what it wants to communicate into a message, which is transmitted to an audience via some channel such as a television or point-of-purchase display. The audience, or potential customer, sees the message and decodes the message. If the decoded message matches the encoded message, accurate communication has occurred. Feedback from the audience to the sender alerts the sender to the success of the message and what, if anything, needs to be modified for future messages. Noise is anything that interferes with the delivery of the message from the source to the audience. AIDA is an acronym for attention, interest, desire, and action. It is the process of developing customers, taking them through the stages of getting their attention, building interest in the product, building desire for the product over competitors, and encouraging them to act, ultimately, to purchase.

4. **Discuss the various factors that affect the relative mix of communication elements in an integrated marketing communications plan.**
The factors that affect the relative mix of an IMC campaign include business versus consumer market, communication objective, push/pull strategy, and product life cycle. Business markets tend to rely more on personal selling, whereas consumer markets rely more on advertising. The communication objectives include increasing demand, differentiating a product, providing information, building brand equity, reducing purchase risk, and stimulating trial. The IMC mix will vary depending on which objective is primary. For push strategies, firms will rely more on trade promotions and personal selling, whereas for pull strategies, advertising and consumer promotions are used. The relative IMC mix will vary with each stage of the PLC, with the maturity stage requiring the highest level of all components of the IMC mix.

5. **Identify the various types of advertising.**
The primary types of advertising are brand, informative, persuasive, pioneer, and comparative advertising. Brand advertising focuses on the brand, with little information. Informative advertising provides the audience with information. Persuasive advertising is designed to convince individuals of the superiority of a particular brand. New products use pioneer advertising to encourage consumers to purchase the new product. Comparative advertising can compare a brand with another, either named or unnamed.

6. **Describe the appeals that can be used in designing an advertisement.**
The advertising appeal is the design a creative will use to attract attention to and interest in an advertisement. The six primary types of appeal are emotional, fear, humor, sex, music, and rational. The appeal chosen will depend on the objective of the ad, the message theme to be used, the target audience, and how the creative wants to convey the message to the intended audience. Almost every product can be advertised using any of the six appeals, and an advertisement will often use two or three appeals.

7. **Differentiate between the three types of message strategies.**
The message strategy is the primary tactic an advertisement will use to deliver a message. The three types of message strategies are cognitive, affective, and conative. Cognitive message strategies are the presentation of

rational arguments or pieces of information to consumers that are cognitively processed. The message focuses on key product attributes or important customer benefits with the goal of developing specific beliefs or knowledge about the brand. Affective message strategies are designed to invoke feelings and emotions within the audience. They are based on the idea that if consumers react emotionally to an advertisement, their response will affect their attitude toward the ad, which will then be projected toward the brand. Conative message strategies are designed to elicit some type of audience behavior, such as a purchase or inquiry.

8. **Discuss the advantages and disadvantages of the primary media (with the exception of digital, addressed in the next chapter).** TV has the advantages of offering high reach, high frequency potential, low cost per contact, high intrusion value, creative design opportunities, and segmentation through cable channels. The disadvantages of TV are a high level of clutter, low recall, short ad duration, and high cost per ad. For radio, the advantages are high recall potential, segmented target markets, flexibility and short lead time in ad production, intimacy with DJs, mobility of radios, and low cost per contact. The disadvantages are a short ad duration, low attention, no national audience, difficulty in buying national time, and target duplication in large metropolitan areas. In the print media, newspapers offer the advantages of high flexibility, high credibility, and strong audience interest. Disadvantages are poor buying procedures, a short lifespan, poor quality reproduction, and limited ad design creativity. For magazines, the major advantages include high target audience segmentation, high reader interest, high color quality, long life, and multiple frequency. Disadvantages are a declining readership, high level of clutter, long lead time, little flexibility, and high cost.

Key Terms

Advertising (348)
Advertising appeal (369)
Affective message strategies (374)
AIDA (356)
Audience (355)
Brand advertising (367)
Cognitive message strategies (372)
Comparative advertising (368)
Conative message strategies (374)
Cost per thousand (CPM) (375)
Database marketing (350)
Decoding (354)
Direct response marketing (350)
Earned media (347)
Encoding (354)
Feedback (355)
Informative advertising (367)
Integrated marketing communications (IMC) (346)
Internet (digital) marketing (350)
Intrusion value (371)
Medium (354)
Message (354)
Noise (356)
Owned media (347)
Paid media (347)
Personal selling (350)
Persuasive advertising (368)
Pioneer advertising (368)
Public relations (PR) (348)
Publicity (349)
Reach (374)
Sales promotions (349)
Source (353)
Trade promotions (349)

Discussion Questions

1. Pick a well-known restaurant, such as Pizza Hut, McDonald's, Outback Steakhouse, or Olive Garden. Discuss how the restaurant integrates all of its marketing messages. What

common theme is used? What types of IMC elements are used? Access the firm's website. Is the website consistent with the television, radio, and other media advertising?

2. Think about purchasing a new car. Identify all of the venues, such as television, radio, magazines, digital media, and so on, that you would use to gather information about the various models and list them. In a second list, include any sources of information an automobile dealer may use to communicate with you but that you would not pay any attention to. What are the most effective means of communicating with you? Where would the automobile dealer be wasting money?
3. List the primary media in a table (television, radio, newspapers, and magazines). Add digital (online) to your list—digital media will be addressed in detail in the next chapter. When you think of viewing or listening to the various media, what percentage of your time is spent with each? The total should add to 100 percent. Create a pie chart showing your media consumption. Write a paragraph discussing each of the media in terms of your personal media consumption.
4. Examine the AIDA model. Go to YouTube and locate advertisements that illustrate each of the steps in AIDA. Explain why you think the ad chosen is a good example of the particular AIDA concept, such as getting attention, building interest, building desire, or promoting action. Provide a link to the four YouTube ads you selected as well as a screenshot.
5. Think about the last major purchase you made. Go through the AIDA concept in terms of what the brand did to get your attention, build interest, build desire, and promote action.
6. Go to YouTube and locate three advertisements you like. Explain why you like the ad. For each ad, identify the type of advertising, such as brand, informative, persuasive, or comparative advertising. Justify your choice. For each ad, identify the appeal used and the message strategy used. Justify these classifications. Provide a URL and screenshot of each of the ads.
7. Review the five types of advertising. For each type, identify an advertisement that you believe is a good example. Explain why you think it is a good example.
8. Review the six types of advertising appeals. Go to YouTube. For each appeal, locate an advertisement that is a good example. Explain why you think it is a good example. Provide a link to the video in your explanation as well as a screenshot.
9. Review the three types of advertising message strategies. Go to YouTube. For each message strategy, locate an advertisement that is a good example. Explain why you think it is a good example. Provide a link to the video in your explanation and a screenshot.
10. On the average, how much time do you spend viewing or listening to broadcast media, TV, and radio? Discuss your viewing habits of broadcast media in terms of time spent with each, shows or programs you like, and impact of advertising on your purchase behavior.
11. On the average, how much time do you spend with print media, magazines and newspapers? Discuss your reading habits of print media in terms of time spent with each, magazines or newspapers you read, and impact of advertising on your purchase behavior.

Review Questions

True or False

1. The process of encoding begins with the interpretation of the meaning conveyed in the marketing message.
2. The abundance of different communication channels and prolific advertising facilitate the communication process and allow customers to select the right message.
3. Marketing managers allocate at least 75 percent of the marketing budget for advertising because advertising has the most direct impact on sales.

4. AIDA is a concept used by advertisers in designing ads and stands for attention, interest, decision, and advertising.
5. Persuasive advertising is the most common form of product advertising.
6. If pioneer advertising worked successfully at the product introduction stage of the PLC, the same ad will most likely be effective in the growth stage.
7. Comparative advertising is designed to build corporate reputation or develop goodwill for the corporation.
8. With most products in the maturity stage of the PLC, advertising is instrumental in the process of developing brand awareness, brand equity, and brand preference.
9. The advertisement appeal defines the manner in which the advertisement will be presented.

Multiple Choice

10. What is the best description of integrated marketing communications?
    a. seamless programs designed to maximize the communication effect
    b. coordination and integration of all marketing communications tools
    c. coordination and integration of all marketing resources
    d. all of the above
11. Promotion of a product directly from the manufacturer or producer to the consumer is
    a. direct response marketing.
    b. database marketing.
    c. Internet or digital marketing.
    d. integrated marketing communications.
12. After seeing an advertisement on TV, a consumer checks the Internet to find the closest retail store or searches for more information on the Web as to where the product can be purchased. According to the AIDA concept, these actions belong to which step?
    a. attention
    b. interest
    c. desire
    d. action
13. Which of the following categories are often used as objectives in the integrated marketing communications plan?
    a. increasing demand and product differentiation
    b. providing information and building brand equity
    c. reducing purchase risk and stimulating trials
    d. all of the above
14. The primary goals of brand advertising include the following, except
    a. build brand awareness.
    b. develop a brand name.
    c. provide detailed information about product features.
15. Comparative advertising is most successful in
    a. building primary demand for a product.
    b. introducing new brands.
    c. developing goodwill for the corporation.
    d. providing more information.
16. What should be a key consideration in creating an advertisement that will get attention and produce results?
    a. advertisement objectives
    b. demographic information
    c. psychographics information
    d. all of the above
17. Which message strategy presents a rational argument or pieces of information to consumers?
    a. cognitive message strategy
    b. affective message strategy
    c. conative message strategy
    d. all of the above
18. Why have magazines become a preferred advertising medium for many consumer products?
    a. ability to precisely target audience segments
    b. high-quality color reproduction capability
    c. long advertising life beyond the immediate issue
    d. all of the above

Answers: (1) False, (2) False, (3) False, (4) False,(5) True, (6) False, (7) False, (8) True, (9) True, (10) d, (11) a, (12) b, (13) d, (14) d, (15) b, (16) d, (17) a, (18) d

Lululemon Athletica, the popular Vancouver-based athleisure company, is growing by leaps and bounds. It recently reached just under $4 billion in revenues, and has enjoyed double-digit growth until 2019; in 2020, after the onset of the COVID-19 pandemic, it continued to post a profit even though it had to close its stores around the world.

Lululemon has always banked on its ability to create a sense of belonging to a community. It is what sets it apart from Nike, whose business is based on huge marketing campaigns with celebrity endorsers. Lululemon, on the other hand, relies on its 1,500 member ambassador program. Its ambassadors are recruited from local store communities and act as influencers in the local communities. Among the higher profile ambassadors, they have recruited the former Superbowl MVP Nick Foles.

The company overcame relatively quickly the negative publicity that engulfed the brand after several misstatements by its founder, Chip Wilson, and stealthy price increases that incensed customers. Instead, today, the company continues to earn points with consumers for promoting healthy living and mindfulness, and for, among others, taking a stance and joining other advertisers pulling their ads from Facebook and Instagram in response to Facebook's handling of misinformation and hate speech.

Its communication initiatives are varied. It launched its first global campaigns, themed "This is Yoga," featuring images shot all around the world, including in Beijing, London, Mexico City, New York City, and Vancouver. The campaign showcased activities that don't necessarily have anything to do with yoga and was intended to broaden the idea of yoga, inviting consumers to practice self-discipline, nonviolence, and deep breathing. The campaign, created by Virtue Worldwide, features Olympic gold medalist Kerri Walsh Jennings, professional surfer Maddie Peterson, and London-based Grime rapper P Money.

Another advertising campaign was aimed at men: in a series of short films, the company celebrated masculinity and strength. The theme of the campaign was "Strength to Be," and it aimed to celebrate the community of men representing their own definitions of masculinity and strength in positive ways. It portrayed men challenging stereotypes by juxtaposing traditional depictions of masculinity alongside more modern interpretations.

As part of its integrated marketing communications campaign, lululemon's grass-roots marketing has promoted its Instagram #TheSweatLife platform, creating a record user-generated content, with more than 1 million posts, with people presenting attainable images of what living lululemon's "sweat life" can help them achieve.

Sources: Pamela Danziger, "Lululemon Is On Fire Thanks To The Power Of Community Retail," December 12, 2019, https://www.forbes.com/sites/pamdanziger/2019/12/12/lululemon-is-on-fire-thanks-to-the-power-of-community-retail/#2ece11f65df8; Jennifer Braun, "Lululemon launches first global ad campaign," Fashion Network, May 16, 2017, https://us.fashionnetwork.com/news/lululemon-launches-first-global-ad-campaign,828099.html; The Drum, "lululemon: Strength To Be by Virtue Worldwide at Vice," https://www.thedrum.com/creative-works/project/virtue-worldwide-vice-lululemon-strength-be, accessed on May 30, 2020.

Case Questions

1. How does lululemon advertising compare to Nike's? Explain.

2. If you were to design a new marketing campaign for lululemon, what type of advertising appeal would you use? Why?
3. What type of message strategy would you use for lululemon? Why?
4. Discuss the media strategy that you think would be appropriate for the athleisure market. Where would you advertise? Justify your choice.
5. Based on the information in this case, design a print advertisement for lululemon.

Endnotes

1. Association of National Advertisers (ANA), Integrated Marketing Definitions, https://thedma.org/integrated-marketing-community/integrated-marketing-definitions, accessed on April 27, 2020.
2. Marketing Dive, "Building, executing and measuring an integrated marketing campaign," April 28, 2020, accessed at https://www.marketingdive.com/spons/building-executing-and-measuring-an-integrated-marketing-campaign/576440.
3. Avi Dan, "Coke Would Like to Teach an Angry World To Chill," *Forbes*, February 28, 2020, https://www.forbes.com/sites/avidan/2020/02/28/coke-would-like-to-teach-an-angry-world-to-chill/#1f47108d3737.
4. 2019 Inmar Shopper Behavior Study, www.inmar.com, accessed February 28, 2020.
5. U.S. Census Bureau: https://www.census.gov/content/dam/ Census/library/publications/2017/acs/acs-37.pdf, accessed on April 27, 2020.
6. Shawn Lim, "Inside Colgate-Palmolive's TikTok-led digital transformation efforts," The Drum, December 12, 2019, https://www.thedrum.com/news/2019/12/12/inside-colgate-palmolives-tiktok-led-digital-transformation-efforts.
7. 2020 Marketing Spending Industry Study, Cadent Consulting Group, https://cadentcg.com/publication/2020-marketing-spending-industry-study.
8. Nitasha Tiku, "Facebook has a prescription: More pharmaceutical ads," *The Washington Post*, March 3, 2020, https://www.washingtonpost.com/technology/2020/03/03/facebook-pharma-ads.
9. Erik Oster, "U.S. Advertising and Marketing Spend to Grow to Nearly $390 Billion in 2020," *AD Week*, January 17, 2020, https://www.adweek.com/brand-marketing/us-advertising-marketing-spend-grow-nearly-390-billion-2020.
10. Business Insider, "10 biggest advertisers that spent more than $1 billion so you'd buy their products," October 4, 2019, https://www.businessinsider.com/10-biggest-advertising-spenders-in-the-us-2015-7.
11. Michael S. Latour and Robin L. Snipes, "Don't Be Afraid to Use Fear Appeals: An Experimental Study," *Journal of Advertising* 36, no. 2 (March/April 1996): 59–68.
12. Kantar Millward Brown, "Does humor make ads more effective?" accessed at http://www.millwardbrown.com/promo/download/does-humor-make-ads-more-effective on May 28, 2020.
13. Jesse Marczyk, "Understanding sex in advertising: getting people to look or buy?" *Psychology Today*, June 26, 2017, https://www.psychologytoday.com/us/blog/pop-psych/201706/understanding-sex-in-advertising.
14. Emanuel Mogaji, "Typology of music in advertising," Proceedings of the 18th International Conference on Research in Advertising Conference (2019 ICORIA) Proceedings. Published by The European Advertising Academy, July 29, 2019, https://papers.ssrn.com/sol3/papers.cfm?abstract_id=3413436.
15. Donald Passman, *All you need to know about the music business,* 10th edition, October 29, 2019, New York, NY: *Simon & Schuster.*
16. eMarketer, US Total Media Ad Spending Share, by Media, https://forecasts-na1.emarketer.com/584b26021403070290f93a2f/5851918b0626310a2c186b4b, accessed on June 15, 2020.
17. Kantar Media, "Cost of a 30 second TV spot during select TV shows in the US, *Advertising Age,* October, https://www.statista.com/statistics/275158/cost-of-a-30-second-tv-spot-during-select-tv-shows-in-the-us; Kantar Media; Advertising Age, October 2019.
18. eMarketer, US Total Media Ad Spending Share, by Media, https://forecasts-na1.emarketer.com/584b26021403070290f93a2f/5851918b0626310a2c186b4b, accessed on June 15, 2020.

Digital and Social Media Marketing

CHAPTER 13

Source: mrmohock/Shutterstock

Chapter Outline

Learning Objectives

Ivelin Radkov/Shutterstock

After studying this chapter, you should be able to:

- Discuss current Internet usage.
- Identify the benefits of digital marketing.
- Discuss the importance of e-commerce.
- Identify and explain the various digital marketing strategies.
- Examine strategies that can be used in social media marketing.

Source: Flamingo Images/Shutterstock

13-1 Chapter Overview

Although marketing has been around for several decades, digital marketing is a more recent phenomenon. The Internet is essential for both consumers and businesses. Having a web presence has become critical, and understanding how to maximize the marketing thrust of a website, Internet marketing and social media is even more important.

In Section 13-2, the makeup of Internet users is presented. Section 13-3 discusses the benefits of digital marketing and functions that are possible with digital marketing. Firms can do more than sell merchandise over the Internet. They can use it for a host of functions that can benefit consumers, other businesses, and even the firm's own employees. Section 13-4 is a presentation of e-commerce and how it impacts buyer behaviors today. Section 13-5 discusses various digital marketing strategies that firms can use. Because of the rapid rise of smartphones, mobile marketing has become increasingly important in the development of digital strategies. In preparing digital content and advertising, firms have to think about the various platforms consumers utilize. The last section of the chapter (Section 13-6) addresses ways firms can utilize social media to engage with consumers.

13-2 Internet Users

Not since the invention of the automobile or computer has any single invention so radically transformed life and changed the way of doing business as has the development of the Internet. Approximately 4.65 billion people around the globe are using the Internet, with over 349 million of those in North America. **Figure 13-1** provides penetration statistics for the major regions of the world. North America has the highest penetration rate, at 94.6 percent, followed by Europe at 87.2 percent. Globally, almost 60% of the world's population use the Internet in some manner. Worldwide, more than 50% of all internet users access it through their mobile decides, and it is predicted that, by 2025, three quarters of world users will do so. Users use phones to access almost 70% of all media, and mobile ad spend has surpassed 250 billion.[1]

13-3 Digital Marketing

The Internet has transformed the way businesses now operate. At the beginning, many businesses jumped onto the Internet and built websites because it was the thing to do. They were not sure how their site would be used or who would use their site. But as Internet usage has continued to increase dramatically, companies have come to realize that the Internet can provide substantial benefits to both customers and the selling firm. Using this information, companies began developing the field of digital marketing.

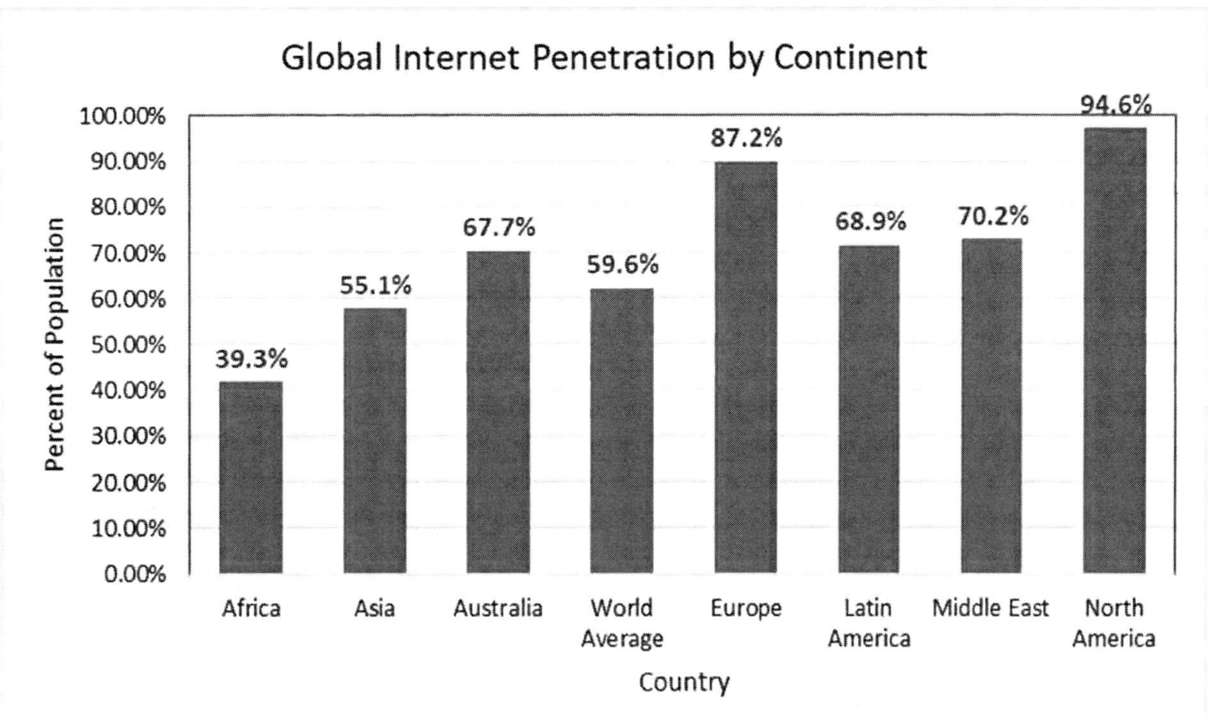

FIGURE 13-1 Global Internet Penetration by Continent
Source: https://www.internetworldstats.com/stats.htm, accessed May 21, 2020

FIGURE 13-2 Company Benefits of Using the Internet for Marketing

The Internet provides numerous benefits for companies, which are highlighted in **Figure 13-2**. The most obvious use of the Internet is for sales. Websites help with the purchase decision, and process the payment: when you buy baseball tickets, you go to the website, see what seating is available and corresponding prices, and then purchase the tickets that best fit with one's interest and budget. If you are not familiar with the baseball park, you can check it out online.

According to the U.S. Department of Commerce, in 2019, U.S. online retail sales of physical goods amounted to 365.2 billion US dollars and are projected to reach close to 600 billion US dollars in 2024. Apparel and accessories retail e-commerce in the U.S. is projected to generate 194.4 billion U.S. dollars in revenue by 2024.[2]

The Internet allows for a dynamic, interactive communication environment, especially through the various social media. Advertising, consumer promotions, trade promotions, and other integrated marketing communications (IMC) efforts are all static and directed toward consumers or other businesses. Only salespeople and the Internet can be interactive.

Attractive graphics and menus guide individuals through a website to the information they want. Yet it can be done at the visitor's own pace. Visitors can skim some sections and read others. They can even bookmark the site or places in the site for future reference **(see Figure 13-3)**. To encourage engagement with the brand, social media and other interactive marketing techniques can be used. The Internet provides a multimedia environment. Sound, pictures, and videos can provide information or entertain. A live cam shot can be used for sites such as a college or resort to show a visitor what the actual campus or facility looks like. At a resort website, a multimedia presentation could show different areas of the resort: the nightclub, restaurants, pool, beach, and any other amenities. A benefit of the Internet is that consumers (or businesses) can examine what they want to see, at the pace they want to see it, and as often as they want. After the COVID-19

FIGURE 13-3 The Internet Allows Users to Read News Headlines, Search for Stories, and Watch Videos
Source: Anton Garin/Shutterstock

pandemic onset, culture moved online to offer customers experiences at their fingertips without having to be physically there. One could live-stream opera singer Andrea Bocelli at the Duomo Cathedral in Milan in an audience-free concert, follow a curator-led tour of a Warhol exhibition at the Tate, or view online exhibits of more than 42,000 works at the National Gallery of Art in Washington, D.C.[3]

Source: vectorfusionart/Shutterstock

Similarly, with medical offices closed and consumers unwilling to go to doctors' offices, worried that they might catch the virus, telemedicine took off, used not just for urgent care, but also for mental health, dermatology, and other specialties. Clearly, there is a great advantage that the Internet provides: flexibility. Content can be changed quickly, often within minutes or hours. New messages can be put up instantaneously. During and after a major snowstorm or hurricane, companies can provide assistance to those impacted. The flexibility means that the Internet can virtually operate in real time. Ads can be placed on the Internet as soon as they are completed, not months later, as would be the case with a magazine. A new product can be highlighted as soon as it becomes available and not have to wait until it passes through the channel and is stocked on store shelves.

The Internet provides an excellent medium to communicate with existing and prospective customers and to provide information to various constituencies. Customers can be provided passwords that will allow them to access website components not available to others. Blogs and newsletters can be used to encourage brand involvement. Brands can engage consumers in dialogue and build stronger loyalty through social media. Apple and Harley-Davidson have built strong brand communities through social media and the Internet.

A major advantage of the Internet deals with cost efficiencies. Most manufacturers spend approximately 20 to 30 percent of the final product cost on sales, marketing, and distribution. What makes the potential of the Internet so exciting is that these companies can use their website to sell directly to customers, potentially reducing these costs by 10 percent or more. The Internet offers cost advantages to bricks-and-mortar retailers as well: when products are shipped directly to customers instead of the store, the retailer saves the costly steps of packing and shipping products to the store, unpacking, and placing the product on the shelves.

An additional benefit of the Internet is also controversial: because of Internet technology, firms can gather information about individuals or businesses that visit the site with or without their knowledge. If used ethically, this information can help a firm better target its products to meet the needs of each person who accesses the website.

Source: Rawpixel.com/Shutterstock

This information can be added to the firm's database to build a more robust profile of its customers. For example, an individual who accesses the baseball equipment component of a sporting goods e-commerce site can be provided with a coupon or premium to encourage a purchase. If the individual accesses the same site on several occasions, the company can safely assume that the customer has a high level of interest in baseball and its products.

13-4 E-Commerce

E-commerce The selling of goods and services over the Internet.

A major use of the Internet is **e-commerce**, the selling of goods and services over the Internet. Retailing can be performed in three ways, illustrated in **Figure 13-4**. The first method is with bricks-and-mortar stores that do not have any presence on the Internet, in terms of e-commerce. These tend to be small stores with regional markets and products that do not lend themselves well to the Internet. In developed countries, bricks-and-mortar firms are a minority and are becoming an even smaller percentage of the total firms every year. However, in lower-income countries, this form of commerce is still the standard mode of operation.

Clicks-only firms Organizations that sell only over the Internet.

In the 1990s, there was a burst of online companies, or **clicks-only firms**, selling only on the Internet. Although they may have an office, they do not have a store that a customer can go to. Shipments are made directly to customer from the manufacturer or distributor. These firms may not even own an inventory but ship directly from producers to customers.

Bricks-and-clicks Firms that operate both a bricks-and-mortar facility and an Internet e-commerce site.

Realizing the impact of the Internet and understanding that it is here to stay, bricks-and-mortar retailers began adopting e-commerce websites. These firms, operating both a bricks-and-mortar store and an Internet e-commerce site, are known as **bricks-and-clicks**. These firms find that e-commerce can provide customers with a different channel of making purchases and that it can be a valuable tool for providing information about the stores' products. Retailers realize that the Internet is essential in building brand loyalty and increased sales.

Bricks-and-Mortar firms: These organizations operate only with traditional physical facilities and do not yet have a web presence. Given the popularity of the Internet, such companies now tend to be few.

Bricks-and-Clicks firms: These organizations recognize the benefits of combining traditional physical facilities with a web presence. Virtually every major firm fits into this category.

Clicks-Only firms: These organizations operate only on the web and do not have traditional physical facilities. This has been a popular format for startup firms over the last decade.

FIGURE 13-4 The Three Forms of Retailing
Sources: Rawpixel.com/Shutterstock (left); Goran Bogicevic/Shutterstock (middle); Primakov/Shutterstock (right)

Rank	Product Category	Online Sales (billions)
1	Computer & Consumer Electronics	$156.50
2	Apparel & Accessories	$135.49
3	Furniture & Home Furnishings	$78.31
4	Health & Personal Care	$72.1
5	Auto & Parts	$51.54
6	Toys & Hobby	$51.23
7	Books, Music, & Video	$42.3
8	Food & Beverage	$41.52

FIGURE 13-5 U.S. Online Retail Sales by Product Category
Source: https://content-na1.emarketer.com/us-ecommerce-2020

The growth of global Internet retail commerce is impressive. In the United States alone, online sales are expected to reach $859 billion in 2020. The top online sales category is computers, electronics, and appliances, at $156.5 billion, followed by apparel and accessories, at $135.49.[4] See **Figure 13-5** for a more in-depth breakdown of U.S. Internet retail sales by product categories.

An e-commerce site has three primary components: a catalog, a shopping cart, and a payment system. Bricks-and-clicks operations must have a fourth component: a location finder. The catalog can be just a few items displayed on the main screen, or it can be a complex presentation of thousands of products embedded within multiple links and pages. The type of catalog used is determined by how many products the firm sells and the objective of the website. Each site must have some type of shopping cart to assist consumers as they select products. The shopping cart can range from just clicking a circle for an item when only a few products are offered to a more complicated shopping cart that keeps records of multiple purchases and previous purchases. Each site must establish some way for customers to make payments for the items they purchase. For consumers, this is often a credit card system or one of the Internet services such as PayPal. For business-to-business operations, payments are normally made through a voucher system. In other situations, a bill is generated or a computerized billing system is used so that the invoice goes directly to the buyer. In more trusting relationships, the invoice is added to the customer's records without a physical bill ever being mailed.

For bricks-and-clicks operations, buyers need some way of finding the nearest location if the merchandise is not being shipped directly to them. A consumer may examine clothes on the Internet but want to go to the retail outlet, where he or she can try on the clothes and then make the purchase. Businesses that offer merchandise in brick-and-mortar locations normally have some type of store locator software that will tell the consumer or business the closest location by typing in the ZIP code.

Although online purchases are growing rapidly, some consumers are still debating whether or not to make online purchases for two reasons: security issues and purchase behavior habits. Many consumers are afraid to use credit cards because of the fear that their credit card number will be stolen. Others are concerned about fraud and dishonest e-commerce websites that will take their money and never ship the merchandise or ship poor-quality merchandise. In terms of purchasing habits, some consumers feel more comfortable purchasing products from retail outlets because that is the way they have always shopped. However, with the COVID-19 pandemic, consumers were forced to overcome their fears and purchase their necessities online. Retailers have been forthcoming, reducing their fears by offering guarantees, and by offering technology to virtually try on clothes or to match make-up color to skin tone. As with any new technology, changing habits will require time and the right kinds of incentives.

Before examining digital e-commerce marketing strategies, it is helpful to review why anyone would shop online in the first place. **Figure 13-6** provides a list of the most common reasons. At the top of the list for both consumers and businesses is convenience. Instead of making a trip to a bricks-and-mortar location, a consumer or a business can place the order while remaining at home or at his or her place of business. More important, the order can be placed at any time, day or night. Seeking information about various products can be quicker and easier on the Internet than using *Consumer Reports*, talking to salespeople, or calling the manufacturer or a retailer. For businesses, ordering merchandise, supplies, and materials over the Internet can save purchasing agents considerable time. In addition to ordering, businesses can check on the status of their orders, shipment information, and even billing data.

FIGURE 13-6 Reasons Consumers and Businesses Shop Online

In most cases, doing so online is considerably quicker than making a telephone call. In this fast-paced world, convenience is a highly attractive incentive for consumers and businesses to shop online.

13-5 Digital Marketing Strategies

Source: fizkes/Shutterstock

As society has shifted from desktop computers to laptops, tablets and mobile phones, marketers need to adapt to these multi-screen formats. Advances in technology create new digital marketing opportunities along with the need to develop campaigns that can be viewed from any type of screen. **Figure 13-7** identifies the primary digital marketing strategies that can be used.

Most Americans (96%) own a cellphone and 81% own a smartphone, up from just 35% in 2011.[5] Mobile phones link individuals to their social networks, allowing them to post comments, photos, and videos and read the thoughts of others. People can check in, tweet, and update their status anytime, anywhere, download deals, look up reviews, check prices, and share information. They can check store hours, get directions to the business, compare prices, and shop. These activities can take place anywhere, even at the retailer's store.

Mobile marketing Refers to the development and application of marketing strategies for smartphones.

The term **mobile marketing** refers to the development and application of marketing strategies for smartphones. Five to ten years ago, mobile marketing strategies were different from digital marketing strategies, with the latter referring to marketing applications geared to desktop and laptop computers. Now, companies realize these cannot be two separate strategies. Thus, the term **digital marketing strategies** refers to all marketing

Digital marketing strategies Refers to all marketing strategies regardless of the device a consumer (or business) uses: desktop, laptop, tablet, or mobile phone.

FIGURE 13-7 Digital Marketing Strategies
Source: Dragon Images/Shutterstock

Source: XanderSt/Shutterstock

strategies regardless of the device a consumer (or business) uses: desktop, laptop, tablet, or mobile phone.

13-5a Geo-Marketing

Mobile phones enable marketers to create advertising campaigns based on a person's geographic location. **Geo-targeting** involves reaching customers where they are located by contacting their mobile communication devices. For instance, by downloading an app, a fastfood restaurant can identify a person's location, show him how far he is from the nearest outlet, and then provide walking or driving directions to that unit. Many smartphone owners have check-in services at Foursquare, Gowalla, Facebook Places, and Twitter geolocation. Starbuck's, McDonald's, Chipotle, Burger King, and others provide restaurant check-ins. When someone checks in, software instantly sends a special promotion and information about the nearest locations. Marketing experts believe this location-based marketing approach will continue to grow. Businesses harness the ability to drive consumers to retail outlets near where they are located, which can be an effective method of engaging consumers with a brand on a one-to-one basis.

Geo-targeting A mobile marketing tactic that reaches customers where they are located based on their mobile device.

Walmart uses geo-targeting: it has a Store Mode that, once an individual is identified as being within a store proximity, it delivers coupons. With one in five Walmart online purchases picked up in store, this system persuades consumers to spend more inside the store.[6]

Creating successful geo-targeting campaigns requires two actions. First, consumers should be in control of the engagement. They opt-in for the app. Second, the brand should provide a discount or something of value to consumers. Campaigns that follow these principles routinely yield engagement and performance measures that are higher than other forms of digital advertising.

13-5b Content Marketing

If you have ever Googled a question on financial investments, you have certainly encountered Investopedia. Their content strategy is persuasive and many consumers find it useful–it brings over 33 million visitors per month. They explain complex issues clearly, with real-world examples in plain English. You want to find out about capital gains taxes or investment trends? They are your go-to information source.[7] Once you are at their website, they can help you build your portfolio, or you hire them to do your financial planning. This approach is called content marketing. **Content marketing**, or *branded content*, consists of providing useful information and product-use solutions to potential customers. Content marketing is not self-promotion or advertising to generate sales. It focuses on developing content that is authentic and of interest to consumers or businesses.

Content marketing Also known as branded content, content that is authentic and useful for businesses and/or consumers.

Source: Sharaf Maksumov/Shutterstock

To succeed, the information provided in content marketing must be relevant and answer problems faced by customers or in some way improve their lives. The goal is to produce information or solutions that visitors to the site want to share with others. Integrating content with the search and social strategies creates synergy. Using key search words in the content and providing content consumers consider to be valuable enhances the chance that a visitor seeking a solution to a problem will share the content with friends through social media. Content should be updated regularly and marketers should avoid the temptation to drift into self-promotion and sales talk over time. Staying true to the mission of the branded content, providing information and solutions is vital.

An alternative to branded content is **sponsored content**, whereby a brand sponsors the content of a blogger or related website. Scrolling down your Facebook, Instagram, or Twitter feed, you may see sponsored content from Samsung advertising the new Galaxy, with loud music and striking graphics. The ad fully matches your feed, it doesn't interrupt your scrolling and site experience, as it is blended in with the rest of the content.

Sponsored content A brand sponsors the content of a blogger or related website.

13-5c Blogs and Newsletters

Blogs are online musings that cover a wide range of topics. Some are interactive and permit visitors to post comments; others do not. Setting up company-sponsored blogs can emulate word-of-mouth communication

Blogs Online musings that cover a wide range of topics.

and engage customers with a brand. Fashion retailers entice customers to visit the company's blog to enjoy postings on new styles, upcoming designers, and fashion faux pas. In the past, customers may have relied on magazines for fashion information. Now, company blogs allow them to obtain information faster, and, more important, interactively. This helps brands engage with customers and establishes a two-way communication channel.

In developing a blog, analysts stress the importance of identifying a specific reason for the blog before launching. It may be to make the company more open to its customers, to humanize the company so customers feel the firm cares. When P&G launched its multi-million dollar campaign, "The Choice," to address racism in America, it launched a blog to coordinate with its ad, which first aired on Oprah Winfrey's town hall on race in the United States. The ad and the blog implore white America to step up to stamp out racism. The blog is educational, urging people to invest time to learn and understand the historical and present-day experiences of Black people in America, persuading readers to ensure that their media and entertainment include diverse voices, to contribute to efforts that advance equity and equality, and to take action as an ally, advocate, activist, and an anti-racist.[8]

Companies have to decide how they will handle negative comments. Most companies have a mechanism for approving comments before they are posted. This policy is to ensure nothing offensive is posted. It should not be to eliminate negative thoughts. Allowing negative comments to be posted shows a company is open and willing to accept feedback, both good and bad. It is important to respond to these negative comments in an honest, straightforward, and polite manner. Customers will respond to brands that are transparent.

Rather than a blog, some companies prefer to offer customers a newsletter. The UrbanDaddy (urbandaddy.com) website emails newsletters to its customers in large metropolitan areas covering news pertaining to nightlife, food, dining, lifestyle, and entertainment. The company is supported by advertising revenue and e-commerce. It organizes free sponsored events for subscribers.[9]

Both blogs and newsletters should follow the same principles outlined as those pertaining to content marketing. Information should be useful and provide solutions to problems customers face. It should be authentic and offer something individuals want to share. It should be integrated with the brand's web content, search strategy, and social media outreach (see Figure 13-14 on page 402).

Source: one photo/Shutterstock

13-5d Email Marketing

Email can be an important part of a company's digital marketing strategy. To be successful, companies need to integrate the email marketing program with other marketing programs. It cannot simply be a program where mass emails are sent to individuals on a list. Most people resent spam, and response rates are extremely low, in addition to damaging the brand's reputation.

Response rates increase when an email message resembles the information on the company's website and coincides with its IMC program. Web analytics can be used to develop email campaigns that offer the greatest chance of response. Emails can be based on the browsing history of an individual on a particular website. Analytics can identify those who made past purchases or items placed in the wish list but never purchased.

Email campaigns may be directed at consumers who abandon shopping carts without making purchases. Overstock, an Internet retailer, routinely emails a 12 to 15% discount coupon to those with an account when they abandon their shopping cart. Web analytics can easily identify the individuals who abandon a shopping basket. Sending an email to these individuals offering free shipping, a discount if they complete the order, or a simple reminder that they have items in their shopping basket can lead to higher sales. Converting these individuals to customers is much easier and more lucrative than sending mass emails.

In Figure 13-8, Holly Betts, an email expert with Marketing Zen, offers a number of suggestions for developing successful email campaigns. It starts with individuals opting-in to the email program. She emphasizes being upfront and honest with subscribers. Companies should tell recipients what they can expect, when they can expect it, and then deliver on those promises. As with branded content, emails should offer subscribers something useful that meets their needs or interests.

Marketing professionals should be sure all emails come from the same source so that subscribers instantly recognize the source and know it is an email they gave permission to receive. Emails should be short, neat, and eye-catching. The message can include links to all of the brand's social media outlets so recipients can increase their engagement with the brand

- Be upfront, honest with subscribers
- Build list for quality, not quantity
- Give subscribers what they want
- Be familiar with your audience
- Keep e-mails neat and clean
- Be eye-catching
- Integrate social media
- Test, test and test

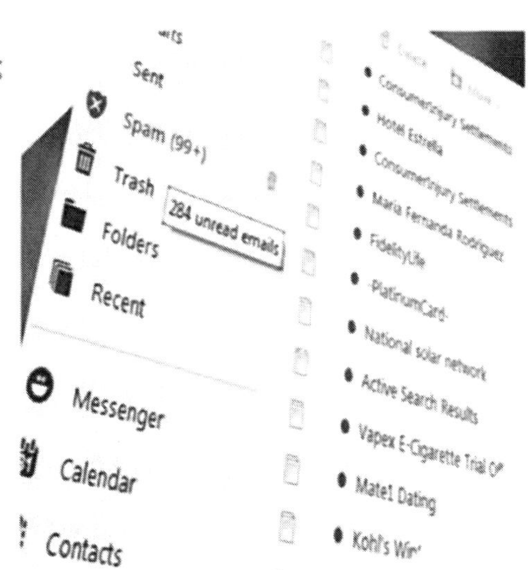

FIGURE 13-8 Tactics for a Successful Email Campaign
Source: Interview with Holly Betts, *Marketing Zen*, February 14, 2014

if they desire. Companies should test every email campaign and keep records of what worked and what did not. These records make it possible to build a file of best practices based on results.

13-5e Digital Advertising

Digital, or online, advertising presents a highly effective method for reaching today's consumers, especially the younger, affluent, and Internet-savvy market. Budgets for digital advertising have steadily increased and are now greater than television advertising. Part of the growth has been fueled by multiscreen advertising, which involves media buys across the various platforms such as the web, mobile, and tablets.

Digital advertising is projected to generate $228 billion in 2024 in advertising revenues. The high growth rate in digital advertising has only been derailed once, at the beginning of the COVID-19 pandemic.[10] See **Figure 13-9**.

Currently, banner ads can be embedded with videos, widget applications, or targeted display ads to increase the chances viewers will see and click the icon. The newest online technology, which has been taken from paid search auction systems, allows advertisers to display a banner ad only to individuals the company chooses. The system is built on a vast warehouse of user Internet data and automated auction advertising exchanges. Advertisers develop messages for specific audiences and set the price they are willing to pay to reach that audience with the banner ad.

When a consumer, such as a 22-year-old female, accesses a particular website with the paid search auction technology, in a microsecond the software searches the auction exchange for advertisers matching the profile

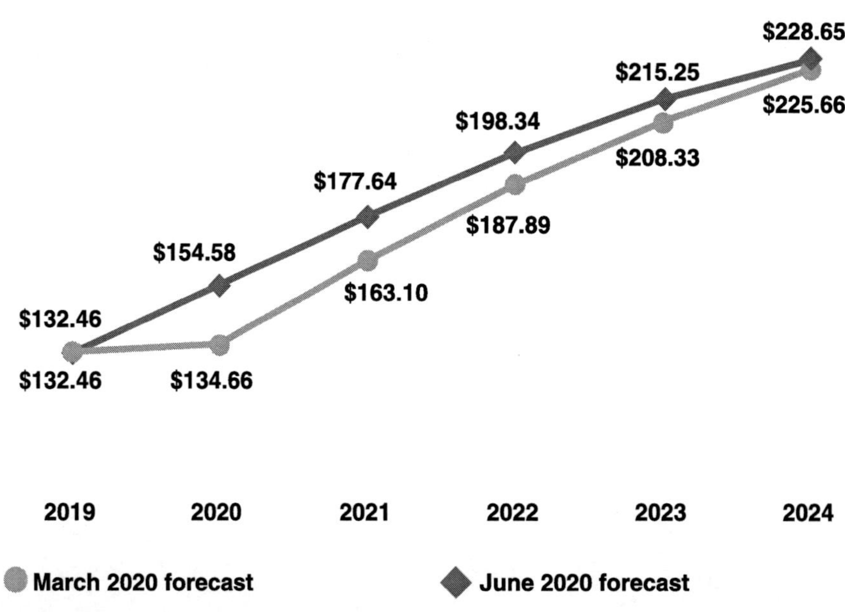

FIGURE 13-9 Digital Ad Spending Forecast (in US$ Billion) Before and After the Onset of COVID-19
Source: e-marketer, "US Digital Spending Update, Q2 2020," emarketer.com

of the individual who logged onto the page and posts the ad on their page. The ad could be for clothing, furniture, or an automobile. If a male with an interest in automobiles logs on, an advertisement for new automobile models may appear. Using a banner exchange program is a free way to get other sites to post your banner ads. However, you give up control over where your ads are posted and what ads are posted on your site.[11]

13-5f Search Engine Optimization

The largest category of online expenditures is for spots on search engines. This makes sense: 93% of online experiences start with a search engine–Google holds 90.1% of total search engine market share. Most B2B marketers (57%) believe that SEO generates more leads than any marketing initiative. On the consumer side, 81% perform some type of online search before making a large purchase.[12] Therefore, making sure that a company's name or brand becomes one of the first ones listed when a person performs a search will be a key marketing goal. **SEO, or search engine optimization**, is the process of increasing the probability of a particular company's website emerging from a search.

Search engine optimization (SEO) The process of increasing the probability of a particular company's website emerging from a search.

Optimization can be achieved in one of three ways **(see Figure 13-10)**. First, a paid text search insertion comes up when certain products or information are sought. The placement of the ad on a search page depends on the price the company pays, the algorithm a search engine uses to determine the advertisement's relevance to a particular search word or phrase, and the bid auction process. The FTC (Federal Trade Commission) now requires that these paid text ads have an "Ad" icon at the beginning of the search result.

Second, a company can increase identification through the natural or organic emergence of the site. This method involves developing efficient and effective organic results that arise from a natural search process. Each search engine uses a slightly different set of algorithms to identify

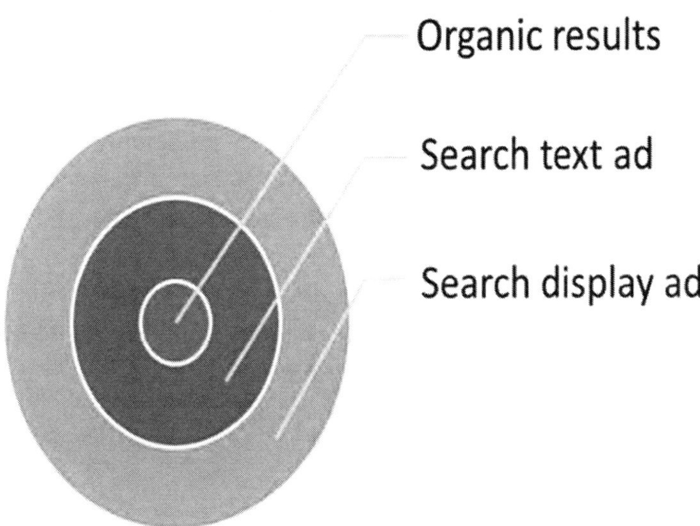

FIGURE 13-10 Forms of Search Engine Optimization

key phrases that match what was typed into the search box. To be listed first in an organic search requires time and effort. Normally, a new website will probably not emerge at the top of the search results. It takes time for the search engine to locate the site.

Studies suggest that the impact of organic listings can be impressive, since 70-80% of people ignore paid search results, choosing instead to click only on organic search results. In addition, 75% never scroll past the first page of search engines.[13]

The third optimization method, paid display ads, are small ads with images located at the top or right of the search results. These search display ads have a strong positive impact on brand awareness, perception, and purchase intentions, even when consumers do not click the paid search ad. The same rules that apply to the search text ads apply to these ads.

Companies spend large amounts on search engine optimization, but they must remember that it is a long-term investment, as effects do not occur quickly. Getting into the top 10 listings of a search can take months or years. It requires optimizing content, programming, credibility, and relevancy that will be picked up by search engines.

13-5g Behavioral Targeting

Behavioral targeting The utilization of web data to target individuals.

Rather than place ads on random websites, companies can target individuals most likely to purchase their products. **Behavioral targeting** utilizes web data to identify these individuals. Behavioral targeting can occur in three different ways, as shown in **Figure 13-11**.

The most common form of behavioral targeting involves tracking a person's movements on the Internet. A cookie is placed on the individual's computer that records data points as she goes from site to site. It records the types of sites visited, the information read, the searches that have been conducted, and products that were purchased. Based on this information, ads will be placed on websites that match this browsing history. If an individual has visited a number of websites about cooking, the individual will see an advertisement for food and cooking-related products. A coupon or other form of incentive can be placed on the ad to encourage the person to click on it.

The second form of behavioral targeting examines an individual's search behavior. It identifies keywords that are typed into search engines and the content that is read based on the keyword searches. If an individual has used a search engine to locate articles and information about new trucks, then he may see an advertisement by Ford or another truck brand. These ads will usually appear on the search engine being used. For example, if you are using Google (**Figure 13-12**) to search for a midsized SUV, you might see an ad for Kia Telluride or other SUV brands.

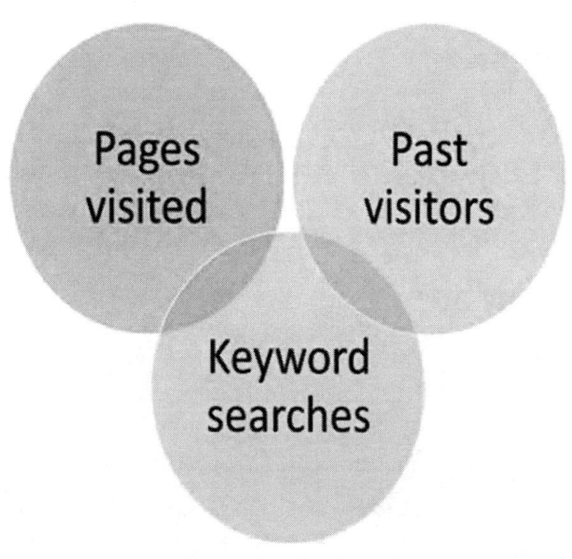

FIGURE 13-11 Behavioral Targeting Methods

FIGURE 13-12 When consumers google keywords such as "Midsize SUVs," they may see advertisements for Kia Telluride or other SUV brands.
Source: Jeramey Lende/Shutterstock

The final form of behavioral targeting is based on past visitors. Amazon uses this form of behavioral targeting to suggest merchandise that may interest a person shopping on the company's website. This form of behavioral marketing typically is triggered when one places a product in a shopping basket or has browsed that product category in the past. An ad will be generated that says "inspired by your shopping trends," or "related to items you've viewed."

Behavioral targeting takes place in micro-seconds without a person even realizing it occurs. Algorithms can be written to trigger these ads as the page loads. Even the brand being advertised rotates or changes based on the bidding process brands use for display advertising. In the above example with keyword behavioral targeting, instead of a Ford ad appearing it may be for a Chevrolet or a Toyota, depending on the result of the bidding process that takes place.

13-6 Social Media Marketing

Social interaction remains the fundamental basis of social media. It is one consumer talking to another, or to many others. Skilled marketers realize the potential inherent in such exchange. The newness of this type of communication has meant that companies are still developing ideas regarding the best approaches to utilize. The primary methods currently being used are given in **Figure 13-13**.

Brand managers develop social media marketing campaigns for a variety of reasons. **Figure 13-14** identifies some of the more common.[14] Two frequently reported rationales are to stay engaged with customers and provide a venue for interactions. Unlike any other marketing method, social media is built on the concept of communications and interactions. Brands have the opportunity to engage fans through the brands' various social media platforms. It offers an active, real-time interaction, 24/7. To be effective, the interaction must be genuine. Both the good and bad must be seen. Brands have to be willing to accept criticism and respond in a humanistic and empathetic manner. It must be two way–both customers

FIGURE 13-13 Social Media Marketing Methods

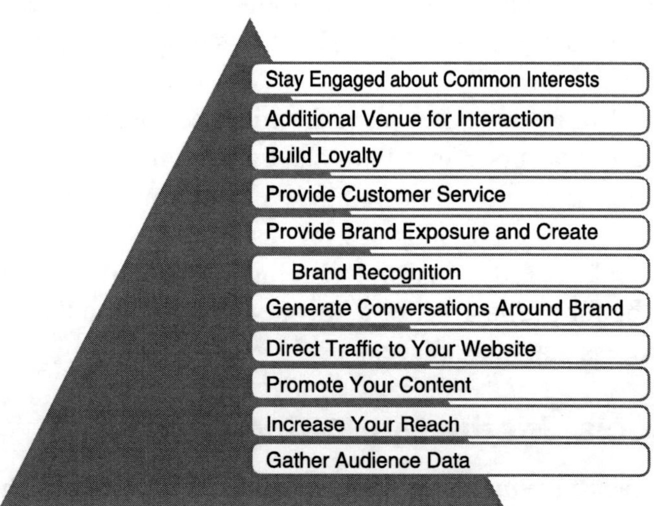

FIGURE 13-14 Reasons for Social Media Marketing

and company personnel talking and sharing. This means brands have to devote dollars and personnel to managing the company's social media efforts.

Social media can provide exposure to the brand. Effective exposure occurs when the social media platform is more than just a sounding board for customers. It should offer a venue for solving problems, gathering useful information, and gaining insights. Social media can drive traffic to a brand's website when visitors click on a URL embedded in a social media post. Marketers utilize social media to lead people to retail locations. In business-to-business programs, social media generates leads that the sales staff could later pursue.

Social media can boost organic search rankings with search engines. These increased rankings occur for two reasons. First, individuals mention the brand name more frequently on social media networks. The search algorithms used by search engines examine numbers of mentions. Second, if content or comments made about the brand fit the search terms, then the quality of those interactions increases and various search engines assign greater credibility to the brand.

Social media can provide valuable information about customers and non-customers. Most companies now engage in listening to social chatter, often called **social listening**. Comments may be negative or positive, but in most cases, visitors render honest opinions. Occasionally, social media buzz creates situations in which the marketing team should react immediately, as in cases when discussions degenerate into derogatory arguments that might reflect negatively on the company's brand. Disabling comments in those situations might be sufficient.

Social listening Listening to social chatter, where comments may be negative or positive, but in most cases visitors render honest opinions.

Social listening offers an excellent source of ideas for company-produced content. Problems consumers face, along with the information they seek, can be presented on various social media pages. By listening, the company appears to be in tune with consumers and seen as striving to meet consumer needs. Social listening can identify customer advocates. These individuals demonstrate a strong commitment to the brand. They make regular, frequent purchases. To these consumers, the brand is the best in the world. Brand managers can recruit these individuals to be advocates. Their recommendations can be extremely valuable in gaining new fans and customers.

Social listening might also involve taking action by temporarily refraining to advertise on social media. Facebook has been criticized for not doing enough to combat hate speech. Civil rights advocates called on businesses to "hit pause on hate" and not advertise on the platform in July, 2020. Adidas, Ben and Jerry's, Coca-Cola, Colgate-Palmolive, Ford, Honda, Levy's, lululemon, and many other brands participated. The boycott has not hurt Facebook's revenues, but it might have consequences for its bottom line: investors started pulling out.[15]

Increasing sales constitute the ultimate goals of any marketing program, but should not be the primary purpose of social media marketing. If customers view a social media outreach program as merely a masquerade

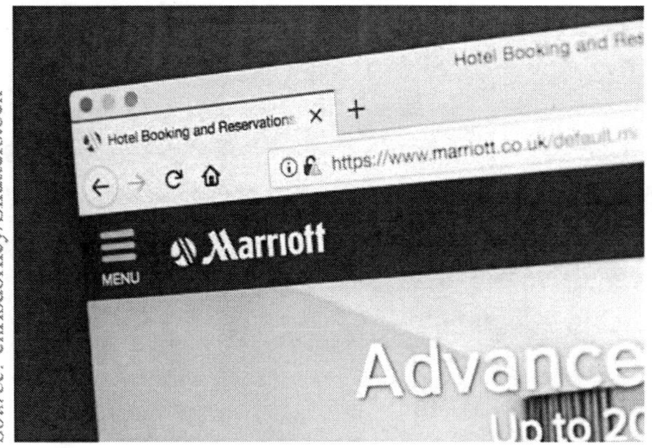

Source: chrisdorney/Shutterstock

for selling, they will likely be alienated. Instead, marketers should design social media programs to engage consumers with the brand. Increasing sales should be viewed as a by-product of social media marketing.

13-6a Content Seeding

Content seeding Providing incentives for consumers to share content about a brand.

People plant seeds into the ground believing that they will germinate and grow into a living plant that bears fruit, vegetables, or flowers. The same concept applies to social media marketing. **Content seeding** involves providing incentives for consumers to share content about a brand. The incentive does not have to be financial, although financial incentives tend to be the most frequently used. An incentive can be information, uniqueness, novelty, or anything that engages consumers with the brand and motivates them to share with others.

Marriott's StoryBooked: Creative Travel Stories documentary series follows artist members of their loyalty program in their journeys around the world, and, in the process, creates much buzz. One story follows an artist exploring his roots in Spain, another follows an artist as she immerses herself in Japanese traditions that had always inspired her. Creating content across Marriott brands has built both awareness, but also communities engaging with the brand, as viewers keep sharing the content on social media.[16]

13-6b Real-time Marketing

The idea of real-time marketing existed prior to the 2013 Super Bowl but it was the infamous blackout during the game in the New Orleans Superdome that legitimized it as a feasible social media strategy. Oreo sent a message via Twitter that it is okay to dunk an Oreo cookie "in the dark." The message was placed on an image of an Oreo cookie, set in light, shadow and darkness. That message became a viral hit, being re-tweeted 15,000 times within the first 14 hours.

Real-time marketing The creation and execution of an instantaneous marketing message in response to or in conjunction with a live event.

Real-time marketing is the creation and execution of an instantaneous marketing message in response to or in conjunction with a live event. The success of Oreos led marketers for other brands to set up "war rooms" during major live events. These war rooms contain top marketing executives, creatives, digital technicians, and attorneys. The group seeks to strike instantly with an approved message when an opportunity occurs.

Effective real-time marketing does not occur on the fly, without any thought. The approach requires upfront strategic planning before assembling a war room and prior to any live event. While seeking to display human emotions and reactions to live events, those actions must be carefully planned to ensure they resonate with consumers (or businesses) and remain consistent with the brand's overall brand image and integrated marketing communications plan. The tone presented in a real-time marketing message is key: it must correlate with the tone present in other company advertisements and other social media efforts. During these pre-planning sessions, company leaders discuss and sometimes even prepare messages and ads to be used for various situations that might occur during a live event. While it may seem that the message was a quick reaction, it may have been discussed and designed weeks earlier.

After luxury brand Baleciaga released a $2,000+ bag that was very similar in design to IKEA's classic blue bag, IKEA responded, much to everyone's amusement, with an ad that offered directions on how to differentiate between the two bags: "how to identify the REAL IKEA FRAKTA bag." Their response went viral on social media platforms and news outlets worldwide.[17]

13-6c Video Marketing

In 2020, the number of digital viewers in the United States was 232 million, and video penetration accounted for 83.8%—meaning that 83.8% of the population watched online video at some point.[18] Marketing professionals recognize that YouTube and other video sharing platforms present unique opportunities and challenges for social media marketing. Figure 13-15 highlights some of the primary tactics.

Because of the popularity of watching videos on YouTube and other video sharing platforms, advertising on videos has grown faster than other forms of advertising. A major reason for this growth is that consumers are more receptive to online video ads.

Ads embedded in videos can be pre-roll (before the video starts), mid-roll (in the middle of the video content), or post-roll (at the end of the content). Advertisements placed at the end of a video experience better click-through rates, because individuals have finished watching the video content. Ads at the beginning of the video result in more impressions while those in the middle have the highest completion rate. Therefore, when creating impressions or enhancing recall constitutes the primary goal, advertisers should front-load ads. When the company seeks to increase brand recognition or enhance brand image, then mid-roll ads represent a better option, because viewers tend to watch the entire ad. Post-roll ads best match direct response–type of advertising with some type of call to action.

Most companies maintain YouTube channels in order to share various types of videos. Marketers post ads prepared for television to video websites. Most Super Bowl advertisers are now posting their Super Bowl commercial or a snippet of it on YouTube prior to the game. Often, the digital ad will be viewed by more

FIGURE 13-15 Video Marketing Tactics

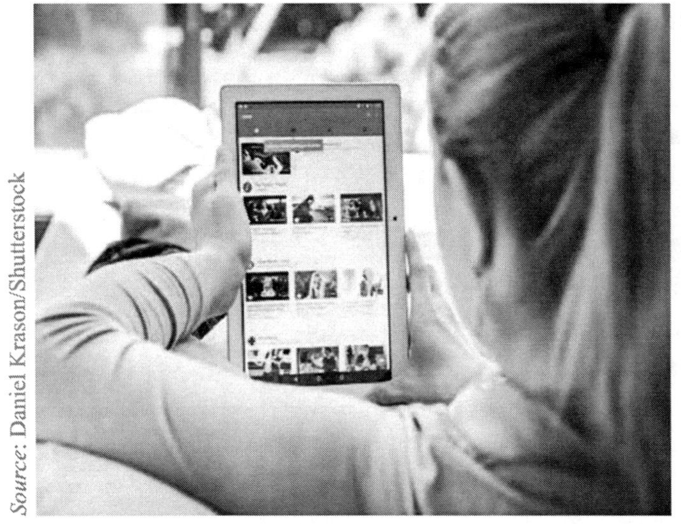
Source: Daniel Krason/Shutterstock

people than those who see the actual commercial during the Super Bowl. In addition to ads, advertisers post background scenes or videos explaining how the ad was produced. Viewers find these interesting, and the approach often increases engagement with the brand.

Companies often will produce informational or instructional videos. These videos are designed to provide useful information to consumers and answer questions they may have about the brand. Providing a tutorial on how to use a product, especially a complex item, can be useful.

Another approach involves posting videos with public relations or cause-related marketing messages. Duracell produced a video about firefighters and emergency personnel telling their personal stories. John Deere produced a video about a Mexican immigrant who came to the United States with nothing and now owns his own business. This type of video seeks to generate goodwill.

Consumers use videos to conduct product research. They often turn to YouTube as a source for product reviews: videos are more engaging because they provide both visual and spoken content.

13-6d Influencer Marketing

Influencer marketing Involves an individual marketing a brand through social media, and is word-of-mouth communication from individuals who are seen as thought or opinion leaders within their social circles or as experts within particular fields.

Messages posted on social media by companies are often ignored. As a result many marketing teams have turned to locating individuals to share information and other facets of a brand. **Influencer marketing** involves an individual marketing a brand through social media. It is word-of-mouth communication from individuals who are seen as thought or opinion leaders within their social circles or as experts within particular fields. A number of agencies now specialize in matching potential influencers with brands seeking to take advantage of influencer marketing.

The size of an individual's social network does not always correlate with the extent of her influence. An individual can have 20,000 followers, but not be seen as an opinion leader within that particular field. The most effective influencers are those individuals that lead conversations and shape opinions. While celebrities have large followings, they are not always the best choices for influencer marketing campaigns.

Source: sergey causelove/Shutterstock

According to famed fitness influencer and author of *The Influencer Code*, Amanda Russell, true influence is built on trust, on establishing genuine connections and building authentic relationships. It is not just about good content, or a slick website, social media presence, or storefront; a truly influential brand involves building a trust with your target audience that moves them to action, requiring a critical balance of creativity, connection, and strategy.[19]

Aligning a brand's message with an influencer's motivation is the key to success. Influencers want to grow their networks of followers. One way to do so is to be viewed as an opinion leader through sharing brand content, especially exclusive or pre-launch content. For instance, a fashion brand can provide influencers access to new fashions before the rest of the public sees them.

To be effective, influencers must be deemed authentic and not as paid spokespersons for companies. Consumers are not opposed to an influencer pitching a particular brand as long as it appears to be genuine praise.[20] Hudda Kattan, the Oklahoma-born makeup expert is the most influential beauty expert, with a wide social media outreach: she has 29 million Instagram followers for her makeup tutorials she puts out. A beauty brand would benefit greatly from having her promote it on her blog.[21]

13-6e Viral Marketing

Preparing a marketing message to be passed from one consumer to another through digital venues or social media is **viral marketing**. It can be an email, a video posted to a personal blog or on YouTube, or a posting on one of the social media platforms. It then evolves into a form of advocacy or word-of-mouth endorsement. The term "*viral*" derives from the image of a person being "infected" with the marketing message and then spreading it to friends, like a virus. The difference is that the individual voluntarily sends the message to others.

Viral marketing Preparing a marketing message to be passed from one consumer to another through digital venues or social media.

Viral marketing messages may include advertisements, hyperlinked promotions, online newsletters, streaming videos, and games. For instance, about a dozen videos were posted on YouTube of a man claiming to be the "world's fastest nudist." He streaks through various locations in New York City wearing only tennis shoes, tube socks, and a fanny pack positioned strategically in front. The links to the videos were emailed from individual to individual. They were posted on popular blogs such as The Huffington Post and Gawker. One appeared on CNN on *Anderson Cooper 360*. The campaign turned out to be a viral video campaign for Zappos.com, an online shoe and apparel store. The viral campaign highlighted that Zappos was selling clothes, because additional videos were posted that showed a van screeching up to the "fastest nudist" and several people jumping out wearing Zappos T-shirts. As the van leaves, the video shows the nudist dressed in pants and a shirt.[22]

Source: one photo/Shutterstock

While companies strive to produce a viral message, in most cases it does not happen. Individuals must have some incentive to pass the message along. A message with entertainment value is one type of incentive. Other incentives may be financial, such as free merchandise or a discount for messages passed along to friends that lead to purchases, logging onto a website, or registering for an e-newsletter. The incentive could also be found in the campaign's uniqueness. A personalized message has a greater chance of being passed along.

The many forms of digital and social media marketing mean that viral marketing has lost some of its luster. Many consumers have lost enthusiasm and are less willing to re-send messages. The marketing team can take advantage of the ability to track the results of a viral campaign and analyze the results to determine whether such a program will have the best chance of being effective.

Summary

1. **Discuss current Internet usage.**
Globally, Internet penetration is at 51 percent. The highest penetration is North America with 88 percent of the population having access to the Internet. Europe and Australia are next, at 80 percent and 70 percent, respectively. Internet access is now available on smartphones and tablets as well as PCs and laptops. Internet usage varies based on the platform that is being used. Email, searches, and texting are the primary activities performed on the Internet by individuals.

2. **Identify the benefits of digital marketing.**
Internet marketing provides the benefits of sales, interactivity, multimedia capabilities, global reach, flexibility, cost efficiencies, real-time information, communication, and database warehousing.

3. **Discuss the importance of e-commerce.**
An e-commerce site has three primary components: a catalog, a shopping cart, and a payment system. Bricks-and-clicks operations must have a fourth component: a location finder. The catalog is a visual presentation of the merchandise to be sold. The shopping cart is some type of mechanism that allows a consumer to select merchandise and put it into a virtual shopping cart until he or she is finished making selections. For bricks-and-clicks operations, where individuals may want to locate or purchase from a bricks-and-mortar site, it is important to include a locator that will provide an address and a map to the facility. Although online purchases are growing at a rapid rate, many consumers are still not sure about making online purchases for two reasons: security issues and purchase behavior habits. Many consumers are afraid to use credit cards because of concerns that their credit card number will be stolen. Others are concerned about fraud and dishonest e-commerce websites that will take their money and never ship the merchandise or ship poor-quality merchandise. In terms of purchasing habits, consumers feel more comfortable purchasing products from retail outlets because that is the way they have always shopped.

4. **Identify and explain the various digital marketing strategies.**
Digital marketing strategies include geo-marketing, content marketing, blogs and newsletters, email marketing, digital advertising, search engine optimization, and behavioral targeting. Because of the GPS embedded in mobile phones, companies can use geo-marketing strategies. These strategies involve sending some type of marketing or text message based on a person's location. Content marketing is the publishing of useful information to the web to connect with consumers and businesses. Blogs and newsletters can be used to engage individuals with a company and provide opportunities for interaction. Email marketing provides a low cost method of reaching consumers. Digital advertising can be through banner ads or search engines. SEO is the process of optimizing search marketing strategies to increase the chances an ad or organic search result appears. Behavioral targeting uses web analytics to send targeted messages to individuals.

5. **Examine strategies that can be used in social media marketing.**
Social media provides a mechanism for firms to interact with consumers and engage them with the brands. Content seeding involves using incentives or placing content in social media that encourages individuals to respond and become engaged. Real-time marketing looks for opportunities during live events to utilize social media to promote the brand. Influencer marketing involves recruiting brand ambassadors to post about a brand in an effort to influence others in a positive manner. Viral marketing attempts to create unique content that is shared from one consumer to another through some digital means.

Key Terms

Behavioral targeting (400)
Blogs (395)
Bricks-and-clicks (390)
Clicks-only firms (390)
Content marketing (394)
Content seeding (404)
Digital marketing strategies (393)
E-commerce (390)
Geo-targeting (394)
Influencer marketing (406)
Mobile marketing (393)
Real-time marketing (404)
Search engine optimization (SEO) (399)
Social listening (403)
Sponsored content (395)
Viral marketing (407)

Discussion Questions

1. Have you used the Internet to research a product before making a purchase? If so, how much time did you spend conducting online research? How did the information influence your decision? Where did you make the final purchase? Provide specific examples.
2. Access Nielsen/NetRatings. What information is available on the website? Report on at least three articles or pieces of information that interest you. Use a screen capture to place the content from the website in your document.
3. Section 13-4 describes three types of retail stores (bricks-and-mortar, bricks-and-clicks, and clicks-only). Discuss each type in terms of your personal shopping experiences. How much shopping do you do at each and what types of products do you buy in each? Talk to your parents and grandparents. Compare your responses to those of your relatives.
4. In Section 13-4, reasons for shopping online are given. Re-order the list based on your personal reasons for shopping online. Explain why you placed them in the order that you did.
5. Pick one of the following product categories. Access three companies that operate in that particular industry. Compare and contrast each company in terms of the e-commerce components and incentives discussed in Section 13-4.
   a. football equipment and fan memorabilia
   b. cheerleading supplies and uniforms
   c. dishes
   d. jeans or another type of clothing
6. What are your thoughts about geo-marketing? Have you personally experienced marketing messages through geo-marketing? If so, provide details. If not, would you be receptive to geo-marketing messages? Why or why not?
7. What are your thoughts about behavioral targeting? Does it influence your purchase decision or thoughts about a brand? Why or why not?
8. Pick one of the following product categories and access two companies that operate in that particular industry. Evaluate their websites based on the information provided in Section 13-5, Digital Marketing Strategies. Which strategies do you believe are being

used? Provide support from the website and explain why you think the brand is using the strategy.
   a. sports equipment and fan memorabilia
   b. electronics such as radios, TVs, or stereos
   c. household appliances such as electric mixers, toasters, or coffeemakers
   d. jeans or another type of clothing
   e. shoes
9. Go to the Internet and locate a company-sponsored blog. Discuss how the blog is being used and the benefit you see for the blog.
10. In your opinion is email marketing effective? Why or why not? What type of email marketing messages work with you?
11. How effective is digital advertising to you personally? Discuss at least two incidents where you clicked on an advertisement or accessed content through a digital advertisement. Explain why the digital ad worked.
12. Do you pay attention to search engine ads? Why or why not? Do you think SEO is important for companies? Why or why not?
13. Identify the social media sites, such as Facebook, Twitter, Instagram, YouTube, etc. that you use. Discuss how much time you spend on each one and what type of activities you conduct with each.
14. For you personally, how effective is social media marketing? Give examples of good social media approaches being used by brands and poor approaches you have seen.
15. What are your thoughts about influencer marketing? Have you had any personal experiences with influencer marketing? If so, provide information and discuss what you liked and disliked. If not, would you be receptive to messages through an influencer? Why or why not?

Review Questions

True or False

1. The global Internet penetration rate is almost 60 percent.
2. A major benefit of the Internet is it has the capability of being interactive.
3. In the United States, online sales are over $800 billion annually.
4. Geo-marketing is possible because of the GPS mechanism in mobile phones.
5. Behavioral targeting consists of providing useful information and product-use solutions to potential customers.
6. Search engine optimization is the process of increasing the probability of a particular company's website emerging from a search.
7. Content seeding involves producing material that is useful to consumers or businesses and posted on a company's website.
8. Viral marketing takes place as one customer passes along a message to other potential buyers.

Multiple Choice

9. The Internet penetration rate in North America is about:
   a. 87 percent
   b. 95 percent
   c. 98 percent
   d. 100 percent
10. The category with the highest online sales is
   a. autos and parts
   b. apparel and accessories
   c. books, music, and videos
   d. computers and electronics
11. Providing useful information or product-use knowledge to consumers on a website or through digital marketing strategies is
   a. content marketing
   b. geo-targeting
   c. email marketing
   d. behavioral targeting
12. Of the three types of SEO results, the best is:
   a. paid search insertions
   b. organic search results
   c. paid search ads

13. Reaching customers where they are located based on their mobile devices is known as:
    a. search engine optimization
    b. interactive marketing
    c. geo-targeting
    d. behavioral targeting
14. All of the following are social media strategies, except:
    a. content seeding
    b. real-time marketing
    c. geo-targeting
    d. viral marketing

Answers: (1) T, (2) T, (3) T, (4) T, (5) F, (6) T, (7) F, (8) T, (9) b, (10) d, (11) a, (12) b, (13) c, (14) c

Case: Bluefly

Founded in 1999, Bluefly.com was created as an online retailer of designer brand clothing and the latest fashion trends. The headquarters is located in New York City, in the heart of the fashion district. The company's fashion buyers are constantly searching for the newest fashions and accessories from more than 350 fashion designers. Everything sold by Bluefly is of the highest quality, but sold for at least 40 percent below other fashion retailers.

The name Bluefly.com was selected because the founders believed that because it was an online retailer, they would have to be hard to catch and always be nimble, fast, and ready to change directions on a dime. The "fly" appeared to be a perfect symbol of these objectives. The idea of "blue" came from the desire to convey the company has a "friendly personality." Because Bluefly has no brick-and-mortar stores, they had to develop ways of enticing consumers to browse and shop at their website. One of the primary incentives used was contests. They have designed several types of contests since their opening in 1999 and always have some type of promotion on their website. The goal of these promotions is to attract individuals to the website and to encourage them to make a purchase.

One contest held by Bluefly.com offered visitors an opportunity to win a $1,000 shopping spree or a much-sought after Hermès Birkin bag valued at $20,000. To enter the contest, individuals had to supply their email address, but they could enter the contest daily to improve their chances of winning. The idea was to get them to access the site on a regular basis. Although they may not make a purchase on the first visit, the founders of the company believed that if they kept coming back, they would make a purchase. The Hermès handbag promotion added more than 100,000 names to Bluefly.com's database. The financial benefit of using this methodology to acquire customers is that the average cost of acquisition for each new customer was only $23.07, compared with an average order of $154.

Another promotion offered by Bluefly was "30 Bags in 30 Days." It was a sweepstakes directed toward fashion-oriented consumers who had the opportunity to win accessories that even celebrities and socialites were waiting months to purchase. The promotion resulted in a 100 percent increase in visits to the website and a 62 percent increase in sales. Some customers asked Bluefly to send them a daily email to remind them to register for the sweepstakes.

Source: IgorGolovniov/Shutterstock

In addition to the contests, Bluefly uses one-time discounts for new customers, followup emails after a purchase, e-newsletters, and personalization of the web software based on the person's past purchases and browsing behavior. The website is attractive and easy to navigate, and the checkout process is among the best. It encourages customers to purchase when they see a product they like because when the inventory is gone, they pull the product from their virtual store. Knowing a particular piece of clothing may not be available tomorrow encourages customers to make a purchase while they are on the website. Another tactic used by Bluefly is the development of a blog called flypaper, which was designed to keep their customers updated on fashion trends.

In advertising, Bluefly has taken a more controversial approach. Its primary target market is women ages 25 to 49 who are fashion conscious and desire to wear the latest fashion trends by fashion designers. But its ads often use naked or scantily clad females that one might expect for a beer commercial. For instance, a recent $3 million campaign featured a TV spot depicting a woman standing nude in front of her closet, which was full of clothes. Unable to find anything appropriate, she goes to the party completely naked. Some TV stations refused to show the ad, others allowed the ad but it had to be edited. In a print ad, a naked woman is shown boarding a train. Bluefly ran a contest asking web browsers to supply the caption. Of the over 1,000 suggested, the winning caption was "I think I forgot to turn off the stove—no wait, that's not it." Before answering the questions that follow, visit Bluefly's website.

Case Questions

1. What has Bluefly done to attract customers to their website and to encourage them to make a purchase?
2. Examine the various digital strategies listed in Section 13-5. Discuss each one in terms of a potential strategy for Bluefly.
3. Because customers cannot try on the clothes before they are purchased, how can Bluefly assure customers to go ahead and make a purchase?
4. What is your opinion of their advertising approach?
5. Examine the social media strategies discussed in Section 13-6. How can Bluefly.com use each of these strategies to promote its website? Provide at least one example for each.
6. What is your evaluation of the Bluefly website and their overall business approach?

Sources: Bluefly.com accessed on April 30, 2020; Lorrie Grant, "Retailers Hope Shoppers Buy Blogs as the Place to Go," *USA Today* (August 25, 2005): Money 5b; Maye Dollarhide, "Bluefly Buzz Bags Shoppers," *Incentive 180*, no. 1 (January 2006): 10; David Sparrow, "Get' Em to Bite," *Catalog Age* 20, no. 4 (April 2003): 35–36; Kenneth Hein and Diane Anderson, "Ads Au Natural a Wise Crack," *Brandweek* 46, no. 38 (October 24, 2005): 38.

Endnotes

1. Andrea Knezovic, "60+ Important 2019/2020 Mobile Marketing Statistics You Need to Know," *Medium*, December 10, 2019, https://medium.com/udonis/60-important-2019-2020-mobile-marketing-statistics-you-need-to-know-2d68d1771c01. Internet world stats, "World internet usage and population statistics," May 20, 2020, accessed on June 10, 2020 at www.internetworldstats.com/stats.htm.
2. Statista, "Retail e-commerce sales in the United States from 2017 to 2024," accessed at https://www.statista.com/statistics/272391/us-retail-e-commerce-sales-forecast on May 28, 2020.
3. A.J. Winningham and Hena Sharma, "All the virtual concerts, plays, museums and other culture you can enjoy from home," CNN, April 10, 2020, https://www.cnn.com/style/article/what-to-do-at-home-streaming

-art-museums-concerts-coronavirus-trnd-duplicate-2/index.html.

4. e-Marketer, "U.S. e-commerce 2020," June 8, 2020, https://www.emarketer.com/content/us-ecommerce-2020.
5. Pew Research, "Mobile Fact Sheet," June 12, 2019, https://www.pewresearch.org/internet/fact-sheet/mobile.
6. Knorex, "Proximity Targeting: What Is It, and How Does It Work For Your Business?" April 27, 2020, https://www.knorex.com/blog/articles/proximity-targeting.
7. SingleGrain, "Companiesdominatingtheworld with content marketing," accessed at https://www.singlegrain.com/content-marketing-strategy-2/companies-dominating-the-wold-with-content-marketing, on June 8, 2020.
8. Doug Zanger, "Powerful P&G Ad Implores White America to Step Up and Help Stamp Out Racism," *AdWeek*, June 10, 2020, https://www.adweek.com/retail/powerful-pg-ad-implores-white-america-to-step-up-and-help-stamp-out-racism; Procter & Gamble, "The Choice," accessed at https://us.pg.com/take-on-race, on June 14, 2020.
9. UrbanDaddy, accessed at https://www.urbandaddy.com on June 10, 2020.
10. E-marketer, "US Digital Ad Spending Update, Q2 2020, accessed at https://www.emarketer.com/content/us-digital-ad-spending-update-q2-2020, June 18, 2020.
11. Tom Harris, "How banner ads work," accessed at https://computer.howstuffworks.com/banner-ad6.htm on June 20, 2020.
12. Pat Ahern, "25 Mind-Bottling SEO Stats for 2020 (+ Beyond)," Junto, January 10, 2020, accessed at https://junto.digital/blog/seo-stats.
13. Ibid.
14. CoSchedule, "20 Important benefits of social media marketing every business should know, https://coschedule.com/blog/benefits-of-social-media-marketing-for-business, accessed on June 10, 2020.
15. Queenie Wong, "Facebook ad boycott: Why big brands 'hit pause on hate,'" Cnet, June 30, 2020, https://www.cnet.com/news/facebook-ad-boycott-how-big-businesses-hit-pause-on-hate.
16. Marriott Bonvoy Traveler, StoryBooked, accessed at https://traveler.marriott.com/storybooked/fidan-bagirova; Jordan Kelley, "These 6 Brand Storytellers Are Paving The Way In Branded Entertainment," *Forbes*, May 9, 2020, https://www.forbes.com/sites/brandstorytelling/2020/03/09/these-6-brand-storytellers-are-paving-the-way-in-branded-entertainment/#727f4d4c7ff8.
17. Charlotte Garner, "The evolution of real-time marketing," September 19, 2018, https://www.minttwist.com/blog/the-evolution-of-real-time-marketing.
18. Millennial Studios, "Online Video Consumption," January 20, 2020, https://millennialstudios.co.uk/blog/online-video-consumption-statistics/
19. Amanda Russell, *The Influencer Code*, Hatherleigh Press, 2020, accessed at https://amandarussell.co/books/the-influencer-code.
20. Blaise Lucey, "In a Fragmented Social World, Influencers Rule," www.adweek.com/socialtimes/626503, accessed March 8, 2016.
21. Digital Marketing Institute, "9 of the Biggest Social Media Influencers on Instagram, accessed at https://digitalmarketinginstitute.com/blog/9-of-the-biggest-social-media-influencers-on-instagram on June 10, 2020.
22. Andrew Adam Newman, "A Campaign for Clothes by a Guy Not Wearing Any," *The New York Times* (www.nytimes.com/2009/10/29/business/media/29zappos.html), October 29, 2009.

Promotions, Sponsorships, and Public Relations

CHAPTER 14

Source: Rawpixel.com/Shutterstock

Chapter Outline

Learning Objectives

Ivelin Radkov/Shutterstock

After studying this chapter, you should be able to:

- Discuss the reasons for a shift in marketing expenditures to promotions.
- Describe the various forms of consumer promotions.
- Explain the importance of in-store promotions in purchasing behavior.
- Discuss the goals of trade promotions.
- Explain the various types of trade promotions.
- Describe the current use of sponsorships.
- Identify the role of public relations in integrated marketing communications (IMC).

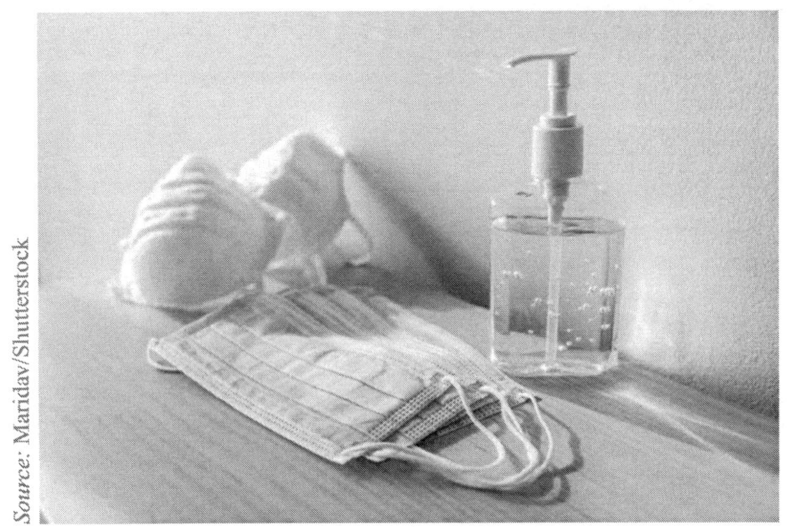
Source: Maridav/Shutterstock

14-1 Chapter Overview

As some businesses reopened after the onset of the COVID-19 pandemic, and others tried to stay in touch with customers and with employees working remotely, companies offered coronavirus-related corporate swag, such as branded sanitizer bottles, "clean key" tools for elevator buttons and, most of all, masks.

Nasdaq ordered masks with its logo and the phrase "NasdaqStrong" for employees returning back to the office. Software firm Atlassian offered gift packages that included masks with a product logo alongside a chocolate bar, a pen and other goodies to their employees, and tech start-up Lemonade had masks branded with its new ticker symbol ready for its executives to wear when they rang the bell for their IPO. A major airline was planning an order of branded masks for its premium-class passengers and ground crew. Companies could be perceived as exploiting the pandemic with people's faces as corporate branding space, commercializing the crisis. Corporations were sensitized to the possibility that people do not want to be walking billboards advertising the brand, so most masks have small logos on the side, with muted colors.[1] Consumer and trade promotions are a critical component of the integrated marketing communications (IMC) effort. Over the past few decades, more and more dollars have been shifted from advertising to promotions. The next section, Section 14-2, examines why this shift in spending has occurred. Promotions can be divided into two types: consumer (or sales) promotions and trade promotions. Section 14-3 examines the major forms of consumer promotion with a focus on couponing—the most pervasive consumer promotion used. Not only are consumer promotions used to stimulate sales, they are also used to generate store traffic because the final decision to purchase a particular brand is often made inside the retail store. Section 14-4 examines in-store promotions that companies use to gain attention and to persuade consumers to make a purchase. Section 14-5, deals with trade promotions. While these tend not to be seen by most people, they are critical for pushing products through the channel and ensuring that products are on retail shelves for consumers to purchase them. Section 14-6 addresses sponsorships, illustrating how companies match the audience profiles with their target markets, and the last section, Section 14-7, addresses public relations, illustrating how companies work to develop strong relationships with their publics to create a positive company image and favorable publicity.

14-2 Promotions

In recent years, firms have shifted more of their communications budgets from advertising to trade and consumer promotions. Trade promotions refer to offers made to channel members, whereas consumer promotions are offers given to end users or consumers. Trade promotions represent 46.1% of the marketing budget, whereas consumer promotions represent 7.3% of the marketing budget, while traditional advertising only represents 12.7% of the marketing budget.[2]

Immediate response
Creates differentiation
Offers a reason to buy in a deal-prone society
Creates communication opportunity
Creates platform to cross-sell and up-sell
Creates greater revenue
Source of product information

FIGURE 14-1 Reasons for Increased Usage of Promotions

This shift toward greater use of promotions has occurred for several reasons[3] **(see Figure 14-1)**. To list a few, promotions have an immediate impact on sales, whereas advertising takes a longer period of time. The impact is not only immediate but is often quite dramatic in terms of increased sales, creating greater revenue. Another reason for the shift is that, with so many product choices, the promotion will create differentiation, offering a reason to buy the product right away. Buyers see little difference among brands; they may have a preference, but will buy the brand offering the best price, style, and fit.

In our deal-prone society, consumers need a reason to buy. Automobiles are purchased with factory rebates, pizza ordered with coupons. Grocery stores have weekly deals, weekend deals, and special deals. It is not unusual for consumers to buy whichever brand has a coupon.

Whatever promotions a company uses, they must be part of the company's IMC program and fit with the advertising that is being done.

14-3 Consumer Promotions

Consumer promotions are used to stimulate some type of activity on the part of a consumer or business. Most of these promotions are aimed at consumers, but the promotions can also be targeted to businesses if the business is the final user of the product. For example, an office supply store may offer a business a special promotion to either make an immediate purchase or place a larger order. If the business purchases the office supplies for its own consumption, then the promotion is a sales or consumer promotion. If, however, it is reselling the office supplies, then it is a trade promotion.

Companies can use ten primary types of sales promotions **(see Figure 14-2, next page)**. It is important that the sales promotions fit into the company's IMC effort and be part of the company's strategic thinking. If not, the message sent to consumers via a consumer promotion may contradict the firm's IMC effort. For instance, if a firm wants to project an image of offering superior quality, using coupons on a regular basis conveys a different message to buyers. Mentally, one would say, "If this product is of such high quality, why do they always offer coupons?" Why is Overstock always pushing 10%, 12%, or 15% off coupons by mail, or on their website? Although coupons can be used, other consumer promotion tools may do a better job of promoting the product while maintaining the higher image desired.

FIGURE 14-2 Sales Promotion Options

Coupons Sales promotion that offers customers some type of price reduction.

14-3a Coupons

Coupons are an excellent strategy for stimulating sales, especially in the short run, because coupons offer a price reduction. The number of coupons has increased from 17 billion in 1970 to more than 321 billion today. Of the 321 billion coupons distributed annually, approximately 2.5 billion, or 0.78 percent, were redeemed. The average face value of the coupons was $1.68, which translates into a savings of $4.2 billion per year. Approximately 92 percent of all shoppers have used a coupon within the last three months.[4]

Direct mail, 1.0%
Check out, 1.0%
Shelf pad/cross ruff, 1.2%
Magazine, 1.8%
Handout, 0.9%
Free-standing inserts, 89.1%
Digital, 3.9%

FIGURE 14-3 Coupon Distribution Methods
Source: 2016 Coupon Trends, white paper, www.inmar.com, accessed November 15, 2019

Figure 14-3 identifies the various methods of distributing coupons and the percentage with which each is used. Manufacturers distribute 80% of all coupons, and the primary method used is print media. Although magazines and newspapers have coupons, 89.1% of all coupons are distributed via **freestanding inserts (FSI)**, sheets of coupons distributed in newspapers, usually on Sunday and Wednesday. The second-highest method is digital at 3.9%, but it is the fastest growing form.[5] Over 50% of consumers select paper/printed coupons to take on shopping trips, 51% look at printed store circulars/ads for a specific retailer before shopping, and 46% look at store circulars/ads to decide which retailer to shop. For online circulars/weekly ads, 40% look for those of specific retailers, and 37% use them to decide where to shop. About 40% load electronic coupons on a loyalty/frequent shopper card.[6] Online grocery shoppers are pros at finding savings: their coupon usage is much higher than that of the average consumer, with 65% using coupons (vs. 45% of all consumers); they use both print and digital sources to find value and plan what and where they will buy.[7]

Freestanding inserts (FSI) Sheets of coupons distributed in newspapers, primarily on Wednesday and Sunday.

Most companies prefer using FSI and print media to distribute coupons because consumers must make a conscious effort to clip or save the coupon. Also, the coupon increases brand awareness even if the consumer does not use the coupon. Manufacturers believe that consumers are more likely to purchase a couponed brand and remember the name when they redeem it, especially if it is an FSI, because they must clip it and take it along to the retail outlet.

Instant redemption coupon A coupon that can be redeemed immediately while making a purchase.

Businesses have a variety of coupons that can be used. **Figure 14-4** lists the different types of coupons with a definition and an example of each. Coupons are often distributed in retail stores by placing them on or near packages. The consumer can immediately redeem the coupon while making the purchase. This type of coupon is called an **instant redemption coupon** and can lead to trial purchases and purchases of additional products. In addition to placing the coupon on the

Source: Pressmaster/Shutterstock

Type of Coupon	Definition	Example
Instant redemption coupons	Coupons that can be instantly redeemed	A coupon attached to a can of coffee for 50 cents off
Bounce-back coupons	Coupons that cannot be immediately used but must be used on the next trip to the store	A coupon inside a can of coffee for 50 cents off the next purchase
Scanner-delivered coupons	Coupons issued at the cash register during checkout	A 50-cent coupon for Folger's coffee issued after the shopper purchased a can of Maxwell House
Cross-ruffing coupons	A coupon placed on another product	A 50-cent coupon for Betty Crocker's cake icing placed on a Betty Crocker cake mix
Response-offer coupons	A coupon issued upon the request of a consumer	A $30 coupon issued to consumers who call a toll-free number after viewing a television advertisement
E-coupons (U-pons)	A coupon issued to the consumer via the Internet	A coupon for 50 cents off a can of Folger's coffee issued electronically

FIGURE 14-4 Types of Coupons

package, coupons are sometimes given with free samples of a product to encourage consumers to try a new brand. Coupons may also be placed in dispensers near various products, which provide convenient access for customers. All of these methods are forms of instant redemption coupons because customers can use them immediately.

Bounce-back coupons Coupons that cannot be used until the next purchase.

Bounce-back coupons are placed inside packages so that customers cannot redeem them at the time of the original purchase. This approach encourages repeat purchases because the coupon cannot be used until the next purchase. Another trend is to have coupons issued at the cash register during checkout. These are scanner-delivered coupons because they are triggered by an item being scanned, usually a competing brand. **Scanner-delivered coupons** are designed to encourage brand switching during the next shopping trip.

Scanner-delivered coupons Coupons issued at the cash register during checkout.

Cross-ruffing coupon A coupon for one product placed on another product.

Another type of coupon is the **cross-ruffing coupon**, which is the placement of a coupon for one product on another product. For example, a coupon for a French onion dip might be placed on a package of potato chips. To be successful, crossruffing coupons must be used with products that logically fit together and that are normally purchased and consumed simultaneously. Typically, a manufacturer uses cross-ruffing to encourage consumers to purchase another one of its products or brands. For example, General Mills might place a coupon on a Honey Nut Cheerios box for another cereal, such as Wheaties. This type of couponing tactic encourages consumers to purchase within the same brand or family of products.

Response-offer coupons Coupons issued following a request by a consumer.

Response-offer coupons are issued following a request by a consumer. Requests might come through a 1-800 number, the Internet, social media, or mail. Coupons are then mailed to the consumer or sent by Internet to be printed by the consumer. Office supply companies and other vendors use response-offer coupons to invite business customers to make purchases or place orders. Firms also distribute coupons through their sales representatives, allowing for instant redemptions because the salesperson also takes the order.

14-3b Premiums

Premiums A promotional tactic of offering consumers some type of free merchandise for purchasing the product.

Premiums offer consumers some type of free merchandise for purchasing the product. Cereal manufacturers have used prizes such as puzzles, games, and toys for years to entice consumers to purchase their brand of cereal. Banks have offered gifts, such as personal organizers, to small businesses that open an account with them. Premiums offer a major benefit not possible with coupons—customers pay full price for the product. If the premium is picked carefully, the premium can actually enhance a brand's equity. Unfortunately, premiums tend to be used by regular customers, rather than new customers. Premiums are not as effective as coupons in encouraging trial purchases.

If a firm wants to reward customers for their loyalty, offering premiums is one way of accomplishing this goal. Premiums can also be used to encourage customers to stock up, which would make promotional offers from competitors less attractive. If a tanning salon offers consumers two free tans with the purchase of ten tanning sessions, it accomplishes two major goals. First, it gets full price for the ten sessions. Second, it encourages current customers to stay with the salon rather than switch to another firm offering a coupon.

To be effective, premiums must be attractive to the customer. If a free gift is offered, the gift must be an item that is desirable and that reinforces the firm's IMC effort. A firm that is marketing upscale products may want to offer a personalized gift, such as an attaché case with the customer's name inscribed on it, as the premium. Such a strategy would be appropriate for a private golf course soliciting new members. Sometimes, premiums are used with another type of promotion, such as a coupon. Using two or more promotions in a single offer is called an **overlay**.

Source: DeiMosz/Shutterstock

14-3c Contests and Sweepstakes

Both contests and sweepstakes offer participants an opportunity to win prizes. The difference between contests and sweepstakes is what a participant must do to win. In a contest, participants may be required to perform an activity or to make a purchase to be eligible to win. In a sweepstakes, participants do not need to make a purchase, and the winners are determined by a random drawing in which every entrant has an equal chance of being selected.

Overlay Using two or more promotions in a single offer.

While coupons appeal to price-conscious consumers, contests and sweepstakes appeal to individuals who enjoy excitement and stimulation. Price-conscious consumers may not participate in contests and sweepstakes because they see the contests or sweepstakes as increasing the cost of the service. To increase the effectiveness of a sweepstakes or contest, firms should emphasize the fun, fantasy, and stimulation aspect. Consumers enter contests and sweepstakes for the experience as well as the hope of winning.

Contests should be structured to provide participants with a challenge as well as excitement. It can be producing a video ad for the brand, a creative recipe using a particular brand's product, or a photography contest at a local art gallery. Most contests are posted online and shared on social media. Here are a couple of examples of contests that ran on Instagram: Domino's Pizza ran a Super Fan contest: contestants did not just have to prove that they were fans, but Super Fans, for a cash reward of $10,000. In another example, Valdo Prosecco offered a trip to Italy. All contestants had to do was to take a photo of a cocktail they made with the prosecco, and share their secret recipe as a caption with a hashtag.[8]

For sweepstakes, consumers are not asked to perform some task. They simply enter and the winners are drawn randomly. Some states allow companies to restrict to one entry per day. In other states you can enter as many times as you wish. Companies cannot require a person to make a purchase to enter a sweepstakes.

Both contests and sweepstakes are effective means for building customer traffic or generating interest in a firm's products. Retailers use them at a grand opening or at other special events to encourage consumers to visit the store. Manufacturers use them to encourage consumers to purchase their products.

14-3d Bonus Packs

Bonus packs Sales promotion that offers customers some type of discount for purchasing multiple items.

Tie-ins Sales promotion of two or more goods or services within the same promotional offer.

Intra-company tie-in A sales promotion involving two or more distinct products within the same company.

Intercompany tie-in A sales promotion involving two different companies offering complementary products.

Bonus packs are additional merchandise offered at the same price or slightly higher price. It may be four bars of soap packaged together and sold for the price of three individual packages. Two containers of potato chips may be packaged together and sold for 50% more than the price of one container. Or a package of Clinique lipsticks, lip pencils, and eye pencils may be sold for less than what it would cost to buy each item individually. The manufacturer's objective in developing a bonus pack is to entice consumers to switch to its brand from a competing brand or to entice current consumers to stock up so a competing brand's promotion is not attractive.

Research found that bonus packs have a greater impact on offline impulse buying than price discounts. They are also a more effective sales promotion than price discounts for expensive products.[9]

14-3e Tie-ins

Promotional **tie-ins** include two or more goods or services within the same promotional offer. The tie-ins can be either intra-company or intercompany. An **intra-company tie-in** involves two or more distinct products within the same company. For example, Mondelēz, with brands such as Nabisco, Ritz, Oreos, and Newtons, could place a 20 percent discount coupon for Oreos on one of its Nabisco products. An **intercompany tie-in** involves two different companies offering complementary products. The St. Louis Cardinals baseball team could provide a 50 percent off coupon to the nearby Gateway Arch with the purchase of an adult ticket to a Cardinals game.

Source: Frank Romeo/Shutterstock

Tie-ins can be an excellent means of stimulating demand for a particular product. It works best if consumers are offered some type of promotional incentive for a high-demand item if the low-demand item is purchased. Another approach is to offer a combination ticket in which the consumer gets two products for a reduced price. For example, tourists can save $30 with a combination ticket that allows them into both Busch Gardens and Adventure Island.

14-3f Frequency Programs

Most sales promotion programs are of short duration and focus on boosting sales immediately, brand switching, or repeat purchase behavior. Few focus on developing brand loyalty and enhancing brand equity, which is the goal of frequency programs. **Frequency programs**, also called loyalty programs, are sales promotions aimed at current customers, designed to build repeat purchase behavior and brand loyalty by rewarding customers for their patronage. Frequency programs have the following advantages, identified in **Figure 14-5**.[10]

Frequency programs Sales promotions offered to current customers and designed to build repeat purchase behavior.

The first frequency program is the American Airlines' frequent-flier program, launched in 1981. Other airlines quickly countered with their versions so as not to be at a competitive disadvantage. At first, the idea seemed great. Airlines gave away free seats. Minimal additional costs were accrued because the seats they gave away would have been empty anyway. The frequent-flier programs turned out to be more popular than expected. In 2019, American Airlines recorded $5.6 billion in loyalty and related revenues, Delta Airlines recorded $9.1 billion in revenues, and United Airlines, $5.3 billion in revenues, contributing to 19% of profits for Delta, and 10% at United Airlines. These numbers do not even take into account the indirect benefits from loyal travelers going out of their way to fly their preferred airline. It is, however, not impossible to consider that airlines, post-pandemic, might declare bankruptcy, in which case, airline miles may disappear with no value returned to consumers.[11]

Source: motive56/Shutterstock

More than 90% of companies have some sort of loyalty program, and, in the United States, there are 3.3 billion loyalty memberships. The average consumer belongs to 14.8 loyalty programs, but is active in just 6.7 of them. Most loyalty program members (84%) have made a redemption from a program.[12]

Frequency programs....

- Increase customer loyalty
- Increase customer lifetime value
- Increase customer retention
- Make customer feel emotionally connected to the firm
- Make it easier for firm to get in touch with client

FIGURE 14-5 Advantages of Frequency Programs

FIGURE 14-6 Starbucks Employee Distributes Free Frappuccino Samples at the Opening of a New Store
Source: rblfmr/Shutterstock

14-3g Sampling

Sampling Sales promotions that include the free delivery of an actual product or portion of a product.

Sampling is used primarily by food and beverage manufacturers but can also be used by almost any type of good or service. An attorney can use sampling by offering a free initial consultation. A fitness center can offer a trial membership for a week. A business-to-business firm could offer the use of a new machine for 30 days or samples of its products. The goal of sampling is to encourage consumers or businesses to try a new product. Sampling is expensive, but it is an effective promotional tool: consumers reduce purchase risk by trying new products. Often, coupons or other consumer promotions are tied with sampling in an overlay to further increase the probability that a purchase is made.

Important events, such as new store openings **(see Figure 14-6)** and holiday promotions are occasions for firms to offer free samples to generate sales. Just before Thanksgiving, Sam's Club usually hosts its annual Holiday Taste of Sam's Club. It was an all-day sampling promotion. Visitors to Sam's could sample holiday dishes, such as citrus grilled pork loin, rosemary and garlic racks of lamb, prime rib, and the traditional turkey and dressing.

After the onset of the COVID-19 pandemic, food sampling practically disappeared, with the Fresh Market no longer offering coffee samples, Costco abruptly ending its abundant sampling, and everyone else following suit. However, sampling gradually came back to delight consumers' senses, placing food in individual serving cups with lids, or individual bags to ensure safety.

14-3h Price-offs

Price-offs A reduction in the listed retail price of a product.

Price-offs involve a reduction in the listed retail price of a product. Price-offs are used to attract consumers, to reduce purchase risk, and to stimulate demand. Price-offs have the greatest impact on price-sensitive consumers and, unfortunately, also with current customers who would usually be willing to pay full price. From a firm's perspective, price-offs are an excellent tool for boosting sales because the impact is almost instantaneous. The disadvantage is that, if used too frequently, customers come to expect the reduced price and are not willing to pay full price for the product.

Retailers use price reductions to attract shoppers into the store and to encourage them to make specific purchases. In addition to purchasing the item on sale, retailers hope shoppers will purchase other merchandise. Price-offs are common during Thanksgiving. Supermarkets often reduce the price of turkeys, sometimes below cost, in the hope that the shopper will purchase other items. In some cases, the price reduction is used to remain competitive and to meet the prices of a competitor. It is also used to discourage customers from taking advantage of a promotion by a competitor. For example, if a particular brand of cookies launches a promotional campaign that includes a sweepstakes and coupons, a competitor may use a price-off strategy to discourage consumers from switching brands.

Source: Corepics VOF/Shutterstock

14-3i Refunds and Rebates

Rather than use coupons to reduce the price of products, firms can use a rebate or refund. Rebates and refunds are cash reimbursements paid to consumers with some type of proof of purchase. Technically, a **rebate** refers to reimbursements for a durable good, whereas a **refund** refers to reimbursements for a soft good or service. However, the words are often used interchangeably today.

Rebates Reimbursements for a durable good.

Refunds Reimbursements for a soft good or service.

The primary objective of offering a refund or rebate is to reward individuals for the purchase of a product. Because the process involves mailing in proof-of-purchase documentation and waiting four to six weeks for the reimbursement, refunds and rebates are not as effective in stimulating a purchase. The exception, however, is in the automotive industry, where consumers expect to get a rebate.

According to J.D. Powers and Associates, buyers expect to receive discounts on new cars. In an example, current Mazda owners can take advantage of a $1,500 loyalty rebate when buying or leasing a new Mazda.[13]

Computer and electronic manufacturers often use rebates to stimulate sales. For instance, Samsung often offers rebates of a few hundred dollars for its big-screen televisions.

14-3j Product Placement

Product placement involves the placement of branded products in movies and television shows. Because of advertising clutter and the fact that many viewers tune out commercials, companies use product placement as a subtle way of advertising. People pay attention to their favorite TV shows and movies, thus, by integrating products, brands can capture attention without distracting viewers from their program. Viewers cannot fast forward their DVR to block product placements; they are the most organic and influential approach to reaching customers. The audience will watch Will Smith riding a Super73 Electric Motorbike or Christina Applegate drinking Empathy wine, and subconsciously has more trust for those brands and will likely purchase them. Coca-Cola has placed its products, logos, and merchandise on the big screen for more than 70 years, from 1946's *It's a Wonderful Life* to 2019's *Stranger Things*.[14]

Product placement Sales promotion technique of placing branded goods or services in movies, on television shows, or in theatrical performances.

Another version of product placement is **branded media**, which is a movie or show that contains a brand name or logo with a story line that intersects the brand's mission or current advertising campaign. The

Branded media A movie or show that contains a brand name or logo with a story line that intersects the brand's mission or current advertising campaign.

Toyota Prius was a central part of the TV show The New Adventures of Old Christine and the environmentally conscious character she played on the show. The Prius automobile was involved in a number of the show's plots and was even featured in a duel with a gas-guzzling Hummer. Similarly, the Toyota Prius was prominently featured in the Larry David show, Curb Your Enthusiasm; in fact, Larry David gave away, with great fanfare, a Prius hybrid used in the show for a charity event. The value of such exposure is difficult for advertisers to measure, but it certainly is effective. For both branded media and product placement, the goal is to get the branded product before the audience in such a way that it is credible and does not appear to be a commercial.[15]

14-4 In-Store Promotions

Although shoppers often compile lists, written or mental, more than two-thirds of purchase decisions are made while in a retail store, and most shoppers walk out with twice the number of products they had planned on purchasing. That means packaging, pricing, point-of-purchase displays, and in-store promotions, such as sampling and coupons, are critically important in swaying consumers to purchase a particular brand. Advertising and sales promotions may get consumers to a retail store, but once in the store, shoppers add items to their shopping lists and could switch brands because of a shelf display (often with a price comparison), a point-of-purchase display, or a product package.

Point-of-purchase displays are an excellent means of reaching consumers. They draw attention to the brand. They inform customers about the benefits of the brand, encouraging them to pick up the product on the spot. They are used, in conjunction with other information, to further build the brand in the mind of the consumer. With a consistent message and imagery, they help create marketing cohesion, to create a consistent message for the product in the mind of the consumer.[16]

With so many purchase decisions made in the store, packaging becomes a critical piece of communication as well and is the last opportunity to convince a shopper to purchase a particular brand. Packaging is tactile, intimate, and provides a tangible experience for consumers, showcasing the brand and its unique identity. A study conducted by the marketing research agency IPSOS and the Paper and Packaging Board found that 72% of consumers agree that packaging design influences their purchase decision—67% are influenced by the packaging material, 63% were more likely to buy products packaged in paper or cardboard because they could reuse the packaging, and 63% believe

Source: Christian Mueller/Shutterstock

that paper and cardboard packaging makes a product seem premium or high quality, making the product look more artisanal or handcrafted.[17]

Although packaging must attract attention, it also must protect the product and make it easy for retailers to stock. Odd-shaped packages may be attractive, but they create difficulties for retailers to place on shelves. It is also important to make sure the packaging stays fresh. Although it is important to maintain some consistency so that shoppers can quickly recognize a brand, it is also important to change aspects of the package over time so that it will generate new interest. Just as ads can wear out over time, so can packaging design.

14-5 Trade Promotions

Trade promotions are the expenditures or incentives used by manufacturers and other members of the marketing channel to help push their products through the channel. Trade promotions can be targeted toward retailers, distributors, wholesalers, brokers, or agents. The primary objective of trade promotions is to build relationships with other members of the marketing channel and to encourage them to sell the firm's products. When a retailer stocks a manufacturer's merchandise, consumers have the opportunity to buy the product. The same is true for distributors, wholesalers, brokers, or agents. It is a two-step process. The first step is convincing the channel member to stock the product; the second is to convince the channel member to push the product.

14-5a Goals of Trade Promotions

For manufacturers, the overarching goal of trade promotions is to increase sales of their brand. Figure 14-7 identifies additional goals that trade promotions can accomplish for manufacturers.[18]

Stimulate initial distribution
Obtain prime retail shelf space
Support established brands
Counter competitive actions
Increase order size
Build retail inventories
Reduce excess inventory of manufacturers
Enhance channel relationships
Support the IMC program

FIGURE 14-7 Trade Promotion Goals of Manufacturers

Retailers, however, seek to increase the market share of their stores and to boost sales of a product category. Retailers are less concerned with which brand sells the most as long as the product line sells. They will promote the brand that is demanded by their customers and that contributes the most to the retailer's gross profit. For example, it does not matter to the retailer which brand of athletic shoes sells as long as the retailer can sell the shoes to customers, and they do not go to a competitor. To accomplish this, retailers will play one manufacturer against another to see which one will offer the best trade promotion and thus put them in a better situation to sell the merchandise to their customers.

Manufacturers such as Cuisinart must use trade promotions to ensure that their products are in retail stores and are pushed through the distribution channel by the various channel members. When a company introduces a new product, enters a new territory, or uses a new channel outlet, trade promotions are needed to push that product through the channel. Without incentives, channel members are reluctant to add a new product. The same is true for obtaining prime locations and shelf space inside a retail store. A typical discount store, for instance, sells more than 40,000 products. Not all can have the best shelf locations. In choosing how to display products and brands, retailers work to maximize their revenue and profits. For a manufacturer to obtain prime space or even more space than it already has normally requires some trade promotion incentives. This is even true for established brands. When a competitor offers a retail chain a trade incentive for extra shelf space, a manufacturer may have to match the competitor's offer just to maintain its current space. If one manufacturer offers a discount on its brand and that brand sells as well as the competitor, then it makes sense for the retailer to offer more space to the discounted brand because the retailer will make more money.

Trade promotions are used to increase order sizes, to build retail inventories, and to reduce a manufacturer's excess inventory. By offering special trade deals, retailers or other channel members can be enticed to increase the size of their order. This serves two purposes. First, it encourages retailers to push the manufacturer's brand because they have a high inventory, and because of the trade incentive, they will probably earn more per item. Second, because of the higher retail inventory, it will reduce the amount of the product category retailers will order from the manufacturer's competitors.

Source: Shuang Li/Shutterstock

Theoretically, trade promotions should enhance relationships with channel members and enhance the firm's IMC program. In reality, neither tends to happen. Retailers and other channel members tend to go with the vendor that offers the best trade promotions, and manufacturers and other channel members tend to use trade promotions to boost sales and prevent competitors from stealing market share, rather than use strategies related to a broader IMC effort. Much like sales promotions, trade promotions normally produce faster and more dramatic results. If sales are down, a trade promotion is often used to get back to the target level. If a competitor is encroaching on a firm's market share, trade promotion is used to counter the competitor's actions and to persuade channel members to stay loyal.

14-5b Types of Trade Promotions

Companies can use a variety of trade promotions, shown in **Figure 14-8**.[19] Choosing the correct trade promotion is an important decision. Each has its own set of advantages and disadvantages. The more a firm ties its trade promotion strategy to its IMC effort, the greater will be the impact of trade promotions, and, in the long run, the less the firm will have to spend on trade promotions. Rather than use trade promotions as a reactive tool, if planned as part of the IMC, trade promotions can become a proactive method of pushing products through the channel.

Trade allowances Some type of financial incentive to channel members to motivate them to make a purchase.

Trade Allowances **Trade allowances** offer some type of financial incentive to channel members to motivate them to make a purchase. The most common trade allowances are off-invoice allowances and slotting fees **(see Figure 14-9)**. An off-invoice allowance is a financial discount or price-off on each pallet, case, or item ordered. These types of trade allowances are common during holidays and promotional seasons and are used to encourage retailers to purchase large quantities. For example, a manufacturer might offer a ten percent discount on fall apparel orders that are received by May 1. In addition to a specified date, manufacturers might also place a minimum order size as a further condition. Off-invoice allowances are also used to encourage retailers to stock up on a particular brand and to meet a competitor's marketing actions. From the manufacturer's viewpoint, the problems with trade allowances are (1) channel members failing to pass along allowances to consumers and (2) forward buying.

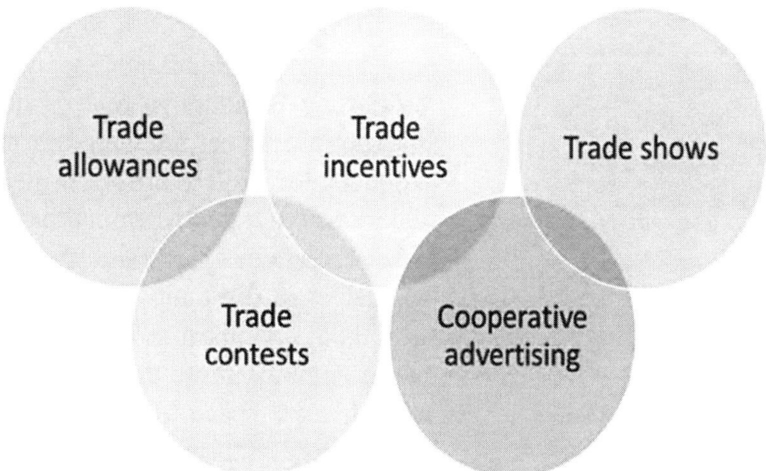

FIGURE 14-8 Types of Trade Promotions

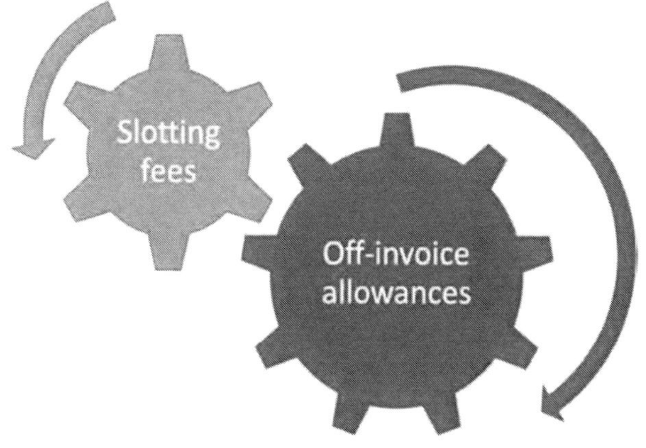

FIGURE 14-9 Types of Trade Allowances

When manufacturers provide a trade allowance to a retailer, they would like to see that price reduction passed on to consumers so it will stimulate sales of their brand. However, retailers often do not pass the savings on to the consumer, charging consumers the same price and pocketing the allowance. One tactic that retailers sometimes use to accomplish this is **forward buying**, which occurs when a retailer purchases excess inventory of a product while it is on-deal to be sold later when it is off-deal. During a "sale period," the savings will be passed on to the consumer, but when the sale is over, the retailer still has merchandise left that was purchased at a lower price, thus generating extra profits. The primary difficulty for the manufacturer is that new orders are then delayed because the retailer has excess inventory and does not need to buy for some time, creating an erratic production schedule for the manufacturer.[20]

Forward buying When a retailer purchases excess inventory of a product while it is on-deal to be sold later when it is off-deal.

Every year, approximately 30,000 new products are introduced, but only 30% of U.S. launches are capable of sustaining or growing their sales during their first two years.[21] Retailers must make a decision on which of these 30,000 items to stock before they know which ones will be successful and which will not. As a result, most retailers charge **slotting fees**, which are funds paid to retailers to stock new products. Retailers justify charging slotting fees because it costs them to add new products to their inventories and to stock the merchandise. If the product is not successful, the investment in initial inventory represents a loss, especially when the retailer has stocked a large number of stores. Also, adding a new product in the retail store means allocating shelf space to it. Because shelves are always filled with products, adding a new product means either getting rid of another brand or product or reducing the amount of shelf space allocated to other products. Regardless of which method is used, the retailer has both time and money invested when making the adjustment for the new product.

Slotting fees Fees that retailers charge to stock manufacturers' brands.

Supermarkets charge significant fees before retailers see their products on shelves. A discount fee to introduce a new ice cream might be as high as $30,000 to appear in just 350 stores. Manufacturers, thus, see slotting fees as tantamount to extortion. In addition, large companies can buy up enough store space to redesign the store's layout. Junk food manufacturers are taking over valuable store real estate, making it difficult for consumers to choose healthier options.[22]

But, because most retailers have low operating margins and markups, slotting fees provide additional funds to support retail operations. Retailers rely on slotting fees and other trade promotions as part of their net profits.

In online retailing, shelf space isn't limited, but attention is. At Amazon, you might have to go through several pages of products before deciding which one to place in your cart. Amazon helps consumers make their decision with its growing suite of ad offerings, which are designed to help brands attract

Source: TY Lim/Shutterstock

customers to their virtual shelf space; these ads are, in fact, a new type of slotting fee. Since over half of consumers first go to Amazon for product related searchers, brands are increasingly sponsoring Amazon ads, enhancing product pages with wide-screen video and interactive multimedia displays—some paying $500,000 per year to enhance all their product pages on Amazon.[23]

Trade Contests In a trade contest, rewards are given to brokers, retail salespeople or stores, wholesalers, agents, or other channel members for achieving a specific goal—the highest sales within a specified time period, or it can be for all channel members to reach a minimum target level. For example, a hardware manufacturer can run a contest among its distributors and offer a grand prize to the distributor with the highest sales, with second- and third-place prizes for runners up. An alternative strategy is to offer prizes to all distributors who reach a certain level, perhaps 100,000 cases or $500,000 in sales. With this latter approach, the prize level is set at a point that only a small number of distributors can reach.

Money or prizes awarded in trade contests are known as **spiff money**. The rewards can be cash or items such as luggage, a television, apparel, or a trip to attractive destinations. Contests can be held at any level of the distribution channel, but most are within an organization and not between rivals. The challenge at the retail level is that buyers in large organizations are often prohibited from participating because they create conflicts of interest and may unfairly influence buyers' decisions. Although the goal of the contest is to influence a buyer to purchase, the buying organization does not want someone making purchases for 2,000 stores based on the buyer winning some sales contest.

Spiff money Monies or prizes awarded in trade contests.

Four Seasons Produce ran a display contest in conjunction with small farmer grown Equal Exchange organic fair-trade avocados. The contest, known as Rock the Guac, took place among smaller retailers in Massachusetts, Connecticut, and upstate New York.[24]

Trade incentives Some type of financial incentive that involves the retailer performing some type of function to receive a trade allowance.

Cooperative merchandising agreement (CMA) A formal agreement between the retailer and manufacturer to undertake a cooperative marketing effort.

Trade Incentives **Trade incentives** are similar to trade allowances; however, instead of price discounts, they involve the retailer performing some type of function to receive the allowance. The most common trade incentive is the **cooperative merchandising agreement (CMA)**, which is a formal agreement between the retailer and manufacturer to undertake a cooperative marketing effort. The agreement may involve advertisements produced by the retailer that feature the manufacturer's brand, the retailer featuring the manufacturer's brand as a price leader in the store, or the retailer emphasizing the manufacturer's brand in the display window, point-of-purchase display, or special shelf display.

Source: Pawpixel.com/Shutterstock

From the manufacturer's viewpoint, the advantage of the CMA agreement over trade allowances is that the retailer agrees to perform some function in exchange for the price discount. With a CMA, the manufacturer knows that either all of the price discount or a specified portion will be passed on to consumers. Perhaps the most important benefit, however, is that it allows the manufacturer to incorporate the CMA into the firm's IMC effort. The CMA is not nearly as attractive to the retailer because some marketing function is tied to the discount. Retailers would rather just have the **off-invoice allowance**.

Off-invoice allowance A financial discount or price-off on each case that a member of the distribution channel orders.

Cooperative advertising program An arrangement whereby a manufacturer agrees to reimburse retailers or other channel members that feature the manufacturer's brands in the ad for a portion of their advertising costs.

Cooperative Advertising Programs Most manufacturers have some type of **cooperative advertising program**, in which the manufacturer agrees to reimburse retailers or other channel members for a portion of their advertising costs for featuring the manufacturer's brands in an advertisement. To receive the reimbursement, the retailer must follow specific guidelines concerning the placement of the ad and its content. In almost all cases, no competing brands can appear in the ad, and in most cases, the manufacturer's brand must be prominently featured.

One of the most well-known co-op advertising programs is by Intel Corporation. Almost everyone has seen the Intel symbol and logo in computer ads by various computer manufacturers. Intel offers financial incentives to PC makers placing Intel logos on their computers. It also partially covers advertisements that feature its "Intel Inside" logo. Intel pumped $4 billion into the cooperative program; as a result, the company's revenue has gone from $3 billion to nearly $30 billion, with nearly 90 percent of the more than 17,000 PC print ads run in the United States carrying the "Intel Inside" logo.[25]

As seen in the Intel example, co-op advertising programs benefit retailers because manufacturers pay a portion of the advertising costs. For most retailers, advertising national brands enhances the retailers' image and attracts customers to stores. Manufacturers benefit because they gain additional advertising exposure at a reduced cost. More important, almost all co-op advertising programs are tied to sales, which means advertising costs are directly related to retail sales. If retailers feature a manufacturer's brand in a store advertisement, they tend to encourage in-store clerks and salespeople to push that brand. So, the manufacturer not only benefits from the advertisement, but also from increased emphasis within the store.

Source: Tada Images/Shutterstock

Trade Shows In the business-to-business market, trade show expenditures are forecast to grow to $18.5 billion by 2023.[26] Although U.S. companies and attendees make few deals during trade shows, it is a different situation with international customers, who tend to be senior executives with the power to make purchase decisions, and who spend more time at each vendor's booth and gather more information. International attendees want to consummate deals, or at least arrange for purchases at the trade show.

Type of Trade Promotion	Definition
Off-invoice allowance	Financial discount (price-off)
Slotting fee	Monies paid to retailers by channel members to stock new products on retail shelves
Trade contest	Contest held among brokers, retail salespeople, retail stores, wholesalers, agents or other channel members
Cooperative merchandise agreement	Formal agreement between retailers and manufacturers to undertake a cooperative marketing effort
Cooperative advertising program	Agreement by manufacturers to reimburse retailers or other channel members a portion of the cost of advertising a manufacturer's brand
Trade show	Shows where buyers and sellers can meet to discuss and transact business

FIGURE 14-10 Forms of Trade Promotions

With disruptions attributed to the COVID-19 pandemic and travel restrictions and bans on large indoor gatherings, exhibitions turned to virtual spaces. Germany's Hannover Messe industrial technology trade show, organized "Digital Days" after canceling the in-person show. Japan's Ceatec consumer electronics fair and the Tokyo Game Show all moved online.

Trade promotions are critical elements of marketing, especially within the distribution channel. Figure 14-10 reviews all of the various forms of trade promotions.

Sponsorship marketing Marketing that involves a company paying a fee to an event, a person, or an organization in exchange for a direct association with that event, person, or organization.

14-6 Sponsorships

Sponsorship marketing involves a company paying a fee to an event, person, or organization in exchange for a direct association with that event, person, or organization. In North America, companies spend approximately billions of dollars on sponsorships ranging from an event like a Little League baseball tournament or a local fall festival to the naming rights of a professional sports arena. The COVID-19 pandemic presented the sponsorship industry with the most serious challenge, with sports and entertainment events and venues shut down indefinitely. Before the pandemic, sponsorships were expected to reach $26 billion (worldwide, over $63 billion), outpacing other forms of marketing in North America. However, the pandemic directly impacted at minimum 120,000 sponsorships and over 5,000 brands in the U.S. Instead, firms decided to switch their spending to social, digital, and branding integration.[27] Figure 14-11 provides a breakdown

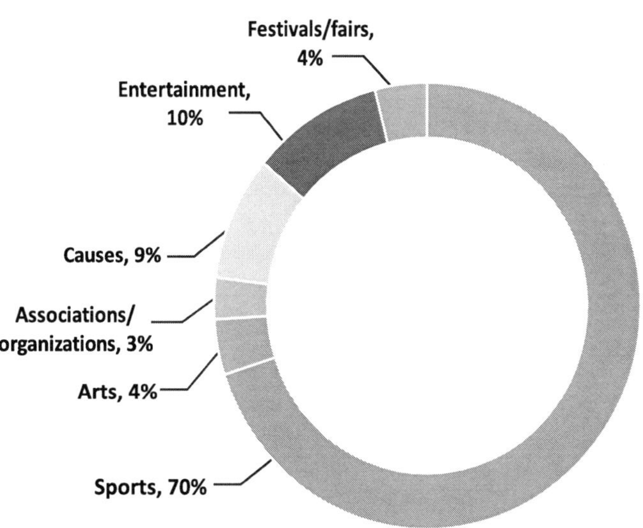

FIGURE 14-11 Breakdown of Sponsorship Spending in North America
Source: Sponsorship Spending Report, IEG, www.sponsorship.com, accessed November 19, 2017

Source: Grindstone Media Group/Shutterstock

of various types of sponsorships in North America. Notice sports constitute 70 percent of all sponsorships.[28]

In choosing a sponsorship, it is important to match the audience profile with the company's target market. A firm whose primary customers are females should examine opportunities to sponsor events that involve females, such as a female softball team, the WNBA, or a beauty pageant. It is also important to make sure the image of the event matches the image the company wants to project. A tuxedo or formal gown retailer sponsoring a dance or beauty pageant is a better fit than sponsoring a rodeo or wrestling tournament.

One of the most effective sports sponsorships has been NASCAR, which has grown from primarily beer, auto parts, and tobacco sponsors in the 1970s to include a wide range of consumer products, business-to-business products, and Internet brands today. NASCAR has a dedicated following that purchases products to support the sport. The NASCAR Cup Series, known as the Monster Energy NASCAR Cup Series, is the sport's premier series. It partnered with Busch Beer, Coca-Cola, Geico and Xfinity in 2020.[29]

Recently, companies have been paying big money for naming rights to ballparks and stadiums. **Figure 14-12** lists a few of the sports stadiums with the average annual cost.

As with the other marketing tools, sponsorships should be integrated with the firm's advertising and IMC plan. The public should easily recognize the link between the person, group, or organization being sponsored and the company involved. It is also important to maximize the sponsorship through advertising, trade and consumer promotions, and public

Stadium Name	Home Teams	Average Yearly Costs
Scotiabank Arena	Toronto Maple Leafs, Raptors	$31.95 million
MetLife Stadium	New York Giants, Jets	$17 million–$25 million
Chase Center	Golden State Warriors	$12 million–$16 million
Citi Field	New York Mets	$20 million
Mercedes-Benz Stadium	Atlanta Falcon, United FC	$12 million
NRG Stadium	Houston Texans	$9.69 million
Suntrust (Truist) Park	Atlanta Braves	$10 million
Hard Rock Stadium	Miami Dolphins	$10 million

FIGURE 14-12 Annual Costs for Naming Rights of Select Sports Stadiums
Source: https://www.sportsbusinessdaily.com/Journal/Issues/2018/04/30/Marketing-and-Sponsorship/Naming-rights-deals.aspx, accessed March 14, 2020

relations. Unless a sponsorship is surrounded by some kind of supporting marketing effort, the sponsorship may not be effective at accomplishing the firm's IMC objectives.

14-7 Public Relations

Public relations are company efforts to develop a strong relationship with its different publics with the goal of creating a positive company image and favorable publicity. The public relations department is responsible for overseeing publicity and communications with groups such as employees, stockholders, public interest groups, the government, and society as a whole. It is important that the PR department work closely with the marketing department and be involved in the company's IMC effort to ensure that every piece of communication produced by the company speaks with one voice. The key functions of the public relations department include:

Public relations Company efforts to develop a strong relationship with its different publics with the goal of creating a positive company image and favorable publicity.

- Monitoring internal and external publics
- Providing information to each public that reinforces the firm's IMC effort
- Promoting sponsorships, event-marketing efforts, cause-related marketing efforts and other image-building activities
- Reacting to any news or emergencies that have an impact on the firm and the IMC effort being conducted

Often, major PR efforts of a firm are handled by an external PR firm for the same reasons that a firm hires an external advertising agency. In some cases, the advertising agency handles the PR function, but usually a separate firm is hired. Because the work of the PR firm is different, it is important that the PR firm understand the IMC effort of the client and how it fits into the picture. Special events, activities, and news releases produced by the PR firm must strengthen the firm's IMC effort.

PR departments monitor various internal and external constituencies, or stakeholders. One of the most important, and most difficult, tasks is the handling of negative publicity. A positive image that has taken years to build can be destroyed overnight. It is the PR department's responsibility to ensure that this does not happen. Crisis management and other techniques are used to help a firm cope with any circumstances that threaten the firm's image, regardless of the cause.

Source: Garagestock/Shutterstock

A crisis might be an opportunity to improve the firm's position and image, if handled properly. For example, PepsiCo encountered some negative publicity about hypodermic needles being found in its products. The management team was quick to respond with photographs and video that demonstrated how bottles and cans are turned upside down while empty before they are filled with any soft drink and how it would have been impossible to put a needle into a soft drink. Pepsi's quick and positive response eliminated negative publicity and at the same time demonstrated to consumers the safety of its products. Unfortunately, not all crises result in positive outcomes. The Takata airbag safety recall, the largest and most complex recall in U.S. history, affected millions of vehicles from 19 vehicle manufacturers and more than 200 models and model years. At least 16 Americans have been killed, and more than 300 individuals have suffered serious injuries allegedly caused by these defective airbags. Not all automobiles were brought in after the recalls, including many Hondas, Acuras, Ford Ranger trucks and Mazda B-Series trucks which are considered higher risk. Automobiles of Fiat Chrysler, General Motors, and Mitsubishi are among those affected in this long-term public relations crisis.[30]

Crisis management involves either accepting the blame for an event and offering an apology, or refuting those making the charges in a tactful manner. Pepsi used the latter strategy. The public accepted Pepsi's explanation because it was supported by hard evidence. Takata accepted the blame, but, due to repeated recalls and the widespread nature of the crisis, the company has lost customers' trust, which negatively affected the automobile manufacturers as well.

Summary

1. **Discuss the reasons for a shift in marketing expenditures to promotions.**
   First, promotions normally have an immediate impact on sales, whereas advertising takes a longer period of time to produce an impact. Second, because of increased brand proliferation and brand parity, consumers and businesses have more choices today and see little difference among firms and among various brands. Third, there is consumer acceptance of promotions, and in some instances, there is a demand for special deals before purchases will be made. Fourth, there is a decline in the impact of advertising. With remote controls and digital video recorders, consumers are zapping out many commercials, and those they do watch, view, or hear are quickly forgotten as a result of the high number of commercials they are exposed to each day.

2. **Describe the various forms of consumer promotions.**
   Firms can use 10 different types of consumer promotions. They include coupons, premiums, contests and sweepstakes, bonus packs, frequency programs, sampling, price-offs, refunds and rebates, and product placement. Coupons offer some type of price reduction and can be instant redemption coupons, bounce-back coupons, scanner-delivered coupons, cross-ruffing coupons, and response-offer coupons. Premiums offer a free gift or a price reduction on additional merchandise, but the consumer pays full price for the initial item. Contests and sweepstakes can be used to increase interest in a brand or company. Sampling is the best method for trying to get consumers to try a product. Bonus packs offer consumers additional product at a lower

price than if purchased separately. Frequency programs involve rewarding individuals for their regular patronage. A price-off is a reduction in the price of an item, and is the best at enhancing an immediate sales boost. Refunds and rebates are cash reimbursements from the manufacturer for a purchase. Product placement is the placement of a brand in a movie, television show, or other type of entertainment.

3. **Explain the importance of in-store promotions in purchasing behavior.**
   Shoppers make approximately two-thirds of all brand purchase decisions while in a retail store, and most shoppers walk out with twice the number of products they had planned on purchasing. This means that packaging, pricing, point-of-purchase displays, and in-store promotions, such as sampling and coupons, are critically important in swaying consumers to purchase a particular brand.

4. **Discuss the goals of trade promotions.**
   For manufacturers, the overarching goal of trade promotions is to increase sales of their brand. Retailers, however, seek to increase the market share of their stores and to boost sales of a product category. Retailers are less concerned with which brand sells the most as long as the product line sells. More specific goals of trade promotions include (1) stimulating initial distribution, (2) obtaining prime retail locations or shelf space, (3) supporting established brands, (4) countering competitive actions, (5) increasing order size, (6) building retail inventories, (7) reducing excess inventories of the manufacturer, (8) enhancing channel relationships, and (9) enhancing the IMC program.

5. **Explain the various types of trade promotions.**
   Companies have a variety of trade promotions that can be used, such as (1) trade allowances, (2) trade contests, (3) trade incentives, (4) cooperative advertising programs, and (5) trade shows. Choosing the correct trade promotion is an important decision. The more a firm ties its trade promotion strategy to its IMC effort, the greater will be the impact of trade promotions, and in the long run, the less the firm will have to spend on trade promotions. Rather than use trade promotions as a reactive tool, if planned as part of the IMC, they can become a proactive method of pushing products through the channel.

6. **Describe the current use of sponsorships.**
   Sponsorship marketing involves a company paying a fee to an event, person, or organization in exchange for a direct association with that event, person, or organization. Sponsorships range from an event like a Little League baseball tournament or a local fall festival to the naming rights to a professional sports arena. Most sponsorships are in the area of sports. Recently, companies have paid big money for naming rights to ballparks and stadiums. Beyond sports, some organizations sponsor cultural events, such as classical music groups, jazz bands, visual art exhibits, dance troupes, and theater performances.

7. **Identify the role of public relations in integrated marketing communications (IMC).**
   The PR department is responsible for overseeing publicity and communications with groups such as employees, stockholders, public interest groups, the government, and society as a whole. It is important that the public relations department work closely with the marketing department and be involved in the company's IMC effort to ensure that every piece of communication produced by the company speaks with one voice. The key functions of the PR department include: (1) monitoring internal and external publics; (2) providing information to each public that reinforces the firm's IMC effort; (3) promoting sponsorships, event marketing efforts, cause-related marketing efforts, and other image-building activities; and (4) reacting to any news or emergencies that affect the firm and IMC effort being conducted.

Key Terms

Bonus packs (422)
Bounce-back coupons (420)
Branded media (425)
Cooperative advertising program (432)
Cooperative merchandising agreement (CMA) (431)
Coupons (418)
Cross-ruffing coupon (420)
Forward buying (430)
Freestanding inserts (FSI) (419)
Frequency programs (423)
Instant redemption coupon (419)
Intercompany tie-in (422)
Intra-company tie-in (422)
Off-invoice allowance (432)
Overlay (421)
Premiums (420)
Price-offs (424)
Product placement (425)
Public relations (435)
Rebates (425)
Refunds (425)
Response-offer coupons (420)
Sampling (424)
Scanner-delivered coupons (420)
Slotting fees (430)
Spiff money (431)
Sponsorship marketing (433)
Tie-ins (422)
Trade allowances (429)
Trade incentives (431)

Discussion Questions

1. Have you had any personal experiences with promotions offered at spring break? What is your evaluation of the promotions that you have experienced personally?
2. Go to the Internet and access three different resorts or vacation destinations for spring break. Discuss the promotions that each offers. Create a screenshot of the promotional offer into your document that you submit along with the URL of each website.
3. From the list of consumer promotions provided in Section 14-3, discuss each consumer promotion as it relates to your personal purchase behavior. Discuss things such as frequency of use, your attitude toward each, how these promotions affect your purchase behavior, and what types of design have an impact on you.
4. Pick one of the consumer promotions identified in Section 14-3 that interests you. Use the Internet and an article database to locate more information about it. Write a summary of what you learn. How are companies using the promotion and what are the most successful strategies?
5. Pick one of the following types of products. Discuss how each of the consumer promotions presented in Section 14-3 could be used. Which ones would be most effective? Which ones would be least effective? Why?
   a. pizza
   b. shoes
   c. dental services
   d. video game
6. List all of the loyalty or frequency programs that you participate in or have a card for. Which ones influence your purchase decisions? Why? Discuss why you joined each one. What frequency or loyalty programs are you a member of, but do not use? Discuss why.
7. What is your opinion of product placements? Do they impact your purchase decisions? Why or why not? Do they have an effect on your image of the brands? Why or why not? Identify at least four product placements you have seen on television or in a movie. How effective do you think each product placement is? Provide support for your answer.

8. The next time you are in a store, make a note of all of the promotions you see, especially point-of-purchase displays. Write a short report detailing the information. What promotions were the most effective? Why? Which promotions were not effective? Why?
9. In Section 14-4, it was stated that two-thirds of all product and brand purchases made in retail stores are not planned. What is your evaluation of this statistic? Talk to at least five other people about how closely they follow a shopping list and how many things they purchase that were not planned.
10. What are your thoughts about sponsorships? Are they effective? Why or why not?
11. A new trend for universities and colleges is naming buildings and sports facilities after brands, that is, accepting naming rights from companies. Do you think this is right? Why or why not? Should public universities accept private money from companies in exchange for naming rights? Justify your answer.

Review Questions

True or False

1. About 89 percent of all coupons are distributed via FSI.
2. Coupons placed inside packages so that customers cannot redeem them at the time of the original purchase are called cross-ruffing coupons.
3. Response-offer coupons are issued following a request by a consumer.
4. The fastest growing method of coupon distribution is digital coupons.
5. The difference between contests and sweepstakes is that, in sweepstakes, participants may be required to perform an activity or to make a purchase to be eligible to win, whereas in a contest, participants do not need to make a purchase and the winners are determined by a random drawing in which every entrant has an equal chance of being selected.
6. Four bars of soap may be packaged together and sold for the price of three individual packages in a bonus pack.
7. An example of an intra-company tie-in would be the St. Louis Cardinals baseball team providing a $10 off coupon to the nearby Gateway Arch with the purchase of an adult ticket to a Cardinals' baseball game.
8. Frequency programs are consumer promotions aimed at current customers that are designed to build repeat purchase behavior and brand loyalty by rewarding customers for their patronage.
9. Sponsorship marketing involves a company paying a fee to an event, person, or organization in exchange for a direct association with the event, person, or organization.

Multiple Choice

10. A reduction in the listed retail price of a product used to attract consumers, to reduce purchase risk, and to stimulate demand is known as a
    a. rebate.
    b. price-off.
    c. promotional tie-in.
    d. none of the above.
11. A movie or show that contains a brand name or logo with a story line that intersects the brand's mission or current advertising campaign is known as
    a. trailer media.
    b. market media.
    c. cooperative media.
    d. branded media.
12. Expenditures or incentives used by manufacturers and other members of the marketing channel to help push their products through the channel are known as
    a. market promotions.
    b. rebate promotions.
    c. cooperative promotions.
    d. trade promotions.

Answers: (1) T, (2) F, (3) T, (4) T, (5) F, (6) T, (7) F, (8) T, (9) T, (10) b, (11) d, (12) d

Case: Ace Air Conditioning & Heating

Alfred (Ace) Jacobs founded Ace Air Conditioning & Heating as a family business in 2004. He worked part-time repairing air conditioners and heating systems for the first five years until he was able to generate enough revenue to quit his job and devote full-time to the small business. Ace Air Conditioning & Heating now generates $1.5 million a year in gross income and employs four service technicians, a full-time secretary, and a part-time bookkeeper.

Ace started his business repairing only residential systems. Then, in 2010, after working on a large air conditioning system for a local business, he decided to offer his services to business customers as well.

The last component of his business was added in 2015, when a local contractor asked Ace to install furnaces and air conditioners in some new homes they were building. Ace found the work easier because the house was not yet completed. He did not have to crawl under structures or go into attics to locate vents and other components that needed repairing. He also found that the new construction was the most profitable. The contribution margins were higher, and the amount of time it took his employees to do the work was less.

Sitting down with his bookkeeper, Ace got a better picture of what he is currently facing. Increased competition in the area has cost him two large business clients and some residential customers he serviced in the past. This has resulted in 12 percent decline in revenues for this past year. The bookkeeper also provided him facts concerning the breakdown of his business in the three areas of residential, business, and new-construction customers, the average margins on each job, and the percentage of gross income each generates.

Source: Carolyn Franks/Shutterstock

Based on the information provided in **Figure 14-13**, Ace realizes that most of his income comes from business customers, yet residential customers make up almost two-thirds of his customers. In addition, the smallest component of his business is new construction, yet it generates the highest gross margins.

Because the level of competition has increased, Ace realizes he may need to use consumer promotions to entice new customers to use his services. He also wonders if he needs to use promotions to in some way reward his current customers and to keep them from switching to a competitor. Lastly, he wonders: Can he use promotions to encourage some customers who are now using one of his competitors to switch to his company?

Case Questions

1. From the information given, which group or groups of customers should Ace Air Conditioning & Heating pursue?

Type of Customer	Gross Revenue ($)	Gross Margin (%)	Percent of Total Customers (%)
Business	675,798	40	27
Residential	407,420	29	62
New construction	433,325	48	11

FIGURE 14-13 Breakdown of Revenue Sources for Ace Air Conditioning & Heating

2. What consumer promotions can he use to attract residential customers? Would the promotions be different for current customers versus new customers? Explain.
3. Should he use consumer promotions for his business customers and the new construction customers? Why or why not? If he should, which should he use?
4. Various manufacturers of heating and air conditions systems, such as Lennox, have approached Ace about cooperative advertising. They have offered to pay 50 to 70 percent of the cost of local advertising in exchange for him using their brand in the homes and businesses that he services? What are the pros and cons of such an arrangement?
5. Every year there is a home and garden show at the civic center in town. About 45,000 local home owners and businesspeople attend. There are usually about 200 exhibitors. The cost for a booth, materials and supplies would be $6,000. Should Ace participate in the show? What are the benefits? What are the disadvantages?

Endnotes

1. AdAge, "Branded face masks hit the market," April 30, 2020, https://adage.com/article/cmo-strategy/branded-face-masks-hit-market/2253366; Jena McGregor, "The new corporate swag: Branded masks, sanitizer spray bottles, and Zoom vanity light rings," June 30, 2020, www.washingtonpost.com/business/2020/06/30/new-corporate-swag-branded-masks-sanitizer-spray-bottles-zoom-vanity-light-rings
2. 2020 Marketing Spending Industry Study, Cadent Consulting Group, https://cadentcg.com/publication/2020-marketing-spending-industry-study
3. Joshua Kennedy, "8 benefits of sales promotion," Mando UK, January 3, 2015, https://www.mando.co.uk/8-creations-of-sales-promotions, accessed on June 10, 2020
4. 2016 Coupon Trends, white paper, www.inmar.com, accessed November 15, 2019; RetailWire, "Will America's love for paper coupons ever die?" April 18, 2019, https://retailwire.com/discussion/will-americas-love-for-paper-coupons-ever-die
5. Ibid.
6. Ibid.
7. 2K19 Valassis Coupon Intelligence Report, https://www.valassis.com/coupon-intelligence-report, accessed on June 12, 2020
8. Julia McCoy, "10 Inspiring Examples of Instagram Contests That Caught Our Attention," *Search Engine Journal,* January 12, 2020, https://www.searchenginejournal.com/inspiring-instagram-contests/337063/#close
9. Xu, Y., & Huang, J.-S. (2014). Effects of price discounts and bonus packs on online impulse buying. *Social Behavior and Personality: An international journal*, *42(8)*, 1293-1302.
10. Gopalakrishnan, Arun and Jiang, Zhenling and Nevskaya, Yulia and Thomadsen, Raphael, Can Non-Tiered Customer Loyalty Programs Be Profitable? (May 6, 2019). SSRN: https://ssrn.com/abstract=2759888
11. Edward Russell, "How much money do loyalty programs make airlines?" June 16, 2020, *The Points Guy*, https://thepointsguy.com/news/how-much-money-do-loyalty-programs-make-airlines
12. Bret Holzhauer, "3 Reasons To Use Your Airline Miles This Holiday Season," *Forbes*, November 13, 2020, https://www.forbes.com/sites/advisor/2020/11/13/3-reasons-to-use-your-airline-miles-this-holiday-season/?sh=56a774a92c09
13. Blake Morgan, "50 Stats That Show the Importance of Good Loyalty Programs, Even During a Crisis," *Forbes,* May 7, 2020, https://www.forbes.com/sites/blakemorgan/2020/05/07/50-stats-that-show-the-importance-of-good-loyalty-programs-even-during-a-crisis/#6dc13e992410
14. Jack R. Nerad and Christian Wardlaw, Automakers Create Coronavirus Car Payment Plans & Programs in Bid to Boost Flagging Sales, J.D. Power, https://www.jdpower.com/cars/shopping-guides/automakers-create-coronavirus-car-payment-plans May 15, 2020
15. Travis Peters, "Why brands should take advantage of product placement," *Forbes,* December 20, 2019, https://www.forbes.com/sites/forbesagencycouncil/2019/12/20/why-brands-should-take-advantage-of-product-placement/#6fe8adbc235d

16. Marc Graser and T. L. Stanley, "10 Favorite Product Placement Deals," *Advertising Age* 77, no. 51 (December 18, 2006): 35.
17. Linchpinseo, "The Beginner's Guide to POP Display to Effectively Use Point of Purchase Displays," June 5, 2020, https://linchpinseo.com/guide-to-point-of-purchase-displays-marketing
18. Paper and Packaging Board, "New Survey Unveils 7 in 10 Consumers Agree Packaging Design Can Influence Purchasing Decisions," May 4, 2018, www.globenewswire.com/news-release/2018/05/04/1496881/0/en/New-Survey-Unveils-7-in-10-Consumers-Agree-Packaging-Design-Can-Influence-Purchasing-Decisions.html
19. Kenneth E. Clow and Donald Baack, *Integrated Advertising, Promotion, and Marketing Communications*, 8th Edition (Upper Saddle River, N.J.: Pearson, 2018).
20. Ibid.
21. Prakash L. Abad, "Quantity Restrictions and the Reseller's Response to a Temporary Price Reduction or an Announced Price Increase," *Asia-Pacific Journal of Operational Management* 23, no. 1 (March 2006): 1–23.
22. Kristin Behrmann, "Bursting with new products, there's never been a better time for breakthrough innovation," Nielsen, December 5, 2019, https://www.nielsen.com/us/en/insights/article/2019/bursting-with-new-products-theres-never-been-a-better-time-for-breakthrough-innovation
23. Phil Edwards, "The hidden war over grocery shelf space," *Vox*, November 22, 2016, https://www.vox.com/2016/11/22/13707022/grocery-store-slotting-fees-slotting-allowances.
24. Patricio Robles, "Is Amazon's ad business the new slotting fee?" Econsultancy, October 20, 2017, https://econsultancy.com/is-amazon-s-ad-business-the-new-slotting-fee
25. Tray Mandara, "2020 Equal Exchange Fair Trade Organic Avocado Display Contest Winners," Four Season Produce, February 27, 2020, https://www.fsproduce.com/2020-equal-exchange-fair-trade-organic-avocado-display-contest-winners
26. Zabanga Marketing, "Intel Inside the Coop Program That Changed the Computer Industry," September 28, 2018, accessed at https://www.zabanga.us/marketing-communications/intel-inside-the-coop-program-that-changed-the-computer-industry.html on June 15, 2020
27. Guttman, "B2B trade show market size in the U.S. 2012-2023," Statista, accessed at www.statista.com/statistics/865283/b2b-trade-show-market-value on June 15, 2020
28. IEG Guide to Sponsorship, Chicago, IL: IEG, LLC, accessed at https://www.sponsorship.com/Latest-Thinking/Sponsorship-Infographics/Sponsorship-Spending-of-Causes-to-Grow-4-6--in-201.aspx on June 20, 2020; IEG Outlook 2020, "Forecasting the future of the sponsorship industry," https://www.sponsorship.com/Outlook-2020.aspx, accessed on June 20, 2020
29. Ibid.
30. Hannah Smoot, "NASCAR signs 4 sponsors for NASCAR Cup Series in 'monumental year' for the sport," *The Charlotte Observer*, December 5, 2019, accessed at http://www.charlotteobserver.com/sports/nascar-auto-racing/article238067789.html#storylink=cpy on June 11, 2020
31. PRNewswire, "Report: More Than 200,000 Dangerously Defective Airbags Remain Unrepaired in Louisiana," August 7, 2019, https://www.prnewswire.com/news-releases/report-more-than-200-000-dangerously-defective-airbags-remain-unrepaired-in-louisiana-300898044.html

Personal Selling and Direct Response Marketing

CHAPTER 15

Source: Prostock-studio/Shutterstock

Chapter Outline

Learning Objectives

Ivelin Radkov/Shutterstock

After studying this chapter, you should be able to:

- Explain the different types of personal selling.
- Discuss the various buyer-seller relationships.
- Identify the steps in the selling process and briefly describe each step.
- Explain the concepts of data warehousing and database management.
- Explain the concept of direct response marketing and list the various methods of direct marketing.

Source: Andy Dean Photography/Shutterstock

15-1 Chapter Overview

Instead of using a real estate agent, Jay and Marcie decided to explore some new houses on their own. Using Realtor.com, Zillow, and other real estate websites, they located three new-construction communities that offered new homes for sale and encouraged new home buyers to see what they had to offer. Arriving at the first appointment, Jay and Marcie were shown a portfolio of new homes that had just been built, with all home construction details described. The salesperson took great pride and stated several times that the company offered the best-quality built homes in the area. Before taking them on a tour of three new homes in the gated community that were almost ready for the market, the salesperson pointed to plaques that hung on the wall, framing awards the company had recently won for innovative home design. As Jay and Marcie toured the three new homes on display, they were impressed. The homes were beautiful. The prices were a little higher than they wanted to pay for a home, but as the salesperson pointed out the quality construction, he reassured them that the higher cost was a small price to pay for the quality that they would be receiving. The salesperson in this story played an important role, informing the prospective buyers about their lifestyle investment, and persuading them that the homes were worth the higher price.

Salespeople are also important when purchasing items at retail stores. They help customers locate merchandise, answer questions, and check out the products. Salesclerks at some retailers have to be hunted down, and they know little about the merchandise being sold, whereas at other stores, the salespeople greet you as you walk in and are eager to assist you in finding just the right item.

Retail sales, however, are only part of the personal selling component of integrated marketing communications (IMC). Business-to-business sales make up a significant component of personal selling. Although consumer and retail sales are discussed in this chapter, the primary focus of the personal selling component of the chapter is on business-to-business selling. Section 15-2 addresses various types of personal selling, buyer-seller relationships, and the selling process. Section 15-3 examines the role of databases in the IMC and how they are used to support personal selling, customer service, and direct response marketing. The concepts of data warehousing and data mining are introduced. The last section of the chapter, Section 15-4, discusses direct response marketing: firms have various methods of direct response marketing that include mail, email, catalogs, the Internet, and mobile.

15-2 Personal Selling

Personal selling is an important component of IMC, especially for business-to-business transactions. Personal selling occurs in many situations, ranging from the salesclerk at a local retail store helping a customer locate a particular item to the field salesperson for Boeing talking to airline companies, the Pentagon, or governments of other nations about purchasing aircraft. Personal selling offers one major advantage not found in the other forms of marketing: two-way communication. The seller is able to interact with the buyer to provide relevant information and to answer any questions or objections the buyer may raise.

15-2a Types of Personal Selling

Personal selling can be classified into three broad categories: order takers, order getters, and support personnel **(see Figure 15-1)**. **Order takers** process routine orders from customers, whereas **order getters** actively generate potential leads and persuade customers to make a purchase. **Support personnel** are individuals who directly support or assist in the selling function, but do not process or directly solicit orders.

Order takers Salespeople who process routine orders from customers.

Order getters Salespeople who actively generate potential leads and persuade customers to make a purchase.

Support personnel Individuals who directly support or assist in the selling function in some manner but do not process orders or directly solicit orders.

Cross-selling The marketing of additional items with the purchase of a particular good or service.

Order takers could have a variety of selling roles. In retailing, they operate the cash register, stock shelves, and answer customer questions. Their role is to assist the customer and to be available when the customer is ready to make the purchase. In manufacturing, an order taker can be in the corporate office taking customer orders online, or by phone, email, or mail.

For a distributor, an order taker may go to retail stores and stock the shelves with the distributor's merchandise. In all of these cases, the order taker does not take an active role in seeking customers or persuading them to make a purchase. The merchandise is presold or selected by the customer. The order taker's task is to assist in completing the transaction.

Order getters, however, actively seek new customers and work to persuade existing customers to purchase more. A salesperson at a car dealership or a furniture store may be an order getter if part of his or her task is to persuade customers to make a purchase. In retail situations where salespeople are paid a commission, they are likely to be order getters because the more customers they can convince to make a purchase, the more the salespeople earn. These salespeople are also more likely to be involved in **cross-selling**, which involves the marketing of additional items with the purchase of a particular good or service. A clothing store salesperson may encourage a customer purchasing pants to purchase a sweater to match. A bank may encourage a customer opening a checking account to open a safety deposit box or apply for a home equity loan.

FIGURE 15-1 Primary Categories of Personal Selling

Source: Nestor Rizhniak/Shutterstock

High-performing salespeople distinguish themselves from others in important ways. Studies have found that successful sales performance is highly correlated with the confidence individuals have in themselves to accomplish their sales goals (this is known as **self-efficacy**); this confidence influences their choice of activities, and determines their level of persistence and effort they put into the job.[1] Skilled salespeople also have important **adaptive selling** skills, altering their sales behaviors during a customer interaction or across interactions based on the perceived selling situation. They readily adapt to customer needs, personalities, social status, body language, and the length of the relationship.[2]

Self-efficacy Confidence individuals have in themselves to accomplish their sales goals.

Adaptive selling Altering sales behaviors during a customer interaction or across interactions based on the perceived selling situation.

Field salesperson A salesperson who is involved in going to a potential customer's place of business to solicit accounts.

Most order getters work in the business-to-business area as field salespeople. A **field salesperson** is involved in going to a potential customer's place of business to solicit business. Field salespeople can be used in the consumer market, but this is limited primarily to high cost items, such as insurance, real estate, and vehicles. Using salespeople in the business-to-business market is feasible because there are fewer buyers and each buyer tends to make a large volume purchase. **Figure 15-2** highlights the primary differences between order takers and order getters.

Online selling involves a marketing agent interacting with a customer. Through search engine optimization, marketing agents can draw in

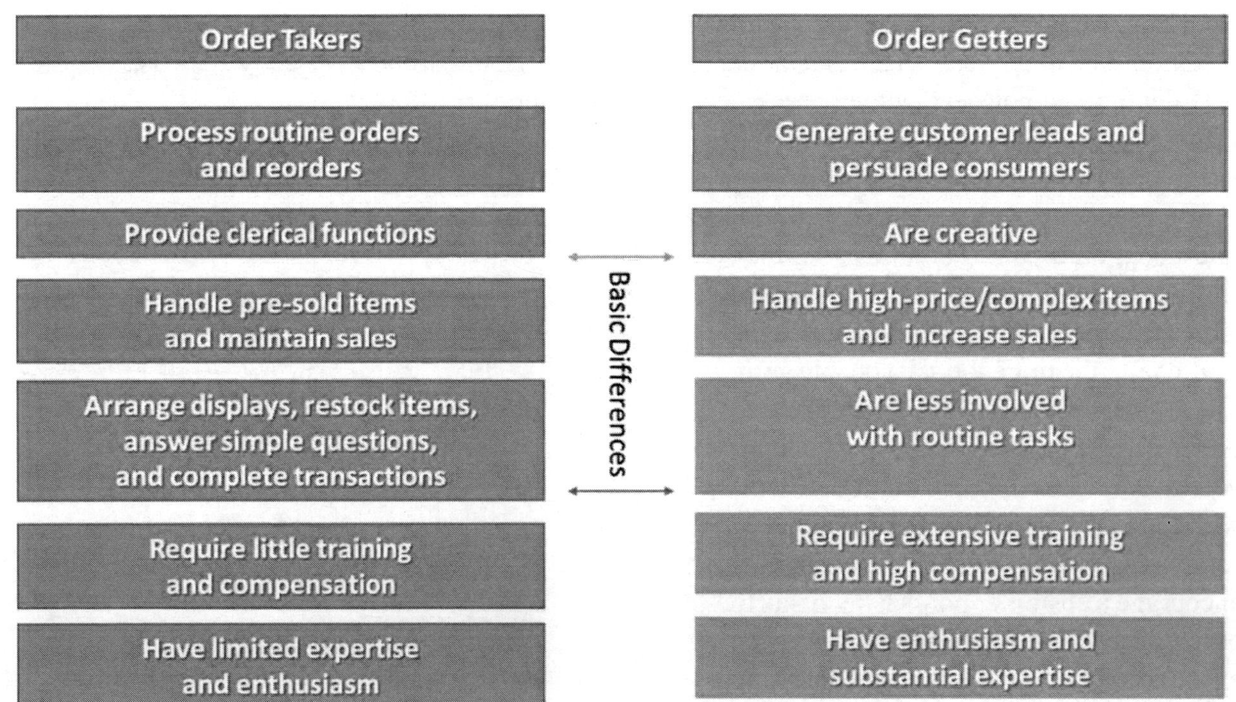

Order Takers
Order Getters
Process routine orders and reorders
Generate customer leads and persuade consumers
Provide clerical functions
Are creative
Handle pre-sold items and maintain sales
Handle high-price/complex items and increase sales
Arrange displays, restock items, answer simple questions, and complete transactions
Are less involved with routine tasks
Require little training and compensation
Require extensive training and high compensation
Have limited expertise and enthusiasm
Have enthusiasm and substantial expertise
Basic Differences

FIGURE 15-2 Differences between Order Takers and Order Getters

Source: Atstock Productions/Shutterstock

customers using persuasive and informative content.[3] Some companies are using telemarketing to sell their products. If the company is calling customers and attempting to persuade them to purchase the product, this is called **outbound telemarketing** and is done by an order getter. If the company is manning telephones that customers call with orders, then it is **inbound telemarketing** and is handled by order takers. Both are used in the business-to-business market and in the consumer market.

The last category of salespeople is the support personnel, with the **missionary salesperson** the most common, tasked with providing information about a good or service. Pharmaceutical companies use missionary salespersons to distribute new drugs and provide doctors with information. The order getter makes the actual sales pitch. For highly technical products, sales engineers address the technical aspects of the product and answer potential customers' questions—usually in conjunction with a salesperson, using a team approach.

Outbound telemarketing The process through which an order-getter salesperson calls prospects and attempts to persuade them to make a purchase.

Inbound telemarketing The process through which an order-taker salesperson handles incoming calls from customers and prospects.

Missionary salesperson A sales support person whose task is to provide information about a good or service.

15-2b Buyer-Seller Relationships

Personal selling allows a buyer and a seller to interact. This two-way communication is called a **buyer-seller dyad** and is illustrated in **Figure 15-3**. Buyers have the opportunity to ask questions, and sellers have the opportunity to provide information. If the salesperson is able to meet a consumer (or business) need, a transaction is likely to occur.

The most basic type of buyer-seller dyad relationship is the **single transaction**, which occurs when the buyer and seller interact for the purpose of a single purchase. This situation may occur in new-buy situations

Buyer-seller dyad Two-way communication between a buyer and a seller.

Single transaction Buyer and seller interacting for the purpose of a single transaction.

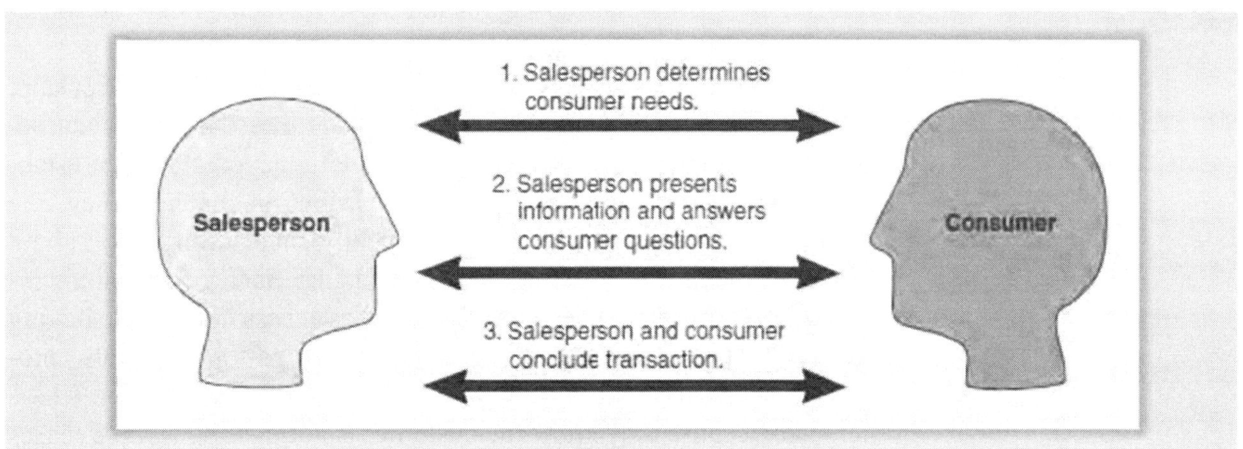

FIGURE 15-3 Contrasting the Buyer-Seller Dyad

in the business-to-business market and for expensive consumer products such as real estate. At the next level are **occasional transactions**, which require an infrequent buyer-seller interaction and may be present in modified rebuy business situations. Occasional transactions may occur in the purchase of equipment, vehicles, computing equipment, and telecommunications equipment for a business. For consumers, the purchase of furniture or vehicles may fall into this category.

Occasional transactions Transactions whereby buyer and seller interact infrequently in the process of making the transaction.

Repeat transactions Buyer and seller interacting over multiple transactions.

Repeat transactions occur when buyers and sellers interact on a regular basis. Gasoline and food purchases involve repeated transactions for consumers, whereas purchases of raw materials, component parts, and maintenance supplies are often repeat transactions for businesses. In most cases, these are straight rebuy business situations. For both consumers and businesses, buyers continue to purchase from the vendor as long as their needs are being met and a more attractive offer does not come along.

For these first three types of buyer-seller dyad situations, transactions are made between the seller and buyer with little or no relationship between the two parties. They meet, they exchange information, and a transaction occurs. There is no commitment or loyalty from either side toward the other party. To ensure a greater commitment from buyers, sellers will often attempt to move the dyad to a higher level, the **contractual agreement**. With a contractual agreement, a written agreement between the buyer and seller is established that states the terms of the interaction, costs, and length of the commitment. With a contractual agreement both the buyer and seller benefit. Buyers are guaranteed a steady supply of a specific product at a predetermined price. Sellers benefit because the buying situation becomes a straight rebuy situation and does not require active selling. As long as they can meet the needs of the buyer, they are guaranteed a sale for the length of the contract and do not have to worry about a competitor taking their client away.

Contractual agreement A written agreement between the buyer and seller that states the terms of the interaction, costs, and length of the commitment.

Whereas contractual agreements represent a more involved form of dyad relationship, they may or may not involve trust. **Trust relationships** in a buyer-seller dyad are based on a mutual respect and understanding of both parties and a commitment to work together. In many countries outside the United States, trust relationships are expected, and company executives are insulted at the suggestion the agreement should be solidified through a written contract.

Trust relationships Buyer-seller dyads based on mutual respect and understanding of both parties and a commitment to work together.

At the next level is the electronic data interchange (EDI) relationship, which expands the trust relationship to include the sharing of data between the buying and selling firms. EDI relationships are often established between intermediaries within the distribution channel. They take place when the buyer and seller electronically share information about production, inventory, shipping, and purchasing. Such relationships involve a high level of trust because the seller has access to all of the buying firm's production information, and the seller ships the materials automatically. Most EDI relationships are with single-vendor sources, which sellers like because they know the customer is not making any purchases from a competitor, and as long as the customer is satisfied, they will keep

Relationship	Definition
Single transactions	The buyer and seller interact for the purpose of a single transaction.
Occasional transactions	The buyer and seller interact infrequently.
Repeat transactions	The buyer and seller interact on a regular basis.
Contractual agreement	A written agreement between the buyer and seller states the terms of the interaction, costs, and length of the commitment.
Trust relationship	The buyer-seller dyad is based on mutual respect and an understanding of both parties, and a commitment to work together.
EDI	This trust relationship includes the sharing of data between the buying and selling firms.
Strategic partnership	The buyer and seller exchange information at the highest levels with the goal of collaboration.

FIGURE 15-4 Buyer-Seller Dyad Relationships
Source: Kenneth E Clow and Donald Baack, *Integrated Advertising, Promotion, and Marketing Communication* (Upper Saddle River, NJ: Prentice Hall, 2002), 454.

the contract. Sellers also know that with EDI it is more difficult for the buyer to switch vendors because of the physical cost of hooking up with a new vendor.

At the highest level of the buyer-seller dyad interaction is the **strategic partnership**. With this approach, the buyer and seller share information at the highest levels. The goal of this relationship is to collaborate on plans to benefit both parties and the customers of the buying firm. In this type of relationship, the seller actively examines ways to modify its products to improve the position of the buying firm in the marketplace. **Figure 15-4** reviews these various levels of the buyer-seller dyad.

Strategic partnership Partnership in which the buyer and seller exchange information at the highest levels with the goal of collaboration.

Personal selling, perhaps more than any of the other components of an IMC program, must be built on trust, honesty, and integrity. Regardless of the type of relationship between buyer and seller, the buyer must have confidence that he or she is given correct and honest information. Yet this is not always the case. Because of the lack of skill, pressure from sales managers, the desire to earn more money, and the need to meet a sales quota, salespeople may be tempted to use unethical techniques ranging from putting pressure on a buyer to make a purchase immediately to telling outright lies. Although high-pressure techniques are not in the long-term best interest for a salesperson and the selling firm, lying and other forms of dishonesty are much worse.

It is important for salespeople to realize that receiving referrals, obtaining repeat business, and building a strong reputation are the keys to successful sales. Success is the result of salespeople being honest with buyers about their products, the products' attributes, and the benefits to the buyer. It is important for salespeople to believe in what they are selling. If they do not, it is impossible to present the product to potential buyers with passion and honesty. Many salespeople are paid a commission on their sales to encourage them to concentrate on selling. Although a commission will certainly encourage a salesperson to push harder for sales, it can also be detrimental if unethical behaviors are used to obtain those sales.

15-2c The Selling Process

The selling process consists of prospecting for leads, preparing a presales approach, determining customer wants, giving a sales presentation, answering questions and objections, closing the sale, and following up. These steps are summarized in **Figure 15-5.** Order getters are involved in all seven steps, and order takers are involved in four or five of the steps. Order takers do not prospect and often do not determine customer needs or follow up after the sale. They may only answer questions and close the sale.

Prospects Potential customers of a firm.

Prospecting for Leads The first step in the selling process is prospecting for leads. **Prospects** are potential customers who have a need for the product being sold and the ability to purchase the product.[4] For example, for a small electric motor manufacturer, prospects are all of the businesses that use small electric motors. They could be other manufacturers, they may be feed mills, they may be government organizations, or they could be distributors of electric supplies. Although all of these firms could be potential customers, salespeople for the small electric motor manufacturer would have to find some way of locating the businesses that would offer the best opportunity for making a sale. The goal of prospecting is to develop a list of viable companies (or consumers) that would be the most likely to make a purchase.

Often, developing a list of potential customers can be the most difficult task in prospecting. Salespeople have several options, and the best method will depend on factors such as the type of product being sold, the expertise of the company, and the competition they face **(see Figure 15-6).** One of the best sources for new customers is the firm's current customers. Often, they can provide the names of decision makers, influencers, and purchasing agents. Having a name and a referral often allows the salesperson to bypass the gatekeepers and talk directly with individuals who would be involved in the purchase decision.

Commercial and government databases can provide potential customers. Commercial sources such as D&B Hoovers can be used, as well as government sources such as the Census of Manufacturers, and the Standard Industrial Classification Code System Search. Also, many marketing research firms sell information about companies that can be used.

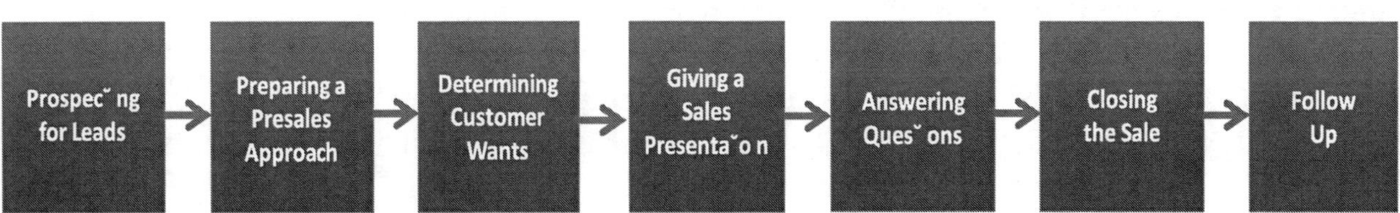

FIGURE 15-5 The Selling Process

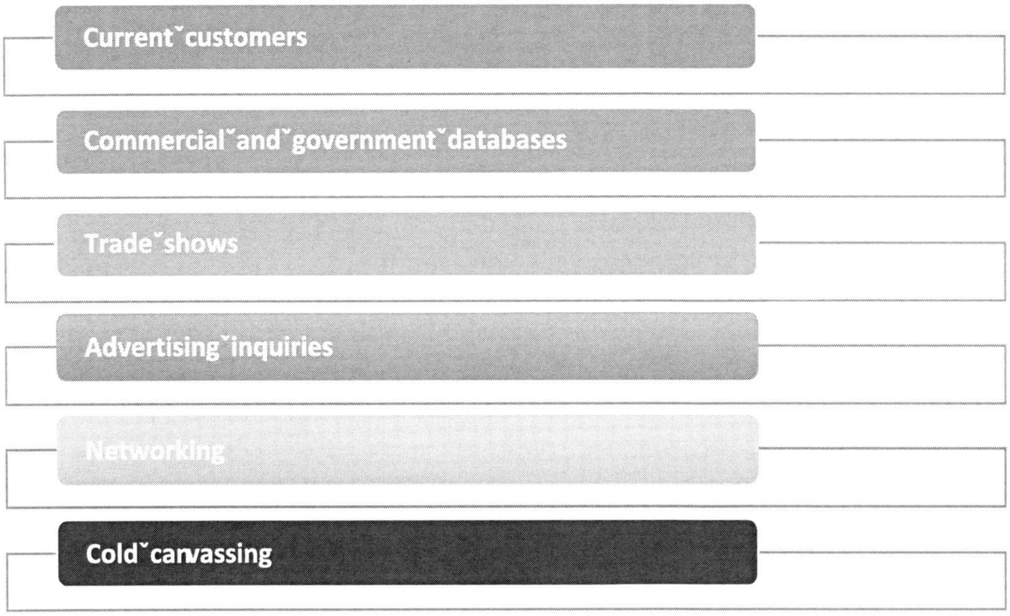

Current customers

Commercial and government databases

Trade shows

Advertising inquiries

Networking

Cold canvassing

FIGURE 15-6 Methods of Prospecting

A business can gather names and information from prospective buyers at trade shows. Most are excellent prospects because the primary reason they attend trade shows is to look at vendors and see what each vendor offers. Contacts can be obtained from advertising and Internet inquiries resulting from the business advertising its products and encouraging interested parties to make an inquiry. In fact, companies are increasingly using online marketing for lead generation, while using the field salesforce for lead conversion: $2 billion is spent on lead generation through Internet advertising, as business-to-business firms spend about 26% of their marketing budget on web content development. Sales leads can then be drawn from web forms, web calls, and emails.[5] Names obtained through this method are almost always good prospects because the potential customers are making the contact and want more information.

For small businesses and consumer services, networking can be used to become acquainted with potential customers. Professional, social, and business organizations are common places for networking. An insurance agent could develop valuable contacts through networking at the chamber of commerce, or other meetings of civic organizations. Business-to-business salespeople often join professional or trade associations to meet potential prospects.

The least-productive method of prospecting is cold canvassing because the buyer knows little about the prospect and a lot of time is spent calling on prospects that have little or no interest. Because of the high cost of making a personal sales call, this method of prospecting is usually not cost effective. Instead of using a salesperson's time, some companies hire missionary salespeople to make cold calls. Their task is not to make a sale but to leave information or a sample of the product. A salesperson would then call only on those whom the missionary salespeople identified as viable prospects.

The second part of prospecting is qualifying the leads. It is important to choose the prospects with the greatest potential or to rank them based on potential. Some questions, for instance, that a small electric motor manufacturer may ask include:

1. What size of electric motors does the company use, and how many does it purchase each year?
2. Who is the company's current supplier?
3. How satisfied is the customer with its current supplier?
4. Does the company purchase from one vendor or multiple vendors?
5. Does the company fit with our current customer base, and do we understand the prospect's business so we can develop a relationship with the prospect?
6. How difficult will it be to get past the gatekeeper and talk with the engineers, users, and decision makers?
7. What criteria will the prospect likely use in making a decision?

Each potential customer can be classified into categories such as A, B, or C based on the responses to these questions. Although a salesperson may not have solid answers for each question, through research he can gather enough information to make an intelligent decision. For instance, suppose a salesperson finds that a prospect purchases a large volume of electric motors in the size the manufacturer produces and that the prospect tends to use a single source vendor. Because of the high sales volume, this prospect is attractive, but key information that is needed is: Who is the current supplier, and how satisfied is the prospect with its current vendor? If the company is very satisfied, this prospect may be classified in the B or C category. However, if the company is not completely satisfied with its current vendor, then this prospect would immediately be placed in the A category and be among the first sales calls the salesperson will make. The better a salesperson does in qualifying prospects, the more effective he or she will be in generating sales because the salesperson will spend more time calling on prospects with the highest probability of making a purchase.

Preparing a Presales Approach In the presales approach, the salesperson gathers information about the potential customer to determine the best sales approach. Useful information would include:

- Current vendor(s)
- Prospect's customers
- Customer needs
- Critical product attributes and benefits desired
- Relative mixture of price, service, and product attributes desired
- Trade promotions used in the past and planned in the future
- Expectations about use of consumer promotions and advertising
- Risk factors in switching vendors

If the prospect's current vendor was not determined during the prospecting step, determining it during this step is essential. Successful salespeople know their competitors, the approaches they are likely to use, and the reasons the customer chose the competitor. Armed with information about the competing firm the prospect is currently using, the salesperson is able to emphasize his or her company's strengths that are perceived as weaknesses for the current vendor. For instance, a salesperson may know that a current vendor has to ship products 1,500 miles by rail to reach the customer. With a facility only 200 miles from the customer, the salesperson is able to emphasize the importance of on-time delivery and how the closeness of the facility will ensure a steady supply without ever revealing that he or she knows the situation the current vendor faces.

Source: Bojan Milinkov/Shuttersock

Having some knowledge of the prospect's customers will enhance the salesperson's ability to make an effective presentation. The salesperson would benefit from knowing which product attributes are most important to the prospect's customers and how the prospect will use the selling firm's products. For example, if you are selling medical supplies or equipment, it is important to understand the doctor's patient base. Does the doctor deal primarily with pediatrics or with adult patients? How will your product or equipment benefit the patient? How will it improve the quality of care that the doctor will provide? Will the new EKG machine be more precise and an improvement compared to the older machine used by the practice? The more salespeople understand about client needs, and about how their company's products can improve clients' performance, the more likely they are to make a sale.

In making a purchase decision, critical product attributes are evaluated from the perspective of the desired benefits. Knowing in advance what benefits are desired and what attributes the prospect will be examining allows the salesperson to have the correct information available. Closely tied with this knowledge is information about the relative mix of price, service, and product attributes. For some customers, price will be the critical purchase decision factor. For others, it will be a service component such as on-time delivery or the ability to handle large fluctuations in orders. Yet for others, it may be some product attribute such as the stress strength of a cable or sheet of aluminum. By knowing the

Source: YAKOBCHUK VIACHESLAV/Shutterstock

emphasis the prospect is likely to put on the price, service, and product attributes, the salesperson is more likely to focus on the points of interest to the prospect and present the information in the correct manner.

For buyers, switching vendors is a risk, depending on the level of relationship they have with the current vendor. If it is only at the transaction level, then little risk is involved and switching is done relatively easily. However, if it is a trust relationship, contractual agreement, or EDI relationship, then switching becomes more difficult and is normally done only if the firm is unhappy with the current vendor. To make a switch otherwise would require a demonstration of some benefit that is significantly superior to the current vendor. Price sometimes can make a difference. For example, if another vendor can offer a component part for 70 cents less and the prospect purchases 300,000 of these parts a year, that would be a savings of $210,000. But making the switch still involves a risk. If the new vendor does not supply the parts in a timely manner, the cost of downtime can quickly eat into the cost savings.

Determining Customer Wants If a salesperson has done a good job in the presales approach, most of the information that is needed for the sales call has already been gathered. All that is needed during this step is confirmation of the customer's needs. The situation, however, is different for order takers. They did not make the initial contact with the customer and did not prospect or use a presales approach. Their first knowledge and contact with the customer occur when the customer makes the contact. Before launching into a sales pitch, the salesperson should first determine the customer's needs.

When shopping for a boat, many buyers may not know what features they want or need. An in-house salesperson should begin by asking individuals questions about how they will use the boat. Will it be for fishing, leisure, or pulling skiers? How much boating will they do? Will the boat be used by just the two owners, or would they be using it for entertaining others? If others, how many others? From these questions, the salesperson can expand to presenting features such as engine size, engine type, and features of the models. By asking the right questions, the salesperson can determine the boat that will best meet the customer's needs and increase his or her chances of making a sale.

Stimulus-response sales approach Sometimes referred to as the canned sales approach, uses specific statements (stimuli) to solicit specific responses from customers.

Source: borevina/Shutterstock

Giving a Sales Presentation After determining a prospect or current customer's needs, the salesperson is in a position to make a sales presentation. The salesperson can use four basic sales approaches, shown in **Figure 15-7.**

The **stimulus-response sales approach**, sometimes referred to as the canned sales approach, uses specific statements (stimuli) to solicit specific responses from customers. Often, the salespeople memorize the stimulus statements (the pitch), and offer memorized or scripted responses to specific questions they are asked. For instance, salespeople may ask prospects if they feel they are paying too much for their car insurance. Most prospects will answer yes (the stimuli), and the salespeople will then explain how they can save the prospects money on car insurance. If, by chance, prospects say no, the salesperson has another question already scripted that will lead into the sales pitch. This sales approach is common for telemarketers, retail salesclerks, and new field salespeople.

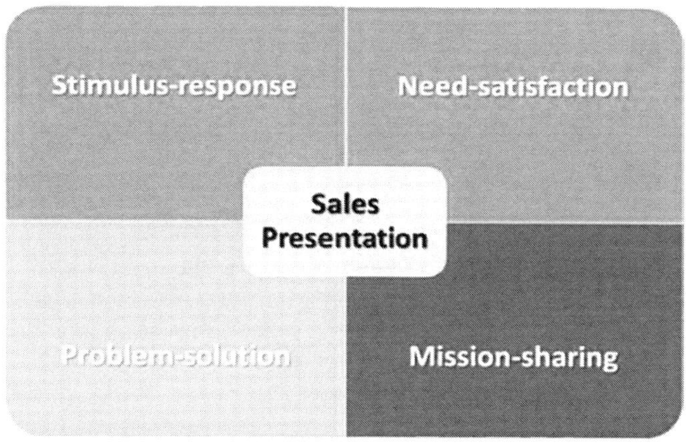

FIGURE 15-7 Sales Presentation Approaches

The **need-satisfaction sales approach** is aimed at discovering a customer's needs and then providing solutions that satisfy those needs. This approach requires the salesperson to be skillful with asking the right questions. The major difference with this approach is that the salesperson does not have a canned list of responses and questions that are designed to lead to the sales pitch. It is an excellent approach for in-house salespeople or order takers who are responding to a prospect's inquiry. Retail salesclerks of complex items like computers will often use this approach. Order getters also use this approach to amplify or clarify information they gathered in the presales approach.

Need-satisfaction sales approach Sales approach aimed at discovering a customer's needs and then providing solutions that satisfy those needs.

The **problem-solution sales approach** requires the salesperson to analyze the prospect's operation and offer a solution that is viable. With this approach, prospects often do not fully understand their needs. They may know their computer system is inadequate for their e-commerce business but not understand what is needed. The selling organization will often use a team approach in this case with engineers and computer experts assisting the salesperson in analyzing the problem and developing a feasible solution. This approach is common in new-buy situations and might be used with a modified rebuy situation.

Problem-solution sales approach Sales approach that requires the salesperson to analyze the prospect's operation and offer a viable solution.

The last approach, the **mission-sharing sales approach**, involves two organizations developing a common mission and then sharing resources to accomplish that mission. This requires the strategic partnership relationship that was discussed previously. In some ways, such a partnership resembles a "joint venture" project. With the increased pressure of global competition, firms have seen the need to cooperate on a higher level. Buyers and sellers that enter into a strategic partnership relationship can use this sales approach to ensure that both the buyer and seller are benefiting from the relationship. The goal is to work together for the benefit of both firms. Figure 15-8 summarizes the four selling approaches.

Mission-sharing sales approach Sales approach that involves two organizations developing a common mission and then sharing resources to accomplish that mission.

The primary factor in determining which approach is used is the form of a buyer-seller dyad. For transaction-type relationships, salespeople are likely to use the first two: stimulus-response and need-satisfaction. Occasional transactions will tend to use either the need-satisfaction or problem-solution. For repeat transactions and the other higher order

Type of Selling Approach	Definition	Example
Stimulus-response approach	Sometimes referred to as the canned sales approach, this approach uses a specific canned sales presentation.	A telemarketer sells aluminum siding for a house, using statements (stimuli) to solicit specific responses from customers.
Need-satisfaction approach	This approach is aimed at discovering a customer's needs and then providing solutions that satisfy those needs.	A salesperson at an electronics store questions a customer about how he or she will be using a camera before offering a particular brand of digital camera with the features that best meet the customer's needs.
Problem-solution	This approach requires a salesperson to analyze the prospect's operation and offer a viable solution.	With the help of computer approach specialists, a salesperson examines the computing needs of a new e-commerce business and then offers a computing network that will meet all of the customer's needs.
Mission-sharing approach	This approach involves two organizations developing a common mission and then sharing resources to accomplish that mission.	A supplier of fiberglass partners with a manufacturer of racing boats to produce a higher quality fiberglass that will withstand the high speeds of boat racing.

FIGURE 15-8 Selling Approaches

types of dyad relationships, problem-solution presentations are the best. The mission-sharing approach is only used with the strategic partnership since higher level personnel are part of the sales process.

Additional factors that determine the selling approach are the dollar value of the sale and the role of personal selling in the IMC plan. If the dollar value of the sale is high, there is a tendency to shift to a higher-level sales approach. The same is true for IMC plans in which personal selling is prominent.

Answering Questions Few sales are closed immediately after the presentation. Prospects will have questions and doubts about making the purchase. Skillfully answering questions and addressing objections and doubts can make the difference between closing a sale and not closing a sale. The disadvantage of the stimulus-response sales approach is that, if prospects raise questions not in the script, salespeople often are not prepared to provide an answer. In fact, most salespeople using this approach skip this step and move directly from the sales presentation to the closing. With the need-satisfaction approach, the salesperson will attempt to relate his or her responses to the needs that were identified earlier in the sales presentation. If this can be done successfully, a sale will often occur. With the problem-solution approach and the mission-sharing approach, few questions and objections are raised if the selling team has done a good job in understanding the problem and developing a joint mission.

A salesperson has the six methods shown in **Figure 15-9** that can be used to overcome objections.[6] With the direct answer method, any

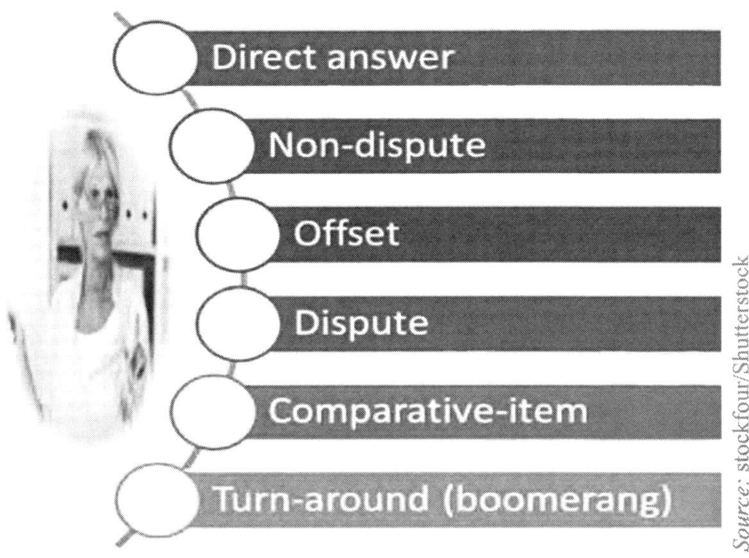

FIGURE 15-9 Methods of Overcoming Objections

objections or questions are met with direct responses. In the non-dispute method, the salesperson avoids or delays any direct answers, or passively accepts the objection without providing an answer or disputing the prospect's claim. With the offset method, the salesperson accepts the objection but offsets it with information about the product's benefits or attributes. Often, the salesperson will use a demonstration, a comparison, or a testimonial to offset the objection.

With the dispute method, the salesperson confronts the objection directly, indirectly, or with a demonstration that shows that the objection is not true or is not founded on correct facts. With the comparative-item method, the prospect is shown two or more products, and when the prospect objects to one, the salesperson will immediately switch to another product to which the objection cannot apply. When using the turn-around, or boomerang, method, the salesperson converts the objection into a reason to make a purchase. If the person says it is too expensive, the salesperson replies that the cost is the very reason it should be purchased.

Which method of handling questions and objections should be used depends on multiple factors, such as the buying situation, the personalities of both the buyer and seller, and the product being sold. Figure 15-10 summarizes each of the methods of overcoming objections with an example of each.

Closing the Sale Although closing the sale is the most important step, for many salespeople it is the most difficult step in the entire process, primarily because of the fear that the prospect will say no. Closings can be classified into the six categories highlighted in Figure 15-11 (see page 459).[7]

With the straightforward close, the salesperson asks for the order in a direct manner and, if necessary, summarizes the benefits for the prospect. With the presumptive close, the salesperson assumes the prospect

Method	Definition	Example
Direct answer	Objections or questions are met with direct responåses.	"We produce all of the sizes you need, and we will make sure they meet your specifications."
Nondispute	Objections or questions are avoided, or the salesperson delays any direct answers or passively accepts the objection without providing an answer or disputing the prospect's claim	"I understand your concern, and it is legitimate." Without responding to the concern, the salesperson goes on, "Let me show you the different sizes we offer."
Offset	The objections or questions are offset with information about the product's benefits or attributes.	"I understand your concern, but let me show you all of the sizes we offer and how we go about ensuring that your specifications are met."
Dispute	Objections or questions are confronted directly, indirectly, or by demonstrating that the objection is not true or not founded on correct facts.	"Somebody gave you incorrect information. We can supply every size you use in your business, and we can meet those specifications. I am confident that our product is stronger than what you are currently using."
Comparative-item	The prospect is shown two or more products and, when the prospect objects to one, the salesperson immediately switches to another product to which the objection cannot apply.	"Because this particular brand does not have the size you need to fit with your product, let me show you this other brand. It comes in the size you need and will meet your specifications."
Turn-around	The salesperson converts the objection into a reason to make a purchase.	"I understand you cannot afford it (boomerang) right now, but with what your competitors have just introduced, you cannot afford not to switch immediately. Any delay will cost you sales and future customers."

FIGURE 15-10 Overcoming Objections
Source: Sean Dwyer, John Hill, and Warren Martin, "An Empirical Investigation of Critical Success Factors in the Personal Selling Process for Homogenous Goods." *Journal of Personal Selling & Sales Management* 20, no. 3 (Summer 2000): 152-161.

is ready to buy and therefore asks a question in terms of how to write up the sale. A retail salesclerk may ask if the person would like to pay with cash, check, or money order. A field salesperson may ask how soon the customer wants the product shipped and in what quantity. With the arousal close, the salesperson appeals to the prospect's emotions or creates a sense of urgency. Insurance agents often appeal to taking care of loved ones before it is too late.

With the minor-decision close, the salesperson seeks approval of small-decision questions throughout the presentation. Then, when the purchase question is asked, the prospect has already responded yes to several smaller-decision questions. If the prospect is almost ready to buy, but has just one objection, a salesperson can use the single obstacle close, which involves answering that one objection within the close. The last closing method is the silent close. With this close, the salesperson says nothing. The salesperson just waits and lets the prospect make the decision. The best closing depends on a salesperson's personality and personal preference, as well as the selling situation. Most salespeople tend to use a particular method more than others but may use all six. It is more likely, however, that they have two or three they tend to use most of the time.

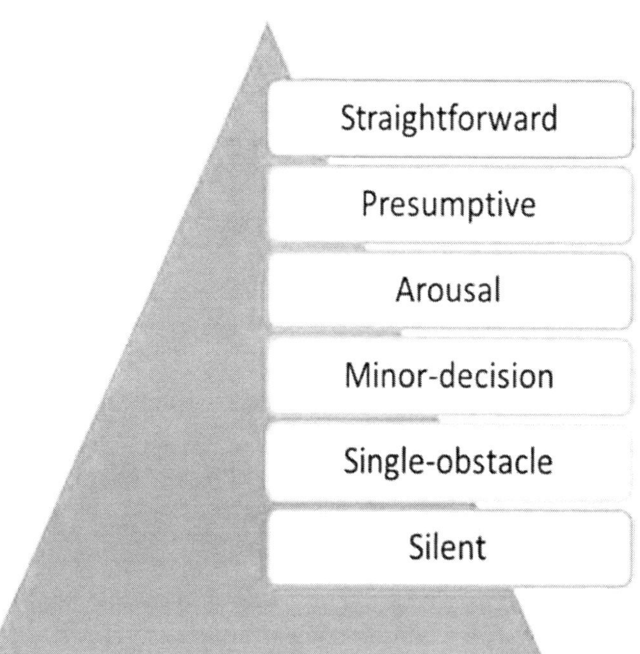

FIGURE 15-11 Methods of Closing a Sale

Following Up Satisfied customers usually purchase again, and, in the business-to-business sector, often develop a strong loyalty to a particular vendor. Unhappy customers, however, not only defect to a competitor, but also spread negative word-of-mouth communication about the firm. Because it is more cost effective to retain old customers than to obtain new ones, follow-up is a critical component of the selling process. The difficulty is that, for many salespeople, it is the least-attractive component of the sale, especially if the salesperson is paid a commission. The salesperson does not want to spend time at activities that do not generate sales.

Source: Dragon Images/Shutterstock

15-3 Databases

Databases are key components of IMC programs. They can be used for a variety of purposes, ranging from providing information to salespeople and other company personnel to direct response marketing. Determining how the database will be used and who will be using it is crucial in the development process.

Service call centers need access to customer records when a customer calls. They need to be easily accessible and easy to understand. Customers expect a service call representative to know what they purchased and be able to answer questions about their account. Salespeople also need ready access to this information. This is especially critical in preparing for a sales call and, sometimes, during a sales call.

Databases are important for marketing departments. Customer data help marketing personnel understand what is being purchased and by whom. These data can be used to develop profiles of the firm's most valuable customers and to determine the best target market for the various products sold by the firm. They are also essential in tracking changes in purchase behavior, alerting marketing personnel to the need to either modify their product offering or alter their marketing communications material.

15-3a Data Warehousing

Data warehousing The process of capturing and storing data within a single database that is accessible to internal personnel for a variety of internal purposes, such as marketing, sales, and customer service.

Data warehousing is the process of capturing and storing data within a single database that is accessible to internal personnel for a variety of purposes, such as marketing, sales, and customer service. It also involves collecting data for decision making and sharing with vendors to improve inventory management. Building a data warehouse involves understanding who will use the data and how it will be used. Too often, companies develop a database only to find that they either have the wrong information, not enough information, or that the information cannot be accessed by the individuals who need it. Collecting the right information for a data warehouse is crucial.

Organizations have two sources of data: internal data and external data. Internal data come from sales transactions by customers. It also can be obtained from salespeople, service personnel, call-center technicians, and others who have contact with customers. To make a database viable, every person who has contact with customers should be able to both access information, as well as add information to a customer's record.

In some cases, internal data are insufficient to develop an optimal data warehouse. Secondary data, such as psychographics, lifestyles, attitudes, interests, media habits, hobbies, and brand purchases, can be collected from external commercial database services. These data can then be attached to a purchase history to create a stronger profile of each customer.

Data mining Computer analysis of customer data to determine patterns, profiles, or relationships for the purpose of customer profiling or predicting purchase behavior.

An important source of data is checkout scanners at retail stores. This technology makes it possible for businesses to track purchasing data on an individual basis. These data can then be tied in with specific customers and used for more efficient marketing programs.

The data warehouse information can also be used by retail store managers, logistics staff, brand managers, and business executives to make better decisions and to improve productivity of operations. To be effective, data warehousing has to be integrated with the other components of the IMC plan.

Source: bleakstar/Shutterstock

15-3b Data Mining

A major benefit of developing a data warehouse is the ability to perform data mining. **Data mining** involves computer analysis of millions of records of customer data to determine patterns, profiles, or relationships for the purpose of customer profiling or predicting purchase behavior.

Through developing profiles of current customers, the marketing team has a better idea of who is purchasing from the company and what they purchase. This information can be used to develop marketing programs aimed at prospects who meet the profile of the firm's best customers. It can also identify customers who may be in that second tier that the company should concentrate on because they match the profile of the firm's best customers but not the purchase history. Because the customers are already purchasing from the firm, it is easier to encourage them to increase their purchases than it is to seek entirely new customers. Amazon, for example, collects data on each customer while using the site, including what pages they browse, reviews, shipping address, etc.; then it uses external datasets, such as census data, to better understand consumers and to forecast future purchases. After examining data mining insights, Amazon could suggest cross-selling opportunities, promoting new products that match the customer's interests.[8]

Data mining also helps companies in the process of product development and innovation. Whirlpool Corporation, a leading home appliance company, uses customer feedback from over a million reviews it receives from 40 websites every month for product development. The data, ranging from reviews, to emails, to different contact forms with sales representatives, address how the products are performing in the market, what features customers like most, etc. It then uses the information to identify different paths to and ideas for innovations.[9]

Firms are also relying on data mining to quickly address any problems that might come up. For example, McDonald's is widely discussed on popular social media channels, such as Facebook and Twitter, which is helpful for fast reactions to negative comments. McDonald's can then react quickly to problems such as mentions of a broken ice cream machine; it can solve the problem instantly and make sure that negative conversations do not spread any further.[10]

Data mining also provides helpful information regarding new store location: by using GIS tools, firms can perform an analysis of local socio-economic data, revealing expectations of the target audience, and locations with high potential that firms were not previously considering. For example, Starbucks uses a data-driven approach to store openings with the help of mapping software that can analyze large amounts of location data, thus identifying the best locations without hurting sales at other Starbucks locations.[11]

15-3c New-Technology Disruption in Sales Management

New sales technologies are changing the structures of sales organizations, untethering sales professionals from organizations and creating new sales roles such as free agent intermediaries and expert brokers. In sales technology, digitization and artificial intelligence are increasing the ease of access to sales knowledge and encouraging sales learning. Artificial intelligence (AI) chatbots are used to improve relationships between salespeople and customers, and 80% of sales teams using AI reported improvements in customer retention.[12]

In the sales profession, automation is improving sales skills, with AI used to provide better training to salespeople, helping them to interface with customers in realistic situations. AI is also changing sales jobs: digital sales channels are thought to lead to the "Death of a B2B salesman," either making salespeople completely unnecessary, or changing their role to more of a consulting role. B2B companies are able to increase selling efficiency, reduce costs, and increase customer value by digitizing sales channels and encouraging online over personal interactions—introducing, for example, self-service technologies such as online shops. Platforms that facilitate these interactions, such as Alibaba, have taken off. For example, to further reduce the need for personal selling and interactions, parts supplier Wurth Industries is using RFID chips and scanners that help customers automatically order items when stocks fall below a certain level.[13]

15-4 Direct Response Marketing

Direct response marketing (or direct marketing), the promotion of a product directly to the consumer or business user without the use of any channel member, is designed to create an immediate customer response, an action on the offer; it is a targeted message, typically personalized and often interactive. The direct response marketing campaign results can be readily measured. People traditionally thought of direct mail, catalogs, and telemarketing when hearing direct response marketing; however, it can be any type of marketing that demands a response, such as direct selling, social media ads, email, text (SMS, which is becoming very popular), and even company landing pages. Direct marketing campaigns are perfect for test-driving a campaign before a larger launch, or for businesses with limited advertising budgets.

Because channel members are bypassed, direct marketing normally allows a producer to earn greater profits or reduce the selling price. More importantly, it can help in developing a stronger brand loyalty with customers. Social media—Facebook, in particular—is often the lifeblood of many direct-to-consumer firms' sales funnel. That is, in many cases, it could be their entire sales funnel.[14]

After the onset of the COVID-19 pandemic, in-home media usage went up, with digital consumption increasing rapidly, more so than network TV viewership. Advertisers have adapted by following consumers, recognizing that the online environment was favorable for direct-response campaigns encouraging quick purchases by consumers.[15]

A key to a good direct response marketing program is the quality of information contained within the firm's database. Not only should it have the basic demographic information, but psychographic and purchase behavior information should also be available. Based on this information, a direct marketing program should begin by dividing each contact into one of three categories: buyers, inquirers, or prospects. Buyers are individuals who have purchased in the past, inquirers are individuals who have requested information, and prospects are individuals who fit the target profile but have not had any previous contact with the firm. The direct marketing message that is designed will vary, depending on which group is being targeted.[16]

Figure 15-12 provides information on the usage rate of the various methods of direct marketing by b2b firms that use direct marketing. It appears that most top performers (those meeting marketing goals) use content marketing (81%), digital ads, pay per click, and retargeting (88%), email(76%), and paid social posts (65%), among others, as do all other marketers (mainstream marketers), even though to a somewhat lesser extent. Interestingly, direct mail is used by 54% of top performers and 37% of mainstream marketers.[17]

Catalogs continue to be an effective approach to direct marketing, used by many of the companies that engage in direct marketing. The number of catalogs have fallen from almost 20 billion in 2006 to less than half.

Tactics US B2B Marketers Plan to Use in 2020, Jan 2020 *% of respondents*

	Top performers	Mainstream
Content marketing	81%	75%
Digital ads, pay-per-click or retargeting	88%	63%
Email	76%	75%
Video	74%	67%
Events	66%	57%
Paid social posts	65%	51%
SEO/organic	55%	57%
Organic social posts	47%	57%
PR	54%	46%
ABM	50%	47%
Webinars	45%	49%
Direct mail	54%	37%
Affiliates or partners	53%	37%
Content syndicators or other third-party sources	39%	17%

FIGURE 15-12 Direct Marketing Methods Used by Companies

Sources: https://chart-na1.emarketer.com/235363/tactics-us-b2b-marketers-plan-use-2020-jan-2020-of-respondents

Note: top performers rated themselves 6-7 (on a 7-point scale) in meeting 2019 marketing goals, mainstream is all others.

ON24 and Heinz Marketing, "Experiences Everywhere: What Top-Performing B2B Marketers Do Differently," March 11, 2020

254289www. eMarketer.com

Source: Hadrian/Shutterstock

However, there are still 10 billion catalogs going to U.S. consumers each year. And, while smaller direct-to-consumer brands have rapidly embraced them recently, it appears that well-established brands are picking up on this trend, adopting them rapidly—they are as effective as advertising on social media, but much cheaper. For example, Walmart embedded its holiday catalog with technology that allows customers to easily buy what they like via the Walmart app when they see it on the page.[18]

Consumers can view catalogs at their leisure, and because most catalogs are kept for a period of time, they have a long shelf life. Days, and even weeks after receiving a catalog, a consumer or business may refer to it for a purchase. One of the attractive features of catalogs is the soft sales approach. Because of the high cost of printing and mailing catalogs, most catalog retailers have gone to more selective distribution lists. Database information about customers and potential customers is used to develop a mailing list of individuals who are most likely to purchase merchandise through the catalog. Rather than one large catalog, companies offer smaller catalogs that focus on a particular line of products like outdoor clothing, children's clothing, hunting and fishing equipment, or kitchen merchandise.

Digital marketing (or Internet marketing) continues to grow rapidly, as seen in the previous chapters. Digital technology allows companies to analyze online purchases, click-streams, and other interactions to develop personalized messages. In addition, the online behavior of a customer can be combined with demographic and psychographic data from either an internal database or an external database firm. Using all of this information, the software can suggest specific products the consumer is most likely to purchase. All of this analysis can occur while the person is still online. For example, a person who is looking at computer games and has purchased a certain type of game in the past may receive an offer for a new game that has just been introduced.

Many companies use email direct response marketing campaigns. Direct marketing emails to customers are used by about 75% of companies.[19] Email makes it possible for the company to deliver customized messages or promotions to customers similar to those sent in the mail. Just before Valentine's Day, Starbucks sends its customers a creative email. In a recent example, it sent "a gift from the heart," with a fun reminder to buy a Starbucks treat for one's valentine.

Telemarketing has been an important medium for direct marketing, although legislation has altered its viability. Both consumers and businesses have grown impatient with telemarketers calling them at inopportune times and selling merchandise that is of no interest. Both the Federal Trade Commission and the Federal Communications Commission worked together to establish a federal do-not-call list that blocks telemarketing calls. Although the law stops some telemarketers, it exempts charities, political candidates, and businesses that already have a relationship with a customer. For example, if you have an ExxonMobil Fleet credit card, then Exxon can call you about other products, even if you are on the no-call list. Although the law has reduced the number of telemarketing calls, this approach remains a viable method of direct marketing.

The mass media may be a part of a direct response marketing campaign. Compared with the other forms of direct marketing, mass media direct response offers tend to be used less, primarily because of a lower response rate. When used, the most common forms of mass media direct response marketing are television, radio, magazines, and newspapers. Television offers the advantage of access to a mass audience and is an excellent choice for products with a general appeal to the masses. Radio does not have the reach of television but still can be used to convey direct marketing messages. However, unless toll-free numbers and web addresses are easy to remember and repeated frequently, consumers will have difficulty retaining the information, because in many cases, they are not in a situation in which they can write down the information. The print media, such as newspapers and magazines, are better for direct marketing programs. Viewers can study ads and write down information.

Summary

1. **Explain the different types of personal selling.**
Personal selling can be classified into three broad categories: order takers, order getters, and support personnel. Order takers process routine orders from customers, whereas order getters actively generate potential leads and persuade customers to make a purchase. Support personnel are individuals who directly support or assist in the selling function in some manner but do not process orders or directly solicit orders. A field salesperson is an order getter who is involved in going to a potential customer's place of business to solicit business. If the company is calling customers and attempting to persuade them to purchase the product, this is called outbound telemarketing and is done by an order getter. If the company is manning telephones that customers call with orders, then it is inbound telemarketing, handled by order takers. A missionary salesperson, belonging to the last category of salespeople, provides information about a good or service.

2. **Discuss the various buyer-seller relationships.**
The most basic type of buyer-seller dyad relationship is the single transaction, which occurs when the buyer and seller interact for the purpose of a single transaction. At the next level are occasional transactions that require an infrequent buyer-seller interaction and may be present in modified rebuy situations. Repeat transactions are at the third level and are characterized by buyers and sellers interacting on a regular basis. To ensure a greater commitment from buyers, sellers will often attempt to move the dyad to a higher level—the contractual

agreement—which is a written agreement between the buyer and seller. Although contractual agreements are a stronger form of dyad relationship, they may or may not involve trust. Trust relationships are based on mutual respect and understanding of both parties and a commitment to work together. At the next level is the EDI relationship, which expands the trust relationship to include the sharing of data between the buying and selling firms. At the highest level of the buyer-seller dyad interaction is the strategic partnership. With this approach, the buyer and seller share information at the highest levels. The goal of this relationship is to collaborate on plans to benefit both parties and the customers of the buying firm.

3. **Identify the steps in the selling process and briefly describe each step.**
The first step in the selling process is prospecting for leads. In this step, viable customers are identified and qualified. Step two is the presales approach, in which the buyer gathers as much information as possible about the potential customer. In step three, the buyer determines the customer's needs to prepare the best selling approach and the strategy involved in presenting the product in its best light. Step four involves giving the sales presentation. Various methods can be used, depending on the ability and style of salespeople as well as the selling situation. Step five is answering any objections or questions the customer may raise. Step six is closing the sale. Various types of closings can be used, depending on the situation. The last step is the follow-up to ensure that the customer is satisfied with the sale.

4. **Explain the concepts of data warehousing and database management.**
Data warehousing is the process of collecting, sorting, and retrieving relevant information about a firm's customers and potential customers. Through a process known as data mining, a company can gather useful information about its customers that can be used for profiling its best customers, developing marketing programs, and predicting future purchase behavior.

5. **Explain the concept of direct response marketing and list the various methods of direct marketing.**
Direct response marketing is the promotion of a product from the producer directly to the consumer or business user without the use of any type of channel members. The typical direct response marketing venues include mail, catalogs, mass media, the Internet, email, and telemarketing.

Key Terms

Adaptive selling (446)
Buyer-seller dyad (447)
Contractual agreement (448)
Cross-selling (445)
Data mining (460)
Data warehousing (460)
Field salesperson (446)
Inbound telemarketing (447)
Mission-sharing sales approach (455)
Missionary salesperson (447)
Need-satisfaction sales approach (455)
Occasional transactions (448)
Order getters (445)
Order takers (445)
Outbound telemarketing (447)
Problem-solution sales approach (455)
Prospects (450)
Repeat transactions (448)
Self-efficacy (446)
Single transaction (447)
Stimulus-response sales approach (454)
Strategic partnership (449)
Support personnel (445)
Trust relationships (448)

Discussion Questions

1. Discuss a recent experience you had with a salesperson at a retail store. Was it a positive or negative experience? Which type of buyer-seller dyad was it?
2. Compare and contrast the various levels of buyer-seller relationships discussed in Section 15-2 in terms of your personal experience. Identify companies or salespeople you have interacted with for each type of relationship.
3. Pick a business that sells to another business, government, or institution. Discuss various ways a salesperson could prospect for new leads. What types of questions would be asked to qualify each lead?
4. For each of the following products and situations, which type of sales approach should be used? Justify your response.
   a. Selling kitchen appliances to a consumer in a retail store
   b. Selling car insurance to a consumer who stops at the insurance office
   c. Selling liability insurance to a business on a cold call
   d. Selling accounting services to a large corporation
   e. Selling a new car to a consumer
   f. Selling a fleet of cars to a business for use by corporate personnel
5. Suppose you were in the process of purchasing a new vehicle. Look through the various methods of handling objections. Discuss each method in terms of how you would relate to a salesperson using that method with you in an effort to handle objections you had in purchasing the new vehicle. Which methods work, which methods do not? Why?
6. Suppose you now work as the account executive for an advertising agency. You have handled the objections of a potential client. Look through the closings. Discuss each close in terms of how you would get this client to agree to hire your advertising agency. Which close do you prefer? Why?
7. Using a database such as EbscoHost or the Internet, do some research on answering objections in the selling process. Write a short paper on what you find.
8. Using a database such as EbscoHost or the Internet, do some research on closing a sale in the selling process. Write a short paper on what you find.
9. Using a database such as EbscoHost or the Internet, do some research on data mining. What did you learn?
10. Direct response marketing is an effective means of reaching consumers. Discuss each method of direct response marketing in terms of your personal experience. Which methods work with you, which do not? Why? What type of offer does it take for you to respond to a direct response marketing offer? Explain.

Review Questions

True or False

1. EDI provides speed and accuracy in buying and selling transactions; therefore, it is advisable that this system should be used with all potential buyers.
2. To meet sales quotas or to earn more money, it is okay for salespeople to use unethical techniques and to persuade the customer in aggressive ways to make an immediate purchase.
3. The least productive method of prospecting is cold canvassing because the buyer knows little about the prospect and a lot of time is spent on calling prospects with no interest.
4. With the presumptive close, the salesperson asks for an order in a direct manner and, if necessary, summarizes the benefits for the prospect.
5. Because it is more cost effective to retain current customers than to attract new ones,

the follow-up is a critical component of the sales process.

6. Databases are important components of an IMC program and direct response marketing campaign.
7. Data mining involves computer analysis of customer data to determine patterns, profiles, and relationships for the purpose of predicting purchase behavior.
8. Direct response marketing is a modern marketing program developed through information gathering from multisource databases and targeted to very broad customer segments.

Multiple Choice

9. Which category actively generates leads and solicits orders from prospects or customers?
   a. order takers
   b. order getters
   c. support personnel
10. In which kind of buyer-seller relationship are the terms of interaction, cost, and length of commitment established in a written agreement?
    a. occasional transaction
    b. repeated transaction
    c. contractual agreement
    d. trust relationship
11. What information will be relevant to determine the best sales approach?
    a. current vendors
    b. critical product attributes
    c. expectations about sales promotion and advertising
    d. all of the above
12. Which sales approach, sometimes referred to as the canned sales approach, applies specific statements to solicit responses from customers?
    a. stimulus-response sales approach
    b. need-satisfaction sales approach
    c. problem-solution sales approach
    d. mission-sharing sales approach
13. Which method is applied when the salesperson confronts the customer objection directly, indirectly, or by a demonstration that the objection is not true or not founded on correct facts?
    a. direct answer method
    b. offset method
    c. dispute method
    d. turn-around method
14. In the context of closing the sale, which category refers to the salesperson's appeals to the customer's emotions or attempts at creating a sense of urgency?
    a. presumptive close
    b. arousal close
    c. minor-decision close
    d. single obstacle close
15. Direct response marketing is focused on which customer category?
    a. buyers
    b. inquirers
    c. prospects
    d. all of the above

Answers: (1) False, (2) False, (3) True, (4) False, (5) True, (6) True, (7) True, (8) False, (9) b, (10) c, (11) d, (12) a, (13) c, (14) b, (15) d

Case: National South Bank

National South Bank has been in business for more than ten years and has expanded to a total of eleven facilities in three different towns. It is a locally owned and managed facility that has built a solid reputation for service, especially with the business community. The retail side of the business, which is directed to consumers, has done well, especially with the baby boomer generation.

National South is one of three locally owned banks, with total assets and facilities approximately equal to the other two locally owned banks combined. The difficulty National South faces is the large regional and national banks in the town. There are eighteen of them, for a city with a population of 95,000 and a county population of slightly less than 160,000. Competition for customers is intense. But National South uncovered

Source: PHTOTBUAY/Shutterstock

one area of town, on the north side, where the market appears to be underserved. The area has grown rapidly during the previous five years, and a bank merger had reduced the number of facilities serving the north side. Eager to establish a presence in this area, National South built a large branch facility. It was now time to develop a marketing program for the branch's grand opening.

The first step National South took was to seek information from Claritas about the geodemographic makeup of the area. Using PRIZM, Claritas located the top market segments in the area that made up 90 percent of the population. These geodemographic groups are described in Figure 15-13.

The second step for National South Bank was to hire a direct marketing firm to handle the opening of the branch facility. National South recognized that it was in a delicate situation because it already had three other facilities in the town. Although it wanted new customers for the branch, it wanted to attract customers from competing banks, not have its current customers transfer their accounts to the new branch.

PRIZM Cluster Name	Size	Description	This PRIZM Cluster Is Most Likely to
Second city elite	30%	Upscale executive families Age group: 45+ Professional Household income: $67,800	Add a bathroom Own a laptop computer Own an Acura Read Bon *Appetit*
Upward bound	24%	Young, upscale, white-collar families Age group: Under 18, 35-54 Professional Household income: $62,100	Be brand loyal Buy a new station wagon Have 401(K) plan Watch *The Tonight Show* Read *Vogue*
Middleburg managers	16%	Mid-level, white-collar couples Age group: 35-44, 65+ Professional/white collar Household income: $42,000	Own a laptop computer Have a home equity loan Watch the QVC channel Read *PC Magazine* Jog or run
Small-town downtown	12%	Older renters and young Age group: 18-44 White collar/blue collar Household income: $22,800	Shop at Target Buy a VCR Have a school loan Watch MTV Read *Muscle and Fitness*
Southside city	8%	African American service workers Age group: 18-34 Blue collar/service Household income: $17,000	Be pro-wrestling fans Buy gospel music Own a Mazda Watch BET Read *GQ*

FIGURE 15-13 Geographic Composition of National South Bank's Market Area

Source: Interview with Graham Morris of Newcomer, Morris & Young, January 9, 2003; Claritas, Inc., available at http://cluster2.claritas.com, February 18, 2003

Although National South Bank was aware that some customers were likely to switch because the new location was more convenient for them, its objective was to ensure that the vast majority of customers were new. To attract these customers, the bank would have to offer some incentives. Some that were suggested included:

- Free checking for six months
- Free safety deposit box for one year
- Free online banking for six months
- A free gift such as a kitchen appliance, briefcase, or makeup kit
- Reduced introductory interest rate on a home equity loan

National South Bank recognized that it could not advertise these incentives on television or in the newspaper without upsetting its current customers, and it could not afford to offer these incentives to all of its current customers. By using a direct response marketing approach, National South felt that it could promote the new facility without many of its current customers knowing what incentives were being offered.

The direct marketing firm that was retained suggested that National South attempt a direct-mail campaign in the area surrounding the new facility, which could be followed up with a door hanger placed at each resident's home. Another suggestion was engaging in some tie-in partnerships with a few of the businesses in the area where they could place free direct response marketing pieces in the business and in the shoppers' bags as they checked out.

Case Questions

1. Which two market segments would you suggest that National South Bank attract? Why?
2. What incentives would you offer to each market segment selected in question 1? Why?
3. Design a direct-mail piece for National South Bank directed to one of the market segments.
4. Discuss a direct response marketing program for National South Bank that would include the market segments you indicated in question 1.
5. Do you think that National South Bank made the right decision in not offering free incentives in television and newspaper ads? Justify your answer.
6. How would you advertise this new branch facility without offending current customers at the other three facilities?

Endnotes

1. Peterson, R. A. (2020). Self-efficacy and personal selling: review and examination with an emphasis on sales performance. *Journal of Personal Selling & Sales Management*, *40*(1), 57–71.
2. Alavi, S., Habel, J., & Linsenmayer, K. (2019). What does adaptive selling mean to salespeople? an exploratory analysis of practitioners' responses to generic adaptive selling scales. *The Journal of Personal Selling & Sales Management, 39*(3), 254-263.
3. Banerjee, S., & Bhardwaj, P. (2019). Aligning marketing and sales in multi-channel marketing: Compensation design for online lead generation and offline sales conversion. *Journal of Business Research*, *105*, 293–305.
4. Anthony J. Ubraniak, "Prospecting Systems That Work," *American Salesman* 48 (November 2003): 25–28.
5. Banerjee, S., & Bhardwaj, P. (2019). Aligning marketing and sales in multi-channel marketing: Compensation design for online lead generation and offline sales conversion. *Journal of Business Research*, *105*, 293–305.
6. Sean Dwyer, John Hill, and Warren Martin, "An Empirical Investigation of Critical Success Factors in the Personal Selling Process for Homogenous Goods," *Journal of Personal Selling & Sales Management* 20, no. 3 (Summer 2000): 152–161.
7. Ibid.
8. Intellspot, "7 Real-World Examples Of Data Mining In Business, Marketing, Retail," accessed at http://www.intellspot.com/data-mining-examples on June 18, 2020.
9. Ibid.
10. Ibid.
11. Ibid.

12. Singh, J., Flaherty, K., Sohi, R. S., Deeter-Schmelz, D., Habel, J., Le Meunier-FitzHugh, K., Malshe, A., Mullins, R., & Onyemah, V. (2019). Sales profession and professionals in the age of digitization and artificial intelligence technologies: Concepts, priorities, and questions. *Journal of Personal Selling & Sales Management*, *39*(1), 2–22.
13. Ibid.
14. Meaghan Graham, "Companies joining the Facebook ad boycott risk their bottom lines to take a stand," CNBC, June 30, 2020, https://www.cnbc.com/2020/06/30/companies-joining-the-facebook-ad-boycott-risk-their-bottom-lines.html.
15. Cathy Lee and Stefan Hall, "This is how COVID-19 is affecting the advertising industry," June 8, 2020, https://www.weforum.org/agenda/2020/06/coronavirus-advertising-marketing-covid19-pandemic-business.
16. Kellee Harris, "What Direct Marketers Know That You Don't," *Sporting Goods Business* 33, no. 15 (October 11, 2000): 12.
17. Emarketer, "Tactics b2b marketers plan to use," Jan 20, 2020, accessed at https://chart-na1.emarketer.com/235363/tactics-us-b2b-marketers-plan-use-2020-jan-2020-of-respondents, June 22, 2020.
18. PYMNTS, "How (And Why) Major Retailers Are Embracing Print Catalogs Again," December 4, 2019, https://www.pymnts.com/news/retail/2019/how-and-why-major-retailers-are-embracing-print-catalogs-again.
19. Emarketer, "Tactics b2b marketers plan to use," Jan20,2020,accessedathttps://chart-na1.emarketer.com/235363/tactics-us-b2b-marketers-plan-use-2020-jan-2020-of-respondents, June 22, 2020.

Appendix: Marketing Plan

OVERVIEW

The marketing plan is an essential element of the company strategic plan, an effort to maintain a fit between company objectives and capabilities and the continuously changing company environment. The approach to the marketing plan presented here addresses this important aspect of planning. You should first focus on corporate planning and, subsequently, on the marketing strategy.

A-1 Defining the Company's Mission Statement

Most organizations prominently articulate their mission statement. If your project involves creating a marketing plan for an existing business, check the company website to identify its mission statement. If you are creating your own new business, then articulate a mission statement that expresses the vision and principles of the company, a guide to what the company wants to accomplish in the marketplace. The mission should underscore the distinctive differentiating aspects of the business and the company's approach to its different stakeholders: consumers, employees, and society.

A-2 Identifying Company Goals and Objectives

A company's objectives stem from its mission statement. Objectives can be expressed in many different terms, including profit, sales, market share, and return on investment (ROI). Company objectives may be to enter new international markets or to increase market share in the national market. Alternatively, they may involve focusing on research and development to bring cutting-edge technology to the marketplace. Objectives can also be expressed in terms of societal outcomes, such as increasing literacy or reducing world hunger, depending on the focus of the business.

As mentioned in Chapter 1, the ultimate organizational goal of the company is creating profit for the firm and wealth for its shareholders. In that sense, increasing productivity and production, maximizing product adoption and consumption, and as a result, increasing sales constitute primary objectives for the company, which can be accomplished with appropriate marketing strategies. In the process of achieving organizational goals, companies offer quality and value to consumers and businesses, engaging customers to create customer satisfaction and loyalty. They compete to offer a wide variety of goods and services and a maximum number of choices for consumers. As they compete, they lower prices that consumers pay for their products to gain market share. Based on your understanding of the company, what are the different goals and objectives it is pursuing? If working with a hypothetical company, you could think about the goals of competition in the process of identifying the goals and objectives of your company.

A-3 Managing the Business Portfolio

The third step in creating the marketing plan involves evaluating the different strategic business units of the company. At this stage, the company must identify the products that have great promise in the marketplace and need additional resources, the products that are performing well in a mature market, and those that are not, which must be divested. Establishing a strategic fit between the firm and the target market is essential. The company may have the resources to support a particular strategic business unit, but if the unit does not fit with the company's long-term goals or if selling the unit would use resources that could be invested more profitably to further the company's goals, the company might consider selling this particular business. Companies periodically review their different businesses in the portfolio and make decisions on whether to acquire new ones or divest those that might be unprofitable or that do not represent a good fit. In the analysis of the portfolio, you will benefit from using the growth-share matrix of the Boston Consulting Group and the product-market matrix introduced in Chapter 8 (especially Section 8-9). Place the different strategic business units in the appropriate categories and comment on their position. Do they need additional resources? Are they performing optimally? Scrutinize them in terms of their market and financial performance and potential.

A-4 Strategic Business Unit Planning

A-4a Developing the Strategic Business Unit Mission

Each business unit must develop its own mission statement, focusing on the strategic fit between strategic business unit (SBU) resources and the company goals with regard to its target markets. At this level, the SBU mission statement should be more specific than the corporate mission statement, focusing on the brand or product itself.

A-4b Conducting the Strengths, Weaknesses, Opportunities, and Threats Analysis

An important step in the analysis process involves identifying the company's strengths, weaknesses, opportunities, and threats (SWOT). First, examine the microenvironment of marketing, addressing its strengths and weaknesses. Here, one must first examine the strengths and weaknesses related to the company, consumers, suppliers, intermediaries, other

Microenvironment	List of Strengths	List of Weaknesses
Company		
Consumers		
Suppliers		
Intermediaries		
Other facilitators		
Competition		

TABLE A-1 Microenvironment Strengths, Weaknesses, Opportunities, and Threats Analysis

Macroenvironment	List of Threats	List of Opportunities
Sociodemographic and cultural		
Economic		
Natural		
Technological		
Political		
Legal		

TABLE A-2 Macroenvironment Strengths, Weaknesses, Opportunities, and Threats Analysis

facilitators of marketing functions, and the competition (see **Table A-1**). Next, examine threats and opportunities in the sociodemographic and cultural environment, the economic and natural environments, the technological environment, and the political and legal environments (refer to Chapters 2 and 3 and **Table A-2**).

A-5 The Marketing Plan

The marketing plan will focus on the SBU (product or brand) you have selected, that you have proposed to analyze. It involves the following steps:

A-5a Identifying Marketing Objectives

Marketing objectives could be defined in terms of dollar sales, units sold, or in terms of market share. They can also be defined, among others, in terms of brand awareness, brand loyalty, or customer traffic, as would be the case for a retail operation.

A-5b Defining the Marketing Strategy

The marketing strategy involves identifying segments of consumers who are similar with regard to key traits and who would respond well to a marketing mix used (market segmentation); selecting the segments that the company can serve most efficiently and developing products tailored to each (market targeting); and offering the products to the market, communicating through the marketing mix the product traits and benefits that differentiate the product in the consumer's mind (market positioning).

At this stage, you should clearly identify the different market segments, selecting those segments that represent the best fit with the company goals and objectives, and designing the strategies aimed to serve these segments more effectively than competitors. Refer to Chapter 6 in your analysis.

An important component of the marketing strategy is the competitive analysis. Identify and describe the products, markets, and strategies competitors are using. Then define your brand's value proposition and position the brand in the consumer's mind relative to competing brands. How are your brand traits and benefits superior to those of competitors?

A-5c Developing the Marketing Mix

After identifying the overall marketing strategy, you can proceed to develop the marketing mix—the four Ps of marketing (product, place, price, and promotion)—that the company can use to influence demand for its products:

- Product—Decide on design, features, brand name, packaging, and service components that will best meet the needs of the target market that has been identified. Refer to Chapters 8 and 9.
- Place—Decide on the types of channels used, market coverage, assortment, transportation and logistics, and inventory management that will be needed to move the product from production to the consumer or business customer. Refer to Chapters 10 and 11.
- Price—Decide on the price, discounts, and credit terms that will be used. Because of brand parity, pricing is an important decision variable in purchase decisions. Refer to Chapter 12.
- Promotion—Decide on advertising, personal selling, consumer and/or trade promotion, public relations (PR), and publicity that the company should pursue. Although the nature of the product will have some impact on which promotions to use, it is also important to consider how competitors are promoting their product. Not only is it necessary to gain the attention of potential customers, it is also necessary to convince them concerning the superiority of the product being offered. Refer to Chapters 13 through 15.

A-5d Marketing Implementation

Suggest how marketing plans can be turned into marketing action programs to accomplish the marketing objectives. For example, the marketing objective may be to increase awareness of a new product among the selected target market. Implementation may involve developing a series of social media and television ads that promote this new product.

Furthermore, identify which social media, websites, or television shows would be the most effective in reaching the projected target market, or which influencer you should tap to pitch your product.

A-5e Marketing Control

Suggest the different procedures for evaluating the outcomes of the implemented marketing strategies and the corrective actions needed to ensure that the previously stated marketing objectives are met. For example, if the objective was to increase product awareness by 30 percent, recall tests could be used to determine whether the objective has been reached. If not, the corrective action could be the purchase of additional television time or the development of a new advertising theme.

A-5f Calculating Marketing Return on Investment (Marketing ROI)

At this stage, it is important to assess your marketing plan by calculating the marketing return on investment (Marketing ROI) on the amount that the company spends on marketing. Divide the net marketing contribution (net sales minus cost of goods sold, minus marketing expenses) by total marketing expenses to measure the degree to which marketing efforts contribute to revenue growth. See Chapter 6. Decide on corrective actions if objectives are not met.

Glossary

acceleration principle An increase or decrease in consumer demand for a product that can create a drastic change in derived business demand.
accessibility The ability to communicate with and reach the target market.
accessory pricing Pricing of accessories and other optional products sold with the main product.
acculturation The process of learning a new culture.
achievers Psychographic group of individuals who are goal oriented, conservative, committed to career and family, and favor established, prestige products that demonstrate success to peers.
actionability The extent to which the target market segment is responsive to the marketing strategies used.
adaptive selling Altering sales behaviors during a customer interaction or across interactions based on the perceived selling situation.
administered channel arrangement An arrangement between intermediaries such that a dominant member of the distribution channel in terms of size, expertise, or influence coordinates the tasks of each member in the channel.
advertising Any form of paid communication directed to an organization's customers or other stakeholders.
advertising appeal The design a creative will use to attract attention to and interest in an advertisement.
advertising effectiveness research Studies conducted to examine the effectiveness and appropriateness of advertisements aimed at individual markets.
affective message strategies Messages designed to invoke feelings and emotions within the audience.
agents Intermediaries who represent buyers or sellers; they do not take possession of or title to the merchandise, and they work based on commission or fees.
AIDA An acronym that stands for attention, interest, desire, and action.
anchor stores Department stores situated at the end (anchor) positions in malls to generate consumer traffic.
aspirational groups Groups that individuals aspire to join in the future—for example, by virtue of education, employment, and training.
assimilation Adapting to and fully integrating into the new culture.
associative reference groups Groups that individuals belong to.
assurance Refers to the knowledge and courtesy of the employees and their ability to inspire customers to trust and have confidence in the service provider.
atmospherics The general atmosphere of the store created by its physical attributes, including lighting and music tempo, the fixtures and other displays, colors, and store layout.
attitudes Relatively enduring and consistent feelings (affective responses) about a good or service.
attribute/benefit positioning Positioning that communicates product attributes and benefits, differentiating each brand from the other company.
attribution theory The process of deciding the cause of a service failure or poor service.
audience Individuals who observe a marketing communication and decode the message.
augmented product A product enhanced by the addition of extra or unsolicited services or benefits, such as a warranty, repair services, maintenance, and other services that enhance product use to prompt a purchase.

baby boomers Born between 1946 and 1964, represent 22.6% of the population in the United States, but they account for almost half of the total spending, and the majority, 60 percent, own their own home; a considerable amount of their income is allocated to mortgage expenditures, home furnishings, and renovation.
bait and switch A marketing tactic in which a retailer promotes a special deal on a particular product and then, when consumers arrive at the store, the retailer attempts to switch them to a higher-priced item.
battle of the brands The conflict between manufacturers and resellers to promote their own brands.
behavioral segmentation The process of identifying clusters of consumers who seek the same product benefits or who use or consume the product in a similar fashion.
behavioral targeting The utilization of web data to target individuals.
beliefs Associations between a good or service and attributes of that good or service.
believers Psychographic group of individuals who are conservative, conventional, and focus on tradition, family, religion, and community. They prefer established brands, favoring American products.
benefit segmentation The process of identifying market segments based on important differences between the benefits sought by the target market from purchasing a particular product.

bid pricing Pricing that involves competitive bidding for a contract, whereby a firm will price based on how it believes competitors will price, rather than based on demand or costs.
big emerging markets (BEMs) Large countries with emerging markets that present the greatest potential for international trade and expansion.
blogs Online musings that cover a wide range of topics.
blueprinting The process of diagramming a service operation.
bonus packs Sales promotion that offers customers some type of discount for purchasing multiple items.
bounce-back coupons Coupons that cannot be used until the next purchase.
brand A name, design, symbol, or a combination thereof that identifies the product or the seller and that's used to differentiate the product from competitors' offerings.
brand advertising An advertisement designed to promote a particular brand with little or no information in the advertisement.
brand awareness research Research investigating how consumers' knowledge and recognition of a brand name affects their purchasing behavior.
brand character (or trade character) A character that personifies the brand.
brand equity (or brand franchise) Brands with high consumer awareness and loyalty.
brand extensions The use of an existing brand name to introduce products in a new product category.
brand logo A distinctive mark, sign, symbol, or graphic version of a company's name that is used to identify and promote the company's product.
brand mark The part of a brand that can be seen but not spoken.
brand name The part of a brand that can be spoken; it may include words, letters, or numbers.
branded media A movie or show that contains a brand name or logo with a story line that intersects the brand's mission or current advertising campaign.
brand-name generation The testing of brand names and logos.
breakeven analysis Identifies the number of units the company needs to sell or the total number of dollars it needs to make on sales to break even with regard to costs, given a particular price.
bricks-and-clicks Firms that operate both a bricks-and-mortar facility and an Internet e-commerce site.
brokers Intermediaries who bring buyers and sellers together; they do not take possession of or title to the merchandise, and they work based on commission or fees.
bundling Pricing of bundled products sold together.
buyer behavior research Research examining consumer brand preferences, brand attitudes, and brand-related behavior.
buyer-readiness stage segmentation The process of segmenting the market based on individuals' stage of readiness to buy a product.
buyer-seller dyad Two-way communication between a buyer and a seller.
buyer's regret A feeling of anxiety related to the consumer's loss of freedom to spend money on other products.
buying When a retailer purchases excess inventory of a product while it is on-deal to be sold later when it is off-deal.
buying center Group of individuals who are involved in the purchase process.

cash cows Products with high market share and slow growth that generate large amounts of cash, in excess of the reinvestment required to maintain market share.
catalog retailers Retailers selling products through mail catalogs.
catalog specialist (Also called category killers): Large specialty stores that carry a narrow variety of merchandise but offer a wide assortment.
causal (experimental) research Research that examines cause-and-effect relationships.
cause-related marketing A long-term partnership between a nonprofit organization and a corporation that is integrated into the corporation's marketing plan.
cause-related marketing A long-term partnership between a non-profit organization and a corporation that is integrated into the corporation's marketing plan.
central business districts Business districts located in the commercial and cultural heart of the city, in the middle of busy downtowns, and close to movie theaters and banks.
channel captain The dominant member of a channel of distribution.
channel performance and coverage studies Studies investigating whether existing channels are appropriate for the marketing task at hand.
channels of distribution The totality of organizations and individuals involved in the distribution process who take title to or assist in the transferring of title in the distribution process from the producer to the individual or organizational consumer.
clicks-only firms Organizations that sell only over the Internet.
close-ended questions Questions that supply possible answers.
co-branding Using the brands of two different companies on one single product.
coercive power Power over channel members based on the ability of one or more intermediaries to remove privileges for non-compliance.
cognitive dissonance An anxiety feeling of uncertainty about whether or not the consumer made the right purchase decision.
cognitive message strategies The presentation of rational arguments or pieces of information to consumers.
community shopping centers Shopping centers with fewer than 40 retailers, containing a department store, a supermarket, and several smaller specialty retailers.

comparative advertising An advertisement that compares the featured brand with another brand, either named or implied.
competitive product studies Pricing studies that determine the price the market will bear for the respective product category based on a survey of competitors' prices.
competitor positioning The process of comparing the firm's brand, directly or indirectly, with those of competitors.
conative message strategies Messages designed to elicit some type of audience behavior, such as a purchase or inquiry.
concentrated marketing The process of selecting only one market segment and targeting it with one single brand.
concept development research Studies that evaluate the viability of a new product and the composition of the other marketing mix elements in light of the product's intended target market.
consequence The degree of importance or danger of the outcome itself.
content marketing Also known as branded content, content that is authentic and useful for businesses and/or consumers.
content seeding Providing incentives for consumers to share content about a brand.
continuous innovations Innovations that have no disruption on consumption patterns and involve only product alterations, such as new flavors or a new product that is an improvement over the old offering.
contractual agreement A written agreement between the buyer and seller that states the terms of the interaction, costs, and length of the commitment.
contractual channel arrangement A contract between intermediaries that defines all the tasks that each channel member must perform with regard to production, delivery strategy and terms of sale, territorial rights, promotional support, the price policies of each intermediary, and contract length.
controlled test marketing Offering a new product to a group of stores and evaluating the market reaction to it.
convenience goods Relatively inexpensive and frequently purchased products.
convenience sample Sample composed of individuals who are easy to contact for the researcher.
convenience stores Small retailers that are located in residential areas, are open long hours, and carry limited lines of high turnover necessities.
cooperative advertising program An arrangement whereby a manufacturer agrees to reimburse retailers or other channel members that feature the manufacturer's brands in the ad for a portion of their advertising costs.
cooperative merchandising agreement (CMA) A formal agreement between the retailer and manufacturer to undertake a cooperative marketing effort.
core product The fundamental benefit, or problem solution, that consumers seek (expected or actual).
cost per thousand (CPM) The cost of reaching 1,000 members of a media vehicle's audience.
cost-based pricing Pricing strategy whereby the firm sets the price by calculating merchandise, service, and overhead costs and then adds an amount needed to cover the profit goal.
cost-plus pricing Pricing strategy that involves adding a target profit margin to total costs.
coupons Sales promotion that offers customers some type of price reduction.
cross-ruffing coupon A coupon for one product placed on another product.
cross-selling The marketing of additional items with the purchase of a particular good or service.
crowdsourcing The act of taking tasks traditionally performed by an employee or an outside service provider and outsourcing them to the community in the form of an open call.
cues Stimuli in the environment, such as products or advertisements, that create individual responses.
cultural values Beliefs about a specific mode of conduct or desirable end state that guide the selection or evaluation of behavior.
cultures A society's personality and a continuously evolving totality of learned and shared meanings, rituals, norms, and traditions among the members of an organization or society. Elements include language, religion, cultural values, and norms.
customary pricing Pricing strategy whereby a firm sets prices and attempts to maintain them over time.
customer lifetime value (LTV) The estimated profitability of the customer over the course of his or her entire relationship with a company.
customer relationship management (CRM) A database application program designed to build long-term loyalty with customers through the use of a personal touch.
customer valuation theory (CVT) Focuses on customer financial contributions to the firm–direct or indirect, or based on their scope.
customer-focus needs segment Market segment willing to pay for higher-than-average service that is tailored to meet users' needs.

data mining Computer analysis of customer data to determine patterns, profiles, or relationships for the purpose of customer profiling or predicting purchase behavior.
data warehousing The process of capturing and storing data within a single database that is accessible to internal personnel for a variety of internal purposes, such as marketing, sales, and customer service.
database marketing The collection, analysis, and use of large volumes of customer data to develop marketing programs and customer profiles.
deceptive pricing Strategy used by sellers who state prices or price savings that may mislead consumers or that are not available to consumers.

decider The member of the buying center who makes the final decision.
decline stage Stage in the product life cycle where products are rapidly losing ground to new technologies or product alternatives, and consequently, sales and profits are rapidly declining.
decoding The process of interpreting the meaning conveyed in a marketing message.
Delphi method A method of forecasting sales that involves asking a number of experts to estimate market performance, aggregating the results, and then sharing this information with the said experts; the process is repeated several times, until a consensus is reached.
demand curve Curve that portrays the number of units bought for a particular price in a given time period.
demand-based pricing Pricing strategy that takes into consideration customers' perceptions of value, rather than the seller's cost, as the fundamental component of the pricing decision.
demands Wants backed by the ability to buy a respective good or service.
demarketing A company strategy aimed at reducing demand for its own products to benefit society.
demographic segmentation The process of identifying market segments based on age, gender, race, income, education, occupation, social class, life cycle stage, and household size.
demographics Statistics that describe the population, such as age, gender, education, occupation, and income.
depth interviews A qualitative research method involving extensive interviews aimed at discovering consumer motivations, feelings, and attitudes toward an issue of concern to the sponsor, using unstructured interrogation.
derived demand Demand for a good or service that is generated from the demand for consumer goods and services.
descriptive research All research methods observing or describing phenomena.
differential pricing Pricing strategy that involves charging different prices based on product features, time of sale or consumption, season, or place.
differential response The extent to which market segments respond differently to marketing strategies.
differentiated marketing A targeting strategy identifying market segments with different preferences for a particular product category and targeting each segment with different brands and different marketing strategies.
digital marketing strategies Refers to all marketing strategies regardless of the device a consumer (or business) uses: desktop, laptop, tablet, or mobile phone.
direct channel of distribution A channel that has no intermediaries; the manufacturer sells directly to the final consumer.
direct response marketing The promotion of a product directly from the manufacturer or seller to the buyer without any intermediaries involved in the transaction.
direct selling Selling that involves a salesperson, typically an independent distributor, contacting a consumer at a convenient location (e.g., his or her home or workplace), demonstrating the product's use and benefits, taking orders, and delivering the merchandise.
dissociative groups Groups that individuals want to dissociate from through their behavior.
distribution centers Computerized warehouses designed to move goods.
distributors Intermediaries whose task is to ensure the convenient, timely, and safe distribution of the product to consumers.
diversification Opportunity for expansion involving developing or acquiring new products for new markets.
dogs Products with low market share and slow growth.
drive (or motive) A stimulus that encourages consumers to engage in an action to reduce the need.
drive to maturity Stage of economic development in which modern technology is applied in all areas of the economy.
dual channel of distribution The use of two or more channels of distribution to appeal to different markets.
dumping Selling products below cost to get rid of excess inventory or to undermine competition.
durable goods Tangible products that have a prolonged use.
dynamic pricing A strategy whereby much higher prices are charged depending on demand.
dynamically continuous innovations Innovations, such as mobile phones, that do not significantly alter consumer behavior, but they represent a change in the consumption pattern.

early adopters Consumers who purchase the product early in the life cycle and are opinion leaders in their communities.
early majority Consumers who are more risk averse but enjoy the status of being among the first in their peer group to buy what will be a popular product.
earned media Media exposure earned through organic search, public relations, and/or influencer marketing.
e-commerce The selling of goods and services over the Internet.
emergency goods Goods purchased to address urgent needs.
empathy The caring, individualized attention the service firm provides to each customer.
encoding The process of transposing the objective or goal of a marketing communication concept into an actual marketing communication piece, such as an advertisement, brochure, or sign.
ethics Philosophical principles that serve as operational guidelines for both individuals and organizations concerning what is right and wrong.
ethnography The study of cultures.
exclusive distribution strategy A distribution strategy that offers a high control of the intermediaries handling the product and thus of the marketing strategy by limiting their number to just one or two per geographic area.
expected (or actual) product The basic physical product, including styling, features, brand name, and packaging, that delivers the benefits that consumers seek.

experiencers Psychographic group of individuals who are young, enthusiastic, and impulsive. They seek variety and excitement, and spend substantially on fashion, entertainment, and socializing.
experiences Personal experiences that consumers perceive as valuable because they fulfill consumer needs and wants.
expert power Power over the other channel members based on experience and knowledge that a channel member possesses.
exploratory research Research conducted early in the research process that helps further define a problem or identify additional problems that need to be investigated.
extended self The idea that possessions contribute to the sense of self, as we learn, define, and remind ourselves of who we are by our possessions.
extensive problem solving Consumer decision making that involves going carefully through each of the steps of the consumer decision-making process.
external secondary data Data collected by an entity not affiliated with the company.

fad A fashion that quickly becomes very popular and just as quickly disappears.
family branding (or blanket branding) Branding strategy whereby one brand name is used for more than one product.
fashion A current style.
feedback The response of the audience to the message.
field salesperson A salesperson who is involved in going to a potential customer's place of business to solicit accounts.
financial risk The amount of monetary loss the consumer incurs if the service fails.
fixed costs Costs that do not vary with the amount of output.
flexible pricing Pricing strategy that allows a firm to set prices based on negotiation with the customer, or based on customer buying power.
focus group interviews A qualitative research approach investigating a research question, using a moderator to guide discussion within a group of subjects recruited to meet certain characteristics.
foreign trade zone (FTZ) Tax-free area in the United States that is not considered part of the United States in terms of import regulations and restrictions. Also called a free trade zone.
freestanding inserts (FSI) Sheets of coupons distributed in newspapers, primarily on Sunday.
freight forwarders Specialized firms that collect shipments from different businesses, consolidate them for part of the distance, and deliver them to a destination, in what is typically a door-to-door service.
frequency programs Sales promotions offered to current customers and designed to build repeat purchase behavior.
functional service quality The process whereby the service was performed.

gap theory Method of measuring service quality that involves measuring the gap between expectations and customers' evaluation of the service.
gatekeeper Individual who is responsible for the flow of information to the members of the buying center.
Generation X A segment of individuals born between 1965 and 1977, whose focus is on family and children, striving to balance family with work, and outsourcing household chores and babysitting.
Generation Y A segment of individuals born between 1978 and 2002; they spend substantial amounts on clothing, automobiles, and college education; they live in rental apartments or with parents.
Generation Z Individuals born after 2001 that makes up approximately 25% of the U.S population, and are the most connected and sophisticated technological generation.
generics Products that emphasize the product, rather than the brand of the manufacturer or reseller.
geographic segmentation Market segmentation based on geographic location, such as country or region.
geo-targeting A mobile marketing tactic that reaches customers where they are located based on their mobile device.
goods Tangible products, such as cereals, automobiles, and clothing.
growth stage Stage in the product life cycle characterized by increasing competition, with new product variants offered to the market, as well as rapid product adoption by the target market.
growth-share matrix Portfolio matrix developed by the Boston Consulting Group and one of the most popular bases for evaluating company product portfolios; it assumes that, to be successful, a company should have a portfolio of products with different growth rates and different market shares.

heterogeneous shopping goods Goods that vary significantly in terms of functions, physical characteristics, and quality.
heuristics Decision rules that individuals adopt to make a decision process more efficient.
high-expectation service segment Market segment that is the most demanding and needs extensive customer focus, placing considerable demands on service providers while also wanting low prices.
high-involvement purchases Purchases that have a high personal relevance.
homogeneous shopping goods Goods that vary little in terms of physical characteristics or functions.
horizontal integration An acquisition or merger with an intermediary at the same level in the distribution channel.
horizontal marketing systems (HMS) Intermediaries at the same level of the distribution channel pooling resources and achieving partial ownership of the system, achieving economies of scale, and playing on their individual strengths.
hub-and-spoke distribution centers Distribution centers designed to speed up warehousing and delivery, by channeling operations to one center (hub) that is

particularly well equipped to handle the distribution of products to their destination.

ideas marketing Concepts that can be used to fulfill consumer needs and wants.
impulse goods Goods bought without any earlier planning, such as candy, gum, and magazines.
inbound telemarketing The process through which an order-taker salesperson handles incoming calls from customers and prospects.
indirect channel of distribution A channel that involves one or more intermediaries between the manufacturer and the consumer.
industrialization The use of machines and standardized operating procedures to increase the productivity and efficiency of a business.
influencer A member of the buying center who influences the decision but may not necessarily use the product.
influencer marketing Involves an individual marketing a brand through social media, and is word-of-mouth communication from individuals who are seen as thought leaders or opinion leaders within their social circles or as experts within particular fields.
informative advertising An advertisement designed to provide the audience with some type of information.
innovators Psychographic group of individuals who are successful, sophisticated, and receptive to new technologies.
inseparability The simultaneous production and consumption of a service.
instant redemption coupon A coupon that can be redeemed immediately while making a purchase.
instrumental values Values related to processes whereby one can attain certain goals.
intangibility The lack of tangible assets of a service that can be seen, touched, smelled, heard, or tasted before a purchase.
integrated marketing communications (IMC) The coordination and integration of all marketing communication tools, avenues, and sources within a company into a seamless program designed to maximize the communication impact on consumers, businesses, and other constituencies of an organization.
intensive distribution strategy A strategy that has as its purpose full market coverage, making the product available to all target consumers when and where consumers want it.
intercompany tie-in A sales promotion involving two different companies offering complementary products.
intermediaries (or middlemen or channel members) The organizations or individuals involved in the distribution process.
intermodal transportation Transportation using two or more different transportation modes—a combination of truck, rail, air, and waterways.
internal secondary data Data previously collected by a company to address a problem not related to the current research question.
Internet (digital) marketing The promotion of products through the Internet.
Internet retailing Selling through the Internet using web-based tools to increase market penetration and market diversification.
intra-company tie-in A sales promotion involving two or more distinct products within the same company.
intrusion value Advertising that has the ability to break through clutter and gain a person's attention.
inventory The amount of goods being stored.

judgment sample A sample of individuals thought to be representative of the population.
jury of expert opinion An approach to sales forecasting based on the opinions of different experts.

keiretsus Japanese families of firms with interlocking stakes in one another.

laggards Consumers who are the last to adopt new products and who do so only in late maturity.
late majority Consumers with limited means likely to adopt products only if the products are widely popular and the risk associated with buying them is minimal.
law of demand Economic law whereby consumers are believed to purchase more products at a lower price than at a higher price.
learning Change in individual thought processes or behavior attributed to experience or new information.
legitimate power Power over the other channel members by virtue of an intermediary's status or position in the firm.
licensing A process that involves a licensor, who shares the brand name, technology, and know-how with a licensee in return for royalties.
lifestyles Individuals' style of living as expressed through activities, interests, and opinions.
lifetime value of a customer A measure of the value of a customer over the typical life span of a firm's customers.
Likert scale A series of statements that asks respondents to indicate their level of agreement or disagreement.
limited problem solving Consumer decision making that involves less problem solving. This type of decision making is used for products that are not especially visible, nor too expensive.
line extension The process of extending the existing brand name by introducing new product offerings in an existing product category.
logistics (or physical distribution) All the activities involved in the physical flow and storage of materials, semi-finished goods, and finished goods to customers in a manner that is efficient and cost effective.
loss-leader pricing Pricing whereby the firm advertises a product at a price that is significantly less than its usual price to create traffic in the stores for consumers to purchase higher-margin products.
low-involvement products Products with limited personal relevance.

loyalty segmentation The process of segmenting the market based on the degree of consumer loyalty to the brand.

macroenvironment Environment of the firm, which includes the sociodemographic and cultural environment, the economic and natural environment, the political environment, and the technological environment.
makers Psychographic group of individuals who are self-sufficient. They have the skill and energy to carry out projects, respect authority, and are unimpressed by material possessions.
manufacturers' agent (or manufacturers' representative) Representative who works as the company's sales representative, representing noncompeting manufacturers in a particular market, and is paid on a commission basis.
manufacturers' brands (or national brands) Brands owned by a manufacturer.
market development The process of developing new markets for the company's existing product or creating new product uses.
market penetration The process of increasing the usage rate of current customers and attracting competitors' customers to sell more products to present customers without changing the product.
marketing Marketing is the activity, set of institutions, and processes for creating, communicating, delivering, and exchanging offerings that have value for customers, clients, partners, and society at large.
marketing analytics Refers to the coordinated collection of data, systems, analysis tools, and techniques designed to make sense of marketing information and to assess and forecast marketing performance.
marketing concept A marketing philosophy that assumes a company can compete more effectively if it first researches consumers' generic needs, wants, and preferences, as well as good- or service-related attitudes and interests, and then delivers the goods and services more efficiently and effectively than competitors.
marketing era Period from 1950 until the present, when the primary focus of marketing shifted to the needs of consumers and society.
marketing intelligence Results obtained from monitoring developments in the firm's environment.
marketing mix Tools marketers use, consisting of product, price, place, and promotion, to deliver value to consumers and profits to the firm.
marketing myopia The tendency of marketing efforts to focus on products, production, or sales and ignore specific consumer needs or important markets.
marketing orientation A firm-wide focus on customer needs and on delivering high quality to consumers in the process of achieving company objectives.
marketing research The systematic design, collection, recording, analysis, interpretation, and reporting of information pertinent to a particular marketing decision facing a company.
marketing return on investment (marketing ROI) A way of measuring the return on investment from the amount a company spends on marketing.
markets All of the actual and potential consumers of a company's products.
markup pricing a variant of cost-plus pricing, with a markup used to cover selling costs and desired profit margin.
mass marketing A shotgun approach to segmentation that involves identifying the product-related preferences of most consumers and then targeting the product broadly to everyone.
maturity stage Stage in the product life cycle characterized by a slowdown in sales growth as the product is adopted by most target consumers and by a leveling or decline in profits primarily as a result of intense price competition.
measurability The ability to estimate the size of a market segment.
media research Studies that evaluate media availability and the appropriateness of the medium for a company's message.
medium The venue the source uses to send a marketing communication message to its intended audience.
merchandise mix The product assortment and brands that a store carries.
merchant wholesalers Independent intermediaries who take title to and possession of products distributed to resellers or organizational consumers.
message The completed marketing communication piece.
microenvironment Environment of the firm, which includes the company, its consumers, suppliers, distributors, and other facilitators of the marketing function and competition.
micromarketing A process that involves a microanalysis of the customer and customer-specific marketing.
missionary salesperson A sales support person whose task is to provide information about a good or service.
mission-sharing sales approach Sales approach that involves two organizations developing a common mission and then sharing resources to accomplish that mission.
mobile marketing refers to the development and application of marketing strategies for smartphones.
modified rebuy situation Occasional purchases or purchases for which the members of the buying center have limited experience.
monopolistic competition Market that consists of many buyers and many sellers with products that vary.
morals Personal beliefs or standards used to guide an individual's actions.
multiattribute segmentation The process of segmenting the market by using multiple segmentation variables.
multibranding Using different brand names for products that the firm sells in the same product category.
multichannel distribution system (hybrid marketing channel) The use of multiple (more than two) channels of distribution, thus offering customers multiple purchase and communication options.

naturalistic inquiry An observational research approach that requires the use of natural rather than contrived settings because behaviors take substantial meaning from their context.
needs Basic human requirements such as food and water.
need-satisfaction sales approach Sales approach aimed at discovering a customer's needs and then providing solutions that satisfy those needs.
neighborhood business districts Business districts that meet the needs of the neighborhood and that tend to be located on a main street of the neighborhood; typically, they have a supermarket, a drugstore, and several smaller retailers.
neighborhood shopping centers Shopping centers that have between five and 15 retailers and that serve the neighborhood, providing convenience in the form of a supermarket, discount store, laundry service, and other smaller specialty stores.
network marketing (or multilevel marketing) An alternative distribution structure, using acquaintance networks for the purpose of distribution.
new buy situation Purchases made by a business for the first time or purchases for which no one in the organization has had previous experience.
noise Anything that interferes with the audience receiving the message.
nondurable goods Tangible products that are consumed relatively quickly and purchased on a regular basis; they last less than two years.
nonresponse The inability or refusal by a respondent to participate in a study.
norms Are derived from values and are rules that dictate what is right or wrong, acceptable or unacceptable.

observational research (or observation) A research approach whereby subjects are observed interacting with a product and reacting to other components of the marketing mix and the environment.
occasion segmentation The process of segmenting based on the time or the occasion when the product should be purchased or consumed.
occasional transactions Transactions whereby buyer and seller interact infrequently in the process of making the transaction.
off-invoice allowance A financial discount or price-off on each case that a member of the distribution channel orders.
off-price retailers Retailers that sell brand-name and designer merchandise below regular retail.
oligopolistic competition Market that consists of few sellers who dominate the market.
open-ended questions Questions with free-format responses that the respondent can address as he or she sees appropriate.
opportunity risk The risk involved when consumers must choose one service over another.
order getters Salespeople who actively generate potential leads and persuade customers to make a purchase.
order takers Salespeople who process routine orders from customers.
outbound telemarketing The process through which an order-getter salesperson calls prospects and attempts to persuade them to make a purchase.
overlay procedure of using two or more promotions in a single offer.
owned media Media owned by the company, such as social media, company websites, customer service, and direct marketing through channels that include email and mobile devices.

packaging All the activities involved in designing the product container.
paid media Media the company pays for such as traditional advertising, direct marketing, and online ads.
penetration pricing Pricing strategy whereby firms initially price the product below the price of competitors to quickly penetrate the market at competitors' expense and acquire a large market share, and then gradually raise the price.
perception The manner in which people collect, organize, and interpret information from the world around them to create a meaningful image of reality.
performance risk The chance that the service will not perform or provide the benefit for which it was purchased.
perishability The inability of a service to be inventoried or stored.
personal selling A direct communication approach between the buyer and seller with the express purpose of selling a product.
personality An individual's unique characteristic patterns of thinking, feeling, and behaving.
persuasive advertising An advertisement designed to persuade viewers' thinking in some way.
physical risk The probability that a service will actually cause physical harm to the customer.
pioneer advertising An advertisement designed to build primary demand for a product.
place (or distribution) The physical movement of products from the producer to individual or organizational consumers and the transfer of ownership and risk; the third P of marketing.
plant/warehouse location study A study that evaluates the appropriateness of plant or warehouse location to ensure that it is in accordance with the needs of the company.
point-of-sale (POS)-based projections Market projections based on the use of store scanners in weekly and bi-weekly store audits.
predatory pricing Pricing strategies used to eliminate small competitors and to deceive consumers.
preference goods Convenience goods that become differentiated through branding and achieve some degree of brand loyalty.
premiums A promotional tactic of offering consumers some type of free merchandise for purchasing the product.
prestige pricing Strategy based on the premise that consumers will feel that products below a particular price

will have inferior quality and will not convey a desired status and image.

price The amount of money necessary to purchase a product; the second P of marketing.

price ceiling The maximum amount that consumers are willing to pay for a product.

price confusion Strategies to confuse consumers so that they do not quite understand the price that they ultimately have to pay.

price discrimination The practice of charging different prices to different buyers of the same merchandise.

price elasticity Buyer sensitivity to a change in price.

price fixing Agreement among channel members at the same level in the channel of distribution to charge the same price to all customers.

price floor The lowest price a company can charge to attain its profit goal.

price leadership The tendency of one firm or a few firms to be the first to announce price changes, with the rest of the firms following.

price/quality positioning A strategy whereby products and services are positioned as offering the best value for the money.

price-offs a reduction in the listed retail price of a product.

price-sensitive segment The market segment that looks for low prices but also has low service requirements. It wants the work done at the lowest possible cost.

primary data Data collected for the purpose of addressing the problem at hand.

private label brands Reseller (wholesaler or retailer) brands.

private warehouses Warehouses that are owned or leased and operated by firms storing their own products.

problem-solution sales approach Sales approach that requires the salesperson to analyze the prospect's operation and offer a viable solution.

product class positioning A strategy used to differentiate a company as a leader in a product category as defined by the respective companies.

product concept A marketing philosophy that assumes consumers prefer products that are easily accessible and inexpensive.

product depth The number of different offerings for a product category.

product development The process of developing new products to appeal to the company's existing market.

product differentiation Identifying an appealing, exclusive, and clear value proposition based on the brand's competitive advantage.

product diffusion Manner in which consumers accept new products and the speed of adoption.

product introduction stage Stage in the product life cycle when the product is available for purchase for the first time.

product length The total number of brands in the product mix—all the brands the company sells.

product life cycle (PLC) The performance of the product in terms of sales and profit over time.

product line The related brands the company offers in the same product category.

product line pricing Pricing that involves creating price differences between the different items in the product line, such that specific price points are used to differentiate among the items in the line.

product mix The complete assortment of the products that a company offers to its target consumers.

product packaging design Studies that evaluate consumers' reaction to a package, the extent to which the package adequately communicates information to the consumer, and the distribution implications of the package.

product placement Sales promotion technique of placing branded goods or services in movies, on television shows, or in theatrical performances.

product portfolio The totality of products the company manages as separate businesses.

product testing Studies that estimate product preference and performance in a given market.

product user positioning A positioning strategy that focuses on the product user, rather than on the product.

product width The total number of product lines the company offers.

production concept A marketing philosophy that assumes consumers prefer products that are easily accessible and inexpensive.

production era Period between 1870 and 1930, when the primary focus of marketing was on producing the best products possible at the lowest price.

product-market matrix A matrix used to identify future products and opportunities for companies.

products Any offering that can satisfy consumer needs and wants; products include goods (tangible products), services, ideas, and experiences; the first P of marketing.

profit-maximization objectives Attempts to maximize the gross margin on each unit of a product sold, while simultaneously providing value to consumers.

promotion Communication with a firm's market through advertising, personal selling, sales promotions, and social media.

promotional pricing Strategy that reduces prices temporarily to increase sales in the short run.

prospects Potential customers of a firm.

psychogalvanometer A physiological instrument that's attached to a respondent's fingers to measure an individual's perspiration level.

psychographic segmentation The use of values, attitudes, interests, and other cultural variables to segment consumers.

psychographics Categorization of consumers according to lifestyles and personality.

psychological pricing Setting prices to create a particular psychological effect.

psychological risk The chance that the purchase of the service will not fit the individual's self-concept.

public relations (PR) A communication venue that addresses issues an organization faces and represents

the organization to the public, media, and various stakeholders.
publicity A form of public relations produced by the news media but not paid for or sponsored by the business concern.
public warehouses Independent facilities that provide storage rental and related services.
puffery When a firm makes an exaggerated claim about its goods or services, without making an overt attempt to deceive or mislead.
pull strategy A strategy whereby the manufacturer first focuses on consumer demand through extensive promotion, expecting that consumers will request the brand through the channel.
pupillometric meter A physiological instrument used to measure eye movements and the dilation of a person's pupil.
purchaser The member of the buying center who makes the actual purchase.
purchasing agents Agents with a long-term relationship with buyers who select, receive, and ship goods to buyers and are paid on a commission basis.
pure competition Market that consists of many buyers and sellers, where no buyer or seller can control price or the market.
pure monopoly Market that consists of only one seller.
push strategy A strategy that focuses on intermediaries, providing the necessary incentives for them to cooperate in selling the product to the final consumer.

qualitative research Research that involves a small number of respondents answering open-ended questions.
quantitative research A structured type of research that involves either descriptive research approaches, such as survey research, or causal research approaches, such as experiments in which responses can be summarized or analyzed with numbers. quantity discount: A discount method where both consumers and intermediaries typically get a price break when they purchase larger quantities of a particular product.
question marks (or problem children) Low market share and high-growth products that require more cash investment than they generate.

rack jobbers Wholesalers that manage the store shelves carrying their products.
radical innovations (or discontinuous innovations) Innovations that create new industries or new standards of management, manufacturing, and servicing, and that represent fundamental changes for consumers, entailing departures from established consumption.
random probability sample A sample in which each individual selected for the study has a known and equal chance of being included in the study.
reach Number of people, households, or businesses in a target audience exposed to a media message at least once during a specific time period.
real-time marketing The creation and execution of an instantaneous marketing message in response to or in conjunction with a live event.
rebates Reimbursements for a durable good.
reciprocity The practice of one business making a purchase from another business that, in turn, patronizes the first business.
reference groups Groups that serve as a point of reference for individuals in the process of shaping their attitude and behavior.
reference price The price that consumers carry in their mind for a particular product or brand.
referent power Power over the other channel members based on the close match in terms of values and objectives that members of the channel share.
refunds Reimbursements for a soft good or service.
regional shopping centers Shopping centers that consist of at least 100 stores that sell shopping goods to a geographically dispersed market.
reinforcement Learning achieved by strengthening the relationship between the cue and the response.
relationship marketing The process of developing and nurturing relationships with all the parties participating in the transactions involving a company's products; the development of marketing strategies aimed at enhancing relationships in the channel.
relationship-seeking segment A market segment that consists of relatively sophisticated service users who believe that the user-provider relationship is important.
reliability The ability of the service firm to perform the service provided in a dependable and accurate (service); the extent to which the data are likely to be free from random error and yield consistent results (scale).
repeat transactions Buyer and seller interacting over multiple transactions.
resale price maintenance Manufacturers requiring retailers to charge a particular price for a product.
response-offer coupons Coupons issued following a request by a consumer.
responsiveness The willingness of the firm's staff to help customers and to provide prompt service.
retailing All the activities involved in the final stage of distribution—selling goods and services to consumers for their consumption.
reward power Power over the channel members based on an anticipation of special privileges, such as a financial reward for conducting a particular behavior.
roles The activities people are expected to perform according to individuals around them.
routine problem solving Consumer decision making whereby consumers engage in habitual purchase decisions involving products that they purchase frequently.

sales era Period between 1930 and 1950, when the primary focus of marketing was on selling.
sales force compensation, quota, and territory studies Different studies pertaining to personal selling activities; they are crucial in helping to determine the appropriate sales and incentive strategies for certain markets.

sales force composite estimates Research studies in which sales forecasts are based on the personal observations and forecasts of the local sales force.
sales promotions Incentives to encourage end users or consumers to purchase a product.
sales-based objectives Attempts to increase sales volume and market share relative to competitors.
sample A segment of the population selected for the study and considered to be representative of the total population of interest.
sample size The number of study participants.
sampling Sales promotions that include the free delivery of an actual product or portion of a product.
sampling frame The list from which sampling units are selected.
sampling procedure The procedure used in the selection of sampling units.
sampling unit The individuals or groups included in the study.
satisfaction A match between consumer expectations and good or service performance.
scanner-delivered coupons Coupons issued at the cash register during checkout.
scrambled merchandising Scrambled merchandising involves retailers adding complementary product categories not included in the existing merchandise mix and more services to create one-stop shopping convenience for target consumers.
search engine optimization (SEO) The process of increasing the probability of a particular company's website emerging from a search.
seasonal discount Discounts offered by retailers to promote off-season sales.
secondary business district Shopping areas, consisting primarily of convenience and specialty stores, that form at the intersection between two important streets.
secondary data Data collected to address a problem other than the problem at hand.
segment marketing A process that involves identifying consumers who are similar with regard to key traits, such as product-related needs and wants, and who would respond well to a similar marketing mix.
segmentation The process of identifying consumers or markets that are similar with regard to key traits, such as product-related needs and wants, and that would respond well to a product and related marketing mix.
selective distortion Consumers adapting information to fit their own existing knowledge.
selective distribution A strategy whereby firms have some control over the marketing strategy by limiting distribution to a select group of resellers in each area, while, at the same time, the company can achieve a reasonable sales volume and profits.
selective exposure The stimuli that consumers choose to pay attention to.
selective retention Remembering only information about a good or service that supports personal knowledge or beliefs.
self-concept An individual's belief about himself or herself, including the person's attributes and who and what the self is.
self-efficacy Confidence individuals have in themselves to accomplish their sales goals.
selling agent Agent that holds an exclusive arrangement with the company, represents all its operations in a particular market, and acts as the sales or marketing department of the firm.
selling concept Assumes that when left alone, consumers will not normally purchase the products the firm is selling or will not purchase enough products.
semantic differential scale Scale that is anchored by words with opposite meanings.
service distribution The availability and accessibility of a service to consumers.
service encounter The second stage of the service purchase process, which is the actual interaction point between the customer and the service provider.
service failures Instances in which a service is either not performed at all or is poorly performed.
service mix The different types of services offered to retail customers.
service recovery The process of attempting to regain a customer's confidence after a service failure.
services Intangible activities or benefits that individuals acquire but that do not result in ownership, such as an airplane trip, a massage, or the preparation of a will.
share of the customer The percentage (or share) of a customer's business that a particular firm has.
shoppertainment Blend of retailing and leisure that increases the length of stay and total spent with a retailer.
shopper marketing Focusing all marketing activities on improving consumers' shopping experience to drive sales in-store or online, at the point of purchase.
shopping centers Groups of stores that are planned, developed, and managed as one entity.
shopping goods Goods that consumers perceive as higher risk but for which they are willing to spend a greater amount of purchase effort to find and evaluate.
simulated test marketing Test marketing that simulates purchase environments in that target consumers are observed in the product related decision-making process.
single transaction Buyer and seller interacting for the purpose of a single transaction.
skimming A pricing strategy whereby the product is priced higher than that of competitors.
slotting fees Fees that retailers charge to stock manufacturers' brands.
social class Relatively permanent divisions within society that exist in a status hierarchy, with the members of each division sharing similar values, attitudes, interests, and opinions.
social listening Listening to social chatter, where comments may be negative or positive, but in most cases visitors render honest opinions.

social risk The probability that a service will not meet with approval from others who are significant to the consumer making the purchase.
societal marketing concept A marketing philosophy that assumes the company will have an advantage over competitors if it applies the marketing concept in a manner that maximizes society's well-being.
sociodemographic and cultural environment A component of the macroenvironment that comprises elements such as demographics, subcultures, cultural values, and all other elements in the environment related to consumers' backgrounds, values, attitudes, interests, and behaviors.
source The organization that originates a marketing communication message.
specialty goods Goods that reach the ultimate in differentiation and brand loyalty in that only the chosen brand is acceptable to the consumer.
spiff money Monies or prizes awarded in trade contests.
sponsored content A brand sponsors the content of a blogger or related website.
sponsorship marketing Marketing that involves a company paying a fee to an event, a person, or an organization in exchange for a direct association with that event, person, or organization.
stability The extent to which preferences are stable, rather than changing, in a market segment.
staples Goods that are bought routinely, such as milk, cheese, bread, and soap.
stars High-share, high-growth products that create profits but require additional investment.
status The esteem which society bestows upon a particular role.
status-quo objectives Pricing designed to maintain a firm's current position in the market.
stimuli Cues in the environment, such as products and advertisements, that create individual responses.
stimulus-response sales approach Sometimes referred to as the canned sales approach, uses specific statements (stimuli) to solicit specific responses from customers.
strategic partnership Partnership in which the buyer and seller exchange information at the highest levels with the goal of collaboration.
stock turnover The number of times a year that the inventory on hand is sold.
strivers Psychographic group of individuals who are trendy and fun loving. They are concerned about others' opinions and approval, and demonstrate to peers their ability to buy.
studies of premiums, coupons, and deals Studies that determine the appropriateness and effectiveness of premiums, coupons, and deals for a given target market.
style A general form of popular expression that could last for a longer period of time or that could be cyclical in nature.
subcultures Groups of individuals with shared value systems based on ethnicity or common background.
substantiality The extent to which the market is large enough to warrant investment.
supermarkets Stores that carry an extensive food selection and drug products, as well as nonfood items (which account for at least 25 percent of sales), combining supermarket, discount, and warehouse retailing principles.
superstores Large retailers, such as combination stores or hypermarkets, that sell food, drugs, and other products.
support personnel Individuals who directly support or assist in the selling function in some manner but do not process orders or directly solicit orders.
survey research Descriptive research that involves the administration of personal, telephone, or mail questionnaires.
survivors Psychographic group of individuals who are concerned with safety and security. They focus on meeting needs rather than fulfilling desires, are brand loyal, and purchase discounted products.

tangibles The service provider's physical facilities, equipment, and appearance of its employees.
target market Consumers or markets that are similar in aspects relevant to the company.
target marketing The process of focusing on those segments that the company can serve most effectively and designing products, services, and marketing programs with these segments in mind.
target profit pricing A pricing strategy used by capital-intensive firms, where the formula used to calculate target profit pricing takes into consideration a standard volume of production that the firm is expected to achieve.
technical service quality The outcome of the service.
time-loss risk. The amount of time the consumer lost as a result of the failure of the service.
television home shopping Retailing through cable channels selling to consumers in their homes, through infomercials, and by direct-response advertising shown on broadcast and cable television.
terminal values Values related to goals.
test marketing Evaluating product performance in select markets that are representative of the target market before launching the product.
thinkers Psychographic group of individuals who are educated, conservative, and practical consumers who value knowledge and responsibility. They look for durability, functionality, and value.
tie-ins Sales promotion of two or more goods or services within the same promotional offer.
time series and econometric methods Methods that use the data of past performance to predict future market demand.
trade allowances Some type of financial incentive to channel members to motivate them to make a purchase.
trade discount A price incentive offered by manufacturers and wholesalers to make a purchase or stock a particular brand.
trade incentives Some type of financial incentive that involves the retailer performing some type of function to receive a trade allowance.

trade promotions Incentives directed toward channel members to encourage them to purchase, stock, or push a product through the channel.
trade-in allowance A form of discounting where an item is purchased with a trade-in of a similar item, thus reducing the price of the new item.
trademark Words, symbols, marks, and signs that are legally registered for a single company's use.
trading companies Complex marketing systems that specialize in providing intermediary service and reducing risk through extensive information channels and financial assistance.
trialability The number of individuals that try a new product or brand for the first time.
trust relationships Buyer-seller dyads based on mutual respect and understanding of both parties and a commitment to work together.

uncertainty The probability that a particular outcome or consequence will occur.
undifferentiated marketing A targeting strategy aiming the product at the market using a single strategy, regardless of the number of segments.
usage rate segmentation The process of segmenting markets based on the extent to which consumers are non-users, occasional users, medium users, or heavy users of a product.
unit pricing Pricing that allows consumers to compare among prices for different brands and for different package sizes of the different brands.
use or applications positioning The process of marketing a precise product application that differentiates it in consumers' minds from other products that have a more general use.
user status segmentation The process of determining consumer status—as users of competitors' products, ex-users, potential users, first-time users, or regular users.
user An individual member of the buying center who actually uses the product or is responsible for the product being used.

value chain (or supply chain) The chain of activities performed in the process of developing, producing, marketing, delivering, and servicing a product for the benefit of the customer.
value proposition Proposition that convinces consumers to buy a firm's products and services over those of their competitors.
values Important elements of culture defined as enduring beliefs about a specific mode of conduct or desirable end state.
variability The unwanted or random levels of service quality customers receive when they patronize a service.
variable costs Costs, such as raw materials, packaging, and shipping costs, that vary with the amount of output.
variable pricing Strategy of changing prices in response to changes in cost or demand.
vertical integration The acquisition or merger with an intermediary in the channel that is either a supplier or a buyer.
vertical marketing systems (VMS) Intermediary marketing systems that consist of manufacturers, wholesalers, and retailers in the same channel who have partial VMS ownership acting as a unified whole.
viral marketing Preparing a marketing message to be passed from one consumer to another through digital venues or social media.

wants Needs that are directed at a particular product—for example, to meet the need for transportation, consumers may purchase an Uber or a bus ride.
warehouse clubs (or wholesale clubs) Stores that require members to pay an annual fee and that operate in low-overhead, warehouse-type facilities, offering limited lines of brand-name and dealer-brand groceries, apparel, appliances, and other goods at a substantial discount.
warehousing The marketing function whereby goods are stored, identified, and sorted in the process of transfer to an intermediary in the distribution channel or to the final consumer.
wheel of retailing A model that describes how stores evolve from innovative low-margin, low-cost, and low-price operations and, in seeking to broaden their customer base, they add services, upgrade facilities, and thus increasing costs and prices; and, in the process, lose their initial customers, who move on to new low-priced retailers, and become conventional retailers.
wholesaling All the activities involved in buying and handling the goods intended for sale to resellers or other organizational users.

Organization Index

V

W

X

Y

Z

Subject Index

Page numbers in italics indicate illustrations and captions.

D

E

F

G

H

I

J

K

L

M

T

U

V

W